AREA HANDBOOK
for the
PEOPLE'S REPUBLIC OF CHINA

Co-Authors

Donald P. Whitaker and Rinn-Sup Shinn

Helen A. Barth
Judith M. Heimann
John E. MacDonald
Kenneth W. Martindale
John O. Weaver

Research and writing were completed October 1971

Published 1972

(This pamphlet supersedes DA Pam No. 550–60, October 1967)

DA Pam 550–60

Library of Congress Catalog Card Number: 72–600022

For sale by the Superintendent of Documents, U.S. Government Printing Office, Washington, D.C. 20402
Price $5.20 domestic postpaid or $4.75 GPO Bookstore

FOREWORD

This volume is one of a series of handbooks prepared by Foreign Area Studies (FAS) of The American University, designed to be useful to military and other personnel who need a convenient compilation of basic facts about the social, economic, political, and military institutions and practices of various countries. The emphasis is on objective description of the nation's present society and the kinds of possible or probable changes that might be expected in the future. The handbook seeks to present as full and as balanced an integrated exposition as limitations on space and research time permit. It was compiled from information available in openly published material. An extensive bibliography is provided to permit recourse to other published sources for more detailed information. There has been no attempt to express any specific point of view or to make policy recommendations. The contents of the handbook represent the work of the authors and FAS and do not represent the official view of the United States government.

An effort has been made to make the handbook as comprehensive as possible. It can be expected, however, that the material, interpretations, and conclusions are subject to modification in the light of new information and developments. Such corrections, additions, and suggestions for factual, interpretive, or other change as readers may have will be welcomed for use in future revisions. Comments may be addressed to:

The Director
Foreign Area Studies
The American University
5010 Wisconsin Avenue, N.W.
Washington, D.C. 20016

PREFACE

In 1971 the People's Republic of China (PRC) was in a state of unprecedented fluidity, accentuated in part by a still obscure but apparently momentous political struggle that occurred in the summer and early fall of the year. This crisis, which appeared to have involved key national leaders, was probably connected with the country's continuing efforts to stabilize the domestic condition and to restructure external relations, both of which had been disrupted by the violent turbulence of the Great Proletarian Cultural Revolution (1966–69). According to fragmentary clues that could be pieced together in November—research and writing for the present *Area Handbook for the People's Republic of China* was completed in October—the political status of Lin Piao may have been affected adversely by this political infighting. Lin Piao, minister of national defense, deputy Party chairman, and Party Chairman Mao Tse-tung's officially designated "successor," was variously reported as either critically ill, purged, or even dead. If true, the implications of this turn of events for the immediate future of the PRC and for the outside world remained unclear. Lack of reliable information imposed a serious limitation on any attempt to outline even the most tentative assessment of this new situation, which was as unexpected as it was dramatic.

Whatever the case, many Western observers increasingly suspected that the PRC's leaders were split in their debates over priorities among major national policies. These debates were apparently focused on, among other things, the Chinese Communist Party's traditional but currently tenuous authority to command "the gun" or the armed forces; the relative emphasis to be placed on economic development as opposed to defense buildup; and the place of the Soviet Union and the United States in post-Cultural Revolution foreign relations. The outcome of debates on any of these issues might well be influenced by the retirement, removal, or demise of any one of the handful of aged national leaders, all of whom had been in positions of power for more than two decades.

The current *Area Handbook for the People's Republic of China* replaces the 1967 *Area Handbook for Communist China*, which was prepared by a team headed by Frederic H. Chaffee and included George E. Aurell, Helen A. Barth, John H. Dombrowski, Neda A. Walpole, and John O. Weaver. The authors of the present volume have found it necessary to redo completely all but a minuscule portion of the earlier edition, partly because the 1967 volume was prepared during the initial phase of the Cultural Revolution and partly because a number of new, critical studies on mainland China became available after 1967.

The *Area Handbook for the People's Republic of China* is an introduction to the very complex and little-known world of mainland China that includes a quarter of the world's total population. It seeks to present the dominant aspects of social, political, and economic life as objectively as the availability and current state of knowledge on this society permit. Sources of information used include scholarly studies reflecting various disciplines and perspectives, current journals, English translations of Communist Chinese materials, and materials in the Japanese language.

Grateful acknowledgment is given to a number of persons for their contribution to the present study: John W. Henderson served initially as team chairman, and Eston T. White wrote Chapter 7, Living Conditions. Special thanks go to Professor Harold C. Hinton of George Washington University, who wrote Chapter 10, Political Dynamics. The authors are also deeply grateful to the following China specialists for their generous help, comments, and advice: Nancy E. Bateman, John Philip Emerson, Robert Michael Field, Edwin F. Jones, Marion R. Larsen, Peter G. Smith, and K. P. Wang. Responsibility for presentation, errors, and omissions is, however, entirely that of the authors.

A glossary is included for the reader's convenience. Wherever possible, transliteration for Chinese words follows the Wade-Giles system for the Mandarin dialect, modified to eliminate diacritical marks but retaining the apostrophe to indicate aspirated consonants. Departures from modified Wade-Giles spelling have been made in the case of a few words—for example, Taiping (Wade-Giles: T'ai-p'ing)— that have long been familiar to Western readers under other romanizations. The United States Board on Geographic Names, United States Department of the Interior, *Gazetteer of Mainland China*, No. 22, Second Edition, Washington, D.C., 1968, has been used for the spelling of Chinese place names.

COUNTRY SUMMARY

1. COUNTRY: People's Republic of China (PRC). Established 1949 after expulsion by force of the Republic of China (Nationalist China) from mainland. The PRC regime is in control of the country with the world's oldest continuous history and civilization dating back to the second millennium B.C. National capital: Peking.

2. GOVERNMENT: Unitary system with nominal division of powers into executive, legislative, and judicial arms. In practice, until the mid-1960s the Chinese Communist Party (CCP) was above the government; ultimate power rested in Party's Politburo (Political Bureau). Extensive breakdown of Party and governmental machinery during the Great Proletarian Cultural Revolution (1966–69) resulted in significant transfer of power to the People's Liberation Army (PLA). In 1971 political situation was highly fluid and volatile.

3. POPULATION: About 800 million in 1971—world's largest, comprising roughly one-quarter of world population. Approximately 80 percent rural, 20 percent urban. Estimated annual growth rate 2 to 2.5 percent, with population expected to reach 1 billion by 1980s. Major ethnic group, Han Chinese (94 percent); some sixty minority groups constitute 6 percent of total population.

4. SIZE: About 3.7 million square miles; third largest in world. China Proper (see Glossary) 40 percent of total area; remainder in Outer China (see Glossary). Approximately 13,210 miles of land borders shared with twelve neighbors; coastline of approximately 3,500 miles bounds east and south.

5. TOPOGRAPHY: Three major regions: northern, extending from the Pamirs and Tien Shan mountain system in the west to Greater Khingan Range in east and encompassing Sinkiang Uighur, upper Ninghsia Hui, and Inner Mongolian autonomous regions and northern Kansu Province—mountains, ranges, plateaus, low-lying basins, and deserts; western, encompassing Tibetan Autonomous Region, Tsinghai Province, and western Szechwan Province—some of world's highest mountains ring great Tibetan Plateau, which has tableland over 12,000 feet high; and eastern, consisting of China Proper and Northeast China—characterized by landscape of fertile valleys interrupted by low mountain ranges. Great rivers flow eastward to the sea.

6. CLIMATE: Great regional contrasts. North China is dry with long, cold winters, much of its rainfall falling in short span in summer.

Northwest China is extremely dry, with great seasonal extremes of hot and cold. In lower Yangtze River valley area, winters shorter than in north, and rainfall greater and more evenly distributed. In southern and southeastern tropical and subtropical coastal areas, annual rainfall high and winters warm and dry. In Southwest China, in Yunnan Province, climate is temperate on the plateau, although area lies partly in the tropics; in Szechwan Province, protected by mountains to the north, climate is warm and moist year round; in Tibet, rainfall is sparse, falling mostly in summer, winters extremely cold, and temperature cool rest of the year.

7. LANGUAGES: The Han speak a number of related Sinitic languages known collectively as Chinese. Major form, Mandarin, is national language; other forms regional, in spoken form for most part mutually unintelligible but using same ideographic writing system. Minority ethnic group languages belong predominantly to Sino-Tibetan, Altaic, and Austroasiatic families.

8. RELIGION: Among Han, primarily folk religion embracing Confucianist, Taoist, Buddhist, and animist elements; Mahayana Buddhism popular in Yangtze valley. Islam practiced by under 3 percent of population, primarily Han but also some minority ethnic groups. Christianity has small following. Among non-Han, many animistic cults. (Proselytizing and many other religious activities discouraged or banned by government, although freedom of religious belief guaranteed by constitution.)

9. EDUCATION: In 1962 about 90 million primary school pupils, 15 million secondary school students, and 900,000 in institutions of higher learning; estimated 60 percent of rural youth and much higher proportion of urban youth were then attending school. After 1962 a major reorganization of education transformed all full-time schools into part-work part-study schools, stressing vocational training with great reduction of time allotted to academic work. All schools closed in mid-1966. Primary and secondary schools resumed after one or two years; higher institutions remained closed four years; some colleges and universities reopened in 1970 with reduced enrollment. Literacy among adults estimated at 40 percent.

10. HEALTH: Life expectancy estimated at fifty-two years in 1971; death rate estimated at fifteen per 1,000 population in 1970. Noteworthy improvement in health of population since 1960 because of large-scale pest and disease eradication campaigns and better sanitation. Health care in rural areas is responsibility of People's Communes, with costs borne by member dues. Severe shortage of modern doctors; since mid-1960s much use made of "barefoot doctors"—medical aides trained in first aid and treatment of common ailments using modern and traditional techniques.

11. JUSTICE: No formal codes of civil or criminal law or procedure since 1949; legal processes are flexible with enforcement dependent

upon current political and ideological considerations; much use made of governmental directives and administrative regulations. Highest formal judicial body is Supreme People's Court, supervising three levels of subordinate courts. Parallel structure for public prosecutors, headed by Supreme People's Procuratorate. In late 1960s and early 1970s PLA had effective control over administration of justice.

12. ADMINISTRATIVE DIVISIONS: Country divided into twenty-one provinces, five autonomous regions (provincial-level areas given special status because they contain sizable minority ethnic group populations), and three municipalities—Peking, Shanghai, and Tientsin—which, because of their populations and importance, are administered directly by the central government. Country is divided into eleven military regions, each having one or more military districts and each military district being coterminous with a province.

13. ECONOMY: Underdeveloped, mainly agricultural. Estimated gross national product (GNP) in 1970 equivalent to US$80 billion or US$100 per capita income. Economy considerably damaged by overmobilization in Great Leap Forward (1958–60); recovered in 1962–65 period to 1957 level through new economic policies. Industry and transportation disrupted in Cultural Revolution, but rural economy apparently not much affected. Recovery to 1966 level and slight further growth in GNP took place in 1969 and 1970.

14. INDUSTRY: Expanded greatly by 1971 from small base inherited in 1949 but remained underdeveloped in relation to country's endowment of natural resources, huge population, and ambitions of leadership. Factories and mines concentrated in eastern third of country. Industry as whole contributes estimated half of GNP. Among Asian nations, PRC second only to Japan in gross industrial output. In per capita output, PRC ranks far behind Japan and other industrialized powers.

15. AGRICULTURE: Most important sector of economy, engaging 75 to 85 percent of labor force; contributes about one-third of GNP and provides substantial foreign exchange earnings. Farm output mainly rice, wheat, other edible grains, and some industrial crops; fisheries, forestry, and grazing less important. Ninety percent of farming carried on by Communes, 10 percent by state farms.

16. LABOR: Labor force estimated about 350 million; only 15 to 25 percent (45 million to 85 million) in nonagricultural employment. Average yearly income of nonagricultural workers and employees stated officially at 650 yuan (2.46 yuan equal US$1) in 1970, about the same as in 1957.

17. FOREIGN TRADE: State monopoly; used to promote industrialization and modernization and also used as tool to implement PRC political and ideological policies. *Principal Imports.* Manufactured goods including: machinery and equipment; iron and

steel; chemicals (of which more than half fertilizers). Raw materials for processing (of which more than one-third rubber), and grains. *Principal Suppliers.* Of industrial commodities, Japan, West Germany, and United Kingdom; Canada main source of grains in 1971. *Value of Imports.* 1970 preliminary estimate: equivalent of US$2,165 million, up 18 percent from 1969. *Principal Exports.* Textile yarns and fibers; animals, meat, and fish; clothing; fruit and vegetables; and crude materials. *Principal Markets.* Hong Kong, Japan, Singapore, West Germany, and United Kingdom. *Value of Exports.* 1970 preliminary estimate: equivalent of US$2,060 million, 2 percent above 1969.

18. FINANCE: Ministry of Finance and banking network, headed by People's Bank of China, major instruments of financial supervision and control of economy. Nation's financial resources obtained primarily via state budget and from state enterprises, institutions, and organizations. No comprehensive budget ever made public through 1971. Over 90 percent of budgetary revenue derived from profits and taxes generated by state enterprises. Balanced national and local budgets favored. Revenue goals determined by expenditure requirements.

19. COMMUNICATIONS: Telephone, telegraph, and postal services operated by state. Most enterprises in urban areas have telephones; all rural Communes reported to be linked by telephone. Telegraph service fairly well developed. Postal services reported dependable, but extent unknown. Radio stations in all provincial and autonomous regional capitals; overseas service in 1970 in thirty-three languages, five Chinese dialects, for over 1,500 hours weekly. Television stations in major urban centers; telecasts limited to certain days and times; estimated in 1971 up to 200,000 television sets in use.

20. RAILROADS: State owned and operated. Estimated 22,000 route-miles in latter 1960s. Railroads largely concentrated in eastern third of country before 1949; since then, considerable expansion to western provinces of China Proper and to Sinkiang.

21. ROADS: Official report in 1969 fixed total highway mileage at 500,000 miles—187,500 miles all-weather roads and 312,500 miles secondary roads. New road construction primarily in inland two-thirds of country.

22. INLAND WATERWAYS: Length of navigable waterways increased from 46,000 miles in 1949 to 90,000 in 1957; 25,000 miles open to steam vessels. In mid-1960s Yangtze River most important inland waterway.

23. PORTS AND PORT FACILITIES: Eight major ports open to foreign trade in 1971: Lu-ta (Dairen); Ch'in-huang-tao; Tientsin; Tsingtao; Lien-yun-chiang (in northern Kiangsu); Shanghai; Canton; and Chan-chiang (in southern Kwangtung). Merchant fleet in 1970 of

248 ships totaling 868,000 displacement tons; also unspecified number of foreign ships under charter.

24. CIVIL AVIATION: State owned and operated; under apparent control of PLA in 1971. In 1966, fifty domestic air routes in service, covering 25,000 miles and connecting seventy domestic cities. International service to several adjacent countries. Several foreign airlines maintained regular service to PRC.

25. INTERNATIONAL MEMBERSHIP: United Nations, by vote on October 25, 1971.

26. INTERNATIONAL AGREEMENTS AND TREATIES: Mutual assistance treaties with Soviet Union, North Korea, and North Vietnam; border agreements with all neighbor states except India, Laos, Bhutan, and Sikkim; treaties of friendship with Albania and several other Eastern European states; economic, cultural exchange, technical cooperation, and trade agreements with many states. Most important aid agreements with Tanzania, Pakistan, Albania, Burma, Egypt, and Ethiopia.

27. THE ARMED FORCES: Named People's Liberation Army (PLA) since 1946; successor to the Red Army, founded in late 1920s, as military arm of Chinese Communist Party. Conceived of as "people's army" with mission to implement domestic Party policies in addition to its military duties. One of world's largest military force with estimated total strength in 1971 of 2.88 million—over 90 percent ground forces; 180,000 air force; and 150,000 navy. About 7 million well-trained militia. PLA manned entirely by draft, with approximately 7 million annually reaching draft age of eighteen. Capacity to wage major offensive operations restricted by limited logistical resources and limited sea and airlift capabilities. Although PRC had nuclear capability, its missiles in 1971 posed no strategic threat to powers outside Asia.

28. INTERNAL SECURITY: Before mid-1960s Ministry of Public Security was main operating element in security system with direct command of People's Police at all levels; during Cultural Revolution, People's Police seriously disrupted and incorporated under command of, or replaced by, PLA. PLA believed to have remained in control of internal security in 1971. Security functions also carried out by various occupational, residence, and social organizations sponsored by, but partly autonomous of, the central government.

PEOPLE'S REPUBLIC OF CHINA

TABLE OF CONTENTS

LIST OF ILLUSTRATIONS

LIST OF TABLES

SECTION I. SOCIAL

CHAPTER 1

GENERAL CHARACTER OF THE SOCIETY

The People's Republic of China (PRC) is the world's most populous country and is the third largest in size after the Soviet Union and Canada. It covers the eastern side of the Eurasian landmass and is rich in natural resources, and its climate is generally temperate. Much of its cultivable land is fertile, but there is an insufficiency of arable land for its population, which is burgeoning at the rate of from 16 million to 20 million a year. The country is overwhelmingly Han Chinese, who all use one written language. The country's culture has always been predominantly secular, although all the world's major religions have gained adherents there.

The PRC is heir to the world's most enduring culture. Nevertheless, its leaders have been more critical about their past than had any of their predecessors. They take pride in some aspects of their country's legacy but reject others that, they assert, interfere with their goal of creating a new, powerful, socialist China.

The government of the PRC was formally established in October 1949 after the Chinese Communist Party (CCP), led by Chairman Mao Tse-tung, defeated the incumbent government forces of the Republic of China (Nationalist China) and installed a new political system. This new system was based on an essentially alien system of ideology rooted in Marxism-Leninism—exemplified at the time by the Soviet Union and its satellite countries. The Nationalist government of Chiang Kai-shek, forced to withdraw to the island province of Taiwan, continued to challenge the PRC's legitimacy. It argued that the Chinese Communists had imposed on the mainland an alien, totalitarian dictatorship against the popular will.

This argument, coupled with the PRC's intervention in the Korean conflict in 1950 (an intervention denounced by the United Nations [UN] as "aggression"), constituted a basis for efforts by many noncommunist nations to block the PRC's representation in the UN for more than two decades. In October 1971, however, the Chinese Communists gained the endorsement of the UN General Assembly for its claim to China's seats in the world organization.

1

The introduction of a revolutionary foreign ideology to a society that has demonstrated a remarkable capacity to resist changes has presented problems. Despite the CCP leaders' rhetoric that "construction begins with destruction," they have paid due attention to the country's heritage, which conditions the people's attitudes, beliefs, and aspirations.

The Chinese Communists have consistently recognized that revolutionary change, to be viable, depends to a considerable extent on its acceptability to the people and that this change cannot be fashioned by decree or coercion alone. They realized that the process of effectuating change in mental attitudes was complex and frustratingly time consuming.

They have had to cope with the inherited centrifugal forces of regional diversity. Marked differences exist among various regions—differences that encourage provincial particularism, foster sectional interests and, when unrestrained, have led to periodic fragmentation. These divisive tendencies often have gained ascendancy and contributed to the rise of local kingdoms and local strong men. The strong forces of cultural homogeneity, a common heritage, one language, and the Confucian system of recruiting government officials kept political discontinuities from seriously impeding continuity of the civilization.

In addition, there has been fragmentation on ethnic grounds. Although only 6 percent of the population is non-Han, this portion in absolute terms is sizable—numbering close to 50 million in 1971. At least ten minority groups have 1 million or more members each. Thus the pace of socialist transformation has had to be flexible in order to account for the idiosyncracies of different minority peoples.

Another portion of the inheritance has been poverty, which is likely to be a very long-term problem because of rising population. Only about 11 percent of the total land area is suitable for cultivation. Rainfall in most of the densely populated eastern part of the country is sufficient for the crops grown (supplemented by irrigation), but years of drought or of excessive rainfall have often occurred and have resulted in reduced harvests and widespread famine. More than four-fifths of the population are peasants, who not only must eke out an existence on this limited acreage but also must provide the state with labor and revenue. The pressure of the population on land and the demands of the state for revenue have been age-old problems.

The strategies of the communist leadership to cope with major issues have been based on two basic approaches. These have been used concurrently, but emphasis on each has varied according to circumstances. They have differed on the means by which to bring about socialist transformation in the shortest possible time. One approach, as exemplified by both the Great Leap Forward (see Glossary) and the Great Proletarian Cultural Revolution (see

2

Glossary), has stressed indoctrination, intensive mass mobilization, moral incentives, and self-sacrifice in the interest of collectivity. The other one, although not neglecting these factors, has emphasized balance between moral and material incentives, between ideological fervor and technical expertise, and between militancy and moderation. The second approach was pronounced from 1961 to 1965 and, more recently, since the subsiding of the Cultural Revolution in 1969.

Efforts to strike a balance between both strategies have frequently caused acrimony. The national leadership has had to take into account conflicting regional interests, tensions between the Party and the armed forces and between old and young functionaries, and the personal ambitions and shifting loyalties of influential figures. Some Western observers have suggested that the PRC's occasional convulsions since 1949 have been surface symptoms of such underlying tensions and frustrations.

Throughout the 2,000-year imperial period, Chinese society was, given its size and territorial spread, remarkable for the homogeneity of its institutions and value orientation. Chief among the factors that contributed to the persistence of Chinese culture was Confucianism, the dominant ideology that influenced all aspects of Chinese life. Sometimes mistakenly regarded as simply a religion, Confucianism was first and foremost a practical system of political and social philosophy. It was essentially a system of thought and a way of life that exalted the dignity of man, stressed harmony in society, and sought the establishment of rule not by the wealthy or the noble but by men of virtue and talent. At the same time, however, the society was notable for the relative paucity of strong social ties connecting individuals to the larger society as against the extensive social obligations deeply felt by members of small groups toward one another—for example, in the numerous and cohesive patrilineages, guilds, and voluntary associations.

Upward mobility was possible for men of superior intellectual ability and education and was not seriously restricted by criteria relating to birth or economic condition. The status of women, however, was low, and many traditional institutions acted to keep it so.

The PRC regime has brought about significant changes in the preexisting social configuration. It has worked to change the value system of traditional China; in particular, it has sought to increase the individual's sense of identification with society as a whole and to reduce his particularistic loyalties to smaller groups. It has also worked, with considerable success, to raise the status of women. It has done so by making women legally the equals of men in rights and obligations and by eliminating practices that had given females an inferior position in society.

3

The most ambitious governmental effort to affect Chinese society in the decade ending in 1971 has been that directed toward changing both the character and values associated with education. Traditionally, scholarship had been the surest route to political power and high social status. It was the accepted duty of the educated to rule and of the uneducated to serve their rulers. The Communists had always opposed this view and, beginning in the early 1960s, the PRC began to reorganize schools and their schedules, curricula, and admissions policies to close the social distance between the scholar and the peasant or worker and to eliminate the age-old gap between mental and manual labor.

Social mobility has been greatly affected by the policies of the Communist regime. "Politics in command" has been the slogan, and political orthodoxy and reliability have replaced Confucian learning as the chief criterion for upward movement. To the leadership the most convincing proof of political reliability has been that the person under consideration for advancement joined the Communists well before the Party had gained control of the Chinese mainland, and thus the effect on upward mobility of the primacy given political reliability has been to severely limit access to high status for persons too young to have played an active political role before 1949. Although purges and reshuffles have periodically eliminated some senior leaders and promoted others, all persons in power in 1971 were, as they had been since 1949, persons who had participated actively on the communist side since at least the mid-1940s, the period of civil war. Some observers have suggested that the frustration of ambitious persons who saw their way to power blocked by the continued tenure of the older generation of leaders contributed considerably to the animus of the early stages of the Cultural Revolution.

Beginning in the third century B.C. an emperor, the personification of the state, ruled through a bureaucracy recruited by an elaborate examination system. The endurance of this form of rule, coupled with imperial China's ignorance of the outside world, led the Chinese to consider their civilization as being at the center of the world—the Middle Kingdom. In time of strength China assumed suzerainty over its weaker neighbors and exacted from them token tributes and pledges of allegiance.

China's self-centered outlook persisted in part because of geography. The towering Himalayas, the Tibetan plateau, steppes, deserts, and highlands, and the sea tended to screen China from the rest of the major centers of civilization in Europe and the Near East. Until the nineteenth century China was deprived of the challenge and the interchange of ideas that come from intimate contact with alien cultures of equal level.

In the middle of the nineteenth century they were suddenly confronted with the industrialized West—first the British and French and later the Americans, Germans, Italians, Dutch, and Russians. Unaware of the dynamic and aggressive elements inherent in the political, economic, and social systems of Western nations, the Chinese ruling class underestimated their capabilities. It regarded the Westerners as merely the most recent of a long line of culturally inferior barbarian invaders.

In the face of a determined Western onslaught aimed at opening the country to economic, missionary, and diplomatic activities, China first reacted by clinging to the traditional attitude of cultural superiority, hoping that the Western tide would recede. Backed by the military strength of their nations, Western traders were able not only to build up a lucrative trade with China but also to obtain for themselves immunity from its laws. This privileged position engendered in many Chinese an intense and widespread antiforeign feeling, despite the considerable good will that missionaries had been able to foster in many areas by their humanitarian efforts. Toward the end of the nineteenth century, many leading members of the scholar-official class began to advocate a policy of compromise, which would adopt Western technology without changing the basic values and structure of Chinese society.

When the Manchu dynasty was overthrown in 1911, Sun Yat-sen and his adherents hoped to set up a republic along Western lines. For two decades, however, China was divided into warlord regimes, and it was not until 1928 that Chiang Kai-shek brought much of the country under the centralized but tenuous control of the Kuomintang (Nationalist Party, often abbreviated as KMT). Chiang tried to carry out the aspirations of Sun to set up a viable democratic government, but his efforts were frustrated by quarrels among warlords, ineffective national administration, the Japanese invasion, and the opposition of the Communists.

Since its takeover in 1949, the communist government has demonstrated tremendous vigor and has, by resorting alternately to force and persuasion, by and large neutralized all forces of opposition. The Communists established a strong and centralized government; embarked upon an ambitious program of economic construction and industrialization; extended the state's political and military influence effectively into the frontier regions for the first time in history; and maintained a considerable degree of stability. Although the regime has not satisfied some of the aspirations of its people, in general popular satisfaction with its achievements appears to have outweighed resentments.

By 1957 the communist leadership had grown confident of its ability to fashion a new society, but at the same time it had become increasingly concerned about the dwindling Soviet aid to the PRC. The interplay of optimism and uncertainty propelled Mao to inaugurate, but not without internal opposition, the ill-fated Great

5

Leap, which was a technologically and economically naïve attempt to accelerate socialization and make the country an industrial power overnight. He also tried to impose the People's Commune system, through which he intended to organize rural life along paramilitary lines and to reform the family system. The family had been the basic social and economic unit on which the imperial Confucian social order was based. The purpose of reform was to do away with family loyalties that had usually taken precedence over the demands of the state.

The Great Leap failed, with disastrous effects, because the peasants were forced to work to exhaustion and were deprived of all material incentives and because two years of adverse weather in many parts of the country brought widespread famine. Moreover, the family structure was torn asunder, and this brought about popular reaction against the regime. The intensive drive was abruptly relaxed: some of the excessive features of Communes were dropped, families were reunited as household units, and supplemental private plots were returned to each peasant family. The communist leadership was also forced to relax the Party's control over all levels of economic life. Mao himself came under muted criticism within the Party, and in 1959 he stepped down from the office of the chief of state, relinquishing that office to his long-time associate Liu Shao-ch'i, who at the time was regarded as a possible successor to Mao.

Through 1965 the PRC followed moderate domestic policies— apparently against Mao's wishes—which succeeded in reinvigorating the economy. These policies were rational and pragmatic, given the circumstances then prevailing, but Mao considered them to be counterrevolutionary. He argued that a true revolutionary should put aside his selfish concerns and should not need the stimulus of material incentives, such as the pragmatists were offering, to induce increased production.

Externally, the PRC's initially very cordial relationships with the Soviet Union have noticeably cooled since 1960 amid signs of a widening rift between the two countries with respect to matters of both doctrine and national interest. It has become increasingly clear that transnational ideological affinity alone is not sufficient to assure neighborly ties when the countries concerned have their own distinct cultures or when the countries have differences stemming from, among other things, territorial disputes.

In 1966 Mao turned his back on some of those who had been his chosen allies since the early 1930s. He initiated the Cultural Revolution with the assistance of Minister of National Defense Lin Piao. His purpose apparently was to punish those who had reservations about his policies, to inject a more revolutionary flavor into the Party and government bureaucracies, and to reverse the country's momentum, which he suspected was skidding toward counterrevolution.

Considerable opposition to the Cultural Revolution became evident soon after its inception and quickly hardened. On one side was the Mao-Lin Piao faction, which was able to control the Politburo (Political Bureau) and the People's Liberation Army (PLA); on the other was a faction headed by Chief of State Liu Shao-ch'i and Teng Hsiao-p'ing, secretary general of the Central Committee of the CCP. The latter faction had its strength in organized labor and most of the Party apparatus below the Politburo level. Premier Chou En-lai, while remaining personally loyal to Mao, tried, apparently, to bring about a reconciliation between the two factions.

Increasingly, Mao suspected that he could not depend on the regular Party apparatus. In mid-1966 he had Lin Piao organize secondary school and university students into an extra-Party organization called the Red Guards that was charged with rekindling the people's revolutionary enthusiasm and with destroying outdated symbols and values.

The result was civil disorder unparalleled in the PRC's career. With the Party and government apparatuses in disarray and the nation's public security system paralyzed, the PLA had to be called in to assume, in 1967, the responsibility of supervising, controlling, and managing a wide range of governmental activities.

Before 1967 the Party's control of the life of the people was all pervasive. In the government and the armed forces all important positions were held by Party members and there was also a parallel system of Party command that took precedence over any other agency of the state.

The PRC after 1967 to at least late 1971 appeared to be instead a military-directed state, a state in which "the gun," or the armed forces, commanded the Party. This reversal posed a host of doctrinal as well as practical questions concerning the formerly preeminent role of the Party in a "proletarian" society. According to the classical Marxist-Leninist doctrine that Mao subscribes to, a socialist political order is based on the premise that the communist party leads the proletariat. Moreover, according to the CCP Constitution adopted in April 1969: "The organs of state power of the dictatorship of the proletariat, the People's Liberation Army, and the Communist Youth League and other revolutionary mass organizations, such as those of the workers, the poor and lower-middle peasants, and the Red Guards, must all accept the leadership of the Party."

The Ninth Party Congress, held in April 1969, signaled a recess of the Cultural Revolution. The ultraleftist rhetoric on both domestic and external issues was toned down considerably. The Cultural Revolution, however, had left in its wake many unsolved problems and new ones as well. The economy was disrupted and stagnating. The people appeared to be disillusioned by a lengthening list of unfulfilled promises.

No sooner had the internal crisis subsided than the PRC had to contend with a major external crisis. In the spring and summer of 1969 the border security forces of the PRC and the Soviet Union clashed at several points. This situation apparently brought into sharp focus the question of whether the PRC, given its limited resources, could undertake both economic construction and national defense buildup simultaneously.

Mainland China has one of the world's largest armed forces, but its military capabilities are reportedly limited because the country's developed resources are not sufficient to support air force and naval arms and a nuclear strike force comparable to those of the Soviet Union and the United States. Thus, during 1969 in particular, the PRC's sense of insecurity was greatly heightened, partly because the Soviet threat was now considered to be real and partly because of the prevailing atmosphere of uncertainty domestically.

The PRC's friendly overtures to the outside world beginning in mid-1969, especially those to the United States in early 1971, can be variously interpreted. Some China specialists sought to explain the PRC's search for an expanded role in world affairs in terms of power struggles inside China between moderates and radicals. The moderates—apparently the dominant force in post-Cultural Revolution years—were said to be arguing that cooperation, not isolation, was the answer to their country's domestic and external problems, but their adversaries insisted on uncompromising struggles against the Soviet Union and the United States. Other observers suggested that the PRC was attempting to break up not only the alleged collusion of the superpowers (meaning the United States and the Soviet Union) against the mainland but also the partnership between the United States and Japan. Among other explanations were that the Communist Chinese were merely seeking to accelerate the pace of United States disengagement from Asia by projecting the image of peace and reasonableness and that the PRC was determined to isolate Nationalist China and exercise its right to participate in the deliberations of the UN.

The PRC's search for internal viability and for world prestige depends in large measure on its economic performance. Considering the debilitating effect of its enormous population on the economy and other adverse factors against the regime, accomplishments in the economic field have been impressive, if sporadic. Initially faced with an economy devastated by more than ten years of foreign and civil warfare, the PRC undertook the economic rehabilitation of the country as its most immediate objective. In this effort, until the mid-1950s, the country was aided substantially by the Soviet Union, but with the termination of Soviet assistance in 1960, the Chinese Communists were forced to rely for the most part on their own internal resources. To the PRC leadership "self-reliance" has since become an article of faith.

As in other socialist countries, the economy is controlled and planned by the state, and all means of production are owned either by the state or by cooperatives. Until the mid-1950s the pattern of planning and development was based mainly on the Soviet model, with emphasis on the development of heavy industries. The collapse of the Great Leap, however, highlighted the centrality of agriculture to the whole economy; the regime thus recognized the need for the industrial sector to be directed into channels that could increase farm production. Another consequence of the Great Leap was decentralization in planning; provincial authorities were given a much wider latitude and responsibility for formulating locally relevant economic plans. This situation remained valid in 1971, except in matters relating to industries directly connected with national defense.

The basis of the country's economy is agriculture, as it has always been. The agrarian sector contributes roughly one-half of the country's gross national product (GNP). It provides employment for three-fourths of the total labor force of the country; raw materials for processing in consumer goods industries; and the savings needed for a steadily rising investment in capital goods industries. The importance of this sector is accentuated by the fact that the inflow of foreign capital into the country has been negligible since the early 1960s.

The industrial sector yields the other half of the GNP. Mainland China has the potential to become an industrial superpower on a scale equal to that of the United States or the Soviet Union. It has adequate natural resources, electric power, and technical knowledge, but the state of their development and utilization is as yet far behind that of other advanced nations. Given this limitation, the country has emphasized the use of substitute materials and new production methods. Nevertheless, the PRC has achieved great technical sophistication in some areas, as best illustrated by its successful nuclear weapons program. It has built and detonated a number of nuclear devices since 1964, but its delivery vehicles program appears to be lagging.

The economy has gone through periods of spurt and stagnation since 1949. Until 1957 it showed signs of vigor and growth, aided in no small part by the combination of Soviet aid, internal peace, favorable weather, improvement of distribution facilities, and redistribution of land. The Great Leap stifled much of this forward progress, and it took several years for the economy to be restored to the level of 1957. Then the Cultural Revolution again caused extensive damage, especially on industry and transportation. Since 1969 economic rationality has been restored, and efforts to raise agricultural production and to expand industry have been assigned top priority, apparently over the protests of military leaders who reportedly argued that defense preparations should be given equal emphasis.

In its economic assessment in 1971, the PRC's leadership appeared to be quite sober. In July Premier Chou En-lai was quoted by a visiting Canadian cabinet minister as having said that mainland China's economy was "still rather weak" and that the mechanization of agriculture was "even more backward." The premier acknowledged that, although food output was the highest in the world in absolute figures, it was "rather low in relation to population." He also reaffirmed the need for continued stress on industrial development, adding that his government would have to persevere in its intensive developmental efforts for "twenty or thirty years."

CHAPTER 2

PHYSICAL ENVIRONMENT AND POPULATION

The vast size of mainland China (the People's Republic of China—PRC) and its population, on the verge of becoming the first of the world's people to number 1 billion, embraces at one time so many complex elements, both of diversity and homogeneity, that generalizations become unreliable. It is a time-honored truism among students of Chinese affairs that anything said about the country is certain to be true somewhere within it; yet, nothing can be said that is true everywhere within it.

The area occupied by the PRC is estimated at about 3.7 million square miles, the exact measurement depending upon the location of a number of ill-defined boundaries. This size makes the country the third largest in the world—much smaller than the Soviet Union with which it shares the bulk of the Eurasian landmass, slightly smaller than Canada, and slightly larger than the United States. Within this area lives the world's largest population, comprising about one-fourth of the world's total.

The last countrywide census to be undertaken was in 1953. This showed a total population of about 602 million, of whom 583 million persons were reported as resident in the PRC, and another 19 million were claimed for Taiwan and the Overseas Chinese groups. Estimates of population increase since then have been derived mainly from birth and death rates that were in themselves primarily educated guesswork. Thus, official estimates by Chinese and foreign demographers vary widely, and there often is no consistency between the total estimates periodically put forward by the PRC and the growth rates estimated by the regime. Many analysts agree, however, that according to the best available estimate in early 1970, the mainland population was about 800 million and was overwhelmingly rural. The variation in estimated growth rates is even wider, but in 1971 most ranged from about 2 percent to about 2.5 percent per year, which would produce a population of 1 billion by the 1980s. All estimates are subject to an unknown percentage of error resulting from dependence on the 1953 census as a base point. The accuracy of the census is widely disputed outside the country and, perhaps, within it.

The rapid growth of the Chinese population has presented leaders with a number of problems. The official Party line originally backed an essentially uncontrolled growth rate. After the 1953 census, however, there was an official change to support birth control. This support was withdrawn in 1958, in part, apparently, because of lack of popular support for the program. A large increase in agricultural production also presumably influenced top-level Party attitudes. The Party's stated position in support of a large population remained unchanged in 1971. Despite this, birth control and planned parenthood have been continuously promoted at lower levels since the 1959–61 food crisis. Until 1965 efforts were concentrated more in urban areas but were expanded to the country beginning with that year.

Although larger than the United States, mainland China possesses only one-third as large an area of cultivated land. Only about 12 percent is under cultivation, and it is estimated that perhaps another 3 percent could be cultivated. Of the remainder, 78 percent is desert, wasteland, or urban area; 2 to 3 percent, inland water, and the balance, forests.

Most of the arable land of mainland China is located in the relatively small eastern segment known as China Proper (see Glossary) and in Northeast China. More than 90 percent of the population is concentrated in these two segments, and two-thirds of these are compressed into a restricted area of alluvial plains, which, added together, are equal roughly to the size of Mexico and comprise only one-sixth of the land area of mainland China (see figs. 1 and 2).

The whole of China Proper makes up about 40 percent of the country's total area. It is favored with a temperate climate, rich productive soils, and usually adequate rainfall and is considered the commercial and agricultural heart of the country. It is divided by the Tsinling range, the northern watershed of the Yangtze River, into two distinct parts—North China and South China—which vary greatly in topography, climate, and agricultural practices. The remaining 60 percent of the land area is known as Outer China and includes Tsinghai Province, and Mongolian, Sinkiang, and Tibetan topographical areas, as well as the northeast provinces, formerly known as Manchuria.

The country has the longest land boundary in the world, a total of 13,210 miles, which it shares with fourteen neighbors. The longest boundary is shared with the Soviet Union and extends for 4,150 miles. The border along the Indian subcontinent, confronting India, Pakistan, Bhutan, Sikkim, and Nepal, is 3,075 miles long; that along Mongolia is almost 2,500 miles; and that along Burma, approximately 1,350 miles. The border along the Democratic People's Republic of Korea (North Korea) is 880 miles, and along the Democratic Republic of Vietnam (North Vietnam) and Laos the lengths are nearly 800 miles and over 250 miles, respectively. The border touching Hong Kong is 155 miles, including the sea frontier—the land frontier is

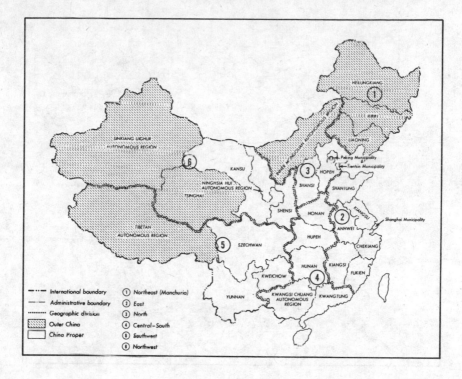

Figure 2. People's Republic of China, Major Geographic Regions.

thirteen miles; along Afghanistan, it is forty-seven miles; and along Macao, a fraction of a mile only. The coastline is almost 3,500 miles in length including islands over ten miles wide but excluding Taiwan.

Both climate and terrain are highly diversified (see fig. 3). Mainland China lies almost entirely in the temperate zone, chiefly between latitudes 30°N and 45°N, with portions of the three southernmost provinces within the tropics. Monsoonal climate is a major influence, with summers hot and humid throughout much of the country, and winters dry and unusually cool or cold for any given latitude. The concentration of rain in the summer months frequently results in torrential downpours and is a major cause of floods, which often have afflicted the country.

Mountains, hills, valleys, plains, some of the world's largest rivers, vast deserts, extensive forests, many lakes, rice paddies interlaced with canals, extensive wheat fields, and an irregular coastline all contribute to a kaleidoscopic physical environment. Mountainous uplands and plateaus account for more than half the total land area. The land slopes downward from the high plateaus and mountains of the west to the shores of the Pacific on the east, a distance of some 2,500 miles. As a result, all major river systems flow into the Pacific drainage basin.

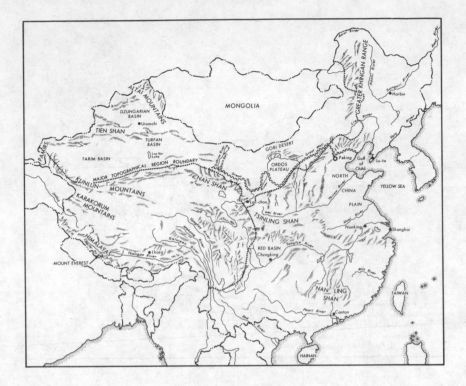

Figure 3. People's Republic of China, Topography.

Although about 94 percent of the total population are Han Chinese, there are many small minority groups; the largest groups live in autonomous areas along the frontiers (see ch. 4, Ethnic Groups and Languages). Despite the relative homogeneity of the population, many cultural and language variations exist between north and south and east and west because of physical barriers, poor transportation, and other factors, which tend to divide the people into isolated groups. One of the illustrations of this diversity best known to foreigners is the great variety to be found in the different kinds of Chinese cookery that have been developed in separate regions.

PHYSICAL GEOGRAPHY

The country can be divided into three major topographical regions: northern, western, and eastern. The northern region extends from the Pamirs and Tien Shan mountains in the west to the Greater Khingan mountains in the east and encompasses the Sinkiang Uighur Autonomous Region (Sinkiang), the upper Ninghsia Hui Autonomous Region (Ninghsia Hui), the Inner Mongolian Autonomous Region (Inner Mongolia), and northern Kansu Province. The region is one of mountain ranges, plateaus, low-lying basins—the Turfan Basin in

Sinkiang is 505 feet below sea level—and deserts. The western region is higher in elevation than the north. In the western region—encompassing the Tibetan Autonomous Region (Tibet), Tsinghai Province, and western Szechwan Province—some of the world's highest mountains ring the great Plateau of Tibet, which has a tableland over 12,000 feet high. East and southeast of the plateau are the headwaters of a number of the major rivers of China, and South and Southeast Asia. The eastern region, consisting of China Proper and Northeast China, is characterized by a landscape of fertile river valleys interrupted by low mountain ranges. In China Proper, all of the great rivers flow eastward to the sea.

There are large fertile plains, particularly in the coastal delta areas of the Liao, Yellow, Yangtze, and Pearl rivers. In between lie masses of hills and uplands, such as the Kirin hills, the uplands of the Liaotung and Shantung peninsulas, the southeastern coastal hill land, and the hills of Kwangtung-Kwangsi along the Pearl River valley. In the southwest the Yunnan-Kweichow Plateau is dissected by a number of foundered lake basins and a series of parallel longitudinal river valleys and mountain ranges.

In the northwest the natural boundaries of China are defined by the Altai mountain system and in the southwest by the Central Asian mountain ramparts that stretch from the Pamir node in Central Asia southeastward along the Himalayan system. The Tien Shan system, running eastward, divides Sinkiang into two parts. To the south, the Kunlun system, also running eastward, branches out over all the country, forming the backbone or skeleton of its topography.

Major Mountain Systems

Lofty mountain massifs and extensive plateaus cover a large part of the country, particularly in the west. There, from the Pamirs, a central mountain knot of all the mountains of Asia, four major limbs of the Central Asian ramparts extend toward mainland China. They are the Altai, Tien Shan, Kunlun, and Himalayan mountain systems. Each consists of several parallel chains, some of which branch out in sharp angles from the main system. These mountain systems form the chief watersheds of all the principal rivers in the country.

The Altai Mountains

Altai is a Mongolian word for gold, which has been found in the ancient crystalline rocks of this system. The mountains have an average height of 6,000 feet, some peaks reaching an altitude of 10,000 feet. They are separated by a series of valleys and basins that provide the basis for agricultural or pastoral economies, combined with lumbering and mining in the surrounding mountains. The mountain gaps in the ranges provide natural routes of communication between China and Mongolia and between Central Asia and Siberia.

The Tien Shan System

The Tien Shan rises abruptly to more than 12,000 feet above the foundered basins of Tarim and Dzungaria, which are situated in southern and northern Sinkiang, respectively. The system consists of a series of parallel chains, trending east to west at an average height of 12,000 feet above sea level. The general level at the foot of the mountains is about 4,000 feet. The principal peak, the Tengri Khan, in the western section, reaches 23,600 feet. The higher summits are snow covered, and at high levels some permanent glaciers exist. Although the Tien Shan does not form a continuous chain throughout, the rift found between the cities of Turfan and Urumchi provides the only natural route across the Tien Shan, between Tarim and Dzungaria, from southern to northern Sinkiang.

The Kunlun Mountains

From the Pamirs the Kunlun system runs eastward, dividing the Tarim Basin of Sinkiang from the high plateaus of Tibet; then, it branches off into three separate chains: the Astin Tagh-Nan Shan ranges in the north, which divide the inland drainage of the Mongolian Plateau from the Yellow River; the Tsinling-Ta-pieh ranges in the center, which form the major watershed between the Yellow River and the Yangtze; and the Thanglha Ri Range in the south, which meets the eastern end of the Himalayan system in western Szechwan and northwestern Yunnan provinces.

The Himalayas

From the great mountain complex of the Karakorum, where the Kunlun and the Himalayas meet the Pamirs in southeastern Tibet, the Himalayan ranges branch off toward the southeast to form a series of parallel concave arcs that rise abruptly above the southern fringe of the plateaus of Tibet until they reach the Thanglha Ri, a massif in southeastern Tibet. From there, the Himalayan chain bends sharply to the south at a right angle to form the Ta-hsueh Shan-Yun Ling system, known as the Chinese Alps.

The Himalayas consist of three gigantic highly folded parallel mountain ranges, of which the central range is the highest, having many peaks over 25,000 feet. Mount Everest, the highest peak, at 29,144 feet, forms the most formidable natural barrier between India and China. The whole width of the Himalayan system is about 300 miles from north to south, with a perpetual snowline and many glaciers among its peaks. Between the northern and central Himalayan chains are high, wide valleys containing numerous lakes and swamps with scanty vegetation. Even the grass is stunted, though occasional clusters of shrubs exist in favorable and sheltered spots.

Other Mountain Groups

In addition to the four major mountain systems, there are two groups of mountains in the northeast and southeast, close to the Pacific coast, that seem to have little relation to any of the major systems in the west. They are known as the Sinic Mountains and are peculiar to eastern China. Between the mountains of the northern group are valley plains, such as the Wei River valley, and the plain between T'ai Shan (4,635 feet) and Lao Shan (3,395 feet) in the peninsula of Shantung. The southern range, the Nan Ling Shan, forms a major geographical divide between the lower Yangtze and the various short independent streams that flow separately into the South China Sea.

Other Features

Among other physical features of the Chinese mainland, giving it a distinctive character, either because of their magnitude or of their unusual nature, is the monumental Great Wall, a manmade, mud-brick barrier stretching about 1,500 miles from the Gulf of Chihli to Kansu and Tsinghai provinces, and dating back as far as the third century B.C. The wall marks a zone of climatic transition from semihumid maritime to arid continental character.

Another conspicuous feature is the loess plateau in the western part of North China, where eroded mountains and hills over a vast area are partially covered by an extensive and deep mantle of fertile, wind-laid silts created by erosion over many centuries. The wind has transferred some of these silts to the North China Plain.

The Grand Canal is an ancient system of north to south water transport begun during the Sui dynasty (A.D. 589 to A.D. 618) to connect the Yellow, Huai, and Yangtze rivers. The canal ran from T'ung-chou, now part of Peking Municipality, to Hangchow, a distance of some 1,200 miles by the time it was finished in the Yuan dynasty more than 600 years later. It was engineered to utilize local streams and lakes, as well as canals, in a unified system of water control across the natural drainage of the North China Plain. Its southern portions are still in use as a transportation artery.

Another natural feature of the country is made up of the limestone areas of Yunnan, Kweichow, and Kwangsi. These areas lack a developed surface water supply and are deficient in good soils; whereas, they abound with caves, sinkholes, and underground watercourses. Steep-sided hills and isolated stone pinnacles are familiar themes in Chinese landscape painting.

Main Drainage Areas and Principal Rivers

Pacific Drainage Area

All the great rivers flow from west to east and belong to the Pacific drainage basin, which accounts for 50 percent of the country's total drainage area. In the northeast the Amur (Heilung) River drains a large part of the Manchurian Plain in its winding course of over 2,500 miles. From its headwaters in northeastern Mongolia, it flows eastward to form the frontier between the Soviet Far East and Manchuria as far as Khabarovsk. Navigation is limited to small steamers and native craft, which can go as far as the confluence of its two upper reaches and even beyond during the flood season. The chief tributary of the Amur is the Sungari, which receives the Nonni River west of Harbin. Together, they drain the core area of the great plain of Manchuria, and a large part of their course is navigable by steamer.

Other rivers include the Liao, the chief river in southern Manchuria, as well as the Tumen and the Yalu, which form the boundary between China and North Korea. The importance of the Yalu lies primarily in hydroelectric power development and in the timber rafts plying its course.

The main river of North China is the Yellow River, the second largest in the country. After it enters Kansu Province, it receives the tributary rivers of a loess plateau, which gives it a yellowish, muddy color and, thus, its name. Winding through the northern provinces from Kansu eastward to Shantung Province, where it empties into the Gulf of Chihli, the Yellow River is 2,980 miles long and drains an area of 600,000 square miles.

The course of the Yellow River can be divided into upper, middle, and lower sections. The upper section, from its source in the uplands of Tsinghai to the mountain massif of southeastern Kansu, is the torrential section, where the gradient of the riverbed drops over 10,000 feet. The course is full of rapids, and upstream navigation is practically impossible. The river's importance at this section lies in irrigation by means of big waterwheels pushed by the flow of the river.

The middle section of the Yellow River, from Kansu to Shensi provinces, forms the great northern bend around the Ordos Plateau. The river first flows through a fairly flat and open valley along the western and northern sides of the Ordos. It is navigable over this stretch for more than 400 miles, and irrigation has been developed quite extensively in some parts. Its lower part, however, between Shansi and Shensi provinces on the eastern side of the Ordos, is not navigable as it flows through a rift valley with many gorges, rapids, and waterfalls. Although there is no possibility of shipping and irrigation, there are some good sites for the development of hydroelectric powerplants, especially at Chi-k'ou, Hu-k'ou, and Lung-men, the three renowned gorges along the rift.

The lower section of the Yellow River begins below T'ung-kuan in Shensi Province and flows through the core area of the North China Plain. At T'ung-kuan the riverbed drops to just above 1,000 feet above sea level, but it soon debouches into the vast flat plain of North

China, where it continues with an average drop of only 1 foot per mile until it empties into the sea. Because of the small change in level, its sediment-transporting capacity is suddenly checked. The heavy load of sand and mud brought down from the middle and upper courses begins to be deposited along its lower course, resulting in ever-increasing silt along the bed. The flow is channeled mainly by a continuous buildup of the embankments along the river; consequently, the present riverbed is 16 feet or more above the general level of the plain, and the river actually flows within manmade embankments on a raised ridge, instead of in a degraded valley controlled by natural levees. As a result of this peculiar feature, floods and course changes have been constant phenomena, particularly during the rainy season in late summer and early autumn, and no important towns have grown up along its banks. The river has practically no tributaries along its lower section through the vast area of the North China Plain.

The Huai, the largest river between the Yangtze and the Yellow rivers, is unique in that it is the only long river without a natural outlet. Hence, it is particularly susceptible to floods, which have occurred quite often and have caused much serious damage.

Sixty percent of China Proper is drained by the Yangtze and its numerous tributaries. The main course of the Yangtze, by far the largest river, is 3,237 miles long and drains an area of over 700,000 square miles. Its source is only 50 miles from that of the Yellow River. From the confluence of its two headwaters in the upland of southern Tsinghai, it flows southward to western Szechwan under the name of Chin-sha River. After winding through a great bend in northwestern Yunnan Province, it then turns sharply to the east and traverses the whole width of South China until it empties into the East China Sea.

Like the Yellow River, the Yangtze can be divided into three parts: torrential, seminavigable, and navigable. The torrential upper course, from the river's source to P'ing-shan in southern Szechwan, includes many rapids and falls, and the flow is too great to permit navigation. The middle course, from P'ing-shan to I'ch'ang in Hopeh Province, is considered seminavigable for 960 miles. Although navigation is possible through the Wu Shan Gorges, it is risky during the flood season because of dangerous rapids and submerged rocky points. Navigation on this stretch is limited to specially made river steamers, propelled from the front, with small loading capacities of at most about 200 metric tons. The lower course, covering a distance of 1,062 miles from I'ch'ang to the sea, is navigable for both coastal and oceangoing vessels. It flows through a series of low, flat lake basins and marshes, which act as reservoirs in time of flood. Close to its mouth, the Yangtze is divided into two channels by Ch'ung-ming Island. The southern channel, known as Woosung, has a deeper entrance and is closer to Shanghai, the leading port of China, from which oceangoing vessels can sail to Hankow, 630 miles inland. The Yangtze has twenty to twenty-five times the annual runoff of the Yellow River.

Among the important rivers that drain the southeastern coastal regions is the Min. It is navigable over most of its course, although upstream navigation is difficult during the flood season. At the mouth of the river, near Foochow, numerous islands are found along the coast, including the Matsu group, somewhat farther out.

The Pearl River, the chief river in Kwangtung Province, is a general name for a network of three waterways: the Tung (East), the Pei (North), and the Hsi (West) rivers. These meet south of Canton to form a big estuary consisting of many channels separated by a number of islets. The main eastern channel, the Hu Men River, enters the sea near Hong Kong, and the main western channel flows close to Macao. The Pearl is the country's fourth largest river, draining an area of 150,000 square miles. The Hsi River, the largest of its three branches, has a total length of about 1,300 miles and is especially important for transportation in Kwangsi and its neighboring areas.

Farther southwest are two independent rivers, whose upper courses only are in Chinese territory. These are the Mekong and the Red rivers, both of which flow southward before they finally enter the sea in the Republic of Vietnam (South Vietnam) and the Democratic Republic of Vietnam (North Vietnam), respectively. Because of steep gorges and fast-flowing waters, they are not navigable inside mainland China.

Other Drainage Areas

Inland drainage accounts for 39 percent of the country's total drainage area, and the Arctic and the Indian drainage make up 5 and 6 percent, respectively. The only Arctic drainage in mainland China is through the upper Irtysh River (a major tributary of the Ob River). Fairly long stretches of the upper tributaries of the principal rivers of the Indian drainage are inside the country, but these rivers enter the sea through other nations' territories. The Salween, the Irrawaddy, and the Tsangpo rivers all have their sources in the mountainous regions of Tibet and western Szechwan. The Tsangpo flows eastward from its Himalayan home to drain southern Tibet; it then bends abruptly south to India, where, under the name of Brahmaputra, it merges with the Ganges River to empty into the Bay of Bengal. The upper courses of both the Salween and Irrawaddy drain a large portion of western Yunnan Province before they reach the sea by way of Burma.

The inland drainage covers a number of upland basins in the vast, dry interior of northern China. Because of the meager rainfall and the difficult terrain, most inland rivers are small and lack outlets to the sea. They generally flow into lakes or gradually die in the desert. Most of them are entirely inside China. The Tarim, the longest inland river in the country, is fed by numerous mountain streams coming down from the Tien Shan, Pamir, and Kunlun ranges in southern Sinkiang. The O-chi-na River in Inner Mongolia is similarly formed by many mountain streams from the Nan Shan in Kansu. A few inland rivers end in other countries, such as the Ili, which flows into Lake Balkhash in Soviet Central Asia.

Although the inland rivers are valuable for irrigation in the dry interior of northern and northwestern China, water from the snowclad mountains is limited. On the other hand, the upper courses of the Red, Mekong, Salween, and Irrawaddy rivers provide potential sources for the development of waterpower in the plateaus of southwestern China. The many torrents and rapids, especially in the summer monsoon season, make navigation impossible. No transportation is available along their courses except on some parts of the upper Red River, the upper Irrawaddy, and the east-west stretch of the Tsangpo River, where small native craft are sometimes seen. At 12,000 feet, the Tsangpo is the highest navigable river in the world.

Coastline and Harbors

The coastline extends in a great arc from the mouth of the Yalu River in the northeast to the mouth of the Pei-lun River in the south, the peninsulas of Liaotung and Shantung in the north and that of Liuchow in the south, protruding into the Yellow Sea and the South China Sea, respectively. The coastline is separated from the Pacific Ocean by a series of islands and archipelagoes, such as the Ryukyus, Taiwan (Chinese name for Formosa), Pescadores (P'eng-hu), Hainan, and the Pratas, Paracel, and Spratly groups. This chain of islands gives mainland China a continuous series of partially enclosed coastal seas—such as the Gulf of Chihli, the Yellow Sea, the East China Sea, and the South China Sea.

About two-fifths of the coast is sandy. These coasts occur principally north of Hangchow Bay, where they are broken only by rocky coasts along the Shantung and Liaotung peninsulas. Smooth coasts also are found to the west of Canton. Such coasts are characterized by regular curves, wide beaches, and a relatively low, flat, and straight shoreline formed mainly out of recent deposits. The country behind the sandy coast is usually low flatland with marshes and lakes. The nearby sea is lined with shoals, and, except at the mouth of the big rivers, there is a lack of good natural harbors. Shanghai, located where the Whangpoo flows into the big estuary of the Yangtze, is an example of such a natural harbor where the river channel is deep enough for large boats.

In contrast, the rocky coasts, constituting about three-fifths of the coastline, are often highly indented with numerous islands and islets along the shore. The land behind them ranges from hilly to mountainous. Along the main rocky coast in southern Chekiang, Fukien, and northern Kwangtung—the parallel northeast to southwest mountain ranges are dissected by transverse rivers. The coasts are bordered by fairly deep seas, conditions that create many good natural harbors, but the characteristics of the hinterlands, which make overland transportation difficult, limit their exploitation. The chief ports along this coast are situated at or near the mouths of the large rivers and include Foochow, Amoy, and Swatow; Canton is the most important southern port.

Ports of importance along the rocky coast in north and northeast China include Antung, at the mouth of the Yalu River, and Lu-shun (Port Arthur) and Lu-ta (Dairen), on the Liaotung Peninsula. Lu-shun is the leading naval base, and Lu-ta, the chief commercial port of Northeast China. Developed ports along the Shantung coast include Chefoo, on the north; Wei-hai-wei, not far from the tip of the peninsula; Tsingtao, lying on its southernmost part at the entrance to the almost-closed Chiao-chou Bay and linked by rail to the north and south trunkline of the Tientsin-Nanking Railroad.

Climate

Extending from latitude 18°N to 54°N (although lying chiefly between latitudes 30°N and 45°N) and with great altitudinal and longitudinal range, the country has great climatic contrasts, especially in regard to length and severity of the cold season and in regard to the amount and distribution of rainfall. The north is much colder than the south in winter, has long, dry winters, and much of its rainfall is received in a short span in summer. The northwest experiences great seasonal extremes of hot and cold, and there is little rainfall and some desert. In the lower Yangtze Valley, winters may have snow but are shorter and milder than in the north. There is more rainfall, and it is more evenly distributed. In the tropical and subtropical coastal area, annual rainfall is high; the winters are relatively warm but dry. Yunnan and part of Szechwan provinces have distinctive climates. Yunnan, though partly in the tropics, has a temperate climate on its plateau, and the Red Basin of Szechwan Province, being protected by mountains on the north, has a moist, warm climate throughout the year.

In winter, temperatures decrease rapidly from south to north. Average temperatures decline from 60°F, south of the Nan Ling Range, to about 40°F, along the middle and lower Yangtze Valley; and about 30°F, in central Manchuria, to 17°F, in northern Manchuria. In summer the temperature is more uniform throughout the country, with a July mean of 80°F, but northern mainland China has much cooler nights and a shorter hot period than the southern regions.

Most rainfall occurs in summer, when the hot, moist air blows gently from the ocean toward the warm interior. Because of the topographical configuration, the amount of precipitation decreases from the south to the north, with an annual average of sixty to eighty inches in the Hsi River valley and the hilly land along the southeastern coast, forty to sixty inches in the Yangtze Valley, and about twenty-five inches over the North China Plain. Southeastern Manchuria has about thirty inches of rain (see fig. 4). Precipitation drops sharply northwestward to less than ten inches in the interior. The late summer rain along the southeastern coast of the country is caused mostly by typhoon influence. Typhoons are also responsible for some cooling and provide a temporary relief from the prolonged summer heat, but they cause damage to crops and also affect types of crops planted. (For example, peanuts and sweet potatoes are grown along the· southeastern coast because the typhoons would damage high-standing crops.)

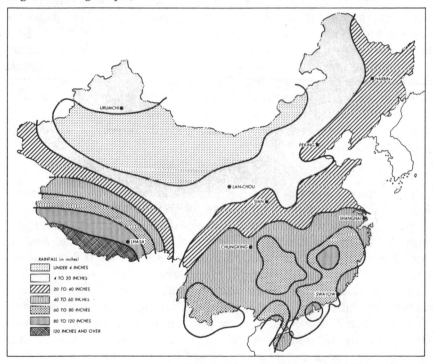

Figure 4.   People's Republic of China, Average Annual Rainfall.

Soils

The soils can be classified into three main groups: the sweet soil of the north; the acid soil of the south; and the neutral, only slightly acid

23

soil of the central part. Because of the flat topography, low annual rainfall, and limited irrigation, the northern region has unleached or slightly leached soils rich in mineral plant food but with little organic matter. The farmers have to apply humus regularly to maintain soil fertility. On the other hand, the acid soil of the south is subject to leaching because of its hilly terrain and abundant rainfall and is generally poor. The deltaic plains, both north and south, are only slightly leached; they contain a fair percentage of calcium and other soluble minerals and are quite fertile.

In general, the northern region with nonacid soil represents the wheat area, and the acid-soil region, the rice area. The belt of neutral, slightly acid soil—western Hupeh, southern Shantung, the Yangtze Delta, and northern Szechwan—is a transitional zone of wheat and rice, the two major crops.

The productivity of the land depends more upon the climate than on the fertility of the soil. For climatic reasons more crops are raised in the southern regions, where the soil is poor, than in the northern areas, where the soil is rich. Broadly speaking, the productivity of the land determines the distribution of the population. The populous areas are the valley plains of the winter wheat and millet area (the loess plateau in the northwest part of the country), the winter wheat and kaoliang area (the North China Plain and Shantung Highland), the Szechwan ricegrowing area (Red Basin), the rice and wheat area (the lower Yangtze Valley Plain), and the double-cropping rice area of the Canton Delta. The Yangtze Delta and the Red Basin of Szechwan, which have slightly leached and weak acid soils, are the most densely populated areas.

Minerals

The country's mineral wealth is impressive. Nearly all minerals are found within the extensive boundaries of the country, most of them in appreciable quantities. In coal mainland China ranks third in the world with reserves totaling one-tenth of those of the United States, one-fifth of those of the Soviet Union, and one-third of those of Canada. Its known reserves of petroleum are reported to be extensive, and new sources are being discovered. Reserves of tungsten, manganese, antimony, and tin are large. Uranium has been reported in many parts of the country, mostly in the northeast and northwest. Other metals present in appreciable quantities are aluminum, mercury, molybdenum, magnesium, sulfur, and bismuth. Chromium, nickel, cobalt, silver, and platinum are almost completely absent (see ch. 15, Industry).

Flora and Fauna

The vast extent, climatic range, and varied terrain of mainland China have produced a complex array of flora and fauna, including species unique to that country. Natural cover ranges from swamps to rain forests and from barren, rocky tundra and desert to tropical vegetation. Broadly speaking, the country is dominated by grasslands and desert in the northwest and extensive woodlands in the southeast.

Some species of animals that have become extinct elsewhere have survived in mainland China, such as the great paddlefish of the Yangtze River and the giant salamander found in the western part of the country. Along the Tibetan border the giant panda is to be found, as are the goat antelope, numerous species of pheasants, and many rare species of other birds. Carp and catfish are among the most common fresh-water food fish. In the extreme southern provinces animal life includes tropical reptiles, amphibians, birds, and mammals.

POLITICAL DIVISIONS

The country, as of late 1971, was divided for administrative purposes into twenty-one provinces, five autonomous regions, and three special municipalities that had essentially the status of provinces. Provinces were subdivided into intermediate level districts (*chuan-ch'u*) that in turn were composed of counties (*hsien*). Below the county level were the People's Communes and areas designated as towns. Provincially administered minicipalities (*shih*) also were found. Some provinces had autonomous districts or counties that were given this special status because ethnic minorities were concentrated there.

The administrative structure generally showed a trend during the 1960s toward standardization and simplification, apparently to strengthen and increase the effectiveness of central control—the Cultural Revolution had an important impact on this structure but the effects, if any, were not known. At the county level little change appears to have occurred, the number in 1971 being about 2,200 for the whole country. An unknown number of new districts was reported set up; presumably these were related to the population growth. The number of such intermediate districts and their equivalents totaled perhaps close to 200 in the early 1970s. Adjustments in the boundaries of first order administrative units were minor until about 1969, when Kansu Province and the three northeastern provinces of Heilungkiang, Kirin, and Liaoning were enlarged at the expense of Inner Mongolia. Information available in late 1971 indicated that Ninghsia Hui had also been enlarged. The divisions in the autonomous regions were similar to those of the provinces.

POPULATION

In the absence of official census figures or even firm estimates by the communist regime, students of the China mainland were forced in

1971 to rely chiefly on educated guesses as to the population of the country and its growth rate. Estimates by 1970 ranged from a low of 720 million to as high as 840 million. The variations were produced chiefly by differing estimates as to the accuracy of the last published census (1953) and differing analyses of vital statistics, as well as the impact of famine and other factors.

Within the range given are estimates made by the United Nations (UN), the United States Bureau of the Census, the United States Department of State, publications within the Republic of China on Taiwan, Japanese sinologists, and Chinese Communist propaganda broadcasts and press releases. The difference between the higher and lower estimates is greater than the population of Japan, Indonesia, or Pakistan; but most authorities, including the Chinese, are in general agreement that the natural increase has been running at 2 to 2.5 percent a year since about 1965. This rate, if continued, would mean a doubling of the population in about twenty-seven to thirty-six years. One United States government estimate placed the birth rate for 1969 at 42.7 per 1,000 and the death rate at 20.6 per 1,000—a natural increase for that year of 22.1 per 1,000. Some other demographers regarded this as much too high an estimate for births. Men reportedly outnumbered women by nearly 3 percent in that year based on the same estimate.

The Chinese growth rate is believed to have exceeded 2 percent in most years after 1953, except from 1959 to 1961, when poor harvests presumably reduced it. The official report of the 1953 census showed a population of 583 million in the PRC and a "total population" of Chinese, including those living in Taiwan or overseas (almost all in Asia), of nearly 602 million. The last detailed population report from Peking covered the period through the end of 1957, at which time the population of the PRC was estimated at 650 million. Detailed monitoring of Peking announcements from 1967 through 1970 showed a total of 730 million in the PRC toward the end of the latter year, but this is without adjustment for the natural increase during the three-year period of the survey (see table 1).

Students of mainland China estimate that the country's population already had reached some 65 million by the late fourteenth century and nearly 150 million by 1600. It may have been 313 million at the time of the American Revolutionary War. Because of the rising population, living standards began to fall, as the nation struggled increasingly to meet expenses.

When the PRC ordered the first modern census in 1953, the results were surprising, not only to the Chinese, but to foreign observers as well. This census is the base point for most current estimates and projections of mainland China's population; these, in turn, are used in many economic analyses in which population is a variable. There is considerable evidence that the 1953 census was understated by a

Table 1. People's Republic of China, Population Estimates, 1967–70

Administrative Divisions	Population (in millions)	Date of Estimate *
Peking Municipality	7.8	August 3, 1968
Tientsin Municipality	4.0	May 22
Hopeh	43.0	February 5, 1968
Shansi	20.0	November 9
Inner Mongolian Autonomous Region	13.6	January 12, 1968
Liaoning	28.6	September 7, 1968
Kirin	20.0	May 23
Heilungkiang	25.0	October 1
Shensi	21.0	September 1
Kansu	13.0	October 5
Tsinghai	2.0	September 9, 1967
Ninghsia Hui Autonomous Region	2.6	February 4, 1968
Sinkiang Uighur Autonomous Region	8.0	October 1
Shanghai Municipality	10.0	July 21
Shantung	57.0	February 10
Kiangsu	47.0	September 12
Anhwei	35.0	July 17
Chekiang	31.0	October 3
Kiangsi	25.0	September 10
Fukien	18.0	October 1, 1969
Honan	50.0	July 31
Hupeh	32.0	April 1
Hunan	38.0	July 17
Kwangtung	42.0	May 28
Kwangsi Chuang Autonomous Region	24.0	July 31
Szechwan	70.0	May 25
Kweichow	20.0	May 23
Yunnan	23.0	May 23
Tibetan Autonomous Region	1.3	October 7
TOTAL	731.9	

* All years are 1970 unless otherwise indicated.

Source: Adapted from China News Summary [Hong Kong], No. 346, November 19, 1970.

significant percentage. The higher estimates for current and projected population proceed from this assumption, whereas the lower ones in general take the census at nearer face value.

Structure

The 1953 census made by the PRC government showed a ratio of over 107 males to 100 females. Some demographers believe the number of females may have been understated. The census also indicated that the population was relatively young, with 15.6 percent under five years of age; 20.3 percent between five and fifteen; 17.3

percent between fifteen and twenty-five; 14.6 percent between twenty-five and thirty-five; 12 percent between thirty-five and forty-five; and 20.2 percent, forty-five or over. By 1966 United States official estimates concluded that about one-half of the population was under twenty years of age.

The United States Department of Commerce estimated in 1968 that the age ratios of the Chinese population would remain fairly stable for some years. It foresaw a range of 36 to 40 percent for the age group under fifteen by 1986, whereas the population between ages fifteen and fifty-nine (which had accounted for between 56 and 57 percent of the total in 1953) was estimated to be at 54 to 57 percent by 1986. The proportion of the population over age sixty was expected to rise from a 1953 range of 5.1 to 6.7 percent to a 5 to 7.3 percent range in 1986. An estimated 28 million to 33 million men were in the prime military age group (eighteen to twenty-two) in 1953, and this number was expected to grow to 65 million by 1986. Economic and educational demands, however, would, as a practical matter, reduce the available military manpower pool substantially.

Distribution of Ethnic Groups

The majority group was the Han Chinese who, according to the 1953 census, constituted about 94 percent of the total population. The remaining 6 percent was made up of various national minorities. The ten ethnic groups with more than 1 million people each were the Mongols, the Hui, the Manchus, the Koreans, the Tibetans, the Uighurs, the Miao, the Yi (Lolo), the Chuang, and the Puyi. The others ranged from less than 1 million to a few thousand (see ch. 4, Ethnic Groups and Languages). Though their numbers are small, the territories in which these ethnic groups live, situated as they are in the vast regions along mainland China's borders, constitute over one-half of the country.

There is considerable variation in the degree to which minority groups have been assimilated. The regime has established controls to keep most of them politically impotent. The most extreme of these measures is the military occupation imposed on Tibet after some 2 million Tibetans rebelled in 1959. There are more Mongols in mainland China than in the independent Mongolian People's Republic on the country's border, but the two groups are politically and physically separated. Three of the largest groups—the Chuang, the Hui, and the Manchus—have become so sinicized that they constitute mere regional and local groupings of Chinese who bear political and social encumbrances of a minority ethnic background.

The Muslims of Sinkiang have traditional affinities with other Turkic-speaking Muslim peoples in Soviet Central Asia, and there is mutual suspicion between them and the PRC regime. Some hill-dwelling southern peoples have avoided assimilation, and their position on the Szechwan, Yunnan, and Kwangsi borders has made them, to some extent, open to outside influence because of the presence of related peoples on the other side. The 1.5 million Koreans in the northeast adjoining North Korea have ties with that country and are resistant to assimilation.

Migrations: External and Internal

The Chinese have a fond attachment to their ancestral homesteads and family traditions, which tends to keep population mobility at a minimum—a tendency reinforced by poor transportation facilities. In past centuries, civil wars, foreign invasions, and natural calamities, such as floods and pestilence, occasionally sent large groups of homeless refugees wandering from one part of the country to another in search of food and shelter. Sometimes economic inducement and the lure of official promotion also prompted the young and able bodied to seek their fortunes in the big cities. On the whole, however, the percentage of such voluntary migrations was small, and, more often than not, such migrants returned eventually to their native villages.

There were three major population movements in the twentieth century before 1949. First, there was a rural-to-urban movement that had been in progress for several decades and became intensified as a result of the growth of the treaty ports into such modern cities as Shanghai, Tientsin, Hankow, and Canton. Because of the steady inflow of foreign capital; the establishment of factories, schools, and modern communications systems; the concentration of banking and other financial institutions; and the protection that the foreign concessions provided for their inhabitants during the time of China's numerous civil wars, these port cities grew rapidly in size and population. A continual stream of migrants from the villages poured into these metropolitan centers to swell the urban population.

There was also migration of the people from the thickly settled agricultural communities to the frontier regions of Northeast China, Inner Mongolia, and Northwest China. These movements started in the late nineteenth century, when the rich unexplored natural resources and the uncultivated arable lands of Manchuria seemed to offer manifold opportunities to migrants from the northern provinces of Shantung, Honan, and Hopeh; peasants from these hard-pressed northern areas were forced to leave their small farmholdings to venture abroad. As soon as restrictions on migration were removed in the last years of the Manchu dynasty, large groups of Chinese peasants from these northern provinces flocked to Northeast China to cultivate its fertile soil and to settle down as agricultural colonists.

As a result of this rapid increase in population, large cities began to grow in Northeast China during the early years of the republic. The Japanese invasion and occupation of Manchuria (in the 1931–45 period) put a halt temporarily to the Chinese migration, but it was resumed after World War II. Some migration also took place during this time to undeveloped arable lands in the northwest.

Between 1860 and 1930 there was widespread emigration from the southern coastal areas to many less populous lands, to Southeast Asia. These immigrants almost universally hoped to return after they had achieved financial success in their new country, where they considered themselves to be merely transients. Nearly all Chinese not living in the PRC live in Asia. As of the end of 1968, within Asia (excluding Taiwan), 77 percent of the Chinese lived in Southeast Asia (see table 2). Ninety percent of Overseas Chinese came originally from the provinces of Fukien and Kwangtung.

Table 2. People's Republic of China, Distribution of Overseas Chinese in Asia, Late 1968

Area	Chinese Population *
Southeast Asia	
Laos	90,700
Philippines	136,641
South Vietnam	1,180,000
Cambodia	260,000
Thailand	4,000,000
Burma	450,000
Malaysia	3,712,183
Singapore	1,499,800
Brunei	40,000
Indonesia	2,750,000
Portuguese Timor	10,000
Subtotal	14,129,324
Other	
Japan	50,445
South Korea	30,810
Okinawa	2,068
Hong Kong	3,892,070
Macao	190,000
Subtotal	4,165,393
TOTAL	18,294,717

* Estimated.

Source: Adapted from Ajia Chosakai (ed.), *Chugoku Soran, 1971* (Survey of China, 1971), Tokyo, 1971, p. 238.

Since the establishment of the PRC, the nature of the internal migration movement has changed. A systematic effort is being made by the government to reverse the rural-urban trend by forcing the unproductive city dwellers to return to the countryside (see ch. 5, Social System and Values). There is also a definite government policy to colonize the frontier regions of Outer China, to use the colonized people in large-scale construction work and industrial projects, and to deal with the population pressure in overcrowded cities and congested agricultural areas by moving a portion of the surplus population to the sparsely settled regions in the west. In addition to economic inducements, it uses mass persuasion, patriotic appeals, and pressure.

Although rural hardship had led to considerable migration to urban areas from agricultural areas in the first decade of Chinese Communist rule, policies of the regime have subsequently reversed this trend. From 1949 to 1959 the urban population increased at an average annual rate of 8 percent but, in the ensuing decade, city population declined at an average annual rate of between 1 and 2 percent.

In addition to directing these internal population movements, the government has also been active in an effort to facilitate the homeward journey of the Overseas Chinese, particularly those who are well established and influential in their own communities. These people are important in the communist propaganda efforts to win the loyalty of the Nationalist Chinese in Taiwan. Among those who have heeded either the appeal of the mother country or the attraction of official positions are educated persons, engineers, and technicians who have been trained in their respective foreign countries and who find useful employment in the industrial development of the country. A sizable number of young men and women have returned to mainland China for advanced education; there are also many small businessmen who have been lured to return with promises of financial rewards. Despite complaints by those who have gone back and experienced the communist way of life, movements for such migration have been widespread in all Southeast Asian countries, particularly in Singapore, Thailand, Burma, Indonesia, and the Philippines.

Population Planning

During its first years the government showed little official concern for the population size, claiming that a large population was a source of national strength and favorable to socialist construction. When the 1953 census showed 583 million persons within the country's borders, it actually pointed with pride to the total, indicating that no problems were envisioned in feeding and caring for them. Shortly after the census, however, public discussion of birth control and planned childbirth began and continued throughout 1954 and 1955. Evidence of increasing official sanction culminated in the August 1956 directive of the Ministry of Public Health, which instructed all health officers to meet popular demands for birth control information.

The first important family planning campaign began in 1956. It consisted of centrally organized propaganda efforts, including films, posters, and public meetings, and efforts to increase the availability of contraceptives. The campaign reached its high point in 1957. Planned parenthood was well received by the better educated and by the cadres (see Glossary) but was generally rejected by the largely illiterate rural population and poorly educated urban factory workers. One obstacle encountered by the campaign was the prevalence of old values in the group then in the peak reproductive years. During 1957 Party opponents of the program, who looked on population limitation as a hindrance to socialist economic progress, took advantage of its poor acceptance to voice gradually stronger criticisms. By late 1957 a change in official attitudes was apparent; the dictum that a large population was an asset was again affirmed in 1958 as the Party line in statements by Mao Tse-tung that a large population was a good thing.

Suggestions have been advanced that the end to the program (in 1958) was also associated with anticipated manpower requirements to be generated by the Great Leap Forward, which began in 1958, and optimism that the Great Leap would make concern with population unnecessary. During the Great Leap period, from 1958 to 1961, however, despite the absence of official approval, limited birth control efforts apparently continued (mainly in the urban centers). Occasional articles providing advice on birth control appeared in the press, and birth control devices could be freely purchased. During this time no restrictions seemed to have been placed on sterilizations or abortions, and birth control devices and medicines were allowed to enter the country duty free.

Three years of poor crops and near famine conditions during the Great Leap period apparently caused renewed concern over population growth and were followed by a renewed and much more vigorous population control effort also mainly in urban areas. Large numbers of Party activists were utilized to disperse birth control propaganda. Social pressures were applied to secure conformity with the official norm, which called for late marriage, a three-year interval between marriage and the first birth, similar intervals between all births thereafter, and small-sized completed families. One propaganda slogan was "Two children is just right, three is too many, and four is a mistake." In some localities, sanctions were reportedly taken against workers who married early or had more than two children; these ranged from denial of ration cards to dismissal from government jobs. Abortion was made more widely available, and male sterilization was encouraged for those with two or three children. As a whole, however, the campaign was more successful in the cities.

In rural areas a new, although indirect, impetus to planned parenthood and birth control was given by Mao's call in mid-1965 for expansion of medical care in those areas. There was a subsequent setting up of mobile medical teams; by December 1965 more than 1,000 such teams were reported (see ch. 7, Living Conditions). The large-scale shift of doctors and medical personnel to rural areas during the Cultural Revolution—particularly after 1967—and the training of large numbers of persons as "barefoot doctors" (paramedical workers, mostly peasants) for rural service further increased the dissemination of birth control knowledge to the countryside, as well as providing the personnel to actually carry out abortions, sterilization, and insertions of birth control devices.

The propaganda and sanctions associated with the second population control campaign were interrupted by the Cultural Revolution in 1966; however, contraceptives, sterilization, and abortions continued to be available without restrictions. After 1968—a year reportedly of record population growth in the PRC—the government actively reasserted itself in pushing population control. Many features of the earlier 1962–66 campaigns were revived. Apparently a very sophisticated contraceptive pill was being manufactured and distributed free at the beginning of the 1970s on an unprecedented scale; a once-a-month pill was also reported in use in some regions. Abortion was being widely performed by the relatively quick and painless vacuum method and at the request of the mother alone. Many women, who were expected to be full participants in society—in politics, in acquiring education, in work—appeared to feel that large families were a burden to be avoided (see ch. 5, Social System and Values).

In 1971, although the Party line apparently still backed the large population concept, there was strong evidence that the government was encouraging birth control without resorting to extensive publicity. This effort appeared to encompass only the Han Chinese. Information available in 1971 indicated that birth control and planned parenthood had not been introduced among the minority peoples (see ch. 4, Ethnic Groups and Languages).

Official data on birth control results on a national scale were not available. A commune in the Shanghai area visited by Western newsmen in 1971 had reported a birth rate between 1.5 and 1.7 percent. A female member of a production team (see Glossary) stated that all married women within her team used some form of birth control. In 1969 the birth rate in Peking was estimated to be 1.6 percent and 3 percent for the city of Sian.

CHAPTER 3

HISTORICAL SETTING

Although earlier civilizations have existed elsewhere and become extinct, China has the world's oldest continuous history and civilization. Samples of archaic Chinese writing, out of which the modern written language evolved, have been found dating back to the second millennium B.C. When those words were written, Chinese civilization—at that time confined to the Yellow River valley of North China—had already acquired many of its distinctive and enduring characteristics (see ch. 8, Education, Intellectual Expression, and the Arts).

The Chinese always have been history minded and have kept voluminous records since very early times. It is largely as a result of these records that information concerning the ancient past, not only of China but also of the rest of Asia, has survived.

Chinese history, until the twentieth century, was written by members of the ruling class and was meant primarily to provide the ruler with established precedents to guide or justify his policies. The official historians confined their accounts almost exclusively to events pertaining to the king or emperor and to the relatively small circle of people with whom the ruler dealt. Their histories told of a succession of dynasties, each one following a cyclical pattern of rising, flourishing, decaying, and falling.

The official historians had a duty to make their history serve the dynasty that patronized them. Nonetheless, they were expected to be accurate and impartial, not mere propagandists. Since the communist takeover, historians in China have been expressly instructed to write history that serves the purposes of the regime. Since 1949 the character of historical writing in the People's Republic of China (PRC) has changed drastically, reflecting the substitution of Marxism-Leninism-Maoism for the traditional Confucian ideology that had provided the philosophic underpinning of the dynastic histories.

In the attempt by communist historians to make Chinese history fit into the authorized Marxist pattern of progression—from primitive communism to slavery to feudalism to capitalism to socialism—most of the imperial period has been termed feudal and given scant attention. The little that has been written by Chinese Marxists about the imperial period (which lasted, with brief interruptions, from 212 B.C. to A.D. 1911) has emphasized the activities of, and conditions among, the common people. The imperial historians had concentrated almost exclusively upon the political elite. The chief concern of the Marxist historians has been the role of the class struggle in China's evolution and, therefore, attention has been focused on peasant uprisings during the imperial period.

Of various recurrent patterns identified by independent historians, an important one has been the tendency of the Chinese to absorb into their civilization the people of contiguous areas by the superiority of their technology, by the refinement of their artistic and intellectual achievement, and by the weight of their numbers. This process continued until virtually all of what is now known as China Proper (see Glossary) had become Chinese and the people of the periphery, especially the Koreans, Japanese, and Vietnamese, had become deeply influenced by Chinese civilization.

A theme related to this tendency of the Chinese to absorb neighboring peoples has been the great and ever-increasing size of China's population. From an estimated 65 million in the late fourteenth century, 150 million in 1600, and 430 million in 1850, the population by 1971 had grown to approximately 800 million, or one-quarter of the world's population. The great size of the country's population and, in particular, the dense settlement over many centuries of the North China Plain and the Yangtze Delta have greatly influenced China's history and society (see ch. 5, Social System and Values).

Another recurrent theme has been the struggle of the Chinese people, who have always been primarily sedentary and agrarian, to deal with the threat posed to their safety and their way of life by predatory foreigners. At first the chief threat came from nomadic tribesmen from the steppes of northern and northwestern Asia, but later it came from traders and missionaries from the Near East and Europe and eventually from modern business, missionary, and military personnel from Europe, America, and Japan.

For thousands of years virtually all of the foreigners that the Chinese ruling class saw came from the less developed societies along China's land borders, and this conditioned the rulers' view of the outside world. For millennia China saw itself as the self-sufficient Middle Kingdom (Chung-kuo—the traditional Chinese name for China), surrounded on all sides by so-called barbarian peoples whose cultures were demonstrably inferior by Chinese standards.

By the time of the first serious confrontation with men from the Western world, China had long taken for granted that it alone was civilized, that its empire included "all under heaven," and that all relations between China and foreigners should be conducted according to the prescribed pattern of patronage and tribute that had evolved over the centuries to govern relations between the emperor and representatives of the lesser states on China's borders. Since the mid-nineteenth century China has been engaged in an effort to reassess its position in respect to Western civilization and to determine what aspects of that civilization could be usefully adapted to serve China's needs. The millennia-old dynastic system of government was brought down in 1911 by its inability to successfully make this reassessment and readjustment.

One historical question about which there has been much debate and little agreement is: to what degree the People's Republic of China has elements of continuity with China's past and to what degree it represents a break with that past. Given the length and breadth of China's history, it is possible for historical antecedents to be found for many contemporary events and conditions. For example, there can be noted since 1949: the persistence of the tendency of Chinese rulers to impose centralized control rather than permit much regional autonomy; the tendency of the rights of the individual to always be subordinated to the needs of the state; and the tendency of the government to seek to control the economy and to keep it subordinate to political and social spheres of activity. The tendency of the communist government to promote an orthodox doctrine that is used to justify and explain policy is also cited by historians.

It is also possible to find many contemporary elements that are without precedent. The denigration of the family and of the past and the admiration of youth, of dynamic change, and of the common man and his work are total reversals of traditional Chinese values. The technological capability of the government—its ability to exert effective control over all of the people at the grassroots level—is also a significant departure from the past.

THE ANCIENT DYNASTIES

Chinese tradition traces civilization back to P'an Ku, the creator, the first in a succession of divine and semidivine beings who taught men the essential skills. Then came a train of legendary rulers, beginning with Huang Ti (the Yellow Emperor), who is alleged to be the progenitor of the Chinese people. Among Huang Ti's successors, the best known are Yao and Shun, who are considered model rulers and whose reigns constituted a golden age. They are reputed to have governed wisely and well, and they also chose the ablest and most virtuous men, rather than their own sons or brothers, to succeed them. As Yao chose Shun, so Shun chose Yu, the hero who is said to have drained off the waters of the great flood of Chinese legend. The legend asserts that Yu left his throne to a son, thus originating the dynastic system of inherited succession to the throne by males of the male line.

The dynasty that Yu founded is known as the Hsia dynasty. No archaeological evidence of the Hsia dynasty has yet been identified, but many scholars believe that the traditional account of it has a basis in fact. The last Hsia ruler is said to have been a tyrant who was overthrown in a popular uprising led by a nobleman named T'ang. This semilegendary event provided a precedent for the ancient Chinese doctrine that the people have a right to depose unjust rulers.

The Dawn of History

The rebel leader T'ang is believed to have founded the Shang dynasty, in which China's known written history had its origin. A wealth of archaeological evidence has been unearthed in the Yellow River valley—also the area of numerous prehistoric sites—that confirms the Shang dynasty's existence during the second millennium B.C. (see fig. 5). The traditional dating for the dynasty is 1766–1122 B.C. (see fig. 6).

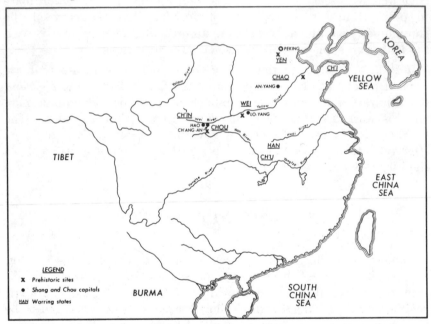

Figure 5. People's Republic of China, China's Beginnings.

In addition to the specimens of archaic Chinese writing found on the oracle bones (animal bones and shells used by priests in divination), there are also inscriptions on a number of ceremonial bronze vessels that date from this period. The workmanship on the bronzes attests to a high level of civilization.

Shang civilization was based on agriculture, augmented by animal husbandry. The Shang kings ruled over much of North China, and

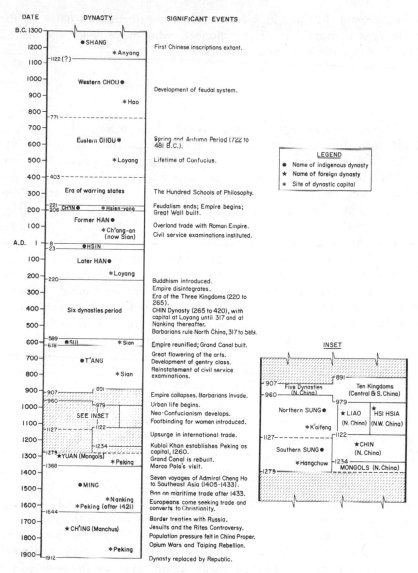

DATE	DYNASTY	SIGNIFICANT EVENTS

B.C. 1300 —
● SHANG
✱ Anyang — First Chinese inscriptions extant.

1200 —
1100 — 1122 (?)

1000 — Western CHOU ●
Development of feudal system.
900 — ✱ Hao
800 — 771

700 —
600 — Eastern CHOU ● — Spring and Autumn Period (722 to 481 B.C.).
500 — ✱ Loyang — Lifetime of Confucius.
400 — 403

300 — Era of warring states — The Hundred Schools of Philosophy.
200 — 221 / 206 CH'IN ● ✱ Hsien-yang — Feudalism ends; Empire begins; Great Wall built.
Former HAN ●
100 — ✱ Ch'ang-an (now Sian) — Overland trade with Roman Empire. Civil service examinations instituted.

A.D. 1 — 8 / 23 ● HSIN
100 — Later HAN ●
200 — 220 ✱ Loyang

Buddhism introduced.
Empire disintegrates.
Era of the Three Kingdoms (220 to 265).
300 —
400 — Six dynasties period — CHIN Dynasty (265 to 420), with capital at Loyang until 317 and at Nanking thereafter.
500 — Barbarians rule North China, 317 to 589.
600 — 589 / 618 ● SUI ✱ Sian — Empire reunified; Grand Canal built.

700 — ● T'ANG — Great flowering of the arts. Development of gentry class. Reinstatement of civil service examinations.
800 — ✱ Sian

900 — 907 ‑ 891 — Empire collapses. Barbarians invade.
960 — Urban life begins.
1000 — 979 — Neo-Confucianism develops.
SEE INSET — Footbinding for women introduced.
1100 — 1127 ‑ 1122 — Upsurge in international trade.
1200 — 1234
Kublai Khan establishes Peking as capital, 1260.
1300 — 1279 ★ YUAN (Mongols) ✱ Peking — Grand Canal is rebuilt. Marco Polo's visit.
1368

1400 — Seven voyages of Admiral Cheng Ho to Southeast Asia (1405-1433).
1500 — ● MING — Ban on maritime trade after 1433.
✱ Nanking
1600 — ✱ Peking (after 1421) — Europeans come seeking trade and converts to Christianity.
1644

Border treaties with Russia.
Jesuits and the Rites Controversy.
1700 — ★ CH'ING (Manchus)
1800 — Population pressure felt in China Proper.
Opium Wars and Taiping Rebellion.
✱ Peking
1900 — 1912 — Dynasty replaced by Republic.

LEGEND
● Name of indigenous dynasty
★ Name of foreign dynasty
✱ Site of dynastic capital

INSET

907 — Five Dynasties (N. China) — 891 — Ten Kingdoms (Central & S. China)
960 —
979 —
Northern SUNG ● — ★ LIAO (N. China) — ★ HSI HSIA (N.W. China)
✱ K'aifeng
1127 — 1122 —
Southern SUNG ● — ★ CHIN (N. China)
✱ Hangchow
1234 —
1279 — MONGOLS (N. China)

Figure 6.   People's Republic of China, Chronological Chart of Main Dynastic Regimes.

Shang forces, often numbering as many as 5,000 troops, fought frequent wars with neighboring settlements and nomadic herdsmen. The capitals—one of which was at Anyang—were centers of glittering court life. Court ritual to propitiate natural spirits and to honor sacred ancestors was highly developed. In addition to his secular powers, the king was the head of the ancestor and spirit worship cult. By the last years of the dynasty the king had become an absolute despot. Evidence from the royal tombs at Anyang indicates that royal personages were buried with much ceremony and with articles of value, presumably provided for use in the afterlife. Perhaps for the same reason, hundreds of commoners, who may have been slaves, were buried alive with the royal corpse.

The Chou Period

The last Shang ruler was denounced as oppressive and was overthrown by Wu, chief of a vigorous people from the Wei River valley in Shensi Province, west of the Shang area in Honan Province. Wu founded the Chou dynasty which, through conquest and colonization, gradually sinicized much of China Proper north of the Yangtze River. The early Chou rulers established their capital at Hao (near modern Sian) in the Wei River valley, west of the right-angle bend of the Yellow River. The Chou dynasty lasted longer than any other—from the twelfth or eleventh century until 256 B.C. Official historians of the Chou dynasty first enunciated the doctrine of the "mandate of Heaven," the notion that the ruler (the "son of Heaven") governed by right of the power divinely invested in him and that, if he were overthrown, his fall from power was proof that he had lost the divine sponsorship. The doctrine permitted them to explain and justify the demise of the two earlier dynasties and, at the same time, provided the chief justification for the authority of China's rulers that would be used by royal apologists from then on.

Chou kings parceled out their kingdom into hereditary fiefdoms granted to royal vassals in a pattern of landholding and personal loyalty relationships similar to that which prevailed during Europe's Middle Ages. In the first half of the Chou period the Middle Kingdom (which in early Chou times corresponded approximately to the region now included in Shensi, Shansi, and Honan provinces) gradually absorbed the peoples and lands to the south and east until all China Proper as far south as the Yangtze and as far east as the ocean was part of the Middle Kingdom. The barbarians of other areas, particularly those of the inhospitable steppes and deserts of the north and west, were hardier and more warlike and successfully resisted the Chinese, even invading the Middle Kingdom whenever Chinese power waned.

In 771 B.C., under threat of barbarian invasion, the Chou court was obliged to abandon Hao, its western capital in the Wei River valley, and move its seat of government eastward to Loyang in the present-day province of Honan. Because of the shift, historians divide the Chou dynasty into Western Chou and Eastern Chou periods. The phenomenon of the capital being withdrawn away from danger in times of dynastic decay and being restored to an advanced position at a time when the central government was strong has occurred repeatedly in the course of Chinese history.

From 722 to 481 B.C. (an era called the Spring and Autumn Period after a famous historical chronicle of the time), the influence of the central government greatly diminished, and warfare between the feudal states increased in violence and frequency. The power of the Chou ruler continued to fade until the dynasty was finally extinguished in 256 B.C.

Although the so-called Era of the Warring States (402–221 B.C.) was one of unceasing warfare, it also coincided with the greatest flowering of Chinese thought and culture. The centuries of civil strife were accompanied by fundamental economic and social changes. Aristocrats became commoners, and commoners rose to high rank. Upward mobility was aided by the spread of education and the development of domestic interregional commerce. Commerce was stimulated by the introduction of coinage and technological improvements. Iron came into general use, making possible not only the forging of deadly weapons of war but also the manufacture of plows and tools. Public works on a grand scale were executed by the various states. Enormous walls were built to fortify long stretches of the northern frontier against horsemen from the steppes. Large-scale irrigation and water control projects were undertaken, and transport canals were dug. These public works were constructed by a huge labor force, drawn from what by the third century B.C. was probably the world's largest population. By that time many of China's domestic arts had also taken their enduring forms. Chopsticks, lacquerwork, and silk were being used.

The Flowering of Philosophy

The increase in government activity, for such purposes as the directing of public projects and the collecting of taxes, had obliged the rulers of the various states to supplement their aristocratic administrative staffs with skilled, literate professionals chosen for their talent, not just their class origins. The new recruitment procedures led indirectly to a revolution in patterns of thought.

So many different ideas arose that the Chinese accounts refer, figuratively, to a "hundred schools" of philosophy. Many of the philosophers were itinerant professional government workers who, besides teaching their disciples, were employed as advisers to one or another of the various state rulers.

The school of philosophy that had the greatest effect on subsequent Chinese thought was the one founded by K'ung Fu-tzu, or Master Kung (551–479 B.C.), known to the West as Confucius. The ablest scholar-teacher of the age, Confucius sought to restore China to the peaceful feudalism of early Chou times but felt that the only way the hierarchical system could be made to work properly was for each person to perform correctly his assigned role. "Let the ruler be a ruler and the subject a subject," he said, but he added that to rule properly a king must be virtuous and set an example of proper ethical conduct. To Confucius, social stratification was a fact of life to be sustained by morals, not force. He laid much stress on the possibility of remolding men's minds through education and taught that proper inner attitudes could be inculcated through the practice of rituals and the observance of rules of etiquette and decorum.

Mencius, or Meng-tzu (372–289 B.C.), developed the humanism of Confucian thought further, declaring that man is by nature good and is corrupted by adverse environment. Mencius also introduced the idea that a ruler cannot govern without the people's tacit consent. If the people successfully depose or assassinate the ruler, this is proof of the fact that he has lost the mandate of Heaven. Thus Mencius took the Chou justification for dynastic conquest and turned it into a justification for popular rebellion.

Taoism, the second most important and enduring stream in Chinese thought, also developed at this time. Its formulation is attributed to a legendary figure, Lao-tzu (Old Master), who is alleged to predate Confucius. Taoism deals with man in nature, not man in society, which was Confucius' sole concern. For the Taoist the goal of life for each individual is to find his own private adjustment to the rhythm and patterns of the natural (and supernatural) world, to follow the Way (*tao*) of the universe. This is achieved by means of nonintellectual disciplines: through mysticism, trance, and periods of solitude in natural surroundings; through spontaneous response to nature; and through the avoidance of action, change, or making distinctions between things. In many ways the opposite of Confucian activism, Taoism proved to many of its adherents to be complementary. A scholar on duty as an official would usually subscribe to Confucian principles but on holiday or in retirement might well seek the harmony with nature of a Taoist recluse.

Another idea that can be traced back to philosophies current in the Eastern Chou period is the belief that all nature is composed of interlocking, mutually complementary opposites: *yang*, which is male, light, hot, and positive; and *yin*, which is female, dark, cold, and negative. Other beliefs that have survived from this period are the concern with numerology, especially the number five—as in the five elements, the five directions (including the center), the five senses, and the five colors. Chinese astrology and geomancy also developed at this time.

One school of thought that originated during this period and has had an enduring influence on China, although it did not attain widespread popularity, is the philosophy of Legalism. According to this belief, man's nature is incorrigibly selfish, and therefore the only way to preserve social order is to impose discipline from above. The ruler should promulgate laws for his own purposes, and these laws must be inflexibly enforced. The punishment for infraction of the law must be so harsh that man's selfish interest will keep him law abiding.

The Legalists exalted the state and sought its prosperity and martial prowess above the welfare of the citizens. They believed that the state should consist of a strong central government overseeing a mass of producers of primary goods, or peasant farmers. Big landholdings were thought to be a threat to the central power, whereas merchants and intellectuals were regarded as nonproductive and therefore not to be tolerated.

Noted Legalists advised the kings of the state of Ch'in and, when a Ch'in ruler became the first emperor of a unified China, Legalism became the philosophic basis for the imperial form of government. In post-Ch'in times the use of Confucian-trained scholar-officials to administer the empire eventually led to a humanizing element being introduced into the administration, which helped to mediate between the people at large and the Legalist imperial framework.

THE IMPERIAL ERA

The First Imperial Period

In the Wei River valley, where the Chou state had begun, there arose, after the Chou capital moved eastward, the state of Ch'in. By the fourth century B.C. the state had established a centralized, nonfeudal administration. The state was divided into prefectures (*hsien*), each under a prefect sent out from the capital, not a local lord or hereditary vassal. All persons were obliged to work in what the regime held to be productive occupations. Conformity to government policy was demanded at the local level. Clusters of families were made collectively responsible for individual actions, and citizens were encouraged to spy on one another.

By 221 B.C. Ch'in armies had gained control of all of the warring states. The king of Ch'in took for himself the grandiloquent title of First Emperor (Shih Huang-ti) and proceeded to apply Ch'in administrative practices to the empire. Provinces, administered by officials appointed by the central government, replaced the feudal system of the warring states. The forms of writing, the codes of laws, the coinage, and even the axle length of vehicles were standardized. Interregional commerce and agriculture were encouraged, and private ownership of land was extended throughout the empire.

To further the standardization of thought and to silence criticism of imperial rule, virtually all books (except technical works) were burned, and many scholars were banished or put to death. To prevent regional concentration of wealth, the population was redistributed; to forestall rebellion, the arms of the people were confiscated; and to fend off barbarian intrusion, the various northern fortification walls were incorporated to make a 1,400-mile-long Great Wall. Ch'in armies pushed forward the frontiers of the empire, and settlers and political offenders were sent to open up virgin lands, especially in South China.

These activities required tremendous levies of manpower and resources from the people. Revolts broke out as soon as the First Emperor died in 210 B.C., and the dynasty was overthrown less than twenty years after its triumph. The imperial system it initiated, however, persisted, with brief interruptions for more than 2,000 years, and the name of the first imperial dynasty survives in the name "China."

Civil war raged until 202 B.C., when a military man of peasant origin named Liu Pang (d. 195 B.C.), who had in 206 B.C. gained the title king of Han, was able to defeat his warlord rivals and gain control of the empire. Under the dynasty of Han (206 B.C. to A.D. 220), which Liu founded, most of the political machinery of Ch'in was retained, although some of the harsher aspects were modified or abolished. The capital was located at Ch'ang-an (now Sian) in the Wei River valley, and Confucian scholars, who had been out of favor during the Ch'in period, were employed in high offices.

Intellectual and artistic creativity revived and flourished and, with Confucianism given official patronage, Confucian ideals began to be adopted by the government. Men of talent were recruited for government service by examinations that stressed the Confucian literature. Technological advances also marked this period. Two of the great Chinese inventions, paper and porcelain, date from Han times. The Han period was such a time of military and cultural prowess that to the present day members of the majority ethnic group of China proudly call themselves "men of Han" (see ch. 4, Ethnic Groups and Languages).

The Han emperors extended their domains westward to include the Indo-European population clusters in small farming oases scattered along the rim of the Tarim Basin, making possible relatively secure caravan traffic across Central Asia to Antioch, Baghdad, and Alexandria. The paths of the caravan traffic are often called the silk route because they comprised the route of importation of Chinese silk by the Romans.

The expansion of the empire into Central Asia came in response to the persistent threat to the plains-dwelling Han Chinese of mongoloid Turkish-speaking nomads from the northern steppes. About 52 B.C. the danger was eliminated. The southern half of the horde submitted to being a tributary people of the Han emperor; others of the group moved westward. Chinese armies also invaded and annexed parts of Korea and Indochina toward the end of the second century B.C.

Han society consisted chiefly of the ruling class and the peasantry. The ruling class was headed by a small hereditary aristocracy. There were also merchants, but the Han rulers regarded commerce as parasitic, and merchants were forbidden to buy land or become officials and were popularly ranked as the lowest in a status hierarchy of the four main occupations, below scholars, farmers, and artisans. Nonetheless, those merchants with great wealth gained considerable power. At the bottom of the scale were some serfs and a small number of domestic slaves.

Han dynastic rule was interrupted early in the Christian Era but was subsequently restored and enjoyed another two centuries of power. In A.D. 220, however, a combination of palace intrigues, internal unrest, and external pressures brought the dynasty to an end.

Imperial rule had already been undermined by the gradual concentration of wealth, especially land, into the hands of a few families whose political influence helped them avoid the imperial taxes. As these landholding families increased in wealth and power, the central government, relying on an ever-diminishing tax base to support ever-rising expenses, grew progressively more odious to the ordinary tax-paying public. This succession of events—concentration of wealth, a diminished tax base, and excessive taxation upon that base—has marked the onset of decay for every major dynasty since the Han period.

The collapse of the Han dynasty may also have been accelerated by the weakening of the intellectual and religious consensus in the empire resulting from the introduction into China of Buddhism, propagated by missionaries from India in the late Han era.

Era of Division

With the collapse of the Han dynasty, the unity of empire dissolved. For 3 1/2 centuries, which Chinese historians call the Six Dynasties Period, the empire remained divided. At first there emerged three kingdoms—one in the north, another in Szechwan, and a third in the Yangtze River valley. The Era of the Three Kingdoms (as this period is traditionally called) is remembered by the Chinese as an age of chivalry, valor, and adventure. The Chin dynasty reunited most of China for a relatively brief period (A.D. 265–420), but it was too weak to hold back the tide of barbarian advance from the north.

Foreign influences were important in this period. North China came under the domination of several successive dynasties of non-Chinese-speaking barbarians, although gradually the various barbarian ruling groups became increasingly sinicized in culture and through intermarriage. The northerners were at first more receptive to

Buddhism than was the conservative population of South China, but gradually Buddhism became a popular religion in both north and south.

Pilgrimages by Chinese converts to the sacred Buddhist sites in India greatly expanded China's knowledge concerning the peoples and countries to be found between India and China. As Chinese knowledge in various fields expanded, major technological advances were made. The invention of gunpowder (at that time for use in fireworks only) and the wheelbarrow and advances in medicine, astronomy, and cartography date from the Six Dynasties Period.

Restoration of Empire

In A.D. 589 a general of Han Chinese family with ties to the barbarian aristocracy brought about the reunification of the Chinese Empire. The Sui dynasty that he founded lasted for only two reigns. Its early demise was the result of the government's excessive demands on the people to carry out ambitious public projects and military adventures aimed at expanding imperial control over much of Central and Southeast Asia as well as Manchuria and northern Korea.

After a chaotic period following the popular revolt that overthrew the dynasty, there emerged the T'ang dynasty (618–907), which is regarded by historians as a high point in Chinese civilization equal, or even superior, to the Han period. A governmental system was built on Sui foundations that was to survive for three centuries under T'ang emperors. Civil service examinations based on a Confucian curriculum, first instituted in Han times, became standard T'ang recruitment procedure. The bureaucratic machinery of the empire was refined, and the T'ang government and its code of laws became models for neighboring states.

The flowering of Chinese culture that occurred during the T'ang period was partly the result of stimuli received from abroad that contributed to a renewal of Chinese creativity in all fields. It was the golden age of Chinese literature and art (see ch. 8, Education, Intellectual Expression, and the Arts). Block printing was invented, making the written word available to a vastly greater audience. Government schools at the regional and national level were introduced.

Foreigners came from afar to receive the polish of a Chinese education, and their presence enhanced the cosmopolitan atmosphere of the T'ang capital, Ch'ang-an. In the tolerant climate of early T'ang, foreign missionaries came to propagate their faiths—Zoroastrianism, Manichaeism, and Nestorian Christianity—and Muslim merchants and soldiers of fortune introduced Islam. Colonies of foreign merchants sprang up in Chinese ports. The Chinese did not hesitate to employ foreigners in their government, to use foreign imported goods in daily life (such as tea, introduced from Southeast Asia), and to gain ideas and technological information from the foreigners.

The most significant development in the social system during the T'ang dynasty was the gradual development of a new social group. This group, which English-speaking Chinese scholars have termed "the gentry," included those persons who passed the Confucianist government examinations, becoming degree holders in literature, the classics, or other fields and thus eligible to be appointed to office in the imperial bureaucracy. The term "gentry" has also been used, more loosely, to describe local landowners who lived in the provincial towns, receiving rents from their rural tenants, and who were members of the families from which the degree holders came. The landowning class supplied the bulk of the scholars because it had the money to pay for the lengthy classical education necessary to pass the examinations.

The presence of the gentry made possible the governing of the great and populous empire by a relatively small group of officials. The gentry, with its enduring status in the local community and its family ties and shared values connecting it to the officialdom, mediated between the rural population and the imperial government from T'ang times until the end of the empire in 1911. It was also the case, however, that candidates who failed the examinations and degree holders who sought but did not obtain official employment constituted an articulate, discontented group within the gentry, ready to support or lead rebellions.

By their military prowess the early T'ang rulers built up a larger empire than that of the Han. In the west they defeated the Turks and established a protectorate over Turkestan. Tibet, unified for the first time in the seventh century, soon came under T'ang suzerainty. In the east the imperial troops vanquished the land and sea force of the Japanese and Koreans. A Chinese-led army even penetrated India.

By the middle of the eighth century T'ang power had ebbed. Military defeats were suffered by the imperial forces at the hands of the Tai people of the kingdom of Nanchao (in modern Yunnan Province) and at the hands of Arabs who were beginning to gain control over parts of Central Asia. Uighurs and Tibetans sacked the T'ang capital.

A barbarian general in the T'ang army, An Lu-shan, led a revolt in 755 that, although quickly crushed, permanently impaired the effectiveness of the imperial government. Regional military commanders came to exert more power at the expense of the central government. The T'ang capital became a center of factionalism and conspiracy. Popular uprisings in the late ninth century further weakened the empire, facilitating the efforts of northern invaders, who brought the T'ang dynasty to an end in 907.

The Sung dynasty was founded in North China in 960. Although in 979 it was able to reunite much of the empire, it was not a total reunification. The advent of barbarian regimes in the north forced the Sung regime to move its capital to Hangchow in the southern coastal area, abandoning the interior provinces.

The Sung period marks the commencement of modern life in China. For the first time private trade overshadowed government enterprise, and urban communities that had begun not as administrative centers but as centers for commerce sprang up. Urban sophistication became characteristic of the Chinese opinion-makers. The landed gentry, although largely dependent upon rural rents for their incomes, lived in the towns alongside the officials and the merchants.

The spread of printing, the increase in the number of schools, and the growth of private trade and of a money economy gave rise to a new group of wealthy and influential commoners. Land and the holding of public office stopped being the chief means of gaining wealth and the sole means of gaining prestige and entry into the gentry class. Industry and commerce were also important sources of income, and the stigma that had been attached to trade since the empire began faded to some extent. Maritime commerce was encouraged and, with the aid of the mariner's compass, the Chinese were able to wrest from the Arabs the Far Eastern leg of the East-West maritime trade.

Culturally, the Sung was a period in which developments that had occurred in late T'ang times were refined. Among these was the T'ang ideal of the universal man who was scholar, poet, painter, and statesman. Another development of the late T'ang period was the decline of interest in, and tolerance for, foreigners and foreign things and concepts. By the mid-ninth century the court had become so antiforeign that it adopted a virulently anti-Buddhist stance on the grounds that Buddhism was a foreign religion.

It was a period of conservatism bordering on reactionism. The chief interest of the late T'ang and Sung intellectuals was to lead society back to the Confucian classics with which the new bureaucracy had become familiar in the course of preparing for the civil service examinations. To the Sung scholars the chief Confucian classics, the Four Books—the *Analects*, *Mencius*, *Great Learning*, and *Doctrine of the Mean*—properly interpreted, could provide all the knowledge of ethics and philosophy necessary to make a good man and an able official (see ch. 8, Education, Intellectual Expression, and the Arts).

Among the Sung Neo-Confucianists who wrote commentaries on the classics, the most famous and influential was Chu Hsi, whose synthesis of Confucian thought and Buddhist, Taoist, and other ideas became the official imperial philosophy. As incorporated into the examination system, Chu Hsi's Neo-Confucianism became by the fourteenth century an unyielding orthodox official creed, which stressed the one-sided obligations of obedience and compliance by subject to ruler, child to father, and wife to husband.

The development of an urban way of life and the emergence of urban amusements and tastes—for example, the appearance of wineshops, teashops, restaurants, theaters, and brothels—were contemporaneous with the development of urban pauperism, as those without land gravitated to the towns. There also began a decline in the status of women. Among the town elite there was a growth in the popularity of concubinage, the taking of secondary wives. A preexisting ban on remarriage of widows also grew more inflexible at this time and, among upper class women, there began the practice of footbinding—the mutilation from childhood of female feet to make them conform to a shape held to be pleasing to Chinese men of the time. The practice of binding women's feet was later to spread to all classes of society.

The growth and development of a refined civil life was accompanied by a decline in enthusiasm for military life. This decline in military capacity left the empire prey to barbarians from the north. After a protracted struggle with the Khitan and the Jurched, the Chinese were in a weakened position when confronted by a stonger enemy, the invading Mongol army.

Mongolian Interregnum

The new invaders already had subjugated North China, Korea, and the Muslim kingdoms of Central Asia and had twice penetrated Europe. Thus Kublai Khan (1214–94), grandson of Genghis Khan, the founder of the Mongol Empire, had the resources of Asia behind him when he began his drive against the Sung. Finally, after having successfully defeated the Chinese army and fleet in the south, the Mongol leader established the first non-Chinese dynasty to control all of China.

The Yuan dynasty (formally created by Kublai Khan in 1271) gained all of China by 1279, after roughly fifty years of Mongol campaigning. By 1267 Kublai Khan had begun construction of a new capital at Peking, which had been his headquarters in China since 1260. Later, the Grand Canal (which had been built in Sui times to connect North China with the fertile Yangtze River valley) was extended to the new capital. His summer capital remained in Mongolia, however, at Shang-tu (Xanadu), north of the Great Wall.

The Mongol regime was never accepted by the "men of Han," as the North Chinese continued to be called, or by the "southerners," as the Mongols called the Chinese of the Southern Sung kingdom. Kublai Khan, who, as the Great Khan, was head of the entire Mongol realm as well as of the Chinese empire, preferred employing non-

Chinese from other parts of the Mongol domain—Russia, the Near East, and Central Asia—in those positions for which no competent Mongol could be found.

The influence of other foreigners upon the Yuan dynasty was also considerable. Related to this time are the first records of travel by Westerners, including both merchants and missionaries, into China after the fall of the Roman Empire. In the last years of the thirteenth century Franciscan monks reached China, and one of them built a church in Peking with the consent of Kublai Khan. The most famous European traveler of the period was the Venetian Marco Polo, whose account of his trip to China and life there astounded the people of Europe. The effect of Europeans upon China, however, was neither as great nor as lasting as that of the peoples and cultures of the eastern half of the Mongol Empire. From this period dates the conversion to Islam, by Muslims of Central Asia, of large numbers of Chinese in the northwest and southwest. At this time also the Mongols acquired Tibetan Buddhism, also known as Lamaism. The Mongols attempted to promote Tibetan Buddhism in China and gave it a favored position at court.

The Chinese Regain Power

Rivalry among the Mongol imperial heirs, natural disasters—especially frequent floods of the Yellow River (which had drastically changed its course in 1194 from north to south of the Shantung Peninsula, reaching the sea through the mouth of the Huai River)—and numerous peasant rebellions against the unpopular Mongol regime led to the collapse of the Yuan dynasty. In 1368 Chu Yuan-chang, a Han Chinese peasant and former Buddhist monk who had become a rebel army leader, emerged as successor to the Great Khan as ruler of China Proper. He founded the Ming dynasty, with its capital at Nanking. After his death the capital was moved, in 1421, to Peking, the city Kublai Khan had built.

The zenith of Ming power was reached during the reign of the third Ming emperor, Yung-lo, who reigned from 1403 to 1424. The Chinese armies reconquered Annam and kept back the Mongols, while the Chinese fleet ranged the China seas and the Indian Ocean, cruising as far as the east coast of Africa. The maritime Asian nations sent envoys to perform the kowtow (formal prostration) in homage to the Chinese emperor. The tribute they sent, together with the gifts China gave in return, were of a volume substantial enough to constitute international trade.

Between 1405 and 1433 the eunuch admiral Cheng Ho led seven separate voyages of the imperial fleet to the Nan Yang (Southern Ocean). After 1433, however, Ming policy was to concentrate its energies on preventing another barbarian land invasion, either by the

Mongols or, later, by a northern ethnic group related to the Mongols, the Manchus. Trade expeditions to the Nan Yang were banned.

The cessation of imperial interest in maritime Southeast Asia may have been in part caused by the development of a conservative climate at court, brought about by pressure from the powerful Neo-Confucianist bureaucracy, which led to the revival of the traditional denigration of trade and commerce. The low esteem in which these occupations were held was enforced by the fact that the path to power and prestige in Ming times was through internal politics and Confucian erudition, not through trade. The stability of the 2 1/2 centuries of the Ming dynasty, which were without major disruptions of the economy, arts, society, or politics, promoted a belief among Chinese that they had achieved the most satisfactory civilization on earth and that nothing foreign was needed or welcome.

This belief in China's self-sufficiency impeded relations with the Portuguese and other European traders and missionaries who began to appear along the coast of China and elsewhere in the Far East during the sixteenth century. The Portuguese were the first to be permitted to establish a trading settlement, in Macao, but all the Western traders were severely restricted in their activities by the emperor. The efforts of the Portuguese missionary Saint Francis Xavier to Christianize China were frustrated by the imperial ban on his entry into the mainland. He died off the coast of China.

The focus of Chinese pride was not as much their ethnic group or territory as it was their way of life, their arts, their government, and their social arrangements. Aware of the Chinese cultural pride, the Jesuit Matteo Ricci (1552–1610) gained a foothold in Peking by familiarizing himself with Chinese customs, institutions, and classical learning so that he could present Christianity in terms comprehensible to the Chinese. The fact that the criteria for being Chinese were chiefly cultural rather than racial was to prove of great importance to the Manchus when they became China's new rulers in the seventeenth century.

Long wars with the Mongols, incursions by the Japanese into Korea, and harassment of Chinese coastal cities by the Japanese in the sixteenth century weakened the Ming dynasty. Its overthrow in 1644 by the leader of the last of numerous rebellions against it, in turn, weakened China so that it was once again ripe for an alien takeover.

The Late Imperial Period

Rivalry among the rebels after the fall of the Ming regime left a power vacuum that the Manchu armies easily filled. In 1644 the Manchus took Peking and became masters of North China, establishing the Ch'ing dynasty (1644–1911). Ming adherents resisted the Manchus for many years, however. By 1683 the last Ming pretender had been taken prisoner, the Ming stronghold on Taiwan had been captured, and the last vestiges of rebellion in South China had been quelled. The empire was to remain in Manchu hands until the twentieth century.

Although the Manchus were not Han Chinese, they had, in contrast to the Mongols, been sinicized to a great degree before coming to power and, realizing the importance of doing things the Chinese way if they were to dominate the empire, they took over many institutions of Ming and earlier Chinese derivation. They buried the last Ming emperor (who had committed suicide) with full honors and claimed that they had come to suppress the anti-Ming rebels and restore order. They also continued the Confucian cult rituals, over which the emperors had traditionally presided.

The Manchus also retained, until 1905, the Confucian civil service examination system for recruiting Chinese officials. Many Chinese found employment with the new regime. Although Chinese were barred from the highest offices, outside the capital Chinese officials predominated over Manchu officeholders, except in military positions. The Manchus retained the Chinese administrative system that had been perfected in Ming times. Under this system the administration was divided among civil, military, and censorial branches, the last branch being a systematized inspector corps assigned to check on the other two and report back to the throne. The Neo-Confucianist philosophy, with its emphasis on obedience by the subject to the ruler, was also retained and was enforced as the state ideology.

The Manchu emperors also patronized Chinese literary projects of enormous scope. Great dictionaries and encyclopedias were compiled; a complete collection of Chinese literature was assembled; and an edition of the twenty-four dynastic histories was published. Since it is known that the dominant concern of the Ch'ing dynasty was to retain its control of China, it has been suggested by historians that the purpose of the emperors in sponsoring these massive literary projects was to keep Chinese scholars harmlessly occupied so that they would not trouble the foreign regime. The imperial literary projects also made possible an official review of Chinese literature. Connected with the review was the imperial suppression of many works on the grounds that they either criticized foreign rule in China or praised the Ming dynasty. Nonetheless, the survival of much of China's ancient literature is the result of the Ch'ing imperial projects.

As part of their policy to ensure Manchu dominance over China, efforts were made by the Ch'ing emperors to prevent the absorption of the Manchus into the Han Chinese population. Han Chinese were prohibited from migrating into Manchuria. No agriculture was permitted in Northern Manchuria, and Manchus were forbidden to engage in trade or manual labor and to bind their women's feet.

Intermarriage between Manchus and Han Chinese was forbidden. Manchu emperors never lost their suspicion of the Han Chinese. In many positions a system of dual appointments was used, the Chinese appointee to do the substantive work and the Manchu to supervise and prevent treachery.

The Ch'ing regime was determined to protect itself not only from internal rebellion but also against invasion from without. From earliest times the chief threat to an established dynasty in China had always come from the barbarians on China's land frontier. The Ch'ing dynasty carried out a policy designed to prevent its being toppled in this way. The Manchus had absorbed the Mongols of Inner Mongolia (present-day Inner Mongolian Autonomous Region) into the Manchu state before they conquered China. After all of China Proper had been subdued, the Manchus conquered Outer Mongolia (now the Mongolian People's Republic) in the late seventeenth century, and in the eighteenth century the Manchus conquered Central Asia as far as the Pamirs and established a protectorate over Tibet.

The Ch'ing thus became the first dynasty to eliminate successfully all danger to China Proper from across its land borders, and during its regime the Chinese empire grew to include a larger area than ever before or since (see fig. 7). In addition, the Ch'ing emperors received tribute from the various states situated just beyond the empire's borders—Burma, Annam, and Korea.

Unanticipated by the Ch'ing emperors, the chief threat to China's integrity and to the continuance of the dynasty did not come overland, as it had so often in the past, but instead it arrived by sea, reaching the southern coastal area first. Western traders and missionaries began to arrive in large numbers. The dynasty's inability to evaluate correctly the nature of the challenge these foreigners posed or to respond adequately to it resulted in the collapse of the Ch'ing dynasty and of the entire millennia-old framework of dynastic rule.

EMERGENCE OF MODERN CHINA

The success of the Ch'ing dynasty in maintaining stability proved a disability when the empire was confronted by the Western powers. The centuries of peace and self-satisfaction with China's civilization dating back to the Ming dynasty had brought about little change within the empire, whereas the same time period had produced major changes in Europe and the United States, culminating in the industrial revolution.

The scholar-advisers who, according to Confucian theory, ought to have been the ones to guide the ruler in coping with new problems, including those arising from the presence of Western interests in the Far East, were seriously restricted by Neo-Confucian orthodoxy.

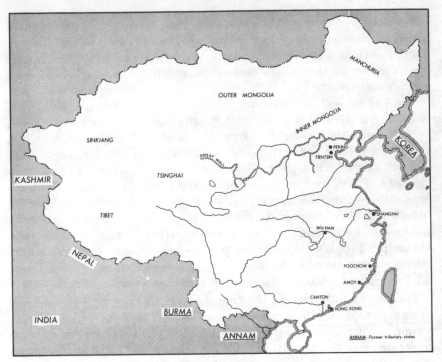

Figure 7. Area Included Within Imperial China in 1911.

According to the orthodox view, obedience to the ruler was the foremost duty of the subject, and virtually no room was allowed for change, for loyal opposition, or for criticism of official policy. The imperial Neo-Confucian scholars accepted as axiomatic the cultural superiority of Chinese civilization and the position of the empire at the hub of the civilized world. To question this assumption, to suggest innovation, or to promote the adoption of foreign ideas would have been tantamount to heresy. Imperial scholastic purges dealt ruthlessly with those who deviated from orthodoxy.

By the nineteenth century the only major change to have occurred in China for 200 years was in the number of its people. By the start of the century there were over 300 million Chinese, as compared to perhaps half that number two centuries earlier, but there had developed no industry or trade of sufficient scope to absorb the surplus labor.

Unemployment and land hunger among the people led to widespread discontent with the regime and a breakdown in law and order, aided by the weakening of the Manchu bureaucratic and military systems through corruption. Localized revolts began to erupt in various parts of the empire in the early nineteenth century in response to deteriorating internal conditions. Secret societies, such as the White Lotus sect in the north and the Hung society in the south, which combined anti-Manchu subversion with banditry, gained ground.

The Western Powers Arrive

Historical accounts show that there had been visits of Westerners to China from Han times, but it was not until the sixteenth century that Westerners came in sufficient numbers or with sufficient resources to make an impact. As elsewhere in Asia, the Portuguese were the pioneers, establishing in the late sixteenth century a permanent foothold at Macao, from which they monopolized the foreign trade at the Chinese port of Canton. Soon the Spaniards arrived on the coast of China, and their flourishing commerce connected the South China coast and Taiwan (Formosa) with Manila, Mexico, and Spain. The currency of the trade was the Mexican trading dollar.

By the mid-seventeenth century the Dutch, who had arrived at the beginning of the century, had driven the Spanish from their base in Taiwan. After the Manchus took the island, the Dutch received permission to trade in Kwangtung and Fukien provinces.

After the Ch'ing pacification of Taiwan the emperor lifted the previously existing ban on maritime commerce, and four customs houses were established at cities in the coastal provinces of Kiangsu, Chekiang, Fukien, and Kwangtung. The British, who by that time had become interested in the China trade, in 1699 opened a factory at Canton, the most prosperous of the Chinese ports. The French also sent traders to Canton and Ningpo and established a trading post in Canton in 1728, but French trade was not of significant proportions until the nineteenth century.

The opportunities to engage in trade with maritime Southeast Asia under the protection of Western trading posts in the area, combined with the lack of opportunity in the overcrowded farming communities of South China, induced many Chinese of the southern coastal provinces to migrate to the Nan Yang. These migrants laid the foundations of Overseas Chinese private enterprises that were later to dominate the domestic economies of Malaysia, Indonesia, the Philippines, Burma, and Thailand.

Trade between the imperial government and the Western powers was carried on in the guise of the tribute. The foreign merchants were obliged to follow the elaborate centuries-old ritual imposed upon envoys from China's tributary states if they wanted the privilege of trading in China. The etiquette imposed on envoys of tributary states included the kowtow before the emperor. There was no ministry of foreign affairs nor any conception at the imperial court that the Western powers would expect or deserve to be treated as equals. The sole exception was in the case of Russia.

The Manchus were fully aware of the need for security along the imperial land frontier and therefore were prepared to be less dogmatic when dealing with Russia, the most powerful inland neighbor. The Treaty of Nerchinsk (1689) with the Russians, drafted to bring to an end a series of border incidents and to establish a border between Siberia and Manchuria along the Amur (Heilung) River, was China's first agreement with a Western power and was in terms of equality between the tsar and the emperor. In 1727 a second treaty with the Russians delimited the remainder of the Sino-Russian border. Envoys from Russia to Peking were obliged to perform the kowtow but, in return, twice in the 1730s Ch'ing envoys were sent to the tsar and performed the kowtow before him, in conformity to Russian court rules for Asian envoys.

The traditional denigration of trade and the age-old habit of ignoring the coastal region in favor of the interior contributed to the dynasty's inflexibility in refusing at first to recognize as other than tribute bearers the European traders who appeared on the coast of China. Diplomatic efforts by the Westerners to expand the trade were rebuffed. An official mission sent by King George III of Great Britain to the Ch'ing emperor to regularize the tariff and increase the number of ports open to British traders received in reply an imperial edict commending the king for his "respectful spirit of submission" but refusing to expand the trade since "our celestial empire possesses all things in prolific abundance." After 1760 all foreign trade was confined to Canton, where the foreign traders had to limit their dealings to a dozen officially licensed Chinese merchants.

Trade was not the sole basis of contact with the West. Since the thirteenth century Roman Catholic missionaries had been attempting to establish their church in China. By the eighteenth century several hundred missionaries, most of them Jesuits, had come to China. Although they had made only a few hundred thousand converts by 1800, the missionaries contributed greatly to Chinese knowledge in a number of fields, including cannon casting, calendar making, geography, mathematics, cartography, music, art, and architecture. European Catholic missionaries served as translators for the Ch'ing court during the negotiations of the Russian treaties and when the emperor received Western envoys.

The Jesuits were especially adept at fitting Christianity into a Chinese framework, but they were condemned by a papal decision in 1704 for having tolerated the continuance of Confucian and ancestor rites by Christian converts. The controversy over the Confucian and ancestor rites resulted in the rapid decline of the Christian movement in China. Emperor Yung-cheng, who reigned from 1723 to 1735, proscribed Christianity as heterodox and disloyal. The most effective missionizing group in China was destroyed in 1773 when the Society of Jesus was dissolved by the pope. By the early nineteenth century a policy of extermination of Christians was being carried out by the imperial government.

The Opium Wars

During the eighteenth century the market in Europe and America for tea, a new drink in the West, expanded greatly, and there was, in addition, a continuing demand for Chinese silk and porcelain. The trade began to be so large that the clumsy fiction of tribute relations was proving unwieldy. An additional problem for the trading powers was the fact that China, still in its preindustrial stage, wanted little that the West had to offer, with the result that the Westerners had to pay for their goods in bullion. In order to remedy the bullion drain resulting from the unfavorable balance of trade, the Westerners sought products that would appeal to the Chinese. Gradually a three-cornered trade developed in which Western ships, predominantly British, exchanged Western merchandise in India and Southeast Asia for raw materials and semiprocessed goods, which found a ready market in Canton.

By the early nineteenth century raw cotton and opium from India had become the staple British imports into China, in spite of the fact that opium was prohibited entry by imperial decree. The opium traffic was made possible through the connivance of the imperial bureaucracy, which had become corrupt and irresponsible.

In 1839 the Chinese government adopted drastic measures to ban the import of opium. In Canton 20,000 chests of opium were confiscated and burned. The British retaliated with a punitive expedition, thus initiating what became known as the First Opium War (1839-42). Unprepared for war and grossly underestimating the capabilities of the enemy, the Chinese were disastrously defeated. At the conclusion of the war, there came a reversal of China's relations with the British, as the emperor acquiesced to the British demands.

Under the Treaty of Nanking (1842), which was the first of a series of agreements with the Western trading nations that the Chinese have called the "unequal treaties," the emperor had to cede the island of Hong Kong to the British; abolish the licensed monopoly system of trade; open five ports—Canton, Amoy, Foochow, Ningpo and Shanghai—to foreign trade; limit the tariff on trade to 5 percent ad valorem; grant British nationals extraterritoriality (that is, exemption from Chinese laws); treat Great Britain as an equal in official correspondence; and pay a large indemnity. In addition, Great Britain was to receive the most-favored-nation treatment, a diplomatic formula meaning that it would receive whatever concessions were granted other powers then or later.

In 1844 the United States and France were able to wrest from the emperor commercial and legal concessions similar to those granted the British, including the most-favored-nation treatment. The Ch'ing court lacked the power to refuse.

The Second Opium War, also known as the *Arrow* War of 1856 to 1860, was undertaken by France and Great Britain jointly against the Chinese government. It was touched off by an incident involving imperial officers and troops in Canton boarding the *Arrow*, a ship flying the British flag but which belonged to a Chinese resident of Hong Kong. The French joined the expedition on the grounds of seeking recompense for the execution of a French missionary who had resided illegally in the interior up to the time of his death.

In 1858 a series of treaties were signed with Great Britain, France, Russia, and the United States that became known as the Treaties of Tientsin. By these treaties the foreigners were granted permission to reside in Peking rather than having to carry on their relations with the emperor always through intermediaries at the ports. Additional ports were opened, and the interference of the Western trading powers in tariff and customs control was reinforced and extended. The Chinese also agreed to pay a large war indemnity to Great Britain and France. Freedom to travel throughout China was to be granted persons with Chinese visas, and unrestricted travel in China was granted for missionaries. The Tientsin agreements had been negotiated after China's military defeat in the Second Opium War. When the Chinese government delayed ratification of the treaties, the British and French armies in 1860 pressed on to Peking, where they burned down the old Summer Palace, including its library of rare Chinese manuscripts. The superior power of the Westerners vis-à-vis the dynasty had been established and was to increase at imperial expense during the remainder of the century.

Expansion of Western Influence

Western influence was at first confined to Hong Kong, Macao, and the treaty ports, where a society of merchants flourished, protected by gunboats, chiefly British. Shanghai in particular was a dynamic center of organized and aggressive commercial competition and soon had special areas of British, French, and United States settlement that competed with each other for Chinese markets and Chinese exports.

Competition also existed among Western missionaries. Protestant missions from the United States and Great Britain arrived in the early nineteenth century, and France secured the issuance of imperial edicts of toleration, in 1844 and 1846, to remove the ban on Christianity. Since the early eighteenth century the Christian church had been classed with subversive secret societies. The Society of Jesus had been restored in 1814 and became very active in China in the mid-nineteenth century. The Catholic priests lived and dressed in the Chinese manner and spoke Chinese, whereas the Protestants tended to introduce Western modes of living as well as Western languages into China. The Catholics penetrated deeper, but the impact of the Protestants was more dynamic and revolutionary.

Some Cantonese, who had first become useful to the Westerners at the port of Canton when that was the sole port open to foreigners, accompanied the Westerners to the newly opened ports and to the newly established colonies and the Straits Settlements. The Cantonese who followed the merchants to Shanghai and Amoy were a nonindigenous element in the new ports, with their own secret societies and guilds, and they became a Westernized and intermediary group between the Westerners and the Chinese at large. Many of them acquired extraterritoriality as part of the foreign merchant establishment. In the late 1840s they cooperated in assembling cargoes of male contract laborers for the worldwide "coolie trade" that was developing to supply labor for mining and plantation industries the world over—in Cuba, Peru, the Pacific Islands, Indonesia, and Malaysia. Although an unenforced imperial ban on emigration existed, other South Chinese migrated freely to the gold mines of California and Australia.

After the abolition of the monopoly system at Canton, the comprador, a new type of Chinese businessman, came into being to handle the Chinese side of the foreigner's business. The comprador, having knowledge of the Chinese language and the Chinese business world, was employed by the foreign firm to hire the entire Chinese staff, to conduct all negotiations with the Chinese business community, and to gather information that would benefit his company. From these beginnings there gradually developed a new Chinese business class, ultimately dependent upon the protection of the foreigner's extraterritorial privileges at the treaty ports but with extensive contacts in the export-producing and import-consuming areas of the interior.

In addition to the encroachments of foreign commerce and missionary activity, there began in the mid-nineteenth century the process of territorial dismemberment of the empire by the foreigners, which was to culminate in the second Sino-Japanese war. The first step in this process was taken by the Russians, who had maintained a small Chinese-language school and an ecclesiastical mission in Peking since the time of the Sino-Russian border treaty of 1727.

The Russians had been expanding into Central Asia in the interim and by the 1850s had invaded the Amur watershed of Manchuria, from which they had been ejected by the Treaty of Nerchinsk (1689). The superior knowledge of China acquired by the Russians through their century-long residence in Peking was used to advantage by their chief diplomat in China, General Nikolai Ignatiev. Ignatiev placed his expertise at the disposal of the other Western powers and, after mediating on behalf of the French and British expedition of 1860 with the Ch'ing court, he was able to elicit on behalf of Russia the cession of all of Manchuria north of the Amur River and east of the Ussuri River. The British also acquired territory at this time. The tip of the Kowloon peninsula, on the Chinese mainland opposite the island of Hong Kong, was permanently ceded to Great Britain and became part of the Hong Kong colony.

The Taiping Rebellion

The reversal of the empire's foreign relations was not the only disaster suffered by China during the mid-nineteenth century. Natural calamities abounded, including droughts, famines, and floods. The most spectacular flooding occurred when the course of the Yellow River shifted again in 1852, returning to the course north of the Shantung Peninsula that had existed before 1194. Government neglect of public works was in part responsible for this and other disasters, and the Ch'ing administration did little to relieve the widespread misery caused by them. The disgrace to the Manchu throne of its military defeats at Western hands contributed to the popularity of anti-Manchu rebellions involving secret societies and other groups. The Nien Rebellion consisted chiefly of imperial efforts to suppress bandit groups that pillaged North China from 1853 to 1868. There was also a rebellion of Chinese Muslims in Yunnan Province lasting from 1855 to 1873. The Tungan Rebellion troubled the northwest from 1862 to 1868.

It was South China, however, the last area to yield to the Ch'ing conquerors and the first place to be exposed to Western influence, that became the center of the most important rebellion in China, the Taiping Rebellion. This uprising was led by, and drew its original support from, the Hakka, a minority group in Kwangtung and Kwangsi provinces. The Hakka (whose name means "guest people") had originally lived in central China and had migrated south during the Sung period. Their dialect and way of life were noticeably different from those of their southern neighbors, and interethnic friction had developed in areas where the Hakka were concentrated. Without strong ties to the local scene, the Hakka were more easily attracted to Christianity and other novel ideas than were the more permanently settled Chinese.

The founder of the Taiping movement, Hung Hsiu-ch'uan (1814–64), was a Hakka from a rural community located near the treaty port of Canton. A village teacher and unsuccessful candidate for degree-holding status, Hung was a visionary who formulated an ideology that combined ancient Confucian and pre-Confucian utopianism with selected Protestant beliefs. He soon had a following for his new religion numbering in the thousands. A military organization to protect against bandits was formed and recruited troops not only

60

among believers but also from other armed peasant groups and secret societies. In 1851 Hung proclaimed himself Heavenly King (T'ien-wang) of the Heavenly Kingdom of Great Peace (T'ai-p'ing t'ien-kuo) and began to openly rebel against the Manchus and prepare for the establishment of the Heavenly Kingdom on earth.

This kingdom was to be a reconstitution of an allegedly ancient ideal state in which the peasantry, organized into units of twenty-five households, owned and tilled the land in common. All property would be held in common, and each such community would have a church and a treasury. Slavery, concubinage, arranged marriage, opium smoking, footbinding, judicial torture, and the worship of idols were all to be eliminated.

Taiping intolerance of the esoteric rituals and quasi-religious doctrines used by the Triad Society and other well-organized secret societies of South China deprived the movement of some able troops, and this, in turn, contributed to the ultimate defeat of the Taiping rebels. Before the Chinese army succeeded in crushing the revolt, however, fourteen years had passed, and well over 30 million people had been killed.

In order to crush the popular rebellion, the Ch'ing court needed a stronger and more popular army than the demoralized imperial forces. These forces had proved barely equal to the challenge posed by the relatively small White Lotus rebellion of 1796–1804. In response to the emergency, the court ordered a Hunan scholar-official, Tseng Kuo-fan (1811–72), to raise a militia to defend his province. The army Tseng created and paid for by local taxes became the nucleus of a new Han Chinese-led modern army.

The Self-Strengthening Movement

The challenge posed by Western imperialism and the Taiping Rebellion stirred the court and scholar-officials to an effort at reversing the dynastic decline. This was to be accomplished through the restoration of the traditional order by a return to Confucian morality. At the same time, Western technology was to be applied where it could provide help in practical matters.

The effort to graft Western technology on to traditional Chinese thought and institutions was known as the Self-Strengthening Movement. In the 1860s, as a result of this spirit of renewal, a semblance of order was restored to the central provinces; agricultural rehabilitation was undertaken; government examination for officeholders, a practice that had lapsed, was resumed; and private schools and libraries were opened. Arsenals of Western-style arms were collected; Western technical works were translated; steamships were built; and an office was created to provide a regular administrative means for dealing with the foreign powers along the lines of a foreign ministry.

Although the chief interest of the reformers was to improve China militarily so that it could defend itself against the twin dangers of foreign aggression and internal rebellion, by the 1870s government-sponsored industrial enterprises were also begun in mining, textile manufacturing, and shipbuilding. Modern communications began with the introduction of telegraph and railroad lines and the building of new harbors.

The efforts at industrialization were severely hindered by the interference of the bureaucracy, which tended to discourage innovation as risky and also tended to take profits rather than reinvest them. There was also a lack of coordination of projects. The leaders of the Self-Strengthening Movement were mostly men like Tseng, who had risen to high position on the strength of provincial popularity and achievement, and their rivalry and regionalism prevented coordinated planning.

Foreign Missionary and Territorial Encroachment

In the last quarter of the nineteenth century foreign imperialism and the disruption caused by the introduction of foreign culture into all parts of China by Christian missionaries contributed to the decline of Ch'ing dynastic rule. By 1894 there were more than 500,000 Roman Catholics and tens of thousands of Protestants in China. More than 2,000 foreign missionaries were active in various parts of China, most of them Protestants from Great Britain and the United States. Their doctrines shook the foundations of Chinese traditional society and were opposed by hundreds of anti-Christian riots, but the missionaries had the protection of foreign gunboats.

The most serious anti-Christian uprising came as the century ended when a fanatical group of anti-Christian and anti-imperialist members of a secret society called the I-ho ch'uan (Righteous and Harmonious Fists), known to the West as the Boxers, killed over 200 missionaries and other foreigners in North China and Manchuria. In the summer of 1900 the Boxers, with the complicity of Manchu princes, laid siege for two months to the foreign legation quarters of Peking. The foreigners were eventually rescued by an allied expeditionary force.

The end of the nineteenth century also brought additional economic concessions to the foreigners. By then, Europeans administered China's maritime customs and postal system and set the schedule of tariffs for the import of their goods into China. They also had the right to establish factories, open mines, operate coastal and inland shipping, construct railroads to funnel commerce through ports under their control, and patrol the rivers and coasts with their warships and gunboats to ensure the execution of the provisions of the "unequal treaties."

The foreign powers also at this time took over the peripheral states that had once acknowledged Chinese suzerainty and given tribute to the emperor. France, victorious in a war with China in 1883, took Annam (Vietnam). The British took Burma. Russia penetrated into Chinese Turkestan (Sinkiang). Japan, newly emerged from its century-long seclusion, annexed the Liu-ch'iu (Ryukyu) Islands and, by defeating the Chinese in Korea (1894-95), began to exert control over that peninsula as well as the island of Taiwan.

The defeat by Japan stripped China of its remaining prestige. Too weak to resist, the Chinese yielded to the foreign powers' plans to carve up the empire. In 1898 the British acquired on a ninety-nine-year lease the so-called New Territories of Kowloon, which greatly increased the size of their Hong Kong colony. Great Britain, Japan, Russia, Germany, France, and Belgium each gained spheres of influence elsewhere in China. The various powers were moving to take control of the communications and industries of whole provinces. The breakup of the empire into colonies seemed imminent for a time.

The United States, which had not acquired any territorial cessions, in 1899 proposed that there be an "Open Door" policy in China, whereby all foreign trade would have equal duties and privileges in all treaty ports within and outside the various spheres of influence. Great Britain, Germany, France, Italy, and Japan agreed to this.

The Hundred Days of 1898

In 1898, in the hundred days between June 11 and September 21, the Manchu court launched a series of edicts aimed at basic social and institutional reforms. These measures reflected the thinking of a group of scholars who had impressed the court with the necessity of making drastic changes if the dynasty were to survive the next few years.

The edicts covered a broad range of subjects and were aimed especially at remaking and revising basic institutions: the school and examination systems, the legal system, the defense system, and the postal system. The edicts also attempted to promote modernization in agriculture, medicine, mining, and other practical studies. To help achieve modernization in these fields, the Chinese government planned to send students abroad to learn from the more technologically advanced countries.

Opposition to the reform movement was widespread among the gentry and the ruling class. With the support of these groups, the Empress Dowager Tz'u-hsi, who had previously exercised power as a result of a palace coup in 1861 but had been in retirement since 1889, engineered a second coup on September 21, 1898. On that date she forced the young reform-minded Emperor Kuang-hsu into seclusion and took over as regent. The Hundred Days of reform ended with the execution of six of the reformers and the flight of the two chief reformers, K'ang Yu-wei and Liang Ch'i-ch'ao, to Japan.

The conservatives then gave clandestine backing to the xenophobic Boxer Rebellion. The rebellion was crushed by expeditionary forces of the foreign powers, and the court was made to consent to the Boxer Protocol of 1901. This agreement provided for the payment of a large indemnity, for the stationing of foreign troops in China, and for the razing of some Chinese fortifications. As a result of the Boxer debacle, the conservative cause lost much of its appeal to the Empress Dowager, and many of the reforms of the Hundred Days were put into effect in the decade that followed.

Educational Reform

In 1905, the year that Japan emerged victorious from the Russo-Japanese war, the civil service examination, with its classical Confucian bias, was abolished. In 1901 efforts had already begun to modernize the education of Chinese and to introduce Western logic, science, political theory, and technology. Thousands of students were sent abroad to study, chiefly to Japan, and an elementary school system similar to the Japanese was begun. The Imperial University at Peking was founded during the Hundred Days of 1898, with a United States citizen as dean of Western Studies. It was expanded in 1902 to include a Western languages department. Later the name was changed to the Peking National University (commonly abbreviated as Peita, from its Chinese name). The university was to play a major role in the popularization of Western ideas during the 1910s and 1920s.

Military Reform

By the late nineteenth century Manchu army techniques were obsolete, and its discipline was poor. An archaic and demoralized Chinese constabulary, the Army of the Green Standard, was also in existence.

Semimodern regional armies had come into being in mid-century and were still in existence, relics of forces organized against the Taiping movement. Tseng Kuo-fan's Hunan army, although it had been formally disbanded, continued to exist. There was also a similar force, the Anhwei Army, that had been created by Li Hung-chang in 1862.

The need to crush the Taiping Rebellion and other rebellions of the mid-nineteenth century had led the Manchu court to rely more heavily than formerly on Han Chinese military leaders. These leaders, many of whom had been active in the Self-Strengthening Movement and who regarded immediate reform as necessary for China's survival, continued to serve as governors general of various regions after the rebellions had ended. They soon acquired considerable regional power resulting from their control of local taxation, administration, and the regional armies.

In an effort to improve the quality of these regional forces, the reform-minded governors general set up military academies in the 1880s, often using German instructors. In 1895, the year China was defeated in the Sino-Japanese War, Yuan Shih-k'ai, a protege of Li Hung-chang of the Anhwei Army, was appointed to train a new imperial army, using German instructors and methods. Yuan's army soon emerged as the most efficient and most modern force in the country and later constituted a formidable weapon in the hands of its ambitious leader. In 1901 the archaic military examinations, with their stress on swordsmanship, archery, and similar other skills, were abolished, and new military academies were ordered established.

The prestige of the Japanese army had increased in China during the Sino-Japanese War of 1894–95 and increased further after the Japanese defeated Russia in 1905. Japan replaced Germany as the chief source of outside military expertise, and many Chinese officer candidates, including Chiang Kai-shek, future president of the Republic of China, then nineteen years old, were sent to Japanese military academies.

Constitutional Reform

One characteristic feature of the Chinese system of government from ancient times had been that all power resided in the emperor or his nominees. The emperor's power, in theory at least, was limited only by his moral principles. Rebellion and conquest were the only means of opposing the ruler. The concept of loyal opposition did not exist, although the scholar-adviser had possessed (in the days before Neo-Confucian thought had rigidified) an obligation to warn the emperor of any danger to the regime, even of the emperor's own making. Since early Ch'ing times, however, the educated people (the degree holders) had been expressly forbidden to make statements concerning policy or to "associate with large numbers of others, or to form alliances or join societies." The only way of opposing the court was to do so secretly.

In the years after the Boxer Rebellion and Japan's victory over Russia, the movement among the leading intellectuals to reform China's basic institutions included an effort to introduce constitutional elements into the dynastic system, as had been done in Japan. In 1906 the ministries were reorganized into a cabinet system. In 1908 the Empress Dowager proclaimed a nine-year program to achieve constitutional self-government, and in the following year consultative assemblies in Peking and the provinces met for the first time. The suddenness and ambitiousness of the reform movement hindered its achievement.

There also came in 1908 a change in the imperial leadership. The Empress Dowager, who had been at the center of power for half a century, died on November 15, 1908. On that day it was also announced that the reform-minded Emperor Kuang-hsu, whom the Empress Dowager had forced into retirement, had predeceased her by one day. The Empress Dowager had named as her successor a three-year-old grandnephew, Pu-yi, whose father, Prince Ch'un, was made regent. The experienced, if autocratic, rule of the Empress Dowager was followed by the rule of inexperienced Manchu princes.

The Republican Revolution

By the time the court began to institute constitutional reform, many Chinese had already become convinced that the only solution lay in outright revolution, in sweeping away the old regime and erecting a new order. As had been the case in the Taiping Rebellion, the leadership and the revolutionary organizational structure came from the Westernized southern coast of China and from the secret society tradition that had grown up there in the period of the Ch'ing conquest. The secret societies, the only organizations through which the common people could seek to bring about a change in conditions, were highly organized in South China, with lodges in several provinces and elaborate systems of passwords and signs used to identify fellow members.

By 1894 a new secret society, the Hsing Chung Hui (Revive China Society), had come into being with branches in the Macao-Hong Kong-Canton area and in Hawaii. The new organization was founded by Sun Yat-sen, the leader of the Chinese republican revolution.

Sun was born into a Cantonese-speaking peasant family living in a village near Macao that had long been in the habit of sending its surplus males to the Nan Yang to seek their fortune. Sun was sent to an Episcopalian boarding school in Hawaii and later attended Queen's College in the British colony of Hong Kong. He became a Christian (Congregationalist) in 1884. His patriotism was aroused by the aggression of the foreign powers in China in the 1880s. From 1886 to 1892 he studied medicine at schools in Canton and Hong Kong and began to practice in Macao, but his medical career was ended when he was forbidden to continue practicing because he lacked a Portuguese diploma. Already a reformer, he became a revolutionist.

In 1895 Sun plotted to seize the Canton provincial government offices. The plot was discovered; several of his associates were executed; and Sun escaped to Japan in disguise. In 1896 he was in London, where he was recognized at the Chinese legation and kidnapped. While he was being held inside the legation building before being sent home to be executed, Sun got a message to Sir James Cantlie, his former medical missionary teacher from Hong

Kong who lived near the legation in London. Cantlie brought pressure to bear upon the British government to intervene. As a result of the publicity attendant upon his rescue, Sun at the age of thirty was an internationally famous anti-Manchu revolutionary.

By 1905, when the reform movement was gaining impetus in the wake of the Japanese victory over Russia, Sun had already begun organizing revolutionary activity among the Overseas Chinese throughout Asia and the Pacific. For this purpose Sun developed his connections with the powerful Triad Society and with the officer corps of the newly modernized imperial army.

In 1905 Sun issued the first statement of his political philosophy, the Three People's Principles (San Min Chu I). These principles were: "nationalism," to achieve political unity so as to resist imperialism; "democracy," the establishment of a centralized government on a popular base; and "people's livelihood," by which was meant improved living standards and popular welfare.

Sun's secret society had grown to over forty branches by 1905, and in that year he reorganized the society and renamed it the T'ung Meng Hui (Together Sworn Society). Japan, where most of the overseas students were, as well as a few reformers who had fled China after the termination of the Hundred Days of reform in 1898, became the headquarters for Sun's revolutionary group. This group took an oath to overthrow the Manchus and establish a republic.

The revolutionaries began publishing and smuggling into China a monthly newspaper aimed at the modern Chinese student group. They also made numerous unsuccessful revolutionary plots. The tenth such effort was discovered in April 1911 in Canton, and the imperial government had seventy-two conspirators executed. Another plot was scheduled for the fall but was accidentally uncovered when a bomb being saved for the event exploded prematurely in a warehouse.

Organized protests had already occurred in the provinces of Szechwan, Hunan, and Kwangtung. These demonstrations were led by shareholders in Chinese companies against an imperial plan to nationalize the rights to build private railroad trunklines, preparatory to mortgaging the lines to foreign powers. By the time of the bomb explosion, fighting over the railroad issue had already broken out in Szechwan. On the night of October 10, 1911, the imperial garrisons at Wu-ch'ang, influenced by Sun's revolutionary propaganda, rose in revolt against the dynasty. This date, often referred to as the double ten—the tenth day of the tenth month—is celebrated by Chinese as the birthday of the republic.

The revolution spread quickly, attracting as adherents various groups who had reason to be dissatisfied with the imperial rule. Sun, who was in the United States on October 10, learned from the newspapers that his revolution had come to fruition. Upon returning to China, Sun was inaugurated on January 1, 1912, in Nanking as provisional president of the Republic of China, but power in Peking had already passed to Yuan Shih-k'ai, commander in chief of the modern imperial army, upon the regent's resignation in December.

In order to prevent division in the country from destroying the new republic, Sun agreed to Yuan's insistence that China be united under a Peking government headed by himself. On February 12, 1912, the Manchu Emperor Pu-yi abdicated, and on March 10 Yuan took the oath as provisional president of the Republic of China.

REPUBLICAN CHINA

Although the Ch'ing regime had been overthrown, the republic that Sun and his associates envisioned did not immediately come into existence. The revolutionists lacked an army, and the power of Yuan, as the new chief executive, began rapidly to outstrip that of parliament. Yuan revised the constitution at will and became engaged in reasserting the central government's control over the civil administration, the provincial military governors, and the peripheral parts of the empire, namely Mongolia and Tibet.

In August 1912 a political party was brought into being by one of Sun's revolutionary associates, Sung Chiao-jen. The new party, called the Kuomintang (Nationalist Party, often abbreviated as KMT), was an amalgamation of small political groups with Sun's revolutionary secret society, the T'ung Meng Hui. During the national elections held in February 1913 for members of the new bicameral parliament, Sung campaigned widely for his party and against the administration in power. The new party gained a majority of seats in parliament. President Yuan had Sung assassinated in March 1913. Yuan already had arranged the assassination of several prorevolutionist generals.

Revulsion against Yuan grew because of his tactics and also because his government signed in April 1913, without parliament's approval, a loan agreement with a consortium of banks from Great Britain, France, Germany, Russia, and Japan for £25 million sterling to maintain his armies and his administration. The agreement with the banking consortium had, in addition to a high interest rate, the pledge of China's salt taxes as security, to be collected by a joint Sino-foreign collection agency. In the summer of 1913 seven provincial governments staged an attempted second revolution against Yuan's government and, when it was suppressed, Sun and other revolutionary leaders fled to Japan.

In October 1913 an intimidated parliament elected Yuan president of the Republic of China, and the major powers extended recognition to his government. To achieve international recognition for the republic, Yuan had to agree to autonomy for Outer Mongolia and Tibet. China was still to be suzerain but would have to allow Russia continuance of its domination of Outer Mongolia and Great Britain continuance of its influence in Tibet.

In November Yuan, legally president, ordered the KMT dissolved and its members removed from parliament. Within a few months Yuan suspended parliament and the provincial assemblies and became the dictator. By the end of 1915 Yuan had proclaimed himself president for life and doubtless would have had himself proclaimed emperor had it not been for the opposition of the provincial military governors. Yuan died of illness in 1916, having failed to found a new dynasty.

The Warlord Era

The central government grew weaker after Yuan's death, and warlords came to power in various parts of China. From time to time they took over control of Peking. The warlords were often men of humble origins who had risen to power through the ability to assemble and lead large and loyal armed bands. With their troops the warlords were able to extract food, money, and labor from the civil population of a given area.

The integrity of China was threatened not only internally by the warlords but also from without by the Japanese. When World War I broke out in Europe in 1914, Japan on the allied side moved to take over German concessions in Shantung Province and in 1915 set before the government in Peking its Twenty-one Demands, which would have placed China under Japanese protection. With United States support, China rejected some of these demands but yielded to Japan's demand that it keep the Shantung territory already in its possession. Great Britain and France confirmed the Japanese claim to the Shantung territory by secret treaties in exchange for Japanese naval support against Germany.

In 1917 China declared war on Germany in the hope of recovering its lost province. The confirmation of the Japanese claim to Shantung at the Versailles Peace Conference of 1919, in spite of the objection of President Woodrow Wilson, brought a storm of protest in China.

Chinese nationalist feeling culminated in a mass student demonstration at the Peking National University (Peita) on May 4, 1919. This was the first time that the new intellectual group, educated along modern non-Confucianist lines, was able to make its mark on Chinese politics. The political activity and the intellectual currents set in motion by these modern students developed into a national intellectual awakening known as the May Fourth Movement.

The demonstration on May 4 was immediately followed by student-led boycotts of Japanese goods. The students mobilized public support and prodded scholars, artists, and journalists into political action against the signing by China of the Versailles Treaty. The

Peking warlord government imprisoned over 1,000 students but had to release them in response to widespread national support for the students. Shanghai merchants and workers closed down business in that great port for a week to demonstrate solidarity with the students. As a result, the Peking government refused to sign the Versailles Treaty.

The political mobilization of the scholarly class was only part of what came to be known as the May Fourth Movement. The more enduring aspect of the movement was the change in the ideology of China's educated group, brought about by the attacks of these modern scholars upon Confucian values. This change had begun before the May 4 incident but gained momentum from it. The subordination of subject to ruler, of wife to husband, and of son to father was condemned as tyranny. The emancipation of women and of youth was promoted, and the dominance of the family over the individual was deplored. Even the authenticity of some of the Confucian classics was brought into question by the new scholars at Peita.

The new thinkers also promoted the use of the Chinese vernacular language as a written medium of communication in all fields, including scholarship, in place of the cumbersome literary Chinese that had continued as the language of literature and scholarship unchanged for millennia (see ch. 8, Education, Intellectual Expression, and the Arts). Using the vernacular, the young writers introduced a new popular literature. The first author to write in the new style, Lu Hsun (1881–1936), in 1918 published a short story that, through satire, launched a bitter attack on traditional Chinese society. The use of the vernacular in writing spread, and popular literature, especially with a political or social message, thrived.

The May Fourth Movement revitalized the revolution. Sun Yat-sen, with warlord help, in 1917 had established Canton as the capital of a separatist KMT government, while the government in Peking, under a succession of warlord regimes, clung to its claims of legitimacy. After the May 4 incident Sun began to reorganize the KMT and built it up as a party capable of taking over all of China.

At that time authoritarian parties were proving successful in Europe. The Fascists came to power in Italy during the period after World War I, and the Russian revolution had just concluded with the triumph of the communist party there. Marxism-Leninism found adherents among many of the leading writers and thinkers of the May Fourth Movement.

The outspoken attacks of the Soviet-sponsored Comintern (Communist International, see Glossary) against "capitalist imperialism" were gratifying to the Chinese revolutionaries. In 1921 the Chinese Communist Party (CCP) was founded by a leader of the May 4 student demonstration. There then began the competition between two groups—the KMT, or Nationalists, and the CCP, or

Communists—for control of China that was to last for many decades. In the year that the CCP was founded, a Comintern agent visited Sun and impressed him with the similarity of his Three People's Principles to the aims of the Soviet Union, then subscribing to its moderate New Economic Policy.

In 1922 the KMT-warlord alliance in Canton was ruptured, and Sun fled to Shanghai in August. The Washington Conference of 1922 restored Shantung to China but too late to win Nationalist gratitude. By then Sun had become committed to seeking Soviet support for his cause. In January 1923 a joint statement by a representative of the Soviet foreign ministry and Sun in Shanghai promised Soviet support of China's national unification.

Soviet advisers, the most prominent being the Comintern agent Michael Borodin, began to arrive in China in 1923 to aid in the reorganization and consolidation of the KMT along the lines of the Communist Party of the Soviet Union (CPSU). The KMT, which had returned to Canton in early 1923, set up local cells, following the Soviet model. The cells elected delegates to congresses at higher levels, which in turn elected executive committees. Party organization culminated in a national party congress and its central executive committee. This system of organization through a progression of indirectly elected bodies was known as democratic centralism. As in the CPSU, party discipline demanded that, once a policy decision had been reached at the highest level, compliance was mandatory for all party members.

The CCP, organized in a similar manner, was under Comintern instructions to cooperate with the KMT, and its members were encouraged to join the KMT as individuals while maintaining their CCP affiliations. The CCP was still small. It had a membership of only 300 in 1922 and only 1,500 by 1925, whereas the KMT in 1922 already had 150,000 members.

In addition to organizing the KMT party structure, the Soviet Union advisers also helped the Nationalists set up a political institute to train propagandists in mass mobilization techniques and gave Chiang Kai-shek, one of Sun's lieutenants, several months' training in Moscow in how to set up a party army. When Chiang returned in late 1923, he began to make plans for the establishment of the Whampoa Military Academy at Canton. In 1924, when he became head of the Whampoa Military Academy, Chiang began the rise to prominence on the basis of his influence with the KMT army that was to make him Sun's successor as head of the KMT and the unifier of all China under the Nationalist government.

Sun died at Peking in March 1925, without having achieved his aim of unifying China, but the Nationalist movement that he had helped to initiate was gaining momentum. Incidents in Shanghai and Canton in May and June of 1925 involving the ruthless suppression by police of anti-imperialist demonstrations led by students inflamed the people and were followed by a prolonged boycott of British goods, Great Britain being regarded by the revolutionaries as the chief imperialist enemy.

Great Britain restored to China its concessions along the Yangtze, and the foreign powers began to evacuate their missionaries and to recruit an international force of 40,000 to defend the foreign settlement at Shanghai.

By early 1926 the communist bloc in the KMT had become powerful, and the KMT itself was divided between left- and right-wing factions. In March of that year Chiang Kai-shek staged a coup in his party, ousting some of the Communists from positions of leadership and emerging as the leader of the KMT. The Soviet Union, for reasons having to do with the rivalry between Josef Stalin and Leon Trotsky, continued to support the KMT army. This helped to make possible the so-called Northern Expedition, launched by Chiang from Canton in July 1926 to unify all of China.

In early 1927 the KMT–CCP rivalry led to a split in the revolutionary ranks. The CCP and the left wing of the KMT had attempted to move the seat of the Nationalist government to Wu-han (see Glossary), but Commander in Chief Chiang, whose northern campaign was proving successful, set his forces to destroying the Shanghai CCP organization and established a government, composed of anticommunist KMT military and civilian elements, at Nanking in April 1927. For the moment there were three capitals in China: the internationally recognized warlord regime in Peking; the communist and left-wing KMT capital at Hankow; and the right-wing KMT capital at Nanking. Nanking had fallen to Chiang's Nationalist troops in March. It would remain the Nationalist capital for the next decade.

The Nanking Government

By mid-1927 the CCP was at low ebb. The Communists had been expelled from Wu-han by their left-wing KMT former allies who, in turn, were toppled by a military regime, and Nanking became the only capital contesting Peking. Chiang was destroying the communist and communist-affiliated organizations, at the same time bringing more Chinese territory under his control. By 1928, as a result of the Northern Expedition, all of China was at least nominally under the control of the Nationalist government at Nanking. The name of Peking, which means Northern Capital, was changed to Peiping (Northern Peace). The Nanking government received prompt international recognition as the legitimate government of China.

The Nanking government announced in 1928 that in conformity to Sun's formulation of the three stages of revolution—military unification, political tutelage, and constitutional democracy—China had reached the end of the first and would embark on the second stage. The period of political tutelage would be under KMT party dictatorship, with the party congress as the ultimate authority. In between sessions of the congress, the central executive committee would be in charge. The government, therefore, was by the party and was responsible to it, rather than to the people directly.

The decade during which Nanking continued as the capital of China was an era of accomplishment by the Nationalist regime. In the diplomatic field success was achieved in negotiations for the return of tariff autonomy, in the recovery of some of the territories alienated from China, and in persuading foreign nations to surrender some of their extraterritorial rights in China. Foreigners were willing to give up many of their special privileges because a semblance of order had been restored in the country. The Nationalist government also acted energetically to modernize the legal and penal systems, stabilize prices, amortize debts, reform the banking and currency systems, build railroads and highways, promote public health, legislate against traffic in narcotics, and augment industrial and agricultural production.

Great strides were made in education. Most remarkable was the progress made in adult education by a mass education movement. Concomitant with this movement was a program to popularize the national language and overcome dialectal variations, as an aid to the unification of Chinese society. The spread of newspapers, magazines, and books, the use of radio and motion pictures, and the improvement of communications facilities further enhanced a sense of unity among the people.

Contemporary with this period of Nationalist accomplishment, there began to emerge the elements that would bring down the KMT government. These were subversion by the Communists and aggression by the Japanese.

Communist Subversion

In mid-1927 the Comintern cause had appeared bankrupt. The Comintern expelled the CCP secretary general from his post and blamed him for its failure. A new policy was instituted calling upon the CCP to foment armed insurrections in both urban and rural areas in preparation for an expected rising tide of revolution. In conformity with the new policy, attempts were made by Communists to take Swatow and Canton, and an armed uprising, known as the Autumn Harvest Insurrection, was staged by peasants in Hunan. The insurrection was led by Mao Tse-tung (b. 1893), the man who would become chairman of the Communist Party and eventually chairman (chief of state) of the People's Republic of China.

Mao earlier that year had presented a report to the CCP leadership advocating that mass revolution in China be based on the peasantry, rather than on the proletariat, as prescribed by orthodox Marxist theoreticians. When the Autumn Harvest Insurrection failed, Mao was temporarily dismissed from the CCP Politburo (Political Bureau—see Glossary), but he continued his work among the Hunan peasantry, turning them into a politicized guerrilla force. Without waiting for CCP approval, Mao also began establishing soviets (communist-run local councils) in southeast China.

Mao, a former schoolteacher but a man of peasant origins and one who had faith in the revolutionary potential of the Chinese peasantry, worked with his military commander, Chu Te, to build up a peasant army. By the winter of 1927–28 the two had recruited approximately 10,000 men into the Red Army, with its headquarters along the Hunan-Kiangsi border. In November 1931, with the help of his Red Army, Mao was able to proclaim the existence of the Chinese Soviet Republic in Jui-chin, Kiangsi Province. The new Chinese Soviet Republic, of which Mao was chairman, was alleged by its leaders to be a "democratic dictatorship of the proletariat and the peasantry," but in fact the proletariat had played no role in its establishment, which had been brought about by Mao's peasant forces. By 1932 the Communists were in control of large pockets of rural areas and mountainous regions of China Proper.

The efforts of the Nationalist government to cope with the communist threat had some success at first. Chiang launched what he termed "bandit extermination campaigns" in late 1931, in May and June and from July to October of 1932, in 1933, and in 1934. In late 1932 the CCP Central Committee fled Shanghai for the Chinese Soviet Republic in Kiangsi. In 1934 the threat of Chiang's army forced the 100,000 people of the Chinese Soviet Republic to move out and begin the famous Long March, the circuitous retreat of the Red Army overland for 6,000 miles through southwest China to the northeast province of Shensi, where refugees from the Kiangsi and other soviets scattered about central China arrived in 1935 (see ch. 21, The Armed Forces). The Communists established their headquarters at Yenan, in southern Shensi Province, in 1936.

Japanese Aggression

In 1931, the year that the Chinese Soviet Republic of Kiangsi was established, Japanese aggression began to threaten China. On September 18 Japanese troops initiated the seizure of Manchuria, a move that was later known as the Mukden Incident. The Chinese authorities were expelled, and a Japanese-dominated state was established. Simultaneously, Japanese forces landed in Shanghai in an attempt to compel China to acquiesce to Japanese gains in the northeast. The League of Nations, established by the Western democracies, was helpless in the face of the Japanese defiance.

With Manchuria as a base, the Japanese began to push down over the Great Wall into North China. Though their efforts to secure secession of the five northern provinces failed, they were able to force the Nationalist government to agree to the creation of the so-called autonomous regimes in North China, in which the Japanese could exploit Chinese resources and markets. The loss of Manchuria was a blow to the Nationalist economy. In 1931 Manchuria accounted for approximately one-fifth of China's trade, and its iron and coal deposits and relatively low population density gave it great potential for industrial development.

About the time that Mao arrived in Shensi Province with 20,000 survivors of the Long March, the Soviet Union shifted its foreign policy from hostility to friendship with the Western democracies. The Chinese Communists, following suit, declared a united front of all Chinese factions against the common enemy, Japan. On December 9, 1935, students in Peking held a mass demonstration to protest the expansion of Japan's domination into North China.

A year after this demonstration, an event took place at Sian that played into communist hands. Nationalist troops stationed at Sian were those who had been ousted from Manchuria by the Japanese. These troops were bitterly opposed to Japan and regarded the Communists as potential allies against the foreign aggressor. In December 1936 the troops at Sian mutinied and kidnapped Chiang Kai-shek. They held him for several days, urging him to accept communist collaboration in the fight against Japan. He was released upon the request of Chou En-lai, his former political commissar at the Whampoa Military Academy and, in 1936, a senior CCP leader, later to become premier of the People's Republic of China.

A United Front and the Sino-Japanese War

On July 7, 1937, a clash took place between Chinese and Japanese troops ten miles from Peking at a site known as the Marco Polo Bridge. This incident initiated open warfare between China and Japan (see ch. 21, The Armed Forces).

An agreement between the Nationalist government and the CCP the same year brought a united front into existence. In joining forces with Chiang, the CCP promised to give up its armed rebellion and its anti-landlord rural campaign, to support the Three People's Principles of Sun Yat-sen, and to put the Red Army (henceforth to be called the Eighth Route Army) under Nationalist government command. Later in the year the CCP received Chiang's permission to build up its New Fourth Army in the lower Yangtze River region, starting with the remnants of the Kiangsi Soviet.

In December 1937 Nanking fell to the Japanese, and in 1938 the Nationalist government headquarters moved westward along the Yangtze River, first to Hankow for a brief period and later in the year to Chungking in Szechwan Province. The government practiced scorched earth tactics, destroying industrial installations and whatever else of value that could not be transported inland to the new headquarters.

By 1940 Manchuria, North China, the coastal regions, and the rich Yangtze River valley of Central China were under Japanese occupation and administered by puppet regimes. Pushing southward, the Japanese succeeded in severing the then existing supply line to China by occupying Indochina. Then, after the bombing of Pearl Harbor, they seized Burma, cutting off China's last line of communication with the outside world. By the time of the United States entry into World War II, China, a partner of the Allies against Germany, Italy, and Japan, was almost completely isolated.

The Japanese occupation of the coastal region cost China 95 percent of its industry and reduced considerably its capacity for war. Industrial development took place in the interior provinces, however; combined with the influx of the coastal population, the migration of students, and the transfer of universities, industrial development advanced the modernization of the inhabitants of the hinterland and instilled in them more national consciousness than ever before.

The economy of the nation was drained by the war; production failed to keep pace with demands; and the overissue of currency and lack of consumer goods resulted in spiraling inflation. The war forced the government to increase its levies on the people and to adopt repressive measures to overcome a growing discontent and war-weariness. Members of the bureaucracy dominated industry and finance through government monopolies and agencies, enriching themselves and a few chosen business partners while stifling the growth of private enterprise. Also, the army had grown too large and was poorly equipped and inadequately officered. Political problems emerged as minority parties demanded a greater voice in the affairs of state, which the KMT was reluctant to grant on the grounds that its political tutelage was still required.

The uneasy alliance between the Communists and the Nationalists had begun to break down soon after it began. Upon moving to Chungking, the Nationalists began to blockade the Shensi Soviet. Simultaneously, the Communists, through the Eighth Route Army, although nominally under Nationalist command, quickly became the chief Chinese power in North China and the focus of patriotic allegiance for Chinese living inside or outside Japanese occupied territory. The New Fourth Army took over much of the Yangtze River valley and by January 1941 had begun to move south of the Yangtze River.

At that juncture the Nationalists, alarmed at the communist territorial expansion, fought an eight-day battle against the New Fourth Army and strengthened its blockade of the main communist area in the northwest near Yenan, the CCP headquarters. The communist expansion continued, and by 1945, when the war with Japan ended, the Communists were in control of over 250,000 square miles of territory scattered throughout China and containing about 90 million people.

The war years, which brought about the demoralization and weakening of the Nationalist regime, were creative and fruitful for the Communists. Free of Soviet Union domination, Mao was able at Yenan to adapt Marxism-Leninism to the Chinese situation and to enlist the rural population to his cause. His theories of how to conduct a guerrilla war—by indoctrinating the troops to regard themselves as the people's army, defenders of the peasants, and dependent upon their good will—became the accepted CCP doctrine, and the CCP official ideology began to be called Marxism-Leninism-Maoism. Thought reform techniques were employed to indoctrinate the party cadres with the new official line.

Communist leadership began to develop a cult of the common man in the places that they called "liberated areas." The CCP worker was taught that to lead the peasants he must learn to live and work with them, eating their food and thinking their thoughts. Artistic and intellectual products were judged to be worthwhile only if they were comprehensible to, and available to, the common man. Woodcuts, folk art, country dancing, choral singing—all with a communist propaganda content—were promoted as the means of reaching the peasant masses.

By 1941 the Nationalists were devoting much effort to fighting the Communists. In late 1941 the United States embarked on a program of massive aid to the Nationalist government so that it could help fight the common enemy, Japan. In January 1943 Great Britain and the United States revised their treaties with China, bringing to an end a century of unequal treaty relations. Within a few months a new agreement was signed with the United States to provide for the stationing of United States troops to aid the Nationalists against Japan.

In 1945 Nationalist China emerged from the war nominally a great power but actually a nation economically prostrate and politically divided. The Nationalist government was unable to cope with the multitudinous problems of rehabilitating the formerly Japanese-occupied areas and of reconstructing the nation from the wreckage of a protracted war. The economy, sapped by military demands of foreign and civil war, sabotaged by the Communists, and undermined by peculations and hoarding, deteriorated despite assistance from the United States. Famine came in the wake of the war, and millions were rendered homeless by floods and the unsettled conditions in the countryside. Because of inflation, which greatly increased in severity in the early postwar years, many officials were driven to accept graft.

The situation was further aggravated by the Yalta Pact, concluded between the United States and the Soviet Union without China's cognizance. This pact brought Soviet Union troops into Manchuria against the Japanese and subsequently enabled them to dismantle and take away the industrial equipment of that region. China was constrained to sign an agreement with the Soviet Union in which the Soviet Union promised to recognize and support Nationalist China, to respect its sovereignty in Manchuria and Sinkiang (Chinese Turkestan), and to establish Dairen as a free port. For its part, China promised to hold a plebiscite to determine the status of Outer Mongolia. The agreement, declared effective for thirty years, was immediately violated by the Soviet Union, which kept Dairen and stayed in Manchuria long enough to enable the Chinese Communists to move in and arm themselves with the equipment surrendered by the withdrawing Japanese army. The plebiscite in Outer Mongolia legalized the alienation of that region from Chinese control.

After the war the United States continued, as it had since 1943, to try to reconcile the two major factions in China. Through the influence and the great personal prestige of General George C. Marshall, United States Army chief of staff, a rapprochement was almost achieved in 1946, but it was illusory. In the end United States intermediaries withdrew, convinced of the hopelessness of the task. The Nationalists thereupon intensified their efforts to eradicate the communist rebellion and put an end to the separatist government. The Communists had continued their aggrandizement during the truce talks and were able to expand the territories under their control.

The Communists were well established in North China and Manchuria. The Nationalists could only enter the main cities. Although the Nationalists had a three-to-one advantage in troop numbers and controlled a much larger territory and population than the Communists, as well as enjoying considerable international support, they had been exhausted by the long war with Japan and the attendant domestic responsibilities.

THE PEOPLE'S REPUBLIC OF CHINA

Establishment and Consolidation

In January 1949 Peking was taken by the communist army without a fight. Between April and November the major cities of Nanking, Shanghai, Chungking, and finally Canton passed from the Nationalists to communist control with only occasional resistance. In most cases the surrounding countryside and small towns had come under communist control long before the cities. After Chiang and a few hundred thousand Nationalist troops fled from the mainland to the island of Taiwan, there remained only isolated pockets of resistance to communist control. In December 1949 Chiang proclaimed Taipei, Taiwan, to be the national capital of the legitimate government of the Republic of China.

On October 1, 1949, Mao already had proclaimed the establishment of the People's Republic of China (PRC). Peking became the capital of the regime. The Soviet Union recognized the PRC on October 2, 1949, and established formal diplomatic relations with it on the following day (see ch. 11, Foreign Relations).

International recognition of the new regime had made considerable strides by early 1950 but was impeded by the involvement of the Chinese Communists in the Korean conflict. The Soviet Union supported the North Korean invasion of South Korea that began on June 25, 1950. United States forces were soon engaged, at the request of the United Nations Security Council, in assisting the Republic of Korea.

On October 7 the United Nations forces, under United States command, crossed into North Korea, and on October 25 units of the Chinese People's Liberation Army (PLA) crossed the Yalu River from Manchuria into North Korea. These units were allegedly a voluntary force answering a North Korean request for aid. The following day the PLA forces also marched into Tibet to reassert Chinese sovereignty over a country that had been, in effect, independent of Chinese rule since the fall of the Ch'ing dynasty in 1911.

In February 1951 the United Nations formally declared the PRC to be an aggressor and in May approved a global embargo on the shipment to it of arms and war materiel. The intervention of the PRC in the Korean conflict against the United Nations eliminated for the time being any possibility of the PRC replacing the Republic of China as a United Nations member and as a veto-holding member of the United Nations Security Council.

In 1950, contemporaneous with the beginning of participation in the Korean conflict, the invasion of Tibet, and a propaganda campaign against the United States, the moderate domestic social and economic policies of the first year gave way to an emphasis on social revolution and an attack on the social groups that were eventually to be eliminated. Deriving from the anti-United States campaign, there developed during 1951 a campaign against the Christian churches, which were alleged to be imperialist links and supporters of counterrevolution and fascism. Christian missionaries were named as United States agents at mass trials. There was also a campaign to forcibly disband a number of Taoist sects at this time.

Beginning in September 1951, the relatively tolerant attitude of the government toward intellectuals that had characterized the early period of communist rule gave way to an ideological reform campaign. Self-criticism and public confessions by university faculty, scientists, and other professional people began to appear in the newspapers. Artists and writers were subject to a similar campaign soon thereafter for failing to give unquestioning loyalty to the CCP.

In the countryside a redistribution of land among the poor peasants, as a first step toward collectivization, was accompanied by a "class struggle" campaign sponsored by the government. The campaign consisted of vilification, and frequently execution, of all landlords and wealthy peasants. This and other campaigns of the period resulted in the killing of millions of people by 1952, according to estimates derived from statements by PRC officials. Millions also were placed in labor camps.

By late 1952 land redistribution had been completed. Land had been confiscated from approximately 20 million landlords, who were allowed to retain only as much land as they could till themselves. The surplus was divided among 300 million poor peasants, thus virtually eliminating rent payments to landlords. Production fell, however, since the smaller plots were uneconomical. Severe food shortages resulted.

The Land Reform Law of June 28, 1950, permitted the retention of private land and property holding until conditions were suitable for agricultural collectivization. Liu Shao-ch'i, at that time one of the six vice chairmen of the supreme organ of state, the Central People's Government Council, promised in a speech given in July 1950 that this would not occur for a "somewhat lengthy time." Nonetheless, as soon as land redistribution had been completed in a given area, great pressure was usually exerted on the peasants to join mutual aid teams and cooperatives.

The drives against the landlords and potential political enemies, including intellectuals and artists, were followed in 1952 by a purge within the CCP and the bureaucracy. In January of that year Mao announced a nationwide campaign against "corruption, waste and bureaucratization," which became known as the "three-anti" campaign. In the course of this campaign the CCP claimed to have discovered a well-organized attempt by businessmen and industrialists to corrupt CCP and government officials. This charge was enlarged into an attack on the "capitalist" class as a whole. Announcement was made of several thousand serious cases in twenty-seven central government bodies, as well as in Shanghai and Canton.

In March 1952 a nationwide campaign against the "five poisons" of the bourgeoisie was at its height. This "five-anti" attack was directed against bribery, cheating on government contracts, theft of economic intelligence, tax evasion, and stealing of government property. The "five-anti" campaign was especially thorough in Shanghai, where only 15 percent of the 163,400 business and industrial establishments were classified as law abiding.

The control of ethnic minority groups was effected through a dual policy of pressure on small or scattered ethnic groups to conform to majority group standards and a program of regional autonomy, promulgated in August 1952, for the non-Han peoples of Outer China (see Glossary). These border peoples were permitted some freedom to maintain their own customs, but this privilege was kept within modest limits (see ch. 4, Ethnic Groups and Languages).

"Transition to Socialism"

The period 1953 to 1957 has been called by Chinese communist theoreticians the "transition to socialism." The period was characterized generally by an increase in efforts to achieve socialist goals domestically, now that the regime's control had been established and the population had been terrorized and indoctrinated into conformity. At the same time efforts were also made to improve PRC relations with the outside world, especially with those nations uncommitted to either side in the cold war between the Soviet bloc and the anticommunist powers.

Domestic Developments

In January 1953 a five-year plan covering the years 1953–57 was inaugurated. Emulating the Soviet model, the PRC plan laid stress on the development of China's industrial capacity. In connection with government economic planning, the first modern census was taken in 1953, and it was discovered that the population had reached nearly 600 million in mainland China, a figure far greater than had been anticipated. A nationwide system of registering births and deaths came into use soon afterward.

In order to carry out the industrial expansion called for by the five-year plan, the Peking regime began to collectivize the agricultural cooperatives and to nationalize commerce and industry. Between 1953 and 1956 the land was collectivized at a rapid rate, and private enterprise in mainland China was virtually abolished (see ch. 14, Agriculture; ch. 15, Industry).

Major political developments included the centralization of government control through the abolition of the six large regional administrations. In addition, elections were held in 1953 that resulted in the choosing of delegates for the first National People's Congress, which met in 1954. The congress elected Mao Tse-tung chairman of the PRC, and Chou En-lai was named premier. They had held these positions since 1949.

The congress also promulgated the 1954 State Constitution. This basic law was based on the Soviet Union model. The promulgation of the new State Constitution had little effect on governmental methods or on popular rights. The legal-judicial system of the PRC remained dependent upon CCP policy rather than on any constitutional principles.

In 1955 there was a new campaign for the suppression of counterrevolutionaries and a new drive to bring all religious elements of the country under stricter government control. Many senior Chinese Catholic clergymen were arrested, and Chinese Protestants were organized under CCP leadership. Catholics, the last religious group to come under control, were brought under strict Party discipline in mid-1957.

In mid-1956 temporary liberalization in the arts and sciences began, under the slogan "Let a hundred flowers bloom, let the hundred schools of thought contend." By mid-1957, however, the movement was suppressed, and an "anti-rightist" campaign was begun (see ch. 8, Education, Intellectual Expression, and the Arts).

Strict rationing of food grains was instituted in all cities between August and December 1955, by which time 1.9 million agricultural collectives containing over 70 million peasant households had been organized. The government also issued an order to stop the widespread slaughter of cattle by peasants.

Foreign Relations

During this period the government was signing trade and aid agreements with neighboring countries that provided for the export of Chinese foodstuffs. By the end of 1956 the PRC was committed to supplying food and other aid to North Korea, North Vietnam, the Mongolian People's Republic (formerly Outer Mongolia), and Cambodia. During 1957 and 1958 further commitments of aid were made to Ceylon, Burma, Nepal, and Yemen.

These treaties were in line with the new international posture of the PRC as friend to the nonaligned nations of the world. In 1953 the Korean conflict ended, and in 1954 Prime Minister Jawaharlal Nehru of the Republic of India and Premier Chou En-lai issued a joint statement of five principles that would guide relations between the two states (see ch. 11, Foreign Relations). PRC participation in the Geneva Conference of 1954, held to conclude the Franco-Indochinese conflict, was the regime's first effort at world diplomacy.

In late 1954 the PRC embarked on a campaign to gain the remaining Chinese islands held by the Nationalists, including Taiwan. By November the military campaign to capture the Tachen Islands (near Hangchow Bay) and the Nanchi Islands (north of the Formosa Strait) was underway. PRC troops took over both groups of islands during January and February of 1955, after the United States Seventh

Fleet had helped to evacuate some 16,000 Nationalist troops defending the islands. A brief campaign against the Nationalist-held islands of Quemoy and Matsu (situated between Taiwan and the mainland) was halted in the face of Nationalist resistance with United States support.

The Great Leap Forward

In February 1958 the so-called Great Leap Forward campaign was formally launched by the government to accomplish the economic and technical development of the country at a vastly accelerated rate. The slogan of the campaign was "Twenty years in a day." Emphasis was placed on steel production, and countless backyard pig iron furnaces were installed to try and make the maximum use of human labor for industrial purposes. The creation of rural People's Communes to replace the 750,000 agricultural collectives began in April. By September 1958, 24,000 had been created. The institution of Communes was a part of the Great Leap Forward campaign since it was expected that the more efficient Commune organization would release manpower for work on such major projects as irrigation works and hydroelectric dams, which were integral parts of the industrialization program.

The Communes, which were self-contained units for agriculture, small-scale industry, schooling, trade, and local administration, each contained as many as 100,000 people. They were organized along labor-saving lines, with communal dining halls and nurseries and, in many cases, large dormitories in place of nuclear family housing. The Communes were organized in a way that constituted a fundamental attack on the institution of the family (see ch. 6, Family).

The Great Leap Forward was an economic failure. Among its consequences were a food shortage (in which natural disasters also played a part); shortages of raw material for industry; overproduction of poor-quality goods; deterioration of industrial plants through bad management; and demoralization of the peasantry and of the intellectuals.

In early 1959 efforts to improve the administration of the Communes were begun. The Commune was broken down into production brigades, each with control over a cluster of villages, and these in turn were divided into production teams based on the single village unit. Whereas the Communes and production brigades were responsible for much administration on a supravillage level, within the production team the farmer worked his land and cooperated with his neighbors in joint projects much as he had before the collectivization had been achieved.

In mid-1959 CCP leaders admitted that the favorable report on production in 1958 that had been issued earlier was seriously exaggerated. The government began to reverse the policy of putting "politics in command" of development. Mao Tse-tung, who bore the chief responsibility for the Great Leap Forward, stepped down from his position as chairman of the PRC in April 1959 and was replaced in that position by Liu Shao-ch'i. Mao still remained chairman of the CCP, however.

By early 1961 the Central Committee of the CCP had devised a plan to cope with the economic crisis that had arisen during the Great Leap Forward campaign. A rectification campaign in early 1961 restored considerable power to factory managers and farmers that had been taken over by Party cadres during the Great Leap Forward. In March the Communes were, in effect, dismantled by new regulations. A large measure of private farming reemerged. By the fall of 1962 the Party had decided to reverse the policy of primacy for industry. The new slogan was "Agriculture is the foundation, industry is the guide."

Problems with Neighbors

Fighting along the borders of the PRC occurred early in 1958. In March an armed rebellion against the communist regime in Tibet was quickly put down by PRC troops. From August through October of that year the PRC carried on its second major bombardment of Quemoy and Matsu. These islands again were effectively defended by the Nationalists.

In mid-1959 relations with India deteriorated as a consequence of the aftermath of the Tibetan revolt. Tibetan refugees fled to India, and the PRC accused India of having abetted the rebels. In addition, the PRC laid claim to nearly 40,000 square miles of territory that India had regarded as within its own borders.

The Soviet Union had, in the meantime, made gestures of conciliation toward its chief enemy in the cold war, the United States, which culminated in a visit of Premier Nikita Khrushchev to the United States in September 1959. The same month the official Soviet Union news agency published its first public attack in what was to become a bitter Sino-Soviet controversy. The attack was a criticism of the stationing of troops by the PRC along the border with India (see ch. 11, Foreign Relations). By mid-1960 the rift had widened to the extent that the Soviet Union withdrew thousands of technicians who were in China to carry out technical aid programs.

In October 1962 PRC troops crossed into India along the Himalayan frontier. They withdrew within a month, although they had gained a clear military victory over the Indian defense forces.

With other neighbors, border problems were peacefully resolved. Border agreements were signed with Burma and Nepal in 1960, with Bhutan in 1961, and with Pakistan and the Mongolian People's

Republic in 1962. The border with Laos was not in dispute, but the PRC expressed support for Laotian neutrality in the early 1960s.

Internal Conflict

After the failure of the Great Leap Forward began to be evidenced, Mao stepped down from his position as chairman of the PRC, in which he was replaced by Liu Shao-ch'i. At the same time, however, the publication of his writings and a government-sponsored Mao personality cult were attempting to make the man and his work the object of national veneration, rather as Confucius and the Confucian classics had been during the imperial period (see ch. 10, Political Dynamics).

From 1963 to 1966 the CCP carried out a socialist education campaign designed to restore ideological purity and revive revolutionary spirit in the Party and the public at large. In connection with this campaign, a thorough reform of the educational system, which had been planned earlier to coincide with the Great Leap went into effect. This education reform had the dual purpose of providing mass education less expensively than previously and of reorienting the values of scholars so that they would no longer despise manual labor. The main feature of the reform program was the combination work-study system in which schooling was programmed to fit in with, and be oriented toward, the work schedules of Communes and factories.

The drafting of intellectuals for manual labor was part of a continuing campaign by the CCP, publicized through the mass media, to remove "bourgeois" influences from the intellectuals and technical experts—in particular, their tendency to have greater regard for their own specialized expertise than for the goals of the Party. Government propaganda accused the intellectuals and professional people of putting "expertise" ahead of "redness."

By mid-1965 Mao had regained control of Party policy sufficiently to launch a campaign to make the study of Mao Tse-tung Thought the chief means of solving all problems. Bolstered by the authority given him by the reverence accorded his published work, Mao attempted to arouse in the public at large a revolutionary fervor to counteract and overcome the conservatism and inertia that he alleged had overtaken the CCP.

The result was the explosive Great Proletarian Cultural Revolution. Triggered by an attack in the press on a contemporary playwright in late 1965, the Cultural Revolution had evolved by mid-1966 into the first mass action in the PRC to have emerged against the CCP apparatus itself. The effects of the Cultural Revolution were still being felt in mid-1971 in all aspects of mainland Chinese life (see ch. 10, Political Dynamics; ch. 8, Education, Intellectual Expression, and the Arts).

In early 1969, however, the internal situation began to stabilize, since the severe disruptions that characterized the 1967–68 period were subsiding. By 1969 the PRC's international prestige had grown as a result of its having remained in power for two decades and also because of the industrial and technological advances it had made. A spectacular example of this progress came in October 1964, when the PRC exploded its first nuclear device. In the late 1960s efforts were begun to improve the PRC's relations internationally (see ch. 11, Foreign Relations).

CHAPTER 4

ETHNIC GROUPS AND LANGUAGES

Although the Chinese people are relatively homogeneous, the People's Republic of China (PRC) comprises diverse ethnic groups and languages whose multinational nature is symbolized in the national flag. This ensign is a solid red field having one large and four small gold stars in the upper left-hand corner. The large star represents the Han ethnic community, which has been dominant in the land for centuries and accounts for 94 percent of the population. The small stars represent Inner Mongolia, Manchuria, Sinkiang, and Tibet—the homelands of major non-Han peoples absorbed by the Chinese state. Within the country as a whole there are over sixty non-Han groups, called minority nationalities, which in 1961 were estimated to constitute about 6 percent of the total population and are believed to have maintained the same proportion since that time. The Han outnumber these national minorities everywhere except in the Tibetan Autonomous Region and the Sinkiang Uighur Autonomous Region (Sinkiang).

The Han Chinese inhabit China Proper and the three northeastern provinces of Heilungkiang, Kirin, and Liaoning (collectively known as Manchuria), where Chinese migrants have been settled for many decades (see ch. 2, Physical Environment and Population). The minority nationalities are widespread but are concentrated mainly in border areas. Most of them inhabit their own autonomous regions, districts, or counties within a larger autonomous region or a regular Han province (see fig. 8).

The Han speak a number of related Sinitic languages that are known collectively as Chinese, of which the major form is Mandarin (Northern and Southern); other forms are Wu, Hsiang, Kan, Min, Hakka, and Yueh (Cantonese). These various forms are mutually unintelligible when spoken but use a common ideographic writing system that enables any literate Chinese to read them all by simply pronouncing the words in his own language. Written Chinese is also read by classically educated Japanese, Koreans, and Vietnamese.

The languages of the minority nationalities also are unintelligible both to each other and to Chinese, resulting in much bilingualism among individuals who deal with the Han. Despite the 1954 State Constitution, which guarantees the minority peoples "freedom to use and foster the growth of their spoken and written languages," the government has been less than scrupulous in this regard.

Although national policy has long been one of assimilating national minorities, it has been intensified under the communist regime as a means of strengthening the unity of the country and of facilitating agricultural and industrial development in minority areas. Qualified observers believe that pledges of autonomy that were given by the Communists when they came to power have been more or less ignored.

Although the authorities have aided the advancement of the minorities through the provision of schools, hospitals, and industries and have permitted some elements of the cultural heritage to be retained, the regime in power in 1971 exercised far more stringent controls than any of its predecessors. Also, all local resources are completely subordinated to the needs of China's national economy. Efforts to impose the national language and to suppress local religious practices and other customs have been carried out since the 1958–59 period despite professions to the contrary. This was particularly true as the result of the Great Proletarian Cultural Revolution of the 1966–69 period.

The official view of the regime is that there is no single Chinese nation but rather a multinational Communist Chinese state—a fraternal cooperative of Han Chinese and minorities, each holding equal rights. Evidence that there is actual or incipient dissidence in the autonomous regions suggests that the implementation of equal status for minority groups varies sharply from the stated objectives (see ch. 9, Political System and Values; ch. 10, Political Dynamics).

THE HAN PEOPLE AND THE MINORITY NATIONALITIES

The origin of present-day Chinese culture is believed to have centered in a people who called themselves Han after the dynasty that ruled China between 206 B.C. and A.D. 221. These people inhabited the Yellow River Valley of North China from which they radiated outward, assimilating other groups, including various Austroasiatic-speaking peoples in the south, Tungusic tribes in the north, and Tibeto-Burman-speaking peoples in the west and southwest. The amalgamated peoples became the Han Chinese—all of whom speak a form of Chinese and have the common social organization, values, and cultural characteristics that are universally recognized as Chinese civilization (see ch. 5, Social System and Values).

As the Han Chinese expanded and assumed control over the area in succeeding centuries, they enveloped a number of other ethnic groups who have more or less resisted being assimilated. These groups differ ·

widely from the Han in language, cultural background, social values, and physical characteristics and have maintained their identities as separate ethnic groups. There has never been a definitive list or satisfactory method of classifying them, and only the vaguest criteria exist for distinguishing them from the Han and from each other. Language, religion, ways of living, and so-called backwardness have sometimes been used as differentiating factors, but they are not always reliable, and some officially designated minority nationalities can be regarded as Han Chinese by any one of these standards. The Hui group, for example, appears to be no more than Chinese Muslims, and the Manchus and Chuang groups have been so completely assimilated that they have virtually lost their separate identities.

Minority nationality groups range in size from the less than 600 Hoche, a Tungusic people who live along the Ussuri River in Northern Manchuria, to the Chuang of South China who, in 1971, were estimated to total almost 8 million. Out of the more than sixty minority nationality groups, only ten are believed to contain more than 1 million members (see table 3).

Table 3. Major Minority Nationalities of the People's Republic of China, 1961 (in millions)

Minority Group	Principal Locations [1]	Group Size [2]
Chuang	Kwangsi, Yunnan, Kwangtung	7.80
Hui	Ninghsia, Kansu, Sinkiang, Tsinghai, Yunnan, Kweichow	3.93
Uighur	Sinkiang	3.90
Yi	Szechwan, Yunnan	3.26
Tibetan	Tibet, Szechwan, Yunnan, Tsinghai, Kansu	2.77
Miao	Kweichow, Hunan, Yunnan	2.68
Manchu	Liaoning, Kirin, Heilungkiang	2.43
Mongol	Inner Mongolia, Ninghsia, Sinkiang, Kansu, Tsinghai	1.64
Puyi	Kweichow	1.31
Korean	Kirin	1.25

[1] People of minority groups are widely distributed throughout China.

[2] Locations cited are only those of their major concentrations. Figures are based on the last census (1953) updated by various sources through 1961. Firm and more accurate figures have not been cited since that year, but the generally accepted annual rate of population increase, estimated to be between 2 and 2.5 percent, would indicate that the figures in the table may be quite low for 1971.

Source: Adapted from Amrit Lal, "Sinification of Ethnic Minorities in China," *Current Scene: Developments in Mainland China* [Hong Kong], VIII, No. 4, February 15, 1970; *Jen-Min Shou-Ts'e (People's Handbook), 1965*, Peking, 1965; and Chugoku Kenkyujo (Chinese Research Institute), *Shin Chugoku Nenkan, 1970* (New China Yearbook, 1970), Tokyo, 1970.

Some minority nationalities can be found only in a single region; others may have settlements in two or more. The Uighurs, for example, are found exclusively in Sinkiang in Northwest China, whereas the Hui have sizable concentrations in all regions except Northeast China. Sometimes a group is large enough to justify the establishment of its own autonomous area administration. Five of these areas are large-scale, provincial-level autonomous regions: the Inner Mongolian, the Tibetan, the Sinkiang Uighur, the Ninghsia Hui, and the Kwangsi Chuang. Many others are smaller and appear as autonomous districts (*chou*) or autonomous counties (*hsien*) that constitute enclaves within the autonomous region of another minority group or within a regular Han province (see ch. 9, Political System and Values).

Historically, the Han Chinese attitude toward the minority nationalities has been that of a highly civilized people toward primitive tribal peoples whom they tried to assimilate to Han culture. This practice provoked much dissension and sometimes open warfare and rebellion (see ch. 3, Historical Setting). In the first half of the twentieth century the incumbent Nationalist (Han) government endeavored to allay anti-Han prejudice and succeeded in achieving a small degree of national unity. The practice of trying to assimilate all minorities to the Han culture, however, continued on traditional terms.

A significant change took place when the Communists seized control of mainland China in 1949. The Communists pledged formally that "all nationalities shall have equal rights and duties." In the 1954 State Constitution, they also declared that Communist China is a "unified, multinational state" and prohibited "discrimination against, or oppression of, any nationality, and acts which undermine the unity of the nationalities."

The change of policy was based on the assumption that minority nationalities could be integrated effectively into the Han-dominated polity only in terms of their own accustomed patterns and habits. This involved bringing minority leaders into closer cooperation with the government, granting them a modicum of self-rule, and training minority youth in Chinese schools to hasten the eventual transformation of their own people. The process was aided and abetted by intense propaganda designed to gain acceptance of the communist ideology by all minority groups.

Official efforts to integrate the minority peoples were stepped up in 1958 and 1959, contemporaneous with the Great Leap Forward, but rebellions broke out, such as that in Tibet, because of resentment over the strict control and the enforced regimentation imposed on the minority people by the central government. Resistance was reported in such fields as land collectivization, efforts to establish literacy in the national language, attempts to reform religious practices, and government-imposed changes in traditional culture.

A foreign communist observer who studied at the Central Institute for National Minorities in Peking and lived and worked with various national groups emerged with a glowing account in 1966 of the equality of status, the right of local self-government, and the freedom to develop individual languages and customs. This observer reported that assistance was given in agricultural work and in health services. Agricultural production was said to have been reorganized and modernized. Supplies were provided by state-owned trading organizations at low, or even subsidized prices.

This same communist observer reported that such diseases as bubonic plague in Inner Mongolia and malaria in the southwest have been nonexistent and that the reduction of venereal disease has helped to increase the national birth rate. The Nationality Institutes, special schools for young boys and girls from minority areas, were established in a half dozen large cities, and a university was set up in the capital of Inner Mongolia. Mass media have been employed in the central government to promote the sinicization of the areas.

Despite such Chinese Communist Party (CCP) accounts of activities aimed at improving the lot of the minorities, there have been fragmentary reports from various Chinese sources indicating that the regime has encountered some resistance to its programs, particularly during the period known as the Cultural Revolution.

Much of the dissidence that appeared during the Cultural Revolution centered in Sinkiang Province, where Muslims saw a threat to their religion in many of the proposed reforms. Armed clashes occurred in 1966 and 1967 and, as a result, the Cultural Revolution was suspended; but as late as 1969 a *Sinkiang Daily* editorial acknowledged the existence of anarchism, individualism, "old customs," and "old influences" in Sinkiang and urged their elimination. Other areas in which violence occurred during this period included Tibet and Inner Mongolia. Intense factionalism is known to have continued in Tibet through 1969.

Regarding the impact of the Cultural Revolution on the minority people, the *China News Analysis* commented in February 1971 that the territories of the minorities were now treated similarly to those inhabited by the Han and went so far as to state, "Today the nationalities, for all administrative and political purposes, no longer exist. ... Instead of the circumspect and shrewd policy in dealing with non-Chinese, with important religious groups, with traditional customs of the nationalities, there is now a single rigid pattern imposed upon all" (see ch. 10, Political Dynamics).

ETHNOLINGUISTIC CLASSIFICATION

China is a land of diverse languages belonging to several of the world's major linguistic families. The national language is Chinese, spoken by the dominant Han peoples in several related but not always mutually intelligible regional versions or dialects. Of these, the most important is Mandarin. In addition, each minority nationality has its own non-Sinitic language.

The various forms of Chinese constitute a branch of a great Sino-Tibetan language family. Languages of other branches of the family, particularly the Tai and Tibeto-Burman branches, are spoken widely. Other minorities speak languages of various branches (Turkic, Mongolian, Korean, and Tungusic) of the great Altaic family. Much less important are languages of the Austroasiatic and Indo-European families.

The great variety of languages and dialects makes bilingualism common and almost mandatory, especially among the non-Han groups. In minority areas, for example, city dwellers usually speak a form of Chinese, and the non-Han people living in surrounding rural villages must learn the national language to market their produce. Even within the Chinese speech community, most government workers, teachers, students, and merchants have to learn more than their own dialect in order to carry on their daily work or studies.

Officials concerned with language reform have considered the establishment of a common national language. Since Mandarin was spoken by more than two-thirds of the entire population, it was a natural choice. Moreover, among the various subtypes of Mandarin, the Peking dialect of the Northern version was considered to be the best qualified and the most appropriate, as it was established as the national medium for writing and speaking. The selection has made it possible for educated Chinese to converse with one another in Mandarin no matter what language or dialect they speak as mother tongues.

In the spring of 1956 the campaign for promoting the use of the new national language was accelerated. It consisted of training language teachers in normal schools and directing that Mandarin be used in all radio programs, newspapers, magazines, books, and films. Mandarin also became a mandatory subject in all elementary and secondary schools.

Chinese

The major form of Chinese is Mandarin (Northern and Southern); among others are Wu, Hsiang, Kan, Hakka, Min, and Yueh (Cantonese). Most are mutually unintelligible.

Mandarin

Mandarin is the form of Chinese spoken by about 70 percent of the total population. A northern language, it spread to the central-east and southern portions of the country and appears in modern times in three main dialects: Northern, Southwestern, and Southern. Northern Mandarin is spoken in the entire Yellow River Basin, in Manchuria, and in Sinkiang. The local dialect of Mandarin peculiar to the area around Peking has been designated the official national language. Southwestern Mandarin, sometimes called Sinan, is a fairly homogeneous group of dialects spoken in a large part of the southwestern hinterland, including the Red Basin of Szechwan, the Yunnan-Kweichow Plateau, and the central Yangtze River plain. Southern Mandarin, very similar to the northern version, is spoken in the lower Yangtze River valley from Hankow eastward to Nanking.

Other Dialects

The Wu language had its origin in Soochow—one of the cultural centers of the imperial period. From there it spread to regions south of the lower Yangtze Rver and gained importance with the rise of Shanghai as a metropolitan center.

The Min, or Fukien, language can be divided into two groups: Northern and Southern. Northern Min, represented by the Foochow dialect, is spoken in northern Fukien. Southern Min is represented by the Amoy dialect in southern Fukien and by the Swatow dialect in northeastern Kwangtung and on Hainan Island. It is also the dialect of the great majority of the pre-1949 Chinese inhabitants of Taiwan and of major Chinese communities in the Philippines, Malaysia, Singapore, Indonesia, and Thailand.

Cantonese (Yueh) speakers include Chinese speakers in Kwangtung and Kwangsi and in many Overseas Chinese communities. It is, for example, the most common form of Chinese heard in Chinatowns of the United States. Cantonese is also the language of major Chinese communities in Southeast Asia.

Three minor dialects of Chinese that occur in the areas south of the Yangtze River are Hsiang, Huichow, and Kan. Hsiang is spoken in central Hunan and is the native language of Mao Tse-tung. It somewhat resembles Southwestern Mandarin. The Huichow dialect is spoken in southern Anhwei Province, and the Kan dialect is spoken in Kiangsi Province.

The Hakka language spreads over an area extending eastward from Kwangsi to Fukien, including southern Kiangsi and northern Kwangtung. It also is spoken in Taiwan, in Hainan Island, and in settlements of the Overseas Chinese throughout Southeast Asia.

There is a great resemblance between the Hakka and Kan languages, so they are sometimes grouped together. In many places in northern Kiangsi, the Hakka and the non-Hakka speech communities have intermingled to such an extent that it is difficult to ascertain whether the dialects they speak are Hakka, Kan, or a mixture of both. When the two dialects are not mixed, however, they are distinguishable. Hakka differs from Kan mainly in tonal system and final consonants.

The Chinese Writing System

The Chinese writing system is ideographic, consisting of an arbitrary set of symbols (characters) that have come to be associated with utterances of the spoken language. The system is identical for all forms and dialects of Chinese and can be read by any person literate in Chinese.

The earliest known forms of Chinese writing are the shell and bone inscriptions called *chia-ku-wen*, which date from the second millennium B.C. During the third century B.C. the characters were standardized in the form known as *chuan-shu*, or seal script. Their basic structure has changed little since then, although there have been changes in stroke styles used in writing them. The form commonly used in 1971 was called *k'ai-shu*, or model script. This form is about 1,000 years old and is characterized by a square shape and exact rendering of each stroke.

In the evolutionary process a tendency toward simplification has occurred. This has included the adoption of simpler variant forms for complicated characters, and the omission of redundant parts. The communist government has taken steps to further simplify many characters. The Committee for Chinese Language Reform, set up shortly after the Communists came to power in 1949, has prepared a number of lists of simplified characters, use of which is required in publications throughout the country except in reproductions of the older classics.

From the mid-1920s Chinese scholars began discussing the possibility of evolving an alphabetized or romanized script. Several systems were developed during the nationalist period, but none received official support. The Committee for Chinese Language Reform was also given the task of producing a suitable alphabetic script. The end product, a phonetic alphabet comprised of the letters of the Latin alphabet, was approved by the communist government in 1958.

The government, however, has been generally cautious in the introduction of this transcription system. Its principal use appears to be as a phonetic aid in the pronunciation of the characters. It has also been used to develop written languages for various minority groups that did not already have one.

Although the new system is sometimes used outside China, Western scholars in 1971 generally used the Wade-Giles system, or a modification of it, for transliterating Chinese names and terms into

English. This system was developed in the latter 1800s by the English sinologists Sir Thomas Wade and Herbert A. Giles.

Languages of the Minority Nationalities

Minority nationality languages are almost all non-Sinitic and unintelligible to each other and the Han Chinese. Some have well-developed and useful written forms; others have scripts that are inadequate to serve the mass of their people; and still others have no written language at all.

The Koreans, Manchus, Mongols, Uighurs, Kazakhs, and Tibetans are among those minorities with well-established written languages and a considerable amount of published material. The Nationalities Publishing House in Peking and the People's Publishing House in Sinkiang produce original works and print volumes of translations in Mongolian, Uighur, Kazakh, and Tibetan. There are also several local-language newspapers in Inner Mongolia and Sinkiang. The Editing and Translation Committee in Tibet also publishes textbooks, histories, dictionaries, and news bulletins in Tibetan. In an effort to expand written forms among the minority groups, the government is improving the imperfect written language of the Tai and Yi; providing revised scripts for the Miao, Chuang, and Puyi; and initiating a totally new script for the Li people and others.

Sino-Tibetan Languages

A great number of the minority languages of Southwest China belong to the Tibeto-Burman branch of the Sino-Tibetan linguistic family and usually are divided into two major subgroups—the Tibetan and the Miao-Yao. Tibetan is spoken not only in Tibet but also in Tsinghai, northwestern Yunnan, and western Szechwan provinces. The earliest records in the Tibetan language date back to the ninth century, when the Tibetan alphabet was first derived from the Hindu alphabet. A large amount of Tibetan literature, mainly Buddhistic, has been preserved in the Lama Buddhist monasteries.

In southern Szechwan Province, in eastern Tibet, and throughout Yunnan and Kweichow provinces there are groups, such as the Yi, Nasi, Lisu, and others, that speak somewhat similar Tibeto-Burman languages. The Yi have their own syllabic writing, which is largely used in religious texts. The Nasi possess two systems of writing, one pictorial and the other syllabic. Several alphabetic systems for the Lisu dialect have been devised by Westerners who have worked among them.

The language of the Pai who live in western Yunnan may belong to the Tibeto-Burman family. It, however, shows a strong Chinese influence in vocabulary and probably in word order so that its status is questionable.

The languages of the Miao-Yao groups are spoken by many peoples in the mountainous areas throughout Southwest China. Formerly it was believed that Miao belong to the Mon-Khmer branch of the Austroasiatic language family and that Yao was related to Tai. Recent studies, however, have established the close relationship between Miao and Yao, as well as their position in the Tibeto-Burman family.

Tai languages are closely related to Chinese. Some scholars place Tai within a separate Tai-Kadai family, but most agree that it belongs to the Sino-Tibetan group. It is spoken by various ethnic groups in Kwangsi, Yunnan, and Kweichow and appears in a number of dialects. These forms can be classified into two larger groups—Northern Tai and Southwestern Tai. Northern Tai consists of some of the Chuang dialects spoken in Kwangsi Province. Southwestern Tai consists of dialects spoken mainly outside China.

In mainland China most Tai dialects have no scripts of their own. The only exceptions are a few dialects in Yunnan that employ either the Shan alphabet taken from the Burmese or an alphabet related to the one used by speakers of the Southwestern Tai dialects. Both alphabets were originally derived from ancient Indian sources.

Altaic Languages

The Altaic languages include Turkic, Mongolian, Tungusic, and Korean branches. The relationship between the branches has not definitely been established, but they have several features in common that justify subsuming them under the general heading of Altaic, derived from the region around the Altai Mountains. Speakers of Altaic languages are spread over a very wide area in Asia Minor, Central Asia, and Siberia, but only a few are found in China.

Speakers of Turkic languages in China include the Uighurs, Kazakhs, and Kirghiz in Sinkiang, Inner Mongolia, and Kansu. Mongolian speakers include the Mongols in Inner Mongolia and several much smaller groups. Tungusic speakers include groups in Manchuria and in the most northeastern part of Inner Mongolia. The affinities of Korean are uncertain, but it is sometimes included among Altaic languages. Its vocabulary, however, has been heavily influenced by Chinese. Mongolians in China use their own traditional Mongolian script, which gives them a feeling of superiority over their ethnic kin in the Mongolian People's Republic who have switched to the alien Cyrillic alphabet. There has been some talk of romanizing Mongolian script, but the Mongols resist its introduction. The well-established written language of the Uighurs uses an Arabic script, as do those of the Kazakhs and the Kirghiz.

Austroasiatic and Indo-European Languages

Only a few minority peoples—the Wa, Palaung, and a few others—concentrated in southern and southwestern areas bordering Burma,

Laos, and North Vietnam speak Mon-Khmer languages of the Austroasiatic language family. Their total numbers are quite small. Only one language, Tadzhik, spoken by a small group in southwestern Sinkiang, is a member of the Indo-European language family.

MINORITY NATIONALITIES AND THEIR REGIONAL DISTRIBUTION

The Northeast Provinces

The major non-Han peoples of Northeast China (Manchuria) are the Manchus and the Koreans. Other minority nationalities of the area are large numbers of Mongols and a few smaller groups of Tungusic origin.

The Manchus

The Manchus are indigenous to Manchuria, allegedly having descended from Tungusic tribes of nomadic hunters, fishermen, and food gatherers, who migrated from northern deserts and plateaus long before the Christian Era. Known to the Han in early times as the Tung-i, or Eastern Barbarians, they founded the Khitan dynasty at Mukden and from time to time invaded and controlled parts of northern China. Their most important incursion was in the seventeenth century when, after changing their name to Manchu, they conquered the Han capital at Peking and established the Ch'ing dynasty that ruled China for over 250 years (see ch. 3, Historical Setting). It was during this time that the pigtail was introduced into China as a symbol of loyalty to the Manchu emperors.

The ancient Manchu language, still spoken in parts of Manchuria and by a branch of the Manchus in Sinkiang, belongs to the Altaic linguistic family, as do the Tungusic languages. Traditionally, the Manchus use a phonetic alphabet adopted from Mongolian rather than the Chinese ideographic system.

For centuries the Manchus in Manchuria maintained their ethnic identity and resolutely resisted assimilation by the Chinese. The Manchu Empire in China Proper (see Glossary) weakened, however, and by the time it collapsed and was superseded by Sun Yat-sen's Republic of China in 1912, Chinese acculturation had already made considerable inroads. Chinese immigrants had entered Manchuria in such numbers that they dominated the region socially and economically; Chinese had replaced the Manchu language as the major medium of communication, and in other cultural matters Chinese institutions and practices engulfed the indigenous group. Ultimately the Manchus became so sinicized that their identity as a separate ethnic group virtually disappeared. In 1971 the Manchus were still classified as a minority nationality, but their estimated 2.4

million people had become an integral part of the Han Chinese cultural group.

The Koreans

The Koreans are fairly recent emigrants from their homeland to the south. These newcomers, estimated to number about 1.2 million in 1971, constitute one of the ten largest non-Han groups in mainland China. They have tended to settle only in areas where they outnumber the native population, and most of them can be found in the Yenpien Korean Autonomous District and the separate Korean Autonomous County in Kirin Province.

The Koreans are a completely unassimilated group who speak and write their native language; operate schools, including a unversity at Yen-chi, where the instructors teach in Korean; and maintain the social organization, customs, and basic culture of their homeland. Most are rural residents, who engage in rice farming and other agricultural activities practiced by the Communes into which they are formed. Manchuria, however, is the most highly industrialized region of mainland China, and increasing numbers of Koreans are employed in the expanding industrial labor force.

North China

The principal minority nationalities of North China are the Mongols and the Hui. The Chinese Mongols are identical to those of the neighboring Mongolian People's Republic. Their homeland is the Inner Mongolian Autonomous Region (Inner Mongolia), located just north of China Proper, where, despite the distinctive title, the Mongols are outnumbered by Han Chinese. Groups of Mongols, sufficiently large to warrant the establishment of their own autonomous districts or counties, are also found in parts of Northeast and Northwest China. Conversely, significant numbers of Manchus and a few other Tungusic immigrants from Manchuria have settlements in eastern Inner Mongolia. Other ethnic groups in Inner Mongolia, most of them in the far northeast, are Tungusic-speaking groups relatively unimportant numerically.

The primary locus of the Hui (Chinese Muslims) is the Ninghsia Hui Autonomous Region, which, until 1952, was a regular province of China. This area is just south of Inner Mongolia. The Hui are the second largest national minority and the most widespread in China, having autonomous areas in many regions.

The Mongols

As an ethnic group of Central Asian origin, the Mongols differ from the Han Chinese in social organization and culture. The Mongols have their own long-established spoken and written language. Moreover, life in an area where rainfall is low and the environment is suited to grazing rather than farming caused them to develop the fundamental social organization and cultural institutions of a nomadic, pastoral people dependent on their livestock for food, shelter, and clothing.

The basic unit of social organization was the mobile camp, or *bok*, a conglomeration of tents on the open steppe. When rapid moving was required, the tents consisted of a simple ridge pole covered with dark cotton cloth. When more permanence was permissible, the simple tent was replaced by a *yurt*. The *yurt*, still common, consisted of a lattice framework about the height of a man, covered with thick felt secured by ropes crisscrossing the lattice. An open hole in the roof permitted smoke from interior cooking and heating fires to escape. Even these structures were designed for mobility and could be dismantled and readied for relocation in a matter of hours.

Their animals provided meat, fats, and milk for the diet. The skins and wool were fashioned into rough but warm and serviceable clothes that used a minimum of cloth from non-Mongolian weavers. Various forms of fermented cow's and mare's milk were favorite drinks. There was virtually no other augmentation to the diet.

In certain areas and at certain times Mongol society has been heavily influenced by contact with alien peoples and cultures. From Tibet, for example, they acquired the Lama Buddhist religion, which introduced the monastery and its supporting congregation and resulted in a more sedentary type of community. From long periods of Chinese suzerainty they acquired a system of fixed administrative units and offices and a more elaborate system of official ranks and titles that, in many ways, was paralleled and supported by Buddhist monastic hierarchies. Eventually there appeared noticeable and more permanent differences in status and wealth between the families of bureaucratic officials and those of common herdsmen and monks.

Mongolian society was further complicated by the direct confrontation of native herdsmen and more highly organized, farm-based, and market-oriented Chinese agriculturalists who immigrated into Inner Mongolia in great numbers and encroached on native grazing lands. In areas where Chinese pressure was slight or nonexistent, the Mongols remained nomadic herdsmen, but in areas of contact widespread changes occurred. Some Mongols decamped to freer areas of the steppe; others who previously had simply traded off their surplus animals and products for Chinese goods were compelled to become more directly involved in a mixed border economy. They developed permanent settlements where forage crops were cultivated for winter fodder and where animal products were regularly collected and processed for Chinese markets. Still others, usually of the poorer classes, took up farming and lived in Chinese style among Chinese farmers.

In modern times, under communism, a third and final series of changes in Mongolian society began. The older civil and administrative bureaucratic structures were destroyed, and their related class distinctions were eradicated. The traditional units of social organization remained, but the cooperative, the Commune, and the state farm were widely introduced over strong Mongolian resistance. Communist Chinese-dominated cadres took political control, and Chinese power in Inner Mongolia became more evident than ever before—despite a semblance of Mongolian autonomy.

Individual Mongols may have benefited from some of these changes, but the old issues remain. They are greatly outnumbered in their own land and, as Chinese pressure mounts, native leaders and spokesmen urge the people to struggle openly or covertly to retain their national identity. Consequently most Mongols, whether living in the pastoral, agricultural, or mixed areas, continue to cling to the Lama Buddhist religion, their distinctive spoken and written language, their nomadic traditions, and the traditions of past military glory under Genghis Khan. The communist regime, recognizing the disruptive potential of these nationalistic forces, has been meticulous in preserving at least the overt symbols of Mongolian identity and culture.

The Hui

The Ninghsia Hui Autonomous Region was designated to be a special area for the Hui, but they also have large concentrations and smaller autonomous areas in Sinkiang and Kansu, Tsinghai, Yunnan, and Kweichow provinces. These people are Muslims but in most other respects are thoroughly Chinese. It is thought that Islam was transmitted to their ancestors by Arab and Iranian soldiers and merchants about 1,200 years ago. An arabic script in their language exists, but few other signs of Middle Eastern influence remain.

Northwest China

Northwest China is one of the most remote and isolated areas of the country. In early history it attracted few Han Chinese migrants and settlers, although under official encouragement they became dominant in the populations of the two inner provinces of Kansu and Tsinghai at an early date. In the outermost segment, Sinkiang (once known as Chinese Turkestan but now officially called the Sinkiang Uighur Autonomous Region), however, the Han in 1971 were still outnumbered by at least fourteen relatively small, indigenous, non-Han groups. This area was one of strategic significance, particularly since the Sino-Soviet rift, because in this region close kinship ties connected peoples on either side of the Sino-Soviet border (see ch. 10, Political Dynamics).

The dominant people in Sinkiang are the Turkic-speaking Uighurs who, with a total membership of about 3.9 million, are the third largest minority nationality in China. Other important peoples of the autonomous region are the Hui, Mongols, Tibetans, Khalkhas, Kazakhs, Kirghiz, Sibo (Manchus), Paoans, Uzbeks, Salars, Solons, and Tadzhiks. All but the Tadzhiks speak Altaic languages of either the Turkic, Mongolian, or Tungusic groups. The Tadzhiks speak an Indo-European language. Except for the Uighurs, who live exclusively in Sinkiang, most of these groups can also be found in Kansu and Tsinghai provinces. In addition, Kansu has significant settlements of Tunghsians and T'us, and Tsinghai has large concentrations of Yukus.

Each minority nationality has its own language, culture, and traditions and occupies its own autonomous districts or counties as enclaves within Sinkiang or the particular province it inhabits. Most are Muslims, reflecting their Turkic origins, but a few are Lama Buddhists or have retained their traditional religions.

The Uighurs

The Uighurs inhabit the Tarim Basin that makes up the southern two-thirds of Sinkiang. It is one of the driest deserts in the world, but the presence of many oases enables the people to live as sedentary farmers. Their small farms, generally of about one to eight acres in size, utilize the land according to their proximity to the centers of the oases. Near the water source the cultivation of garden crops is intensive. As the distance outward increases, however, hardier crops, such as potatoes, millet, and kaoliang, are grown. North of the Tien Shan mountain range where there is some rainfall, winter wheat is important; here, cotton is grown as a cash crop, as are melons, grapes, peaches, and apricots. Silkworms also are raised.

The intense nationalism of the Uighurs is closely tied to Islamic symbols, and their religious leaders are as important for preserving the cultural heritage as for their spiritual role. Historically, the group has been the only literate element in the population. Most of their works, written in Arabic, are religious in character.

The Uighurs are Sunni Muslims who maintain ties with other Muslims and think of themselves as members of a world Muslim community. They are not strict in their observance of ritual practice, such as the daily ablutions and prayers, or in abstaining from alcohol. Few women are veiled, and many go about unescorted. Muslim dietary habits are followed only to a certain extent.

There are numerous Muslim shrines, but their names betray evidence of older ancestor worship. The shrines are associated with curing disease and with childbirth. Disease is attributed both to Allah and to evil spirits that are identified with Muslim *jinns* (see Glossary). There is a strong belief in ghosts, and witch doctors were traditionally among the chief medical practitioners.

The family group, often including married children living together under one roof, is the basic producing unit in the Uighur agricultural society. Despite the pressure on limited landholdings, large families are considered desirable because the water available to the family depends on the quantity of communal labor supplied in the cooperative irrigation enterprises. Families living together in a single community thus are bound together more by economic necessity than by kinship. A family man is respected and esteemed, and it is a disgrace for a woman to be childless.

Polygamy was traditionally permitted, but the status of Uighur women was not as low as in some Muslim communities, and wives did not tolerate rivals. The few men who could afford two or more wives therefore usually kept them in different parts of the community or even in another town.

Traditionally, wealth gained through efficient irrigation and farming practices was the basis of the Uighur class structure. The landed gentry, who held title to fifty or more acres, was socially and politically at the top of the social structure. Small holders made up about two-thirds of the society. The clergy and merchants made up the other classes. The economic base of social stratification was destroyed, for all practical purposes, with the introduction of communes in 1959.

The Kazakhs

The term *kazakh*, like its Slavic form *cossack*, originally meant a fugitive and masterless man. Such people were formed into a specific ethnic group when the Mongol Empire of Genghis Khan collapsed in the sixteenth century. Most of them had been part of the Golden Horde and were of Uzbek origin. They continued as independent nomadic herders until subjugated by the Russians during the nineteenth century. Only a small fraction found themselves in China when the Russian and Chinese empires met in Central Asia. There were estimated to be more than 500,000 Kazakhs with grazing grounds in Sinkiang in the 1960s. They occupied northeastern Sinkiang along the Soviet border adjacent to their counterparts in the Kazakh Soviet Socialist Republic.

Principally nomadic herdsmen tending flocks of sheep, goats, horses, cattle, and camels, the Kazakhs are also familiar with agricultural techniques. Poor herders usually spend part of the year cultivating hay, grains, and potatoes; wealthier Kazakhs hire others to do this for them. Milk, cheese, grain, and potatoes are the staple diet; herds of horses are prestige symbols; and *kumis*, fermented mare's milk, is a special luxury.

Winter quarters are usually permanent earthen or wooden structures in the foothills of mountainous areas. Felt-covered tents are used in the summer. Winter quarters belong to specific families, but summer pastures belong to the clan as a whole. Disputes over winter quarters are a common cause of friction among Kazakhs and between them and other ethnic groups, especially aggressive Uighurs and Han Chinese farmers.

Kazakhs consider themselves to be Muslims, but they are lax about hours of prayer, seasons of fasting, and dietary laws. They do not, however, eat pork. Their way of life prevents either veiling or secluding their women. Pre-Muslim folk religion continues to play an important role in their daily lives, and they are quite tolerant toward nonbelievers.

The Kirghiz

The Kirghiz are nomadic herdsmen who inhabit the Tien Shan mountains, the Pamirs, and the Karakorum Mountains. Their economy is similar to that of the Kazakhs, except that they depend more on agriculture and their herds have a higher percentage of cattle and yaks. Unlike the Kazakhs, however, who spread out in various directions from their winter quarters, the movement of the Kirghiz is mainly vertical. They inhabit lower slopes in the winter and move to pastures at higher altitudes when the snows recede.

The Kirghiz language is more closely related to Changhatai Turkish and to Uighur than to Kazakh. The literacy rate of the Kirghiz is very low, and the only written form was in Arabic until the Cyrillic alphabet was introduced among the Soviet Kirghiz.

Their religion is a variant of Islam, modified greatly by customs associated with their way of life and by survivals of their original beliefs and practices. Nevertheless, they feel more strongly about being exemplary Muslims than do other Muslim groups in Northwest China, and they are less tolerant of nonbelievers.

Other Northwest China Minority Groups

Other minority nationalities in Northwest China are smaller and so dispersed that none of them plays a dominant role above village level. The Khalkhas, Sibo, Paoans, Uzbeks, Tatars, Salars, and Solons are Turkic in origin and language and Muslim in religion. The Tadzhiks are also Muslim and have ethnic origins stemming from Southwest Asia. The Mongols, Tibetans, Yukus, and T'u are Lama Buddhists.

Southwest China

There are more different ethnic groups in the southwest than in any other region of China, at least twenty-two of which are large and prominent enough to be recognized as distinct minority nationalities. Five of these groups (Chuang, Hui, Yi, Miao, and Tibetans) are among the ten most numerous minority nationalities in the country.

All Southwest China groups except the Hui represent peoples of the kind found in Vietnam, Laos, northern Burma, and northern

Thailand. Each has its own language (although not always with a written form) and its own cultural heritage. Most are sedentary farmers but some, especially those in Tibet and Szechwan Province, may be nomads and herdsmen.

Seventeen of the twenty-two groups are native to Southwest China. Five are segments of minority nationalities principally located in other regions—the Chuang, Miao, Yao, and Puyi from South China and the Hui from North China. They range in size from the Pumi of Yunnan, who have less than 2,000 members, to the Yi of Yunnan and Szechwan, who number about 3.26 million.

The Tibetans

The Tibetan Autonomous Region lying to the extreme southwest in the high mountains and plateaus of the Greater Himalayan Range is the homeland of the Tibetans, but the group also has many autonomous areas in Sinkiang, Kansu, and Tsinghai. About 80 percent of the population in the homeland are sedentary farmers who cultivate the poor, sandy soils of the southern and southeastern parts of the area. The other 20 percent are nomadic herdsmen who occupy the northern plateau regions. A few Tibetans are traders, craftsmen, government officials, and clerks in towns.

Sedentary communities of the Tibetans are usually tightly knit villages consisting of related families living in adjacent permanent houses. Each community is administered by an elected village headman and a council of elders. The soil of their surrounding farms is fertilized mainly by human and animal excreta and, since rainfall is scarce, is sometimes irrigated by primitive, inefficient systems. Crop rotation is known but is not systematically carried out. The principal crop is barley, but turnips, potatoes, wheat, and millet are also grown. Peas are raised as fodder for horses. Some beef and dairy cattle are raised as a sideline, but they are generally poor. Yields of milk and butter are small but are highly valued.

The basic form of communal organization among the nomads is the encampment, or tent-circle, of five to eighty families banded together for protection and cooperative effort in handling their herds. These encampments are designed for mobility, since they must move with the seasons. From late spring through summer, community herds are grazed in successively higher pastures because of the short growing season at each level. In winter the community descends into river valleys and changes its patterns of living from herding to trading, repairing equipment, and weaving yak haircloth. Winter, a time when little cooperative labor is required, is also a period of intensified social life.

The basic social unit is the family, characterized by a varying and complex composition. Several forms of marriage are customary and acceptable. Monogamy is the most prevalent, but variations, including polyandry, in which one woman cohabits with several men, and polygyny, involving the mating of one man with several females, are common. The precise form of marriage followed in individual cases seems to be associated with a desire to maintain family landholdings intact—a motivation that underlies many other cultural values and practices.

The eldest son in the paternal line is the head of the family. His younger brothers do not have the right to marry formally and, customarily, enter a monastery when they reach a certain age. In large families, however, one or two may remain home and, unable to marry, cohabit with a brother's wife. Any issue from such an arrangement is always considered to be an offspring of the family head.

When the eldest son marries or has his first child, he displaces his father, becoming the family head and assuming the taxpaying and labor service burdens that accompany the family's landholdings. The father moves to a smaller house on the property, accompanied by his wife and any unmarried daughters.

If the new head of the family is not capable of having children, he informs his younger brother in the monastery, and they may agree that a child be adopted to continue the family line. It is far more common, however, for the younger brother to leave the monastery, replacing his brother as head of the family, and taking his wife without the necessity of a formal marriage ceremony. Sometimes when there are no brothers, an additional wife is taken into the household if the first wife is childless, and even a third wife is taken if the second one remains barren. At other times two additional husbands (in addition to brothers of the original husband if they are available) may be called in before turning to adoption as a last resort.

The formal or state religion of Tibetans is Lamaism, an adaptation of Buddhism in which the concepts of *karma*, *nirvana*, transmigration, and reincarnation have remained basic. It has been seriously weakened by the Communists, and thousands of its monks have been forced to work as laborers on road construction or to perform other menial tasks. The prevailing sect is the Yellow Hat, of which the Dalai Lama is the de facto head. The Dalai Lama, who resided in Lhasa until he fled to India in 1959, formerly was also the political leader of Tibet. A lama of secondary importance, the Panchen Lama, thereupon was installed by the Communists on the throne vacated by the Dalai Lama but was deposed by them five years later for statements supporting the traditional head.

Both the Dalai Lama and the Panchen Lama are believed to be reincarnations of their predecessors. When either dies, the priesthood has to determine in which newly born child the Lama has been reincarnated. This could occur anywhere, often in a peasant family. Such a family automatically becomes a member of the noble class.

The basis of Lamaism is the monastery system, and monastic institutions are found everywhere in Tibet. Some monasteries house more than 5,000 monks or lama priests. Many also have associated colleges and are centers of learning and repositories of Buddhist literature. Others have huge grain storehouses that are used to alleviate hunger during crop failure, and until 1959 no major region had experienced famine.

In substance, the belief embraces elements of a much older religion, the Bon or Bon-pa, involving belief in nature spirits, evil spirits, practices of propitiation, and magic. This form is still practiced among tribesmen who are more remote from the influence of formal Lamaism. Among them, illness is attributed to evil spirits and must be cured by magical means. Lamas sometimes cure illness by chanting Buddhist *sutras* or religious incantations. Divination, or fortunetelling, is also popular and takes many forms.

Until the communist annexation of Tibet in October 1950, land was divided equally among peasants, although in principle it remained the property of the Dalai Lama. Technically, the actual landholder merely used his portion in return for assuming various obligations, such as paying taxes and providing labor services as requested. Over the centuries parcels of land changed hands, often being consolidated into large tracts occupied and controlled by certain aggressive individuals or families.

At the top of the social structure traditionally was the noble class, whose members lived in cities and were the largest landholders before the advent of communism. Included among the nobility were descendants of former Dalai Lamas and former monarchs, or descendants of individuals who had performed meritorious political or military service. Their present-day influence is minimal, especially since the central government introduced in 1959 a series of "democratic reforms" in administration, land tenure and industry. By late 1960 land redistribution had been about 90 percent completed; the remainder had been probably redistributed at the latest by the time the Cultural Revolution receded in 1969.

Very little is known about class structures among the nomadic herdsmen. In agricultural areas, however, there were, at least until the 1960s, several categories of peasants at the apex of which were the heads of families and other individuals who controlled sizable land tracts on which they paid taxes. Below them were lesser peasants, mainly younger sons and others who had no land in their own right. Many of this class entered monasteries, but many others became dependent landholders on the property of a noble or a taxpaying tenant. Upon death the land they cultivated reverted to its primary holder.

Probably those who benefited most from the communist rule were many landless rural laborers and household servants who formed the lowest class. In the past, they could not enter a monastery and could not legally marry, so they perpetuated themselves primarily by informal cohabitation and therefore could not hope to raise themselves to a higher class level. From this group, the Communists have recruited many cadres on the assumption that, having nothing to lose, they are most likely to be loyal to the new regime.

The Yi

Traditionally, the Yi, sometimes called the Lolo, were divided into castes. The dominant caste was the Black Yi, which owned all property and had political control of the villages. The lower caste had two divisions in early times: the White Yi and Chinese slaves. Both were regarded as chattel property by the Black Yi and were required to do all domestic and agricultural work. As captured Chinese became assimilated to the group, they acquired status as White Yi and could improve their status by renting land from their Black Yi masters. There was no mobility between the Black Yi and the lower castes, but barriers between the White Yi and Chinese slaves were less rigid.

The clans in Yi society are patrilineal, each being made up of members claiming descent from a common ancestor. Clan organizations tend to be fairly large, having several main and auxiliary branches. Members of a clan live in a village, but larger clans sometimes occupy a number of adjacent villages. The villages are highly cohesive, being tied together by kinship as well as by proximity and matters of common security. There is no formal system of succession to village leadership, as the leader is chosen by common consent and on the basis of personal characteristics. Wealth may be a factor, but desirable personal qualities such as leadership are more important.

The main economic activity of the Yi is agriculture, which is looked down upon by the Black Yi who supervise the necessary labor performed by the White Yi. The major crop is corn, which is stored in a room of the house after harvesting. The fields are then planted in wheat and beans, which, in turn, are harvested in time to replant more corn. Buckwheat, the second most important crop, is cultivated by slash-and-burn methods. After sowing, the fields are unattended until harvest. The practice of double cropping buckwheat quickly exhausts the soil, and the fields must be abandoned for several years. Some potatoes, oats, and vegetables are also grown, as is a little rice.

Agricultural land was owned in the past by the clan but was allotted to individual Black Yi families, who treated it as private property. Those having excess arable lands rented them to White Yi, taking a major percentage of their produce for rent.

Pasture and forest land were communally owned and used. Sheepherding and goatherding, although economically less important than agriculture, are looked upon as suitable occupations by the Black

109

Yi who tend their own herds. Wool is cut three times annually and is woven into cloth for their characteristic long overcoats. Shearing time is a big social occasion when several clans may bring their herds together.

Yi dwellings are mud or stone structures enclosed within a mud outer wall. Animals, including horses and oxen, are penned within this enclosure. Construction of the house and compound is a cooperative venture involving the whole clan.

The basis of Yi religion is a conception of a world peopled with good and bad spirits. Evil spirits are numerous and have their own names and special functions—including responsibility for all misfortune and disease.

The chief religious specialist, called a *pimu*, combines the functions of a priest and a sorcerer. The position is hereditary and is passed down from father to son. A *pimu* performs cures by exorcising evil spirits and brings rain by propitiating mountain spirits. A second specialist, the *simu*, acquires his power by recovering from serious illness when a spirit allegedly attaches itself to him and gives him unusual capabilities. He is primarily a curing specialist.

The concept that destiny—good or bad—is controlled by the world of spirits is a fundamental Yi belief. Divination is therefore a necessary procedure for foretelling the future. No major activity is undertaken without first resorting to it, and all Yi wear amulets that are believed to protect the wearer in hunting and warfare.

Other Southwest China Groups

The other lesser minority nationalities of Southwest China are all native to Yunnan except for the Chiang who inhabit Szechwan. They include the Pai, Hani, and Tai, each of which has more than 500,000 members; the Lisu, Wa, Lahu, Nasi, and Chingpo, who number between 100,000 and 300,000 each; and the Achang, Chiang, Pulang, Nu, Penglung, Tulung, and Pami, none numbering over 50,000. Most of these groups are segments and branches of peoples who, because of the Han Chinese pressure in the distant past, were forced to migrate southward from their homelands in the Yangtze River valley. The Nu and the Tulung, closely related to the Tibetans, are a possible exception.

The major religion of the area is Buddhism, modified in some groups by intrusions of pre-Buddhist belief and practice. A few groups adhere almost entirely to local religions. In some of the more assimilated communities subjected to communist ideology, formal religion is weakening and is being replaced by atheism.

The form of social organization varies among the different groups. Some, such as the Lisu, that are classified as branches of the Yi family, are organized into clans based on descent from a common male ancestor. The Nu and the Tulung have structures closely paralleling the Tibetans. The Chingpo, located on the Yunnan-Burma border, are similar to the Kachins of Southeast Asia. Others, such as the Tai, have organizational structures based on the small, independent bilateral family.

Virtually all groups are farmers who live in small villages from which they go out to cultivate their surrounding fields. Their houses are built of wood or bamboo or a combination of these two materials. The small farms produce good yields of dry rice, corn, and buckwheat, except in river valleys where wet rice is predominant. Small numbers of cattle are raised for food.

South China

The most prominent minority nationalities in South China are fourteen in number and, except for the Hui, are closely akin to groups in Southwest China and to the various peoples of Southeast Asia. They include the Chuang, Miao, Yao, Puyi, T'ung, Tuchia, Li, She, Shuijia, Molao, Moanan, Kolao, and Ching, in addition to the Hui. Their languages, all mutually unintelligible, are either of the Tibeto-Burman or the Austroasiatic linguistic families and have been strongly influenced lexically by Chinese.

The Chuang

The Chuang, who live primarily in the Kwangsi Chuang Autonomous Region but also have autonomous settlements in neighboring Kwangtung and Yunnan provinces, are the largest minority nationality in China; however, material on them is fragmentary. Moreover, they have been so thoroughly assimilated by the Han Chinese that their separate identity is fading, and it is difficult to distinguish between the two.

The Chuang are agriculturalists like the Chinese and have adopted many Chinese farming practices. They grow rice in irrigated paddies, using water buffalo for plowing. These animals, however, are chiefly important as a measure of wealth and not as a means of production. Settlements are generally situated near water, and dwellings are elevated on piles or stilts.

In some of their customs, the Chuang resemble the neighboring Miao groups. They have a clan organization, although clan exogamy is not rigidly followed. Marriage is arranged through the services of a middleman and is usually performed at festival times. The bride remains with her parents until a child is born and only then goes to live with her husband. Polygamy was quite common in the past.

Little has been recorded of Chuang religious beliefs and practices, but a reliance on spirits and magic is known to exist. There is a spring festival characterized by fertility rites, sexual license, dancing, and singing. Magicians are prominent, and a form of sorcery using doll images is practiced.

The Miao and Yao

These two groups are separate and distinct from one another, are widely scattered geographically, and exhibit considerable cultural variation, but they are usually considered together because they have certain major cultural characteristics in common. Both are primarily agriculturalists who use techniques and tools influenced by centuries of contact with the Han Chinese, and both speak variations of Tibeto-Burman languages and have similar religious systems.

In Kweichow, where the Miao are most numerous, there is little arable land, and what there is must be used intensively. Slash-and-burn cultivation is practiced on higher slopes too steep for fertilization and produces corn, millet, barley, kaoliang, and beans. At lower levels and along riverbanks wet rice is the major crop. Even in good years the harvest is barely adequate for subsistence; in bad years there is likely to be much starvation.

Cash crops include tea, tung oil seeds (the oil of which is used in industry), tobacco, sugarcane, and indigo. Fishing is economically important, as are the numerous cows, horses, pigs, sheep, ducks, and chickens that are raised.

Handicrafts are favorite home occupations, particularly the production of bamboo mats, hats, baskets, boxes, and fishtraps that are traded or sold. Cloth is also woven at home, and many men augment the family income by becoming silversmiths, blacksmiths, or carpenters.

Traces of clan organization are said to remain among the Miao, but the Yao have no kin groupings larger than the family. The nuclear family, consisting of husband, wife, and unmarried children, is the primary social and household unit. The family owns its own fields, house, animals, and furnishings. Both men and women work in the fields.

The predominant form of marriage is monogamy, although concubines may be kept in separate household establishments. Children are encouraged to marry by the time they reach seventeen or eighteen years of age. Considerable sexual license is permitted among young, unmarried people. Some Miao villages have youth houses where young people can meet to sing and to establish liaisons.

Settlements are generally found on mountain slopes and along streams, with villages surrounded by mud or stone walls. Houses are strewn irregularly along twisting streets or alleys within these enclosures. Rooms of the houses are separated by pillars rather than walls and have provision for storing grain and stalls for domestic animals.

The religious systems of these groups are characterized by a belief in supernatural beings—all referred to generically as ghosts, whether they be ancestral or nature spirits. There are many such ghosts, at least forty of which are objects of special ritual observances marked by a mixture of religious and magical elements. The attendant ceremonies are quite long, involving a large body of paraphernalia and a long procession of precise activities, including animal sacrifice. Nearly every village, especially among the Miao, has one or more shrines to an earth god where special rituals are performed twice yearly.

The soul is believed to leave the body during sleep. At other times, when it is enticed away by evil spirits, the absence generally is believed to be a cause of sickness. At death, the soul is thought to ascend to the skies, and some souls may be converted into evil spirits.

The Puyi

The Puyi, located almost entirely in Kweichow Province are the ninth largest minority nationality in the country. Their culture differs little from that of the neighboring Han. This fact has made them readily assimilated to Chinese communities. In villages where they live together with the Chinese, the two groups are not easily distinguishable.

Puyi men and women dress like the Chinese except for the older women who tend to favor the traditional tight-fitting jacket and long skirt. Originally a Tai-speaking people, most of them have adopted Chinese, in which the greater proportion are literate.

The Puyi essentially are peasants, and only a few settle in towns and cities to engage in trade. The women work in the fields and have a relatively low social status. The Puyi usually own the land they cultivate and are well-to-do; because of this they have not accepted collectivism in agriculture as readily as the communist regime would like.

Religious beliefs and practices among the Puyi are more or less similar to those of their Chinese neighbors in Kweichow Province. There is, however, a residual belief in a plurality of gods and spirits among a large segment, and others are Buddhists, like other Tai groups in southwestern China. Since the beginning of the twentieth century Western missionaries have penetrated into interior Kweichow Province, and many Puyi peasants, for a time at least, embraced Christianity.

Other South China Minority Nationalities

None of the southern minority groups are large enough to exert a significant social, economic, or political impact on the region outside their individual local areas. They usually occupy their own autonomous administrative areas, although some of the areas may be jointly inhabited by two or more groups. Primarily, all groups are farmers who produce crops native to their respective areas on small farms similar to those of the Chuang or the Miao and Yao peoples. Their languages are mutually unintelligible, although all are rooted in either the Tibeto-Burman or the Mon-Khmer linguistic families and have become strongly modified by centuries of contact with the Chinese.

The groups are widely distributed throughout the south from Kweichow eastward to the coastal provinces. The T'ung, Tuchia, and Kolao are concentrated in Kweichow Province, although some T'ung are found in Kwangsi and some Tuchia are in Hunan and Szechwan provinces as well. The Molao and Moanan live among the Chuang in Kwangsi Province; the She are in Fukien and Chekiang provinces; the Ching and Li are in Kwangtung Province, including Hainan Island; and the Shuijia are in Kwangtung Province.

CHAPTER 5

SOCIAL SYSTEM AND VALUES

A high level of uniformity of social patterns has been characteristic of China since ancient times. Approximately 94 percent of the population belongs to a single ethnic group, the Han (see ch. 4, Ethnic Groups and Languages). Although there are marked regional variations in language and customs, the similarities among the Han have always been far more striking than the differences.

Between 80 and 85 percent of the people live in rural areas, where they are engaged primarily in subsistence farming. Urban areas, however, rose early and, since the eighth century A.D., there have been cities with populations of 1 million or more. Marketing and social networks have developed over the centuries to the extent that country and city people came to share approximately the same social values, although urban residents have always had higher social status and better living conditions than rural people.

Since coming to power the Communists have been engaged in carrying out a social revolution to bring into being eventually an ideal classless society in which there is no exploitation of one person by another and one in which the basic needs of all the people are met. To achieve this transformation, the government of the People's Republic of China (PRC) has worked toward the eventual abolition of all forms of private ownership and of all autonomous social institutions, whether occupational, religious, or other—that is, all except for those that are controlled by, and serve the interests of, the collectivity. Whereas, traditionally, loyalty to the kin group had been dominant, the PRC has attempted to reorient individual allegiance so that society as a whole has primacy.

As a result of the government's efforts, by the early 1970s autonomous social institutions had been weakened or destroyed. The nuclear family has remained the basic social unit but appears to have somewhat less cohesion than formerly. Beyond the family household, the social system has an unprecedented fluidity, as old institutions recede or disappear and new ones begin to emerge under official sponsorship.

Because of the dominance of the state over social institutions, the main criteria for social stratification has apparently become virtually exclusively political, and only the state-controlled channels offer significant opportunities for social advancement. Within these channels, upward mobility has been slight since 1949 and, from time to time, the stress given the different criteria determining upward mobility—experience, technical expertise, and political reliability—has fluctuated (see ch. 9, Political System and Values; ch. 10, Political Dynamics; ch. 8, Education, Intellectual Expression, and the Arts). Information concerning the dynamics of society in the PRC as of the early 1970s is lacking. Chinese social scientists have not published works in this field, and foreign social scientists have been denied the opportunity to do fieldwork since 1949.

The characteristic technique used by the Chinese Communist Party (CCP) leadership to carry out the social revolution has been the mass campaign (see ch. 12, Public Information and Propaganda). At the start of such a campaign, trained agitators are placed at various levels in the society and within various social organizations. Their job is to mobilize others to act in certain ways and to oppose certain people and institutions. The agitator seeks to evoke an emotional commitment on the part of the masses to the goals of the campaign. Eventually a so-called high tide of emotion and activity is reached. The masses have been mobilized. This stage may lead to a local breakdown in law and order, which is tolerated for a period. There then follows governmental restoration of order, retrenchment and, finally, demobilization.

The pattern followed by the government's social campaigns has become familiar to the Chinese people and, to a limited extent, they have learned to judge how to behave in order to be in tune with, or preferably slightly ahead of, the phases of a campaign. In this way they seek to avoid public humiliation and threats to personal safety and job security.

The mobilization phase of a campaign upsets the various social hierarchies and provides opportunities for advancement to socially ambitious persons with highly developed sensitivity to political nuances. Especially for junior personnel, the periods of mobilization provide opportunities for advancement within the power hierarchies. Such periods, however, carry high risk of purge for senior personnel in the governmental, Party, and mass organizational bureaucracies. They are also dangerous times for intellectuals, artists, and professional people. In periods of retrenchment and demobilization, opportunities for social advancement within the political bureaucracies are reduced, and senior cadres (see Glossary) are more secure. At such times persons whose primary concern is with technical and other nonpolitical considerations have greater freedom to do and say what they wish.

By the late 1950s the pattern of the mass campaigns appeared to have become set and predictable and did not bring about the same severe social disruption and emotional upheaval that had occurred during earlier campaigns. The Great Proletarian Cultural Revolution

(1966–69—see Glossary), however, was carried out with a revolutionary fervor reminiscent of the violent campaigns of the early 1950s.

The preexisting power hierarchies were threatened and, in some cases, destroyed. The mass social organizations that the regime had created were greatly damaged. The sudden collapse of some of the mass organizations in 1966 and 1967 suggests that these organizations had failed to gain the wholehearted support of their members, although other factors were also important in damaging them at this time (see ch. 10, Political Dynamics). For some time the Party bureaucracy itself ceased to function. Information was lacking in mid-1971 concerning whether or not certain mass organizations, such as labor unions, professional organizations, and women's associations, had survived the hectic years from 1966 to 1969. What was apparent was that the People's Liberation Army (PLA), as a result of its role in the Cultural Revolution, had become the dominant organization in PRC society and had representation in the leadership group of virtually all social organizations down to the grassroots level (see ch. 10, Political Dynamics; ch. 21, The Armed Forces).

CHINESE SOCIETY IN THE EARLY TWENTIETH CENTURY

The Chinese social system, which had endured for millennia, underwent a revolutionary transformation during the twentieth century. As the century opened, Chinese society was headed by the emperor and the imperial family. Below this inherited elite was the gentry, a class headed by persons who had passed the government civil service examinations and were therefore eligible for appointment to positions in the imperial bureaucracy. Membership in the gentry class was open, in theory at least, to all those who could pass the national examinations, which were based on a syllabus that stressed the Confucian literature as interpreted by imperial officials (see ch. 8, Education, Intellectual Expression, and the Arts). In practice, some degrees could be purchased. Civil servants were drawn chiefly from the wealthier landowning families, often referred to as the landed gentry, since only the wealthy could afford the requisite schooling or the purchase of degrees and since the merchant class was disbarred. With its ties both to the capital and to the local area where its tenants dwelt, the gentry functioned as the mediating class between the rural population and the central government from the seventh century A.D. until the collapse of imperial rule in 1911 (see ch. 3, Historical Setting).

Below the gentry were three main classes of commoners: farmers, artisans, and merchants, in order of diminishing status. Members of the merchant group were forbidden to take the civil service examinations that qualified candidates for gentry status. In practice, however, class distinctions were not completely clearcut. Many members of the landed gentry also engaged in business. Farmers were often artisans in the slack season, and artisans in towns and cities often marketed their own goods. Nonetheless, the prejudice against merchants helped to keep the nonlanded middle class relatively small and ineffectual.

In the late nineteenth and early twentieth centuries a new urban middle class began to emerge. This group consisted of those who participated directly or indirectly in the foreign concessions and international settlements at the treaty ports (see ch. 3, Historical Setting). Unlike the merchants and artisans of the interior, the new business group was relatively free of official interference and arbitrary taxation since it operated under the protection of the foreigners' extraterritorial status.

The new urban middle class included persons of a wide range of income, social status, and living styles. By the start of the twentieth century this group was headed by Chinese industrialists, bankers, and other big businessmen who shared the living standards and, to some extent, the values and social position of the Western businessmen. Below them in wealth and prestige were the compradors, the Chinese business agents of the Western firms. The next lower group consisted of small storekeepers and retail traders. A small but expanding industrial working class had also emerged.

In 1905 the civil service examination system was abandoned, and the empire began to train a new educated class to replace the Confucian-educated scholar-gentry. After the abandonment of the Confucian curriculum the social philosophy that had served as the justification for the Chinese hierarchy of classes came into question. Confucianists had looked upon social differences as the reflection of differences in moral rectitude, education, and self-discipline. Persons allegedly achieved ruling-class status by virtue of moral and intellectual superiority. Thus the authoritarian structure of Chinese society was justified. The new intellectual class that emerged from educational institutions in Europe, the United States, Japan, and modern Christian missionary and secular schools in China denigrated the Confucian social philosophy as having kept the empire economically and socially backward for centuries.

A revolution headed by Chinese who had been exposed to the Western concepts of nationalism, social equality, and political democracy brought down the dynastic system of government in 1911. Thus, within the space of a few years the traditional ruling group of China, consisting of the emperor, the nobility, and the scholar-gentry, had lost its position in society.

Within the rural villages, however, where more than 80 percent of the people lived, little had changed. The central government had never impinged more than slightly upon the peasantry. A traditional rural proverb states that "Heaven is high and the emperor is far away."

The loss of control over the bureaucracy by the gentry had little immediate effect upon rural China. Although no longer connected to the national leadership, the landed gentry still retained its dominance over landownership, and population pressure in the countryside assured the landed gentry of continuing influence among, and deference from, the land-hungry farmers who competed for the right to become tenants.

The lineage organizations (*tsu*) also retained their position as the most important social institutions influencing village life (see ch. 6, Family). The lineage was the largest social group toward which a villager felt strong allegiance. Cutting across class lines, it included all villagers who were connected patrilineally and their wives. In southern and southeastern China, where it was common for all villagers to belong to the same lineage, kin ties and village allegiances were synonymous, and kin relationships governed village social interaction. In the north and west, where villages tended to contain members of various lineages, social rivalries tended to develop out of, and reinforce, lineage group loyalties.

The lineage was the unit that established and maintained the temples and rituals necessary for ancestor worship, sponsored the education of its gifted members, supported orphans and the elderly, and provided for burial of the dead. In many instances, the lineage leaders settled disputes among kin group members. Interference by the government was considered detrimental to lineage interests. It was also a reflection on the government official if the people under his jurisdiction were unable to settle their differences without his frequent intervention.

Villagers' social relations were not limited to the village, however. The marketing area, including from fifteen to twenty-five villages, or about 1,500 households, interacted on market day (once every three or six days) at the market town. The marketing areas encompassed a social community of great importance to villagers. Although the area utilizing a single market was too large to permit close relationships among all members, the typical peasant usually was at least on nodding acquaintance with all the adults of the marketing community. Socializing at teashops, meetings of regional secret society officials, payment of rent by tenants to landlords, meetings of government representatives with lineage elders and local landowners, meetings of guilds and benevolent societies, contact between farmer and merchants—all these activities at the market town involved the rural dwellers in social relations with persons outside their villages. The primary marketing area was connected, through tiers of higher level marketing networks with headquarters at the larger towns, to the cities.

Loyalty to one's home village, market area, and province had always been strong in imperial China and was probably accentuated in the years immediately following the collapse of the Ch'ing dynasty, as a result of the growth of warlord regimes in the 1910s and 1920s. These, in effect, broke the empire into regional units, each under the control of a military leader and his armed followers. Depredations by, and rivalry among, warlords caused unrest and insecurity in rural areas, with the result that villagers flocked to the towns and cities. There the migrants tended to seek social and economic support from persons with family ties to the same geographic and language dialect areas as themselves.

The chief social institution for the urban migrant was, as it had been for centuries, the provincial or district club, an association of persons from the same locality created to carry on those burial, relief, educational, legal aid, mediation, and other functions that lineage organizations fulfilled in the villages. These organizations helped to maintain the loyalty of their members to the home region and its customs and values.

Secret societies also drew membership from the rural and urban people. As in lineage organizations, the solidarity of these voluntary associations was cemented by shared religious observances, but their chief purpose was to promote the attainment of economic and political benefits for their members. Little was known about the social composition of such voluntary societies since they were clandestine and were regarded as subversive by the government. Beggars, robbers, prostitutes, demobilized soldiers, and other groups of low social status organized secret societies for mutual aid and support. The more politically oriented and permanently established societies were located chiefly in the south of the country and included in their membership many prosperous townspeople and suburbanites of the coastal cities. The southern societies maintained connections with Chinese emigrants to Southeast Asia and the Southwest Pacific. It was among these societies that Sun Yat-sen first gained the financial and organizational backing that made possible the republican revolution of 1911.

SOCIAL INNOVATIONS IN THE NATIONALIST PERIOD, 1927 TO 1948

In the 1920s and 1930s the Nationalist Party (Kuomintang—KMT) began to exert a tighter control over Chinese society than had ever been achieved by a single organization (see ch. 3, Historical Setting). The KMT was organized according to the principles of democratic centralism (see Glossary) into a tightly disciplined network of members obedient to instructions emanating from above (see ch. 9, Political System and Values). KMT local cells were set up under central control down to the village level, at which point use was made of an age-old institution for social control, the *pao-chia* system.

This system involved the mutual guarantee and surveillance of members of household groups for and by one another. Roughly one hundred families formed a *chia*, and ten *chia* made one *pao*. The KMT leadership envisioned the *pao-chia* system as a means of gradually introducing the villagers to democratic institutions. A number of *pao* constituted a village or town community, and each *pao* was to choose two representatives to serve on the town or village assembly. The assembly would assist the head of government at the local level, who would be an elected official.

Another innovation of the Nationalist period was the change in the social status of soldiers. The Nationalists, with the help of advisers from the Soviet Union, created a modern party army. Because of its technical and political training, the KMT army enjoyed a degree of prestige that had not accrued to the military in many centuries. Whereas formerly a well-known saying was that "one does not make a nail out of good iron or a soldier out of a good man," a military career began to be an attractive one for many of the country's educated youth. KMT military men emerged as admired national leaders, the foremost being Generalissimo Chiang Kai-shek, president of the Republic of China. Several prominent CCP leaders, among them Chou En-lai, also belonged for a time to the KMT army.

There also emerged during the Nationalist period a new social group composed of wealthy government officials with connections in banking, commerce, and industry. This group came into existence as a result of the KMT effort to control industry and finance through various governmental mechanisms, and it gradually overshadowed the private capitalist group.

During the 1930s the modern intellectual group gradually became politically partisan. The KMT sought to gain the support of the students and teachers. Branches of the Kuomintang Youth League were established in the schools to promote the official ideology and to help in the policing of student and faculty activities. The KMT organizations acted to suppress whatever was detrimental to the regime, which was by then fighting for its life against the Japanese and the Communists. Many intellectuals, alienated by the KMT's efforts at control of their activities, were drawn to the communist cause.

Much of the peasantry, too, became alienated, for the new regime was more socially distant from the rural masses than the ancient ruling class had been. Over the millennia, the Confucian ruling class values had filtered down through the gentry and through folk tales,

Chinese drama, and other means until a general consensus of values could be said to exist throughout all classes of Chinese society. The ruling group under the Nationalists, however, consisting of modern non-Confucianist intellectuals and military and business people with Westernized concepts and urban orientation, had little in common with the rural peasantry who remained loyal to the values that had been shared by ruler and ruled in the imperial period.

The CCP and the Red Army, which, like the KMT, had been created with the help of advisers from the Soviet Union, began in the late 1920s to court peasant support. All Red Army soldiers were indoctrinated in the need to regard themselves as a people's army and as the defenders of the peasants. Red Army soldiers gained a reputation for paying for their supplies and helping the villagers among whom they lived to carry out local projects.

Exploiting antagonisms between landlords and tenants and helping the peasants establish new modes of cooperation for such purposes as land reclamation, labor exchange, and small-scale industry, the Communists gained the allegiance of millions of farmers. It was upon this peasant base that Mao Tse-tung was able to engineer the rise to power of the CCP.

CLASS CATEGORIES

The Chinese Communists have considered a variety of criteria in determining a person's class status. Beginning with the land reform campaign of the late 1940s and early 1950s, persons were given as many as four separate class-related labels. Two dealt specifically with the past—family background and individual background—and two—family status and individual status—were meant to cover the present and were subject to review in five years. Thus, for example, an individual might have parents who had been poor peasants and might himself have been a factory worker. These would be his family's and his own class backgrounds. His present family status, however, might be that of lower middle peasant and, if he had later acquired a secondary or higher level education and was making use of this education in his work, his current individual class status might be that of intellectual. Whereas one's own status and that of one's family might change, the "background" classification remained permanently on the individual dossiers, and, in the late 1960s and early 1970s, continued to affect one's privileges and vulnerabilities. Persons of landlord, rich peasant, or bourgeois family backgrounds, for example, have since 1949 generally been denied access to positions in the state-controlled hierarchies through which upward mobility is achieved.

The concepts used in classification derive originally from two main sources: Mao's early writing on analysis of classes in the 1920s and

1930s that, in turn, are based on the writings of Karl Marx; and Mao's later use, as in the 1957 essay "On the Correct Handling of Contradictions Among the People," of functional and ideological categories.

According to a 1939 textbook entitled *The Chinese Revolution and the Chinese Communist Party*, written by Mao and others, Chinese society of that time was classifiable into the following Marxian categories: the landlord class; the big bourgeoisie or comprador class, involved with foreign capitalists; the national bourgeoisie, with domestic control of trade and commerce; the petty bourgeoisie of small merchants, artisans, professional people, most intellectuals, and the more affluent peasants; the semi-proletariat, consisting of lower middle and poor peasants; and the genuine proletariat of urban workers, shop assistants, and farm laborers. The lowest class consisted of vagrants—urban and rural people who, lacking legitimate employment opportunities, had such unsavory occupations as robber, gangster, beggar, or prostitute or "live[d] upon superstitious practices." Since the mid-1950s, however, Mao and other PRC officials have more commonly described Chinese society as consisting of "workers," "peasants," "intellectuals," "others," and "enemies of the people." They have not, however, abandoned the earlier social category terminology.

Workers

The working class consists chiefly of industrial laborers—the true Marxian proletariat—and for that reason has always been the favored group in the PRC in spite of the fact that the peasants have always been the Party's chief supporters. According to the official ideology, the proletariat is the most progressive of all groups in society, and the interests of the working class are identical with those of the state and the Party. In 1962 workers made up about 15 percent of the CCP membership, as they did of the nation at large (see ch. 17, Labor).

Peasants

The peasants constitute approximately 80 percent of the PRC's population and made up, in 1961, about two-thirds of the Party membership. Since 1949 peasants in positions of power have tended to come from the lower middle and poor peasant categories.

Intellectuals

The classification "intellectual" applies to only a small group. In 1956, out of a total population of well over 600 million, only 3.84 million (well under 1 percent) were officially classified as intellectuals. The criteria for this classification have tended to be vague. In general, anyone with better than average education may be labeled an intellectual. Thus, in the countryside junior middle school graduates are often classified as intellectuals, whereas in the cities senior middle school graduates and college students are called intellectuals and the category "higher intellectual" is used for college graduates, university faculty, doctors, engineers, editors, and similar groups.

Intellectuals are a small minority and are regarded as politically less reliable than workers or peasants, but they are nonetheless well represented in the Party and in other governmental hierarchies. Their superior skills enable them to fill a disproportionate number of positions in the middle and high echelons of the national bureaucracy. Intellectuals, especially "higher intellectuals," have been particularly subject to indoctrination campaigns and to demands that they participate actively in group criticism and self-criticism sessions (see ch. 8, Education, Intellectual Expression, and the Arts).

Others

In 1957 Mao also acknowledged the continued existence of a small national bourgeoisie. These are former owners of private enterprises who have been kept on as managers when their companies were converted into joint state-private enterprises (see ch. 13, Character and Structure of the Economy). According to Mao, these former owners, who were in 1966 reported to be still receiving a fixed rate of interest on their share in the capital of joint state-private enterprises, were in the process of being transformed into "working people living on their own labor" but had "not yet cut themselves loose from the roots of exploitation."

Beginning in the mid-1960s there developed a tendency for official PRC pronouncements to refer to "workers-peasants-soldiers" as a social category of politically reliable working people, as distinguished from "intellectuals." The intellectuals had been out of favor since the antirightist campaign of 1957, following the Hundred Flowers Campaign (see Glossary). The social category of "soldier" includes PLA members (and perhaps veterans). Members of the PLA and of the militia, according to the 1970 draft state constitution, are "children of workers and peasants" and thereby qualify by family origin for working class status.

The introduction of "revolutionary armymen" as a separate category in the CCP Constitution of 1969 is indicative of the high status gained by soldiers as compared to other elements of the "people" during and after the Cultural Revolution. As of 1971 there were approximately 3.15 million soldiers (PLA members) in the country. The proportion of members of the armed forces in the Party had been only 6 percent in 1961, but by the late 1960s PLA members were reported to be dominating the higher ranks of the Party and of the civilian bureaucracy (see ch. 10, Political Dynamics; ch. 21, The Armed Forces).

Enemies of the People

The division of Chinese society by the regime's leadership into the categories of "people" and "enemies of the people" has been an important technique of social control from the earliest days of the land reform campaign up to the 1970s. As of the mid-1960s, for example, class enemies and their spouses were not permitted to vote or become Party members or cadres. As Mao explained in his 1957 essay, "On the Correct Handling of Contradictions Among the People," the decision as to who falls within the category of the "people" must depend upon tactical considerations. During the war with Japan, for example, all those who opposed the Japanese were "people." At the time of the founding of the PRC the "people" consisted of the national bourgeoisie, the petty bourgeoisie, the peasants, and the workers.

Within ten years of coming to power, the regime had come to classify as "enemies of the people" the "five bad elements": landlords; rich peasants; counterrevolutionaries; bad elements (thieves, murderers, and vandals); and "rightists." In urban areas a series of class struggle campaigns in 1952 succeeded in eliminating compradors, "bureaucratic capitalists," most private businessmen and traders of the national bourgeoisie class, and many professional people and intellectuals who had been taken over as government staff from the KMT regime. Many targets of the struggle campaigns were executed; some killed themselves; many of the survivors were classified as "enemies of the people." Not all of the "five bad elements" were executed or sent to labor camps. Many worked side by side with the "people" in farms, factories, and offices.

Before the Cultural Revolution those whose enemy status was the result of being counterrevolutionary or rightist or having other illegal political bias amounted to approximately 20 million people. A person acquired such a label usually after having been brought before his colleagues for a series of "struggle" meetings, during which incriminating evidence was produced by his accusers.

In the latter half of 1966, however, at the time of the most disruptive stage of the Cultural Revolution, Maoist rebel groups organized attacks indiscriminately on all the so-called leading cadres of their units. The cadres counterattacked, and the result was that many people on both sides of the ideological conflict of the Cultural Revolution were hastily issued "enemy element" labels. When the dust settled, correction of mistakes in conferring labels began to be made. Special "reception stations" throughout the country were set up to take charge of "reversals" of labels.

When the new administrative machinery for reversing verdicts came into being, large numbers of persons who had long had enemy status, enemy family status, or enemy family background labels sought to appeal for official reconsideration of these verdicts. Few of these appeals were heard and, in general, reversal proceedings were held only for those who claimed that mistakes had been made since the beginning of the Cultural Revolution.

The efforts to get labels reversed in the late 1960s brought to public attention an unresolved issue concerning the role of family origin in determining an individual's political or class label. In late 1966 and early 1967 the theory of being "naturally red" gained currency in the Party. This theory held that persons of working class and lower middle or poor peasant family backgrounds were naturally more politically reliable than intellectuals or others. This theory was attacked by others in the Party who claimed that the idea of someone being "red" by birth was merely a perpetuation of the so-called feudal practice of imperial China by which the elite was selected on the basis of heredity. The attackers of the "naturally red" theory held that one's own achievement must be the criterion by which classification is made, not family background.

Since 1949 persons of "landlord" or "rich peasant" family background (provided they have acceptable current individual and family statuses) have been "people" with full civil rights, although some job opportunities have been denied them. They have been, however, highly vulnerable to attack by rivals and by those seeking appropriate targets for mass criticism. Information covering the period up to 1971 suggests that such persons are the first to be purged from the Party and from other governmental and mass organization posts at times of heightened class awareness.

Mao has expressed concern since the late 1950s that, even though the transition to socialism has been achieved, class struggle must not be abandoned. Speaking in May 1963, Mao said that if the existence of classes and class struggle were forgotten, "then it would not take long, perhaps only several years or a decade, or several decades at most, before a counterrevolutionary restoration on a national scale inevitably occurred. The Marxist-Leninist Party would undoubtedly become a revisionist party or a fascist party, and the whole of China would change its color . . . what a dangerous prospect!"

By 1971, however, a generation had grown to adulthood that had no direct memory of the time when there were still landlords and private businessmen in China. Perhaps as a result of this fact, there began to appear in the PRC press occasional statements indicating that children of landlords and other "enemy elements" would no longer be excluded automatically, as they had formerly been, from holding cadre positions or from such key jobs in the People's Communes (see

Glossary) as accountants, recorders of work points (see Glossary) and inventory controllers.

PRIVILEGED GROUPS

Cadres

The functionaries who work in the Party, governmental, and mass organizations are known as cadres (*kan-pu*) and constitute the ruling elite of the PRC. The broadest definition of cadre includes all personnel who hold any responsible position in the bureaucratic hierarchy. In general, however, persons in the most junior ranks of the government service and the bureaucracies of mass organizations are not called cadres. The lowest ranking cadres are the regime's representatives, agents, and "activists" in schools, farms, and factories who have the task of carrying out Party policies and reporting back to the leadership at the next higher level. Cadres of this type usually remain in their home villages or towns and perform the same jobs as their neighbors.

Within the ranks of the cadres there are significant status differences and other cleavages. State cadres—that is, cadres in the Party, government, and some mass organizations that receive their salaries from the state—have higher status generally than do local cadres, whose salaries are paid by a factory or other local organization. Urban cadres have higher status than rural cadres.

Party members have higher status than non-Party cadres and, within the Party group, important cleavages exist based on seniority. Whether one joined the Party before 1949 or afterwards is a major consideration in allocation of prestige. A senior Party official in the mid-1960s complained that Party solidarity was beginning to fractionate along generational lines. In 1971 virtually all of the senior-most positions in the Party and the government were filled by cadres who had been active in the communist cause before 1949, so that the highest echelons were manned almost exclusively by persons close to or above age sixty. (Although many senior cadres were purged during the Cultural Revolution, their replacements share these credentials.)

Within the "old cadre" group, finer distinctions are often made by the membership to specify whether a given cadre had joined the Party in time to participate in the Long March (see Glossary) or had joined in the Yenan period, the Anti-Japanese War period, or other periods. In general, the earlier one joined the Party, the greater his prestige. Members of the Party generation that was recruited in the early 1950s and given responsible positions in the rural areas during the Great Leap Forward (see Glossary) were subsequently blamed for the failure of that campaign.

As in bureaucracies elsewhere, salaries and titles indicate social status differences among cadres. Salaries for state cadres are paid on a standard nationwide ranking system involving more than two dozen salary grades. In the mid-1960s the bottom ranking state cadres received one-tenth the salary of heads of ministries. A corresponding title hierarchy existed. In one ministry in the 1960s personnel were categorized as minister level cadres, bureau-chief level cadres, division-chief level cadres, section-chief level cadres, and ordinary cadres. Job title distinctions were reflected in various perquisites and privileges, such as housing, dining facilities, office furniture, and access to official transportation facilities. Although ranks were abolished in the armed forces in 1965, status distinctions based on salary, function, and rights to various perquisites were reported to still exist in the early 1970s among military cadres as among civilians.

In determining social status among cadres, education is of some importance. A certain level of literacy and academic knowledge is regarded as necessary for incumbents of senior positions. To be called an "intellectual," however, is not regarded as desirable since the term carries with it a connotation of bourgeois class origins or values. Intellectuals among the government or mass organizational cadres are more likely to be non-Party members than are cadres who started out as workers or peasants. A notable exception in 1971 was Premier Chou En-lai, who not only received a university education but also studied abroad, in Japan and France.

Among cadres, social status of PLA cadres has always been high. The political, organizational, and technical training received while in the PLA is regarded as a good preparation for a cadre career. Demobilized military personnel often take up cadre positions in their hometowns and villages upon release from military service. More prestigious, however, are those PLA cadres who, while still on active service, are assigned to civilian jobs in the Party and governmental hierarchies.

Since the Cultural Revolution PLA cadres have dominated the higher cadre positions in the PRC. A social scientist's biographical analysis of the careers of the top 1,000 PLA personnel in the late 1960s indicates that, as among the Party cadres, differences in status reflect when people "joined the revolution" and that seniority is a major consideration in achieving high status. The persistence was noted of informal loyalty groups shaped by associations among officers who served together in regional units. For example, the career histories of the leadership of the PRC in mid-1971 indicated that the Politburo (Political Bureau—see Glossary) and the Central Committee of the CCP have been dominated since the end of the Cultural Revolution by veterans of two army field units that served in certain areas more or less continuously for forty years.

Cadres known to be trusted by the Party or its agents at higher levels have high prestige in their village or neighborhood. The highest status in rural society in mid-1971 appeared to belong to members of the Commune and production brigade revolutionary committees. These committees had been formed as a temporary measure in the middle of the Cultural Revolution, when the Party and governmental bureaucracies were under attack by Red Guards and other Maoist organizations (see ch. 10, Political Dynamics). They have been retained and serve as replacements for previous governmental and administrative organizations, including Commune administrative committees and production brigade committees.

The prestige of civilian rural cadres was presumably adversely affected by the collapse of the Party apparatus during the Cultural Revolution and by the primacy of the PLA since then. Many cadres were purged; however, a senior PRC official was quoted as saying in mid-1971 that no more than 1 percent of the country's Party members would be permanently purged as a result of the Cultural Revolution. If this proves to be true, the more than 20 million cadres at the production brigade and production team levels (most of whom are Party members) can be expected to continue in their work with a position in rural society similar to that held before the social eruption of 1966 to 1969.

The local rural cadres are drawn chiefly from the poorest elements in the pre-1949 peasantry—the poor and lower middle peasants. Because of the ostracism and disenfranchisement of the more affluent rural groups, the poorer peasants have become the rural leaders at the hamlet and village level and represent their communities at the Commune level.

In theory, the local cadres are obliged by the requirements of the so-called "mass line" policy to allow no social gap to come between them and the people they lead and represent (see ch. 12, Public Information and Propaganda). Cadres are not supposed to accept any gift and must share in the work, thought, and living conditions of the people among whom they work.

Hsia fang (send down) campaigns have been held periodically since 1957 to move middle- and high-ranking cadres from the cities to the rural areas. During the Cultural Revolution many cadres were sent, or volunteered, for stints of manual labor in the fields alongside the peasants. Nonetheless, the middle and upper ranking cadres have remained predominantly urban in residence and orientation, and the social gap between them and the masses of working people, rural and urban, has remained great. All cadres have high status in relation to the masses by virtue of their political connections and their authority, which carries with it the threat of potential sanctions. Except for the lowest ranks, cadres are looked up to by the masses because they hold positions in which mental rather than manual labor is utilized.

Occasional editorials in the PRC press in 1970 and 1971 deplored the misbehavior by "bourgeois elements" among the cadres, including their permitting the continuance of clan and religious activities. A PRC press account in August 1970, for example, noted that in some rural villages the cadres were permitting old "feudal superstitions" and customs to revive. Great banquets were being held to celebrate the harvest at which offerings were made to the gods. Cadres have also been accused of allowing a social gap to exist between them and the masses. There were reports of cadres using their authority to obtain the use of collective property and labor for their personal gain.

Activists

Socially ambitious youths who aspire to cadre status become "activists" (*chi chi fen-tzu*) or links between the Party and the people of their community or organization. An activist is one who, taking his cue from the leadership, agitates on its behalf. Working with the masses, of which he is a member, the activist is able to help in mobilizing the community to full participation in campaigns initiated from above. The rewards for activism are opportunities to become members of the political leadership of the group. Mao, in a 1943 article on leadership, wrote that "the activists who come forward in the course of the struggle must constantly be promoted to replace those original members of the leading group who are inferior by comparison or who have degenerated."

Other Privileged Groups

High social status accrues to intellectuals, professional people, managerial and technical personnel of industrial enterprises, and white-collar workers who live in the urban areas. Although many are cadres, their social positions are based chiefly on nonpolitical criteria; they are regarded by the regime leadership as less politically reliable than workers or peasants and are therefore lower in prestige in the official view, although superior in privileges.

Although members of this group are especially vulnerable to purge and public humiliation, they receive relatively high incomes. Factory managers, college professors, and scientists can earn as much money and have as high living standards as high-ranking governmental and military officials. Those whose expertise is needed for industrial production or national defense have high prestige and better than average job security (see ch. 8, Education, Intellectual Expression, and the Arts; ch. 16, Science and Technology).

Before 1949 high prestige had always been popularly bestowed upon persons of superior education who engaged in mental, rather than manual, labor. It was not known in the early 1970s, however, to what extent such persons could retain the high regard of the people if they lacked adequate political credentials. The regime has worked to devalue mental work, to raise the prestige of manual labor, and to make political reliability the paramount criterion for receiving the esteem of the masses. A work-study school system was instituted in the mid-1960s with the aim of replacing within a generation, this professional, intellectual, managerial, and technical staff with an educated group of skilled personnel who had worker or peasant family backgrounds, personal experience of manual labor, and a firm adherence to proletarian social values.

Students at urban middle schools and universities are privileged in the sense that only they have the opportunity to acquire skills that can fit them for careers not wholly dependent upon political criteria. Members of this group, however, have suffered a decline in status as a result of the fact that for the first fifteen years of the regime the educational system trained students at a faster pace than the economy or the bureaucracy could absorb them, producing an unemployment problem for graduates in urban areas.

Tens of millions of these unemployed young people were sent to the countryside during the 1960s. In 1964 former middle school students recruited for service in rural Communes by Canton street committees were told that they would remain in the countryside for a limited period—alleged by some to be three years. By 1965, however, the policy reportedly changed to one of permanent transfer. When the Cultural Revolution began, the resettlement program was halted, and millions of the youths and others who had been resettled in the rural areas crowded back into the cities in the guise of participating in the Cultural Revolution rallies. The number of urban unemployed increased. In mid-1967 Shanghai alone had an estimated 400,000 persons out of work. In 1968 the resettlement program was revived at an accelerated pace.

THE MASSES

Urban Residents

The masses in urban society consist of industrial workers, their dependents, and the unemployed. Since 1949 industrial workers have probably earned at least two or three times the income of the average peasant and have been entitled in addition to various pension, health, and other social services that, unlike those of the rural people, have been paid for by the state (see ch. 17, Labor).

During the mid-1960s, however, the privileged position of the workers vis-à-vis the rural masses began to be undermined by a worker-peasant labor system, introduced in 1964, designed to convert many industrial workers into farmers and to replace them with short-term recruits from the rural Communes. Under this system, the differences in rewards between industrial and agricultural employment began to be gradually lessened. Peasants were recruited to work either part of the year in seasonal industries such as sugar refineries or, in nonseasonal industries, they were to be employed for a term of from three to seven years. They would then return to their agricultural Commune. Displaced industrial workers were sent to rural Communes. The peasant-workers who replaced the permanent staff would continue to remain on the Commune rosters and surrender to it their salaries minus living expenses. They were not entitled to take their dependents with them to the cities or to receive the high wages and expensive fringe benefits of the permanent staff.

Dissatisfaction was reported to be great among the discharged permanent workers as well as among the recruited worker-peasants, most of whom sought to become full-time industrial workers, with all of the benefits granted permanent staff. In January 1967 Shanghai and some other cities were experiencing labor strikes in the transportation industries, and on January 5, 1967, 100,000 temporary or contract workers in Shanghai protested publicly against the "irrational system of temporary and outside-contract labor. ...." It was not known to what extent the worker-peasant system was being implemented in 1971.

Rural Masses

The approximately 80 to 85 percent of the population that lives in rural areas has experienced a number of reorganizations of its social and economic structures since the 1940s. The CCP land reform campaign, begun in 1946 in areas then under its control, attempted to "awaken the class consciousness of the peasants" by urging them to wage a "fierce class struggle" against local landlords. As part of this effort and the 1950–52 nationwide land reform campaign and also as part of the continuing effort to make class consciousness replace kin group loyalty and other traditional allegiances among the peasants, class labels were given to the rural people by the Party. Questionnaires were circulated and, on the basis of the replies, each villager was assigned a class label.

Landlord status was given those who owned land and lived chiefly from the rent of that land rather than from their own labor. Whereas being a landlord had been a prestigious occupation in earlier times, under the Communists landlords were "enemies of the people;" as such they did not qualify as "people" and were explicitly denied political rights.

The label "rich peasant" was applied to the person who owned all or part of his own land or who owned none but had working capital of some sort and derived at least part of his income from "exploiting" the labor of others. Below this category were the "middle peasants," a classification subsequently (during the mid-1950s) subdivided into upper middle, middle, and lower middle groups on the basis of living standard and relative freedom from exploitation. The lower middle peasants had relatively little personal access to means of production and were subject to exploitation—that is, they had to work for others or borrow money at interest to make ends meet.

The next category, "poor peasant," included persons living under conditions similar to those in the lower middle peasant category, except that the standard of living of the poor peasant was so low as to involve real hardship. It was estimated by Mao that approximately 70 percent of the peasants were in the lower middle or poor groups.

During the several class struggle campaigns, conducted during the first half of the 1950s, accusation meetings were held under the direction of cadres recruited from among the poor peasants and farm laborers. The object of the particular local "struggle" had to bow his head before the crowd of his accusers and publicly confess his errors or crimes and apologize for them. Many landlords were executed at the climax of struggle meetings in the early campaigns. The landlord who personally survived the campaign lost prestige, and almost all his land and other goods were confiscated and redistributed among the rural poor. By November 1952 about 20 million landlords had been eliminated as a class through death or through confiscation of the property. Rich peasants were eliminated in a similar "struggle" in the course of the rural cooperative campaign of the mid-1950s.

In the course of these campaigns, class loyalty and ideology were made paramount. Insofar as they conflicted with these, lineage solidarity and relations among household members were disrupted. Landlords and peasants of the same kin group were set against each other. The young were encouraged to accuse their elders if they were not politically or socially correct. The distribution of confiscated land, being made without regard to sex and age, favored women and young persons who would never have received property in their own right under the traditional family system (see ch. 6, Family).

During the campaign to create the collectives, the "middle peasants" also came under attack, but not to the extreme that had been the case with the landlords and rich peasants. Those who refused to join the cooperatives were subject to various forms of pressure and persuasion. For example, schools and welfare benefit schemes were set up for cooperative members and were not available to others. Also, the tax collectors tended to be more exacting of nonmembers.

A major attack on the traditional rural social structure occurred in 1958, with issuance by the Party Central Committee of the *Resolution on the Establishment of People's Communes in the Rural Areas* on August 29, 1958, when the Great Leap Forward campaign was launched in the countryside. A chief feature was the consolidation of the collectives into Communes. Within less than a year, the rural population had been reorganized into 24,000 Communes.

The Communes brought together an unprecedented number of people into a single community. A typical Commune in Hopeh Province, for example, had 4,700 households and 25,000 people. Such a unit was three times the size of the average rural marketing area, the largest unit with which the peasantry had previously had extensive social contact. It was intended that the Commune become the basic unit of the social structure, combining industry, agriculture, trade, education, and military affairs. Communal dining halls and, to a lesser extent, dormitories were established for the Commune population, and nurseries and kindergartens were set up to free women from domestic responsibilities so that they could join the labor force. Homes for the elderly and other collective welfare institutions were also established.

The Communes soon proved too big for detailed administration and unwieldy as units of collective social activity. Reorganization was effected in the early 1960s, however, and the Commune has remained a unit of social organization in rural society. The Communes were divided into production brigades, corresponding roughly in size to the natural village. By 1961 the production brigade had begun to surrender the function of serving as the accounting unit in remuneration of labor to the hamlet or neighborhood organization—a subdivision of the brigade called the production team (see Glossary). In addition, by 1963 the average Commune, which was still the headquarters for some administrative purposes, had been reduced to one-third its original size.

The Commune since 1963 has tended to be roughly coterminous with the traditional administrative area known as the *hsiang* (township or administrative village). This traditional administrative unit had usually corresponded to the primary rural marketing area.

Thus, in the early 1970s the rural society's traditional units of hamlet, village, and marketing area were still being utilized as the basic administrative units, although under new names. At the hamlet, or production team, level members of from twenty to thirty households pool their labor and are remunerated according to work points. Individuals earn work points on the basis of the quantity and quality of their labor (with some bonus or diminution based on political criteria, age, and sex) (see ch. 17, Labor).

At the village, or production brigade, level members of the production teams interact frequently. Members of different teams staff and make use of the brigade's schools, health centers, and other community facilities. In mid-1971 there were approximately 750,000 production brigades, and each had about 100 households. Although after 1960 the compulsory communal dining halls and certain other social innovations of the original Commune were abandoned, the

Commune has continued to be the administrative headquarters for rural industry and also has remained the site of rural secondary schools, hospitals, and other important social services.

The family household is the basic social unit of Chinese peasant society. Although no national statistics have been published since 1960, available information suggests that the average size of a rural household is slightly more than four persons. The rural household most often contains only the nuclear family—parents and dependent children. Where space permits, the household may also contain other relatives, most commonly a parent of either the head of the household or his wife. Income is usually pooled by household members.

Very little was known in 1971 about social stratification within rural communities. It is not known to what extent one's family background affects an individual's social status. It is also not known to what extent relative prosperity is translated into social prestige or the reverse. Information from one Commune in Fukien Province in 1963 reveals that labor in one brigade was remunerated at substantially different rates, depending upon whether the laborer was classified as a first-class, second-class, or third-class worker. It is presumed that quality of labor was a factor in this rating system, but other factors may also have been involved. At Tachai, a nationally promoted model production brigade in Shansi Province, in the late 1960s work points were allotted not on the basis of a systematic accounting of work hours and quality of work but rather on the basis of popular consensus of the working group membership. In evaluating the performance of their members, this brigade gave stress to rewarding those who showed "progressive" attitudes and behavior. Continued propaganda during the late 1960s and early 1970s was directed toward having rural society "learn from Tachai." It was not known to what extent Tachai practices were being followed nationally in the early 1970s.

The campaign to tie income to political reliability has been intensified since the late 1960s. Efforts have been made to limit private income sources, such as peddling, handicrafts, and private plot crop cultivation, and to induce persons who engage in these activities to turn over all the earnings to the collective for yearend redistribution according to work points. If these efforts prove effective, control over the distribution of wealth will be effectively limited to the politically reliable segment of rural society. Judging by the scanty information available, politics is already the chief source of social prestige, in the sense that persons well connected to politically powerful persons at the supravillage level are respected and are influential in their home communities.

Resettled Urbanites

Urban personnel have been resettled in rural areas by governmental initiative since 1957. The aims of these campaigns have been manifold. The first *hsia fang* (send down) campaign was designed primarily to rid the upper and middle leadership organs of excess cadres, at the same time reinforcing the basic-level leadership. This method of reducing the size of the bureaucracies at their urban headquarters had been employed several times since, most recently in the early 1970s.

During the periodic cadre rectification campaigns and purges, the *hsia fang* campaign was the most commonly used disciplinary tool. In addition—because of the high value in Chinese Marxist ideology placed on manual labor and on the need to eliminate social gaps between leaders and followers, mental and manual workers, and town and country—numerous campaigns have been launched to induce cadres to periodically gain personal experience of rural farm life. The May 7 cadre schools instituted in the late 1960s, are designed to provide cadres with such experience as part of their leadership training (see ch. 8, Education, Intellectual Expression, and the Arts).

Urban school graduates have also been sent to rural areas in large numbers. A small minority of these are selected, after several years of productive labor on the farms, to return to the cities to attend institutions of higher learning. Most are supposed to be permanently resettled on the farm.

The result of these resettlement programs has been the sudden appearance in villages scattered throughout the PRC of large numbers of urban persons of better than average education, little or no experience of farming or manual labor, and a wide range of political beliefs. Teachers in disgrace with the regime for their bourgeois views are sent, together with rising young Party cadres gaining valuable rural experience and discredited extremist Red Guards. A PRC press report in 1970 noted that the cadres, teachers, doctors, and students were being sent to villages in Kiangsi Province in mixed groups; the urban cadres handled the administration of the urbanites, and the villagers were charged with reeducating the group politically. The urbanites were reported to have kept apart from the villagers; also, the urban cadres refused to allow Commune and production brigade personnel to take over the administration of the resettled group. In one Commune the problem was solved by dividing the urban group into smaller units and assigning each student, or cadre, or intellectual to the tutelage of a peasant whom the ex-urbanite was to revere as he would a teacher.

Many of the resettled personnel have been sent to parts of the border regions where non-Han peoples predominate (see ch. 4, Ethnic Groups and Languages). No information has appeared concerning the social effects of the resettlement program on minority group communities.

There are indications that the *hsia fang* campaigns are highly unpopular, at least among the resettled urban youths. Many resettled students have reappeared in the urban areas from which they originally came. Lacking authorization to return, they cannot get ration cards. They have a difficult time providing for themselves and are a drain on their families. There has also been a rise in the number of refugees entering Hong Kong. Between 12,500 and 15,000 persons entered Hong Kong in the first eight months of 1971. Most of these refugees were urban students who had been sent to rural areas.

SOCIAL MOBILITY

There is a dearth of information concerning the dynamics of society in the PRC. The official PRC press releases, the main source of information, are concerned less with describing present social patterns than in presenting the regime's social policies and goals. To seek to rise in the social hierarchy is not an acceptable ambition to the regime's policymakers. There is, therefore, no acknowledgment in the press of the existence of social mobility except for occasional editorials deploring the ambitions of a few "self-seeking opportunitists" who are "taking the capitalist road."

The PRC had been in existence only twenty-two years in 1971, and there had been as yet no opportunity for anyone brought up from childhood under the communist regime to have reached the highest positions of political power and social prestige. Virtually all the senior-most persons in the political and military bureaucracies, education, science, industry, the arts, finance, or commerce were already in their thirties and forties in 1949. Most of these leaders have held senior positions more or less continuously since the first years of the PRC. There was, therefore, no indication of how high status is to be achieved under the new regime. There is also no information that reveals to what extent parental achievements will prove an asset to children of the present leaders.

Urban persons have easier access than do rural persons to higher education of the sort that permits social mobility not wholly dependent upon political criteria. Persons of working class or peasant family backgrounds have the preferred credentials for memberships in the Party and the PLA and for leadership positions in mass organizations.

The limited information available suggests that the chief common characteristic shared by the top leaders at national, military regional, and provincial levels is that of having joined the Party or having actively supported the communist cause before 1949. Virtually all those who have risen to the top of the political power hierarchies started out as young men in the Red Army or the CCP in the 1920s and 1930s; it has not been possible for persons to achieve nonpolitical status first and then enter the political hierarchy at a high level.

Moreover, within the power hierarchy there is little lateral mobility. The top leaders are almost all persons who have remained within their own organization, branch, or stream for decades.

Observers have noted that, in order to stay in power and survive the various purges and rectification campaigns that have been conducted during the two decades since 1949, members of the leadership in 1971 have had to develop certain skills. Chief among these are political skills, especially the ability to understand and interpret political affairs, to recognize promptly the imminence of major policy shifts, and to anticipate the waxing and waning of periods of heightened concern with ideological and class considerations. Social skills are also necessary. These include the ability to get along well with superiors without losing one's own identity; being able to speak clearly and persuade others; and being able to avoid making enemies or relying too much upon friends. These skills involve careful timing and calculation, especially within the small group criticism and self-criticism sessions that are an almost daily occurrence among highly placed cadres.

Other kinds of skills can also be useful for helping one stay in power. Persons with specialized skills of immediate use for production have a better chance of not being purged or of being restored to their positions after purge than do educators. Nonetheless, senior personnel in education are usually reinstated eventually. For example, during the Cultural Revolution there were large-scale purges of university faculty, but most of these persons had been restored to their positions by 1971.

Those whose special talents have a less obvious practical utility, such as artists and writers, however, are more vulnerable to attack by activists and political power groups and are less likely to be subsequently reinstated. The prestige and security of persons with special skills, such as research scientists, technicians, economists, factory and commercial establishment managers, educators, and artists, are greatest immediately after a campaign has run its course and the consolidation phase has begun. Such phases occurred in 1954, from mid-1956 to mid-1957, and in 1961 and 1962.

For the vast majority of the population that reached adulthood after 1949, career mobility, and therefore social mobility, has been extremely limited. Most Chinese born into peasant families have no opportunity to pursue a different career from that of their fathers. Persons born in rural areas are prohibited by government regulation from migrating to the urban areas. The only way for a rural person to legally become an urban resident is by official assignment, which results from membership in the PLA, the Party, or the governmental administrative hierarchies. Persons of landlord, rich peasant, or bourgeois family origins are generally denied access to these hierarchies. Persons from poor or lower middle peasant families have

138

the preferred social background, but many cannot afford to pay the primary and middle school fees. Some rural people feel that they cannot afford to relinquish the labor of their school-age children. Lacking sufficient academic qualifications, persons of peasant origins are often qualified only to serve as rural cadres in their home communities.

Of an estimated 60 percent of rural school-age children who attend primary school, only a minority go on to middle school (grades seven through twelve). Although more rural children than formerly have been able to receive primary schooling since the reform of the educational system in the mid-1960s, they have also been denied the opportunity to attend urban middle schools. This has meant that they have been cut off from college preparatory training since the rural middle schools offer only agricultural vocational training.

Urban children have a much better chance of receiving a middle school education, and some of these receive the academic training that can fit them for further study at an institution of higher learning. Thus urbanites have a better chance of acquiring the academic and technical skills that can make them eligible for careers that are not wholly dependent upon political considerations.

There are indications that children of highly placed cadres have special education opportunities unavailable to others. In early 1967 a Red Guard publication printed an exposé entitled "The August First School System for Children of High-Ranking Cadres." According to this article, an illegal school system had grown up catering exclusively to children of high-ranking cadres, in spite of the fact that since 1955 the State Council and the Party Central Committee have issued periodic directives demanding that such schools be abolished. The article was chiefly concerned with a school of this type in Peking, but it also stated that other such schools existed in various provinces and municipalities.

While still in his teens, the ambitious person must decide whether or not to seek PLA or Chinese Communist Youth League membership —the two main paths to Party membership and political power. The competition to enter these organizations has been so great that only those youths who have been consistent enthusiastic supporters of Party policies and campaigns from early adolescence can expect to be selected. Having become an activist, however, he must continue to be conspicuously enthusiastic, whether or not he achieves PLA or league membership; otherwise, he runs the risk of being attacked as a revisionist or a politically unreliable person.

For the person without special skills or advanced education who seeks to achieve high status, Party membership is virtually obligatory. Membership is open, according to the 1959 Party Constitution, to "any Chinese worker, poor peasant, lower-middle peasant or revolutionary armymen or any other revolutionary element who has reached the age of eighteen" provided that he is recommended by two Party members and endorsed by the Party branch in his area after examination and that this endorsement is approved by the next higher Party committee. Membership in the Party is confined to a small proportion of the population, estimated as under 3 percent in the early 1970s.

Entry into the Party is no guarantee of upward mobility or even security. In fact, Party members are often the first to be adversely affected by changes in national policies and, the higher a person's status within the power hierarchies, the greater the risk of his losing that position as the result of ideological purges or periodic reductions in the size of the staff at middle and upper ranks. Such a reduction in staff was occurring in the early 1970s, and some ministries were reportedly losing as much as half their personnel. Persons in politically sensitive or strategic positions are especially vulnerable to attack on ideological grounds and must adhere to more stringent ideological requirements at all times than those persons in less strategic or controversial posts.

The social opportunities for women have increased greatly since the communist takeover. The PRC has consistently supported equal rights and equal opportunities for women. As of the early 1970s Chinese press reports estimated that 55 million housewives had been freed from domestic chores to work on farms and in factories. Women are reported to constitute between 30 and 40 percent of the national labor force. By 1958 they formed over 15 percent of the nonagricultural work force—more than double the percentage in 1949. As of the early 1960s it was estimated that women comprised 25 percent of college faculty and 45 percent of secondary school teachers. In the 1956/57 academic year one-fourth of the total student enrollment at colleges and universities were female, and in medical colleges and universities the proportion of female students was in some cases higher than 40 percent. Indications were that the proportion of female students has continued to rise since then.

A political elite group of women also has come into existence. Out of the 3,000 deputies elected in 1964 to the Third National People's Congress, 542 were women. The CCP Central Committee, as of early 1971, had thirteen women full members and ten women alternate members. Some of these women were wives of important leaders. For example, Chiang Ch'ing (Mao's wife) and Yeh Ch'un (Lin Piao's wife) were in the Politburo.

For most women, however, opportunities for upward social mobility are less available than for men. Women are underrepresented at all levels of administrative and Party hierarchies, a tendency that has presumably increased with the domination since the mid-1960s of these hierarchies by PLA members. As of 1961, the last year for which

140

information is available concerning the social composition of the CCP, women constituted only about 10 percent of the membership.

In addition to education, place of residence, class background, age, sex, and political and social skills, an individual's upward mobility within the PRC political hierarchy is affected by the class status and political activity of his spouse, friends, and residential and occupational associates. The purge of a senior man often is accompanied by the purge of those who worked directly for him. It is of great importance for the ambitious to avoid association with, and, most important, marriage to, persons with political credentials inferior to their own. A person who does not put political and ideological considerations first when choosing a friend or a spouse shows that he has not put "politics in command" of his personal life, as he is officially urged to do. Thus activists marry activists, and Party members associate with Party members.

SOCIAL CONTROL

Before 1949 kinship groups had been responsible to higher authorities for the good behavior of the people. Since 1949, however, various so-called mass organizations have performed these surveillance and enforcement services for the regime. These mass organizations are theoretically voluntary and autonomous of the state, but they perform a quasi-governmental role in exacting conformity of their members to the demands of the regime. Numerous mass organizations exist, including associations for youth and women, and others are organized according to occupation or residence.

Some of these organizations suffered great disruptions during the Cultural Revolution. An example was the Chinese Communist Youth League, a mass organization with over 25 million members in the early 1960s that had served as the cadet organization of the CCP. The youth league came under attack by a new mass organization, the Red Guards, in 1966 for allegedly supporting PRC Chairman Liu Shao-ch'i against Party Chairman Mao. For nearly three years it was not mentioned in the PRC press. Then there began to appear scattered references to attempts to consolidate and rebuild the youth league. In some factories it was reported that former members of the youth league were reluctant to rejoin it since "they had taken the wrong side in the early stages of the Cultural Revolution." In September 1971 the Shanghai newspaper *Chieh Fang Jih Pao* devoted an editorial to recounting the story of a "revolutionary martyr and outstanding League member." This suggests that the rehabilitation of the youth league was continuing. Information is lacking concerning many other mass organizations that were disrupted or destroyed during the Cultural Revolution.

Almost everyone participates in at least one mass organization. In rural areas, production team and production brigade organizations include virtually all villagers. In urban areas, wage earners participate in mass organizations at work, students join the Young Pioneers Brigade or the Chinese Communist Youth League at school, and the unemployed family members of urban wage earners are encompassed by urban residents' committees.

One of the major functions of the residents' committees, as of all organizations, is the surveillance and mobilization of the membership in conformity with the changing requirements of the state. To this end much use is made of small study groups (see ch. 14, Agriculture; ch. 20, Public Order and Internal Security).

The study group has become the basic unit of social control within the Party and within the various mass organizations. Weekly and, in some cases, daily meetings of the small study groups are common in many mass organizations and places of employment. At study group sessions approximately fifteen persons assemble to study Mao Tse-tung Thought, to expose one another's faults, and to confess their own. The leader of the discussion, either a Party cadre or activist who has the backing of the authority and the potential sanctions of the government, attempts to cultivate a willingness in the group to attack faults frankly and to work to transform the guilty parties through the social pressure of the group upon the individual.

The use of face-to-face criticism and public self-criticism by the Communists, when it was first introduced during the land reform campaign of the early 1950s, had a devastating effect upon those who took part in it. The avoidance of overt hostility or of public humiliation had been an age-old value in Chinese society. Many persons attacked in those campaigns committed suicide. By the early 1970s, however, the Chinese people had become much more experienced and sophisticated with respect to public criticism and self-criticism.

Schoolchildren in the PRC are obliged to write their autobiographies, with emphasis on political ideas and activities, beginning at age eight. Cadres, persons of importance, and persons under suspicion of heterodox beliefs or activity are required to write autobiographies at frequent intervals—in some cases, annually. A life history of this type includes all errors and omissions committed by the individual, as judged by his present understanding of current Communist ideology.

THE ROLE OF RELIGIOUS INSTITUTIONS IN CHINESE SOCIETY

Popular religion in China has for centuries drawn from three main religious streams—Confucianism, Taoism, and Buddhism. These were commonly referred to as the "three ways to one goal."

Confucianism, although it had certain ancient rites that theoretically served to connect the emperor with the forces of the supernatural, was primarily a system of ethics and did not concern itself in a systematic way with theology or the supernatural. The imperial cult rites were abolished when the Ch'ing dynasty fell in 1911. After the collapse of the social structure upon which Confucianism had been based, the vitality of Confucianism as a system of belief began to decline during the twentieth century.

Connected to Confucianism was ancestor worship, the veneration of patrilineal ancestors involving offerings of incense, food, and other objects at domestic shrines, lineage and clan halls, and gravesites at specified times during the year. Ancestor worship, although it probably is more ancient than Confucianism, has been connected in the popular mind with the chief Confucian virtue of filial piety. Confucian values, especially the concern with the so-called three bonds—connecting subject to ruler, child to parent, and wife to husband—permeated all of Han Chinese society and have been retained among the peasants, according to available information.

Taoism is the term used to denote two interrelated, but distinct, traditions. Philosophic Taoism, a quietistic creed that dates back to the late Chou period, favors mystical, nonrational efforts at union with the natural pattern of the universe, the Way (*tao*) (see ch. 3, Historical Setting). Popular Taoism, which has a far larger following than philosophic Taoism and is the predominant strain in the folk religion of the Chinese peasantry, is practiced under the direction of diviners, demon exorcisers, geomancers, alchemists, and magicians. At least until 1949 such practitioners were regularly consulted by the peasants in cases of sickness, when burying the dead, or when deciding on the auspicious location of a new building or the appropriate time for a wedding. Taoist belief acknowledges the existence of many gods, spirits, powers, and deified historical figures but is chiefly concerned with appeasing and manipulating these spirits for the benefit of the living. As is the case with Confucianism, Taoism—whether philosophic or popular—lacks a systematized theology or clerical organization (although there are Taoist monks) and, like Confucianism, puts stress on this world rather than on the next.

Popular Taoism was always deplored by educated people in imperial times, partly because the Confucianist ruling class was contemptuous of what it regarded as the superstitious practices of the Taoists and partly because Taoist secret societies often harbored lawbreakers and rebels. The KMT shared this view and worked during its final years on the mainland to suppress the activities of fortune tellers, astrologers, geomancers, magicians, and secret society members.

Mahayana Buddhism (see Glossary) is the third major stream in Chinese religion. It is of Indian derivation, but by the ninth century A.D. it had been thoroughly sinified and had given birth to a variety of new sects. Some of these, for example, Ching-t'u and Chen-yen, were popular sects that eventually became part of the syncretistic folk religion. These stressed the attainment of paradise through the relatively mindless worship of benevolent Boddhisattvas (Buddhas-in-the-making). There were also highly intellectualized and meditative sects that attracted members of the educated elite. One such sect, Ch'an, is well known in the West by its Japanese name, Zen.

Buddhism declined in importance in later centuries. In South China and the Yangtze River valley, however, Buddhist elements were still important in popular religion in the twentieth century, until the communist takeover. Marriages, funerals, and other family ceremonies there were usually conducted by Buddhist monks.

Strains of Buddhism distinct from the syncretistic folk religion also exist. Buddhists of this type refrain from eating or slaughtering animals, attend the various ceremonies commemorating events in the life of the Buddha, and contribute regularly to the maintenance of monasteries and temples. In 1956 PRC official estimates, Buddhists in this category numbered 55 million, or slightly under 10 percent of the population at that time. This figure included not only Han Buddhists (the vast majority) but also Tibetan and Mongol adherents to Lamaism, a minority sect of Mahayana Buddhism introduced from Tibet in the thirteenth century (see ch. 3, Historical Setting). Buddhism is more highly organized and systematized than are Confucianism and Taoism and, unlike them, it is a universal religion with millions of adherents in the countries of eastern, southern, and Southeast Asia.

By the time of the communist takeover the popular religions of China were in decline. Confucianism was no longer the official cult, and its basic tenets were challenged by the new ruling group. Popular Taoism, although widely practiced by the common people, was universally disdained by the educated elite and was coming under attack in the rural areas by the Communists who, like the Nationalists, regarded popular Taoism as sheer superstition without ethical justification and as politically subversive because of its historic connection with secret societies. Buddhism had begun to revive in the late nineteenth and early twentieth century as a result of improved communications with Buddhists of other countries. This revival, however, was limited for the most part to a small group of educated monks, devotees, and pious laymen of the middle class who frequently attended activities at the monasteries.

There also exist numerous minor religious communities in the PRC. Of these, the largest and most important is the Islamic. Like Buddhism, Islam has adherents among the Han Chinese and is also the religion of certain minority peoples of Outer China, namely the Turkic-speaking nomads of Sinkiang Uighur Autonomous Region (see ch. 4, Ethnic Groups and Languages). Ninghsia Hui Autonomous Region and Kansu, Shensi, Tsinghai, and Yunnan provinces all have large numbers of Han Chinese Muslims (Hui). It was officially estimated in 1956 that there were approximately 14 million Muslims, of whom only 4 million were non-Han. Like Buddhism, Islam was introduced from outside China and is an organized, universal religion with many overseas adherents. This was of importance in moderating government policy toward Muslims.

Christianity is the foreign religion most recently imported into China and has gained relatively few adherents. Estimates made by PRC authorities in the mid-1960s, before the Cultural Revolution, indicated that there were then approximately 3 million Roman Catholics and 700,000 Protestant Christians.

Unlike the other foreign religions—Buddhism and Islam— Christianity tended to be dominated by foreign missionaries and the sponsorship of overseas organizations. Major cleavages separated groups of Christians largely as a result of the persistence of ties to different foreign missionary organizations. Roman Catholicism in China was spread by Portuguese, French, and Spanish priests, whereas Protestantism was propagated chiefly by British, United States, Dutch, and German missionaries. The different sects, using different foreign languages, kept apart. Another reason for division was that Roman Catholicism came centuries earlier to China than did Protestantism.

The policies of the national leadership with respect to religion and religious institutions reflect the Marxist thesis that religion originated in primitive society as an explanation of natural phenomena and, when class divisions arose, religious beliefs and institutions became tools in the hands of the exploiting classes to oppress the common people. The thesis concludes with the prediction that, as ignorance and exploitation are eradicated, religion will wither away. Until the mid-1960s it was the official policy that any attempt to suppress religion prematurely would be foolhardy and would not work, although events since 1965 indicate that this policy may have changed.

Freedom of religious belief is guaranteed by the 1954 State Constitution and is included in the 1970 draft state constitution, but in practice this has been interpreted to limit religious observances to within the walls of churches and temples. The Religious Affairs Bureau, set up in the early years of the PRC, has kept the personnel and activities of religious organizations under close surveillance. It was officially instructed to "strike at politically obstinate reactionaries in churches," to mobilize religious communities to cooperate in the national political and social campaigns, and to arrange for the entertainment of foreign guests, chiefly Buddhists and Muslims.

Official propaganda against organized religion, theism, and so-called superstitious practices has been carried out continuously by the regime since 1949 as part of the effort to hasten the demise of religion through education of the masses. Confucianism—with its ties to the imperial social and political structure, its emphasis on family loyalty, and its justification of the domination of youth by the aged and of women by men—is utterly condemned. Since Confucianism has no formal institutions, however, it has been difficult for the regime to attack Confucianist beliefs. The lineage and clan ancestral temples have been destroyed for the most part, but such Confucianist practices as sweeping the graves on the occasion of the Ch'ing Ming festival and family offerings to the Kitchen God on Lunar New Year's Eve have persisted into the 1970s, according to reports attacking these practices in the PRC press.

Taoism, fundamentally an unstructured folk religion with an immense popular following among the peasantry—the group in society that has most consistently supported the communist regime—has proved difficult for the regime to suppress. Taoist monasteries have been taken over and their landholdings confiscated; the temples have been stripped of their religious paraphernalia and burned; and members of Taoist associations have been made to register as "belonging to reactionary associations and [following] Taoist superstitions." Taoist activities have continued nonetheless.

The secret society tradition within Taoism has apparently helped it resist efforts at suppression, and there were reports in the 1950s that new monasteries and secret societies arose even as old ones were destroyed. The situation in this respect in 1971 was not known, however. In 1957 the government set up the Chinese Taoist Association, the first such national association in history, in an effort to establish organizational control over Taoists.

The government attitude toward Taoist institutions has not been uniformly negative, however. Although many shrines have been destroyed, a few Taoist temples of major historic or artistic importance have been preserved and restored with the help of government funds because of an official PRC policy that has as its goal the preservation of important relics of the national cultural legacy. There has also been considerable official support for folk medicine, including acupuncture and other techniques used by Taoist medical practitioners (see ch. 7, Living Conditions).

The official policy toward Buddhism has been ambivalent and has fluctuated between periods of strong official support for some of its activities and institutions and other periods when official disapproval of Buddhism as a relic of feudalism and an obstacle to production has predominated. During the land reform campaign the Buddhist monasteries were deprived of their holdings, and many former patrons, coming from the bourgeoisie and landowning classes, were no longer in a position to support Buddhist monks and institutions.

The Chinese Buddhist Association was established in 1952 as a quasi-official mass organization for all Chinese Buddhists, including Lamaists. The tasks of this organization have been to mobilize Buddhists for national campaigns, to indoctrinate Buddhists in the state ideology, to provide facilities for supervising the activities of Buddhists, and to handle the entertaining of Buddhist delegations from other countries in Asia.

As part of the program indoctrination in state ideology, leaders of the Chinese Buddhist Association have attacked basic Buddhist doctrines. For example, a basic belief of Buddhists has been that, since to live in the world is to suffer, the ultimate goal of man must be to gain release from the cycle of birth-death-rebirth and thereby avoid the sufferings of the world. This is to be achieved through meditation and through detaching oneself from worldly affairs and cutting all ties to this world. In 1960, however, the president of the Chinese Buddhist Association praised the majority of Chinese Buddhists for having "discarded their tolerant, transcendental, negative attitude of rejecting the world, which has been handed down from the past," and having taken a new "positive attitude of entering the world."

The fact that Buddhist institutions had in ages past been important patrons of the arts has helped to preserve some shrines and relics of Buddhism. A number of shrines have been restored through the sponsorship of the PRC government as part of the national policy of preserving the country's cultural legacy.

Of even greater importance to the preservation of Buddhist institutions has been the fact that Buddhism is a religion practiced in countries with which the PRC has sought friendly relations. In the early 1960s efforts were made for the PRC to win control of the World Fellowship of Buddhists, the main international Buddhist organization. In addition, in 1963 and 1964, the Chinese Buddhist Association held conferences to which delegates from a number of Asian countries were invited. Foreign Buddhists were also invited to participate in 1963 and 1964 in various Buddhist celebrations. The high point of this religious activity came in the spring of 1964 when, in March, elaborate ceremonies were held, with the participation of Japanese Buddhists, to mark the anniversary of the death of Hsuan-tsang, a famous T'ang dynasty Buddhist pilgrim. In May the birthday of the Buddha was celebrated with the customary bathing of Buddha images in Shanghai, Peking, and Lhasa. The next month a tooth relic of the Buddha was transferred from Kwangchi monastery to a new pagoda built with state funds in 1963 to replace a pagoda burned down during the Boxer Rebellion of 1900. The transfer of the tooth was witnessed by delegates from nine countries that have sizable Buddhist populations.

Since 1965, however, Buddhism has apparently come under renewed attack by the regime. According to one foreign student of Chinese Buddhism, the last reference in the press to Buddhism was in August 1966, the month that the Cultural Revolution was officially launched. In 1965 the official organ of the Chinese Buddhist Association, *Hsien-tai fo-hsueh*, ceased publication. The same year the new *People's Handbook*, published in Peking, did not list the names of officers of the Chinese Buddhist Association as it had in previous editions.

Some observers regard 1965 as the year when a major shift in PRC policy toward religion occurred. In October of that year an article appeared in the journal *Hsin chien-she*, which contradicted the Marxist thesis concerning the ultimate waning of religion:

> Religion ... will not disappear of its own accord. ... It will rely on the force of custom to prolong its feeble existence and even plot to make a comeback. When a dying cobra bites a man, it can still wound or kill him. Therefore, no matter how little of religion's vestigial poison remains, it is necessary to carry on a rigorous struggle against it on all fronts and to pull up and destroy all of its poisonous roots.

The Red Guard attacks on the "four olds" in 1966 and 1967 had especially great impact on religious practices, institutions, and objects (see ch. 8, Education, Intellectual Expression, and the Arts). By 1969 there were reports by visitors to the PRC, however, that indicated that some Buddhist monasteries were continuing to function. In one large coastal city, a famous monastery was reported to have fourteen resident monks. Although these monks worked at a nearby Commune and wore ordinary secular apparel, they resided in the monastery and ate vegetarian food. Another visitor in 1969 to a rural area in the Buddhist heartland of Central China observed a number of monasteries in operation. The monks there grew their own food and were self-supporting, but they also carried out rites for the dead on behalf of the laity.

Islam has received the mildest treatment by the PRC of any religion. During the civil war period Red Army personnel were instructed in Islamic dietary laws. They were taught not to smoke, eat pork, or drink spirits in the homes of Muslims or to bathe at Muslim bathing places.

Like Buddhism, Islam is a world religion with adherents in countries with which the PRC has sought friendly relations, and this fact has influenced the government's policy toward Muslims. Unlike the Buddhists, the Muslims have in many cases been allowed to retain land to provide for the maintenance of religious buildings. The Chinese Islamic Association was organized in Peking in 1953 to serve as a liaison body between the government and the Muslims, oversee Muslim activities, and promote friendly relations with Muslims abroad.

An observer writing in a foreign Muslim publication in 1966, just before the Cultural Revolution, noted that there were a number of mosques that were well maintained, that celebrations at various times in the Muslim religious calendar were being carried on, and that Muslims were well represented in the national people's congresses. He also noted, however, that many mosques in rural areas had been converted to other uses; that many old textbooks on Islam had been banned; that Muslim religious officials were being compelled to engage in manual labor and in some cases were replaced by communist-trained Muslim cadres; and that efforts were being made to get the religious leadership to interpret the Koran from the Marxist-Leninist point of view.

During the Cultural Revolution Islam came under attack along with other religions. Mosques in the cities were closed down. A Red Guard group was formed that called itself the Revolutionary Struggle Group for the Abolition of Islam. Members of this organization beat and humiliated Islamic leaders and propagandized in wall posters against the study of the Koran, Islamic marriage laws, circumcision, and other Muslim practices. By 1969, however, at least one urban mosque had reopened.

The policies of the PRC leadership toward Christianity have been influenced by their belief that the foreign connections of the Christian churches are remnants of the imperialist aggression upon China dating back to the nineteenth century and earlier. Since 1949 the main thrust of PRC policy toward Christians has been to take over control of missionary-supported schools, hospitals, and orphanages and to sever the Christian churches in the PRC from their foreign ties.

During the land reform campaign Christian churches were temporarily closed, and their landholdings were confiscated. By the end of 1952 the PRC had either closed, nationalized, or otherwise removed from church control all Catholic and Protestant schools except for a few seminaries; these closed in the late 1950s. A Franciscan Sisters of Mary school for children of foreigners in Peking survived as the last remaining Christian school until 1966 when it was closed.

The efforts to separate the Christian churches from their foreign sponsors was complicated in the case of the Roman Catholic Church. Although the foreign priests and nuns were variously expelled, deported, imprisoned, or killed during the 1950s, the problem of foreign connections persisted because of the obligation of all Roman Catholics to acknowledge the supremacy of the pope at Rome. The Chinese Roman Catholic clergymen were caught between conflicting obligations to their government and to the Vatican, which has demanded that all Catholics oppose communism. During the mid-1950s the PRC promoted the creation of the Chinese Catholic

Patriotic Association under the leadership of an excommunicated vicar-general of Nanking, who had assumed the title of bishop of Nanking. This mass organization developed into a so-called patriotic church, which performed Roman Catholic rites but did not acknowledge the authority of the pope.

In 1965 an archbishop and leader of the Chinese Catholic Patriotic Association claimed that there were at that time seventy bishops, 2,000 priests, and 3 million Catholics in the PRC. Information from the mid-1960s indicated that infant baptism was forbidden by the government but adult baptism was still being permitted and that religious instruction for candidates for confirmation was being carried out, provided that the candidate was at least eighteen years old. No one listed with the Office of Religious Affairs as being an enemy of the people—landlord, counterrevolutionary, or culprit who had undergone labor reform—could receive baptism or religious instruction. Clergymen had to guarantee that the adults they baptized would not subsequently commit any offense against the state.

The Protestants were subject to similar restrictions. In December 1949 announcement was made in the form of the *Message from Chinese Christians to Mission Boards Abroad* demanding that finance, administration, and policy be placed entirely in indigenous hands. The so-called Three-Self Movement was organized soon thereafter under PRC sponsorship to bring about self-government, self-support, and self-propagation in the Chinese Protestant churches. During the Korean conflict a campaign against foreign missionaries was launched, and many were convicted of conspiring on behalf of the United States. Some were imprisoned, and others were expelled, and by late 1951 most of the foreign missionaries were gone.

The number of Christian churches of all types decreased and the size of their congregations declined during the early 1960s. At the time of the Cultural Revolution all churches were reported closed. By mid-1971 there was as yet no reliable word of any Christian churches having reopened.

SOCIAL VALUES

The CCP has been engaged since its formation in the 1920s in an attempt to educate the Chinese people to discard their traditional values and replace them with others regarded by the Party as progressive. It was not possible, from the information available in 1971, to estimate to what extent the Party had succeeded in its tasks after more than twenty years in power. Scattered press references, however, indicate the persistence of traditional values.

Newspapers, motion pictures, dramatic presentations, wall posters, and loudspeakers continuously exhort the public to conform to the new value system (see ch. 12, Public Information and Propaganda). The stress is on civic virtue above all. Encouragements and awards are given to persons who practice the Five Good Model. The "five goods" are to be a good advocate: first, for labor and production; second, for a frugal and simple life; third, for sanitation and hygiene; fourth, for service and selfless sacrifice for the masses; and fifth, for scholarship and education.

Numerous references to the "five goods," the "three-eight working style," and the "five loves" continually keep before the public the various ethical formulas that they are expected to follow. Stories of heroic behavior by PLA soldiers, peasants, and factory workers provide models for emulation. In the mid-1960s, during the height of the Mao personality cult, an effort was made to evoke a personal allegiance to Chairman Mao as a means of promoting the national values. People were encouraged to confess their wrongdoings or bad thoughts during the day to Mao's image, which occupied the position on the household altar formerly occupied by ancestral tablets.

The Individual, the Family, and Society

Individualism as understood in the West has never been highly valued in Chinese society. The term used for individualism, *ko-jen chu-i*, is a modern construction that carries the antisocial connotation of "each-for-himself." Traditionally, the individual's social identity was determined by his family's position in the social hierarchy and by his own rank within the family (see ch. 6, Family). The individual owed loyalty chiefly to his parents and persons of the senior generations in his patrilineage. Religious observances and ethical considerations also stressed the primacy of the familial bond. A child was taught that "gratitude to your parents for bearing you is as great as heaven." In traditional China, the emphasis on loyalty to the family acted to limit allegiance to society at the suprakinship level. The welfare of the bloodline was of far greater importance to the individual than was the welfare of neighbors or society as a whole.

The regime in power in 1971 has worked to shift this primary loyalty of individuals from the family to the wider society—the class, the Party, and the country. To serve the people is the highest goal, according to Mao and the Party propagandists. High value is placed on honesty, hard work, asceticism, frugality, and sacrificing for production. These beliefs derive from the basic contention that society must come first and that the individual must not allow his individual appetites to rob society of its necessities. Foreign observers have noted that these values are being adhered to in the PRC. In marked contrast to traditional behavior, there is reportedly comparatively little graft or theft and very little conspicuous display of wealth. Goals, such as those outlined by famous modern

151

philosopher Feng Ting in the 1950s in his definition of happiness as "peace and no war, good food and fine clothing, a spacious and clean house, love and harmony between husband and wife, parents and children," are rejected; to follow them is to "take the capitalist road." The Communists have also worked to make people put the collective good ahead of their concern with their own social status or reputation. The traditional Chinese concern with maintaining a decorous public image, or face, has been attacked through the mass criticism and self-criticism sessions instituted by the Communists. These have been designed in part to habituate people to disregard concern for their own image or that of others and consider only their duty to society.

There are scattered indications in the PRC press and in reports of foreign observers that some Confucian values persist, especially those in regard to the family. For example, a 1970 PRC newsletter editorial notes that, although the Confucian family system has been abandoned, "its shady spirit has not dissipated." Earlier, in 1969, there were reports of people grouping themselves by clan rather than by class in Honan Province. The PRC report states that people in one county there had been heard to say "family ties cannot be broken; no man can lift his hand against his own people." The veneration of the family, lineage, and clan as an institution that connects the individual with a vast span of history has apparently also continued. A 1969 PRC press release deplored the fact that people are still saying "Clans last for hundreds or thousands of years; a government does not last so long."

Young and Old

In the course of the various campaigns that have been launched since 1949, youth has been urged to put political loyalty to the state ahead of loyalty to kin and to disregard the traditional obligation to show respect toward persons of the older generation in this respect. Children have been urged to be loyal to their class rather than to their parents and, if necessary, "draw a demarcation line" between themselves and reactionary parents; however, the regime in 1971 was urging upon youth respect for elders within the family unit.

Moral authority appears less attached to age than in the past and more tied to political reliability. In some villages in Hunan in late 1968, according to a Hunan radio report, new family heads were reported to have been elected by the household members on the basis of political reliability and knowledge. Young people are regarded as more politically reliable than their elders because they have no personal experience of the old regime.

Leaders and Followers

The traditional concepts of the relationship between ruled and ruler are based on the authoritarian family pattern in which children owe complete obedience to parents. The pattern was projected to the relationship between emperor and subject. The clear-cut traditional division between leader and followers, with the leader taking the initiative and the followers passively obeying, has been continuously attacked by the Communists. It is not sufficient to accept passively the orders of the leadership. People are constantly barraged with exhortations urging them to "actively grasp the revolution," to be energetic and decisive, and never to compromise the revolution or class interest for the sake of personal advantage or social harmony. They are also exhorted to take initiatives, to dare, as did Mao and his cohorts when they challenged the established regime during the civil war. Thus, the prestige of those who opted actively for the communist cause in the days before it became powerful is far greater than is that of persons who waited until later to "join the revolution" (see ch. 9, Political System and Values).

The traditional passivity of the lower class Chinese, as caricatured in Lu Hsun's *The Story of Ah Q* (1921), has been attacked. Ah Q, who became a nationally known comic figure, was a man of little intelligence and less will power, passively accommodating to the winds of change. He habitually used phrases such as *ch'a-pu-to* (more or less) and *mei yu pan fa* (nothing can be done), which indicated his fatalism and willingness to make do with, rather than strive to improve, any situation. Even the utterance of these phrases has been banned in the PRC, and the attitudes they represent have been virulently attacked.

The Communists have also devoted considerable efforts to attempt to prevent cleavages from developing between leaders and followers. Cadres are exhorted to stay close to the masses, to learn from the workers and peasants, and to participate in manual labor in order not to lose the sense of belonging to the working class. In the early 1970s revolutionary committee members in the governmental bureaucracy, the farms, and the factories were doing regular stints of manual labor in order to periodically renew their sense of belonging to the working class. To reduce status consciousness in the PLA, the government abolished formal military ranks in 1965. Although there is evidence that there is a social gap between leaders and followers in the PRC, observers agree that these techniques have helped to make the gap much narrower than in earlier periods in China.

Males and Females

One of the most spectacular changes to come about in the twentieth century has been that of liberating women from the position of inferiority they had held in traditional China. Traditionally female infanticide was common among the poor, and women's inferior status was continuously reinforced by such widespread practices as

153

concubinage, female footbinding, child marriage, the forbidding of widow remarriage, and the dominance of the patrilineal kin groups. Many of these practices were losing popularity among the Western-educated Chinese as early as the 1910s; their demise was hastened by the strong action of the PRC government in enforcing the equal-status provisions for women of the PRC Marriage Law of 1950.

Equal status in the PRC applies to marriage, divorce, and inheritance and carries with it equal obligations to become part of the national labor force. Women are expected to put the needs of production ahead of the demands of husbands and children. Nurseries and homes for the elderly are designed to free women from the need to stay at home. Women in rural areas are expected to participate actively in farmwork. In case of conflicts between the needs of the family—for example, illness of dependent children—and production, the admired woman in the PRC press is the one who chooses to stay at work rather than "selfishly" nurse her child. It is not known to what extent such behavior is emulated. Women are encouraged to wait to age twenty-five to marry and to have no more than two children. The wedding should be simple, not extravagant, and should take place after working hours.

The needs of production sometimes require the separation of husbands and wives for long periods, especially if the wives have jobs. This is often the case in cadre households. As in all aspects of life, the emphasis is on serving the people at the expense of more personal attachments.

Articles, letters to the editor, and editorials in the PRC journal *Women in China* indicate that many women in nonagricultural employment have had difficulty reconciling the needs of their husbands and children with the demands of their careers and that many found it a great hardship to be sent to work and live away from their families. Urban women also were apparently concerned that, if they did not work outside the home, they would be regarded as parasites.

Evidence of women receiving lower wages for equal work on Communes; the tendency for women to be given "female" jobs, such as home handicraft, flyswatting, and manure collecting; and their relatively low representation in the Party and on decisionmaking bodies leads to the conclusion that true equality between the sexes has not yet been achieved in the PRC. The status of women is, however, immeasurably higher than at any earlier time.

Friends and Comrades

Although friendship has never been as binding a relationship as has the patrilineal relationship, it has been of great importance in traditional Chinese society. To a great extent the rules of friendship were patterned after family obligations. One's loyalty to a friend was necessarily stronger than to a stranger or to society at large. Bonds of friendships were formed between persons who shared an important experience or who were fellow members of an organization. The relationship tended to be activated when the friends met again in a new setting. Former schoolmates, for example, could expect to receive extensive support and assistance from one another in adult life. One's obligations to act as a friend were, to a certain extent, an automatic result of having once been associates, without regard to one's feelings for the other person.

Allegiance to friends often took precedence over the public welfare. Such particularistic loyalties have therefore come under attack by the Party. In study sessions much pressure is exerted upon friends to expose each other's faults. It is regarded as disloyalty to one's class to allow a friend's faults to go unchastised. As a result of experience of small group criticism sessions, people have learned not to burden their friends with confidences.

To give special help to a friend is officially equated with cheating society, but to show helpfulness toward others, especially toward persons with whom one is not intimate, is encouraged. Comradeship, in the sense of friendly and responsible relations between equals and between fellow citizens is admired. This is a marked innovation in ethics. Before 1949 a disregard for the welfare of persons unconnected by ties of kinship or friendship was a notable feature of Chinese social behavior.

Man, Nature, and Time

The traditional, Taoist-derived concern of Chinese to be in harmony with nature, rather than to control it or overcome its power, is in conflict with the Maoist belief that man, given the right thoughts, spirit of determination, and time, can conquer nature. The new attitude is best illustrated by one of the so-called three constantly read essays of Mao, a retelling of an ancient Chinese fable, *The Foolish Old Man Who Removed the Mountains* (see ch. 8, Education, Intellectual Expression, and the Arts). This tells of a foolish old man whose doorway was blocked by two enormous mountains. He led his sons in digging up the mountains with their hoes and, when derided for his foolishness in so doing, replied, "When I die, my sons will carry on; when they die, there will be my grandsons, and then their sons and grandsons, and so on to infinity. High as they are, the mountains cannot grow any higher and with every bit we dig, they will be that much lower. Why can't we clear them away?"

Although the fable is used by Mao to illustrate his belief that, traditional beliefs notwithstanding, man can overcome any obstacle, the fable also indicates the persistence of traditional concepts concerning time and especially the way in which every person is connected to, and has obligations to, generations before and after his own. Ancestor worship rites in the past helped keep alive the Chinese sense of involvement with at least five antecedent generations and, in the absence of other institutions, parents and senior kinsmen felt a great obligation to provide for the future needs of their descendants. Although under the communist regime public institutions provide welfare, educational, and other facilities that were formerly the responsibility of kin group organizations, the popularity of this fable in the PRC in the early 1970s suggests that the individual's sense of involvement with many generations of his family, past and future, has persisted.

CHAPTER 6

FAMILY

Until the seizure of political control of the country in 1949 by the communist regime, the extended family for over two millennia had been the single most important social institution in society, performing, in addition to its inherent natural role, a wide variety of functions that in modern states are usually considered rights and duties of the state. The extended family was roughly coextensive with a localized patrilineage. Such a patrilineage included all males in the community who were related to each other by virtue of their descent through males from a common ancestor. The patrilineage also encompassed the wives and unmarried daughters of these men. The patrilineage supervised the moral and political behavior of its members, educated its young, regulated and sanctioned marriages, provided the basis of religious belief and practice, and determined the social identity of everyone connected with it. It maintained peace and order, owned property in the name of its members, and controlled land use and inheritance. It was, in fact, the center of almost all social, economic, religious, and political activity. The state, for its part, allowed the patrilineage considerable autonomy in these matters, regarding the institution as a form of subadministrative organization capable of taking care of itself (see ch. 5, Social System and Values).

In the latter nineteenth century contact with the West and the introduction of Western cultural influences caused Chinese intellectuals to question the values of the old family system (see ch. 3, Historical Setting). In the early 1900s rising industrialization started the formation of a new labor force that was independent of patrilineage sponsorship and increasing urbanization afforded, particularly to young persons, greater opportunities for social relationships outside the restricted family circle. Rural areas were relatively untouched, but in large urban communities demands for reform began to appear.

The revolutionary movement of Sun Yat-sen, which resulted in the formation of the new Republic of China in 1912, was largely led and supported by young people, including many women. During the second and third decades of the twentieth century, popular movements for the emancipation of women from restrictions of the past and for young people of both sexes to be accorded greater

157

freedom, social mobility, and the right to participate in social, economic, and political affairs rose and flourished. Although these early movements had few practical results, they did focus public attention on the need for reforming the old family system and gave stress to the nuclear family (parents and dependent children) as the basic social unit and, within it, greater freedom for women and children.

The first attempts to legislate reform was the Kinship Relations Law promulgated in 1930. This act embodied most of the demands for reform, but although it had great revolutionary potential it was not effectively enforced, and its direct impact on Chinese society as a whole was slight. Change continued, however, in the urban areas during the war with Japan (1937–45), and the new family model was carried to other parts of the country by refugees from the coastal cities.

On coming to power, the communist regime announced its intention to remold the entire structure of China's social, economic, and political life; this included the destruction of the patrilineage. The initial major action, as far as the family was concerned, was the new Marriage Law of 1950. Determined enforcement of this law, which contained many of the provisions of the earlier Kinship Relations Law, during the ensuing twenty years, appeared in 1971 to have effectively changed the family institution. Little information on these changes was available, however; Western scholars were generally unable to carry out studies in mainland China during the period from 1949 to 1971, and it appears unlikely that any objective research on the family institution occurred within the country during that same time.

Various reports indicate, however, that the traditional authority and responsibilities of the extended family have been stripped away and taken over by various agencies of the state, and the family in essence has been reduced to the nuclear unit concerned chiefly with certain consumption and recreational activities, child care, and normal emotional functions. To this extent, it resembles the present-day Western family unit. At the same time the retention of some of the older values is indicated in the stress placed by the regime on the care of older persons by adult children, harmony between husband and wife, and the need for respect by children.

There is also evidence, although fragmentary and frequently indirect, that other concepts associated with the old, traditional extended family system still persisted despite efforts of the regime through its cadres (see Glossary) to eliminate them. These included attitudes connected with clan and lineage, the tradition of arranged marriage, and ancestor worship.

THE TRADITIONAL FAMILY

Within the traditional family pattern relationships were based on the supremacy of males over females and of age over youth. The status of women in particular was low. They were required to be submissive and obedient to their husbands and deferential to all males within and outside the family. They had no authority or voice in the management of vital family affairs and no right to participate as individuals in social, political, or economic activities. They were secluded within the home; bore children; performed household chores; and, in wealthier families, supervised the servants. In poor families they helped men till the fields when necessary.

Youth occupied a subordinate position in relation to their elders, including older brothers (not sisters) or any male of a preceding generation. They were expected to remain at home contributing their labor to the family enterprise and to subjugate their personal desires to the will of their elders and the welfare of the extended family.

The Chinese family traditionally has reckoned its descent in the male line; not all present-day minority nationality peoples, however, are patrilineal (see ch. 4, Ethnic Groups and Languages). The head of the family was always a male. In a nuclear family it was the father; in an extended family it was the oldest male of the most senior generation. When the family head died he was succeeded by his eldest son or, if he had no sons, by his eldest brother.

The authority of the family head was theoretically absolute. He represented the family in dealing with the state or with other families, and his decisions were binding on the entire household. At the same time he was responsible for the support, education, marriage, and behavior of each member. If any one of them committed an offense against the state or society, the family head was held to account. Each member, in turn, was answerable to the family and had to accept family authority, to be loyal to the head, to contribute labor and substance to support the entire group as necessary, and to subjugate his personal desires to the greater good and advancement of the family as a whole.

The family name and property were handed down only from father to son. Daughters might be accepted and loved, but they had no inheritance rights. They were looked upon as only temporary family members since when a daughter married she left her home and became completely a part of her husband's family. Sons, therefore, were very important and were desired intensely, to ensure the continuity of the family. If the family head's wife produced only daughters or if she were barren, the father could take a second wife or a concubine, or both, to give himself a male heir. If these measures proved unfruitful, he could adopt a son for the purpose.

Although patterned relationships were the same in all cases, the family's social structure differed according to social class. Among the peasantry the family tended to take the form of a nuclear family, that is, a husband and wife and their children. Among the gentry or elite it tended to consist of a number of nuclear families in a multigenerational unit or extended family.

The Nuclear Family

The nuclear family consisted of a man and his wife or, sometimes, wives (or, in the case of the elite, concubines) and their unmarried offspring. It was the primary unit of consumption, education, and recreation. Ordinarily a peasant nuclear family lived in its own farmhouse of one or two rooms. In an extended family the house was one of a complex of similar houses within a compound that accommodated the combined organization. Storekeepers and artisans in the towns usually lived in their shops or in separate buildings adjoining them.

Middle-class and even poor nuclear families often had dependent relatives or unrelated laborers living with them. In the towns apprentices and employees who were not relatives lived with members of the household and ate with the family. In these cases the nuclear family and the household were not identical. This was also true when an extended family was divided but continued to live under one roof. Individual nuclear families cooked, ate, and managed their finances separately, although they remained physically together within one large household. To a certain degree, this practice has continued despite communist attempts to collectivize urban manufacturing quarters.

The Extended Family

The extended family was an ideal for all classes of the traditional society and served as a functional means of securing political and economic advantages for a selective kinship group with corporate property to protect. For reasons that were largely economic, this kind of family organization rarely occurred unless some of its members were at least moderately well off.

The extended family included the patrilineal grandparents, their unmarried children, and all of the married sons and their families. All ideally lived under one roof, usually in separate parts of the house or compound. This was rare, however, except among the wealthy. Because the family as a group functioned as a coordinated income and consumption unit, ideally the larger it was the more successful it was likely to be. It was rare, nevertheless, to have more than three generations in one house or compound.

The head of the extended family was the oldest male of the oldest generation. This was usually the paternal grandfather, whose prestige and authority derived from his advanced age, as well as from his position as family head. When the grandfather died, he was succeeded by his oldest brother or by his oldest son.

The extended family system was to all intent destroyed in the rural areas during the land reform of the early 1950s as a result of the breakup of large landholdings and the imprisonment or execution of many wealthy landowners and peasants. Collectivization of industry and commerce in urban areas by the mid-1950s had also removed much of the economic base needed to maintain an extended family in the cities. There appeared in 1971 to be some evidence of observances but no definite evidence of economic activity undertaken by lineages (see ch. 3, Historical Setting; ch. 5, Social System and Values).

Patterned Relationships

Internal relationships were similar in nuclear and extended families but underwent some alterations in the extended family because of the combined group's complex nature and greater size. The father-son relationship was one of authority-submission but usually warm and cordial. The son had to revere and support his parents. Mourning and worship after their deaths were integral parts of a son's duty. Conversely, a father was obliged to support his son, train or educate him, and provide a wife for him. Regardless of the age or maturity he might reach, a son never attained equal adult status with his father during the sire's lifetime. In one sense, however, father and son were identified in that a son's economic and social position was largely defined by that of his father. Even during the lifetime of his father, the eldest son was regarded by outsiders as the heir to his father's prestige, property, and family leadership.

The relationship between father and daughter was less formally defined and usually not close. Girls did not contribute to the vital continuation of the paternal line. Moreover, after marriage and movement to her husband's home, a daughter's contacts with her original family were infrequent, especially if she lived some distance away.

The husband-wife relationship was one of authority-submission. After he died she could not remarry but had to submit, theoretically at least, to the authority of his family or of her eldest son, who became the new family head. A husband owed his wife her support, even when there was no affection between them. If she were treated too badly, a wife might return to her parents' home, but they were likely to send her back. In the last extreme she might commit suicide, which would bring disgrace both upon her own family and that of her spouse.

The mother-son relationship was important; a wife's status depended upon her producing a male to ensure continuity of the family. Since the arrival of a son gave her improved status and security, the mother naturally felt much warmth for him. Her authority over a male child never equaled that of the father, but while he was an infant she was with him constantly, catering to his every need and training requirement. Even after infancy, when a son ordinarily moved to his father's side of the house, the mother sometimes interceded for him with his father and often played a strong role in the selection of his wife.

Mother and daughter had a closer relationship as a result of the practice of segregation by sex. A daughter remained with her mother, learning household tasks and feminine arts. The mother, thus, was the dominant influence in determining a daughter's development and behavior.

Brothers and sisters did not associate closely in the family, even in play. A brother was dominant over his sisters regardless of their respective ages. After a sister married and moved away, there was little contact between her and her brothers. In times of natural disaster and civil war, however, it was common for the sister's family to seek refuge with the brother's family, or vice versa.

The older-younger brother relationship was similar to that between father and son. An older brother had authority over his younger brother or brothers although not as great as the father's. All were supposed to live in harmony, and much emphasis was placed upon the idea that they were from a common source.

The relationship between sisters was completely informal among peasants, and contacts among them might disappear almost completely after they were married. After the emancipation of women in the early 1900s, this pattern was modified among educated women of elite families. A well-known example was the famed Soong sisters (Madame Chiang Kai-shek and her sister, Soong Ching-ling, the wife of Sun Yat-sen and later an official of the communist regime in Peking). Educated women of elite families were allowed to play strong roles as public figures, and their families encouraged them to have broad contacts among kinsmen as a mark of social prestige.

Relations between sisters-in-law were informal and considered unimportant, but a husband's natural sisters sometimes caused conflict. Such conflicts gradually lessened as the natural sisters married and moved away. The wives of brothers who were permanently attached to the household did not become close despite their common unfavorable situation. Instead, the older brothers' wives tended to exploit the most recently added sister-in-law to consolidate their own positions in the family.

Certain relationships that were relatively minor in a nuclear family became important in the extended family system. The most significant were those that had to do with contacts between and among the various forms of in-laws. Prominent among them was the relationship between parents-in-law and daughters-in-law. A wife's primary duty was to her husband's parents rather than to her own spouse. She had to serve them and to mourn for them as their own son was expected to do. Because of the pattern of sex segregation, a daughter-in-law had little contact with her husband's father; in fact, their relationship was almost one of avoidance. The relationship with her mother-in-law, however, was critical as she worked at household tasks under the mother-in-law's direction and was in constant daily contact with her. Generally this relationship was one of the most strained in the extended family.

A daughter-in-law's relations with her husband's brothers varied in accordance with the principle of age. Those with his older brothers, like those with her father-in-law, approximated avoidance; those with his younger brothers could be freer, although they too were generally distant.

Factors Affecting Family Structure and Dynamics

The life of a Chinese was viewed as developing through a general sequence of five age periods. The first was infancy, covering roughly the first four years of life. During the first two years the child was coddled, pampered, and subjected to no formal training or discipline. The mother was in constant attendance throughout this stage, although the care of the child might be shared by older siblings and other members of the family and, in wealthier families, by servants. There was little distinction between the physical treatment of boys and girls during this time. If the family were too poor to support many children, however, a girl baby might be sold or traded away. If their poverty was extreme and there was no other way to dispose of a girl, female infanticide might occur.

The next age grade was childhood, which lasted from about four until the child was fifteen or sixteen years of age. During this period the real discipline of family life was brought to bear upon the children, and differentiation on the basis of sex began in earnest. The change from infancy to childhood marked the advent of rigorous training in a boy, who might be subjected to discipline from a source outside the family. Girls remained with their mothers and began learning to take over household duties. They had few nonfamily contacts and were confined largely to the home.

The next age group was youth, referring to the years between sixteen and thirty years of age for males and to a somewhat shorter and earlier period for females. Youth was a more or less intermediate period during which a person could no longer be called a child but was not yet accepted as a full-fledged adult. Most Chinese were married before the end of this period, an event that terminated their classification as youths.

Full-fledged adulthood began when an individual was married or, if single, when he became thirty years old. Adulthood was divided into two parts. An individual was simply an adult up to about forty years of age, after which he was referred to as middle aged until roughly his fifty-fifth birthday, when he reached the stage of old age.

As an elder, the individual was treated with great respect and veneration and was allegedly invested with considerable authority. The formal deference, respect, and security accorded old people were very real, but the actual authority and control might be more formal than real.

The lack of a natural male offspring to continue the family line and perform necessary rites for the ancestors might have led to adoption. Near relatives were virtually under obligation to provide a boy when adoption became necessary. If none were available among close relatives, a search would be made among those that were more distant. In any case, the boy would have to be the son of a generation corresponding to the adopting parents. Adoption of a nonrelative was rare.

If a family had daughters but no sons, a husband might be adopted for one of the girls. He then came to live with her family, took its name, and abandoned his own family. Such matrilocal marriages were often looked upon as degrading in most parts of China because only an admittedly poor man and one who was shiftless would abandon his ancestors in this manner. Nevertheless, it served its purpose of providing a male heir, who was not the adopted husband but the first son born to the union.

Economic, Social, and Religious Functions

All family property and all income earned by members of the traditional nuclear family belonged to the male head of the family. The nuclear families of peasants, artisans, and small merchants were units of production in which the men and boys cultivated the fields and the women and girls performed household tasks and made the family clothing. To a large extent, these families were self-sufficient. In the case of artisans and small merchants, sons were expected to follow the father's trade; and female members, to do the household tasks. If absent members of the family were wage earners, they were expected to send home all their income except that required for actual subsistence. An individual who attempted to keep his earnings for himself was considered to be unfilial.

Economically, the extended family acted as a corporation, holding a variety of material and personal resources for the common good of its members. Property was individually owned, but the right to manage it and the budget rested in the hands of the extended family head. Each family member turned over all his income to his family head, who allocated it according to need among all members. Income supporting the extended family was usually derived from rents, commercial enterprises, salaries, and professional services. The extended family was basically a unit of consumption; its members were not usually engaged in production.

Social contacts of an individual in the poor nuclear family were generally not limited to his family and close relatives, but the closest ties were with them, and the family was his first recourse in times of stress or trouble. The family provided education which, in the case of the poor, usually was practical and consisted of the parents teaching the children whatever skills and lore they knew.

The social functions of the extended family were similar to those of the nuclear type. As the unit was larger and the number of persons involved was greater, however, it tended to provide more social contacts and recreation for its members, particularly with regard to the women. These women had servants to attend to outside errands and consequently were more secluded; their social contacts for the most part were limited to members of the household. Education was usually provided by hiring a tutor or by sending the child to a school.

One of the most important functions of the family—and a basic factor underlying its solidarity and unity—was the performance of ancestor worship. Families were regarded as continuing entities, some of whose members were deceased, some living, and the rest as yet unborn. The deceased were not thought to be dead but to live in another realm where they could influence, and be influenced by, the living. Thus, it became the duty of the living to perform certain rites and ceremonies at specific intervals to ensure the continued well-being and protection of all ancestors. Should a family neglect these duties the living and future generations would surely suffer. Conversely, suitably cared for ancestors were capable of rendering material aid to their descendants (see ch. 5, Social System and Values).

Memorial tablets for the immediate ancestors in the nuclear family were usually located in a shrine within the family dwelling house. In the extended family, tablets of the immediate ancestors of the entire group were kept in a shrine in the main hall of the family head's house. The tablets for ancestors of the wife remained in her father's home. When she entered her husband's home a wife venerated his ancestors, and when she died she was considered to be a member of his family. Future generations, then, included her with the ancestors of the husband.

Kin Groups

Kinsmen comprised those persons related through one's father, through one's mother, and through marriage. Under the rules of ritual and ceremonial conduct, certain relatives from all three groups were considered mourning relatives, or relatives for whom one was expected to mourn at their death.

The circle of paternal relatives in the category were the children, grandchildren, and great-grandchildren of the deceased. Collaterally, they included a brother's family and the family of his progeny. The obligation to mourn ceased with the descendants of a common great-great-grandfather. In the case of his relatives, a man wore mourning for his mother's parents, her brothers and sisters, and his wife's parents. The mourning period required to be observed varied with the distance of the relationship. A woman was expected, however, to mourn her husband's parents as long as her own. A woman who had gone through the proper mourning period for her husband's parents could not be divorced.

The circle of mourning relatives was composed of a close group of kinsmen from within the lineage and the clan. This was reflected in the greater degree of solicitude and mutual aid expected from its members than from either of the larger groupings.

Clan and Lineage

The clan and the lineage are often confused by an overly loose translation of the Chinese word for lineage (*tsu*) to mean both groups. The lineage was actually a local descent group tracing its ancestry through males to a first male ancestor who settled in a given locality. Only patrilineal descendants were considered lineage members. Marriage within a lineage was not permitted, so a woman married outside her father's lineage, and her children belonged to the lineage of her husband.

Lineages usually included wealthy and poor families that crosscut class lines and represented several social strata. They lost many of their integrative functions in larger cities where class distinctions were sharp and where guilds and other organizations took over some of their protective functions. The importance of lineages also varied from one region to another. They were generally strongest in the south where a whole village might be composed of only one or two dominant lineages. When this was the case village organization became identical with lineage organization, and lineage leaders became the major village functionaries.

A clan included many lineages and referred even to all persons having the same surname. At practical levels a clan was a group of lineages from different localities that recognized a common ancestor.

Although families within a clan bore the same surname, they were not necessarily related; the clan simply imputed to them a common ancestor. It was not uncommon for families who desired to increase their prestige to make use of a specialist in forging or manufacturing family pedigrees to enable them to claim membership in a successful clan. The great extent to which this occurred was evidenced by the fact that there were roughly 470 surnames in use in China, whereas in the past there had been five times that many.

The most conspicuous function of both clans and lineages was to unite in social bond larger numbers of related people than could have been achieved by the family alone. Lineage members, for example, were reminded of their unity by the use of kinship terminology to address fellow members and to expect from them the prescribed patterns of behavior associated with these terms. The expected behavior patterns were more attenuated than in the family, but they stressed similar respect for the older generation and for old age.

In areas of strong lineage development the lineage had economic, educational, judicial, and political functions in addition to the religious role. Wealthy members donated land and property, and through investments and rents some lineages and clans were able to amass considerable wealth. These resources were used to build and support lineage temples, defray the expenses of ancestral rituals, pay for court litigations involving members, assist younger members in attaining an education, help orphans and indigent elderly members, and provide burial space for the dead.

Concomitant with this concentration of wealth was a concentration of power. Leaders of both types of organization were drawn from those members who were able to enhance the standing of the group vis-à-vis outsiders, such as the government. These leaders enjoyed certain rights and privileges not available to lesser members. Certain rites and banquets were reserved for them and, like family heads, they had a proportionate authority over the members of their respective groups. Matters concerning the group at large were referred to the appropriate head and his advisers; cases were heard and punishments were meted out in the ancestral hall or temple according to tradition and lineage rules. Criminal offenses, such as homicide, were supposed to be under the jurisdiction of the government, but in areas of strong lineage development government authorities found it impossible to interfere. The lineage or clan preferred to deal with its own and was strong enough to ignore government authority. Often the government official would make a face-saving investigation, but the group retained the real power.

Usually neighboring kinship organizations were on good terms because ties of intermarriage and friendship connected them. Nevertheless, by the very nature of their makeup, some rivalry was inevitable. In some areas this took the form of competition in the education of members or in the construction of ancestral temples. In other areas, especially southeastern China, the rivalry sometimes broke out into feuds involving fighting over extended periods of time. Sometimes several lineages banded together for mutual benefit, thereby forming a bloc that government authorities found impregnable.

THE FAMILY UNDER THE REPUBLIC

The New Culture Movement

The revolution in 1911 embodied within it a questioning of the concept of kinship dominance in the operations of the state. At the same time, the overthrow of the monarchy resulted in the abolition of the old imperial laws that compelled conformity to the traditional family institutions (see ch. 3, Historical Setting). These factors and the spread of Western cultural influences helped to initiate during the ensuing several years a gradually widening discussion of the position of the family in the social and political life of the country. Led by a group of young faculty members of Peking National University, the discussions, which covered not only the family but also the problem of general social and cultural reform, culminated in 1917 in what is called the New Culture Movement, or Chinese Renaissance (see ch. 8, Education, Intellectual Expression, and the Arts).

During the movement, which reached full force in 1919 in the May Fourth Movement, the term *family revolution* came into use. Drawing support particularly from young people, both male and female, the movement had no organized platform, but its general objectives were evident from its slogans and the content of an expanding volume of literature. Greater equality between the sexes was demanded, as well as freedom of social association, a stronger voice in the selection of marriage partners, and the right to break away from the family group in pursuit of better opportunities. In essence, a new family institution generally similar to that found in the West was implied.

The New Culture Movement expanded and grew in influence during the 1920s. Open attacks on Confucianist orthodoxy became highly fashionable among the intellectuals, and a further weakening of the traditional family institution resulted (see ch. 5, Social System and Values). The movement did not gain many adherents in rural areas, where family organization remained strong, but in the urban areas it drew an increasing number of recruits from among the young and among educated people of both sexes in the upper and upper middle classes. During the decade many of these families, despite strong opposition from the older generation, experienced fundamental changes in structure. The total strength of the movement was small in relation to the overall population, but it was able to formulate and publicize a coherent group of ideas that focused public attention on the problem and ultimately enabled the government to pass the Kinship Relations Law of 1930.

The Kinship Relations Law

The Kinship Relations Law of 1930 made a number of radical reforms in the old family system. Probably the most important of its features was its failure to include any reference to ancestor worship. This delivered a blow to the heart of the traditional institution as it implied that a male heir was no longer a necessity to the family. Although the family continued to be centered on the husband's home, the previous powers of the family head were curtailed. The law made consent of the parties concerned a requirement for a marriage contract. This constituted a shift from the idea that marriage was a contract between families to the notion that it was one between individuals. It also declared that men and women were equal with regard to divorce, remarriage, property rights, inheritance, and even the right to be family head, attacking the old principle of male superiority. The law further made the position of children more secure by prohibiting a father from killing them, something he could previously do without interference from the state. The law also provided that gifts and inheritances received by a child became his own personal property after he attained his majority at the age of twenty years.

The new legislation did not mention concubinage but tacitly recognized its existence by providing liberally for illegitimate children. Since concubines were not recognized as legal wives, their children were regarded as illegitimate, but the law made it easy for them to achieve legal status.

Many radical changes other than those noted in the law specifically had taken place in the position of women in the interim after the revolution in 1911. One was a movement sanctioned by the government against the binding of women's feet, which helped contribute to freeing women from seclusion in the home. Another was the increasing employment of women, leading to more educational facilities being made available to them. These included the first government-established public school for girls, which resulted in an influx of women into professional work.

The Law of Kinship Relations was radical in concept and revolutionary in its provisions but, despite its liberality, the immediate effect on the traditional family system throughout the country was slight. Potentially, it weakened the old family institution by providing the legal authority for extensive changes, but the Nationalist government was apathetic about its actual implementation, and the great mass of people generally ignored its provisions. Only in urban areas and among the educated strata of the population were its provisions really understood, and for them it merely gave legal sanction to practices many had already adopted with their espousal of the New Culture Movement. In rural areas the old system may have been challenged legally but, in fact, it underwent little or no alteration.

THE FAMILY UNDER COMMUNISM

The changes that occurred in the traditional family system after the revolution in 1911 until the assumption of full state power by the Communists in 1949 had taken place largely as the result of evolutionary processes. The total number of persons affected by the changes, however, was comparatively small, and the traditional system in 1949 still constituted a major competitor with the state for the allegiance of the people. The continued existence of this system represented a serious barrier to attainment of the social, economic, and political goals of the new regime, and as one of its first reform acts it promulgated a new marriage law on May 1, 1950.

The Marriage Law of 1950

The new Marriage Law was the first civil code produced by the Communist regime. Some of its provisions had been introduced originally in the Kinship Relationship Law of 1930, but, whereas acceptance of these under that law was generally left to the individual, adherence to the new law was compulsory; and pressures of various sorts, including well-organized mass movements, were used in an effort to achieve conformity.

Although many of the provisions of the new law were not actually new, the communist regime carried them further, introducing innovations that were revolutionary in their impact. The old law, for example, merely recognized that the agreement of the parties concerned was important to a marriage contract, whereas the new measure stipulated that such agreement was an essential factor that could not be set aside by any agreement or pact concluded exclusively by the families of the young couple. Thus marriage, which traditionally had been a contract between families, was transformed into a contract between individuals. Additionally, a valid marriage, previously legitimized merely by having the sanction of the families, was required to be registered and legitimized by the state, which thereby replaced the family as the controlling agency. Other provisions included firm proscriptions against child betrothals, polygyny, concubinage, and the practice of selling, trading, or giving daughters to another family to be reared by them as future brides for their young, often as yet unborn, sons.

Under the new law's definition of intrafamily relationships, the relationship between husband and wife, which traditionally had been characterized by the complete submergence of the woman's personality in that of her husband, was recast in terms of individual equality. The law accorded both marriage partners equal rights to own and manage family property and the right to free choice of occupation and to participate in work or social activities outside the home. The relationships between parents and children (including children who were illegitimate, adopted, or stepchildren or the issue of parents who became divorced) were altered from blind adherence to the demands of filial piety to a willing sense of mutual responsibility for the care and support of each other. The relationships of other family members were similarly equalized without regard to differences in their ages or generation.

The concept of divorce was an important part of the family revolution of the precommunist period, although acceptance was generally limited to the newer intellectuals. The matter of divorce was given elaborate attention in the new law. Grounds for divorce were liberalized, and wives were guaranteed equal rights in seeking a decree. These rights had been included in the earlier Kinship Relations Law, but at that time they had provided only formal equality since the idea of the inferior social status of women was retained. In the new version the equality became real, and if a wife encountered resistance from her husband or family, she could count on help from the local communist cadre. In like manner, divorced wives and widows who previously were faced with bleak and lonely futures were authorized and encouraged to remarry.

The Modern Chinese Family

The purpose of the Marriage Law and other social and economic measures appears not to have been destruction of the nuclear family as such but, rather, elimination of the extended family structure and lineage bonds. There is some evidence that, included in the concept of the Communes established in 1958 in conjunction with the Great Leap Forward, party theoreticians envisioned a certain amount of impersonalization of family relations (see ch. 5, Social System and Values; ch. 14, Agriculture). The communal social aspects of the program were found unworkable, however, at least for the time, and their functions reverted to the individual nuclear family.

Western correspondents who visited the country near mid-1971 found evidence that the family had been definitely retained as an essential social institution and that family bonds, for both social and economic reasons, were being encouraged by the state. Family life appeared to be relatively intimate. Divorce was also found, but the state appeared to be making efforts in such cases to effect reconciliations wherever possible.

171

CHAPTER 7

LIVING CONDITIONS

The strain of a large population on limited land and other resources was in the early 1970s, as it had been for nearly two centuries, a dominant factor in mainland Chinese life. The per capita share of the gross national product (GNP) in 1970, according to the estimates of Western economists, did not exceed the equivalent of US$100. For most people it was necessary to labor long hours at hard work to maintain a standard of living that was barely above subsistence level. The paucity of food, fuel, and construction materials required strict economy in consumption and the recycling of waste materials to the fullest possible extent.

There were indications that the population as a whole was better off materially in 1971 than it had been for several decades. The improvement resulted mainly from the reduction or elimination of social and economic inequities and not from any substantial increase in goods available. The standard was improving most rapidly for the poorest elements of the population. Cadres (bureaucratic functionaries —see Glossary) who promoted the interests and programs of the Chinese Communist Party (CCP) continued, however, to enjoy special advantages and better than average living conditions.

Urban dwellers continued to enjoy a higher standard of living than the peasants, despite increased emphasis beginning in the mid-1960s on improving the welfare of the rural population, which consisted of more than 80 percent of all families and which lived in approximately 600,000 villages. There was improvement in living conditions, particularly in health, in rural areas. The movement of city population, including professional-level personnel, to rural areas was a contributing factor, but the peasants were required to provide most of the funds for any improvement schemes (see ch. 5, Social System and Values).

Patterns of living, which before 1950 had been strongly influenced by family, clan, and customs, were changed or modified at an unusually rapid pace by actions promoted by CCP leaders. Government agencies and social organizations controlled by the CCP attempt to guide and direct every facet of life in order to have individual identification with and loyalty to the socialist cause prevail over traditional family and community influences. Although the efforts to dispense with old customs and relationships sometimes met with resentment, the trend since the early 1950s has been toward stern controls, increased regimentation of the social, economic, and political life of the individual, and loss of privacy.

The seasonal cycle of work sets the pattern of economic life for the rural population and has remained basically unchanged. The collectivization of agriculture under the CCP and the elimination of individual peasant farms, however, brought striking changes in social and economic relationships, greatly reducing the time available for work and leisure activities of personal choice (see ch. 14, Agriculture).

Although the system for distributing food appeared to have improved, continued population growth at an annual rate of over 2 percent during the 1960s caused strains on available food supplies. Housing in 1971 remained critical despite construction of some new developments, particularly by state industrial enterprises. Improving health, resulting from large-scale campaigns to eliminate pests and other causes of diseases, better sanitation, and provision of basic health services to the rural population, has been one of the most notable developments in recent years.

PATTERNS OF LIVING

In the early 1970s the influences of CCP and state-controlled organizations were felt in nearly every facet of everyday life. Many work and social activities that in the precommunist period had centered on the family and the individual farm or enterprise were shifted to cooperatives, state enterprises, and mass social organizations. The family continued to have a place in the socialist system, but the clan, once a powerful institution, was eliminated. Ties within the nuclear family were weakened deliberately by channeling work and leisure activities into state-controlled institutions (see ch. 5, Social System and Values; ch. 6, Family).

In rural areas the peasant's life was largely in the context of the collective organization within a People's Commune (see Glossary). The main source of income was from a production team consisting of from twenty to thirty households and was calculated on work points earned. Welfare benefits were paid by the collective and cooperative systems, of which the production team was the basic unit. Another facet of rural economic life encompassed the small plot allotted by the collective and a few head of livestock, which the peasant could utilize as he desired. Social life in rural areas took place mainly in organizations and groups under the direction of CCP cadres. These included the Peasants' Union, the Women's Federation, youth groups, and others. There was little time for family life, but mutual dependence and the need to share burdens tended to maintain close relationships within the nuclear family.

The life of the city worker is tied to the state enterprise where he works and its associated cooperatives and social organizations under CCP and state control. Most workers are members of a small group, formed at their place of employment, of from eight to fifteen persons. Wives and young persons also form groups. Cadres give guidance and direction to these groups during their discussions on their work and on social or political matters. The range of choices left open to the family is limited, but the family continues as a basic consumption unit and a vehicle for pooling resources and sharing goods and services used in common by family members.

In the countryside the rhythm of village life is largely established by the seasonal cycle of farming activities. In North China agricultural work is geared to the growing of wheat, millet, and kaoliang (see Glossary) and the need to maximize the use of moisture accumulated in the soil during the fall and winter rains. In the spring, as winter-wheat fields dry, water from wells is applied, frequently by hand methods, to bring the crop to maturity. Other fields that were lying fallow throughout the winter are fertilized, utilizing waste material from the household pit, and tilled and planted in April and May. Newly planted fields also are irrigated. The harvesting of the winter wheat and the preparation of the fields for a second crop, such as soybeans, bring another very busy period for production-team households. The pace slackens briefly and then toward the end of the summer again intensifies, when the fields planted in the spring are harvested. Preparing the soil and planting winter wheat extend the period of heavy activity into the autumn. In the late fall and winter, when there is no field work, various housekeeping chores are accomplished, such as repairing implements and buildings, spinning and weaving cloth, and making and repairing clothing. Generally during this period the family pig is slaughtered and frequently sold as a means of obtaining cash. The new year brings festivities and a letup in work activities.

South of the Yangtze River peasant life is closely tied to the growing of rice, the dominant crop of the region. The cycle begins in early spring with the chores attendant to growing rice plants in nursery beds. This work is followed by cultivation of the soil, application of fertilizer, usually in the form of night soil, and other tasks concerning preparation for transplanting the young rice plants from the nursery beds. The spring season of difficult work is completed with the transplanting of the young rice shoots, which requires crouching in the water.

During the summer growing season weeding and cultivating are required, but peasant life is somewhat easier. The harvesting and threshing of the rice in late summer again calls for intensification of work. The harvest season is followed with continuing requirements for hard work as the fields are prepared for another crop. In some areas two and even three rice crops are grown in a single year; in other parts of South China the rice crop may be followed by winter wheat or rape. During the winter season the peasant works on maintenance and repair chores and handicrafts. The demands by the government for contributions of labor for public improvements, such as irrigation and roads, tend to reduce to a minimum the amount of time the rice farmer of the south as well as the wheat grower of the north has available for personal tasks.

National holidays provide opportunities for celebration and a break in the routine of work. Except for the Spring Festival, which is established by phases of the moon, all national holidays fall on specific dates according to the Gregorian calendar. They are: Spring Festival, the first to third days of the first moon of the lunar calendar (usually in late January or in February); May Day, May 1; Army Day, August 1; and National Day, October 1 and 2. The government has additionally fixed March 8 as Women's Day, May 4 as Chinese Youth Festival Day, June 1 as Children's Festival, and December 9 as the anniversary of the 1935 Shanghai Student Demonstrations. January 1 is the occasion for an editorial in the leading newspapers to extol the regime's accomplishments during the past year and to further support for the leadership's objectives, but otherwise the day passes without celebration.

The CCP regime's efforts to eliminate ceremonies involving superstitions and ancestor rites have largely reoriented and decreased the significance of some traditional festivals once widely celebrated. Those that appear to have declined include: the Feast of the Dead, during the third lunar month (usually in the beginning of April); the Dragon Boat Festival, the fifth day of the fifth lunar month (usually in late May); and the Autumn Festival, the fifteenth day of the eighth lunar month (usually in September).

The Spring Festival, formerly China's New Year, is the most important feast day. It is a time for celebration and general relaxation. Many of the ceremonies in early years related to ties between the living and the dead, but they have been replaced by group activities that are acceptable to CCP leaders. Celebrations include displaying pictures and slogans, preparing special dishes, and engaging in group social activities. Romanticized portraits of Mao Tse-tung and other Chinese Communist heroes dominate the displays of New Year's pictures once devoted largely to the deities. Slogans in keeping with CCP aims have taken the place of paired mottoes that expressed wishes for long life, happiness, and wealth. Social activities, once restricted to family and friends, have been broadened to make them community affairs. Dramatic groups organized by the local element of a mass social organization or traveling troupes perform an approved repertoire for the villagers. Cadres sponsor lectures and provide instructive films. Authorities allow extra food for the New

Year, but the period of festivities, which earlier had continued for fifteen days, has been abbreviated. For many families this is one of the rare occasions when meat is served. Foods considered special for the season may vary from province to province; in the north *chiao-tze* (meat dumplings) is a favorite, and in the south *nien-kao* (New Year cakes) is a specialty.

May Day, in honor of workers, and National Day, the anniversary of the People's Republic of China (PRC), are given the greatest emphasis by the government. For these celebrations there are collective festivities that extol the accomplishments and virtues of the CCP regime. On National Day there is a large parade with representations from agriculture, industry, the military, the arts, and other facets of Chinese life. On Army Day special tribute is paid to the military for their important role in establishing the regime and maintaining its security.

Pastime and social activities are largely under the guidance of organizations controlled by the CCP. Community culture centers are the focal point for many activities. Among the most popular games played by adults are two forms of chess. One resembles Western chess; the other is best known in the West by the Japanese name *go*. Walks and picnics, emulating the Long March (see Glossary), are a favorite diversion for family and other groups. Community recreation includes skits, drama, and musical performances approved by the government.

Youth and other social group activities frequently include exercises that are designed to improve physical fitness. Marching and other physical activities that contribute to military proficiency are commonplace. Games entailing little expense are most common because there is a dearth of money available for recreation. Basketball is most popular, but table tennis, a game in which the Chinese are particularly skillful, is played throughout the country. Volleyball also is a favorite group game. Although athletics and military training are frequently combined, sports, such as boxing, that involve physical contact have been outlawed by the CCP government.

FOOD

The quantity of food available in the early 1970s was little improved over that of the years just before the Great Leap Forward (see Glossary) because of a high rate of population growth and only a slight increase in crop production. The importation of wheat annually in the 1960s added only a small, but perhaps critical, margin to domestic supplies (see ch. 14, Agriculture). Although firm data are lacking, reports indicate that government controls, including the rationing of some basic commodities, improved the distribution of available food and that there is less chance of mass starvation when regional famines or crop disasters occur.

In 1970 per capita daily intake was estimated at 2,150 calories, whereas the average for the 1964–70 period was estimated at 2,000 to 2,100 calories. Poor crop years from 1959 to 1961, however, caused serious food problems, and in 1960 and 1961 the average daily intake probably did not exceed 1,850 calories; deaths resulted from lack of food in some disaster areas, and scattered reports indicate that the toll was in the millions.

An average per-day intake of 2,000 calories, according to Western authorities on Chinese food and agriculture, is adequate to maintain the population in reasonably good physical condition. Intake of food below this level is likely to result in loss of body weight for the average adult and reduced productivity in work activities. Estimates also indicate the need for a daily intake of about 2,200 calories to perform heavy work. The rationing system for urban residents takes energy requirements into account and provides the largest ration to persons engaged in heavy physical labor. The rice ration in 1970, for example, varied from thirty to forty-five pounds per month.

The diet generally is heavy in carbohydrates and lacks balance. Of the total per capita daily intake of 2,150 calories, it was estimated that 1,650 calories were from cereal crops, and 500 were from other foods. Wheat and millet are the main foods in the north, and rice is the staple in the south. Sugar, animal proteins, and minerals such as calcium are generally lacking. Even in normal years there are signs of malnutrition.

Meals are simple and offer little variety. Soup consisting of water and a few vegetable leaves or stems, seasoned with soy sauce, is served twice daily, in addition to the main dishes made from cereals. Meat is scarce, and meat dishes are usually reserved for special occasions.

CLOTHING

The almost universal costume for men and women is trousers, a loose tuniclike jacket, and a cap. Usually made of a drab blue, green, or khaki color, the clothing gives the appearance of a uniform. Most people own only one suit of clothing at a time. The ration of cotton material is about six square yards per year. Old garments and every bit of material are utilized for patches and to make footwear. Synthetic fibers are not rationed, but they are purchased mainly by persons with above-average incomes. The once-common practice of wearing brightly colored clothing with ornate needlework has largely disappeared. Children, however, sometimes wear bright colors. In cold areas garments are heavily padded to give warmth.

Manufactured shoes made of heavy cotton with rubber or synthetic bottoms are most commonly worn. Shoes are sometimes handmade, and the number of persons who are without shoes has been greatly reduced. A sewing machine is a prized possession because most people continue to make their own clothing.

HOUSING

A critical shortage of housing continued to exist in 1971. Estimates of available living space varied, but indications were that the per capita share did not exceed 3 square yards. As a result of a study of housing in Shanghai in 1967, a Western scholar estimated that 85 percent of the city's population lived in pre-1949 quarters and had less than 2.5 square yards per person and that the remaining 15 percent had about 4.8 square yards per individual. In the villages most families lived under very cramped conditions, and sometimes as many as ten persons lived in a single room.

Village houses vary in type of construction and materials according to the climatic conditions. In the north houses tend to be clustered, but in the south they are farther apart and more open. Many are situated on a roughly north-south axis to take advantage of the warming effects of the sun in the cold season. Earth, stone, and bamboo are most commonly used for construction. Wood is scarce and beyond the means of most peasants. In the warmer areas, walls are usually made of bamboo laths plastered with mud, and roofs are tile. Thatched roofs made of wheat are widespread in northern areas. Nearly all houses have earthen floors and tend to be damp. There are few windows, and glass is seldom used because it is expensive.

Most rural homes have only one or two rooms. One room generally serves as a kitchen and bedroom, and the cooking stove, the main source of heat, is used to warm the family brick bed. Fuel is scarce, and peasants usually wear additional clothing or padding constantly in cold weather. Little space is available for furniture, and most homes have only the barest essentials.

Quarters for the mass of city dwellers were little better than those in rural areas. The construction of housing projects after 1949 by factories and industrial complexes resulted in more comfortable quarters for some, but it was not on an adequate scale to alleviate the pressure for living space resulting from population growth. The quality of the new housing developments varied from airy garden apartments surrounded by playgrounds and open space to austere barracklike buildings. A family in a new apartment generally has one or two rooms with private lavatory and use of public bathing facilities. Kitchen facilities are frequently shared by several families. Furnishings are sparse in most city homes. The political elite and others in higher income categories, however, usually have adequate space and well-furnished accommodations.

Illumination of Chinese houses is generally poor. Most peasant houses and many city homes are illuminated by oil lamps. Usually there is only one lamp in a room. Kerosine is generally used, but the poorest families frequently use a cheaper substitute, such as vegetable oil. Electric lighting increased gradually as new housing areas were constructed, and small generators, some producing only 200 to 300 kilowatts, were installed in the rural Communes. Consumption of electricity countrywide remained low, in 1968 reaching only 56 kilowatt-hours per capita.

Water supplies in areas with substantial population are generally adequate for household use. Sources are generally contaminated because of the extensive use of night soil and the improper disposal of other waste. Drinking water must be boiled. Many families have their own wells, but a community source, such as a well or spring, frequently is used by ten to fifteen families. Modern waste systems have been installed in many cities, but frequently families in the lower income categories cannot afford to have lines extended to their homes and must pay charges for water consumption.

A pit located near family living quarters usually serves as a collection place for human and other wastes. Periodically the stored materials, known as night soil, are applied to cultivated areas. Beginning in the 1960s campaigns to improve sanitation and eradicate causes of disease have included chemical treatment of waste pits. In those areas of cities where there is a municipal water system, liquid waste is disposed of through sewers. Solid waste materials in cities are collected by municipal authorities. Reports indicate that garbage collection has improved substantially as a result of organized community efforts to eradicate rats and other disease-carrying pests.

CONSUMPTION PATTERNS

Data were not available in 1971 to make accurate estimates of personal consumption. Indications, derived from estimates of the growth of gross national product, were that personal incomes had increased slightly during the period from 1958 to 1971. Still, in 1971 the average worker had little cash remaining after procuring basic necessities for his family. It was necessary for more than one family member to work in order to procure a radio, sewing machine, bicycle, or other goods over and above basic essentials. Government controls have maintained monetary stability since 1950, and prices of consumer goods were generally kept low. Cereals, cooking oil, and cotton cloth were rationed, but government controls in pricing in effect regulated the availability of many other items. It was difficult for the average family to accumulate either goods or monetary savings beyond its immediate needs.

Only scattered reports were available on peasant incomes, but indications were that the bulk of farmers received 20 to 30 yuan (2.46 yuan equal US$1) a month. All, or nearly all, peasants were members of collectives, and their income depended largely on the number of work points earned in the production team efforts. Part of their earnings also came from the private plot allocated by the production team. A plot was usually only a few square yards. Within the collective as a whole the private sector could not exceed 5 percent of the total cultivated area. Privately owned livestock, such as a pig and a small number of poultry, was usually maintained as a part of the family economy.

The urban worker was somewhat better off than the farmer. Estimates, based mainly on reports from travelers, indicated that the ordinary industrial laborer received 40 to 60 yuan per month in early 1970. City residents also frequently had the advantage of public transportation and other facilities that were not available in the villages. Maoists supported the policy that persons who performed valuable services and produced above-average output should receive higher pay. There were, therefore, differentiations in incomes and levels of consumption. Top-level specialists earned about 250 yuan, and ranking cadres received 350 yuan or more a month.

Prices varied from place to place somewhat because of transportation costs, but basically they were uniform throughout the nation, according to Chinese officials. Data obtained mostly from foreign traders indicated approximate prices of commodities in early 1971 (see table 4).

Table 4. People's Republic of China, Approximate Prices of Commodities, as Reported by Foreign Traders, Early 1971

Item	Unit	Price in Yuan	Equivalent (in US dollars)*
Rice	pound	0.17	0.07
Wheat flour	—do—	0.12	0.05
Fresh vegetables	—do—	0.05	0.02
Fresh beef	—do—	0.70	0.28
Cotton tunics	each	7.00	2.80
Trousers	pair	7.00	2.80
Sweaters	each	10.00	4.00
Shoes			
Leather	pair	20.00	8.00
Cloth	—do—	5.00	2.00
Bicycles	each	100.00	40.00
Wristwatches	—do—	120.00	48.00

* 2.46 yuan equal US$1.

HEALTH

Improvement in the health of the masses of people has been one of the most noteworthy developments since 1960. The death rate is estimated to have dropped from 25 per 1,000 population in 1960 to 15 in 1970. In 1971 life expectancy was estimated at fifty-two years, and it was continuing to increase at a moderate rate. Expansion of basic medical services to the rural population and large-scale campaigns to improve sanitation and personal hygiene and to eliminate disease-causing pests and parasites were major positive influences. On balance, longtime problems, such as crowded living quarters, improper diet, and shortages of skilled medical personnel and modern drugs, continued in 1971 to present obstacles to the maintenance of good health.

Prevalent Diseases

Indications were that most diseases that had once swept over large areas leaving a trail of dead and disabled had been brought under control in the 1960s. A measles epidemic occurred as late as 1960, and there were unofficial reports of meningitis in South China in the winter and spring of 1966. The most feared diseases, which in past years had taken heavy tolls, were bubonic plague, cholera, Japanese B encephalitis, measles, scarlet fever, and typhoid.

Data were not available on the incidence of diseases or the number of deaths resulting from particular afflictions for the 1960s and early 1970s. The most prevalent diseases from 1949 to 1958, as reflected by data on work absences, were tuberculosis, schistosomiasis, malaria, Japanese B encephalitis, typhus, bacillary and amebic dysentery, and ancylostomiasis (or hookworm).

Tuberculosis was probably still one of the most common diseases in 1971 because of dietary deficiencies, overcrowding, and unsanitary practices, such as spitting in public places and improper cleaning of utensils. The number of cases was believed to have been reduced by government campaigns to encourage the wearing of facemasks by those afflicted with respiratory illnesses, to induce people to use eating utensils, and to promote the use of spittoons. Inoculation, particularly of babies born in city hospitals, was also being used to combat the disease.

Trachoma, once a common affliction, is believed to have been reduced by improvement in standards of hygiene. Typhus occurs mostly in the north, where in winter people bathe infrequently and seldom change clothing. Lice, the primary carrier of the disease, thrive on the human body and on rats. Campaigns to improve hygiene and eradicate rats reportedly have reduced the incidence of this disease.

Improperly balanced diet and deficiencies of protective foods cause some maladies, such as rickets, and tend to weaken resistance to disease generally. Lack of calcium, particularly in central and South China, causes rickets and contributes to poor teeth. Animal's milk is seldom consumed, and only a little over 5 percent of food intake comes from leafy vegetables.

Endemic parasitic diseases sap the energy of millions, lower resistance to infection, and sometimes result in death. Government leaders claimed during the 1960s that the incidence of these afflictions was being reduced, and by 1971 some reportedly had been almost eliminated.

Schistosomiasis, is most prevalent along the Yangtze River and to the south of it. It is caused by a snail parasite that enters the bloodstream in the form of a fluke. Striking results from drugs to break the cycle of the fluke have been reported, but the organizing of massive campaigns to clear areas of snails indicated that the disease continued to be a threat in the early 1970s.

Filariasis is found in approximately fourteen provinces, especially in the south of Shantung and Shensi. An insect-borne disease, it attacks the circulatory and lymphatic systems. Fumigation of areas infected by the vectors has reduced the number of cases.

Ancylostomiasis, once common in South and eastern China, has been reduced by the use of drugs and the wearing of shoes by larger numbers of people. The hookworm, after entering the body, lives in the small intestine and saps strength by feeding on the blood.

Kala azar affects both humans and dogs and is endemic in the area north of the Yangtze River. The parasite is a blood-sucking type. The principal carrier, a flea, appears seasonally and can be destroyed by one thorough application of insecticide on walls of dwellings in early summer. From 1949 to 1964, according to reports, 700,000 persons were rid of the parasite by use of sodium gluconate.

Malaria has occurred in nearly every part of China but is mostly found in the rice region south of the Yangtze River and in western Yunnan Province. The use of therapeutic drugs combined with new measures to destroy mosquitoes, according to mainland China press reports, have diminished this affliction that in the 1930s infected over half the population in some areas.

Infant mortality, estimated at 39 per 1,000 live births in 1970, continued to be relatively high despite some improvement in the 1960s. Infection resulting from unsanitary practices by midwives and other unskilled personnel was a primary cause of death. The establishment of maternity stations and health centers for women and children and the training of midwives and medical assistants were much publicized and probably contributed to the reduction of infant mortality.

Types of Medicine

Medicine and measures to maintain health include traditional methods developed in China over more than 2,000 years and Western practices adopted mainly since 1900. After the mid-1950s Chinese political leaders attempted to integrate the two systems. By 1971 both systems were frequently employed side by side, sometimes on the same patient, but it appeared that they tended to retain their distinctive identities.

Chinese traditional medicine is basically a philosophy of nature, a set of hypotheses about the individual as a microcosmic arena in which the elemental forces of the universe contend. Very early it adopted a primitive scientific approach, but it has not adopted modern scientific physiological methodology. In the context of the whole of medical history, some of the achievements of early Chinese practitioners were remarkable. Anesthetics, for example, were used in the Han period (206 B.C.–A.D. 220), and inoculation, not vaccination, against smallpox was practiced in the Sung period, A.D. 960–1279.

The authoritative source on traditional practices is *The Yellow Emperor's Classic of Internal Medicine*, compiled between 1000 B.C. and 200 B.C. It treated in detail various steps that are still fundamental in the prognosis of ailments, such as inspection of the general physical state of the patient, analysis of body odors and monitorship of sounds arising within organs, review of medical history, and analysis of the pulse at various points. Also, social influences were studied, thus making the Chinese one of the earliest people to take psychosomatic factors into account. According to this system of medicine, the meticulous palpitation of the pulse is the central feature in determining the causes of diseases.

Good health, according to traditional practitioners, is dependent upon maintenance of harmony in the interaction of forces within and outside the body. One set of forces known as *yin* is cold, dark, female, and moist; the other set known as *yang* is warm, bright, masculine, and dry. Natural phenomena—elements of special importance to the Chinese—wood, earth, fire, metal, and water, as well as social factors, are given consideration.

Traditional medicine makes much use of herbs and such substances as iodine, kaolin, sulfur, and mercury as preventatives or cures. Formulas frequently have many ingredients; some contain a hundred or more substances. Medicines are classified as *yin* or *yang* and are prescribed to maintain or restore proper balance.

Tonics containing ginseng root and powder from antlers and horns are among the most popular. Ginseng, it is believed, prolongs life and helps to cure a wide range of disorders. Powdered antlers and horns are regarded as sources of strength and as aphrodisiacs. Camphor and a substance produced from the Chinese variety of the lovage plant are also widely used. The government encouraged the growth of herbs on Communes, particularly after the early 1960s, and urged the use of native medicines.

Human dissection never became a part of traditional medicine, having been forbidden since the second century because the body was necessary for ancestor worship and thus sacred. Two therapeutic techniques, acupuncture, the insertion of needles into specific parts of the body, and the application of burning sticks to these points, have held an important place for over 2,000 years. The Chinese mainland press in the 1960s and early 1970s claimed cures by acupuncture for afflictions that were considered beyond the capabilities of Western medicine. These included the restoration of hearing to deaf mutes. Traditional practitioners reportedly cured a wide variety of common diseases and serious disorders. Visiting foreign scientists in 1971 claimed to have witnessed the effective use of acupuncture for an anesthetic in open-heart surgery performed by modern doctors.

The technique of acupuncture is based on the assumption that needle penetrations at certain points and in a particular manner have therapeutic effects. Some doctors in the Western hemisphere have accepted that, in certain cases, the use of acupuncture has resulted in a patient's improvement, but as of 1970 no satisfactory scientific explanation had been found to account for its effects.

Traditional practitioners are concerned with both the prevention and cure of ailments. They have used massage and gymnastics in addition to tonics and acupuncture and other techniques.

There was almost total lack of contact with the advances of Western medicine until the first quarter of the twentieth century. Western medicine was largely confined to the work of missionaries before 1913, when the first modern autopsy was performed in China. The establishment of the Peking Union Medical College, with the aid of the Rockefeller Foundation, in 1914 was an important boost to the introduction of scientific medicine. Chinese Nationalists and Communists alike supported the adoption of Western medical practices and opposed traditional medicine in the 1920s and 1930s as one means to modernize institutions. The shortage of trained doctors and limited funds for facilities and equipment tended to confine the development of modern medicine to urban areas. In 1949 the number of modern physicians probably did not exceed 40,000.

Western doctors who visited mainland China in the 1960s and early 1970s observed some of the most modern equipment available in the largest cities. Chinese physicians who had completed the full program of medical education of five or more years of higher education were considered to be competent even by Western standards. Various measures after 1965, such as the curtailment of long-term medical programs for prospective physicians and increased emphasis on political training for doctors, tended to have an adverse effect on the quality of Western medical practice in China. Some of the most outstanding work, such as the grafting of limbs and other extremities, was that of modern doctors.

Governmental Attitudes and Medical Care

Communist leaders appear to have favored the development of the scientific side of modern medicine from the beginning, but they were suspicious of, and after the mid-1950s openly hostile to, the social and political attitudes of doctors who practiced Western medicine. In the 1940s CCP leaders began to look to traditional practitioners as a means of overcoming the severe shortages of modern doctors.

In 1951 they provided year-long courses to improve the work of traditional doctors, but it was not until the mid-1950s that they made an abrupt policy change and advocated the integration of traditional and modern medicine. Membership in the Chinese medical association, previously restricted to regular physicians, was opened to traditional doctors. Modern doctors were increasingly subjected to criticism for their social and political attitudes, and traditional practitioners were praised for their correct attitudes. During the Great Leap Forward the establishment of public health centers under Commune control forcibly brought both kinds of doctors together. A new kind of doctor, competent in both Chinese and Western medicine and possessing a communist consciousness, was held to be the ideal.

A speech by CCP Chairman Mao Tse-tung on June 26, 1965 was the beginning of a major effort to expand medical care in rural areas and to increase political activity by medical personnel. Criticizing the urban orientation of medical care and the doctors' practice of giving priority to prominent persons, Chairman Mao called for a radical reorientation of medical resources in which trained medical personnel, equipment, and supplies would be shifted from the cities to rural areas.

Measures during the 1965-71 period brought many revisions throughout the medical system. Especially after 1967, doctors and other medical personnel were shifted to rural areas on a large scale, leaving urban hospitals, medical schools, and other medical facilities with fewer specialists. Some of the former city doctors served on mobile medical teams; some taught classes of medical assistants; others served in rural medical facilities.

The Chinese for many years had widely utilized a medical assistant, but after 1965 a new type of medical aide called the barefoot doctor, deployed in rural areas, became the most publicized figure in implementing Maoist directives. They received about three months of training from medical teachers and Mao Tse-tung Thought Propaganda Teams, which were usually composed of People's Liberation Army (PLA) political cadres. These barefoot doctors

186

perform first aid, treat common diseases, and practice acupuncture, at the same time disseminating Maoist propaganda. Medical aides, called worker doctors, perform similar functions in the large industrial complexes.

The PLA played a leading role for propaganda purposes in the extending of medical care to the villages. It helped to train medical aides and provided various medical services. In 1969, 80,000 soldiers, organized into almost 7,000 teams, were engaged in medical work. In the late 1960s and early 1970s the medical work of the PLA was held up as a model to be emulated by other organizations.

The Ministry of Public Health administers health activities under central government control. Quasi-official organizations concerned with health, such as the Chinese Welfare Association and the National Red Cross Society, also operate under ministry direction. The Academy of Medical Sciences, founded in 1957 but closed during the Great Proletarian Cultural Revolution, heads research and development activities. In the late 1960s a center for acupuncture was established to further enhance the prestige of traditional medicine. There are many medical institutes, and one is situated in nearly every province.

Governmental medical organizations function at province, district, and county levels to give direction and control, but primary responsibility for health care is placed on the Cooperative Medical Service System, which operates within the Commune. This scheme was instituted on a broad basis after the break between Maoist elements and Liu Shao-ch'i (see ch. 10, Political Dynamics). It follows the Maoist philosophy that Communes should finance their own programs to provide at least minimal low-cost medical services rather than the policy attributed to Liu, that the central government should underwrite rural health programs.

Under the cooperative system each production team member pays annual dues equal to about 2-1/2 days' earnings and for each occasion when services are rendered at the local dispensary a fee of 5 fen (1 fen equals US$0.004). When costly treatment is required, the production brigade or other element of the Commune is called upon to bear additional expenses. The central government is not charged with the responsibility to provide funds to the cooperative for individual medical services rendered under the cooperative system.

Although the central government directed the efforts of millions of medical workers, particularly after 1965, budgetary allocations for public health and sanitation appeared to be very modest. During the 1953-57 period about 2 percent of the national budget was spent on health and sanitation. Data are lacking, but indications are that the percentage for subsequent years probably did not exceed the 1953-57 level. One of the government's arguments for traditional medicine was its low cost and availability.

The number of persons engaged in medical work and public sanitation programs reportedly increased vastly after the mid-1960s, but in the early 1970s there were no meaningful data to provide a basis for estimates of the number engaged in these activities. By the end of 1966, according to Western estimates, 200,000 persons had completed higher medical education, and there may have been as many as 150,000 modern physicians, 30,000 dentists, 20,000 pharmacists, over 500,000 traditional doctors, and 3,500,000 full-time medical workers. After 1966 masses of medical assistants and aides were trained, and whole communities were sometimes organized on a part-time basis for public health and sanitation campaigns. On the other hand, the longer medical curricula of five or more years for training modern doctors were eliminated during the Cultural Revolution, and other programs were revised. In the early 1970s the training programs for modern doctors included more traditional medicine than previously and were heavy with indoctrination in Maoist thought.

SOCIAL WELFARE

The CCP regime has attacked social problems mainly by the leveling of social and economic classes through government actions. It has placed responsibility for welfare programs primarily on collective organizations within the Commune and on enterprises rather than on the central government. The Chinese Welfare Association and the National Red Cross Society, whose members usually work on a part-time basis, assist in mobilizing local resources for welfare purposes.

Government action against elements considered to be undesirable has largely eliminated prostitution and begging. These practices, once widespread in urban areas and in part the result of disparities in economic well-being, are controlled by placing offenders in corrective labor projects.

CCP leaders have attempted to channel the enthusiasm of youth against old ideas, customs, and habits as a means to avert juvenile delinquency. They have weakened the strong family ties and discipline, which had been major factors in maintaining high standards of behavior among children, and at the same time have strengthened the hold of the state on youth. Various pressures, including the use of informants, are employed to preclude the formation of gangs or dissident groups either inside or outside state-controlled youth organizations.

The overwhelming majority of the population, those living in rural areas, rely on welfare funds maintained within the Commune for assistance in old age, sickness, or other contingency. A percentage of the total annual earnings of the production team was set aside each year for welfare purposes within the Commune. In 1971 the rate was reportedly 2 percent. Also, deductions for other purposes were made before collective members received their shares of income calculated upon work points earned (see ch. 14, Agriculture). Members of the production teams are the main source of these funds. Sometimes families are called upon to take care of members who are in need when funds within the Commune are inadequate.

The social insurance system for industrial and other nonagricultural workers, first set up in 1951 and similar in some respects to that of the Soviet Union, places responsibility for administration and financing on the enterprise where an individual works. Benefits are provided in case of sickness, injury, disability, maternity, and old age. The enterprise takes 3 percent of the payroll for welfare purposes and then places 70 percent of the amount set aside in the fund from which benefits are paid. The remaining 30 percent is paid to the central trade union organization for its welfare programs. Since benefits are paid by the enterprise in which an individual was last employed, long-term consecutive service at the place of last employment is advantageous. For example, persons retiring after thirty years' total service receive a higher percentage of their wages if they had been ten years at their last place of employment than if they had worked there only five years. Funds at some factories have not been adequate to meet requirements for medical and other benefits, and therefore workers have sometimes formed cooperatives to help meet expenses (see ch. 17, Labor).

Old age pensions vary, but under ordinary conditions male workers at the age of sixty and women at the age of fifty who have twenty years' total service, of which fifteen are consecutive at their last place of employment, receive 70 percent of their last monthly wage. Benefits for periods of sickness and other reasons also varied.

In 1971 a system was reportedly in effect to help establish minimal acceptable family incomes. The central government published a schedule setting forth the per capita cost of living in each region. If family income fell below the minimum, the enterprise was required to pay the worker a subsidy to maintain the standard or, in the case of a farm worker, the Commune was charged with providing payments to maintain the standard. This, in effect, served also as a means to reduce the need for welfare and as an economic leveler.

CHAPTER 8

EDUCATION, INTELLECTUAL EXPRESSION, AND THE ARTS

A contemporary Chinese scholar has remarked that, although Confucianism was never an organized religion with a priesthood, it could be said that traditional Chinese intellectuals functioned as its priests and that all Chinese philosophy, history, and literature, at least until the twentieth century, reflected the Confucian system of values (see ch. 3, Historical Setting; ch. 5, Social System and Values). In their determination to erase Confucian values and replace them with those of Marxism-Leninism-Maoism, the Communists have become engaged in a struggle against the entire millennia-old educational, artistic, and intellectual tradition of China. Pride in China's cultural legacy and national patriotism, however, has made the Communists unwilling to discard the whole Confucian inheritance.

The dilemma of the Communists—one that has confronted Chinese intellectuals since the end of the nineteenth century—has been how to be modern and yet still be Chinese. Beginning with the Self-Strengthening Movement of the nineteenth century, which aimed at grafting Western technology onto traditional Chinese institutions, Chinese intellectuals have attempted to solve this dilemma by various means. By 1919, the time of the May Fourth Movement, the prevailing attitude among the young intellectuals was pro-Western and antitraditional. The Chinese cultural heritage was accused of being bankrupt and of having contributed to social injustices, such as the subjugation of youth, women, and the common people.

Some iconoclasts of the 1920s and 1930s recommended the wholesale abandonment of the cultural legacy. Others felt that it was possible to separate and preserve those traditional arts, institutions, and ideas that were consistent with rationalism, social equality, material progress, and other modern values and to discard the rest. Since the Yenan period (1936–47) the Chinese Communist Party (CCP), under the leadership of Chairman Mao Tse-tung, has subscribed to the latter policy. It has attempted to avoid wholesale acceptance or rejection of China's cultural heritage and has attempted to weed out that which it regards as "reactionary" or "feudal" while cultivating and preserving that which in its essence is deemed "democratic" or "progressive." During the more than two decades

191

since the CCP came to power, there has been, at different times, considerable variation in interpretation of the Party's cultural policy. What was labeled "democratic essence" at a time when a comparatively liberal attitude prevailed might suddenly be called "feudal dross" when the policy implementation underwent a shift toward greater stringency.

Since 1949 there has been, similarly, an ambivalent attitude toward academic education and toward highly educated people. Policies have tended to fluctuate between a concern that China develop as quickly as possible the technical expertise in all fields that would make it an advanced industrial nation of the stature of the United States and the Soviet Union and an equal but conflicting concern that the elitist flavor of education in China, which had been present through two or more millennia, be scrapped in favor of genuine mass education, by and for the peasants and workers, to create a unified society loyal to the CCP and its goals.

In the first two years of the People's Republic of China (PRC), virtually every product of the imperial artist and intellectual tradition was condemned as feudal and, of the traditional culture, only the folk arts were promoted by the regime. By the mid-1950s the policy had become liberalized, and many arts that had reached a peak under imperial patronage, such as traditional painting, classical poetry, and traditional drama, were revived and supported. The peak of liberalism in education, scholarship, and the arts was reached in the year from mid-1956 to mid-1957, the period of the so-called Hundred Flowers Campaign (see Glossary). By late 1957 this policy had been reversed by the "anti-rightist" campaign. "Politics in command" became the slogan applied to education and the arts during the Great Leap Forward (see Glossary) campaign that began in 1958.

By mid-1959, however, when the Great Leap Forward had already begun to prove a disappointment to many senior Party leaders, the cultural policy began to grow more liberal again. Ch'en Po-ta, at that time vice director of the Propaganda Department of the CCP, articulated the Party's efforts to strike a balance. He criticized the "leftist infantilists" who took a "scornful attitude" toward the cultural legacy and also condemned the "rightist deviation" of devoting too much attention to past history, art, and institutions.

This middle path was followed until 1962; during this time all aspects of artistic and intellectual expression flourished. In January 1963 an editorial in the official journal of the CCP Central Committee, *Red Flag* (Hung Ch'i), signaled the end of this policy. The editorial reminded the people of Mao's statement that they must "place the political criteria first and the artistic criteria second."

The Great Proletarian Cultural Revolution that erupted in 1966 brought into effect a government policy toward education, literature, and the arts that was more politically stringent and less tolerant of the heritage of the imperial past. The assault on the educational system was particularly severe. Beginning in 1966, the primary schools suspended operations for a year; secondary schools (middle schools) closed for two years; and institutions of higher learning ceased functioning for four years and did not begin to revive until 1970.

Teenage Red Guards (see Glossary), released from schoolwork and given the support of Mao and the People's Liberation Army (PLA) against the more conservative group in the government led by Liu Shao-ch'i, who was chairman of the PRC, began in mid-1966 an iconoclastic attack on all remnants of traditional China (see ch. 10, Political Dynamics). They changed the names of historic places—streets, buildings, and shops—allegedly to wipe out traces of feudalism, superstition, or imperialism. In obedience to a Mao dictum, that "in the contemporary world, all culture or art and literature belongs to a given class and a given political line," the Red Guards broke into people's houses and into libraries, temples, and churches to destroy and eliminate anything that showed an affiliation to social classes other than the working class. Much that had been preserved because it was regarded as beautiful, elegant, comfortable, or sacred was attacked, denounced, and destroyed in a wave of iconoclasm, which was intense for a few months before it gradually subsided.

The implementation of government policy in educational, artistic, and intellectual fields since 1949 has been carried out by the appropriate ministries, by units of the CCP in the schools and places of employment, and by numerous temporary committees created during various ideological and social campaigns instituted by the national leadership. There also exist other organizations that implement national policy in these fields. In the schools there are the junior organizations of the CCP—the Chinese Communist Youth League and the Young Pioneers Brigade—that mobilize students to carry out Party policy. Purged during the Cultural Revolution, the Youth League was being rebuilt in the early 1970s; its membership consisted of young Party trainees, roughly between fifteen and twenty-five years of age. The Young Pioneers Brigade, for children age nine through fifteen, had a reported membership in mid-1966 of 100 million.

In the arts, government control has been enforced in other ways. The first All-China Conference of Literary and Art Workers was convened in July 1949. Out of this congress emerged the All-China Federation of Literary and Art Circles. This federation supervised various specialized organizations, such as the All-China Association of Writers, and these in turn supervised associations down to the district level. This pyramid of organization has been tightly controlled from the top by senior Party personnel or their trusted associates.

During the Cultural Revolution nearly all the senior personnel who were employed in supervision and production in the fields of education, intellectual expression, and the arts were either temporarily or permanently forbidden to continue in their work. By mid-1971 there was as yet no information available to foreign observers as to who, if anyone, was minister in charge of education and higher education or who was director of the Propaganda Department of the CCP, a position that formerly had included in its responsibilities the supervision of education and culture. An outside observer's report in early 1970 indicated that there was only one literary magazine, a PLA publication, being published at that time for the domestic audience. The many other literary journals had suspended publication during the Cultural Revolution and had not yet resumed operation.

Since the beginning of the Cultural Revolution there has been a tendency for the PLA to assume leadership in educational and cultural activities. An early indication of this was the convening in February 1966 of the Forum on Work in Literature and Art in the Armed Forces, held in Shanghai and presided over by Mao's wife, Chiang Ch'ing. A summary of the results of the forum was released in June 1967, with a forward by Lin Piao, minister of defense, stating that Chairman Mao had read it three times and made revisions.

In the field of education, the PLA began to take over control of the schools in August 1968, midway through the Cultural Revolution, by means of Mao Tse-tung Thought Propaganda Teams composed of workers and peasants under PLA leadership. According to information available, the PLA was retaining its position of leadership in supervising education, intellectual expression, and the arts as of mid-1971.

EDUCATION

Evolution of Modern Education

From the time of Confucius the Chinese have regarded education as a means of bringing about significant change in individuals and in society. Schools have been sponsored since ancient times by public and private agencies. Education provided the means for participating as a member of the bureaucratic elite since before the beginning of the empire. Until 1905, for more than two millennia, the government recruited its officers from those who had received a Confucian education and were therefore able to pass the nationwide civil service examination. Education was the main avenue to power and prestige and was, in theory at least, open to all Chinese regardless of social background (see ch. 3, Historical Setting).

Through its control over the civil service examination system, the imperial government could determine the content of education. The curriculum was based on Confucian philosophic precepts as interpreted by the imperial scholars and concentrated on the study of the Confucian classics. The scholar-officials kept alive the knowledge of the ancients and tried to apply the accumulated wisdom of the ages to the management of the state. Gradually, however, the examination system degenerated. Instead of providing the humanistic education that Confucius had advocated, it became an exercise in the writing of highly stylized essays and poems in which content and comprehensibility were sacrificed to formal elegance. Proficiency in reading and writing literary pieces of this type was the major consideration in determining whether or not one achieved a position in government service. As a result, the educational system of the late imperial period produced graduates who, though educated and literate, had little knowledge of practical use and no comprehension of the social and political problems that beset the state.

Government policy began to change in the late nineteenth century, largely as a result of the challenge posed by the territorial and other demands of the Western trading powers and Japan. In 1898 the court founded Peking National University (commonly abbreviated as Peita, from its Chinese name) as an institution of modern, non-Confucian studies. In addition, by the beginning of the twentieth century thousands of students annually were being sent overseas to study, primarily to Japan but also to the United States and Europe. Returning scholars began to play an increasingly important role in government.

In 1905 the civil service examination was eliminated, and Western science and other non-Confucian subject matter were introduced into the curricula of public and some private schools at all levels of education. Many new schools were founded. Teacher training schools were also introduced as part of the effort to establish a modern school system. Missionaries from Great Britain, the United States, and other countries established schools from primary to university level in different parts of the country.

Peita became the center of an intellectual movement that was gradually to renovate and revolutionize Chinese education, intellectual and artistic activity, and eventually, politics and government. This movement began with the Hundred Days of reform in 1898 and gained momentum after the establishment of the Republic of China in 1912. In 1917 it became the New Culture Movement or Chinese Renaissance. A key event in this movement was the appearance in 1915 of a new magazine, *New Youth* (Hsin Ch'ing Nien), published by Ch'en Tu-hsiu, dean of the faculty of arts at Peita. Ch'en later became a leader in the May Fourth Movement of

1919 (which marked the political debut of the new intellectuals) and in 1921 was named first chairman of the CCP.

Contributors to the magazine included many professors at Peita who had been hired by the reform-minded chancellor of the university, T'sai Yuan-p'ei. In *New Youth* and other magazines founded in this period new intellectuals advocated the use of the scientific method and the liberation of language and literature. Many aspects of Chinese traditional thought and institutions were attacked. The two decades of intellectual ferment and liberal education that began in 1905 was the period during which Mao and many of the senior Party leaders active in 1971 received their academic education.

Beginning in 1927 the Nationalist government, from its headquarters in Nanking, began to exert control over the newly emerged modern schools. Previously autonomous missionary-run schools and universities had to register with the government and had to be headed by a Chinese. All curricula, syllabi, and textbooks, graduation examinations in the lower schools, and entrance examinations to the universities had to be approved by the government's educational authorities.

The first decade of Kuomintang (Nationalist Party, often abbreviated as KMT) government was fruitful in the realm of education and scholarship. The new government established universities that greatly surpassed, in both quantity and quality of facilities, the previously existing institutions. Among the KMT's achievements in this decade was the founding of a new national library and a medical college and the establishment of a national research organization, named the Academia Sinica, to sponsor pure research in a number of fields.

Gradually during the 1930s, as the Nationalist government faced the dual threat from the Chinese Communists and the Japanese invaders, the KMT became active in efforts to hold the political allegiance and support of the students and faculty and to eliminate criticism of the government by members of the educated group. The Kuomintang Youth League, founded in 1938 with official support, established branches in the schools and universities. The KMT had to approve all members of student government organizations. Indoctrination in the San Min Chu I (Three People's Principles) propounded by Sun Yat-sen became obligatory in all schools. Advocacy of communism was prohibited by law.

The war years 1937 to 1945 brought serious disruption to the schools. Universities, most of which were forced to abandon their campuses and move inland in flight from the Japanese, had to leave behind much of their equipment and libraries. The runaway inflation of the war years compelled many students and faculty members to sell their remaining books for food and other necessities. Lower and middle schools were also affected.

196

Nonetheless, throughout the KMT period of control over mainland China school enrollment and the number of educational institutions increased rapidly. By 1948 there were more than 200 universities and institutions of higher learning with a faculty of approximately 20,000, an enrollment of 155,000, and a yearly graduating class of 25,000. There were also nearly 6,000 secondary schools (grades seven through twelve) with over 140,000 teachers, about 2 million students, and an annual graduating class of nearly 400,000. There were nearly 300,000 primary schools (grades one through six) with approximately 785,000 teachers, about 24 million pupils, and nearly 5 million graduates each year. Roughly 20 percent of school-age children were attending primary and secondary schools at the time.

The Nationalist government also made efforts to reduce illiteracy—which had been estimated at about 80 percent—and to reach those over school age through adult education programs. Experiments were carried out to find ways to simplify the Chinese script in order to make basic literacy easier for the nonscholar to master. A "little teacher" movement was begun whereby schoolchildren were utilized as teachers to illiterates. In spite of these efforts, roughly 80 percent of the population remained illiterate in 1949 as a result of disruptions of war and of the growth of population.

In the 1930s and 1940s there also began to develop the educational system that would later be imposed by the Communist regime of the PRC. By 1934, three years after the establishment of the Chinese Soviet Republic in Kiangsi, more than 3,000 primary schools had been established in communist-controlled areas in Kinagsi, Fukien, and Kwangtung provinces (see ch. 3, Historical Setting). Tens of thousands of literacy classes had also been established. In addition, three universities–Red Army University, Soviet University, and Marxist-Communist University–had been founded to train Party and educational cadres (see Glossary).

In 1934 Mao Tse-tung, soon to become the chief theoretician of Chinese Communist educational policy, wrote:

> Our general line is to educate, in the communist spirit, the broad masses of laboring people, to use culture and education to serve the revolutionary war and class struggle, to unite education with labor, and to make it possible for the broad masses of Chinese people to enjoy culture and happiness. ... Our central task is to ... launch large-scale socialist education, to vigorously eliminate illiteracy and to create a large number of high-level cadres to lead the revolutionary struggle.

From 1936 to 1947, when Yenan functioned as the national communist headquarters, Mao's thinking about the role of education in a communist society developed along the lines indicated in his 1934 statement. In particular, stress was laid on the necessity of uniting education with labor and for theory to be connected with practical and productive work. The necessity for all aspects of education and cultural activity to serve politics and the class struggle was also emphasized in Mao's writing of the early 1940s.

Educational Policies and Problems of the People's Republic of China

Soon after October 1, 1949, the day Mao formally proclaimed the establishment of the PRC, the new regime issued, as part of its interim constitution (the so-called Common Program), the following pronouncement:

> *Article 47:* In order to meet the widespread needs of revolutionary work and national construction work, universal education shall be carried out, middle and higher education shall be strengthened, technical education shall be stressed, the education of workers during their spare time and education of cadres who are at their posts shall be strengthened, and revolutionary political education shall be accorded to young intellectuals and old style intellectuals in a planned and systematic manner.

As is suggested by the wording of Article 47, the practical necessity of carrying out reconstruction in a country devastated by war and revolution made expedient the utilization of educated persons who had received their training at noncommunist schools in and outside of China before the PRC came into existence. Such persons were regarded by PRC leaders as politically unreliable, however, since they came chiefly from upper and middle class backgrounds. Beginning in 1951, various campaigns were waged by the government to politically reeducate the intellectuals, especially teachers and university students, and to reduce the influence of "old style intellectuals" on the educational system. During the early 1950s the majority of private schools, including the many missionary-run establishments, were also closed down or taken over by the government. The influence of educational practices of the Soviet Union was great in this period.

Debate within the Party concerning educational policy has focused on the balance to be struck between producing graduates who are "red," that is, politically reliable, and turning out "experts," that is, technically qualified personnel. While maintaining always that the goal is an educated mass that is, in Mao's words, "both red and expert," the decisionmakers in the PRC have alternated between periods in which expertness is stressed and other periods when "redness" was the chief goal of the educational system, even at the expense of educational quality.

Although there have been various campaigns to convert intellectuals to the Party view since 1949, until 1958 the tendency was to promote the development of a new skilled corps, necessarily small in membership, of technicians and intellectuals. Overly stringent criteria of Party loyalty and working class origin were avoided in order that utilization could be made of some educated personnel leftover from the KMT regime. A reversal of these policies came with the Great Leap Forward from 1958 to 1960, during which period "politics in command" was a slogan frequently repeated in reference to education in speeches and newspaper editorials.

During the Great Leap period, in connection with the setting up of rural People's Communes (see Glossary), an effort was made to decentralize the educational system and to unite theory and practice more closely in the student's school-hour activities. Part-work part-study schools, in which roughly half the student's time was devoted to work in the fields or factories, were promoted by government efforts. Factories and Communes were set up in the schools, and schools were established within factories and Communes. Although half of the time was spent in nonacademic occupations, the amount of time allotted to complete a course remained what it had formerly been. At the level of higher learning, so-called "red and expert universities" were established along similar work-study lines. As a result of the proliferation of these part-work part-study institutions, the number of colleges and universities rose from 229 in academic year 1956/57 to 1,065 in 1957/58.

The quality of academic education declined markedly during this period, as did faculty and student morale. A return to emphasis on educational content and the building up of a corps of well-trained personnel occurred in 1961 in the wake of Party dissatisfaction with the results of the Great Leap. In August 1961 Ch'en I, the foreign minister, in a speech before 20,000 college graduates in Peking said that, "At present, we should stress specialized studies because failure to do so will keep our country perpetually backward in science and culture." He also criticized the practice of making college students spend too much time on political study and manual labor at the expense of their special subjects.

In the fall of 1962 the Socialist Education Campaign was begun throughout the country to reeducate Party cadres and intellectuals and working people through the study in depth of the writings of Chairman Mao. Politics was once more in command. Also in the fall of 1962 the government cut enrollment in the schools. Although official figures are generally lacking for the 1960s, estimates have been made by students of the subject that enrollment dropped from 900,000 to 750,000 in institutions of higher learning, from over 15 million to 12 million in middle schools, and from 90 million to approximately 80 or 85 million in primary schools. The number of universities and colleges fell to 277 from the 1958 inflated figure of over 1,000.

As part of the Socialist Education Campaign, urban middle school graduates, of whom there was thought to be a surplus, were sent to rural areas, which were short of low-level technicians. By 1964 PRC officials announced that 40 million students had been sent to the countryside, many of them to remote border areas of Outer China (see Glossary).

In 1964 the political pressure on the educational system increased. Party cadres were sent to live and work with teachers. Students were given reduced academic loads to allow for extracurricular activities—

that is, political activities—and the work-study movement was revived in a new campaign begun in mid-1964. Farm-study schools were promoted and were justified in the press on the basis of the need for more schools to meet the demand. It was pointed out, for example, that only 40 percent of school-age children in Kiangsu Province had attended school in September 1964 (at the beginning of the school year) but that by early 1965, when the second school term began, this percentage had increased to 75 percent as a result of the establishment of new farm-study schools.

The saving in the cost of education to the government was also a consideration. Mao had written earlier that "part-work and part-study, running schools through the practice of working while studying, does not cost the state a cent." A *People's Daily* editorial in September 1965 stressed the advantages to be derived from having two concurrent educational systems: the full-time school system, financed and administered by the ministries of education and higher education; and the half-study system, financed and administered by Communes and other local administrative units. This dual system, with its continuation of full-time schools, remained in effect until the Cultural Revolution began; it was then denounced as a product of the efforts of Liu Shao-ch'i to restore capitalism (see ch. 10, Political Dynamics).

The socialization of education, of which the work-study movement was an important part, apparently did not move fast enough for Mao and Lin Piao, the two foremost Party advocates of putting "politics in command" of education. In May 1966 the *Circular of the Central Committee of the Chinese Communist Party* went out to Party cadres calling for them to "follow Comrade Mao Tse-tung's instructions, hold high the great banner of the Proletarian Cultural Revolution, thoroughly expose the reactionary bourgeois stand of those so-called 'academic authorities' who oppose the Party and Socialism, thoroughly criticise and repudiate the reactionary bourgeois ideas in the sphere of academic work, education, journalism, literature and art and publishing and seize the leadership in these cultural spheres."

On May 7, 1966, Mao issued a directive that was to govern the reform of the educational system during the Cultural Revolution. The directive, which circulated informally among Party cadres before being published and was in the form of a letter from Mao to Lin Piao, called for school curricula to include industrial work, farming, military affairs and criticism of the bourgeoisie in addition to academic study. Mao also stated that "the period of schooling should be shortened, education should be revolutionized and the domination of our schools by bourgeois intellectuals should by no means be allowed to continue."

The policy enunciated in the May 1966 directive was reinforced in a statement by Mao on July 21, 1968. Later referred to in the press as the July 21 Directive, it stated that it was still necessary to have universities and colleges of science and engineering but that it was essential to shorten the length of schooling and revolutionize education. Students should be selected from among workers and peasants with practical experience, and they should return to production after a few years' study.

The May 7 and July 21 directives were the key documents constantly quoted in the press when reference was made to the reform of the educational system in the late 1960s. They were still the main statements of government education policy in mid-1971.

Actual implementation of the Cultural Revolution campaign began at Peita, on May 25, 1966, with a denunciation of Lu P'ing, the university's president, led by a philosophy teacher and party cadre. Similar denunciations in other institutions of higher learning soon followed. Within two weeks Lu P'ing had been dismissed from his university position, and the purging of educators and intellectuals had begun all over the country.

On June 13 the government announced that enrollment for the new academic term would be postponed for six months in order to "carry out the Cultural Revolution thoroughly and transform the educational system completely." The announcement was in reference only to universities and senior middle schools (grades ten through twelve) but, in fact, by mid-July all schools, including junior middle schools (grades seven through nine) and primary schools (grades one through six), had closed down.

Policy disagreement within the Party was evidenced, however, as PRC Chairman Liu Shao-ch'i sent teams in June 1966 to combat the "rebels" at Peita and elsewhere. By the end of July these teams were withdrawn, accused in the press of having become "divorced from the masses."

On August 8 the Cultural Revolution received the endorsement of the Central Committee of the CCP, and on August 18 the Red Guards, a revolutionary mass organization set up under the Cultural Revolution by Peking's university and middle school students, made their debut at a mass rally in Peking (see ch. 10, Political Dynamics). This rally was the first of a series in which millions of teenagers from Red Guard units formed throughout the country participated. Each wore a red armband imprinted with the words *Hung Wei Ping* (Red Guards) and waved a copy of the little red book *Quotations from Chairman Mao*. Some 11 million Red Guards are estimated to have traveled to Peking by November 1966 to bear witness to their regard for Mao and to their support of the Cultural Revolution. The Red Guard movement was notable chiefly for the fact that it was the first movement involving students and youth in the PRC that did not derive its leadership from the Party cadet organizations, the Chinese

Communist Youth League and the Young Pioneers Brigade (see ch. 10, Political Dynamics).

For several years political activism replaced formal schooling. In February 1967 students were officially ordered to return to school, but most did not comply. The primary schools reopened in late 1967, but the Red Guards as of mid-1968 still had not complied with the government demand that they return to their middle schools and colleges. In August 1968 it was announced in the press that worker Mao Tse-tung Thought Propaganda Teams with PLA backing would enter the schools and take charge of education. These teams, led by PLA cadres, eventually set up revolutionary committees that took over control of the schools, replacing the previous administrative hierarchies. The Red Guards were ordered to "accept the leadership of the working class."

In September 1968 a double purge of the schools began. The more militant and rebellious Red Guards in urban schools were sent to the rural areas to engage in manual labor in Communes and local factories, a move that helped to dampen the social and political conflagration of the previous two years. Many teachers and educational staff who were deemed not sufficiently revolutionary were also sent to the rural areas in order to be reeducated by self-criticism and manual labor. By mid-1971, however, a high proportion of members of the second group had been restored to their jobs in the schools, having been reeducated and reformed.

The Educational System Since the Cultural Revolution

Since the Cultural Revolution the emphasis on political education, as opposed to academic studies and curricula, has been as great or greater than it was during the Great Leap. Moreover, in the political education field, the PLA has attained primacy as the best interpreter of Maoist thought. This has resulted from the work of PLA cadres in the workers' propaganda teams and revolutionary committees that have dominated the secondary schools and universities since the reopening of the schools in the late 1960s.

A social transformation of the schools has been effected by new policies governing admission to secondary schools and institutions of higher learning, which assign little importance to academic criteria but instead give preference to young persons of working class origins and older persons with considerable military or manual labor experience. Status relationships in the schoolroom have shifted radically from the pre-Cultural Revolution period in which teachers were in command to that in the early 1970s, when teachers were expected to accept political education from the students (see ch. 5, Social System and Values).

The new student body, because of its predominantly working-class background, apparently is assumed to be more politically reliable than the faculty. Even in academic work, the practical experience of the students is alleged by commentators in the press and elsewhere to be equal or superior to the book learning of the teachers. Students are exhorted to correct and lead the teachers toward the "unity of theory and practice."

A resultant morale problem of considerable dimensions among faculty throughout the nation in the early 1970s is suggested by the widespread press criticism of faculty members for their alleged complaints that it is "a calamity" to be a teacher and that it is preferable and safer to become a farmer or factory worker than to continue in such a sensitive profession as teaching. At the same time a shortage of teachers at all levels has been reported.

The new structure of the educational system had not been made public by mid-1971 but, beginning in the late 1960s, various proposals appeared in the press. Widespread coverage was given particularly to model schools, factories, and Communes and to the results of efforts to emulate these models. Since the press is an instrument of the regime's public information and propaganda program, the appearance of such proposals implied the tacit endorsement of the government's leaders (see ch. 12, Public Information and Propaganda).

Chinese and Western press accounts have indicated that by mid-1971 the chief results of the reform in education were: decentralization, with the costs borne chiefly by local factories and Communes; restructuring of all administrative hierarchies connected with education in order to place members of the PLA and the working class and other politically reliable personnel in positions to determine educational policy and to administer the schools; replacement of old textbooks with new texts compiled jointly by teams of workers or peasants and soldiers, revolutionary technicians, and teachers; abolition of entrance and graduation examinations; reduction of the time required to complete courses and of the number of years spent at each level of schooling; emphasis on the integration of theory with practice, implemented in such a way that practical application is stressed at the expense of theory; and the integration, at all levels, of study with productive labor.

Administration and Financing

The educational bureaucracy was destroyed during the Cultural Revolution as a result of the dismissal from office of most of the senior educational personnel in the ministries dealing with educational matters, the closing of the schools for from one to four years, and the implementation of the new policy of decentralization, by which schools are financed by local funds. Information available in mid-1971 indicated that the administrative structure of the educational system had probably not yet been replaced.

On August 25, 1968, Mao issued a directive that urban education was to be supervised by workers and rural education by "poor and lower middle peasants." In November 1968 a plan proposed in Shantung Province received publicity as a model for rural educational organization. According to this plan, primary education was to be paid for by the production brigade, and the teacher was to be remunerated in work points (see Glossary). Rural teachers were to return to their home areas and teach in their own production brigades. In May 1969 these ideas were further refined in a *People's Daily* report of an educational program suggested by educators in Kirin Province in which production brigades run the primary schools and the Communes run the secondary schools.

Preschool Education

Kindergartens (ages four to seven) and nursery schools (for infants to three years old) are considered an important component of the school system. They introduce the child at an early age to the ideals on which his thought processes should be based and also serve to release women from child care, thus allowing them to engage in productive work. In most areas the development of preschool education is associated with child welfare programs. Recent enrollment figures were unavailable; however, nursery schools in the rural areas alone took care of 67,700,000 children in 1959.

The chief content of nursery and kindergarten education has been the teaching of correct social attitudes—to develop group consciousness and loyalty to peers, school, and society. The child is taught to put loyalty to these groups ahead of loyalty to self or family. Literacy is not taught, although oral expressive ability is practiced.

Primary and Secondary Schools

Official enrollment statistics have not been released since the late 1950s. Estimates derived from PRC official statements in the early 1960s were that approximately 85 percent of all primary school age children but only 60 percent of those in rural areas were receiving schooling. Fragmentary reports suggest that the number of primary and secondary schools in urban areas and their enrollment may have declined since the Cultural Revolution but that primary schools in the rural areas, especially in the remote border regions, may have expanded in number and enrollment. Schooling is not compulsory or universally available. At the primary and secondary levels, a small fee is charged each student.

Students start primary school at age seven. Until 1966 primary school lasted for six years, but in 1971 the course was five years. Classes number between forty and sixty pupils. In rural areas most pupils in 1971 were attending combined primary-secondary schools that provided a total of seven years' schooling. In urban areas, and sometimes at Commune headquarters in rural areas, more complete secondary schooling was provided in 1971 at middle schools. Rural middle schools provide agricultural vocational training only. Before 1966 academic middle schools had provided six years of schooling to qualified primary school graduates, divided equally into junior and senior middle schools. By 1971 the duration of middle school had been reduced to four or five years.

The academic content of primary and secondary schools has been greatly diluted by the transformation of the full-time schools into part-study schools. As the name indicates, pupils at the part-study schools spend part of their school time in productive labor on farms or factories attached to the school or to which the school is attached. The addition of political content has also been at the expense of academic work. A December 1968 account of the lesson time in a secondary school in Kweichow Province estimated that 58 percent was devoted to Maoist thought and class struggle; 21 percent, to learning from the workers, peasants, and soldiers; and the remaining 21 percent, to basic subjects. In addition to the labor requirement of the part-study school program, urban middle school students generally spend one month per year in full-time factory work and another month in a rural area, participating in farm labor.

The conversion of the formal full-time school system into a part-study system has been one of the most significant results of the Cultural Revolution. It is in conformity to the Maoist demand that education not be divorced from labor. Its advocates have promoted the system as a way of permanently eliminating the age-old status differences of China that were based on whether an individual was educated or worked with his hands (see ch. 5, Social System and Values).

A textbook shortage during the Cultural Revolution was caused by the purge of books that allegedly advocated bourgeois values. Much press coverage was being given in mid-1971 to the compilation of new textbooks by teams of workers, peasants, soldiers, revolutionary technicians (by which was meant Party cadres), and teachers. Foreign journalists reported in the early 1970s, however, that memorization and group recitation of material to be learned was, as it had always been, a major pedagogical techniques in the schools.

The content of primary education was unknown in 1971. On the eve of the Cultural Revolution in the first four primary grades language, speech, and the writing of Chinese consumed half the time allotted; arithmetic took one-quarter (the abacus was introduced in the fourth year), and the remaining time was devoted to handicrafts, drawing, and singing. The last two years of primary school also included nature study, history, geography, and physical education.

Similar subjects presumably were being taught in 1971. Reports indicated that academic work was being presented where possible in terms that carried a political content or that had immediate practical applicability. Reading, writing, and history texts stressed political themes, such as reviling class enemies and promoting Mao's thought. Arithmetic problems were often couched in political terms. For example, pupils were given the problem of calculating the exorbitant rents and taxes allegedly paid landlords by poor peasants before 1949.

At the secondary educational level, before the Cultural Revolution, there had existed three types of full-time schools—the general academic middle school, the normal (teacher training) school, and the vocational and technical school. The general academic type had the greatest enrollment and was designed to provide college preparatory education. Since the Cultural Revolution this type of school has apparently been either abandoned or greatly reduced in enrollment as compared to normal and vocational and technical schools. •

In mid-1971 a foreign newspaperman's account of a typical middle school indicated that practical application was stressed in all academic courses. Physics, chemistry, and other scientific subject matter were integrated into a course called industrial knowledge, in which practical application was emphasized. Zoology and biology were part of a course called agricultural knowledge. Mathematics courses included study of farm accounting. Subjects that did not have obvious practical value such as history were dropped in the higher grades.

The practice of modeling school administration after that of the PLA has reportedly also been widespread since the Cultural Revolution. Another foreign journalist's account of a middle school in 1970 noted that the student body of 1,700 was divided into twenty-nine classes of 50 students each. Four classes formed a "company," with a company commander and a political commissar. Attached to this school was an automobile spare parts factory, and outside of town there was a farm connected to the school. Students and faculty were expected to work one month each year at the factory and six weeks on the farm.

Although many schools have reportedly dispensed with grades and examinations, this school had both. Examinations, of the open-book type, were graded jointly by the teacher and the entire class. The journalist also reported that no student had received a failing grade so far but that less than half the graduating class would eventually be allowed to attend higher level schooling.

In 1971, upon completing middle school, all pupils were expected to spend two or more years working, primarily as manual laborers, before becoming eligible to apply for higher education or advanced training. Graduates of urban middle schools are usually assigned to agricultural communities in rural areas. Estimates of the number of students and other urban unemployed or otherwise undesirable persons who were resettled in rural areas between late 1968 and late 1970 range as high as 20 to 25 million persons.

Some of the millions of urban middle-school graduates who have been assigned to remote rural areas have been utilized in their new communities as teachers in newly established primary schools. By this means, primary schools have come into existence where none had been before. Rural resettlement of urban Chinese has also encouraged the spread of the national language (Mandarin), based upon the Peking dialect of Northern Chinese, to areas where it had previously not been used (see ch. 4, Ethnic Groups and Languages).

Institutions of Higher Learning

Throughout the period of the Cultural Revolution, which first erupted into action at Peita in 1966, the discussion of educational reform was focused primarily on higher education. Of the more than 250 institutions of higher learning that had been in operation before the Cultural Revolution, only a handful had reopened by mid-1971. The academic year 1970/71 was the first in which Peita and Tsinghua University—both located in Peking and in many ways the models for university education throughout the country—functioned since the closing of schools in 1966.

Tsinghua, a technical university, and Peita, a comprehensive science and arts university, each had an enrollment of over 2,000 new students in the 1970/71 academic year. This number was approximately one-fourth of the total new annual enrollment of the two schools in the years before 1966, but it was anticipated that a larger group would be admitted in the 1971/72 academic year. At this rate, the schools would return to their pre-Cultural Revolution enrollment levels in four years or less. Unlike lower level schools, tuition was free at institutions of higher learning.

Members of the university student body in 1970/71 were older than their predecessors, but most were under twenty-four years of age. They had several years' work experience and, as a minimum academic requirement, had completed junior middle school. A special category existed to encompass a group of older students, who had had ten or more years of work experience and the correct class origins; they were admitted, without having to meet any academic criteria, to receive higher training in technical fields. No degrees were awarded graduates. Like middle school graduates, they had to accept whatever employment they were assigned.

The social composition of the university student body has undergone a significant change. In 1971 Tsinghua University claimed that, of its students, 45 percent were from workers' families, 40 percent were from peasant families, and 15 percent were members of the PLA. Before the Cultural Revolution the average institution of higher learning recruited only about half of its students from such backgrounds.

Indications are that university curricula are emphasizing practical application of knowledge. For instance, in January 1971, at Tsinghua University there was apparently no work being done in nonapplied science or in pure research. The time to complete a course had been reduced. For example, a chemical engineering student was expected to complete the course in two or three years, as compared to the five or six years required before 1966. A fairly typical daily schedule for a student at Tsinghua in 1971 included six hours of lectures, laboratory work, and labor in the attached antibiotic drug-producing plant; one hour of organized recreation; and one hour of study of Mao Tse-tung Thought.

Emphasis in the humanities appears also to be on their practical aspects. At Sun Yat-sen University in Canton, for example, it was reported in mid-1971 that, out of 547 students enrolled, there were 127 studying the humanities and social sciences. The Chinese classics, however, are mentioned only as negative examples, and literature courses are oriented primarily toward producing persons competent to write summaries and commentaries for use in practical fields. The course of study in these fields was of two years' duration, down from five years before 1966. Peita was reported in March 1971 to be retaining literature and humanities courses, but little was known about their content. In some sensitive subjects, such as political economy, teaching had not been resumed at Sun Yat-sen University as of mid-1971. It was not known in mid-1971 whether various specialized institutions of higher learning, such as the Cultural Institute of Fine Arts at Peking and the Central Conservatory at Tientsin that train artists and musicians, had resumed or would reopen soon.

Special Education

The regular school system is supplemented by a variety of spare-time programs that offer studies supplementary to full-time employment. These special programs aim both at providing the needed trained manpower for agriculture and industry and at giving the masses of the population the ideological education required for the transformation of Chinese society. They are intended mostly for the adult population but are also important for those young people who cannot be accommodated by the regular school system. The number of persons taking spare-time studies was unknown in mid-1971. Official statistics for 1958 claimed 71 million persons enrolled in spare-time classes, including 40 million in literacy classes.

A new type of special school, known as the May 7 cadre school after Mao's May 7, 1966, directive, came into existence in 1968. The first such school was set up in Heilungkiang Province in May 1968, and by early 1969 cadre schools had been established at county and higher levels by the provincial revolutionary committees in most parts of the PRC. District revolutionary committees also run cadre schools, as do branches of some national organizations, such as the People's Bank of China. Central government ministries and various branches of the CCP, as well as the Party Central Committee have also set up May 7 cadre schools.

The schools are organized along military lines, with cadres grouped into platoons and squads. They are situated primarily in rural settings and are expected, insofar as possible, to be self-sufficient and self-supporting through farming, forestry, fishing, and small collective enterprises of various types. The goal of the schools is ideological reeducation of cadres who have become "detached from the three things" (by which is meant labor, the masses, and reality). The training reportedly is for the purpose of producing a new generation of Communists who can handle both military and civilian affairs, engage in both industry and agriculture, work at both higher and lower levels, and hold official posts while remaining as common people.

In the first year these schools were populated chiefly by cadres who had become redundant as a result of the recent administrative reorganization or had fallen into disfavor during the Cultural Revolution. Beginning in mid-1969 efforts were made to broaden the scope of the cadre schools, making them part of standard training, at one time or another, for all cadres, including new ones. Some of the cadres who have completed the May 7 school course have been returned to official posts; others, however, have been settled as farmers in the rural areas.

Literacy

Literacy programs have been pursued with varying intensity since the early days of the republic. The extent of illiteracy has never been accurately determined, but most sources estimate it as being around 80 percent at the time of the communist takeover. Literacy programs since then have been aided by efforts to simplify the written language and by the promulgation in 1958 of a set of roman letters for the spelling of Chinese characters as aids to their pronunciation (see ch. 4, Ethnic Groups and Languages).

The extent of success of literacy programs has been difficult to determine. A *People's Daily* report in January 1964 estimated that 20 percent of factory workers were illiterate or semiliterate. A continuing problem has been the tendency of the newly literate to relapse into illiteracy for lack of practice.

Education for Ethnic Minorities

The 1949 Common Program, predecessor to the 1954 State Constitution, guaranteed the freedom of the national minorities to preserve their languages, religions, and customs (see ch. 4, Ethnic Groups and Languages; ch. 9, Political System and Values). In September 1951 a national conference on national minorities education decided that primary and secondary schools for minority group members in minority regions would be conducted in the native language of the people of the region. If the language had no adequate script, one would be developed, or an existing one would be improved, in order to teach literacy in the mother tongue.

By the mid-1950s various types of schools had been established that were attended exclusively by members of certain minority groups. In areas where the minority population was intermixed with Han Chinese, however, minority group members attended ordinary Han Chinese schools. Special Nationality Institutes were also established in major centers to create and train national minority leaders in politics, culture, and other fields. A high proportion of the students at the institutes were members of the CCP or the Chinese Communist Youth League.

Beginning in 1959, during the Great Leap Forward, the PRC press claimed that the minority ethnic groups who spoke minority languages were showing a "high tide" of interest in learning both spoken and written Chinese. Courses conducted in the national language were added to minority group schools at that time. During the Cultural Revolution, purges of many educational leaders of minority ethnic groups were justified on the basis that the purged individual had opposed Mao's statement that "the nationality problem in China is a class problem" or had in other ways shown "regional nationalism." In the campaign to combat "regional nationalism," the efforts to accelerate the use of the national language in minority schools were intensified. These efforts were aided by the great increase in numbers of Han-speaking urban middle school graduates in the border autonomous regions as a result of the massive resettlement campaigns of the 1960s (see ch. 4, Ethnic Groups and Languages).

Enrollment in minority schools has increased greatly. The quality of education available to ethnic minorities in the early 1970s was thought to be comparable to that generally available in the country. It suffered from the same problems—shortages of teachers, textbooks, equipment, and facilities.

LITERARY AND INTELLECTUAL EXPRESSION

To the Chinese, the educated man has always been the man who could write, and writing has remained the most important cultural legacy from ancient times. For thousands of years the art of writing Chinese characters has been the distinguishing accomplishment of persons of elite social status, and until the twentieth century the ability to write was a prime indicator of ruling class membership. Calligraphy was regarded as one of the arts, and a fine example of it would often be displayed and preserved as if it were a painting.

The difficulty of mastering the written language, involving both comprehension and transcription of many thousands of characters, confined true literacy to a very small group. Efforts in the twentieth century have been made, with considerable success, to simplify the forming of ideographs and to reduce the number of characters used in modern writing to less than 3,000 (see ch. 4, Ethnic Groups and Languages). Nonetheless, Mao, a noted calligrapher, in his formal writing has generally eschewed the simplified characters in favor of the classical characters that he had learned in his youth.

Literature has been produced and preserved in great quantities in China over a longer period of time than in any other country. For many centuries—from Ch'in times (third century B.C.) down to the early twentieth century—all serious literature (except novels and some drama) and all official writings were in literary Chinese. Literary Chinese differed markedly from spoken Chinese and was therefore difficult to write or to comprehend. It was the written language of the gentry and of the court.

It was not until after the thirteenth century that colloquial literature, conforming more closely to the style and word choice of the spoken language, began to be written down and preserved. The colloquial literary style owes its beginnings to the work of professional storytellers and for centuries was restricted to prose fiction and to traditional Chinese drama (often called Chinese opera), which uses a mixture of literary and colloquial styles. Beginning in the early decades of the twentieth century, however, the literary style began to be displaced in all fields of writing by the colloquial style.

A foreign newspaperman, writing in mid-1971 of a recent trip to the PRC, noted that he saw no works of old Chinese literature on sale, that no traditional dramas were performed, and that the works of the ancient Chinese authors in the university libraries were not being taken out and read. Nonetheless, Chinese literature of the past, written in the classical style, has played a formative role in Chinese culture and remains a source of national pride and inspiration.

The Confucian Classics

An ancient body of literature, preserved to modern times, that has been studied and revered by Confucian scholars for 2,500 years or more is known as the *ching* [classic(s)]. This collection includes the *I-ching* (Book of Changes), which scholars believe may have been written as a diviner's manual and has come to be used by adherents to Chinese folk religion as an aid in astrology, numerology, and other forms of prophesy (see ch. 5, Social System and Values). The *Shih-ching* (Book of Odes), also known as the Book of Poetry, is a collection of folk songs, religious poems, and ceremonial hymns, many of which date to early Chou times and perhaps before. The *Shu-ching* (Book of Documents) is a collection of documents and speeches alleged to have been written by rulers and officials of the early Chou period. Another historical classic is the late Chou work *Ch'un Chiu* (Spring and Autumn Annals). A classic collection called *Li* (Rituals) deals, among other things, with a description of ancient rituals and rules of conduct.

Also usually included in the list of classics are the so-called Four Books: the *Lun-yu* (Analects [conversations] of Confucius); *Meng-tzu* (Book of Mencius); *Ta-hsueh* (Great Learning); and *Chung-yung* (Doctrine of the Mean). The last two books have a central place in Neo-Confucian philosophy (see ch. 3, Historical Setting). Another work often included is the *Hsiao Ching* (Book of Filial Piety).

Philosophy

Traditional Chinese philosophy is based primarily on Confucius' teachings but also owes much to later commentators in the Confucian tradition and to Taoism, Buddhism, Legalism, and other ancient philosophies, many of which were formulated in the late Chou dynasty era (see ch. 3, Historical Setting). Central to traditional Chinese philosophy is the concept that society is, and should be, hierarchically stratified, and that proper and harmonious relationships grow out of loyalty to superiors, benevolence to inferiors, and harmony with nature. Each person, being a mere link in the chain of generations, should subordinate his desires to the needs of the family, as articulated by the family head, the senior male (see ch. 6, Family). As the individual subordinates his wishes to those of his family and accepts the authority of the senior male, so the people should subordinate their wishes to the needs of the state and accept the authority of the emperor.

The Confucian classics, which provided the materials from which the Confucian philosophy was derived, were regarded as authoritative by the Confucianists. Similarly, the sayings attributed to Lao-tzu and the body of Buddhist literature were sacred and authoritative to the Taoists and Buddhists, respectively. This tendency to regard all literature either written or approved by, or otherwise connected to, a venerated sage as being philosophic truth has persisted into the communist era. The Chinese Communists regard Marx, Lenin, and Mao as the sources of philosophic truth instead of Confucius, Lao-tzu, and the Buddha, but the tendency to justify and explain policy and events by means of citing the relevant passage from a revered author's works has continued. As in traditional times, when failure was explained as having been caused by not following correctly the precepts enunciated by the ancient sages, so in 1971 failure in any endeavor is explained as having come about through not properly reading and understanding Mao Tse-tung Thought.

The triumph of Mao's ideas, which evolved out of the attempt to apply Marxism-Leninism to the Chinese situation, followed several decades of philosophic debate in China among innovators of the New Culture Movement of the 1910s and 1920s. During this period Confucianism and other traditional ideologies were attacked, and efforts were made to find philosophic backing for the social, political, and economic changes that the reformers thought essential to China's well-being. In this, the thinkers of the New Culture Movement tended to look to philosophers of the West for inspiration.

Some of the more attractive philosophies to the young Chinese intellectuals of the period were: positivism, that is, the belief in the applicability to all subjects of the so-called scientific method of inquiry; pragmatism, or the testing of the meaning of an idea primarily by its effects if acted upon; and materialism, the belief that matter exists separately from man's consciousness and that thought is a reflection of matter.

The two leading Chinese intellectuals of the New Culture Movement were: Hu Shih, who had studied philosophy at Columbia University under John Dewey, a leading pragmatist philosopher, and had returned to be Dewey's leading disciple in China; and Ch'en Tu-hsiu, dean of the faculty of arts at Peita and founder of the magazine *New Youth*. Ch'en and many other leading intellectuals were attracted to Marxism. In 1921 Ch'en became the founder and first chairman of the CCP, which subsequently attracted many artists and writers of the 1920s and 1930s.

By the mid-1930s, however, Ch'en had been expelled from the CCP. Mao, at that time a young disciple of one of the Party's cofounders, Li Ta-chao (d. 1927), who was a professor and librarian at Peita, became the chief exponent of the communist philosophy in China.

The key documents of the official PRC ideology of Marxism-Leninism-Maoism in 1971 were the essays "On Contradiction" and "On Practice," formulated by Mao during the Yenan period (1936–47). The central tenet of Mao's thought, his theory of contradictions (also known as the law of the unity of opposites), expounded in these essays, was further elucidated in February 1957 by Mao in a speech entitled "On the Correct Handling of Contradictions Among the People."

According to Mao, contradictions—that is, conflicts of interest or polarities—exist always. Therefore, struggle, not harmony, is a universal principle. Contradictions are of two types. The first is antagonistic and is overcome only when one side combats and overpowers the other. The second type of contradiction is nonantagonistic and can be resolved peacefully, being between persons, classes, or categories that are, for one reason or another, on the same side of a major cleavage. Whether a contradiction is antagonistic or nonantagonistic depends upon the circumstances. During the second Sino-Japanese war (1937–45), for example, bourgeois members of the united front were in nonantagonistic contradiction with the working class, whereas at various other times these two classes have been engaged in antagonistic class struggle.

The lack of consistency and the twists and turns in Party policies that observers have noted in the PRC's policies find their ideological justification in the emphasis in Mao's thought that is given to practical considerations. Thought, according to Mao, is the result of combining theory (Marxism-Leninism)—which is alleged to be universal and permanently true—with practice, that is, ever-changing circumstances. Thought therefore changes as permanent theory recombines with new, impermanent practice. Thus, anxious not to be out of step when the Party ideology changes to meet new circumstances, the literate public scans the newspaper editorial pages and other public media each day, alert for ideological nuances that might indicate new lines of cleavage emerging and widening in the constant struggle by the PRC leadership to identify and resolve contradictions.

History, Research, and Scholarship

Much of the literary output of Chinese writers from ancient times has been devoted to history and to the pursuit of knowledge in various fields. Historical literature is especially plentiful and has occupied an important position in Chinese writing. The *Shu-ching* is perhaps the earliest historical work to survive to the present. The dating of this work has been a cause for scholarly controversy for 2,000 years, but parts of it are alleged to be documents produced in early Chou times.

The *Shih-chi* (Memoirs of a Historian) is often regarded as the masterwork of Chinese historical writing. Written by the Han historian Ssu-ma Ch'ien (145–90 B.C.), it is a comprehensive history of the sinicized world up to the author's lifetime. With its topical essays, charts, and brief biographies of notable persons, the *Shih-chi* became a model for subsequent historical writings. During the mid-1950s, at the time of a more liberal attitude toward China's literary heritage than any since the PRC began, Ssu-ma Ch'ien received the Party's praise for the factualism and realism of his account; he was later treated as a feudal historian.

Beginning in Han times, a tradition was established that obliged each new dynasty to compile an official account of the preceding dynasty, which, if acceptable to the presiding regime, became the official version. By the eighteenth century twenty-four standard histories of this type had been officially recognized. (In 1921 another version of the history of the Mongol Yuan dynasty was given official status by the president of the republic, bringing the total number of standard histories to twenty-five.) No history of the Ch'ing dynasty ever received official endorsement.

The habit of dealing with history in dynastic units, coupled with a veneration of the past, helped give rise to a cyclical theory of history among the Chinese. In the traditional historical accounts each dynasty rises, flourishes, decays, and falls. Decay and fall may be delayed but never prevented; progress does not exist. This theory of history is in conflict with Marxist theory, which maintains that, in accordance with the laws of historical materialism, history is an account of the linear progression of society, from one stage to another, as the result of class struggle. At what dates China passed through the various Marxian stages—from primitive communism to slavery to feudalism to capitalism to socialism—is a cause of considerable debate among contemporary Chinese Marxist historians but that these stages did occur, and in the prescribed sequence, is held to be a universal truth and therefore not open to question or debate.

According to PRC historians, almost the entire imperial period belongs to the feudal stage and therefore is unworthy of much scholarly attention. Archaeology, however, is popular with the regime because it can provide evidence, notably lacking in the official dynastic histories, of the life of the common man. Archaeological research has been enthusiastically sponsored by the PRC, and much new evidence was uncovered in the 1950s and 1960s relating to prehistoric and early historic China that may greatly add to, and revise, world knowledge of these periods. Much scholarly writing since 1949 has been devoted to providing evidence to buttress the Marxist theory of historical progress. For example, there has been much concern to show how archaeological sites of the Shang period indicate that it was a slave-owning society. Another example is the quantity of recent historical writing devoted to proving that China would have developed capitalism on its own, even if Western capitalists had not intervened.

The demand by PRC authorities that all scholarship, as all other aspects of modern Chinese life, put "politics in command" and that all educational, artistic, and intellectual endeavor stress practical applicability and contribute to production has tended to limit the pursuit of knowledge to a few fields. In addition to the constraints upon historians, the necessity for total conformity to PRC ideology and goals has limited the scope of scholarship in the fields of economics, political science, and other social sciences. The social sciences, considered politically and ideologically more sensitive and also of less direct practical applicability for production, have far lower status than do the natural and applied sciences.

An additional problem that confronts the social sciences and the humanities is the shortage of qualified senior research and teaching personnel, resulting from the fact that, unlike Western-trained physical scientists, Western-trained scholars in these other fields have had great difficulty finding employment in the PRC. Scholars in the social sciences and humanities were also complaining in the 1960s of a lack of suitable texts and of being denied access to foreign publications. During the 1950s, before the Sino-Soviet rift, there had been a heavy reliance on material from the Soviet Union and Soviet bloc countries, but by the 1960s this source had been denied scholars. By contrast, the scholars working in the physical sciences have had access to scholarly literature from all over the world.

University students are usually required to write a thesis on a research project carried out individually or with others. Especially since the mid-1960s, such projects have tended to be ones that purported to be immediately useful in agriculture, industry, or technology.

Research carried on outside the universities and colleges generally falls under the jurisdiction of the Chinese Academy of Sciences and the Scientific and Technological Commission (see ch. 16, Science and Technology). Thousands of monographs and scholarly articles in learned journals have been published since 1949 by societies belonging to the Academy of Sciences. Since 1966, however, much of the literature has been devoted to accounts by author-scholars of concrete personal experiences that showed how study of Mao Tse-tung Thought had benefited them in their research. It was not known in mid-1971 whether the various institutes of archaeology, history, ethnology, and other social sciences belonging to the Department of Philosophy and Social Sciences of the Academy of Sciences had resumed operation after the Cultural Revolution.

Creative Writing and Literary Criticism

Poetry

In prerepublican China every educated man was expected to be able to write poetry. One of the questions on the examination for the imperial civil service demanded the writing of a poem. As a result, the body of Chinese poetry is immense. A list of the most famous poets would include Ch'u Yuan, a semilegendary figure of the early third century B.C., who is credited with the authorship of a number of long, ornate, and highly emotional poems included in the collection called *Songs of the South*. Also included would be T'ao Ch'ien (A.D. 376–427), who wrote terse descriptions of nature in lyric form of five-syllable meter; Li Po (701–762), a T'ang dynasty lyricist who is the best known outside of China of all Chinese poets; and Tu Fu (712–770), another T'ang poet renowned for the poignancy of his work.

Most of the poetic forms were originally conceived of as being set to music. As a result, meter is the dominant stylistic concern, and there is usually also rhyme. The influence of Taoism, with its emphasis on communion with nature, is strong in Chinese poetry. The general tendency in Chinese literature toward a profusion of similes, metaphors, and allusions to other literary works is most pronounced in poetic writing.

One feature virtually obligatory to poetic creation since T'ang times has been parallel writing. Parallel writing of *lu shih* (regulated verse) demanded symmetry in images, word choice, and other stylistic features between the first and second lines of every couplet; for example, if the first line referred to a mountain, the next line should mention a river.

A more flexible poetic medium exists in the *tz'u*, a poetic form based on popular song tunes, some of which were of Central Asian origin. The *tz'u* was developed to its fullest by the poets of the Sung dynasty (960–1279).

As the *tz'u* gradually became more literary and artificial after Sung times, the *san-ch'u*, a freer form based on new popular songs, developed. The use of *san-ch'u* songs in drama marked an important step in the development of vernacular literature.

The use of classical forms of poetry has continued. Mao has written poems in the *tz'u* and other classical forms. Nevertheless, Mao has indicated that he does not approve of the promotion of old styles of poetry among the young, giving as his reason that the old style "restricts thought and is difficult to learn." Poems by Mao in the classical style received little attention in the PRC in the late 1960s and early 1970s as compared to the attention given his philosophic works and his shorter prose pieces, especially *The Foolish Old Man Who Removed the Mountains, Serve the People,* and *In Memory of Norman Bethune.*

In the period of intellectual and literary ferment that took place in the early decades of the twentieth century, Western influences on poetry were substantial. Nationalism and wartime patriotism in the 1930s and 1940s led to an increased interest in patriotic themes and the revival of uniquely Chinese forms, particularly folk songs and ballads. These forms had lacked respectability as vehicles for serious literature during the imperial era but were revived and encouraged by the Party as being examples of poetry by, for, and of the masses.

A new development during the Great Leap Forward campaign in the late 1950s was the launching of a mass poetry movement. The government urged that production in poetry, as in all other fields, meet unprecedented target figures. Hundreds of thousands of poems were produced, written by peasants, workers, and soldiers and edited by PRC literary specialists before publication in magazines and newspapers.

This mass poetry movement lost momentum during the 1961–62 period of revived interest in quality production in the arts. It regained some of its importance thereafter as part of the Socialist Education Campaign from 1963 to 1965, however, and later became part of the renewed campaign during the Cultural Revolution to see that the arts be produced for the masses.

Prose

Early prose was written in the literary style which, like that of poetry, was largely concerned with parallel imagery, parallel sentence structure, tonal euphony, and other arbitrary conventional elements. In the Sung dynasty period, *ku-wen* (ancient style), a literary prose that did not follow any set of arbitrary rules for rhythm and ornamentation, developed. Colloquial fiction became popular after the fourteenth century A.D., although it was never esteemed in court circles.

Covering a broader range of subject matter, longer, and less highly structured than literary fiction, vernacular fiction includes a number of masterpieces. The greatest is the eighteenth-century domestic novel, *Hung lou meng* (Dream of the Red Chamber). A semibiographic work by a scion of a declining gentry family, *Hung lou meng* has been generally acknowledged by students of Chinese fiction to be the masterwork in its field.

As a result of the efforts of Lu Hsun (1881–1936), China's first major stylist in vernacular prose (other than the novel), and of the literary reformers and leaders of the New Culture Movement, Hu Shih and Ch'en Tu-hsiu, the literary writing style came to be replaced by the vernacular in all fields of literature. Literary journals and societies espousing different artistic theories proliferated in the 1920s and 1930s, but gradually during the 1930s and 1940s, as the Sino-Japanese war and the civil conflict came to dominate life in China, political and social concerns began to dominate literature. The interest in purely artistic problems and criteria faded.

The League of Left-Wing Writers was founded in 1930. Including Lu Hsun in its leadership, by 1932 it had adopted the Soviet doctrine of socialist realism, the insistence that art must concentrate on contemporary events, in a realistic way, exposing the ills of nonsocialist society and promoting the glorious future under communism.

The late 1920s and 1930s were years of creativity in Chinese fiction. Among the major writers of the period were Kuo Mo-jo, who was a poet, historian, essayist, and critic. (In 1971 Kuo was a high-ranking Party official.) Mao Tun, Kuo's contemporary, was the first of the novelists to emerge out of the League of Left-Wing Writers. His work reflected the revolutionary struggle and disillusionments of the late 1920s. Pa Chin, a novelist whose work was influenced by Ivan

218

Turgenev and other Russian writers, produced a trilogy in the 1930s that depicted the struggle of modern youth against the age-old dominance of the Confucian family system. Another major writer of the period was the gifted satirist and novelist Lao She. Many of these writers became important as administrators of PRC artistic and literary policy after 1949. Most of those still alive in the mid-1960s were purged or had to submit to public humiliation during the Cultural Revolution.

After the communist takeover socialist realism became the uniform style of Chinese authors whose works were published. Conflict, however, soon developed between the regime and the writers. The ability to satirize and expose the evils in contemporary society that had made the writers useful to the Party before its accession to power was not welcome once the regime was installed. Even more unwelcome to the party was the persistence among writers of what was deplored as "petty bourgeois idealism," "humanitarianism," and an insistence on freedom to choose subject matter.

At the time of the Great Leap Forward the government insistence on socialist realism was broadened to combine so-called revolutionary realism and revolutionary romanticism. Authors gained permission to write not only of contemporary China but could also deal with other times during China's modern period. Nonetheless, the political restrictions discouraged many writers. Although increased production of literature was being urged, in 1962 only forty-two novels were published.

According to students of the field, among the best novels published since the regime came to power is Ai Wu's novel entitled *Steeled and Tempered*, published in 1958. A selfless worker, an able Party secretary, a factory manager, and a KMT saboteur are the main characters in this novel set in a steel factory.

A novel in the new revolutionary romantic genre that was greatly praised when it first appeared in 1958 is *Keep the Red Flag Flying* by Liang Pin, a novel about two peasant families caught in the turmoil of early twentieth-century war and revolution in China. *Three Family Lane*, published in 1959 and written by Ou-yang Shan, has been called the finest novel of the period. Its plot, although set in the 1920s and 1930s, closely resembles that of the famous *Hung lou meng*.

Although they were published with Party approval, many modern novels, including *Keep the Red Flag Flying* and *Three Family Lane*, were subsequently condemned, and their authors were punished for exhibiting traits that were not in conformity with the current literary policy of the regime. In the chief document of literary policy issued during the Cultural Revolution, the *Summary of the Forum on the Work in Literature and Art in the Armed Forces*, various "theories" or deviations from approved policy are specifically condemned, and some authors who advocated them are named. The "theory of 'truthful writing'" is condemned for wanting to show the "seamy side" of life in socialist society. The theory of "the broad path of realism" is condemned for insisting that "each author should write whatever he pleases," abandoning the worker-peasant-soldier orientation in favor of exploring "new fields which would give unlimited scope to their creativeness." Class struggle and the serving of proletarian politics are asserted to be the only worthwhile themes of literature. Specific authors are condemned for wanting to write about "middle characters," people in an "intermediate state" vacillating between socialism and capitalism or unconcerned with the class struggle. Others are accused of wanting to write works dealing with "human interest" or "love of mankind" or about "insignificant people" and "minor events."

During the mid-1960s, as the entire literary and artistic leadership of the PRC was criticized and purged, the PLA began to gain the initiative in this field. PLA teams were organized and instructed to produce literature—biographies, novels, and other works—to supplement the study of Mao thought. Most of these works are about model soldiers who sacrificed their lives for their country and their Party. The most ambitious of the PLA literary efforts of the 1960s was the novel by Chin Ching-mai, one of the PLA team authors, entitled *Song of Ou-yang Hai*. It is a fictional work published in 1965 and modeled on the life story of PLA hero Lei Feng.

Literary criticism is published in magazines and newspapers (all of which are government controlled) and is often written by prominent artists, intellectuals, and government and Party officials. The criticism generally does not concern itself with aesthetics or other purely literary attributes of the work but only with its political significance and meaning. The plot, the characters, and the style are analyzed in order to determine whether they illustrate correct behavior and attitudes on the part of the author and of the hero. During periods of reduced revolutionary fervor, debate may develop in the press concerning the meaning and value of a given work. More frequently, however, differences in interpretation reflect a change in the regime's policy.

To enhance the educational value of any literary work and to ensure that the reader will interpret it in the desired manner, sessions for reading and discussing literary works have been organized in factories, schools, Communes, and various social organizations under the guidance of Party or PLA cadres.

Criticism of the literary legacy of the precommunist era has vacillated between nearly total rejection of the past and efforts to incorporate at least some of this rich heritage into the body of acceptable literature by indicating its class consciousness, realism, popular origin, or uniquely Chinese character. For example, Tu Fu, the great T'ang poet who suffered poverty himself and wrote feelingly of the hardships of the people, is the object of qualified CCP admiration, whereas his equally gifted contemporary Li Po, a bibulous libertine, is not.

PERFORMING ARTS

Traditional Drama

Traditional Chinese drama, often called Chinese opera, is a synthesis of spoken dialogue (in relatively colloquial idiom) and song (in a more literary language), together with dance and theatrical gesture and accompanied by an orchestra of traditional Chinese instruments. Drama of this type had its original development during the Yuan dynasty. During the Ming period the city of Soochow was the center of the most popular and most highly regarded school of Chinese drama, but by the mid-nineteenth century Peking opera became the favorite with audiences and with the critics and has remained so in 1971. Regional drama styles, which differ from Peking opera primarily in dialect and secondarily in musical styles, plots, and some of the theatrical conventions, have also continued to be popular.

The drama is highly artificial, full of conventions that provide, for the initiated, a code by which to decipher developments in the plot and the behavior of the protagonists. The orchestra, by the use of its different instruments (the flute and strings for subtle emotions and the percussion instruments, gongs, cymbals, and drums for moments of vigorous activity or high drama), indicates the emotional atmosphere desired. Certain orchestral passages signal changes in scenes or acts or announce a wedding, a funeral, or the entrance of a high imperial official.

The four main roles to be found in most operas of this type are the male lead, female lead, painted-face actor, and comic. Makeup and costume are not supposed to be realistic, but they provide an indication of the character the actor is portraying. The acting of female roles by male impersonators is common. Plots of plays in the traditional repertory are chiefly historical and are concerned with the triumph of heroism, filial piety, and loyalty to Confucian values.

The PRC government has shifted its policy regarding Chinese traditional drama several times. The enormous popularity of the theater among the people and its distinctively Chinese character have made the formulators of cultural policy unwilling to eradicate it. Premier Chou En-lai in his youth was a clever amateur actor of female roles and is reported to be one of traditional drama's champions. Government sponsorship in the mid-1950s and early 1960s made possible the revival of plays, domestic and overseas performances by excellent touring companies, and experimentation with new techniques to make the drama easier for rural audiences to comprehend.

Nonetheless, because the content of the drama is so thoroughly interwoven with the imperial past and the highly stylized nature of acting is so far removed from the realism enjoined upon socialist artists, deep suspicion of the Peking opera has always been present in official PRC circles. Perhaps because of the great popularity of the Chinese drama, it has usually been the first of the arts to receive the impact of changes in artistic policy. In the mid-1950s, for example, the traditional theater was the first of the arts to be encouraged to flourish under the slogan "Let a hundred flowers bloom, let the hundred schools of thought contend." Likewise, the attack a decade later, in November 1965, on Wu Han and his historical play the *Dismissal of Hai Jui* was the first indication of the start of the Cultural Revolution. The attack on the Wu Han play, written in 1960, was not so much that it was feudal but that Wu Han was following the practice of satirists of earlier times—directing a veiled attack on the present regime through analogy with a historical event.

Since the mid-1960s, Mao's wife, Chiang Ch'ing, has been active in a movement to replace the traditional repertoire with new plays that conformed more closely to socialist reality. During the Cultural Revolution, as a result of the purge of contemporary playwrights who wrote for the traditional stage, much of the postwar drama was dropped from the repertoire. In May 1971 a foreign newspaperman noted that no dramas of the traditional repertoire were being performed and that only about ten recently written plays—many of them produced under the patronage of Chiang Ch'ing—were being seen.

The best known and most successful of the modern plays written for the traditional stage that was still being performed in mid-1971 was *The Red Lantern*, written in 1964. Since 1967 performances of *The Red Lantern* have used the innovation of piano accompaniment instead of the traditional orchestra.

Dance and Music

Growing out of the reform movement in the traditional theater, there has also developed an interest in ballet. One of the new Peking dramas, *The White-Haired Girl*, a tale of the sufferings of peasants under the old regime and the triumph of the peasants and the Party over feudalism and landlordism, was adapted to the Western-style ballet form and in the late 1960s was being performed more often as a ballet than in its original dramatic version. Another of the new ballets is entitled *The Red Detachment of Women*. These ballets, which take their themes from the revolutionary struggle that eventually culminated in the rise to power of the CCP, are artistically an innovation in China, being based on Western dance forms that were until recently unfamiliar to most Chinese.

Chinese-style dance, formerly subordinated to the theater, has become an independent art form. Folk dancing has been popularized throughout the country as part of the cultural heritage of the peasants. It provides opportunities for group participation and mass attendance. The *yang-ko* (harvest dance), based on a very old harvest ritual dance from northwest China, was adopted and popularized by the Communists during the Yenan period. The simple steps of the dance, the rhythm being emphasized by cymbal accompaniment, became known all over China and were associated with liberation, unification, and the national spirit. Regional and ethnic dance troupes are encouraged and patronized. Dance festivals with competitions and prizes attract large audiences. Professional troupes perform in the large cities, and some have toured abroad.

Chinese vocal music has traditionally been sung in a thin, nonresonant voice or in falsetto and is usually solo rather than choral. All traditional Chinese music is melodic rather than harmonic. Instrumental music is played on solo instruments or in small ensembles of plucked and bowed stringed instruments, flutes, and various cymbals, gongs, and drums. The scale has five tones. Although new and foreign instruments and vocal styles have been in use in the twentieth century, traditional music has predominated into the 1970s.

During the mid-1950s and early 1960s, official sponsorship of traditional Chinese music was considerable. The Institute for Research in Traditional Chinese Music, founded in 1954, revived the music of ancient instruments, among them the *ch'in* (a seven-stringed lute), the *erh-hu* (a two-stringed fiddle) and the *p'ip'a* (Chinese guitar).

Since the New Culture Movement of the early twentieth century, there has also been considerable interest among educated people in the Western symphony orchestra, individual Western instruments, and the Western musical notation system. Chinese symphony orchestras have played hundreds of concerts in the cities and over the radio. Western-style melodies and techniques were adapted for use in patriotic songs during the Yenan period. Among these were the *March of the Volunteers*, which was made the national anthem.

The tightening of restrictions upon the arts to make them conform more closely to the government's ideology and social policies has been felt in music as elsewhere. During and immediately after the Cultural Revolution both Western symphonic music and traditional Chinese music were out of favor, at least temporarily, and only modern revolutionary music was performed.

Domestically produced records disseminate the approved music throughout the country. A longplaying record released in the late

1960s had the title *Warmly Hail the Communique of the 12th Plenary Session of the 8th Central Committee of the Chinese Communist Party*. Songs on the record included "The Party's Communique is the Beacon Light," "Down with Liu Shao-ch'i," and "The State of the Proletariat Will Last Forever."

The Chinese record industry has expanded its repertoire greatly since 1949 in the fields of traditional music as well. Recordings have been made of numerous traditional dramas, ballads, instrumental music, and folk music of the Han and minority nationalities.

Folk Drama: Puppet Plays and Storytellers' Tales

During the Yenan period and in the early years after the CCP takeover, the emphasis in all fields of art in the PRC was on encouraging and reviving the folk arts while condemning and suppressing those that had been prized by the imperial ruling class. As a result of this official sponsorship of folk art forms, the puppet theater received more wholehearted support by the government than the Peking opera. In April 1955, for the first time in history, an all-China puppet show festival was held.

Puppets of various types exist: glove puppets, marionettes, rod puppets (some of them life-size), and shadow puppets. Although the puppet theater predates Chinese traditional drama of the Peking opera type, most plays in the traditional puppet repertoire are adaptations of classical drama. Puppet players, however, have adapted some of the new revolutionary dramas to their medium in recent years.

In the early 1960s the Shanghai Communist League Committee and the Shanghai Cultural Bureau organized classes to train rural storytellers. Within three years they had trained more than 10,000 peasants from nearby rural Communes in the techniques of storytelling and provided them with a repertoire that had, according to a *Peking Review* article of November 1965, "a clearcut orientation [to] propagate the Party's policies." Thus an oral tradition that had been an important source of peasant entertainment in the days when literacy was confined to members of the ruling class had found a new use.

Modern Drama and Motion Pictures

Although it remains less popular than traditional drama, modern or spoken drama based on Western forms has become very popular with the educated people of the bigger cities. Western plays with a social message began to be popular in China in the 1920s and 1930s. The works of Henrik Ibsen were particularly well received.

At first, subject matter in the Chinese spoken dramas tended to be on contemporary themes, but historical material eventually came to be used as well. Since the attack in the mid-1960s on plays that allegedly used historical themes to criticize the contemporary regime, plays on historical subjects have become unacceptable. A campaign has been launched to promote plays with themes drawn from the so-called democratic revolution of Sun Yat-sen, the socialist revolution of the CCP, and the contemporary scene.

The film industry started in China in 1917. It has grown considerably since 1949, and by the early 1960s there were approximately three dozen studios; twelve produced full-length films, and the remainder produced short documentaries, public information films, and newsreels (see ch. 12, Public Information and Propaganda). Peking and Shanghai are the chief centers for the making of feature films. Great advances have been made since 1949 in photography, color, sound, continuity, and editing. The first wide-screen film appeared in 1960.

Film subjects include original screenplays and adaptations of modern fictional and historical writings, traditional and modern dances and mimes, musical films of traditional drama, and films of the dances and dramas of minority nationalities. Cartoon films are very popular. Before 1949 cartoon films from the United States were shown in all the major Chinese cities, and Chinese cartoon films at first tended to imitate Western models. In the post-1949 period a national style of cartoons began to develop, using puppets, shadow puppets, scissored silhouettes, and other Chinese folk art elements. The plots have often been adapted from Chinese folk tales and famous novels but revised to conform to contemporary political guidelines.

VISUAL ARTS AND HANDICRAFTS

Although the PRC since 1949 has guarded and preserved ancient relics of Chinese arts and crafts, it has by and large discouraged the production and study of those arts that had imperial, upper class associations. It has also attempted to revive and spread those folk arts and crafts that had peasant origins.

The Legacy of the Past

The arts and crafts of China have developed over four millennia and have made notable contributions to the art of the world in numerous fields. The technical skill evident in ceremonial bronzes of the Shang and Chou dynasties of the second and first millenia B.C. has never been surpassed; this is also true of the porcelain of the T'ang and Sung periods. Chinese silk, brocades, and embroidery;

porcelain vessels and ornaments; and cups, bottles, and figurines carved from jade, semiprecious stones, ivory, and bone have been prized throughout the world since Han times.

Painting, Calligraphy, and the Graphic Arts

In imperial times painting and calligraphy were the most highly appreciated arts in court circles and were produced almost exclusively by amateurs—aristocrats and scholar-officials who alone had the leisure to perfect the necessary technique and sensibility to produce great brushwork. Calligraphy was thought to be the highest and purest form of painting. The tools were the brush pen, made of animal hair, and black inks made from the soot of burned wood. In ancient times writing, as well as painting, was done on silk but, after the invention of paper in the first century A.D., silk was very gradually replaced by the new and cheaper material. Original writings by famous calligraphers have been greatly valued throughout China's history and are mounted on scrolls and hung on walls in the same way that paintings are.

Painting in the traditional style involves essentially the same techniques as calligraphy and is done with a brush dipped in black or colored ink; oils are not used. The most popular materials on which paintings are executed are paper and silk. The finished work is then mounted on scrolls, which can be hung or rolled up. Traditional painting is also done in albums and on walls, lacquerwork, and other media.

Beginning in the T'ang era, the primary subject matter of painting was the landscape, known as *shan-shui* (literal meaning: mountain and water) painting. In these landscapes, usually monochromatic and sparse, there was no attempt to reproduce exactly the actual appearance of nature, but rather an effort was made to grasp an emotion or atmosphere to catch the rhythm of nature. In Sung times landscapes with a more poetic range appeared; immeasurable distances were conveyed through the use of blurred outlines, mountain contours disappearing into the mist, and impressionistic treatment of hills and trees. Certain pictorial conventions also evolved to represent natural phenomena. This was concomitant with a concentration on the spiritual qualities of the painting and on the ability of the artist to reveal the inner harmony of man and nature, as perceived according to Taoist and Buddhist concepts.

Beginning in the thirteenth century there developed a tradition of spare paintings of simple subjects—a branch with fruit, a few flowers, or one or two horses. Narrative painting, with a wider color range and a much busier composition than during the Sung period was immensely popular at the time of the Ming Dynasty.

During the Ming period the first books appeared that were illustrated with colored woodcuts. With the perfecting of the techniques of color printing, illustrated manuals on the art of painting began to be published. The *Manual of the Mustard Seed Garden,* a five-volume work first published in 1679, has been in use as a technical textbook for artists and students ever since.

Sculpture

A fondness for miniature sculpture—carvings in jade, quartz, soapstone, ivory, bone, and precious stones and workings in ceramics —has continued from ancient times. Sculpture and miniature sculpture were not practiced by members of the ruling class or recognized artists but were done by anonymous artisans in the service of the court, religious foundations, or wealthy gentry families. The art of sculpture was never as highly regarded as painting, nor did it ever achieve the peak of perfection that painting reached. The best period in Chinese sculpture was during the time Buddhism was most influential in China, before and during the T'ang period. Buddha images of monumental size and whole caves chiseled into thousands of Buddhist images date from this period.

Architecture

The principal feature of traditional Chinese architecture, both secular and religious, was a massive roof, with upcurving edges, resting on a post and lintel system of beams supported by columns (usually of wood). Buildings were usually of one story, additions being made horizontally on a symmetrical plane. Although pagodas and other towers abound, the emphasis in Chinese traditional buildings is on horizontality. Side buildings, courtyards, and pavilions were often disposed axially around the main structure, the whole forming a symmetrical arrangement enclosed by a high wall. The roof of a palace or temple was usually covered with tiles in brilliant colors. Dragons, phoenixes, and other ornamental designs were often fixed to the crest of the roof, to the eaves, and to the corner ends. The walls, which were nonstructural, were usually lavishly painted and decorated and pierced with windows, doors, and decorative niches.

The most famous example of Chinese traditional architecture, a product chiefly of the Ming period but also incorporating work done in the Yuan and Ch'ing periods, is the Forbidden City, the complex of buildings of the Imperial Palace enclosure in Peking. This complex of palatial buildings, enclosed by great walls and ornamental gates, covers a rectangular area of 250 acres.

Handicrafts and Folk Arts

From the most ancient times the Chinese have had a rich tradition of handicrafts. These include: weaving and embroidery of fabrics for decoration or use; lacquerware and cloisonné dishes and trays; an unmatched tradition of ceramic manufacture for every conceivable purpose; and decorated, inlaid, and ornately carved furniture, chests, and screens. These objects were produced by artisans patronized by members of the ruling class.

Folk art, like other Chinese art forms, also follows long-established traditions. It is mainly the product of village artisans for their own use or for others of their class and includes such objects of daily use as ceramic vessels, textiles, objects woven of bamboo fiber and reed, toys, dolls, and lanterns. It also fills the decorative needs of rural households. In parts of northern China, cutout pictures of red tissue paper are pasted on the white translucent paper windows of peasant houses as a year-round decoration. The designs are usually flowers, plants, insects, animals, and human figures; some also represent events and persons from legend and history.

Archaeological Excavations, Museums, and Monuments

Construction of museum buildings, recovery of relics from archaeological and construction sites, and restoration of historic monuments have been carried out on an unprecedented scale since the Communists came to power in 1949. Although the purpose and form of socialist artistic expression are quite different from traditional art and much of the old art is condemned as decadent, the PRC from its inception has promoted a policy of preserving ancient art objects and monuments and of sponsoring the recovery of relics of historical significance.

In 1950 the government published regulations calling for the registration with the Ministry of Culture of all historic art objects, artifacts, and books. Numerous private and public collections of books and objects were shipped to Peking to be deposited in state libraries and museums. The export of art objects was strictly regulated. Some monuments, such as the Great Wall, have been restored, and others, such as the Forbidden City in Peking, have been maintained in their original splendor and made accessible to the public for the first time. Museums have been opened all over the country, some of enormous size. The new Anhwei Provincial Museum, for example, has 15,000 square feet of floorspace.

During the great construction activity in the 1950s numerous sites of historic and artistic interest were uncovered, and the excavated articles were carefully preserved and placed in museums throughout the country (see ch. 3, Historical Setting). The most ambitious archaeological project since 1949 was the location and opening of one of the Ming imperial tombs near Peking. Thirteen Ming emperors were known to have been buried in the Valley of the Tombs. The gravesites and their approaches are noted examples of architecture and sculpture. The tombs themselves, however, had been set deep in the hills, and their exact location was not known. In the early 1950s, after decades of archaeological efforts to locate the tombs, the first one was found and opened. The tomb contained a treasure hoard of gold and silver bars, precious stones, and ceremonial implements made of costly materials and encrusted with gems. Some of these treasures were removed from the site for placement in museums and have been replaced there by copies. The tomb was electrified, and a stairway was put in to make it accessible to tourists.

In 1968 the tomb of a former Han dynasty prince and his wife was excavated in the mountains of Hopei Province. The tomb complex, which was as big and elaborate as an underground palace, contained thousands of funerary objects. Included in the find were the first known examples of jade corpse cases, the two halves of each case joined by fine gold wire that had been threaded through the four corners of the cases. Other major finds, in 1969 and 1970, included a mammoth granary dating from Sui and T'ang dynasty times (sixth to tenth century) at Loyang, and an eighth-century tomb belonging to a prince of the T'ang dynasty that was uncovered near the site of ancient Ch'ang-an, the T'ang capital.

Archaeology first became important in China in the 1920s and 1930s with the major discovery of Peking man, a possible precursor of Homo sapiens, and the material confirmation of the existence of the Shang dynasty through the discovery and identification of oracle bones (see ch. 3, Historical Setting). Many of the country's most valuable relics, however, were removed from China during the period before 1949. This outflow of relics has since ceased, and construction personnel, peasants, and others who find them or other evidence of the existence of archaeological sites are under orders to report their finds to the government.

In late 1966 during the most violent stage of Red Guard activity in connection with the attack on the "four olds"—old things, old ideas, old customs, and old habits—there were reported to be serious assaults on works of art, museums, public statuary, and monumental buildings of the imperial period. Foreign journalists subsequently have reported that China's most valuable treasures appear to have survived this attack, some of them having been protected from the Red Guards by regular troops of the PLA.

In mid-1971 foreign journalists noted that the museums and art galleries that had been closed during the Cultural Revolution had not yet reopened. One source reported that they were being rearranged so that the exhibits would conform more closely to Maoist precepts. The great Buddhist and Taoist temples of Peking that had attracted sightseers in the early 1960s were reported to be barred in mid-1971, and their religious images and other furnishings had been removed.

Modern Trends

Kuo Mo-jo, a top Party official and head of the Chinese Academy of Sciences, articulated the PRC policy as of mid-1971 concerning the arts: "In China, the arts are instruments of the revolution. We feel that there is no such thing as non-political art anywhere. Art that serves politics is revolutionary; and art that does not serve politics or that pretends to be apolitical is counter-revolutionary."

Soon after the PRC was established, the Central Academy of the Fine Arts was founded in Peking to train artists of the working class. Artists were directed to use current political and educational campaign subjects for their theme and to promote by their art the construction of a socialist society. Traditional landscape painting gave way to scenes of iron mines, steel mills, dams, and agricultural collectives. In some cases oils and other nontraditional materials that had first come into use during the New Culture Movement period have been used. Much of the contemporary art, however, follows the traditional style in form and techniques.

Artists usually teach and also accept commissions for work. When his work is published and reproduced, the artist reportedly receives royalties. Artists are relatively well paid by PRC standards but, in order to assure the maintenance of the working-class point of view, they are periodically sent to do manual labor at farms, factories, mines, and production projects. Workers and peasants are encouraged to express their creative urges and patriotic fervor through art works, which are exhibited either in the place of work or in the local cultural center.

By far the greatest part of visual art created under the communist regime has been illustrative—posters, cartoons, woodcuts, and picture story books. The enormous output in these fields serves a vast audience of illiterates and semiliterates. Small serial cartoon books for both children and adults are used in education and propaganda programs (see ch. 12, Public Information and Propaganda). Many traditional tales have been illustrated and brought up to date to express useful contemporary moral messages.

The woodcut, a centuries-old medium, is the most frequently employed for book illustrations. Artists have been urged also to seek their inspiration from the traditional folk art of the masses. Some painters of the traditional court style continue to paint insects, fish, flowers, and other works in the ancient genre under the sponsorship of the PRC government.

In architecture, efforts were made in the early years of the PRC to continue an earlier trend of synthesis of Western and traditional Chinese architectural features into a national style. In the 1950s and early 1960s Soviet influence led to the building of bulky structures of great size. Since then, a utilitarian tendency has been noted, with all decorative features deprecated.

Sculpture has also tended to follow Soviet realism, and the subject matter has been generally didactic. The most highly praised work of sculpture in the PRC as of mid-1971 was a group of over 100 life-sized figures called the *Rent Collection Courtyard*. The figures, modeled in clay, are arranged in six scenes dramatizing the sufferings of the peasants of Tayi County in Szechwan Province under the merciless domination of a tyrannical landlord. A portion of the original manor house complex belonging to the landlord has been turned into a museum, in which the original sculptural group has been placed. The display is designed for the purpose, according to a PRC official publication, of reminding the people "never to forget class struggle." Over 100 reproductions of the *Rent Collection Courtyard* group have been made for display in other parts of the country.

Small pottery figurines of PLA heroes and peasant boys and girls and busts of Chairman Mao Tse-tung have been made in massive quantities for domestic dissemination. One of the kilns that was producing works of this type in 1971 was the 800-year old Shekwan kiln at Foshan (twenty miles outside of Canton) famous in the past for its statuettes of Buddhist and Taoist images and characters from Chinese literary works.

Craft production in all fields has been encouraged by the PRC, and workers interviewed by foreign newsmen have indicated that wages and working conditions of artisans and craftsmen have improved since 1949. In May 1971 a foreign journalist visited a craft factory in Peking, one of many that make a wide range of craft products, including lacquerware; cloisonné; carvings in jade, quartz, semiprecious stone, ivory, and bone; inlaid screens and chests; and ornately decorated furniture. Traditional designs are used for export products, but new socialist themes, for example, a carving in ivory of the huge new bridge across the Yangtze River at Nanking, are primarily made for local consumption.

SECTION II. POLITICAL

CHAPTER 9

POLITICAL SYSTEM AND VALUES

In 1971 the People's Republic of China (PRC) was still recovering from massive dislocations caused during the convulsions of the 1966–69 Great Proletarian Cultural Revolution. Although the personal preeminence of Mao Tse-tung (chairman of the Chinese Communist Party, head of state, and former PRC chairman) appeared to have been assured by means of both Red Guard campaigns and the intervention of the People's Liberation Army (PLA), the formal machinery of government remained in a state of flux. Whereas some parts of the machinery appeared to be working as defined in the 1954 State Constitution, others were operating under the personal instructions of Chairman Mao and his deputy Lin Piao or under the provisions of the 1970 draft state constitution that had yet to be officially adopted and promulgated. The emerging picture was not clear, but to qualified foreign observers, policies and actions were affected more by the response to day-to-day exigencies of those holding power in Peking and provincial capitals than by constitutional principles.

The political system was dominated, as from the origin of the PRC, by the Communist Party. The Party dictated government policy and its execution through a small group of leaders concurrently holding high office in both the Party and government. In a narrow sense the Party was operating outside the formal structure of government but, viewed in a larger political context, it was operating as a government within the government and as the nucleus of the entire political system (see ch. 10, Political Dynamics). Although there was no mention in the 1954 State Constitution of the Communist Party as an integral part of the government, the 1970 draft document was more explicit on this point, stating that the National People's Congress, "the highest organ of State authority," should function "under the leadership of the Chinese Communist Party." Moreover, the 1970 draft declared that to support "the leadership of the Chinese Communist Party" was a fundamental right and duty of the citizens.

A significant new trend since the mid-1960s has been the growing influence of the PLA in the governing process as administrator, soldier, and ideological specialist. The PLA has been the chief instrumental force behind the regime's continuing efforts to change the mental attitudes of the population in accordance with Mao Tse-tung Thought (Mao Tse-tung szu hsiang), the ultimate source of political values and legitimacy and, in Lin Piao's phrase, "the peak of Marxism-Leninism."

Political values as sanctioned by Marxist-Leninist-Maoist teachings and as applied to China contain many tenets, including love of country, loyalty to the Party and Chairman Mao, subordination of self to the collectivity, love of manual labor, austerity, self-reliance, political activism, the primacy of human will over material forces, and universal applicability of Mao's teachings.

Efforts to inculcate these values in the people were particularly intense during the height of the Cultural Revolution. They were continuing in 1971, albeit on a lower level of intensity, in order to sustain a highly tension-charged structure of human relations. The people were being constantly told of the necessity of "uninterrupted revolution" in a socialist society. The aim of this ideological remolding exercise was, according to the Party, to train a new generation of Communists who were proficient in both military and civil affairs and would engage in both industry and agriculture and cultural activities, political work at both higher and lower levels of the government hierarchy, and hold official posts while behaving like humble, ordinary workers.

CONSTITUTIONAL BACKGROUND

The Communist Chinese constitutional evolution started with the adoption in November 1931 of a constitution for the first Chinese Soviet Republic, established in the remote mountain districts of southern Kiangsi (see ch. 3, Historical Setting). The 1931 version was replaced in 1949 by a second document that lasted until 1954. A new permanent constitution went into effect in late 1954 and in mid-1971 still remained in force, but its status was somewhat uncertain. There were indications in 1971 that a new constitution might be introduced soon to reflect the realities of the post-Cultural Revolution years.

The 1931 Constitution, as did later versions, accepted the Marxist-Leninist view of history regarding class struggle as the primary ideological basis for reconstructing Chinese society. It sought to introduce "the democratic dictatorship of the proletariat and peasantry in the Soviet districts and to secure the triumph of the dictatorship throughout the whole of China." The aim of this dictatorship was, among other things, to limit the development of capitalism, to foster class consciousness, to improve the living conditions of the working class through redistribution of lands and the

234

enforcement of a new labor code, and to terminate political and economic privileges obtained in China by foreign powers. The constitution granted political rights and freedom to the "people"—peasants, workers, Red Army soldiers, and the toiling masses but not to the "enemies of the people"—counterrevolutionary elements, such as the capitalists, landlords, gentry, warlords, reactionary officials, village bosses, and monks.

As the Communists gradually expanded the areas in which they operated and gained in techniques of civil administration, they followed an expedient policy of appealing to broader segments of the population, toning down their doctrinaire attitudes and policies. In his 1940 work *On the New Democracy*, Mao Tse-tung called for the establishment of a "new democracy" under the "joint dictatorship of all Chinese revolutionary classes headed by the Chinese proletariat." Neither capitalist nor socialist, the new democracy was to be achieved during the first phase of what Mao described as a two-stage revolution, the democratic and the socialist. The government of the new political order was to be guided by the principle of democratic centralism (see Glossary) and through a hierarchy of people's congresses.

In July 1949, with the communist victory almost certain, Mao advocated a "people's democratic dictatorship" that he said would be different from the pure proletarian dictatorship of the Soviet Union type. The people were defined as an alliance of four classes—the workers, peasants, intellectuals, and national bourgeoisie (see ch. 5, Social System and Values). The democratic dictatorship was to be led by the workers but in alliance with the other three classes; its aim was to wipe out feudal vestiges and so-called lackeys of imperialism, such as landlords, bureaucratic capitalists, and the Kuomintang (Nationalist Party, often known as KMT) reactionaries and their henchmen. In foreign policy Mao said that China should "lean to one side," that is, favor the camp of socialism as opposed to the camp of capitalism.

In September 1949 a constituent body called the Chinese People's Political Consultative Conference (CPPCC) was convened in Peking in order to formulate a new constitutional framework. The conference adopted a set of three important documents: the Organic Law of the Central People's Government, which defined the functions of the various state organs and their relationships to one another; the Organic Law of the CPPCC, designating the CPPCC as the supreme organ of the state empowered to exercise legislative functions pending the convocation of a national people's congress; and the Common Program of the CPPCC, a detailed statement of general principles relating to the philosophy, goal, and program of the Chinese Communists for the transitional period ending in 1954. The conference also elected Mao Tse-tung chairman of the People's Republic of China.

In 1953 the People's Republic of China accelerated the pace of transition from the first stage of political consolidation and economic rehabilitation to the second stage, which was to lead to the arrival of socialism. The government's announcement of the "general line of the state during the period of transition to socialism" was followed in that year by the inauguration of the country's first five-year plan and the formation of a committee to draft a new permanent constitution.

The constitution drafting body was chaired by Mao Tse-tung and consisted of thirty-two members, of whom nineteen were Communist Party members, mostly from the Party Central Committee and the Politburo (Political Bureau). In September 1954 the final draft of the constitution, which was in fact a document originally written by the Party Central Committee, was adopted by the National People's Congress, formed earlier in the same month.

The State Constitution of 1954

The 1954 document is based on the Common Program of 1949 and is officially described as an improvement on the program. In style and substance the document resembles the Soviet Union's Constitution of 1936 but with certain modifications to suit the realities of China as the leadership perceived them.

The People's Republic of China is defined by the Constitution as "a people's democratic state led by the working class and based on the alliance of workers and peasants" and "a single multinational state" in which all minority peoples are said to be integrated into one great family of free and equal nationalities. Autonomous areas inhabited by these minorities are declared as inalienable parts of the PRC. Cultural freedom is granted to these people with respect to their languages and customs; in actuality, the government has followed a policy of sinicizing these areas (see ch. 4, Ethnic Groups and Languages).

The Constitution declares that the state will, by peaceful means, gradually abolish systems of exploitation and build a socialist state. It recognizes four basic forms of property ownership during the transitional stage: state ownership or ownership by the whole people; cooperative ownership or collective ownership by the working masses; ownership by individual working people; and capitalist ownership. The state was directed to transform private and partial collective ownership to the complete collective type as a transitional step toward the establishment of the state-controlled economy. For agriculture and handicrafts, the socialist transformation was to start by organizing the elementary agricultural producers' cooperative; the capitalist industry and commerce were to be transmuted into the socialist economy through "various forms of state capitalism."

The fundamental law deprives feudal landlords and capitalist members of the bureaucracy of political rights for a specified period of time. It recognizes, however, that these "undesirables" could be reformed and become "citizens who earn their livelihood by their own labor."

The 1954 State Constitution contains sections defining the powers and functions of the National People's Congress, the chairman of the People's Republic of China, the State Council, the local people's congresses and local people's councils, the organs of self-government of national autonomous areas, and the people's courts and the people's procuratorates (see fig. 9). The manner in which these agencies functioned remained generally stable until it was disrupted during the Cultural Revolution (see ch. 10, Political Dynamics).

The Draft State Constitution of 1970

In November 1970 the Republic of China on Taiwan published a text of a new draft state constitution that it said was an authentic copy of the document then being circulated among top Party and military leaders on the mainland. Although as of mid-1970 the genuineness of this document had yet to be verified, news reports emanating from the mainland seemed to point to its authenticity.

The draft contains only 30 articles, as compared with 106 in the 1954 State Constitution. It has no preamble such as that in the previous document that referred to China's "indestructible friendship with the great Union of Soviet Socialist Republics." The nature of the post-Cultural Revolution China is described as "a socialist state of proletarian dictatorship led by the working class," and Minister of National Defense Lin Piao is explicitly named as "Chairman Mao's close comrade-in-arms and successor."

The People's Republic is still called "a unified, multinational state," and all minority nationalities are accorded "freedom to use their spoken and written languages." In contrast to the 1954 State Constitution, however, the freedom of minority nationalities to preserve or reform their own customs or ways is not mentioned, thus suggesting in part that these customs or ways, representing feudal relics, became a main target of Red Guard attacks during the Cultural Revolution.

The draft recognizes only two forms of property ownership: socialist ownership by the whole people and socialist collective ownership by the working masses. For the latter purpose, the draft identifies three levels of ownership: by the People's Commune, the production brigade, and the production team. Unlike the 1954 version, the right of peasants to own land and the right of handicraftsmen to own means of production are not contained in the 1970 draft, which,

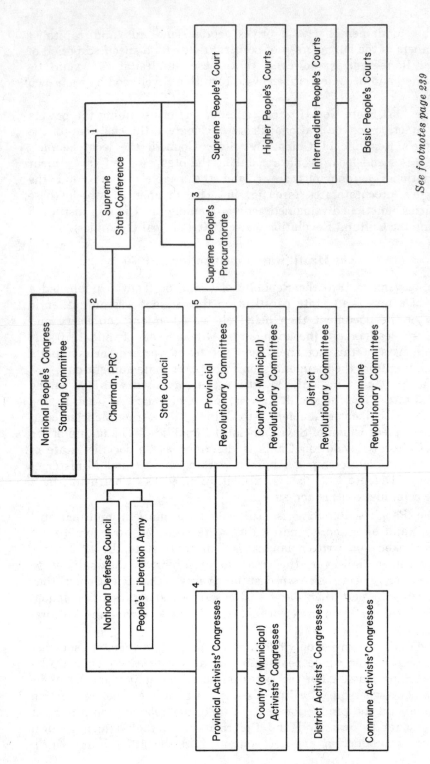

National People's Congress
Standing Committee

Supreme
State Conference¹

Chairman, PRC²

National Defense Council

People's Liberation Army

State Council

Supreme People's
Procuratorate³

Provincial
Revolutionary Committees⁵

County (or Municipal)
Revolutionary Committees

District
Revolutionary Committees

Commune
Revolutionary Committees

Provincial Activists' Congresses⁴

County (or Municipal)
Activists' Congresses

District Activists' Congresses

Commune Activists' Congresses

Supreme People's Court

Higher People's Courts

Intermediate People's Courts

Basic People's Courts

See footnotes page 239

*Figure 9.   People's Republic of China, Formal Governmental Structure,
December 1970.*

however, provides that "the members of the People's Commune may operate a small amount of private plots."

In an attempt to legitimize the new power alignment of the post-Cultural Revolution years, the draft document exhorts all state organs to enforce the revolutionary three-way alliance of the army, cadres (see Glossary), and masses. Mao's apparent desire to unify the generations is indicated in part in this draft, which calls for another tripartite alliance, between the old, middle-aged, and young.

As for the state organs, the draft has no mention of the chairman of the PRC but retains provisions concerning the National People's Congress, the State Council, the local people's congresses (called local activists' congresses since 1971), local revolutionary committees (formerly local people's councils), and judicial organs and procuratorates.

CENTRAL GOVERNMENT

National People's Congress

Both the 1954 and 1970 documents describe the National People's Congress (NPC) as the highest organ of state authority, but the latter document differs from the former in stating that this body is "under the leadership of the Chinese Communist Party." The 1954 State Constitution empowers the NPC to supervise the enforcement of the Constitution; to enact laws; to elect the chairman and the vice chairman of the People's Republic; to examine and approve the state budget and the financial report; to decide on questions of war and peace, to appoint and recall ambassadors and ratify or abrogate treaties with foreign states; and to exercise such other functions and powers as it considers necessary.

The NPC members are elected for a term of four years (five years under the 1970 draft) at the ratio of 1 deputy for every 800,000 persons from a province, 1 for every 100,000 persons from a centrally administered municipality, and 1 from each provincially administered municipality with a population of more than 900,000; a total of 150 deputies from the national autonomous regions, 60 from the armed forces, and 30 Overseas Chinese are elected. The 1970 draft states that

[1] In mid 1971 all indications point to the dissolution of this conference first created under the 1954 State Constitution.

[2] Party Chairman Mao Tse-tung is, for all practical purposes, holding this position as "the head of state of our country ... and the supreme commander of the whole nation and the whole army" (as phrased in the 1970 draft state constitution). The title of chairman of the PRC was not used after October 1968, when Liu Shao-ch'i was ousted from this position.

[3] The status of this organization remained unknown.

[4] Known as people's congresses until end of 1970. Reference to "activists' congresses" became infrequent after early 1971.

[5] Known as people's councils until the end of 1966.

in case of necessity a certain number of patriotic personalities may be invited to attend.

By law, citizens over the age of eighteen are entitled to vote and to be elected to office, unless disqualified as a member of the traditional landlord class, as a bourgeois reactionary, or as a supporter of the KMT. Direct voting exists only at the base level, where villagers elect their deputies to the Commune congresses. Deputies to higher congresses at district, provincial, and national levels are chosen by indirect election by lower congresses. They are elected through secret ballot. Candidates are screened and nominated usually by the Party, and there is seldom more than one nominee on the ballot for each single-member constituency.

In actual practice the NPC has no significant power. It usually meets once a year, on the call of its Standing Committee, and acts mainly as a sounding board for the Party and as a transmitter of Party and government policy to the lower levels of organs and the people. The NPC sessions are short; voting has been characterized by "unanimous decision"; and speeches invariably have echoed the Party line. Its deputies, as in lower congresses, are subject to the policy direction and control of the Party and are required to assist actively in the execution of the laws and policies of the state. The NPC has not met since early 1965, when it was attended by over 3,000 deputies.

Constituted as the NPC's permanent body, the Standing Committee is to interpret the laws and adopt decrees; to supervise the work of the State Council, the Supreme People's Court, and the Supreme People's Procuratorate; to annul decisions and orders of the State Council that contravene the Constitution, laws, or decrees; to exercise powers relating to the conduct of foreign relations; and to perform such other functions and powers as vested in it by the NPC. The Standing Committee is elected by the NPC and usually meets twice a month. The top leaders of this body are all high-ranking members of the Party or leaders of other major mass organizations. The last public meeting of this committee took place in April 1966. Nevertheless, messages to foreign countries were still sent out, in the 1970–71 period, jointly in the name of the Standing Committee and the State Council.

The Chairman of the People's Republic of China

Under the 1954 State Constitution the chairman of the PRC, elected by the NPC for a term of four years, is the head of state, representing the government in its relationships with foreign states and receiving their diplomatic envoys. He is the supreme commander of the armed forces and presides over the National Defense Council and the Supreme State Conference. In the name of the NPC or its

Standing Committee, he also exercises powers to promulgate laws and decrees; appoint or remove the premier, vice premier, and cabinet-level officials; proclaim martial law and a state of war; and order mobilization. He is assisted by a vice chairman, who succeeds him in case of death or resignation and acts in his behalf if the chairman is incapacitated by sickness for a prolonged period of time.

The chairmanship is not provided for in the 1970 draft constitution, which instead presents Mao as "the head of state of our country under proletarian dictatorship and the supreme commander of the whole nation and the whole army." According to the 1970 document, foreign diplomatic representatives present their credentials to the Standing Committee of the NPC. The chairmanship remained vacant after October 1968, when Liu Shao-chi, who had held this position since 1959, was publicly vilified by Red Guards and was stripped of all Party and government positions (see ch. 10, Political Dynamics).

According to the 1954 State Constitution, the chairman of the PRC convenes the Supreme State Conference and submits the views of this conference on major policy issues to the NPC, its Standing Committee, the State Council, or other bodies concerned for their consideration and decision. As a consultative body responsible to the chairman only, the Supreme State Conference held its sessions only infrequently; those invited to attend its sessions represented a cross section of the senior members of the state ministries and agencies, and participants ranged in number from 60 to over 1,000. The last known sessions of this body were held in December 1964. The 1970 draft makes no references to this organization.

Also not mentioned in the 1970 document is the National Defense Council, headed by the chairman of the PRC. The council is concerned with high military affairs, but in practice it has functioned more as an honorific, consultative body. It has met only rarely, and many of its 100-odd members were non-Communists, almost one-third of them being former Chinese Nationalist generals. In 1971 all important deliberations on military matters were made, as in the past, by the Military Commission (formerly Military Affairs Committee) of the Party Central Committee (see ch. 21, The Armed Forces).

The State Council

The 1970 draft, as does the 1954 State Constitution, describes the State Council as the Central People's Government. The highest executive organ of the state, the council (or the cabinet as it is known in most Western countries) is composed of the premier (Chou En-lai since October 1949), vice premiers, ministers, and heads of commissions and is responsible and reports to the NPC or its Standing Committee (see fig. 10). The State Council coordinates and

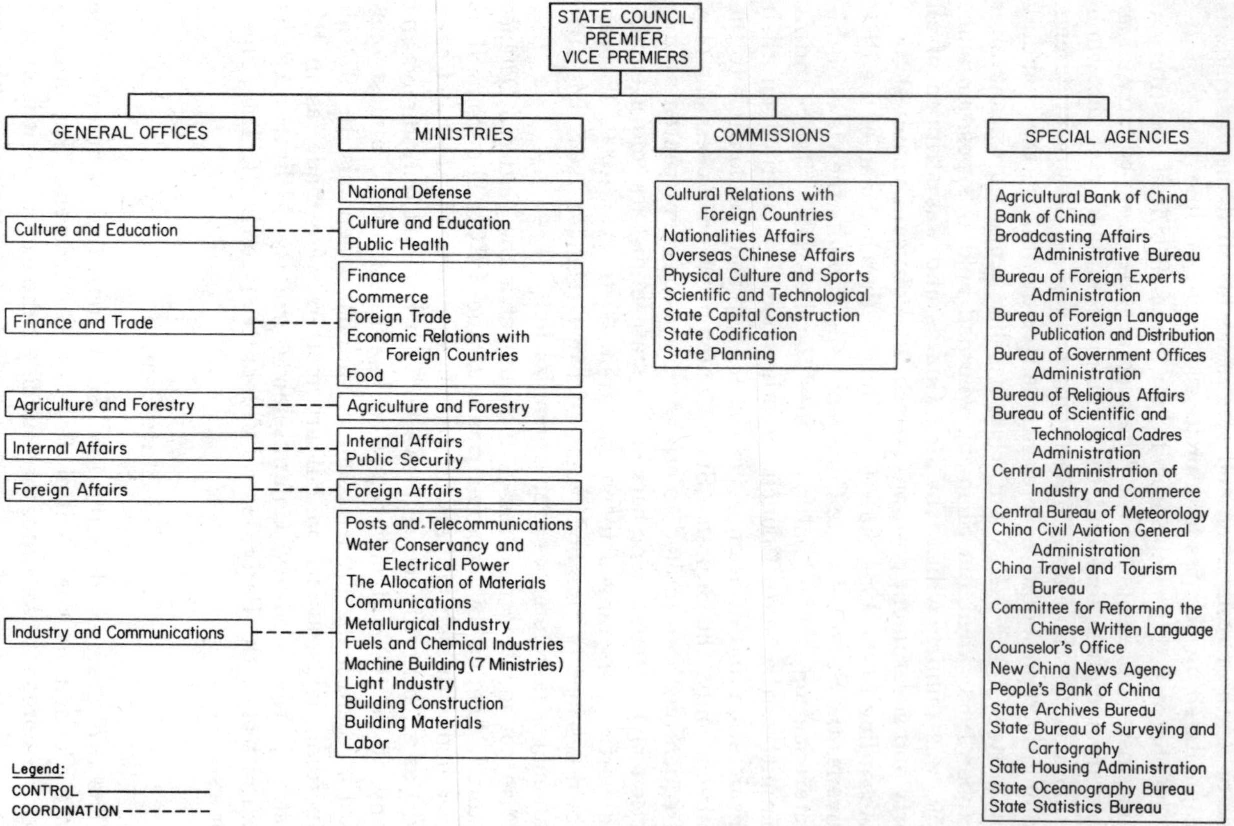

STATE COUNCIL
PREMIER
VICE PREMIERS

GENERAL OFFICES

- Culture and Education
- Finance and Trade
- Agriculture and Forestry
- Internal Affairs
- Foreign Affairs
- Industry and Communications

MINISTRIES

- National Defense
- Culture and Education
- Public Health
- Finance
- Commerce
- Foreign Trade
- Economic Relations with Foreign Countries
- Food
- Agriculture and Forestry
- Internal Affairs
- Public Security
- Foreign Affairs
- Posts and Telecommunications
- Water Conservancy and Electrical Power
- The Allocation of Materials
- Communications
- Metallurgical Industry
- Fuels and Chemical Industries
- Machine Building (7 Ministries)
- Light Industry
- Building Construction
- Building Materials
- Labor

COMMISSIONS

- Cultural Relations with Foreign Countries
- Nationalities Affairs
- Overseas Chinese Affairs
- Physical Culture and Sports
- Scientific and Technological
- State Capital Construction
- State Codification
- State Planning

SPECIAL AGENCIES

- Agricultural Bank of China
- Bank of China
- Broadcasting Affairs Administrative Bureau
- Bureau of Foreign Experts Administration
- Bureau of Foreign Language Publication and Distribution
- Bureau of Government Offices Administration
- Bureau of Religious Affairs
- Bureau of Scientific and Technological Cadres Administration
- Central Administration of Industry and Commerce
- Central Bureau of Meteorology
- China Civil Aviation General Administration
- China Travel and Tourism Bureau
- Committee for Reforming the Chinese Written Language
- Counselor's Office
- New China News Agency
- People's Bank of China
- State Archives Bureau
- State Bureau of Surveying and Cartography
- State Housing Administration
- State Oceanography Bureau
- State Statistics Bureau

Legend:
CONTROL ————
COORDINATION --------

Figure 10. People's Republic of China, The State Council, December 1970

242

Powers and functions of the council as listed in the 1970 draft are considerably fewer than those in the 1954 version. Apart from its supervisory and coordinating functions, the council is empowered to formulate administrative measures and issue decisions and orders, in accordance with the Constitution, laws, and decrees. It may also formulate and implement the national economic plan and the state budget and exercise such other functions and powers as are entrusted to it by the NPC or its Standing Committee.

In 1970 and 1971 some ministries and commissions under the State Council were being reorganized through mergers in order to simplify administrative operations. For example, the former ministries in charge of culture, education, and higher education were absorbed into the new Ministry of Culture and Education; the three separate ministries dealing with agriculture, forestry, and state farms and land reclamation were incorporated into the single Ministry of Agriculture and Forestry; the Ministry of Communications absorbed the old Ministry of Railways; and the Ministry of Fuels and Chemical Industries took over the ministries of chemical industry, coal industry, and petroleum industry. In addition, the Ministry of Light Industry combined the former first and second ministries of light industry; the former Eighth Ministry of Machine Building was taken over by the First Ministry of Machine Building; and the Ministry of Economic Relations with Foreign Countries was known until December 1970 as the Commission for Economic Relations with Foreign Countries.

The Judicial System

As constituted in 1954 the court system, responsible to the NPC or its Standing Committee, consists of the Supreme People's Court at the top, located in Peking; higher people's courts, in provinces, autonomous regions, and centrally administered municipalities; intermediate people's courts, in special districts, provincial municipalities, and autonomous districts (chou); and basic people's courts, in counties, autonomous counties, and towns. There are also special people's courts that include military courts.

The basic people's courts usually act as the court of first instance, from which appeal could be addressed to intermediate courts. Depending on the nature of cases, however, intermediate or higher courts may assume direct jurisdiction, the cases so tried being subject to appeal to the Supreme People's Court. In highly important cases the Supreme People's Court is empowered to act as a court of first instance, in which case no further recourse to appeal would be possible.

In 1971 the court system remained basically intact, although it was disrupted in some instances and attacked by Red Guards as hampering the Cultural Revolution. The Red Guards set up their own "private courts" and sometimes organized "trial rallies," although they were forbidden to do so by the authorities. That the system was considerably politicized during the Cultural Revolution is indicated in the 1970 draft constitution. This document insists that the "mass line" must be carried out in court proceedings and that the masses must be aroused to hold discussion and criticism in the handling of counterrevolutionary criminal cases.

The position of the procuratorate in the judicial system was not clear in 1971 because the Supreme People's Procuratorate is omitted in the 1970 draft. Under the 1954 State Constitution the Supreme People's Procuratorate is responsible to the NPC or its Standing Committee and supervises local people's procuratorates as well as military procuratorates. Members of these bodies represent the state as prosecuting attorneys in all courts and are not subject to interference by other state organs.

The Supreme People's Procuratorate exercises investigative authority over all central and local government organs, including courts, and over all persons working within and outside the state organs. It also checks the decisions, orders, and measures of all state organs to ensure their conformity with existing statutes and examines the adjudication procedures of local people's courts.

LOCAL GOVERNMENT

The country had, as of mid-1971, a total of twenty-nine administrative divisions: three centrally administered municipalities (*chih hsia shih*); twenty-one provinces (*sheng*); and five autonomous regions for minority peoples (*tzu chin ch'u*) (see ch. 2, Physical Environment and Population). Municipalities were subdivided into districts (*ch'u*) and counties (*hsien*); provinces, into counties, provincially administered municipalities, towns (*chen*), and People's Communes (*jen min kung she*); and autonomous regions, into districts (*chou*), counties, People's Communes, and towns.

In most provinces there were also special districts (*chuan ch'u*) operating between provincial and county levels. These districts served as coordinating centers for two or more counties and thus had no separate local administrative organs.

Although administrative divisions remained unchanged from those of the pre-Cultural Revolution years, local administrative bodies in them changed somewhat. In 1971 the old local people's congresses and local people's councils were known as the local activists' congresses and local revolutionary committees, respectively. Moreover, the way in which these bodies worked differed from one region to another; in any given region, variations appeared to be more pronounced at county or Commune, rather than provincial, level.

Activists' Congresses and Revolutionary Committees

The 1970 draft state constitution declares that the local activists' congresses and the local revolutionary committees ensure the execution of law and order in their respective localities, examine and approve the local budgets, maintain "revolutionary order," protect civil rights, and "bring the enthusiasm of various localities into full play." Duties and powers are not spelled out further, but it appeared in 1971 that these local organs were performing essentially the same functions as their predecessors but under different names.

Under the 1954 State Constitution the local people's congresses at all levels are defined as the highest organs of state authority in their respective areas, and local people's councils act as the executive organs of these congresses at corresponding levels. The duties of the congresses include formulation of plans and policies, approval of local budgets and financial reports, and election and recall of local people's council members and presidents of local people's courts. The sessions of the congress are called by the respective people's councils.

Deputies to the congresses of provinces, autonomous regions, municipalities, districts, counties, and People's Communes are chosen by the people's congresses of the next lower level. Deputies to those municipalities not divided into districts or counties are elected directly by the voters.

The term of office of the congresses of provinces and centrally administered municipalities is extended, in the 1970 draft, from four to five years; and of districts, ordinary municipalities, and counties, from two to three years. Commune- and town-level congresses are to be elected, as before, for terms of two years.

Local revolutionary committees were established first in January 1967 by the leadership group directing the Cultural Revolution as "temporary organs of power." They continued to exist in 1971 more as a permanent feature of local government. As an instrument of power controlled by the three-way alliance of military representatives, revolutionary cadres, and representatives of mass organizations, these committees were operating in all administrative divisions, as well as in factories, in schools, and even in larger production brigades.

The presence of military representatives was conspicuous in many of these committees. Military influence varied from one region to another and was felt especially at the provincial level and in those security-sensitive areas facing Soviet borders (see ch. 10, Political Dynamics).

In mid-1971 information regarding the actual relationships of local revolutionary committees to activists' congresses at the same level was fragmentary. Under the 1954 State Constitution these committees would have functioned not only as executive organs of the corresponding level congresses but also as executioners of orders and decisions of higher level committees, or people's councils as they were formerly called. They also had the responsibility of directing the work of lower level councils.

The Commune System

In the years after 1958 the People's Commune remained the basic administrative unit, each comprising several former townships (*hsiang*), the size of population ranged from 20,000 to several hundred thousand persons. As of the end of 1963, the latest date for which officially released information was available, there were about 74,000 Communes in the country, up from 24,000 in 1958. The Communes consist of 700,000 production brigades and 5 million production teams.

The Commune is an outgrowth of the agricultural production cooperatives but much larger in scope and with a much higher degree of collectivization (see ch. 14, Agriculture). As originally conceived, the Commune was to become a basic social, political, and economic organization engaged not only in agriculture, local industry, banking, trading, and distribution but also in running rural educational and cultural systems and in organizing a militia. In the more advanced Communes centralized dormitories, public messhalls, and nurseries were to be provided so that female, as well as male, labor could be more efficiently utilized. According to the government the worker, peasant, trader, student, and militiaman were to be mobilized into the so-called five-in-one collectivity operating essentially along military lines.

This method of highly regimented social mobilization did not last long. The peasants were exhausted by the unremitting pressure of the Great Leap Forward (see Glossary) with which the Commune scheme was integrated; they grew intensely resentful over the loss of their land tenure that they had gained in the early years of communist rule. Confronted with this peasant discontent and the sharp deterioration of agriculture, the state retreated in 1959, decentralizing political and economic controls. Portions of land on which to grow crops and livestock to be sold on the free market were returned to individual peasant families.

Administratively, the production brigade became "the basic accounting unit," but because of continuing rural difficulties a further decentralization took place in November 1961, when the Party decided to make the production team the basic accounting unit. Under this incentive-stimulating measure, each production team of thirty to forty households emerged as a cohesive social and economic unit, since each team was more or less coterminous with a single natural village (see ch. 14, Agriculture).

The extent of changes at the Commune level in the wake of the Cultural Revolution had yet to be fully assessed in 1971. In broadest terms it appeared that restrictions were being reimposed on peasant life and that in some cases peasants were being urged "voluntarily" to return at least a portion of their private plots to the Commune. Economic self-sufficiency was another aspect of new trends stressed and was being accomplished by merging smaller inefficient production brigades and production teams into larger units. Attempts at consolidation, however, aroused antagonism in many areas, and more productive brigades or teams were unwilling to join those having an inferior production record. Another noticeable trend was the attempt by the state to let production brigades assume more financial responsibility for agriculture, trade, rural education, and medical care, thus seeking to reduce the state expenditure.

Autonomous Regions

There were in 1970 five province-level autonomous regions, twenty-nine district-level areas, and sixty-nine county-level areas for minority peoples in the country. Some of these areas were in predominantly Han Chinese-populated provinces. Before 1949 the central government authority scarcely extended below the county level and, in the case of Tibet, seldom outside the capital city of Lhasa. Until then most of these areas had been ruled by native hereditary tribal chieftains nominally under the jurisdiction of central, provincial or, sometimes, county authorities.

The purpose of these regions and areas was to safeguard and promote the interest of minority nationalities through local self-government. Broad guidelines were contained in the 1949 Common Program and in the three separate decrees issued in 1952: the Regulations on the Protection of the Right of All Scattered National Minority People to National Equality; the Regulations on Measures for the Establishment of Local Democratic-Coalition Governments of Nationalities; and the General Program of the People's Republic of China for the Implementation of Regional Autonomy for Nationalities. The 1954 State Constitution also contains provisions aimed at the protection of national minorities.

With the exception of the Inner Mongolian Autonomous Region, which obtained special status in 1947, other regions were granted autonomous status after 1949: the Sinkiang Uighur Autonomous Region in 1955; the Kwangsi Chuang and Ninghsia Hui autonomous regions, both in 1958; and the Tibetan Autonomous Region in 1965. According to the 1954 State Constitution, the organs of local government in these regions may be determined based on "the wishes of the majority of the people of the nationality or nationalities enjoying regional autonomy in a given area"; in practice, however, the central government has had wide latitude in its gradual but persistent policy of socialist transformation for these areas. The central authority has been able to extend its socialist as well as Han influences through the Communist Party cadres and their auxiliary organizations, through an extensive program of training for youths from minority nationalities conducted at the Central Institute for National Minorities in Peking and its counterparts in various localities, through a large-scale "voluntary" migration of Han Chinese to these regions, and through assigning key posts in local administration to Han cadres.

As a result, the governing bodies of the autonomous regions are identical to those in regular administrative divisions. They are authorized to organize local public security forces, manage local finance, and enact local regulations but always subject to tight control by the central government. For example, local organs may "draw up statutes governing the exercise of autonomy or separate regulations suited to the political, economic, and cultural characteristics of the nationality or nationalities in a given area," but such statutes and regulations can be vetoed by the Standing Committee of the NPC.

The autonomy of the minority peoples meant, at least until the mid-1960s, the right to uphold their own customs and to use their own language instead of the Chinese language. During the Cultural Revolution, however, all manifestations of old customs in these autonomous areas were labeled as localism and feudal vestige, and the communist efforts to bring Mao Tse-tung Thought to the non-Han people were accentuated.

THE BUREAUCRATIC SYSTEM

The Chinese Communist bureaucracy performed in 1971 much the same functions as before the mid-1960s, despite extensive disruptions brought on by Red Guard activities. Many government officials of all cadres had been publicly vilified, humiliated, and sometimes beaten for their alleged revisionist sins or for lack of fidelity to Chairman Mao. Although some had been rehabilitated, others had disappeared from the public scene altogether. From late 1968 on, still others were being reeducated at the so-called May 7 cadre schools as part of a massive Down to the Countryside movement.

The May 7 cadre schools, first established in 1968, took their name and inspiration from Mao Tse-tung's directive dated May 7, 1966, in which he outlined a scheme for transforming state and Party cadres, soldiers, students, workers, peasants, technicians, intellectuals, and traders into a new generation of experts in agriculture, industry, politics, and administrative and military affairs. For the bureaucracy, the cadre school idea took on added importance in October 1968, when Mao was said to have issued a "supreme directive," urging state cadres to take part in the schools set up in the countryside.

According to the Communist Party, the purpose of this cadre training method, first instituted in 1957, is to heighten the revolutionary consciousness of those in authority, to narrow the traditional psychological distance that existed between the authorities and the people, and to propagate Mao's saying that "the cadres of our Party and State are ordinary workers and not overlords sitting on the backs of the people."

In the first few years after the communist seizure of power, the bureaucracy expanded manyfold because of multiplying social, economic, and political activities of the new regime. Loyal supporters, old and new, of the communist government were rewarded with official positions, often without adequate screening. Indiscriminate hirings boosted the number of state employees from 720,000 in October 1949 to 3,310,000 by September 1952, most of them being peasants. A limited number of "retained cadres" from the KMT bureaucracy were also employed. These employees included those working in state organs and enterprises but not those in cooperatives, military units, the Party, and mass organizations. By 1958 the number had risen to 7,920,000. The number of state employees has not been officially released since 1959.

With the initiation of the first five-year plan in 1953, there was the growing need for qualified administrators, scientists, technicians, engineers, teachers, and managers for many types of specialized work, but selective hiring was still not possible because of the shortage of educated middle school or college graduates. Many inadequately schooled personnel had to be given intensive administrative and technical training in hastily set up cadres schools to fill the urgent personnel requirements. By 1955, however, the pressure for quality recruitment had eased considerably because young cadres could be drawn from among recent secondary school and college graduates. With passage of time, these young cadres gradually replaced many of those who had joined the public service before 1953.

A key feature of state cadre training was political indoctrination, designed to familiarize cadres with the doctrine of Marxism-Leninism, Mao Tse-tung Thought, and the program and policies of the Party. Weekly study classes, symposia, and discussion groups organized by local propaganda units of the Party in various functional organizations and at all administrative levels served as a major means of raising the political awareness of these trainees.

Another standard practice, especially after 1957, was the government policy of transferring central state cadres to the countryside on either a permanent or a temporary basis. The objectives of this policy, among other things, were: to strengthen leadership at local levels; to help eliminate the traditional gap between urban and rural areas; to educate or reeducate cadres through physical labor in rural Communes; and, sometimes, to punish errant cadres.

As officially defined in 1958, state cadres (*kuo chia kan pu*) were those public employees from the clerical level and above, including generalists in government and Party organs (excluding the armed forces and mass organizations) and technical personnel in industry, agriculture, maritime transport, science, the news media, and publishing houses. Teachers, medical personnel of middle rank and above, translators, and artists were also called cadres. State employees working at the Commune, production brigade, and production team levels were usually referred to as local cadres (*ti fang kan pu*).

The cadre system was ranked, as announced in 1955, into twenty-six grades: state and Party cadres were assigned ranks from grades one to twenty-six, as were judicial personnel in courts and procuratorates. Technicians and engineers were graded into seventeen classes. General service personnel, such as messengers and janitors, ranked from twenty-seven to thirty, were not called cadres. Cadre rankings automatically indicated great differentials in prestige, status, and salaries.

The assignment of ranks and positions in state and Party organs, depended on, in order of importance, seniority in the Party hierarchy; loyalty to the Party and Mao Tse-tung; expertise; discipline; suggestions, innovations, and inventions contributing to national welfare; and actions protecting state property. The highest cadre ranks were reserved usually for persons of long revolutionary history, such as the Long March (see Glossary) cadres, who joined the Communist Party before 1934 and had survived the ordeals of this epic event. Less prestigious cadres were those who joined the Party after the completion of the Long March but before the early 1940s and those non-KMT elements who joined the Party in the post-1945 civil war struggle.

Personnel management was under the dual responsibility of the General Personnel Bureau of the Ministry of Internal Affairs and departments of the Party Central Committee. In the mid-1960s the ministry handled lower ranking cadres in matters of appointment, promotion, transfers, and dismissals; the Party departments controlled middle and higher level cadres.

SOURCES OF POLITICAL VALUES

Dominant political values in the country are derived, for the most part, from the ideological system combining Marxism-Leninism and Maoism but to an extent also from China's own historical heritage.

Since the early 1960s Maoism, or Mao Tse-tung Thought, as Communist Chinese propagandists describe it, has become increasingly important as the guiding code of thinking and behavior for all occasions; this phenomenon has been particularly noticeable since the mid-1960s.

Before the nineteenth century the Chinese took for granted that their cultural achievement was the highest in the world, but the impact of the West after the opium wars precipitated an unprecedented crisis of confidence in their own system of beliefs and institutions (see ch. 3, Historical Setting). Although many conservative scholar-officials continued to cling to the self-conception of China's being the center of the universe and to the old ways of life, some began to modernize their country by combining the best of both traditional China and the modern West, especially in science and technology. Others began advocating that nothing short of fundamental change would accomplish the task of building a modern and powerful China and that the Confucian system of sociopolitical ethics and practices had to be totally repudiated.

This demand for a new China was a direct reaction to the weaknesses of Chinese society. A growing number of students, youths, and intellectuals realized the urgency of building a strong and stable national government to bind together a divided people and to withstand the encroachment of foreign influence. Their immediate problems were to acquire an organized political-military power as an instrument of national unification, to convert a sprawling agrarian society into a modern industrial power, to undertake sweeping social reforms, and to bring the country into the family of nations as a sovereign and equal member.

The KMT government sought to find the answers to these problems. Its inability to find successful solutions, despite significant progress, was not entirely of its own making because the Japanese invasion and World War II thrust China further into chaos. The resulting cultural, spiritual, economic, and political dislocations had the most unsettling effect upon the attitude of many Chinese intellectuals, who in a desperate search for order, unity, and discipline became susceptible to all forms of ideology that seemed to promise a total solution.

The first modern foreign ideology ever to take root in China, communism was introduced to the country shortly after the Bolshevik Revolution of 1917; it had gained, by the early 1920s, a limited number of converts from among middle-class Chinese youths who, first as Nationalists, saw in Marxist-Leninist doctrines a vision of a powerful intellectual force to stimulate a new way of thinking about the future of China. These adherents grew in number only slowly, however, because communism was scarcely congenial to the Chinese family system and because the KMT government was determined to wipe out communism by force of arms. It was not until after World War II, when the KMT defeat appeared certain to most people, that the Communist Party was able to draw broad popular support. Even then, for fear of alienating Nationalists, the Party continued to emphasize the importance of all progressive and nationalist elements participating in the Chinese "people's democratic dictatorship."

Thus at the time of takeover in 1949, the operating values of the communist regime derived from nationalism, Marxism, Leninism, Stalinism, and Maoism. As the Communists gradually consolidated their power, nationalist themes decreased, albeit still a potent force. References to Stalinism decreased sharply after 1956 when the Communist Party of the Soviet Union launched its de-Stalinization campaign.

In general, the post-1949 system of ideology was similar in some respects, but dissimilar in others, to Confucianism, the orthodox state ideology in imperial China. Both systems are highly authoritarian, prompting some Sinologists to express the view that popular acceptance of, or acquiescence in, communism was aided by the Confucian, autocratic political culture that placed high value on conformity with orthodoxy, occasional deification of emperors, and recruitment of ruling elite based on mastery of doctrinal texts.

Harmony and struggle are two of the more conspicuous features that separate the two ideologies. Whereas Confucianism exalts social harmony, the status quo, and the compatibility of loyalty to both the state and the family, communism stresses conflict and change through class struggle, accepting the loyalty to the Party as the only legitimate form of political expression. Moreover, unlike the Confucian sociopolitical order, which recognized the five class distinctions according to functional categories of scholar-officials, peasants, artisans, merchants, and outcasts, communism preaches a single-class supremacy of the workers-peasants. Communism and Confucianism also differ sharply in that, unlike in traditional China, intellectual excellence in itself has little ideological value in mainland China, where the virtue of manual labor is placed above book learning.

IDEOLOGY AND STATE

The PRC is a state in which ideology—or the way and content of thinking unique to a group or class, as the term is commonly defined —plays a key political role. In this society the whole range of human activities and thinking processes is defined, explained, and rationalized in the language of Marxism-Leninism as interpreted by Mao and of Mao Tse-tung Thought. Endowed with the sanctity of an unchallenged truth, these schools of thought constitute the basis, as well as substance, of political values and are buttressed by the fullest extent of coercive powers inherent in a sovereign political system. Few in China are able to ignore the all-pervasive influence of ideology.

Propagation of ideology is thus a premier function of the Communist Party acting on behalf of the state. Party and state organs, schools, armed forces, mass organizations, and production units are all mobilized and used in the Party efforts to create a new "rational man" or "Maoist man." These efforts are regarded as a continuous process to be accentuated by ideological remolding or "rectification" campaigns that were started first in 1942 and were repeated in later years, the turbulence of the Cultural Revolution in the 1966–69 period being the latest example.

Ideology has performed various functions in mainland China. It has given the founders of the Chinese Communist movement a sense of common purpose and a common world view, which has had as its aim the substitution of a classless, proletarian-dominated society for the Confucian way of life. The Chinese leaders accepted the idea, as a matter of religious faith, that a myriad of old and new problems could be resolved only through a radically different, total approach, drawing their intellectual strength from the doctrinal certainty of dialectical conception of history. They took the view that the era of imperialism would inevitably be replaced by the era of socialism but then only through relentless class struggle tempered by the recognition of the primacy of human will as a determining force in revolutionary processes.

The Marxist conception of class struggle as a major motivating and determining force of human drama has tended to produce an aggressive frame of mind. In China this tendency was reinforced by the experience of the Communist Party, which was forced to fight against formidable odds in its early years. Compromises and reconciliations were to be accepted only as a last resort, as a tactical expediency designed to gain two steps forward by one step backward.

The infallibility of Party leadership has been another feature of the Chinese Communist ideology. It has encouraged the notion that devout and unquestioning acceptance of Party authority and spontaneous participation in the Party movement would help to impel the people toward the height of communist virtue, that is, the selfless man motivated only by the desire to work for the good of collectivity. Apart from serving as a basis of a political value that stresses total commitment to the Party and its leader, Maoist ideology has given the people personal assurance of security; this assurance has been especially meaningful in a society such as mainland China where tensions and mutual vigilance are deliberately engendered as a policy of the state in order to prevent the population from becoming indolent.

Efforts to sweeten personal sacrifice constantly demanded by the Party have also been undertaken through ideological exhortations. The people have been promised that hard work and self-denial will be rewarded abundantly. Thus the extolling of the so-called revolutionary optimism has been a means of reassuring that perseverance in adversity will be richly rewarded in later years.

The rhetoric of Marxism-Leninism-Maoism has been the single most important medium of communication between the authorities and the people. The Party and government cadres convey their intentions and policies in Marxist-Leninist-Maoist idioms both to elicit desired popular responses and to ensure uniformity of thinking and behavior. Communication occurs by means of intensive study sessions, self-criticism, and mutual criticism sessions. Ideology has thus served at the same time as ends and means in the Party's massive undertakings designed to create an exclusive, self-contained world of ideas in which total allegiance would be focused on the Party and its leader. As a parallel process, it has been the Party's policy to root out all manifestations of old-fashioned family loyalty (see ch. 5, Social System and Values).

Legitimizing communist rule has been another key function of ideology. The authority of the state as wielded by the Party has been rationalized as a logical consequence of the spontaneously expressed will of the people. According to Party propagandists, every phase of Party and government policies is projected as promoting the interests of the working class. The people are encouraged to believe that they are actually participating in the political process through the operation of democratic centralism, meaning the combination of mass political involvement and the centralized Party leadership. A logical corollary of this legitimizing function has been the determination of the Party and government to conceal failure or discontinuity of a given policy and to emphasize only the positive.

MAO TSE-TUNG THOUGHT

Mao Tse-tung Thought (Mao Tse-tung szu hsiang) takes its basic ideas from Marxist, Leninist, and Stalinist categories but is restated to account for Mao's own contributions in light of China's revolutionary experiences. The difference between Mao's thought and its foreign prototypes is apparent more in the method and form of applying Marxist and Leninist revolutionary prescriptions than in substance on dialectical and materialistic assumptions relating to history, class struggle, proletarian dictatorship, and imperialism.

Principal Themes

The primary expression of Mao's thought is found in the four-volume *Selected Works of Mao Tse-tung* (the first three volumes appeared in Chinese in the 1951–53 period; the last, in 1960), which presents in chronological sequence most of his essays and speeches dating back to the 1920s. Mao's political ideas also appear in an abridged form known as *Quotations from Chairman Mao* (also called Little Red Book), which was published first in 1964, initially for circulation within the PLA and later reissued in 1965 and 1966. In his foreword to the 1966 edition, Lin Piao states, "Once Mao Tse-tung's thought is grasped by the broad masses, it becomes an inexhaustible source of strength and a spiritual atom bomb of infinite power."

The evolution of Mao's thought corresponds closely to the development of the Chinese Communist movement. Since Mao considered Chinese situations to be different from those of the Soviet Union, he stressed the need for creatively applying Marxist-Leninist doctrines to his own country. In calling for the "Sinification of Marxism" as early as 1938, Mao stated:

> What we call concrete Marxism is Marxism that has taken on a national form, that is, Marxism applied to the concrete struggle in the concrete conditions prevailing in China, and not Marxism abstractly used. ... Consequently, the Sinification of Marxism ... becomes a problem that must be understood and solved by the whole Party without delay. ... There must be less repeating of empty and abstract phrases; we must discard our dogmatism and replace it by a new and vital Chinese style and manner.

In official publications, and especially in those intended for glorification, of Mao as "the greatest Marxist-Leninist of our era," the most frequently cited works of Mao are, with some exceptions, those published before the 1949 takeover. Among these are: *A Single Spark Can Start A Prairie Fire* (1930); *Strategic Problems of China's Revolutionary War* (1936); *On Practice* (1937); *On Contradiction* (1937); *On Protracted War* (1938); *The Role of the Chinese Communist Party in the National War* (1938); *The Chinese Revolution and the Chinese Communist Party* (1938); *On the New Democracy* (1940); *Talks at the Yenan Forum on Literature and Art* (1942); *The Foolish Old Man Who Removed the Mountains* (1945); *On Coalition Government* (1945); and *On the People's Democratic Dictatorship* (1949). Most frequently mentioned post-1949 works include: *The Socialist Upsurge in China's Countryside* (1955); and *On the Correct Handling of Contradictions Among the People* (1957).

Major themes that thread Mao's writings are: a new and powerful China, anti-Japanese armed struggles, revolutionary heroism, frugality, self-reliance, the centrality of man in history, the supremacy of spirit over material forces, disdain for leisure, the infallibility of Party leadership, uninterrupted revolution, antagonistic and nonantagonistic forms of contradictions in class relationships, and the perfectibility of ideology through rectification.

The Cult of Mao

The deification of Mao's thought and his person was not a major preoccupation of the regime until the early 1960s. It may be noted that Mao was admired and praised for more than two decades within the Party as the object of highest national esteem. Already in the mid-1930s, when the Chinese Communists completed their legendary Long March, Party cadres were chanting, "The East is Red, the sun rises. China has brought forth a Mao Tse-tung." In 1942 the cult of Mao was set in motion, but the level of adulation in Yenan days scarcely bore any resemblance to the rising crescendo of official acclamations about him after the mid-1960s. The Party Constitution of 1945 stated that, "the Chinese Communist Party follows the Thought of Mao Tse-tung, the thought that unites the theory of Marxism-Leninism with the experience of the Chinese revolution"; this statement, however, was omitted in the Party Constitution of 1956, which, taking its cue from Soviet Premier Nikita Khrushchev's antipersonality campaign launched early in that year, instead called on the Party to make decisions by collective leadership and not "by any individual."

According to evidence that emerged during the height of the Cultural Revolution, the crisis of leadership precipitated by the failure of the People's Communes and the Great Leap in the 1958–60 period impelled the drive to glorify Mao for fear that otherwise the authority of the Party and government might be questioned and weakened (see ch. 10, Political Dynamics; ch. 14, Agriculture). For the first time, after he established himself as undisputed Party leader in 1935, Mao was confronted with internal questioning of his domestic policies and leadership style. Mao was known to have been criticized by opponents for his reckless "guerrilla methods" of economic development. Humiliated, Mao was forced to give up his chairmanship of the state to Liu Shao-ch'i in 1959; his retreat in the 1960–61 period was accompanied by a relaxation of the drive for ideological indoctrination, the return of private plots to peasants, and a liberalized policy on art and literature (see ch. 10, Political Dynamics). As it turned out, however, the retreat was a calculated expediency designed to recoup his forces. In 1962 Mao initiated a major indoctrination drive in the form of the Socialist Education movement (see ch. 8, Education, Intellectual Expression, and the Arts).

At the forefront of this drive was the PLA. In 1963 army cadres were placed in commercial and industrial enterprises to strengthen the work of studying Mao's thought, and in early 1964 the so-called "Learn from the PLA" movement was officially launched. *Quotations from Chairman Mao* was first published in May 1964 to coincide with the opening in the following month of yet another thought remolding campaign designed to "revolutionize" the youths.

Mao Tse-tung Thought was given its highest, almost fanatical expression of praise in the 1966–69 period as the people's "food, weapon, and compass." Mao's being "the Red sun in our hearts" and "the never-setting sun" became an everyday exclamation; his birthplace in Hunan came to be worshiped as "the place where the

Red sun rose." The people were told not to serve meals without reverence to Mao or go to bed without evening reverence.

Mao's revolutionary past was recreated, reinterpreted, and transmuted, in the words of a Western scholar, into "a psychodrama of heroic triumph, of epochal swims across great rivers, of fierce struggle against authority, of celebration of the eternal victories of the past. ..." The infinite complexity of all historical and contemporary circumstances was reduced to a few emotionally appealing slogans. Abstract doctrinal discourse was not encouraged unless it was presented in such a way as to confer mystical virtues and powers on Mao's thought. Many Party theoreticians came under attack and were purged for not having correctly followed or interpreted Mao's thinking. Theoretical writings ceased to be published without prior clearance from the PLA. In August 1970 the Hong Kong-based *China News Analysis* commented: "Today Marxism is the Marxism of the barracks. There is no longer a single Marxist scholar in evidence" in China.

There were certain aspects of Maoism that were especially magnified during the Cultural Revolution. The frenzied adulation leveled off considerably after 1970, but these tenets remained very much in evidence as operating political values of the post-Cultural Revolution years.

Foremost among those tenets was the primary importance of putting "Politics in command" of everything, a slogan first popularized during the Great Leap; this emphasis was said to be in tune with Lenin's axiom, "Politics cannot but have precedence over economics." According to Mao-Lin apologists, politics was in effect Mao Tse-tung Thought synonymous with "spirit" or "soul," all of which were declared to be superior to all material things and thus the supreme motive force that energizes the material forces. Not to have a correct political view and attitude, it was insisted, was not to have a soul. With the right spirit colored by Mao's Red Thought, it was argued, the soldiers could fight well, the workers and peasants could produce more, technicians could design better machinery, and Party and state cadres could serve the people more effectively.

The virtuous man in Mao's China was supposed to possess many qualities—so many that it would be impossible for one man to display all or most of them. The first quality was always the active studying of Mao's "living ideas" (as opposed to ideas in books) and its application to reality. Others were willingness to accept hardships, emulation of the Red heroes of the PLA, and readiness to crush both internal and external enemies. According to the *Kiangsi Daily* of July 1969: "The Thought of Mao Tse-tung paints a man's thoughts red and makes him ready 'One, not to fear hardship, Two, not to fear death'. ... A man who has this knows nothing of insurmountable obstacles, invincible enemies. ... The revolutionary elan depends on the spirit of man. The power of the spirit can be seen particularly in extreme difficulties."

The idealized Maoist man was acclaimed as the decisive factor in revolution and in war, more powerful than any weapons of mass destruction. This kind of man was idolized as the living symbol of personal sacrifice, as one who would disdain material things, one who would consider demanding a wage increase to be morally evil and counterrevolutionary. A true Maoist man was supposed to make no distinction between manual and mental labor; he would voluntarily go down to the university of labor, or the countryside, to perform physical labor. According to Chinese exhortations, his highest purpose in life was to serve the collectivity and to struggle for the complete victory of communism at home and abroad.

The concept of "uninterrupted revolution" was also prominently stressed after the mid-1960s. It was predicated on Mao's assumption that class contradictions or conflicts would persist even in a socialist society and that proletarian dictatorship should therefore prevail indefinitely, or at least until the goal of communism was realized. Revolutionary vigilance against bourgeois and revisionist tendencies must not be relaxed under any circumstances during the period of transition to communism.

In May 1966 Mao was quoted in a Party Central Committee circular as saying, "Put destruction first, and in the process you have construction." Destruction was said to be criticism and repudiation; it meant revolution. The idea of destruction-construction formed the basis of Lin Piao's clarion call for launching the Red Guard rampage at a rally held in August 1966; it was at this rally that Mao's heir apparent called for a Four Olds movement—against old customs, old habits, old thinking, and old ideology (see ch. 10, Political Dynamics). The thrust of this iconoclastic drive was to eliminate tangible evidence of old things, ranging from old books and old art objects to old ways of dress and traditional weddings. Nothing was to be spared from this revolutionary antithesis against the old order, even against "those in authority." Suddenly few things were left sacrosanct any more. Among those publicly vilified was T'ien Han, who wrote words for the national anthem that was adopted in 1949 along with the Common Program; the anthem itself was repudiated by the Red Guards allegedly because it failed to reflect Mao's thought.

China's quest for undisputed leadership of the world proletarian revolution, as well as competition with the Soviet Union for doctrinal preeminence within the socialist commonwealth, also had a bearing on the way in which Mao's thought was related to the outside world (see ch. 11, Foreign Relations). In articulating Mao's concept of "People's War" in September 1965, Lin Piao put forth the strategy of encircling cities from the countryside, a legacy of the Chinese Communist guerrilla warfare that Mao and Lin now considered to have universal application. Likening the urban-rural dichotomy of China to the world, Lin Piao declared: "Taking the entire globe, if North America and Western Europe can be called 'the cities of the world' then Asia, Africa, and Latin America constitute the 'rural areas of the world'." He emphasized, however, that, although his country had the obligation to support revolutionary people's war wherever possible, the war itself had to be fought by the local people themselves without depending on outside assistance. This, he said, was the historical lesson of the Chinese revolution, a revolution accomplished through Mao's idea of self-reliance.

CHAPTER 10

POLITICAL DYNAMICS

Communist Chinese politics in 1971 was in a state of transition punctuated by uncertainty and anomaly. The Chinese Communist Party (CCP), its previously sacrosanct authority badly impaired by the political convulsion of the Great Proletarian Cultural Revolution from 1966 to 1969, was still recovering from this near fatal experience. In 1967 the CCP was, in effect, displaced from its customary position of political preeminence by the People's Liberation Army (PLA), the only cohesive public institution to emerge from the Cultural Revolution more or less unscathed by the violence of Red Guards (see Glossary). With the Party in disarray, the military establishment became the de facto caretaker government at both national and provincial level, controlling and exercising a wide range of political, administrative, and economic powers. The PLA's extramilitary involvement was so extensive that Mao Tse-tung's political principle that "the gun must never be allowed to command the Party" was all but meaningless.

National leaders of both radical and moderate persuasions continued to recognize the necessity of restoring domestic peace and of rebuilding, as quickly as was practicable, the organizational infrastructures that were dislocated during the Cultural Revolution. Nonetheless, they were embroiled in late 1971 in an intense yet subdued struggle evidently centered on the question of under whose direction and in what way this stabilization should be achieved.

On one side of the struggle was a group of radical leaders, or Maoists, who were deeply committed to the purification of the whole society through an uninterrupted process of politicization according to Mao Tse-tung Thought. To this group, stabilization was acceptable only when it was accentuated by a high level of political zeal and by the spontaneous popular demonstration of self-sacrifice, hard work, self-discipline, and devotion to the interest of collectivity. On the other side was a group of moderates that, while accepting the importance of extolling conflict and ideology as basic motivating forces of a revolutionary, was at least equally concerned with the importance of pragmatic and flexible approaches in solving a myriad of issues facing the nation. Given the integrative force of ideology in a communist society, the moderates were also amenable to Mao's scheme of "uninterrupted revolution," but only to the point where

261

any prearranged political ferment would not endanger established authority and external security (see ch. 9, Political System and Values).

After 1969 the moderate group, associated with Premier Chou En-lai, appeared to have won the first round of political struggle. Whether this group could sustain its momentum toward pragmatism at least through the mid-1970s was uncertain because of the still fluid post-Cultural Revolution situation marked in part by what seemed to be a succession crisis that began to unfold in September 1971. The immediate outcome of this crisis was difficult to foresee in part because of the circumstantiality of the evidence. A number of conflicting forces were at work, generated by the interplay of personality clashes, individual power ambitions, doctrinal differences, and most of all the division of national leaders into the radical and moderate factions with their conflicting loyalties.

The confrontation between the two groups was only the latest manifestation of policy differences dating back to the 1920s but especially to the circumstances surrounding the disastrous Great Leap Forward (see Glossary) of 1958–60. In fact, the underlying continuity of Communist Chinese political dynamics after the mid-1950s was the challenge-response pattern of interaction between the two intra-Party factions. Thus, whereas the Great Leap was the result of Mao's imposition of his overpowering personality on a reluctant Party bureaucracy, the politics from 1961 to the end of 1965 was dominated, except in Lin Piao's PLA, more by pragmatic bureaucrats with their preference for routine and tangible results than by Party ideologues whose main concern was to ensure popular adherence to Party lines and Mao's political thought. Then in 1966, Mao launched the Cultural Revolution in an attempt to prevent what he considered the ossification of China into the deadening routine of bureaucratism, to shock the Party bureaucrats out of their supposedly growing complacency, to revive the revolutionary spirit of the Yenan days, to train "revolutionary successors," and to reassert his full control of the Party bureaucracy by purging those who had taken exception to his brand of policies and leadership style.

Mao's revolt against the political system over which he in theory presided unleashed many forces, some latently divisive and others apparently unforeseen. It widened the longstanding chasm between the Maoists and their moderate adversaries, making reconciliation based on mutual trust, bargaining, and compromise more difficult, if not impossible. What remained of the Party was confronted with the crisis of authority: the mystique of its infallibility was shattered; and the symbol of political legitimacy as well as efficacy that the Party had represented for more than two decades were no longer exclusively identified.

262

The power vacuum left by the Party's difficulties could be quickly and effectively filled by the PLA, but it too was not impervious to divisive internal wranglings; some of its leaders became allied with the Maoist faction, whereas others supported the moderate group, and still others chose to remain unattached to either. Mao destroyed much of the old political order, which he had suspected was becoming infected with a Soviet-style bureaucratism, but he failed to offer workable substitutes. Moreover, the puritan revolutionary milieu that Mao had set out to create through the vehicle of the Cultural Revolution was not evident in the post-1969 years. Communist China in 1971, for all intents and practical purposes, was very much where it had been in the mid-1960s, still groping for the best possible mix of priorities and policies in attempting to solve the multiplying, diverse problems of managing the world's most populous society. It appeared to be in effect under even greater tensions and stresses than in 1966, most likely because there were fewer economic resources available on a per capita basis (see ch. 13, Character and Structure of the Economy).

Despite the limits and chaotic effects of the Cultural Revolution, Mao himself emerged from this deliberately produced crisis probably with enhanced personal prestige and influence both among the leadership and with the public. This seemingly paradoxical phenomenon could be attributed mainly to his vast hold on popular loyalty; his charismatic appeal to the masses of the people was powerful enough to withstand even the virtual collapse of the organizational basis of his political power, the Party. Although there was an apparent toning down of the adulation accorded him—reportedly at his own request—Mao remained unchallenged publicly in 1971. His leadership and the correctness of his "thought" continued to hold the country together, providing the limits for and the terms in which the power struggles in the country were carried on.

Nonetheless, the post-1969 politics was essentially a counterreaction to the frenzied rhetoric of Maoism that peaked during the Cultural Revolution. The nature of policymaking, for both domestic and external purposes, was far more moderate and pragmatic than that between 1966 and 1969. This trend apparently had Mao's personal, albeit reluctant, endorsement, but over the loud protests of his wife and her radical supporters.

POLITICAL DEVELOPMENTS FROM 1949 TO THE CULTURAL REVOLUTION

In an important document published on June 30, 1949, and entitled *On the People's Democratic Dictatorship*, Party leader Mao Tse-tung made it clear that the Chinese Communist regime, which was formally proclaimed on October 1, 1949, as the People's Republic of China (PRC), would follow, with significant modifications to fit Chinese conditions, the essentials of Stalin's formula for developing the Soviet Union: the fastest possible expansion of heavy industry (with Soviet, not Western, aid), socialization of agriculture to provide a suitable base for the industrialization program, and terror to the extent necessary to curb opposition. Mao stated, however, that 90 percent (the percentage was later announced as having increased to 95) of all Chinese accepted the "leadership" of the CCP and therefore qualified as "people," and only 10 percent (later, 5 percent) were enemies on whom an admitted "dictatorship" would have to be imposed (see ch. 5, Social System and Values). In spirit at least, this attitude that "those who are not against us are with us" constituted a significant modification of the more doctrinaire Stalinist model. The Party has not resorted to police terror on the scale that Stalin did, nor has it treated its own rural population as harshly as Stalin did during his collectivization campaign of 1929 to 1932.

In a relatively modest way at first, but with growing intensity, Mao's Thought, as embodied in such documents as *On the People's Democratic Dictatorship*, had become the official ideology of his Party since as early as 1942. It was also widely propagated as the official ideology of China, a major piece of invisible cement helping to hold the country together and confer legitimacy on the new regime. Mao's colleagues, accepting this trend as a necessary, if not entirely agreeable, one, were left later in a weak position to oppose the burgeoning "cult of personality" focused on Mao. Mao put himself in effect in a position from which he could appeal directly to public opinion when necessary against dissenters among his colleagues, when his usual approach of playing them against each other proved ineffective.

Initially the CCP benefited from, and made effective use of, a number of favorable political conditions. Through prolonged warfare it had established internal peace and unity in China for the first time in several decades—an achievement that evoked widespread public pride and support also because Mao restored self-respect to the people after a century of humiliation at the hands of foreign powers. Various regional strongmen or warlords had also been defeated or had accepted the leadership of the new regime. Real or suspected opposition, notably pro-Kuomintang (KMT) elements and the rural landlord class, was virtually eliminated, although not always physically. In the course of the 1950–52 land reform campaign and the 1951–52 campaign against counterrevolutionaries, between 750,000 and 2.8 million persons were reportedly executed.

A noteworthy feature of the land reform drive was the manipulation of the peasantry in attacking the landlord system. This method helped the Party avoid the onus of direct responsibility for its repressive measures against the "nonpeople" and, in fact, helped to create the impression of mass spontaneity.

Along with these blows at the internal enemy went major "democratic" reforms, for example, under the Agrarian Reform Law of June 28, 1950, and the Marriage Law of 1950 (see ch. 3, Historical Setting; ch. 6, Family). Moreover, in efforts to facilitate the intensive mobilization and control of the people under the Chinese Communist political principle of the "mass line" ("from the masses, to the masses"), practically everyone was enrolled in one form or another of mass organization, such as peasant associations, labor unions, youth groups, and women's groups, formed and led by Party cadres (see Glossary).

In the urban sector Chinese Communist controls were as real as in the countryside but were somewhat mitigated by a recognition of the need to secure the cooperation of specialists, such as businessmen and intellectuals, who had served under the preceding regime. These were still expected to show loyalty to the new order, and those who were suspect were frequently subjected to varying degrees of "thought reform" (brainwashing), usually ending in the signing of humiliating "confessions."

Because the Party came to power after a prolonged civil war, its armed forces played an important though diminishing political role in the early years. Although the government and the Party leadership—both presided over by Mao Tse-tung—were the most effective control authority that China had known for perhaps a century and a half, there also existed six regional governments, only one (North China) of which was completely controlled from Peking. In addition, there was a powerful regional bureau of the CCP Central Committee for each of these and, except in Northeast and North China, there were powerful corresponding regional military commands known as field armies.

This decentralized power structure not only posed a threat to central control but also tended to impede centralized economic planning and military modernization—both of which got underway in earnest, and with extensive Soviet aid, when the Korean conflict ended in 1953. The abolition of the regional machines was hastened and facilitated by a sharp but brief crisis within the Party leadership at the beginning of 1954, centering on Kao Kang, the head of the Northeast (Manchurian) regional organization. Kao apparently made an attempt at that time to make himself Mao's principal deputy by means that were extraneous to the Party constitution, at a time when Mao was seriously ill. Kao's purging, in the spring of 1954, coincided approximately with the abolition of all three types of regional power, so that the center at that time had direct contact with and control over the provinces.

In 1955 Mao was confronted with a serious politicoeconomic problem because of rural tensions stemming from the agricultural socialization campaign launched in 1953, floods in the Yangtze River valley, and the resulting food shortages in the cities. The Party leadership was divided over the best means of handling this problem. The majority favored moderating the projected rate of agricultural socialization, and this principle was embodied in the First Five Year Plan when it was finally published in July 1955. Mao, on the contrary, opted for an acceleration of the rate. He prevailed by the irregular method (that is, against the CCP's own principle under which the minority is required to abide by the decision of the majority) of taking his case personally to the propaganda apparatus of the Party, over which he nearly always managed to maintain close control, and to an ad hoc conference of secretaries of provincial Party committees. As a result agriculture was almost completely socialized between the fall of 1955 and the end of 1956, and similar measures of socialization were introduced in the fields of handicrafts and private business (see ch. 14, Agriculture). The episode was important not only because of its revolutionary impact on the country but also as a precedent for later, even more drastic, efforts by Mao to impose his will on an indifferent or even adverse Party leadership.

Tensions among the elite thus created were sharpened by Nikita Khrushchev's denunciation of Stalin at the Twentieth Congress of the Communist Party of the Soviet Union (CPSU) in February 1956. Some of Mao's more moderate colleagues, even while agreeing with him in criticizing some aspects of Khrushchev's performance, apparently saw it as an opportunity to curb Communist China's own version of the cult of personality centered on Mao. Meanwhile, through a series of initiatives, Mao himself set out to reaffirm his creativity and prove his innocence of the charge of having promoted a cult of personality. These initiatives included an unsuccessful proposal in April 1956 for a two-thirds cut in the Party and state bureaucracies and, in the following month, the implementation of the famous Hundred Flowers Campaign (see Glossary), which, despite the reservations of Mao's more cautious colleagues, encouraged free discussion of public issues but within certain limits and was implemented directly through the Party propaganda apparatus.

Despite his efforts, Mao appears to have been on the political defensive at the Eighth Party Congress in September 1956. All references to him and his "thought" were removed from the Party constitution, and a number of new features were introduced into the Party charter that tended to work against Mao. For one thing, he was deprived of effective control over the important Central Secretariat, which came under the direction of General Secretary (a newly created title) Teng Hsiao-p'ing. On the other hand, the Party constitution created a new top policymaking body, the Standing Committee of the Politburo (Political Bureau—see Glossary), and Mao was promptly elected its chairman.

In February 1957 the Hundred Flowers Campaign was stepped up, partly as a result of the Hungarian revolt in October and November 1956. It seemed advisable to create a safety valve in Communist China to avoid a possible similar outburst. Moreover, Mao was apparently eager to prove both the superiority of his own creativity as compared with most of his colleagues and the allegedly superior popular support his regime enjoyed as compared with that of the Soviet Union. Unexpectedly for both Mao and his colleagues, once free public discussion began at last in May 1957, it promptly erupted in a barrage of criticisms of nearly all aspects of the system of CCP dictatorship. The campaign was abruptly terminated at the end of May and was transformed into a campaign designed to stamp out principal critics, or "rightists," as the Party labeled them. The entire leadership was shaken by this episode, but the shock was especially severe for Mao, who had been the main promoter of the idea of free public discussion.

Mao's situation was complicated further in 1957 when long-term Soviet industrial credits ran out. For reasons having to do mainly with the need to assert freedom of action with respect to Moscow, Mao, supported by most of his colleagues, had to chart a new strategy of economic development—one that was to rely more on using indigenous resources and methods than Soviet credits and the Soviet economic model. Party leaders agreed that this strategy, supplemented by whatever Soviet aid might be available on a current, as opposed to long-term, basis, should make it possible for Communist China to catch up with Great Britain in fifteen years in the output of major industrial products. In agriculture the size of cooperative farms would be reduced, and large numbers of local light industrial enterprises would be started.

During the winter of 1957–58 Mao's mood grew increasingly radical, not only because of confidence and optimism stemming from the Party's success in a massive mobilization of peasant labor for public works conducted at that time but also because of differing Sino-Soviet perspectives on international situations (see ch. 11, Foreign Relations). In early 1958 the Party began to speak of the Great Leap, which was officially proclaimed in May 1958, but not before a number of reluctant Party officials were purged in many of the provinces (see ch. 3, Historical Setting; ch. 14, Agriculture).

In August 1958 the Party leadership proclaimed as a general model for rural Communist China the People's Commune (see Glossary), which had already become widespread since the previous spring (see ch. 14, Agriculture). The announcement was apparently timed to take advantage of the tense atmosphere created by the Peking-initiated crisis in the Formosa Strait, which made it easier for the regime to mobilize popular support. Communist Chinese propaganda at that time clearly implied that Communist China was "building communism" like the Soviet Union and not merely "building socialism" and that by virtue of its superior leadership and policies it was ahead of the Soviet Union. There was a further implication that Communist China had found the key to rapid development of all agrarian societies.

The Great Leap soon ran into difficulties. Production statistics were consciously inflated, on the theory that accuracy mattered less than political effect, and resulted in extravagant claims. Much of the population, especially the peasantry, was worked virtually to the point of exhaustion. Disruption of agricultural activity and transport produced food shortages in the cities. Beginning in October 1958 the leadership responded by modifying the worst excesses of the Great Leap, such as the "backyard furnaces," most of which were closed down. Demands for labor were moderated.

The modified version of the Great Leap appears to have been backed by a virtual consensus of the Party leadership, except for Minister of National Defense P'eng Te-huai. P'eng, who was already in trouble with Mao because of his opposition to the original version of the Great Leap, strongly argued that the Great Leap had adverse effects on the country's long-term economic development, on the PLA's morale and efficiency, and on the outlook for Soviet military aid and the Soviet nuclear shield. With at least a degree of Soviet support, he demanded at the Party Central Committee Plenary Session held in August 1959 an abandonment of the Great Leap and even challenged Mao's fitness to continue leading the Party. There was, however, a virtual closing of ranks against P'eng, and he was outvoted and purged with little difficulty. He was succeeded as defense minister by Mao's military favorite and P'eng's rival, Lin Piao (see ch. 21, The Armed Forces).

In 1960 the modified version of the Great Leap met with near disaster. For purely political reasons connected with the growing Sino-Soviet dispute, Khrushchev canceled all industrial aid in the summer and recalled its technicians and advisers. Also, the 1960 harvest was a poor one, in some considerable part because of bad weather but largely stemming from the effects of the Great Leap; the regime, however, preferred to blame errors by local cadres, bad weather, and Soviet betrayal (see ch. 14, Agriculture). By the first months of 1961 the Great Leap for all practical purposes had been brought to an end. Relatively, Mao retired into the background where domestic economic policy was concerned, while Liu Shao-ch'i and other Party leaders sought economic recovery through retrenchment, restoration of material incentives, and limited relaxation of the Party's centralized control. The regional bureaus of the Party, which had been abolished in 1953 and 1954, were revived to supervise the implementation of the new program and soon acquired considerable power and autonomy. After about two years of stringency and near famine, a good winter wheat harvest in early 1962 showed that the bottom of the crisis, China's worst from 1949 to 1971, had been rounded.

At that point a debate broke out between Mao and Liu, each backed by his own supporters, as to the best course. Liu contended that the moderate policies that had just proved so successful should essentially be continued (in fact, they were continued until 1966, since the Party apparatus sympathetic to Liu retained effective control over domestic policy, especially its crucial economic component). Mao, on the other hand, maintained that the prolonged downgrading of the Great Leap could be justified only as a last resort because of its stifling impact on the revolutionary spirit in Communist China and thus urged a return to something like the original version of the Great Leap. He was unable to carry a majority of his comrades with him on this, but at about the time of a Central Committee Plenary Session held in September 1962 he was able to get agreement to a less extreme measure, a "socialist education movement" to be conducted in the rural areas, initially among the Party cadres and subsequently among the peasants. The movement had relatively little impact on the rural areas and served only to widen the rift between Mao and Liu (see ch. 3, Historical Setting).

Of greater practical importance was a successful effort begun in 1963 by Mao and Lin Piao to place military personnel—some active and some recently demobilized, but all presumably loyal to Mao and Lin Piao—in various civilian agencies, notably economic enterprises, and to build around them political departments modeled on those in the PLA. This effort was expanded in 1964 in the form of a "learn from the PLA" campaign for the whole country and another to train a generation of "revolutionary successors" from among the youth (see ch. 21, The Armed Forces). Mao could hardly have failed to conclude that he stood a better chance of attaining his revolutionary political goals through working with the army than through working with the Party apparatus, if only a suitable format for doing so could be devised.

THE CULTURAL REVOLUTION

For the outside world the chaos precipitated by the Cultural Revolution beginning in 1966 helped to shed new light on the little-known world of Mao's political preferences and prejudices. Various accusations leveled by Mao and his supporters in the course of that revolution indicated that, by 1965, Mao had been increasingly concerned over the direction of events in his country. Mao had concluded, for example, that the Communist Chinese revolution was in danger of losing momentum and that some of his closest associates,

Liu in particular, had become infected with a Soviet-style "revisionist" (see Glossary) tendency to emphasize "bureaucratism," status, and material incentives. He also concluded that the revisionist infection would spread rapidly unless firmly checked. Mao thought that the current generation of youth was insufficiently motivated and needed to be given a kind of synthetic revolutionary experience, as similar as possible to the pre-1949 one that his generation had undergone, if the future of Chinese revolution as he envisioned it were to be safeguarded.

By 1965 Mao had also concluded, with considerable justification, that he had been deprived of much of his power, especially over domestic policy, by Liu and other relatively moderate colleagues in the Party's central apparatus; his suspicion that Liu and others had been actively conspiring against him, as reflected in charges made to this effect during the Cultural Revolution, appears to have been without foundation, however. Moreover, Mao had apparently taken exception to a number of allegorical criticisms, some of them in published form by noted literary figures, that had been leveled at him since 1961 for the failure of the Great Leap and his treatment of P'eng; he was determined to refute and punish his critics and vindicate his own record as a revolutionary statesman. Fragmentary evidence also indicated that since about 1962 Chiang Ch'ing, Mao's wife, had exerted an increasingly radicalizing influence on the Party leader not only in cultural affairs (for instance, the politicization of Peking opera) but also in politics (see ch. 8, Education, Intellectual Expression, and the Arts). Evidently, Liu objected to Chiang Ch'ing's political involvement, and she in turn resented his attitude; her long-felt animosity toward Liu's attractive wife, Wang Kuang-mei, was further aroused as a result.

Mao's attempt to change the direction of events in Communist China was probably delayed until 1966 because of the escalation of the conflict in Vietnam in 1965 and the resulting necessity for the leadership to devote a large share of its time and energy to external affairs. Thus during 1965 the Party leadership had to address itself to a major strategic question involving Vietnam. In this debate some individuals, notably Chief of Staff Lo Jui-ch'ing, argued for the desirability of more direct support for Hanoi but stressed at the same time not only the need to be prepared against the possibility of United States strategic attack on Communist China but also the desirability of a limited rapprochement with the other nuclear superpower, the Soviet Union. Consequently, Lo and others opposed, as did like-minded officers before P'eng Te-huai's dismissal in 1959, Mao's and Lin Piao's program of further politicizing the PLA at the expense of combat training as inappropriate to a time of crisis (see ch. 21, The Armed Forces). Lo's view was overridden by a dominant school led by Mao and Lin Piao that successfully argued for merely indirect support for Hanoi, minimized the likelihood of an American attack, and ruled out the possibility of a Sino-Soviet rapprochement. Lin Piao insisted that if an American attack occurred it would take the form of an invasion and could be dealt with by the standard Maoist strategy of guerrilla warfare, or "people's war."

As events unfolded, the crisis in and over Vietnam proved to be an opportune external diversion (as long as Communist China did not become directly involved), which permitted Mao to press ahead with his political plans. At a Party conference held in September and October 1965 he demanded, over the reservations especially of Politburo member P'eng Chen, the launching of the Cultural Revolution in literary and academic circles. This was a highly controversial demand because P'eng Chen, mayor of Peking and the powerful boss of the Party's Peking municipal committee, had close ties with and acted as a patron of many leading Party figures. The result was a compromise amounting to a watered-down version of what Mao had sought, yet something that senior Party leaders thought would be acceptable to Mao. Mao, dissatisfied, retreated in November for six months to the Yangtze River valley, where he waited for P'eng Chen to make a misstep. Meanwhile, Mao began to line up political support for a counteroffensive and to publish propaganda attacks on some of his critics in the literary world.

Of the crucial seven-man Standing Committee of the Politburo, Mao probably had little trouble in getting at least the conditional support of Chou En-lai, who resented the efforts of the Party ideologues to influence his State Council.

Lin Piao, on the other hand, appeared to have had some initial reservations because of the crisis in Vietnam, but in April 1966, when the chances of a Sino-American clash over Vietnam had seemed remote, his *Liberation Army Daily* began to increase its level of support for the Cultural Revolution. For purposes of domestic political mobilization, however, Mao and his supporters tried to maintain the image of a Sino-American war, or even a third world war, as possibly imminent. Mao's May 7, 1966, directive to Lin Piao (unpublished at that time) instructed him to make the PLA a "great school" for politics, military affairs, and agriculture, on the grounds that such a step was necessitated by the danger of war (see ch. 21, The Armed Forces). By implication Lin Piao was to make the PLA a major, if not the only, locomotive of the Cultural Revolution. Since this directive conveys the spirit of the Cultural Revolution perhaps more than does any other single document, the fact that it is addressed to Lin Piao suggests that by that time Mao had gone far toward choosing Lin Piao as his successor. Indeed, such a choice may have been the price for Lin Piao's wholehearted support for the Cultural Revolution. General Secretary Teng Hsiao-p'ing, very likely motivated by personal rivalry with his fellow secretariat member P'eng Chen, appears to have been won over in early May 1966.

With his plans complete and a kind of personal staff created to direct the Cultural Revolution, Chiang Ch'ing being one of its most influential members, Mao returned to Peking in mid-May 1966. He purged P'eng Chen, probably with the aid of some threat of military force, and installed a more compliant municipal leadership in Peking. At that time units of Red Guards began to emerge on high school and college campuses in Peking and soon afterward in other cities.

Mao's idea was to use the most exploitable elements of the youth as the major instrument for promoting the Cultural Revolution and for establishing a direct link between himself and the masses. This move was not warmly received by Liu and Teng since it smacked strongly of the cult of Mao and worse still of "spontaneity," a bugbear of orthodox Leninists for many decades. Seeing this basic conflict of views, Mao again retired, in early June 1966, to the Yangtze River valley, leaving Liu and Teng to cope with the rising Red Guards and probably to fall into a political trap in the process. This did indeed happen, since work teams of cadres sent by the regular Party apparatus leadership had serious controversies with the emerging and obstreperous Red Guards, whose role was facilitated by a suspension of regular educational activities from June 1966.

Meanwhile, both Mao and Liu (who with his supporters can from this point be termed the opposition) began preparing for a forthcoming session of the Party Central Committee, where the future of the Cultural Revolution and of the Red Guards in particular would be thrashed out. Mao enjoyed the advantages not only of the support of Lin Piao and the mainstream of the army leadership and Chou En-lai but also of control over the Party's reconstituted propaganda machine, which he purged repeatedly to ensure support at each stage of the Cultural Revolution. In late July 1966, after a much-publicized swim in the Yangtze River designed to dramatize his political reemergence, Mao returned to Peking.

In early August 1966, with the crucial support of Lin Piao, Mao's views prevailed over those of the opposition at the Eleventh Plenary Session of the Party Central Committee. The Cultural Revolution and the Red Guards were sanctioned, at least in general terms, although Chou En-lai, who basically supported Mao, succeeded in extracting from him a pledge not to unleash the full vigor of the revolution on technicians and others with specialized skills needed by the state, as long as they were deemed competent and patriotic. This pledge, however, was by no means fully kept.

Shortly after the session Red Guard activities—such as denunciation meetings, putting up *tatzupao*, or wall posters, and attacks on "bourgeois" elements—were intensified. A series of eight huge rallies were held for the 11 million Red Guards then in Peking, taken there by rail transportation provided by the PLA. At several of these, Mao and Lin Piao, who was clearly Mao's chosen heir, appeared together with other members of the leadership. Between August and November 1966 the central Party apparatus was effectively put out of action and almost out of existence by the Red Guards, and propaganda attacks on its leaders began to appear in the Red Guard press, although not in the official press.

In the late summer and fall of 1966, partly to reduce the congestion in Peking but more importantly to facilitate the "remolding," although not necessarily as yet the complete destruction of the powerful regional and provincial machines of the Party apparatus, Red Guards were ordered out of Peking into the provinces to unite with their counterparts there. It was hoped, especially by Chou En-lai, that in the process of attacking the local Party leaders the Red Guards would not disrupt the working of agriculture and the other sectors of the economy. They tended to take their cue, however, not from moderates like Chou En-lai but from the so-called Cultural Revolution Group created by Mao at the end of 1965 as his personal staff and, above all, from its most outspoken member, Chiang Ch'ing, who was assumed to know better than anyone else what her husband was thinking.

The Red Guards ran into difficulties, however. Not only did they tend to split into quarreling factions but, despite reinforcement by adult groups of Maoists (mostly workers) known as revolutionary rebels, they encountered formidable and effective resistance offered by the entrenched provincial Party apparatus. This was particularly true in Szechwan, which because of its size and remoteness has always been a problem for Chinese central governments. The only major local success for the Maoists at this stage was the establishment of a short-lived and poorly organized "commune" in Shanghai in January 1967, inspired evidently by the pre-Leninist Paris Commune of 1871. Although not sufficient in other cases to produce a "power seizure"—a favorite term during the Cultural Revolution—the efforts of the Red Guards were strenuous enough to threaten many urban areas with chaos.

In the hope of preventing such an undesired outcome, but still more in order to push the Cultural Revolution ahead, the Cultural Revolution Group in Peking, probably after some bargaining with Lin Piao, ordered the PLA to intervene in the Cultural Revolution, to "seize power" from the Liu-Teng opposition, and to form revolutionary committees (see ch. 21, The Armed Forces). These committees were new-style local and provincial governments based on "three-way alliances" among "revolutionaries" (mainly Red Guards), "loyal cadres" (actually or supposedly pro-Mao defectors from the opposition), and representatives of the PLA (see ch. 9, Political System and Values). There were a number of "false power seizures" during the ensuing months that Peking refused to recognize, evidently because "revolutionary elements" were accorded insufficient representation in the ensuing three-way alliances. In this unaccustomed role the army, being essentially in favor of order and discipline, tended in many cases to repress Red Guard activities rather vigorously. Under these conditions revolutionary committees with recognition from Peking were formed at the provincial level in Shanghai and in Heilungkiang, Shansi, Shantung, and Kweichow provinces in early 1967; one was also formed in Peking at the municipal level in April 1967.

Protests from local revolutionary elements against the army's behavior, and a shift to the left that occurred at the center in the early spring of 1967, resulted in a directive of April 6, 1967, to the PLA not to repress the "left," as well as a propaganda campaign in the official press against Liu (not yet by name, but as "China's Khrushchev"), by way of creating a revolutionary atmosphere. Then and later there was a fairly extensive purge by Lin Piao of PLA officers who were considered insufficiently loyal to the Cultural Revolution or who were formerly too close to P'eng or Ho Lung (another rival of Lin Piao's who had been purged at the beginning of 1967) or both, in favor of officers closely associated with Lin Piao himself. As the army accordingly eased its pressures for order, Red Guard violence escalated in the spring and summer of 1967; one of its more spectacular forms was antiforeign demonstrations in Peking, Hong Kong, and Rangoon and along the Sino-Soviet border. The local military and other stability-oriented elements viewed this trend with disfavor but in most cases were inhibited by Peking's attitude from taking effective action against it for the time being.

The turning point of the Cultural Revolution was the so-called Wu-han Incident. One local military leader who had continued to repress Red Guard turbulence was Ch'en Tsai-tao, commander of the Wu-han Military Region. To mediate between him and the protesting Red Guards of his area, Peking sent a special mission to Wu-han (see Glossary) in July 1967. These emissaries were seized and briefly held captive at Ch'en's instigation, if not on his direct orders. Pressure from Peking soon secured their release.

Enraged by this episode and anxious to capitalize on it to enhance their own influence, extreme leftists, such as Chiang Ch'ing, demanded and to some extent gained the arming of Red Guard units from military stockpiles and, less successfully, a purging of the army leadership. That was evidently too extreme. The military leadership dug in its heels after sacrificing Ch'en and succeeded in persuading Mao and Lin Piao to purge the principal extremists of the Cultural Revolution Group (except for Chiang Ch'ing and Ch'en Po-ta) instead of the army and to authorize the latter to take a somewhat firmer line in dealing with disorderly Red Guards. As a result, extremists were thrown out of the Ministry of Foreign Affairs, where their brief "power seizure" had led to the burning of the British diplomatic mission's compound on August 22 (see ch. 11, Foreign Relations). To make this shift to the right intelligible if not acceptable to the Red Guards, Mao and Chiang Ch'ing made themselves, probably with reluctance, the spokesmen for the new, more moderate line. Under these conditions a substantial number of revolutionary committees was formed, largely under military domination, in the last few months of 1967 and the first few months of 1968.

This trend naturally aroused resentment on the part of the extremists (especially Chiang Ch'ing) who began in the spring of 1968 to concentrate their fire on Chou En-lai. He, however, protected his own position effectively, although not always those of his subordinates. He seems to have formed an informal alliance with Huang Yung-sheng, the able and clearly stability-oriented former commander of the Canton Military Region, who was appointed chief of staff in March 1968. Then, probably to impose some semblance of order on this confused and potentially dangerous situation, Mao in late April 1968 created a new and informal leading group of fourteen members, with a majority of moderates including military men but also with a substantial minority of extreme Maoists including Chiang Ch'ing. The new group functioned as a "collective leadership" of sorts until the Ninth Party Congress of April 1969, performing the duties of the old Politburo and its Standing Committee, which, although reconstituted in August 1966, had been inoperative since the spring of 1967.

In the late spring and summer of 1968 there was a resurgence of Red Guard violence, although not on the scale of 1967. The Kwangsi Chuang Autonomous Region was particularly affected, and the disorder there was especially serious because it included raids by Red Guards on trains carrying military equipment to North Vietnam, for the purpose of acquiring weapons with which to fight other Red Guards. This episode, coupled with Peking's repeated but unsuccessful efforts to stop it and the rapid degeneration of the Red Guard movement into squabbling factions that were seemingly capable of plunging the country into chaos, compelled Mao in late July 1968 to authorize, with great reluctance, the suppression of the Red Guards as an organized political force.

Officially rationalized on the ground that the Red Guards, being largely students, were essentially "bourgeois" and that leadership of the Cultural Revolution ought to rest with the "working class," the suppression was carried out during the late summer and early fall by the army and by teams of workers and peasants apparently controlled by the army. Red Guard units were disbanded, and many of their members were sent to the countryside to do manual labor. This major turn to the right, which meant the effective, although unadmitted, end of the Cultural Revolution, permitted agreement between Peking and the local elites involved on the composition of the remaining provincial revolutionary committees, which were accordingly proclaimed in August and early September 1968. The urgency of these efforts at stabilization was heightened by Peking's nervousness after the Soviet invasion of Czechoslovakia; however, the latter event occurred after Mao's decision to authorize the suppression of the Red Guards and therefore could not have been the cause of it.

The Twelfth Plenary Session of the Party Central Committee in October 1968 symbolized the virtual end of the Red Guard movement —and to that extent of the Cultural Revolution itself—but Mao was still determined to maintain some sort of revolutionary momentum, if in a different form. Exploiting the tension over Czechoslovakia and the Brezhnev Doctrine (see Glossary) as part of his rationale and in view of the need for an appropriately militant atmosphere for the forthcoming Ninth Party Congress, Mao during the next six months implemented a program of transferring large numbers of people (perhaps as many as 30 million) from the cities to the countryside.

The move served as a means both of easing the burden on the cities and possibly of energizing and revolutionizing the rural areas, which had not been much affected by the Cultural Revolution (see ch. 14, Agriculture; ch. 17, Labor). This program leveled off in the spring of 1969, by which time it had begun to threaten the countryside with serious disruption, and a more moderate phase set in. Other moves that were probably initiated and almost certainly favored by Mao during this period, partly at least as contributions to the desired tense atmosphere for the Ninth Party Congress, were the cancellation almost at the last minute of ambassadorial talks with the United States at Warsaw scheduled for February 20, 1969, and a clash with Soviet units on the Ussuri River on March 2, 1969 (see ch. 11, Foreign Relations).

The Ninth Party Congress was finally held from April 1 to 24, 1969. It brought to Peking some 1,500 delegates, many of them chosen in irregular and informal ways, from all parts of the country. Under these circumstances, control by the Party leadership over the proceedings was apparently established less easily than is usual at such congresses. The major report, by Lin Piao, was devoted mainly to rationalizing and defending Mao's leadership and the Cultural Revolution. A new Party constitution, which had been approved in draft form by the Central Committee the previous October, was formally adopted. A new and cumbersome Central Committee was elected, with a great deal of window dressing in the form of obscure Maoists who could not possibly wield any real influence; but the Central Secretariat that had been the stronghold of Mao's opposition before 1966 was eliminated. In reality, power at the top remained where it had been during the last stages of the Cultural Revolution, in the hands of a coalition composed of civilian and military moderates like Chou En-lai and Huang Yung-sheng and a substantial but less important group of extreme Maoists like Chiang Ch'ing and presided over by Mao and Lin Piao.

POST-CULTURAL REVOLUTION TRENDS

The remainder of 1969 after the Ninth Party Congress saw continuing emphasis on political and economic stabilization. In July 1969, soon after the election of the new Politburo and as befitted an era of relative calm after the turmoil of the Cultural Revolution, the cult of Mao in Chinese propaganda, both domestic and external, began to be reduced approximately to pre-Cultural Revolution levels. After the Ninth Party Congress a long series of "latest instructions" from Mao to the Chinese people came to an end. Mao later stated privately that he had become disgusted with the lengths to which the adulation of himself had been carried during the Cultural Revolution and had personally directed the deemphasis. Even so, his cult and the influence of his thought remained very great, but in practice he appeared to be delegating primary responsibility for concrete decisions, in domestic and foreign policy alike, to Chou En-lai.

The year 1969 was dominated by the repercussions of the Sino-Soviet border crisis and Soviet politicomilitary pressures on Communist China. The Communist Chinese response to these influences took the form of diplomatic moves, directed by Chou En-lai, that were designed to stall off a Soviet attack, to resume and improve relations with friendly countries aimed initially at maximizing foreign support in the face of Soviet pressures, and to strengthen conventional military defense. In addition, especially after the beginning of Sino-Soviet talks on the border issue in Peking in October 1969, the regime undertook extensive measures of mass mobilization and civil defense designed to enable the country to fight a "people's war," if necessary, and to enhance the regime's authority over the people at a time of low morale after the Cultural Revolution. To a considerable degree, in fact, an atmosphere of Sino-Soviet tension was consciously fostered in Communist China, on the one hand, by the moderates for domestic political effect in order to enhance the local political authority of the PLA and, on the other, by the radicals, although with less success, to cultivate a revolutionary atmosphere.

The last few weeks of 1969 and the first two months of 1970 were a period marked by a prolonged nonappearance of Mao, perhaps because of illness. Possibly as a consequence there was official silence on most major questions relating to political reconstruction. In the spring of 1970 a sense of forward movement reappeared with the aid of propaganda stressing the centennial of Lenin's birth (April 22) and the orbiting of Communist China's first earth satellite (April 24).

After officially admitting the existence of a "fierce debate" between moderates and radicals, the Second Plenary Session of the Ninth Party Central Committee (from August 25 to September 9, 1970) called for acceleration of the process of rebuilding the damaged Party apparatus (this process began in December 1970). The session adopted but did not publish a draft of a new state constitution and called for the convening of the National People's Congress (the fourth) "at a suitable time" (see ch. 9, Political System and Values). It apparently also concluded that the time had come to deemphasize the campaign of war preparations that had been underway for the past year.

In early 1971 the regime made another effort to create a revolutionary, or at least a quasi-revolutionary, atmosphere by capitalizing on the orbiting of a second earth satellite on March 3 (but announced on March 16) and by celebrating, amid great propaganda fanfare, the centennial of the Paris Commune on March 18. Nevertheless, the tone of the celebration of the Party's fiftieth anniversary in July was a rather subdued one, probably reflecting the complexity and difficulty of the contemporary political situation. The anniversary editorial devoted most of its wordage to general historical and ideological questions from a Maoist standpoint and contained nothing new regarding contemporary problems.

Like other aspects of the post-Cultural Revolution political situation, the power and leadership question is complex and obscure. The regular membership of the new twenty-one-man Politburo elected by the Central Committee immediately after the Ninth Party Congress in April 1969 includes twelve members of the fourteen-man leading group that had existed for a year before the congress. More precisely, the Politburo consists of Mao and Lin Piao, and then the remaining nineteen members are officially listed in the order of the number of brushstrokes in the family names (in other words, in the Chinese equivalent of alphabetical order), with the effect and probably the purpose of introducing qualitative distinction between the top two and the formally undifferentiated remainder of the leadership. It soon became clear, however, that Chou En-lai retained his third-ranking position in the hierarchy. The listing by the brushstroke order, instead of the previous practice of listing in the descending order of seniority, seemed to reflect, if anything, the still unsettled power alignment at the top and thus the harbinger of things to come if either Mao or Lin Piao or both depart the scene under foreseeable circumstances.

Categorized by functions these nineteen included, in mid-1971, three Party elders or "aged comrades" of little real political importance (Chu Te, Tung Pi-wu, and Liu Po-ch'eng), five radical Maoists (Ch'en Po-ta, Chiang Ch'ing, Yao Wen-yuan, Chang Ch'un-ch'iao, and Yeh Ch'un), two administrators (Chou En-lai and Li Hsien-nien), two Party control and security specialists (K'ang Sheng and Hsieh Fu-chih), five central military leaders (Huang Yung-sheng, Li Tso-p'eng, Ch'iu Hui-tso, Wu Fa-hsien and Yeh Chien-ying), and two regional military leaders (Ch'en Hsi-lien and Hsu Shin-yu). At the same time, the Central Committee elected a five-man Politburo Standing Committee consisting of Mao, Lin Piao, Chou En-lai, Ch'en Po-ta, and K'ang Sheng.

The only discernible pattern of political leadership after 1969 was the semblance of continuity as symbolized by Premier Chou. Chou En-lai made many of the major decisions, often in consultation with Mao himself in order to fend off a variety of pressures from the Maoist radicals and proceeded to rebuild his governmental (as opposed to Party) bureaucracy, including the public security apparatus, which had been badly damaged by the Cultural Revolution (see ch. 20, Public Order and Internal Security). The number of central government cadres had been substantially reduced as a result of the Cultural Revolution, and the ministries were correspondingly streamlined and in some cases merged (see ch. 9, Political System and Values).

By mid-1970 new ministerial appointments began to be announced —the personnel involved typically having military backgrounds. In other fields as well, including the Party apparatus, Chou En-lai appeared to be influential if not decisive in making key appointments, again choosing frequently men with military backgrounds. The explanation is not some sort of takeover of the civil bureaucracy and the new Party organization by the PLA, whether at Lin Piao's initiative or not, but rather the fact that Chou En-lai during the Cultural Revolution had broadened and deepened his contacts with, and support among, several critical groupings, including central and regional military leaders, and therefore was in a far better position than before to select promising candidates for the next leadership generation.

In October 1971 it was difficult to ascertain with assurance the manner in which the five Standing Committee members exercised their power, in both formal and informal capacities—be it individually, collectively, or in coalition. The state of Mao's health remained a matter of conjecture, as was Lin Piao's. Lin Piao seldom appeared in public without Mao and gave few signs of having sufficient political stature to be a worthy successor. Whether his relative inactivity was attributable to his poor health or to other factors was not readily ascertainable. It appeared that his actual political influence in 1971 consisted to a large extent in his preeminent authority, through his de facto chairmanship of the Military Commission of the Party Central Committee, over the Party network within the PLA. Despite an extensive internal purge in the latter half of 1967, the PLA was probably the closest body that Communist China possessed, after 1967, to a functioning nationwide structure holding the country together in an organizational sense (see ch. 21, The Armed Forces). By 1971 the provincial military leaders, presumably with the approval of their superiors in the PLA, had shown signs of an intention to retain power indefinitely, but it was not certain whether they had the unqualified endorsement of Mao, Chou En-lai, and other veteran remnants of the Party.

Apart from the trio of Mao, Lin Piao, and Chou En-lai, the status of other leaders was unclear and shifting. Ch'en Po-ta was not seen in public after August 1, 1970. K'ang Sheng also disappeared from public view for six months beginning in mid-November 1970.

It appears probable that Mao and Lin Piao gave at least passive consent to the dominant trend toward stabilization, at the same time trying to prevent it from going so far as to stifle all revolutionary momentum. On the other hand, whether with or without their approval, the radical faction, notably Chiang Ch'ing and the two leading figures in Shanghai, Chang Ch'un-ch'iao and Yao Wen-yuan, clearly objected to the trend and tried with little success to resist it. They not only aired their views in propaganda articles and such other sources as the revised, very militant versions of Peking operas that were published in late 1969 and early 1970 but also attempted to capitalize on anti-Soviet feeling to obstruct the holding of the Sino-Soviet border, as well as to urge opposition to the moderate establishments in the provinces. Here and there, as in Shansi for example, radicals, including former Red Guards, engaged in violent disorder. More constructively, both central and local extremists tried to counter the rising influence of the moderates by continually citing and trying to turn to their own advantage Mao's various pronouncements on the importance of uninterrupted revolution even in a socialist state; but these activities failed to thwart the efforts of the moderates.

One of the more persuasive indications that the moderates were gaining in domestic politics as well as in foreign policy was in Peking's invitation of July 1971 to President Richard M. Nixon to visit Communist China (see ch. 11, Foreign Relations). No matter what the foreign policy arguments are in favor of the invitation, it seems highly probable that the radical Maoists objected to it on both ideological and political grounds. The fact that they obviously lost can be viewed as indicating that the center of political gravity has moved farther to the right than had been generally assumed.

In the absence of any effective countervailing political organizations, the PLA as of mid-1971 was by far the strongest single political force in the country. This preeminence was maintained by the considerable and pragmatic influence of Lin Piao and Chief of Staff Huang Yung-sheng. Together, Lin Piao and Huang have staffed the central and regional military leaderships with officers associated at some time with them and presumably still loyal to them. This process has been carried on with due regard for current realities, including the still considerable influence of the radical Maoists. In September 1970, for example, it was disclosed that the once powerful General Political Department of the PLA Headquarters, which had been inconspicuous and relatively inactive for two years (1967 to 1969), had been given a new director, General Li Te-sheng, a man with a somewhat leftist reputation and hailing from Anhwei Province, where Chiang Ch'ing had acquired considerable influence during the Cultural Revolution.

The search for domestic tranquillity clearly implies an effort to revive, if in modified form, the usual functioning of the state bureaucracy, which virtually ceased to operate during the Cultural Revolution, partly because it was associated with Liu Shao-ch'i as chairman of the PRC. After the Ninth Party Congress, senior Vice Chairman Tung Pi-wu began to function as acting chairman, mainly for the purpose of appointing and receiving ambassadors. Junior Vice Chairman Soong Ching-ling (Mrs. Sun Yat-sen) began to share these functions in late 1970. But this was only a small beginning, and any comprehensive normalization in the state field would require the election and convening of the Fourth National People's Congress and the adoption of a new state constitution (see ch. 9, Political System and Values). This in turn would require a greater degree of stability at the provincial level than had been achieved by late 1971.

The Cultural Revolution has resulted in a considerable, although far from total, devolution of centralized political power to the provincial level. From the Ninth Party Congress to the end of 1970 the main authority in the twenty-nine major administrative jurisdictions was the revolutionary committees, whose post-Cultural Revolution leaderships were prominently recognized, at least in terms of prestige, at the central level; thus about 120 members of provincial-level revolutionary committees, including all chairmen of the provincial revolutionary committees, were elected to the 279-member Ninth Central Committee.

Generally speaking, in mid-1971, the revolutionary committees did exercise effective authority, and this was increasing despite some fairly serious disorder and political violence reported in some areas—mainly in Shansi and Kweichow provinces and to an apparently lesser extent in Szechwan and Tibet. In nearly all cases, by far the largest single share of political power at the provincial level was exercised, informally if not always formally, by the leadership of the corresponding military districts or military regions. The political commissars in these divisions since the Cultural Revolution had usually been professional officers rather than, as before, essentially civilian officials of the local Party apparatus. In several cases the chairmen of the revolutionary committees were replaced, usually without announcement. The cadres of the pre-1966 Party apparatus at the provincial level did not all emerge unscathed from the Cultural Revolution. Of the many who survived, a substantial fraction, usually after intensive reindoctrination, was allowed by both Peking and the local military authorities to play an active role in the post-Cultural Revolution politics, sometimes after transfer to another area.

Together the military and the "revolutionary" cadres on the revolutionary committees at the provincial level and below (most organizations, including factories, had revolutionary committees) silenced and squeezed out many of the representatives of the "revolutionary masses"—Red Guards and others—who made up the third element of the "three-way alliances" on the ground that they were "troublemakers." On the other hand, other representatives of the "revolutionary masses" made their peace with the two dominant elements or for some reason, possibly as window dressing, were allowed by the latter to remain politically active in one capacity or another. For their part, the military components of the revolutionary committees, at the upper levels, were subjected to considerable reshuffling during 1969 and 1970, the new appointees, especially in the south and southwest, generally having records of association with, and presumably a sense of loyalty toward, Lin Piao and Huang Yung-sheng.

It was within this framework (that is, under the direction of the revolutionary committees—in most cases under the effective control of the local military) that, under prodding from Peking, the Party apparatus began to be rebuilt at the provincial level and below. Once rebuilt, the Party apparatus at least in theory would give leadership to the revolutionary committees, especially since there was a tendency for the military to withdraw from civil functions below the level of the province; actually much appeared to depend on the particular personalities and power relationships in a given area. It was not until late November 1969, however, that the first Party Committee on the county (*hsien*) level was formed—in Hunan, Mao Tse-tung's native province. After that the formation of other county-level Party committees got underway, but rather slowly; only/about 120 of the 2,200-odd counties had formed Party committees by December 1970.

Party committees at the provincial level also began to be formed in December 1970, after Party congresses. Again, the first province to enter the lists was Hunan. The process of forming Party committees for the provinces proceeded fairly rapidly, far more so than had the earlier process of forming revolutionary committees, and by late August all provincial-level political divisions had organized Party committees. In all cases the Party committee was headed by a first secretary who was concurrently chairman of the revolutionary committee; before the Cultural Revolution, it was also common for the chairman of the provincial government, or governor, to serve as first secretary of the provincial Party committee. Six of these first secretaries were the commanders of the military regions whose headquarters were located in those provinces.

There was a considerable, although by no means complete, overlap between the memberships of the revolutionary committees and the Party committees. There was no precise uniformity among provinces as to the number or titles of the secretaries of the new Party committees, an indication of the relative decentralization prevailing in the post-Cultural Revolution political order. Nor was there any uniformity regarding the size, composition, or procedures of the Party congresses that elected the Party committees. Very likely to disguise the embarrassingly small number of representatives of the "revolutionary masses" in the Party committees at the provincial level, the committees were said to be based on a new type of "three-way alliance" composed in theory of "old, middle-aged, and young people," although it was hard to find much evidence of the presence of youth. Honan experimented briefly with a formula combining the older and newer versions of the "three-way alliance," but this did not gain favor as a model and was dropped in favor of the newer version.

As with the revolutionary committees, the largest single share of power by far in the Party committees, with only one clear exception (Shanghai), lay with the military, whose growing power and occasional arrogance generated resentment and sometimes criticisms both in Peking and in the provinces. An example of the essentially pragmatic and locally oriented character of the policies pursued by the provincial military leaderships within the revolutionary committees and Party committees was the fact that, whereas the Peking press gave a good deal of publicity to the alleged revolutionary significance of the Paris Commune centennial (March 18, 1971), the provinces (except for Shanghai) gave virtually none.

The revolutionary committees had been formed in an essentially random fashion; this formation pattern tended to reflect the length of time required locally to work out a leadership group acceptable both provincially and in Peking. Provinces of strategic importance had tended to be slow in forming these bodies, indicating possible reluctance by the local military commanders to become involved in setting up such bodies—at any rate on a basis politically acceptable to Peking—rather than maintaining an informal version of martial law. The decision of late July 1968 to dissolve the Red Guards presumably broke the deadlock with respect to those areas that had still not formed revolutionary committees at that time.

The general emphasis on stabilization has been reflected in the policies of the central and local authorities toward the population. Harsh measures, including some executions, have been carried out since the end of the Cultural Revolution for the purpose of restoring order. Students have been regarded with suspicion, and in some cases former Red Guards have been forced to pay, or help pay, for damage caused during the Cultural Revolution. There has been a revival of emphasis on organized sports, which were neglected and even frowned on during the Cultural Revolution. Although the Maoist emphasis on local "self-reliance" as opposed to direction and financial support from the center is maintained to a considerable degree, there seems to be some backing away in practice from the Maoist emphasis on substituting ideological incentives and political slogans for material rewards, an emphasis conspicuously exemplified in the famous Tachai model commune in a poor region of Shansi (see ch. 5, Social System and Values). Social welfare is receiving increased attention (see ch. 7, Living Conditions).

The dominant political temper of the military leadership, although not necessarily that of Lin Piao, appeared, at least in mid-1971, as quite pragmatic. Chauvinism and expansionism, to the extent that they exist, are largely propaganda themes for internal consumption, not attitudes governing Peking's actual external behavior. Expansionism seemed unlikely to engage the attention of a leadership that was weak in economic and military capabilities and confronted by the colossal task of building a powerful Communist China at home (see ch. 11, Foreign Relations).

Despite the appreciable political decentralization since the Cultural Revolution, the center in 1971 was by no means powerless, if only because it was still presided over by Mao, Lin Piao, and Chou, and, continuing internal tensions notwithstanding, the country appeared unlikely to fall apart. There were, moreover, strong nationalistic barriers to disintegration, since most politically conscious Chinese were well aware that in Communist China's modern history excessive disunity had led, through national weakness, to foreign pressures and even invasion. Other factors militating against a breakup were the somewhat improved, as compared with the pre-1949 era, nationwide communications, and the fact that modern arms were produced in only a few major installations that appeared in mid-1971 to be under effective central control. On the other hand, the country appeared unlikely in the political field, as in any other, to overcome its problems and weaknesses dramatically enough to attain the status of a superpower, a status that in any case its leadership claimed not to aspire to, since it was alleged to connote oppression of weaker states (see ch. 11, Foreign Relations).

THE CHINESE COMMUNIST PARTY

From the standpoints of organization and functioning, the CCP before the Cultural Revolution fell well within the permissible limits of the Leninist model and the Party constitution of 1956, despite the overpowering personality of Mao Tse-tung and its corrosive effect on the principle of collective leadership. Major decisions within the Politburo were made frequently by compromise and consensus, although less so after the mid-1950s, sometimes after informal discussion and preliminary resolution below the Politburo level. These decisions were then transmitted for implementation to the Party apparatus through the Central Secretariat, or to the PLA through the Military Commission of the Party Central Committee, or to the State Council, or to the Standing Committee of the National People's Congress, or some combination of these, depending on their nature. During the 1960s an informal body known as the Central Work Conference played an important role in the decisionmaking process.

The Central Committee elected the Politburo and the members of the Central Secretariat. It ratified (and sometimes debated) their decisions at its Plenary Sessions, four of which were held between October 1949 and the Eighth Party Congress in September 1956, twelve between the eighth and ninth Party congresses, and two since the Ninth Party Congress. For their part the Party congresses elected the members and alternate members of the Central Committee— alternates being entitled to attend and speak, but not to vote, and forming a panel from which vacancies in the regular membership were usually filled. Both members and alternates were important Party functionaries in practically all fields of public life.

All these elections were managed to a considerable extent from above. The operation of the vast pyramid of territorial and functional organs, such as Party committees and Party branches, that made up the CCP as a whole was supervised by an elaborate bureaucracy composed of departments under the Central Secretariat. One of the most important of these, the United Work Department, dealt with noncommunist organizations. Electoral mandates of a contrived kind flowed up from the bottom in indirect fashion, each body electing delegates to the next higher level, and directives flowed from the top down within prescribed channels of command. At the bottom of the pyramid stood the ordinary Party cadre, which served in and supposedly led or helped to lead some organization outside the Party apparatus—a Commune, a factory, a military unit, or similar organization.

This elaborate structure was badly disrupted during the Cultural Revolution, especially at the top. Although only about 1 percent of the Party's total pre-Cultural Revolution membership of 20 million was purged during the Cultural Revolution, the victims included a substantial percentage of the top ranks of the Party apparatus. About 30 percent of the Eighth Central Committee elected in September 1956 was reelected to the Ninth Central Committee in April 1969. Although by no means all of the 70 percent were purged during the

Cultural Revolution, this high turnover conveys at least a rough idea of the havoc wrought by the Cultural Revolution in the upper ranks of the pre-Cultural Revolution elite.

As early as the latter part of 1967 authoritative indications began to appear in Peking that the Party as an institution would have to be rebuilt as soon as feasible. The process began in 1968, more at the local level than at the center, and proceeded roughly parallel with the formation of revolutionary committees, in most cases, under the supervision and control of the local military authorities. The argument between the radicals and the moderates over the composition of the new model Party that accompanied the rebuilding process was therefore decided essentially in favor of the moderates. The main issue was whether Red Guards and other militant activists should be admitted en masse into the Party. By and large this did not happen, although essentially as window dressing some Red Guards, model peasants and workers, and others were admitted, and a few were even elected to the Ninth Central Committee.

The process of Party reconstruction was far from finished by the time of the Ninth Party Congress, although the list of provincial revolutionary committees had been completed seven months earlier. In fact, not a single provincial level Party committee had been formed or a single provincial Party congress held by April 1969. The provincial delegates to the congress were therefore selected in an informal manner, evidently under the supervision of the revolutionary committees. When the Ninth Party Congress finally met, it elected a Central Committee, 170 regular members and 109 alternates, roughly twice the size of its predecessor.

The greater structural informality and the more antibureaucratic flavor (as compared with the preceding 1956 Party constitution) were reflected in the new Party constitution that was adopted by the congress on the basis of a draft that had been earlier debated and adopted at the Twelfth Plenary Session of the Central Committee in October 1968. The two versions differed somewhat; unlike the 1968 draft, the final version contained no reference to any need for further renewal of the Party along Cultural Revolution lines.

The constitution names Mao Tse-tung as the leader of the Party (for life, by implication) and Lin Piao as his successor, a highly irregular feature for a document of this kind. Maoist thought is acclaimed as the Party's ideological basis. Unlike the preceding Party constitution, this one does not even refer to the desirability of good relations between the Han and the non-Han minorities or between the CCP and the "democratic" minor parties. It is easier than before for new members to enter the Party; there is no specified probation period. In the event of disagreement with his superiors an individual Party member is authorized to communicate his views directly to the Central Committee and even to Mao, a provision presumably intended to ensure against a possible reemergence of entrenched, expertise-first (as opposed to politics-first) bureaucratic machines within the Party.

The procedure for choosing the membership of executive bodies, including the Central Committee, is very vague; these bodies are said to be "produced," rather than elected. No central Party organs other than the National Party Congress, the Central Committee, and the Politburo and its Standing Committee are explicitly provided for; there is no mention of a Central Secretariat or of regional bureaus. Even provincial Party committees are not specifically mentioned, although there is a brief, rather vague, passage covering "local" Party organizations. The 1969 Party constitution, in short, retains much but not all of the antibureaucratic flavor of the Cultural Revolution, places much stress in theory on the roles of Mao and Lin, and leaves the actual structure and functioning of the new model Party vague, indicating they were probably to be determined, over time, largely in accordance with the real balance of power—outside as well as within the formal Party apparatus.

After the Ninth Party Congress the pace of Party reconstruction accelerated somewhat, to a considerable extent under the direction of the Party apparatus within the PLA. There was an apparent tendency, in view of the important role played by the army since January 1967, for at least some of the eleven military regions to act as de facto regional Party bureaus. Little was known in 1971 regarding the rebuilding of the central Party apparatus. The United Work Department of the Central Committee was mentioned in the press in May 1970, and the International Liaison Department, which handles relations with foreign communist parties, was mentioned in March 1971 as being headed by Keng Piao, an able military man who had just returned from a brief tour as ambassador to Albania. There have also been repeated references in the press to unspecified "departments under the Party Central Committee" (see fig. 11). These references suggested that the Central Committee departments continued to exist on a skeleton basis during the Cultural Revolution and in 1971 were being cautiously revived with some injection of new personnel not connected with the old Party apparatus, yet there was no indication when they might fully regain their formerly great power and prestige.

The Chinese Communist Youth League, which felt the brunt of the early stages of the Cultural Revolution along with its parent organization, the regular Party apparatus, was apparently also being cautiously revived, as a replacement for the Red Guard organizations. There was also some evidence that Maoist radical leaders were trying to revive the Red Guards under the guise of the Chinese Communist Youth League but with little success. Contact between the new model Party and Mao Tse-tung Thought on the one hand and the masses on

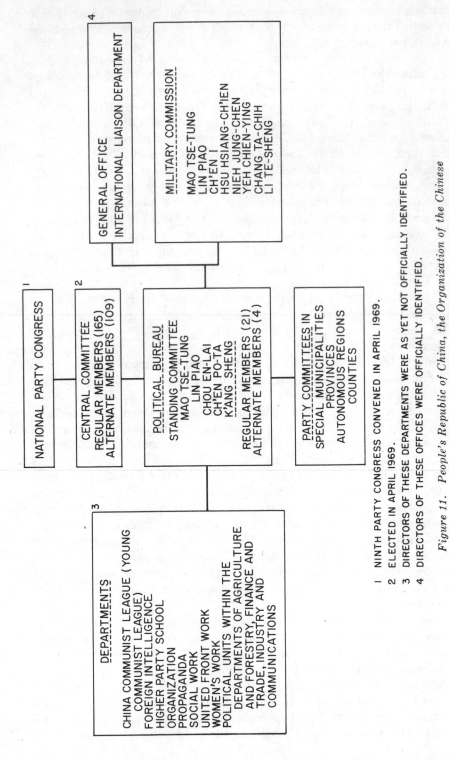

NATIONAL PARTY CONGRESS [1]

CENTRAL COMMITTEE [2]
REGULAR MEMBERS (165)
ALTERNATE MEMBERS (109)

POLITICAL BUREAU
STANDING COMMITTEE
MAO TSE-TUNG
LIN PIAO
CHOU EN-LAI
CH'EN PO-TA
K'ANG SHENG

REGULAR MEMBERS (21)
ALTERNATE MEMBERS (4)

PARTY COMMITTEES IN
SPECIAL MUNICIPALITIES
PROVINCES
AUTONOMOUS REGIONS
COUNTIES

DEPARTMENTS [3]
CHINA COMMUNIST LEAGUE (YOUNG
   COMMUNIST LEAGUE)
FOREIGN INTELLIGENCE
HIGHER PARTY SCHOOL
ORGANIZATION
PROPAGANDA
SOCIAL WORK
UNITED FRONT WORK
WOMEN'S WORK
POLITICAL UNITS WITHIN THE
   DEPARTMENTS OF AGRICULTURE
   AND FORESTRY, FINANCE AND
   TRADE, INDUSTRY AND
   COMMUNICATIONS

GENERAL OFFICE
INTERNATIONAL LIAISON DEPARTMENT [4]

MILITARY COMMISSION

MAO TSE-TUNG
LIN PIAO
CH'EN I
HSU HSIANG-CH'IEN
NIEH JUNG-CHEN
YEH CHIEN-YING
CHANG TA-CHIH
LI TE-SHENG

1 NINTH PARTY CONGRESS CONVENED IN APRIL 1969.

2 ELECTED IN APRIL 1969.

3 DIRECTORS OF THESE DEPARTMENTS WERE AS YET NOT OFFICIALLY IDENTIFIED.

4 DIRECTORS OF THESE OFFICES WERE OFFICIALLY IDENTIFIED.

Figure 11. *People's Republic of China, the Organization of the Chinese Communist Party, Mid-1971.*

288

the other was being maintained by a widespread network of May 7 cadre schools, which were attended by many categories of Party members and non-Party individuals and in which the emphasis was on political indoctrination and manual labor (see ch. 8, Education, Intellectual Expression, and the Arts; ch. 9, Political System and Values).

Since the Ninth Party Congress, there was mounting evidence that Mao Tse-tung had increasingly assumed the role of elder statesman and left most concrete decisions to others, notably Chou En-lai. Mao has said that he thinks of his current role as primarily one of teacher —of his own Party and people and perhaps of the world at large to the widest extent possible. He appeared in mid-1971 to be reading fairly widely and writing something in the nature of a political testament. He still received foreign visitors, but only rarely. His role, in short, appeared to be that of a man who thought that most of his active work was done and needed mainly to be rationalized for public consumption.

OTHER PARTIES AND MASS ORGANIZATIONS

Since, according to Mao, 90 to 95 percent of all Chinese accept the leadership of the CCP but only 2 to 3 percent belong to it, the CCP has necessarily followed the policy of constructing a united front—an elaborate organizational means to assist the Party apparatus and the regime in exercising leadership over the people. The united front (including the CCP) is technically represented by a large and unwieldy body known as the Chinese People's Political Consultative Conference (CPPCC), whose National Committee resembles the National People's Congress in size and composition and usually met more or less simultaneously with it before the Cultural Revolution. Like the National People's Congress, the CPPCC and its National Committee have been in a state of suspended animation since the beginning of the Cultural Revolution. Since the Ninth Party Congress, however, the Communist Chinese press has published an increased number of references to the united front, suggesting that the CCP leadership is anxious to repair the damage done in this field during the Cultural Revolution and to revive the united front in a new form, the nature of which was not yet clear in 1971.

Among the most important aspects of the united front are the "democratic" parties. Strictly speaking, the CCP claims to be democratic and therefore should be included in the collective term *democratic parties*. No one in Communist China, however, has any doubt when the term *party* is used without qualification as to which is meant. Moreover, everyone understands the term *democratic parties* to refer generally to the minor, noncommunist parties that the CCP tolerates because of their utility in maintaining a democratic facade and exercising leadership over noncommunist elements. There were originally eleven minor parties, all of which adhered to the CCP before 1949, in some cases very shortly before. Three were dissolved or compelled to merge with others soon afterward, so that for most of the years since 1950 there have been eight. By communist standards, all are bourgeois in social origin, including such individuals as former KMT members, former businessmen, and intellectuals. The CCP itself monopolizes formal representation of the industrial working class (or proletariat) and the peasantry.

Largely because of the unusually broad character of its united front, the CCP at first resisted accepting such Soviet-style terms for its political system as *proletarian dictatorship* or *people's democracy* and used instead Mao's term *people's democratic dictatorship*. The Twentieth Congress of the Communist Party of the Soviet Union, held in 1956, invited the CCP to interpret the term *proletarian dictatorship* as it liked, as long as it used the term, which the CCP proceeded to do. Since the term clearly implied the exclusion from political activity of certain classes, including the bourgeoisie, and since there was a short-lived flurry of talk in China in 1956 about attaining "socialism" (a state of affairs in which only the working class and the peasantry still exist as classes), the minor parties expressed some anxiety that they might be dissolved. They were officially assured, however, that this would not happen, perhaps because at that time ideological neatness seemed less important to the Chinese Communists than the practical advantages of keeping the minor parties in existence. In fact during the Hundred Flowers Campaign they were allowed to recruit new members as a form of insurance against dying out, and some of them survived.

Some minor party members, as well as other non-Communists and Communists, were at the forefront in criticizing the CCP during the brief "rectification campaign" in the spring of 1957. Like other critics, they were promptly made the targets of an "anti-rightist struggle" waged by the CCP, on the theory that although their economic base had been liquidated in 1955 and 1956 through the transformation of private businesses into joint state-private enterprises, their ideological base obviously required further remolding. Even though the leaders of the minor parties made a great show in late 1957 and early 1958 of "giving their hearts to the Party," their representation in the government was reduced below its already low level, and they were no longer permitted to expand their membership. In general they simply kept quiet and had to be satisfied with bare political survival, which they still managed to do even during the Cultural Revolution when there were loud Red Guard demands for their abolition.

Mass organizations, many with large memberships, serve as so-called transmission belts for the regime and its "mass line." They are divided broadly into two types: those that have nearly universal memberships within the urban or the rural sector, as the case may be, but do not have a national organization, because they exist mainly to facilitate the activities of the local governments; and those that have much less than universal membership but have national organizations that are in direct touch with the central CCP apparatus. Both types concern themselves mainly with the organization and mobilization of the people, so that the central and local governments can mainly devote themselves, at least in usual times, to administrative matters.

The main examples of the first type of mass organization are the residents' committees in the urban areas, each composed of one to several hundred families living in a contiguous section, and in the rural areas the production teams, the lowest units under the three-tiered People's Communes (see ch. 9, Political System and Values). These basic organizations are much influenced by personal relationships, local conditions, and traditional patterns, as well as by the directives issued to them from above (see ch. 5, Social System and Values).

The second type of mass organization can be subdivided into three categories. The most important is the mass membership organization, of which the principal examples are the Chinese Communist Youth League, the All-China Federation of Trade Unions, the Women's Federation, and the Students' Federation; these organizations are led by CCP members, operate under the principle of democratic centralism (see Glossary) (like the CCP itself), and have an elaborate structure of local organizations. Of these four organizations, the All-China Federation of Trade Unions has been the only one to challenge Party policies in the interest of its members; perhaps as a result its leadership has been subjected to repeated purging. The other three have been more consistently cooperative with the Party. The second category consists of a much smaller kind of organization, concerned with foreign affairs (although one of these, the moribund Sino-Soviet Friendship Association, once claimed a mass membership), mainly with propaganda and international visits. The third category includes the professional or technical associations for journalists, scholars, and artists.

NATIONAL MINORITIES

Considering its huge size, the population of Communist China is remarkably homogeneous from the ethnic point of view; only about 6 percent of the total population, or a little over 40 million, are non-Han (see ch. 4, Ethnic Groups and Languages). Although not numerous by comparison with the vast Han majority, these peoples, or at least some of them, have considerable political importance.

Generally speaking, they are tough fighters and live thinly scattered over the strategically sensitive and mineralogically rich western half of the country, where the Han population also is relatively sparse, although it is becoming less so through sponsored migration.

Since well before 1949 the CCP had promised the minorities autonomy, but it became clear in 1949 that no right to secede would be allowed, and the 1954 State Constitution described the minority areas as inalienable parts of Communist China. The minorities in 1971 were firmly tied to Peking, not only by the Constitution but by the fact that, even though autonomous, their territories were just as much subjected to unified, centrally controlled Party and government administration, economic planning, military command, and educational and propaganda activities, as any other in Communist China. Key posts were usually held by Han communist cadres, and the general policy, in spite of the official use of local languages alongside Chinese in the minority areas, was essentially one of assimilation. Han colonists have been introduced into minority areas, especially since the start of the Great Leap. Local cultures are being gradually squeezed out, and both Buddhism and Islam have been intermittently persecuted. Nomadism is being eliminated because of Peking's dislike of uncontrolled movement on the part of any significant sector of the population.

Under these conditions, the term *autonomous* is almost meaningless, constituting little more than a designation for the contiguous piece of territory where some significant number of people of a given minority nationality live. If the territory is relatively small, it is placed under the Han-dominated province in which it is located and labeled an "autonomous *hsien* (county)" or an "autonomous *chou* (district)." In such cases "autonomy" consists of little more than a limited freedom to practice traditional local customs—subject to such temporary interference as by Red Guards during the Cultural Revolution and to varying enforcement of Party policies.

Broadly speaking, policy shifts in Peking have been applied to the minority areas as well as to the Han areas but have evoked somewhat greater resistance in the former. Land reform in Han areas had its parallel in the minority areas in the abolition of "feudal" privileges of tribal chiefs. Socialization was applied, to some extent, in the mid-1950s and still more intensively during the Great Leap to the newly "liberated" former "serfs" of the minority areas. The frequently violent response evoked periodic campaigns of repression, sometimes military, against "local nationalism." During the Cultural Revolution the minorities were particular targets of the Red Guards, who despised them both because they were not Han and because they were thought to be generally nonrevolutionary. Red Guard violence in minority areas was mitigated, however, although not entirely prevented, by precautionary measures taken by local military

292

commanders anxious to avoid conflict. The lot of the minorities since the Cultural Revolution has apparently been at least as difficult as it was before.

Of the several autonomous regions, Inner Mongolia, Sinkiang, and Tibet are politically the most important for Peking. Until 1967 Inner Mongolia had the advantage of being under the leadership of a member of the local minority, the Mongol (although a sinicized Mongol) Ulanfu. He identified himself to a considerable extent with the interests of his own people, who were heavily outnumbered in Inner Mongolia by Han after the merger of the province of Suiyuan with the autonomous region in 1954, as against his colleagues in Peking. He tried to protect the Mongols from having their grazing lands colonized by Han farmers (a process that has been going on since the beginning of the twentieth century) and to avoid driving the Mongols to slaughtering their livestock, as happened in many cases in the mid-1950s when socialization began. His moderate policy was at its height in 1963 through 1966, when the retreat from the Great Leap was still in progress, and presumably it met with the approval of the Party apparatus leaders in Peking.

Ulanfu was also a major target of the Cultural Revolution and of Red Guard violence, even though he went through the motions of introducing the Cultural Revolution into Inner Mongolia himself in the hope of remaining in power and protecting his people. He was removed from office in the spring of 1967 by a combination of Red Guard violence and military intervention from outside the region. A regional revolutionary committee was set up in November 1967 headed by T'eng Hai-ch'ing.

The Han in 1971 were still a minority, although a growing one, in Sinkiang. Peking has paid special attention to this vast region because of its remoteness, its poor communications with China Proper (see Glossary), its historic vulnerability to Russian and Soviet pressures, and its traditional tendency toward local secessionist movements. From the beginning Peking encountered difficulties in imposing its will on local Turkic leaders (especially Kazakhs), who were often very harshly dealt with. Peking's control was considerably facilitated when the Soviet Union returned in the spring of 1955 the holdings of the two large "joint" companies, one for petroleum extraction and one for nonferrous minerals (especially uranium) that had been operating in western Sinkiang for the previous five years. Peking then began to promote Han migration to Sinkiang and set up semimilitary "production and construction" units on a large scale. Socialization and pressure on "local nationalism" produced a serious crisis in 1958 and another in 1962. The one in 1962 was especially serious, because by that time the Sino-Soviet dispute had assumed major proportions, and Soviet authorities had apparently encouraged, or even conspired, the flight of some 50,000 Kazakhs and Uighurs across the border into Soviet Central Asia.

One of Peking's most unpopular measures in Sinkiang has been the effort to replace the Arabic script with another one (first Cyrillic, later Latin). Red Guard violence and general turbulence were severe in Sinkiang during the Cultural Revolution and led to the taking over of regional leadership in 1968 by General Lung Shu-chin from Hunan and the ousting of Wang En-mao, the formerly powerful pre-Cultural Revolution boss of the region. Conditions were very tense in Sinkiang in 1969 because of the Sino-Soviet border crisis and Soviet efforts to propagandize the minorities. They remained tense in 1971 but apparently were less so than during 1969.

Of all the minority areas Tibet has the strongest separate tradition and sentiment and the best claim to be an independent nation, even though no foreign government recognizes it as such. For much of its history, including the several decades before 1949, Tibet Proper was not effectively controlled by China. Peking has followed the Nationalist practice of keeping the province of Tsinghai separate from Tibet but has divided the former Nationalist province of Sinkiang between Tibet and Szechwan. Tibet is especially sensitive in Peking's eyes because of its contiguity with India.

After their "liberation" by Communist Chinese troops in 1950 and 1951, the Tibetans were promised autonomy, with special reference to Lamaism, in a formal agreement resembling a treaty, but its terms were soon violated as Peking began to apply essentially the same socialist and assimilationist policies as in other regions. Peking made a puppet of the Panchen Lama, traditionally the second ranking dignitary of the Tibetan church, and played him against the more independent-minded Dalai Lama. Tibetan grievances were not redressed and if anything seemed to be intensified when Peking established a Preparatory Committee for the Tibetan Autonomous Region in 1955. Revolts broke out about that time among the Khambas and Goloks, warlike peoples on the eastern fringes of Tibet. These risings had some effect on the more peaceable Tibetans farther west in the Lhasa area. In 1957 Peking thought it wise to promise an indefinite postponement of further "democratic" reforms and socialization and to withdraw most of its Han cadres, although not the PLA garrison, from Tibet. Unrest continued, nevertheless, and by March 1959 the Khamba guerrillas had been pushed by the PLA into the vicinity of Lhasa. In that month disorder broke out in Lhasa itself as Tibetans became fearful that Peking planned some harm to the Dalai Lama, who was persuaded by his followers to flee to India. The ensuing crisis, which included a sharp upsurge of border tension with India, was harshly suppressed by the PLA, although some guerrilla resistance continued to 1971.

After a period of accelerated socialization (the 1957 pledge was officially repudiated), Tibet became an autonomous region in 1965. The Panchen Lama, who appears to have become increasingly alienated by Peking's Tibetan policy, got into difficulties during the Cultural Revolution, which produced the usual turmoil in Tibet; his fate is obscure.

CHAPTER 11

FOREIGN RELATIONS

In October 1971, for the first time since 1949, the government of the People's Republic of China (PRC) gained multilateral, international endorsement of its status as the only lawful and competent spokesman of the Chinese people in the community of nations. This was made possible when a majority of United Nations (UN) members decided in effect that the PRC, rather than the government of the Republic of China (Nationalist China) on Taiwan, had the right to be seated in the UN. This development opened the way for the PRC to restructure its relationships with the outside world, from which it was largely cut off during the Great Proletarian Cultural Revolution (1966–69).

Western observers have differed in their view of the PRC's foreign relations since 1949. Broadly stated, there have been two main schools of thought in attempting to explain the PRC's motivations, objectives, policies, and actions. The first of these has tended to view Chinese foreign policy behavior in terms of what is said to be the PRC's aggressive impulse generated by communist ideology. Those who subscribe to this school have cited as proof the PRC's continuing hostile attitudes toward the West, its direct and indirect "aggression" into neighboring countries, and its support of insurgent movements wherever opportunities presented themselves.

By contrast, the second school has presented the PRC policy and behavior essentially as defensive, nationalistic, and pragmatic. It has maintained that the major Chinese objective is to preserve its independence and territorial integrity by taking necessary measures but without incurring risks of a major war with either the United States or the Soviet Union.

A critical review of events since 1949 indicates that neither of these two approaches alone provides an adequate framework for understanding the complexity of the PRC's external relations. Aggressiveness and prudence have not been mutually exclusive; rather, they have complemented each other flexibly according to twists and turns in internal and external situations. Aggressiveness has been tempered by caution when confronted with the likelihood of military retaliation by other powers. Caution has been balanced by verbal hostility so that China would not be vulnerable to foreign coercion or deprivation.

China specialists generally agree that, despite variations in emphasis, nationalism and communist ideology have both figured importantly in the conduct of Chinese foreign relations. The PRC's leaders have been the first to admit that they are not only nationalistic but communist as well, with concurrent obligations to serve their own country and to spread communism the world over. On the other hand, Mao Tse-tung, Chou En-lai, and their associates started their revolutionary careers as nationalists, intensely aware of the need to bring an end to nearly a century of national frustrations, humiliation, and defeat suffered at the hands of foreign powers, Japan and Czarist Russia in particular (see ch. 3, Historical Setting).

In their determination to modernize and revitalize China, the PRC's leaders adopted the alien Marxism-Leninism-Stalinism as the basic guide to their program for sweeping change. Not content with accepting the foreign ideology in its original form, Mao has modified some aspects of it to fit China's own conditions and in time has revised it in the form of Mao Tse-tung Thought (see ch. 9, Political System and Values). Ideological modification almost immediately has posed a challenge to the Soviet Union's status as the repository of doctrinal truth; mutual suspicions, accentuated by historical border conflicts and cultural differences between the Chinese and the Russians have led to what is commonly known as the Sino-Soviet dispute. This dispute has had far-reaching consequences in the conduct of foreign relations in both countries.

The PRC's foreign policy has shown underlying continuities, despite tactical shifts appropriate to changing domestic and external situations. Its policy objectives have been to preserve territorial integrity, to secure universal recognition for the PRC as the sole legitimate representative of the Chinese people, to enhance international stature, to establish the PRC as the preeminent power in Asia, and to gain leadership of the world communist movement and of the third world to counterbalance the power of the United States and the Soviet Union.

In pursuing these ends, the government has sought to develop economic and defense capabilities and to translate its tangible power into a foreign policy instrument of persuasion, both peaceful and coercive. It has also attempted to isolate Nationalist China internationally, to broaden and diversify its foreign contacts, and to play an enlarged role in world affairs commensurate with the size of its population and its potential power. At the same time, the PRC has exerted pressures on neighboring countries, especially Japan and India, in an effort to convert Asia into its sphere of influence; this effort has entailed a set of policies designed to establish friendly states along Chinese borders and to exclude the military, economic, and political influences of the United States from Asia and weaken the Soviet position in the region.

Central to the PRC's foreign policy strategy has been the assumption that the poor nations of the world emerging from colonial oppression have a common interest and a duty to cooperate with one another in their common anti-imperialist struggles. The PRC has found it expedient to stress the theme that it too was a poor country once under foreign aggression but that it successfully freed itself from foreign rule through revolutionary armed struggle. It has claimed to be "the most faithful and reliable comrade in arms of the oppressed peoples and nations" and has in fact told foreign revolutionary organizations, to emulate Mao's successful revolutionary experience. In June 1963 the Chinese Communist Party (CCP) openly accused the Soviet Union of not paying sufficient attention to pressing problems of revolution in underdeveloped countries; it also declared that "the attitude taken towards the revolutionary struggles of the people in Asian, African, and Latin American countries" was "an important criterion" for determining whether one was a friend or foe of these countries.

The PRC's division of the world into opposing camps of poor and affluent countries has an important bearing on its strategy toward the United States and the Soviet Union. Minister of National Defense Lin Piao in September 1965 asserted that "North America and Western Europe," which he called "the cities of the world," could ultimately be defeated by Asian, African, and Latin American countries, or "the rural areas of the world." Implicit in his statement was the notion that the PRC regarded the Soviet Union as belonging to "the cities" and that the PRC and "the rural areas" should heighten vigilance against the "Soviet-United States collaboration for the domination of the world."

The PRC's often-expressed fear of Soviet-United States collusion against itself is reflected in its exhortation that small and medium-sized nations should unite and resist bullying by superpowers. The PRC government has attempted to create the impression that superpowers are essentially aggressive, are prone to interfere in the internal affairs of other smaller countries, and are engaged in nuclear threats and nuclear blackmail. In mid-1971 Premier Chou En-lai told foreign visitors that his government "neither now nor ever in future" would assume the role of superpower. He said his country was against sending troops abroad and produced nuclear weapons only in the hope of ending the nuclear monopoly of superpowers. To underscore the defensive nature of its own nuclear weapons program, Chou's government has reiterated its position that "at no time and under no circumstances will China be the first to use nuclear weapons." Its suspicion of "the two superpowers" is also shown in its rejection in 1971 of the Soviet proposal for a five-power nuclear summit conference; its argument was that "the problem of complete prohibition and destruction of all nuclear weapons" should be solved not by a few big powers but by "a summit conference of all countries, big and small."

Since 1949 the PRC's foreign relations have shown shifts in priorities in reaction to internal and external exigencies. In the broadest terms, the PRC's main concern from 1949 to 1953 was to defend the country's borders, strengthen its ties with other socialist countries, and learn from the advanced experiences of the Soviet Union.

Between 1954 and 1957 peaceful coexistence was the dominant theme. China subscribed to Prime Minister Jawaharlal Nehru's five principles of peaceful coexistence as set forth in the preamble to the 1954 Sino-Indian agreement on Tibet. These principles were: mutual respect for each other's territorial integrity and sovereignty; mutual nonaggression; mutual noninterference in each other's internal affairs; equality and mutual benefit; and peaceful coexistence. The PRC's moderation was based on the realization that militant attitudes toward other Asian countries would force the latter to seek the protection of Western powers.

The combination of optimism, nationalistic assertiveness, and frustration marked the third phase of foreign relations between 1958 and 1965. This period started with Mao's unsuccessful efforts to press the Soviet Union into a more militant anti-United States posture. It continued with his humiliation of India in 1962, weakening India's claim to be the spokesman for the third world, and making a bid to replace Nehru as the leader of the Afro-Asian bloc; but this period ended on a bitter note in 1965 when many Afro-Asian nations refused to back the PRC's efforts to exclude the Soviet Union from the second Afro-Asian People's Solidarity Conference scheduled for June of that year.

The Cultural Revolution from 1966 to 1969 precipitated the country's virtual isolation from the outside world and a sharp decline in its prestige abroad. Although the overriding concerns of the government during this period were domestic, excesses of the Red Guards (see Glossary) overflowed into the country's foreign affairs, disrupting its relations with more than thirty countries. The height of this disruption was reached in 1967 when the PRC not only attempted to export "the great red banner of the invincible thought of Mao Tse-tung" abroad but also lashed out at any country, noncommunist or communist, said to have committed real or imaginary slights against the Cultural Revolution.

Beginning in mid-1969 the PRC government became less vitriolic and sought in earnest to restore friendly relations with other countries and to cultivate new contacts wherever possible. The spirit of the post-Cultural Revolution foreign relations was aptly described by the *People's Daily* in January 1970: "It has always been our persistent policy that our relations with other countries are to be developed on the basis of the five principles of peaceful coexistence."

MECHANICS OF FOREIGN RELATIONS

The towering figure in the PRC's foreign relations since 1949 has been Premier Chou, who once headed the Ministry of Foreign Affairs (from 1949 to 1958). His successor, Ch'en I, stayed on until mid-1967, when he was criticized by Red Guards and was ousted by a group of extremist junior officials within the ministry. These radicals were later thrown out and were replaced by officials of more moderate persuasion. In 1971 Chi P'eng-fei was serving as acting minister, but indications were that Premier Chou was actually in command of the nation's foreign affairs.

As far as can be ascertained, the Ministry of Foreign Affairs had, in 1971, four geographical departments: Asian Affairs; Soviet Union and East European Affairs; West Asian and African Affairs; and West European, American, and Australasian Affairs. Its functional units included the General Office and departments relating to protocol, information, political affairs, general services, international affairs, personnel, treaty and law, training, consular affairs, and translation. Of these, only the General Office and the information and protocol departments had their directors and "responsible persons" identified publicly.

Although the foreign ministry is the principal organization responsible for the conduct of foreign relations, other agencies have some responsibilities in this area. These include the Ministry of Foreign Trade, the Ministry of Economic Relations with Foreign Countries, the Commission for Cultural Relations with Foreign Countries, the Overseas Chinese Affairs Commission, and the Foreign Affairs Section of the Ministry of National Defense, which supervises military missions abroad (there were twenty-six such missions in the mid-1960s). The Chinese Academy of Sciences also plays an auxiliary role in matters relating to scientific and technological cooperation with foreign countries. The China Committee for the Promotion of International Trade maintains a number of "unofficial" trade missions abroad, and the Chinese People's Association for Friendship with Foreign Countries handles matters concerning friendship societies, student and cultural exchanges, and related "nongovernmental" contacts.

The far-flung network of the official New China News Agency (NCNA) in foreign capitals also plays an important role as both disseminator and collector of information useful to the formulation and conduct of foreign policy in Peking (see ch. 12, Public Information and Propaganda). Some NCNA "correspondents" are

301

known to have taken part in clandestine, antigovernment, or pro-Communist Chinese activities in foreign countries; a number of them have been expelled from various countries, especially in the second half of the 1960s.

During the Cultural Revolution the operation of these agencies was virtually suspended as a result of indiscriminate Red Guard attacks on their ranking officials. At the peak of the Red Guard frenzy in 1967, the Ministry of Foreign Affairs was actually taken over by a group of radical officials, and the government, having lost control of the ministry, was unable to conduct normal diplomatic relations with foreign governments. All but one of the PRC mission chiefs were recalled for "reeducation," and many of them were denounced by Red Guards for their "bourgeois" attitudes and disappeared from public life. The radical elements denounced diplomatic immunity as a "remnant of bourgeois institutions," harassed scores of foreign diplomats and nationals, sacked the British mission, and attacked the Indonesian, Burmese, and other embassies, all in Peking. Pro-Mao Chinese residents in foreign countries also provoked incidents, in protest against foreign government bans on wearing Mao badges or distributing propaganda materials. Since mid-1969, however, diplomatic relations with foreign governments have been gradually restored to normality; some of the ablest diplomats have been returned to their overseas posts.

The PRC's external relations are carried on through three distinct but sometimes overlapping channels. The first channel is the formal government-to-government diplomacy dealing with state visits, economic and technical aid, military assistance, and trade. Activities in this category are overt and are sanctioned under bilateral government agreements.

The second channel is the semiofficial people-to-people intercourse, or "people's diplomacy" as the PRC calls it. This channel is commonly used in contacts with countries that do not formally recognize the PRC. It includes trade, cultural and scientific exchanges, and sports competition, as well as cultivation of sympathetic or dissident groups within the target country. Technically, these activities take place between nongovernmental groups. From the PRC's point of view, "people's diplomacy" is regarded as a transitional step toward eventual mutual diplomatic recognition and as a very important tool for influencing domestic political opinion in a given foreign country.

The third form of relationship is maintained between the CCP and Communist parties or other leftist groups in noncommunist countries. The PRC may or may not have formal diplomatic or semiofficial contacts with the countries where PRC-supported antigovernmental or insurgent activities take place. This party-to-party channel is

302

under the direction of the Party's International Liaison Department instead of the Ministry of Foreign Affairs.

Of particular interest in the PRC's efforts to cultivate international contacts has been the extension of economic and technical assistance to a growing number of less-developed nations. This aid program, which began in 1956, averaged less than the equivalent of US$30 million annually through 1959 but rose to an annual average of about US$125 million between 1960 and 1965. By 1965 PRC aid to these countries had totaled almost US$850 million in credits and grants; about 50 percent of this amount to Asia, 32 percent to Africa, and the remainder to the Middle East. This sharp increase was attributable to the intensifying Sino-Soviet competition for influence in the noncommunist world, as well as to PRC's stepped-up efforts to counter Nationalist China's much publicized aid activities in Africa.

During the 1956-65 decade, recipient countries utilized only about 15 percent of the aid offered them. The low ratio of utilization was attributable, among other factors, to the economic difficulties and politically inspired suspicions of recipient countries as well as to the PRC's inexperience in administering foreign aid activities.

Much of the Chinese aid was focused on small-scale light industrial projects and was extended mostly interest free. The aid was to be repaid over ten years with a ten-year grace period. About 20 percent of the aid was extended in the form of grants, but indications after 1965 were that emphasis was shifting from grants to loans. The repayment was to be made in commodity exports of the recipient country or in indigenous or convertible currency.

Under its technical assistance program, the PRC provided skilled and semiskilled technicians for projects relating to roadbuilding and bridgebuilding, agricultural activities, and dam construction. A number of foreign students and technicians were also brought to mainland China for a variety of training with the PRC providing for their expenses.

During the Cultural Revolution the PRC's aid was drastically reduced, but in 1970, in line with Premier Chou En-lai's renewed post-Cultural Revolution bid for a greater role as a world power, aid was greatly increased, totaling the equivalent of nearly US$710 million in that year alone. (Tanzania, Zambia, and Pakistan accounted for the bulk of this amount.) The PRC thus emerged in 1970 as the largest single donor among the communist countries of nonmilitary foreign aid to developing nations, far outstripping the Soviet Union that in 1970 pledged about US$200 million in economic aid. The PRC's 1970 total represented about 43 percent of all the aid it had extended in the years after 1956.

THE REPUBLIC OF CHINA ON TAIWAN

The PRC's political competition with the government of the Republic of China (Nationalist China) took a new turn in October 1971 when Nationalist China was voted out of the UN by a majority of its members. Although this new situation represented a major foreign policy achievement for the PRC, it did not immediately bring about any change in the hostile relationships that had existed between those on the mainland and Taiwan for more than two decades. The PRC's goal of "recovering" the island province remained unfulfilled in 1971, and its legitimacy as the sole government of China was still challenged by Nationalist China. From all indications, it appears that Nationalist China would remain a major problem in the PRC's foreign policy and relations.

The PRC attempted to incorporate Taiwan initially by military means, but this effort brought the United States, which is committed to the defense of Nationalist China under a mutual assistance treaty, into a position of active political and intermittent military counteraction. In 1971 Communist Chinese artillery continued to shell the islands off Amoy that were in the hands of the Nationalist Chinese; the PRC and Nationalist China remained at an impasse in their territorial confrontation.

Apart from its military threat of "liberation," the PRC used the familiar techniques of diplomatic, people-to-people, and party activities to effectuate the isolation of Nationalist China in the international community. It was apparent that the PRC's tactic was to strengthen the case for its status as the only legitimate government of China by treating the question of Nationalist China as a domestic concern and by asserting that Taiwan was "an inalienable part" of China. This tactic worked without problems in the case of nations that had no bilateral relations with Nationalist China—for example, some of the newly independent African states—but countries that had maintained diplomatic ties with Nationalist China presented difficulties. Thus in negotiations with Canada and Italy that resulted in diplomatic recognition of the PRC in 1970, the PRC agreed, for expediency, to wording markedly less stringent than previously. In their joint communiques with the PRC, Canada and Italy merely took note of the Communist Chinese position that Taiwan was an integral part of its territory. The PRC's acquiescence to this wording appeared to suggest that it was more interested in gaining immediate recognition of its legitimacy than in the immediate recovery of the island province.

THE UNITED STATES

The PRC's relations with the United States were on the verge of change, potentially dramatic, in October 1971. The rapid succession of events in the preceding six months—the PRC's invitation to a United States Ping-Pong team and its acceptance of a visit to Peking, the relaxation by the United States of its unilateral barriers to trade with mainland China, the joint United States-PRC announcement of a trip to Peking by President Richard M. Nixon, and the decision of the United States to support the PRC's entry into the United Nations General Assembly in October 1971 (but rejecting the expulsion of Nationalist China) presaged some thaw in the PRC's attitude toward the United States. The PRC's public posture was certain to be altered in some way, but the manner in which this new policy would be translated into specifics remained unclear. The process might well be slow, as the PRC groped for new policies in its withdrawal from a period of virtual isolation, self-imposed during the Cultural Revolution. One of the important elements in both the substance of the policies and the pace of their implementation might well be the state of the PRC's relations with the Soviet Union.

In 1971 the complex of factors that had previously conditioned the PRC's policy toward and relations with the United States appeared likely to remain unchanged in the immediate future. These factors were the PRC's perception of national interest (sovereignty, territorial integrity, and economic benefit), the shifting scheme of great power relationships, the imperatives and constraints of ideology, and the strong historical sense that pervades Chinese thinking. Up to early 1971 these factors had produced a strong animosity—stridently expressed toward the United States. Its behavior, however, has been cautious. Whether this characteristic would remain was one of the many questions that remained to be answered.

The nature and course of the PRC's relations with the United States as a practical matter has been strongly conditioned also by United States actions. Since 1950 the product of this interaction was an almost diametrical opposition. The likely points of major difference would be continued United States recognition of and association with Nationalist China, United States efforts to reach agreement on arms control with the Soviet Union, and on the Vietnam conflict with the government of the Democratic Republic of Vietnam (North Vietnam).

The PRC in its early days saw the outer world clearly in terms of the Leninist conception of contradiction between socialism and imperialism. This perception led the Communist Chinese to "lean to one side," toward the Soviet Union, and to label the United States as the leader of the imperialist camp when the United States blocked by threat of force the PRC's completion of its revolution by taking over Taiwan. Though circumstances had changed, especially because cooperation with the Soviet Union had become open competition, these concepts remained the cornerstones of PRC foreign policy in 1971.

The newly established communist government considered that the United States had a favorable image in China. Once its policy toward the United States had been set, it proceeded to try to destroy the image, with what long-term effects could not be determined. Although almost any obstruction to the attainment of PRC goals could be exploited for this purpose, the most prominent were connected with the wars in Korea and Vietnam. The United States government, as the PRC's chief enemy, is presented in the country's propaganda both as being a "paper tiger" strategically and thus to be scorned and as representing the interests not of the friendly and oppressed (especially nonwhite) people of the United States but of the ruling monopoly capitalist class.

The PRC has, without doubt, felt vulnerable to and genuinely feared pressures and threats from the United States from the beginning of its active concern with international affairs. Its reaction was clearly reflected in the Sino-Soviet treaty of February 1950, which was an alliance against "Japan or any other state" (meaning the United States) joined with Japan.

Formal contacts between the PRC and the United States took place at the Geneva conferences of 1954 and 1961 to 1962, which were convened to deal with the Indochina war and Laos, respectively. Communist Chinese behavior in both instances was restrained, in contrast to accompanying hostile rhetoric. At the first conference, the PRC and the United States agreed to establish direct official contacts. The dialogue between the PRC and the United States continued at irregular intervals, first in Geneva and later in Warsaw, until 1970.

THE UNITED NATIONS

On October 25, 1971, the United Nations General Assembly voted favorably on a resolution sponsored by Albania and others to seat the PRC and to expel Nationalist China. The voting showed seventy-six in favor, thirty-five opposed, seventeen abstaining, and three absent (see table 5). Earlier the General Assembly had defeated a resolution declaring the expulsion of Nationalist China an "important question" and thus requiring a two-thirds rather than a simple majority for passage (see table 6). The outcome of voting on the two resolutions signified the major initial step toward the PRC's efforts "to restore all its rights" and to gain recognition of its stand that its representatives are "the only lawful representatives to the United Nations." After the voting the PRC announced its decision to send delegates to the United Nations.

The PRC's case for representation in the UN was made public almost immediately after its conquest of the mainland. In November 1949 the PRC sent a note to the president of the UN General

Table 5. *People's Republic of China, United Nations Vote on Resolution to Seat PRC and Expel Nationalist China*

In favor—(76)

Afghanistan	Denmark	Laos	Singapore
Albania	Ecuador	Libya	Somalia
Algeria	Equatorial	Malaysia	Southern Yemen
Arab Republic of	Guinea	Mali	Soviet Union
Egypt	Ethiopia	Mauritania	Sudan
Austria	Finland	Mexico	Sweden
Belgium	France	Mongolia	Syria
Bhutan	Ghana	Morocco	Tanzania
Botswana	Guinea	Nepal	Togo
Bulgaria	Guyana	Netherlands	Trinidad-Tobago
Burma	Hungary	Nigeria	Tunisia
Burundi	Iceland	Norway	Turkey
Byelorussian SSR	India	Pakistan	Uganda
Cameroon	Iran	Peru	Ukrainian SSR
Canada	Iraq	Poland	United Kingdom
Ceylon	Ireland	Portugal	Yemen
Chile	Israel	Romania	Yugoslavia
Congo (Brazzaville)	Italy	Rwanda	Zambia
Cuba	Kenya	Senegal	
Czechoslovakia	Kuwait	Sierra Leone	

Opposed—(35)

Australia	Dahomey	Japan	Philippines
Bolivia	Dominican	Lesotho	Saudi Arabia
Brazil	Republic	Liberia	South Africa
Cambodia (Khmer	El Salvador	Madagascar	Swaziland
Rep.)	Gabon	Malawi	United States
Central African	Gambia	Malta	Upper Volta
Republic	Guatemala	New Zealand	Uruguay
Chad	Haiti	Nicaragua	Venezuela
Congo (Kinshasa)	Honduras	Niger	
Costa Rica	Ivory Coast	Paraguay	

Abstentions—(17)

Argentina	Fiji	Lebanon	Spain
Bahrain	Greece	Luxembourg	Thailand
Barbados	Indonesia	Mauritius	
Colombia	Jamaica	Panama	
Cyprus	Jordan	Qatar	

Absent—(3)

China (Taiwan)	Maldives	Oman

Note. Resolution voted on October 25, 1971, sponsored by Albania, Algeria, Ceylon, Congo (Brazzaville), Cuba, Equatorial Guinea, Guinea, Iraq, Mali, Mauritania, Nepal, Pakistan, Romania, Somalia, Southern Yemen (People's Democratic Republic of Yemen), Syria, Sudan, Tanzania, Yemen (Arab Republic of Yemen), Yugoslavia, and Zambia.

Source: Adapted from *New York Times*, October 26, 1971, p. 1.

Table 6. People's Republic of China, United Nations Vote on Resolution Declaring the Expulsion of Nationalist China an "Important Question"

In favor—(55)

Argentina	Dahomey	Jamaica	Paraguay
Australia	Dominican	Japan	Philippines
Bahrain	Republic	Jordan	Portugal
Barbados	El Salvador	Lebanon	Rwanda
Bolivia	Fiji	Lesotho	Saudi Arabia
Brazil	Gabon	Liberia	South Africa
Cambodia (Khmer	Gambia	Luxembourg	Spain
Rep.)	Ghana	Madagascar	Swaziland
Central African	Greece	Malawi	Thailand
Republic	Guatemala	Mauritius	United States
Chad	Haiti	Mexico	Upper Volta
China (Taiwan)	Honduras	New Zealand	Uruguay
Colombia	Indonesia	Nicaragua	Venezuela
Congo (Kinshasa)	Israel	Niger	
Costa Rica	Ivory Coast	Panama	

Opposed—(59)

Afghanistan	Cuba	Ireland	Sierra Leone
Albania	Czechoslovakia	Kenya	Singapore
Algeria	Denmark	Kuwait	Somalia
Arab Republic of	Ecuador	Libya	Southern Yemen
Egypt	Equatorial	Malaysia	Soviet Union
Bhutan	Guinea	Mali	Sudan
Bulgaria	Ethiopia	Mauritania	Sweden
Burma	Finland	Mongolia	Syria
Burundi	France	Nepal	Tanzania
Byelorussian SSR	Guinea	Nigeria	Trinidad-Tobago
Cameroon	Guyana	Norway	Uganda
Canada	Hungary	Pakistan	Ukrainian SSR
Ceylon	Iceland	Peru	United Kingdom
Chile	India	Poland	Yemen
Congo (Brazzaville)	Iraq	Romania	Yugoslavia
			Zambia

Abstentions—(15)

Austria	Iran	Morocco	Togo
Belgium	Italy	Netherlands	Tunisia
Botswana	Laos	Qatar	Turkey
Cyprus	Malta	Senegal	

Absent—(2)

Maldives	Oman

Note. Resolution voted on October 25, 1971, sponsored by Australia, Bolivia, Costa Rica, Dominican Republic, El Salvador, Fiji, Gambia, Guatemala, Haiti, Honduras, Japan, Liberia, New Zealand, Mauritius, Nicaragua, Philippines, Swaziland, Thailand, United States, and Uruguay.

Source: Adapted from *New York Times*, October 26, 1971, p. 1.

Assembly denying the authority of Nationalist China to speak in the UN on behalf of the Chinese people. In December 1949 the Soviet representative on the UN Security Council supported the PRC's claim and challenged the competence of the Kuomintang (Nationalist Party, often abbreviated as KMT) group. The Security Council took no action. In January 1950 the Soviet Union again supported the PRC's request that the Security Council expel the KMT group. This move was also defeated, causing the Soviet Union to walk out and to remain absent from the Security Council until August 1950. When the Soviet representative returned and assumed the presidency of the Security Council in regular rotation, he ruled the exclusion of the Nationalist Chinese representatives from the council, but his ruling was challenged and overruled.

The PRC's first and the only appearance in the United Nations (through October 1971) occurred in November 1950, when the PRC presented its case on the outbreak of war in Korea and the entry of PRC troops into the war in the preceding month. The purpose of this appearance was to accuse the United States of "aggression" in Korea, and not to plead the PRC's case for being seated in the UN. The General Assembly adopted a resolution in February 1951 condemning the PRC as having "itself engaged in aggression in Korea." In May 1951 the General Assembly passed a resolution imposing an embargo on the export of "strategic materials" (specifically "arms, ammunition and implements of war, atomic energy materials, petroleum, transportation materials of strategic value and items useful in the production of arms, ammunition, and implements of war") to the PRC.

The PRC's case was presented and argued by others in successive UN sessions, notably by the Soviet Union and India, at various times depending on their relations with the PRC, and by Albania. The Soviet Union consistently supported the admission of the PRC. Since December 1950 the matter has been considered in the General Assembly rather than in the Security Council.

During the 1960s, after the experiences with the UN in the preceding decade, the PRC did not seem eager to join the UN. In a statement made in October 1963, its foreign minister said that the PRC had no intention of seeking a UN seat because under circumstances at the time "China had no role to play in the United Nations." In 1965 the PRC's foreign minister stated his government's conditions for entry into the UN: ousting of the "Chiang clique"; cancellation of the 1951 aggressor resolution and adoption of a resolution condemning the United States as an aggressor; review and revision of the UN Charter; and inclusion of all independent states in the UN and expulsion of all "imperialist puppets."

By the mid-1960s the increase in UN membership, mostly of newly independent former colonial territories, had resulted in generally greater support for the PRC in the voting on the several kinds of proposals put forward. This favorable trend was halted during the Cultural Revolution because of adverse foreign reactions to the PRC's attempts to export the Maoist version of revolution. The PRC's more conciliatory approaches from 1969 on were, however, generally well received in foreign capitals, and in the fall of 1970 for the first time a majority in the General Assembly supported a motion to seat the PRC in the UN, but this support fell short of the two-thirds plurality required for formal adoption. In 1971 the leaders of the PRC showed greater interest than ever before in playing a role in the UN, prompted in no small measure by the prospect of modification of United States policy toward the PRC.

THE SOVIET UNION

When the PRC formally stated its foreign policy, in late 1949, it emphasized the fundamental importance of close and friendly relations with the Soviet Union. According to Mao Tse-tung, the PRC was to "lean to one side"—toward the Soviet Union. Soon afterward, Mao made his first trip outside China, going to Moscow where he participated in the negotiations for a treaty of friendship between the PRC and the Soviet Union, which was concluded on February 14, 1950. Two other agreements were signed at the same time: one for the return to the PRC no later than 1952 of Soviet rights in Manchuria; and the other for a long-term credit to the PRC for the purchase of capital equipment in the Soviet Union.

The treaty of friendship, alliance, and mutual assistance between the two countries remained in effect in 1971 and continued to be observed for certain aspects of their relations, such as Soviet support for seating the PRC in the UN. Its terms made no provision for denunciation by either party before the last year of its specified validity of thirty years. The PRC and the Soviet Union agreed on the affirmative and negative aspects of their future cooperation, consultation, and mutual respect as sovereign states, without reference to their "fraternal" communist relationship.

The period of closest friendship and cooperation between the PRC and the Soviet Union lasted from 1949 to 1955. The Soviet Union provided technical assistance, plans, and capital equipment for the industrialization of mainland China's economy and assistance for the organization of the Chinese Communist system generally. In the conduct of their foreign relations the two countries usually acted in concert, as in support of the North Koreans in the Korean conflict.

Beginning in about 1956, Sino-Soviet disagreements widened gradually, initially over doctrinal issues, and progressively greater importance was attached to their respective national interests. These conflicts of national interests, however, usually took the form of dispute over ideology.

The apparent root of differences was in Premier Nikita Khrushchev's policy of de-Stalinization announced in February 1956 —without any prior consultation with the PRC leadership. To the Chinese Communists, this was "revisionism" (see Glossary); to the Russians, the rejection of their view was "dogmatism." At stake was the immediate and fundamental question of doctrinal overlordship within the communist world, whether by the Communist Party of the Soviet Union (CPSU) or by the CCP.

Differences in the national interests of the PRC and the Soviet Union first appeared when the latter remained neutral during the Sino-Indian border clashes in 1959. Another difference combining theory, practice, and national attitudes emerged when Mao Tse-tung's socialist transformation began to diverge from its Soviet model after Mao approved the policies that resulted in the Great Leap Forward (see Glossary) and the system of People's Communes (see Glossary) (see ch. 13, Character and Structure of the Economy; ch. 14, Agriculture). Khrushchev was reported to have described the Commune system as "reactionary."

Controversy came into the open in the 1960–62 period. At this stage the PRC publicly accused the Soviet Union of being "revisionist," and the Soviet Union countered that the Communist Chinese were "dogmatic" and "reckless," especially in their view on nuclear war. In their mutual recriminations, neither named the other, referring instead to Yugoslavia and Albania as the holders of the views being criticized. In 1960 the Soviet leadership unilaterally withdrew technical aid, an action deeply resented by the PRC, which was at that time in dire need of foreign aid because of the disastrous Great Leap Forward. Moreover, much to the dismay of the PRC, in early 1963—in the wake of the Sino-Indian border war in late 1962—the Soviet Union gave aid to India, including MIG-21 jet fighters.

In the 1963–64 period the conflict intensified as acrimony mounted, the PRC indicting Khrushchev and the Soviet Union, accusing the Communist Chinese of being nationalist and Stalinist. Each country took actions in its foreign relations of which the other disapproved; one instance was bitter Communist Chinese denunciation of the Soviet acceptance in 1962 of compromise with the United States and removal of its missiles from Cuba.

In 1963 there was in one exchange the first indication of the possibility of renewed conflict over territorial claims, a source of friction since the seventeenth century. In the post-Khrushchev period of 1965 and early 1966 the two countries exchanged allegations of border provocations, and the first popular demonstrations were staged by the Communist Chinese as the change in Soviet leadership brought about no more than a temporary respite. In April 1966 for the first time the CCP stayed away from a congress of the CPSU.

The breach in the party-to-party relations, as distinct from the government-to-government relations, widened enormously during the Cultural Revolution period of 1966 to 1969. The main issues were hostility to "Soviet revisionism" and refusal to cooperate with the Soviet Union on aid to North Vietnam on the terms proposed. In December 1966 the Soviet party's Central Committee used Mao's name for the first time in condemning his policies. Both countries increased their border forces, and each accused the other of starting the fighting that took place at disputed points. The PRC accused the Soviet Union of collusion with the United States against the PRC, and the Soviet leadership countered by accusing the PRC of provoking conflict between the United States and the Soviet Union. The most serious difference between the two countries arose from the suppression in 1968 of the reform-oriented regime of Alexander Dubcek in Czechoslovakia by Soviet-led military action. The PRC charged the Soviets with the crime of aggression, and the latter justified its action by proclaiming the "theory of limited sovereignty" (see Glossary).

A series of clashes along the border in early 1969 raised tensions to a high level, to the point of rumors of impending war. In October 1969, however, the two countries began negotiations on the border problem. The talks continued through mid-1971, unofficially reported as at a stalemate, but no border incidents had been reported since the talks started. Polemical exchanges took place in the latter half of 1969 but virtually ceased for a year after April 1970. There was improvement in government-to-government relations in 1970, evidenced by the exchange of ambassadors (withdrawn in 1967), the conclusion of a Sino-Soviet trade agreement for tripling the value of bilateral trade, and the unusually warm tone of messages exchanged on the national days of the two countries in that year.

The improvement of PRC-United States relations in early 1971 brought renewal of charges by both the PRC and the Soviet Union that the other was acting in collusion with the United States. Relations between the PRC and the Soviet Union were tense in 1971, and the two remained still deadlocked in their dispute over a wide range of problems. One Western observer stated that, even if tensions between the two were reduced, there would be little likelihood that the alliance could be restored to the cordiality of the 1949–55 period. The conflict of interests, resentment, and suspicions between the PRC and the Soviet Union were too deeply embedded. He noted that the Sino-Soviet conflict has affected the foreign policies of all major states with respect to Asia. The PRC appeared to be groping for new policies while preoccupied with domestic matters and the threat of actual war with the Soviet Union. The effect of the Sino-Soviet dispute upon the worldwide scheme of power relationships was to effectuate a shift to multipolarity from United States-Soviet Union bipolarity. The dispute also provided the United States with an opportunity to move in new directions in overall policies toward East Asia.

THE OVERSEAS CHINESE

Since 1949 the Overseas Chinese have constituted not only an important target of the PRC's foreign policy but also an instrument of its "people's diplomacy." About 97 percent of the estimated 18.3 million Overseas Chinese (at the end of 1968) are scattered in enclaves from the Philippines to Burma and south into Singapore and Indonesia (see ch. 2, Physical Environment and Population). The PRC has shown much interest in the Chinese abroad for both political and economic reasons.

There has been considerable intermarriage with local people throughout Southeast Asia, but most Overseas Chinese have preserved their language and traditions and their own neighborhoods, schools, and voluntary organizations. They have retained close links with their kinship groups in mainland China, chiefly in the coastal provinces of Fukien and Kwangtung, from which more than 90 percent of Overseas Chinese emigrated.

Industrious and frugal, Overseas Chinese have amassed great wealth and control a sizable portion of the economic activity of the countries in which they live; this isolation and wealth have often caused local resentment and have prompted their host countries to initiate measures designed, on the one hand, to hasten their assimilation and, on the other, to weaken their formidable economic power.

With the exception of Singapore, the Overseas Chinese as a whole have avoided becoming involved in local politics but have often found it necessary to make payoffs in order to preserve or promote their economic interests. Within their own communities, competition for control of power and influence has been intense and sometimes acrimonious but has seldom involved ideological issues. In all these communities there is a hard core of Communists or pro-Communists, usually among the younger element, who, for both idealistic and nationalistic reasons, are impressed by the advancement the PRC has made toward world power status. The vast majority of Overseas Chinese, however, have tended to be fence sitters in political matters affecting the PRC and Nationalist China. Many owe their affluence to free-enterprise economies, but they have tended to refrain from publicly criticizing the PRC for fear that their relatives on the mainland might be persecuted. Expressions of PRC sympathy or allegiance, wherever they exist, have tended to derive more from particularistic factors such as kinship loyalty than from ideological preference.

The PRC, as was true of its predecessor governments, considers that all persons of Chinese blood are Chinese citizens regardless of where they were born or reside. Both the Common Program of 1949 and the 1954 State Constitution stated that the PRC would protect the "legitimate interests and rights" of the Chinese residents abroad; in addition, the 1954 constitution provided for a representation in the National People's Congress of thirty Overseas Chinese. The 1970 draft state constitution also contains a similar provision but without referring to the number of reserved seats.

The PRC's policy toward the Overseas Chinese changed according to shifting internal and external priorities. From 1949 to 1953 the PRC was generally militant in its efforts to infiltrate, influence, and control Overseas Chinese communities, often to the point of antagonizing some of the Southeast Asian governments. It was through the manipulation of these Chinese that the PRC attempted to influence the policies of their governments to be favorable toward the PRC. In 1954 it shifted to a more circumspect line in keeping with its newly enunciated principle of peaceful coexistence; the Overseas Chinese were asked by Premier Chou to refrain from interfering in local politics and to work for the improvement of relations between their countries of residence and the mainland. The PRC also vigorously sought to capture the loyalty of the Overseas Chinese by appealing to nationalist and patriotic themes and considerably toning down communist propaganda.

More important, the conciliatory approach was dictated by the increasing need to attract Overseas Chinese capital and channel it into the mainland economy. In 1955 the Overseas Chinese Investment Corporation was established, with branches in seven provinces and six larger cities, and issued a preferential investment policy by which Overseas Chinese investors were guaranteed an annual 8-percent return on their investments (as compared with 5 percent for domestic investors). Despite this policy, remittances to mainland China, a major source of foreign exchange earnings for the PRC, continued to decline from the peak of the equivalent of US$150 million in 1952 to about US$52 million in 1958; after the disastrous Great Leap and the Commune experiment, the sum dropped in 1959 to an all-time low of about US$36 million. By 1962 the remittances, which were viewed more or less as an indication of Overseas Chinese attachment to their homeland, had increased to about US$62 million, an amount that was believed to have remained fairly stable through the mid-1960s. Remittances dropped sharply during the chaotic years of the Cultural Revolution; during 1966 alone, those from Hong Kong declined 30 percent from the previous year, and those from Bangkok, 80 percent, according to a Japanese source.

A sizable number of people in the southern coastal province of China are financially dependent on these remittances. In 1957, according to an official mainland source, there were at least 10 million persons whose livelihood depended directly on this financial source. That this situation still prevailed in 1970 was indicated by the "three overseas movement" underway late that year in the province of Kwangtung. This movement was aimed at discouraging "the imitation of overseas trends," "dependence on overseas remittances and goods," and "admiration of the overseas way of life." According to an official directive, the ultimate objective of this drive was to stamp out the corrosive effects of foreign influence seeping in through the Overseas Chinese and to render the country less dependent on foreign technology and products.

During the Cultural Revolution, especially in 1967, Red Guards attempted to use Overseas Chinese communities in other Asian countries as a conduit for exporting Maoist thought. Many Chinese residents were encouraged to return for revolutionary activity on the mainland or for training for future assignment in foreign countries. Beginning in mid-1968, however, the PRC's line shifted from militancy to moderation; Overseas Chinese were told to stay in their countries of adoption and work for revolution there. Red Guard attacks on the relatives of Overseas Chinese ceased, and the authorities inaugurated a propaganda campaign designed to discourage dependence on remittances from abroad.

RELATIONS WITH SELECTED ASIAN COUNTRIES

Japan

As of October 1971, the PRC had no diplomatic relations with Japan, but the two countries had extensive trade and other unofficial contacts, despite the PRC's *pro forma* ideological insistence that trade and politics should be inseparable. Japan countered that trade was one thing and political relations another.

China and Japan had close historical ties, but their relations began deteriorating after the last decade of the nineteenth century as a result of Japan's military and economic thrusts into China (see ch. 3, Historical Setting). The legacy of bitter memories has therefore continued to underlie the Chinese Communist view of Japan. This has been especially the case with the PRC's concern about a revival, real or imagined, of Japanese militarism.

The PRC's fear of Japan has grown in proportion to the latter's rapid recovery from the ravages of World War II, its emergence as the preeminent economic power in Asia, its economic penetration into Southeast Asia, its steady development of defense capabilities, and the deepening of its ties with the United States. Japan has come to be regarded as the principal obstacle to the PRC's efforts to establish itself as the most influential Asian power.

Communist Chinese foreign policy toward Japan has been to prevent Japan from rearming, to gain a political foothold in Japan by aiding the "peace-loving" leftist opposition to the Liberal Democratic Party (LDP), to remove United States military and economic influence from Japan, and to seek the establishment of a neutral Japan friendly to the PRC. The Communist Chinese have sought to achieve these objectives by exerting economic, political, and psychological pressures through trade and "people's diplomacy."

The PRC first enunciated its "three political principles" in 1958 as a basis for improving Sino-Japanese relations. These principles, reaffirmed repeatedly and still in effect in 1971, were that the Japanese government must not be hostile toward the PRC, must not join in any conspiracy to create two Chinas, and must not obstruct any effort to restore normal relations between the two countries. Later in that year the PRC also called on the Japanese government to adopt a nonaligned foreign policy.

In its continuing attempt to check the alleged resurgence of Japanese militarism and to cause the breaching of Japanese-United States ties, the PRC in 1959 indicated to a visiting Japanese Socialist delegation its willingness to conclude a mutual nonaggression and collective security pact involving the PRC, Japan, the Soviet Union, and the United States if Japan repudiated its 1952 Treaty of Mutual Cooperation and Security with the United States. It also stated that, upon the conclusion of such a pact, the military clauses against "Japan or any other state allied with her" as contained in the Sino-Soviet treaty of 1950 would be expunged from that document. The PRC's peace pact offer was repeated in August 1960, when Premier Chou proposed the establishment of a nonnuclear zone in Asia and the Western Pacific.

Commercial exchanges were carried on under the "three trade principles" announced by Premier Chou in 1960. This set of principles provided for three types of exchanges: trade based on formal government agreements; private contracts sanctioned indirectly by governments; and special consideration in individual cases. The last of these types came to be known popularly as friendly trade—trade allowed by the PRC only to those Japanese firms that it considered to be friendly to the PRC. It was through this friendly trade, which was opened in late 1960, that the Communist Chinese government attempted to create a friendly Japanese political climate toward the mainland.

Because the PRC's generally militant attitude toward Japan from 1949 to 1960 tended to antagonize Japan, Premier Chou in 1962 announced a more flexible line emphasizing "gradual and cumulative methods" in developing Sino-Japanese economic and political relations. His government began toning down its anti-Japanese propaganda in an apparent effort to promote a long-term semiofficial trade. In the same year Liao Ch'eng-chih, a senior official of the PRC Ministry of Foreign Affairs, and Tatsunosuke Takasaki, a senior member of the LDP, signed a five-year trade memorandum (1963–67), the Liao-Takasaki Agreement, known as the L-T trade. In early 1968 the so-called L-T trade was renamed Japan-China Memorandum Trade or M-T trade (see ch. 18, Trade and Transportation).

The PRC's political attitude toward Japan stiffened after the mid-1960s, allegedly because of Japan's anti-PRC policy, its growing influence in South Korea and Nationalist China, its close military ties with the United States, and its rapid defense preparations. The PRC reacted in part by switching the emphasis from M-T trade to friendly trade. Propaganda attacks on Japan were particularly accentuated after November 1969, when the United States and Japan agreed on the terms for the return of Okinawa to Japan in 1972; this agreement provided that "the United States would retain under the terms of the Treaty of Mutual Cooperation and Security such military facilities and areas in Okinawa as required in the mutual security of both countries." The PRC charged that Japan was intensifying "its collusion" with the United States as well as the Soviet Union in an attempt to embark on aggression and expansion abroad.

Relations between the PRC and Japan have been complicated by Japan's attitudes toward Nationalist China, with which it had diplomatic ties after the signing of a Nationalist Chinese-Japanese peace treaty in 1952. The PRC asserted that this treaty was "illegal." Japan maintains a thriving trade with Nationalist China and also has considerable investments there. Its reluctance over the years to grant any long-term credit to the PRC arose from its fear of an adverse reaction from Nationalist China and to an extent also because of strong pro-Nationalist Chinese pressures within the ruling conservative party in Japan. The PRC in 1971 appeared to be gravely concerned about the possibility of Japan's return to Taiwan. It accused Japan of attempting to occupy the island permanently. In August 1971 Premier Chou asserted that if "Japanese militarim" was to assert itself abroad, it would first aim at Taiwan and Korea or "these two things" as he put it.

Beginning in the late 1960s the PRC quickened the tempo of "people's diplomacy" seeking to force the Japanese government to revise its China policy. The LDP government, already under pressures from the "doves" within the ruling group as well as from an assortment of opposition parties, gradually adopted a more conciliatory attitude toward the PRC; its conciliatory attitude was accentuated further after President Nixon announced in July 1971 his plan for a forthcoming visit to Peking.

Nevertheless, Japan's reluctance to forsake Nationalist China was made clear in Prime Minister Eisaku Sato's statement in July 1971: "If the condition for establishing diplomatic relations with China is to be the abrogation of the peace treaty with the Republic of China or the ouster of the Republic of China from the United Nations, we cannot help adopting a very cautious attitude." On the other hand, it also became clear that his government no longer opposed the seating of the PRC in the UN. Thus, in September 1971 Japan declared its intention of voting to seat both the PRC and Nationalist China in the UN but expressed the view that the China question should be solved "through peaceful dialogue" between the PRC and Nationalist China.

The PRC's reaction was predictably hostile and demanded the Japanese acceptance of "four principles" proclaimed in 1970. These called for Japanese recognition of the PRC as the sole legitimate government of the Chinese people; the recognition that Taiwan is an "inalienable part" of the territory of the PRC; the abrogation of "the Japan-Chiang treaty"; and the replacement of Nationalist China by the PRC in all UN organs and the expulsion of Nationalist China from the UN. In an apparent attempt to make these principles more palatable to the Japanese and also to capitalize on a growing Japanese mood of reassessing their view of China, a Communist Chinese spokesman is said to have told a visiting delegation of the Japanese Diet in September and October 1971 that his government would foreswear war reparations (to which the PRC had made claim) if Japan severed its treaty ties with Nationalist China and established diplomatic relations with the PRC.

Pakistan

Sino-Pakistani relations are focused on Pakistan's manifest feeling of insecurity with respect to India. Thus, although Pakistan became allied in 1954 with the United States and other Western powers through the Southeast Asia Treaty Organization (see Glossary), the Communist Chinese government has tended to view this alignment as a function of Indo-Pakistani confrontation and not as an indication of hostile Pakistani intentions toward the PRC. Beginning in the mid-1960s, the PRC became Pakistan's principal supplier of arms and developed a very friendly relationship with that country.

Relations with Pakistan had become somewhat tense during 1959 because of Communist Chinese encroachments into border areas that Pakistan claimed were within its jurisdiction. Pakistan also proposed to India a possible joint defense policy along the northern frontier in light of what was said to be a common threat from the north. The Sino-Indian border conflict of 1962, however, resulted in a marked improvement of ties between the PRC and Pakistan. In March 1963 three years of border negotiations ended with the signing of a frontier demarcation. A civil aviation agreement and a telecommunications agreement were also concluded during the year, as were trade and barter agreements. In 1964 the PRC offered a long-term, interest-free loan equivalent to US$60 million.

The PRC's increasingly pro-Pakistan orientation was clearly reflected in its attitude toward the Kashmir dispute, which is at the heart of Indo-Pakistani relations. Whereas until 1963 its position on this issue was ambivalent (as against the Soviet position that Kashmir was "an integral part of India"), a joint communiqué issued in 1964 by Premier Chou and President Mohammad Ayub Khan stated that the dispute should be solved "in accordance with the wishes of the people of Kashmir," thus unequivocally siding with Pakistan against India.

When fighting broke out between Pakistan and India in 1965, the PRC predictably supported Pakistan for its "just action in Kashmir to repel Indian armed provocation," declaring at the same time that "India's aggression against any one of its neighbors concerns all its neighbors." In late 1965 it began its delivery of tanks, MIG-19 fighters, and ground equipment to Pakistan.

In 1969 the ancient Sinkiang-Gilgit caravan route (traditionally known as the silk road) was reopened after twenty years. In early 1970 the first ordnance factory built with Communist Chinese assistance was opened near Dacca, in East Pakistan, and the PRC agreed to provide financial and technical assistance for several industrial projects. In November 1970 the two countries signed an economic and technical cooperation agreement under which the PRC extended an interest-free credit equivalent to US$200 million, reportedly as the first installment for Pakistan's Fourth Five Year Plan (1970–75); the terms of this loan call for repayment in twenty years (including a grace period of ten years), to be made in kind by exporting goods to the PRC. The 1970 loan brought the total Communist Chinese foreign aid to Pakistan from 1954 to 1970 to the equivalent of US$307 million.

In a joint communique issued in November 1970, the two countries noted that their friendly relations provided a good example of peaceful coexistence between "states practicing different social systems." Premier Chou also indicated in this communique the PRC's willingness to render further assistance within its means and capacity "to help make the economy of Pakistan self-reliant" and reaffirmed its support for Pakistan's struggle "for the defense of national independence and against all forms of outside aggression or foreign interference."

Despite its profession of friendship with the PRC, the government of Pakistan has generally refrained from taking sides in the Sino-Soviet dispute. Nonetheless, in November 1970 the PRC's NCNA made a point of recalling that a certain "superpower" had proposed a scheme for regional economic cooperation and collective security in Asia—in allusion to the Soviet Union's proposal made public in June 1969. The NCNA approvingly referred to Pakistan's previously announced reservations about this cooperative scheme and asserted that this proposal, without naming the Soviet Union, was an attempt "to control the Asian countries and further push its aggression and expansion in Asia and oppose China."

The latest of many indications of Sino-Pakistani cordiality was the opening in February 1971 of a new road link, a gravel-surfaced highway over the 15,420-foot Khunjerab Pass (Hung-chi La Shan-K'ou), about 170 miles northwest of the Karakorum Pass.

India

Sino-Indian relations have been affected by such factors as border tensions, regional rivalry, balance-of-power politics, and great power competition for influence in South Asia. These relations in 1971 were polite but strained, despite apparent desires on both sides to restore their historically close ties (see ch. 3, Historical Setting).

From 1949 to 1958 the Sino-Indian ties were very good, although India was disturbed by the PRC's annexation by force of Tibet in 1950 and there were occasional but unpublicized border clashes beginning in the mid-1950s. Relations during this period were conducted under the five principles of peaceful coexistence that they formally proclaimed in 1954. Prime Minister Nehru and Premier Chou exchanged visits, and trade and cultural exchanges flourished. India actively advocated that the PRC should be admitted to the UN.

Nehru's policy of nonalignment was interpreted by the PRC as compatible with, and in fact contributing to, its own aim of keeping Asia free of Western influences. The PRC appeared to appreciate Nehru's efforts to bring the communist regime into the world community, initially through the Afro-Asian conference at Bandung in April 1955. For its part, India needed the friendship of its powerful neighbor to secure peace along the northern frontier and, more important, as a potential ally to be counted on in its armed confrontation with Pakistan. Its assumption in the mid-1950s was that the PRC and India marching together would serve as "the most effective stabilizing factor in Asia."

Relations grew somewhat tense beginning in late 1958 when it became known that the PRC had built—in 1957 without India's knowledge—a segment of its Sinkiang-Tibet road across the Aksai Chin area in the northeastern sector of Jammu and Kashmir. This revelation, coupled with other indications of border tensions, led to a series of inconclusive negotiations, with India insisting that the Sino-Indian frontier had been defined by treaty, agreement, and custom but the PRC contending that it had never been formally delimited.

320

This bilateral effort was complicated by the outbreak of Tibetan revolt in 1959, which brought Communist Chinese accusations of Indian complicity after India had agreed to grant sanctuary to the Dalai Lama, the spiritual head of the Tibetan population.

Relations between the two neighbors were ruptured upon the outbreak of large-scale border fighting in October 1962. According to critics of Nehru's pre-1962 China policy in New Delhi at that time, India was said to have been militarily humiliated, and its national prestige suffered greatly as a result. India and its sympathizers almost immediately accused the PRC of aggression; others argued, however, that the Communist Chinese military action was prompted by Nehru's "forward policy" (meaning his policy of reinforcing Indian military buildup along the northern border between 1959 and 1961). Whatever the case, the Sino-Indian relations worsened, as much because the United States and Great Britain responded favorably to India's call for urgent military assistance from these countries as because the Soviets proved to be less than anxious to support the PRC during the border conflict.

Relations worsened in 1965 when the PRC declared its support of Pakistan during the Indo-Pakistani war of that year. The government of India countered by measures aimed at curbing Communist Chinese activities in Calcutta and Bombay. In 1966 the PRC protested that India was not only engaged in a two-China plot but also was giving aid and comfort to Nationalist China. Relations deteriorated further during the Cultural Revolution; the PRC embassy in New Delhi and the Indian embassy in Peking were besieged in June 1967, but diplomatic ties remained unbroken. Still another source of tensions was the PRC's propaganda support of terrorist activities undertaken by pro-Maoist extremists in West Bengal and elsewhere in India.

With the subsiding of the Cultural Revolution in 1969, the PRC began softening its truculent anti-Indian rhetoric. In March 1970 a visiting Communist Chinese envoy at Katmandu, Nepal, attended an Indian embassy reception held there and had friendly talks with the visiting Indian president, Varahgiri Venkata Giri. This was the first renewing of contact between Communist Chinese and Indian embassies at Katmandu since the border fighting of 1962. Two months later, Mao himself was reported to have suggested to the Indian chargé d'affaires in Peking the desirability of improving relations between the two countries; in October 1970 the Communist Chinese ambassador in Cairo called on his Indian counterpart, apparently to signal the PRC's intention to resume normal relations.

Meanwhile, India continued to reiterate its policy of friendship and cooperation with its communist neighbor, especially since the late 1960s. Its spokesman made it clear in early 1969, however, that its peaceful coexistence policy would not be pursued at the cost of India's national honor and territorial integrity. In September 1971 Indian

Minister of External Affairs Swaran Singh reaffirmed his government's desire to "normalize and improve" ties with the PRC. The government of India accepted an invitation for its table tennis team to compete in an Afro-Asian friendship table tennis tournament in Peking. According to some observers, the lack of any appreciable progress toward a Sino-Indian rapprochement was attributable to India's concern that overtures to the PRC might have an adverse effect on its relations with the Soviet Union.

Democratic People's Republic of Korea

The PRC and the Democratic People's Republic of Korea (North Korea) have generally maintained friendly and cooperative relations since 1949 except for a period of minor tension in the second half of the 1960s. The PRC's policy toward this fraternal country has been to preserve the northern half of Korea as a buffer state and to seek its assistance in removing the influence of both the United States and Japan from the Korean peninsula. This policy is based on the assumption that the peninsula, if subject to hostile foreign influence, would pose a major threat to the security of Northeast China (Manchuria); this apprehension stems in part from Japan's pre-1945 use of Korea as a corridor in the execution of expansionist policies toward the mainland and in part from Japan's growing economic influence in the Republic of Korea (South Korea) since the mid-1960s.

The PRC intervened in the Korean conflict when it appeared imminent that North Korea would be defeated completely. After ensuring the survival of Premier Kim Il-sung's regime at great cost to itself, the PRC aided North Korea's recovery and reconstruction in post-1953 years with generous help. Moreover, in an effort to win over Premier Kim it signed the Treaty of Friendship, Cooperation, and Mutual Assistance with North Korea in July 1961; North Korea had signed a similar treaty with the Soviet Union only a few days earlier.

From 1962 to the ouster of Soviet Premier Khrushchev in late 1964, the PRC and North Korea generally shared the same views on issues underlying the Sino-Soviet conflict. Both disagreed openly with the Soviet Union on such issues as de-Stalinization, peaceful coexistence with the West, limited detente with the United States, and the nuclear test ban. The PRC welcomed North Korean moral support in the Sino-Indian border conflict and its opposition to the Soviet attempts to isolate the PRC and Albania from other communist nations as well as from the world communist movement. It was reported that in 1963 the PRC and North Korea settled an old border dispute over Mount Pai-t'ou (Paektu-san in Korean), apparently in North Korea's favor. These developments were accompanied by continuing emphasis in both capitals on the theme of national self-reliance, which was in effect intended as much for internal consumption as it was for asserting freedom of action from the Soviet Union.

After 1965 the Sino-North Korean relations became less cordial because North Korea, already troubled economically and feeling insecure militarily, turned to the post-Khrushchev Soviet leadership for much needed assistance. Equally important, Premier Kim became disillusioned with Mao's obsession with the antirevisionist struggle, which in his view prevented the formation of any effective Sino-Soviet united front against the United States in Vietnam. During 1966 Premier Kim stated obliquely that, although struggle against revisionism was important, struggle against "United States imperialism" was even more crucial and also in effect declared that he would no longer take sides in the Sino-Soviet dispute.

PRC displeasure with North Korea's new attitude was publicly indicated during the Cultural Revolution, a campaign that Premier Kim did not publicly support. In early 1967 a group of Communist Chinese war veterans who had fought in the Korean conflict called Kim a "fat revisionist" and "Khrushchev's disciple" and accused him of ingratitude for Communist Chinese aid during the 1950s and of slandering the Cultural Revolution. Mutual recriminations, albeit low keyed, continued for several months, culminating in the heightening of border tensions in early 1969.

Beginning in mid-1969 the PRC sought to resume friendly relations, partly to counteract increasing Soviet influence in Pyongyang and partly to thwart Soviet attempts at the formation of a system of Asian collective security; it regarded the Soviet move, first made public in June 1969, as a step toward the encirclement of the PRC. In April 1970 Premier Chou paid a friendly visit to Pyongyang, his first diplomatic trip since the beginning of the Cultural Revolution. The Sino-North Korean entente deepened as a reaction to Japan's expanding regional role in the economic sphere and because of indications after late 1969 that Japan's influence might extend also to the military sphere.

In September 1971 the PRC and North Korea signed a military aid agreement. Most observers viewed this agreement as the PRC's reassurance of its determination to support Premier Kim's foreign policy objectives relating especially to the United States, South Korea, and Japan.

Democratic Republic of Vietnam

The PRC was the first to extend, in late 1951, military aid to the Vietnamese Communists fighting against the French. It played a major role in the Geneva Conference of 1954 that defined the terms of

323

armistice for Indochina and also fixed the provisional military demarcation line that became the de facto boundary between the Democratic Republic of Vietnam (North Vietnam) and the Republic of Vietnam (South Vietnam). Beginning in the mid-1950s the PRC continued to exert an important, though not decisive, influence on the internal and external affairs of North Vietnam, in both the economic and the military spheres.

In December 1961 the PRC sent a military mission to Hanoi and pledged its support for the Vietnamese struggle against United States "intervention and aggression" in South Vietnam. Its propaganda support increased from late 1964 onward with assertions that United States "aggression" against North Vietnam was "aggression" against the PRC and that the Chinese people would not ignore the situation. Communist Chinese leaders also indicated their willingness to send "volunteers" to Vietnam if they were asked to do so by North Vietnam and to intervene in North Vietnam if United States forces crossed the seventeenth parallel.

With the intensification of the Vietnam war in 1965, PRC-North Vietnam relations became complicated for a number of reasons. Despite its public declaration of "powerful backing" for North Vietnam, the PRC was apprehensive that the war in Vietnam might spill over into its own territory. From all indications, it appeared that mainland China was exercising caution, confining its support for the most part to a low-risk policy of supplying small arms and materials. In July 1965 the two countries signed an agreement under which the PRC pledged economic, technical, and military assistance to North Vietnam. Similar agreements were renewed annually thereafter. The PRC's measured restraint was highlighted in Minister of National Defense Lin Piao's statement in September 1965 "Long Live the Victory of People's War." According to Western analysts, this statement sought to convey, among other things, a message to North Vietnam that it should fight the "people's war" in Vietnam with minimal outside help, just as the Communist Chinese themselves had done against the Japanese in pre-1945 years.

Communist Chinese relations with North Vietnam were affected also by the Sino-Soviet dispute. In essence, the Communist Chinese followed a policy of aiding North Vietnam independently, without coordinating with the Soviet Union. In April 1965 they rejected the Soviet proposal for joint action in Vietnam on the argument that such an action would not only aid the "Soviet-American collaboration for the domination of the world" but also obstruct the struggle against "modern revisionism." This rejection, coming as it did on the heels of the escalation of the Vietnam conflict and the Soviet decision to step up its aid to North Vietnam in reversal of the pre-1965 Khrushchev policy of minimal involvement, caused North Vietnam to question the propriety of Mao's anti-Soviet and anti-United States attitudes and to veer away from its pro-PRC position of the 1963–64 period.

The Cultural Revolution had its impact felt also in North Vietnam. Shipments of arms and supplies from the PRC to North Vietnam were disrupted by Red Guard activities. The Mao leadership also urged the Vietnamese to persevere in their "people's war," warning them not to accept any peace initiatives proposed by outsiders. In 1968, when North Vietnam announced its decision to open peace talks with the United States in Paris, the PRC maintained disapproving silence for several months.

In 1971 the North Vietnamese leadership issued a number of statements, intended at least in part for the Communist Chinese leadership, expressing its reservations about Premier Chou's friendly overtures to the United States. These statements indicated a rising curve of suspicion in North Vietnam that the PRC might bargain with the United States on the settlement of the war in Vietnam, a problem that North Vietnam declared should be solved by the Vietnamese themselves and not by outsiders. In July, for example, it warned the PRC indirectly that the United States was plotting not only to divide "the socialist countries, winning over one section and pitting it against another in order to oppose the national liberation movement," but also to "achieve a compromise between the big powers in an effort to make smaller countries bow to their arrangements." This theme was repeated later with the assertion that the Vietnamese people should "uphold the spirit of independence and sovereignty." In response, Premier Chou publicly indicated that his government had no intention of playing any intermediary role concerning the war in Indochina and that the Vietnamese war should be solved by the Vietnamese themselves.

Mongolian People's Republic

Communist Chinese relations with the Mongolian People's Republic (Outer Mongolia) are complicated in part by the historic Mongolian fear of the Chinese and in part by the PRC's activities in that country aimed at enhancing Communist Chinese influence at the expense of the Soviet Union (see ch. 3, Historical Setting). The result has been Outer Mongolia's tendency to support the Soviet Union in the Sino-Soviet dispute. Relations between the PRC and Outer Mongolia have been polite but hardly cordial.

The PRC and Outer Mongolia signed an agreement concerning economic and cultural cooperation in 1952 and a treaty of friendship and mutual aid in 1960. In 1962 a dispute over the status of the entire Outer Mongolian-Chinese frontier was brought to an end with the signing of a border demarcation agreement. Meanwhile, Outer Mongolia's pro-Soviet attitude remained unchanged and, in light of growing Communist Chinese pressure to neutralize this attitude, it tightened security along the Chinese border and expelled a number of Communist Chinese technicians.

The Communist Chinese became further irritated in 1966 when Outer Mongolia signed a treaty of friendship, cooperation, and mutual assistance with the Soviet Union; this treaty provided for "all necessary measures, including military steps" to be taken by both countries in the event of an attack on either by a third party. This pact was directed ostensibly against the West, but the PRC's chilly reaction to it suggests that the PRC government interpreted the treaty as unfriendly.

In 1966 Outer Mongolia publicly indicated its disapproving attitude toward the Cultural Revolution, and as a result its embassy in Peking was sacked by Red Guards in 1967. This incident, coupled with deteriorating Sino-Soviet relations, led to intensification of mutual recriminations and protest demonstrations in both countries. In 1969 tensions along the Chinese-Outer Mongolian border rose sharply, and in May of that year Outer Mongolia issued a joint communiqué with the visiting Soviet president, Nikolai Podgorny, denouncing the great power chauvinist course of the Communist Chinese leadership. The PRC countered with the charge that Outer Mongolia had been turned into a Soviet colony, complete with Soviet military bases and troops. As of mid-1969 Western sources indicated that the Soviet Union had more than 100,000 troops in Outer Mongolia. Strained relations between the PRC and Outer Mongolia were also felt in their economic intercourse. By early 1969 the number of Communist Chinese technicians engaged in a variety of aid projects in Outer Mongolia had dwindled from a peak of 40,000 in 1959 to about 300. In addition, the volume of trade decreased substantially over the years; according to a Soviet source in August 1969, the PRC was said to have cut its trade with Outer Mongolia by 40 percent between 1961 and 1967, causing considerable inconveniences for the Outer Mongolians, who depended heavily on the PRC for consumer goods. A Western reporter returning from Ulan Bator reported in mid-1969 that, as of early that year, trade between the two countries "dwindled almost to nothing."

Indonesia

Relations with Indonesia have been affected both by the presence in that country of a sizable Overseas Chinese community and by the presence of an important indigenous communist movement, in the mid-1960s the largest in a noncommunist country. Measures taken by the Indonesian government and by private Indonesians against ethnic Chinese have caused strains in relations between the PRC and Indonesia, although the PRC, anxious to maintain close cooperation with Indonesia's Communist Party, tended to react mildly.

In 1950 there were estimated to be 2 million Chinese in Indonesia who, although they lacked political power and were subjected to various official restrictions on their activities, were disproportionately influential in the economy, especially in domestic trade, causing the majority group to resent them. The Indonesian government was concerned that many claimed dual nationality and thus eluded government regulations that they found onerous. In April 1955, while Chou was in Indonesia to attend the Bandung Conference, a treaty was negotiated with Indonesia to deal with the problem of dual nationality among Overseas Chinese.

By 1959, however, the enforcement of Indonesian regulations designed to reduce the control of rural trade by resident Chinese was again causing strain in the relations between Indonesia and the PRC. In February 1960 the PRC sent ships to evacuate all Chinese who wished to leave for the mainland. In July President Sukarno suggested that certain amendments be made to the dual nationality treaty; these were accepted by the PRC, and relations between the two countries improved steadily and were not significantly affected by a new outbreak of violence against resident Chinese in Java in 1963.

By that time, the Indonesian Communist Party had become extremely powerful and was the party upon which President Sukarno relied most heavily for guidance and support in his foreign policy. In April 1963 Liu Shao-ch'i, then chief of state of the PRC, went to Indonesia to pay his first visit to a noncommunist country, accompanied by Foreign Minister Ch'en I. While there, Liu gave public support for Indonesia in its avowed determination to "crush Malaysia."

In October 1963 an agreement with the PRC helped make possible Indonesia's serving as host to the Games of the New Emerging Forces the following month. Sukarno conceived of the New Emerging Forces as consisting of the communist countries and selected other countries in Asia, Africa, and Latin America that opposed the colonialist, neocolonialist, and imperialist practices of the so-called Old Established Forces. (Whereas Sukarno was noncommittal on this subject, the Indonesian Communists classed the PRC in the New Emerging Forces category and the Soviet Union in the Old Established Forces group.) In 1964 PRC collaboration with Indonesia on the international scene in Afro-Asian bodies increased, and in January 1965 the PRC lauded Indonesia's action in resigning from the UN in protest over Malaysia's election to a nonpermanent seat on the Security Council.

Numerous visits were exchanged by high officials during the early and mid-1960s, and various treaties of friendship and agreements on technical, economic, and cultural cooperation were signed. In March 1965 an agreement for scientific and technical cooperation was signed providing for the exchange of scholars, technologists, and scientific information. At that time Indonesia also gave permission to the Communist Chinese to set up a powerful radio transmitter on Java.

In the next six months there were dozens of Indonesian delegations sent to the PRC for various reasons, and Chou and Ch'en I attended tenth anniversary celebrations of the conference in Bandung in April; the same month a delegation from the CCP attended the forty-fifth anniversary celebrations of the Indonesian Communist Party in Djakarta. In August more Communist Chinese delegations arrived for Indonesian National Day celebrations. Sukarno referred to the tie with the PRC as a so-called antiimperialistic axis. The same month Singapore separated itself from Malaysia, and Ch'en I returned to Indonesia to discuss the implications of this separation.

On September 30, 1965, the NCNA announced the signing of seven documents covering economic and technical cooperation with Indonesia. On the same day, however, in Djakarta, there began an attempted coup by the Indonesian Communist Party in which it tried to eliminate the anticommunist army leadership, considered to be its chief rival for power if the ailing Sukarno were to die soon. The coup backfired, and many thousands of Indonesian Communists and also many resident Chinese were killed.

General Suharto, an anticommunist army man who had led the counterattack on the Communists, assumed power in March 1966; next, the NCNA was expelled, the local Communist Party was banned, the PRC ambassador left Djakarta, and many Overseas Chinese enterprises and schools were closed down. In September 1966 several thousand Chinese returned to the mainland.

In 1967 one effect of the Cultural Revolution was to worsen relations further; the Indonesian government was angered at PRC diplomats who, influenced by the Cultural Revolution in the mainland, distributed Mao badges and disseminated Maoist propaganda among Indonesian Chinese. In August the Communist Chinese embassy in Djakarta was sacked, as was the Indonesian Embassy in Peking. In October 1967 relations between the two countries were suspended.

As of mid-1971 Indonesia continued to refer to the relations between the two countries as "suspended," not "severed," and its prime minister and foreign minister continued to affirm Indonesia's willingness to have normal relations restored if the PRC would recognize the Suharto government, not interfere in internal affairs—especially in the small but continuing communist insurgency in West Kalimantan (Borneo)—and cease its Indonesian-language propaganda broadcasts. Beamed from a powerful transmitter in southern China, the broadcasts continually referred to the Indonesian government as a "fascist military clique." In May 1971 Indonesia's foreign minister, Adam Malik, addressing a domestic audience, suggested that it would be in his country's interest for local businessmen to establish trade ties with the PRC, even though diplomatic relations had not resumed.

In October 1971 at the UN Indonesia voted in favor of the "important question" resolution that would have required a two-thirds vote on the Albanian resolution to seat the PRC and to expel Nationalist China. It abstained on the Albanian resolution itself.

Malaysia and Singapore

Relations with Malaysia have been affected by that country's experience of communist insurgency. Malaysia (including Singapore from September 1963 until August 1965) has been engaged in suppressing communist terrorist activities for many years. On the Malay Peninsula these efforts go back to 1948, and there has been a separate small-scale communist insurgency in Sarawak (in the Borneo territory) since the 1950s. Both insurgent movements are, and have always been, virtually exclusively ethnic Chinese in membership and have received constant propaganda support from the PRC. During the 1948–60 period of greatest danger to the state from the communist insurgency, Chinese Communist cadres were introduced into Malaya. In the late 1950s the communist terrorists on the peninsula withdrew into the jungles along the border with Thailand. Joint Thai-Malaysian expeditions have been launched periodically against them, but the movement was showing signs of renewed strength in 1971.

In East Malaysia (the Bornean portion of the country) in early 1970 there were estimated to be about 10,000 sympathizers and about 150 armed terrorists operating on both sides of the Sarawak-Indonesia border; their numbers were being reduced by efforts of Indonesian and Malaysian forces. Propaganda support from radio broadcasts in Malaysian languages, purporting to emanate from Malaysian communist headquarters but in fact beamed by a South China transmitter, were continuing in 1971.

The PRC did not recognize the state of Malaysia (which had come into being in September 1963 from the union of the Federation of Malaya, Sarawak, Sabah, and Singapore), and it also did not recognize the secession of Singapore from Malaysia in August 1965. In 1964, during the period when the PRC was endorsing Indonesia's armed "confrontation" against Malaysia, a Chinese consulate was opened in Kuala Lumpur. In January 1966, still the confrontation period, the NCNA announced the establishment in Peking of a mission of the Malayan National Liberation League.

Malaysian relations with China have been complicated by the fact that ethnic Chinese constitute nearly half of that country's population. Most of these have been loyal to their host government and have found the Malaysian communist activity of a minority of ethnic Chinese to be an embarrassment. The Malaysian government has avoided diplomatic relations with either Nationalist China or the PRC. In the mid-1960s consular missions were exchanged between Kuala Lumpur and Taipei, Taiwan. Nonetheless, the Malaysian government has always favored "in principle" the admission of the PRC to the UN, and it has always permitted Malaysian Chinese to make short visits to the mainland to visit relatives and has also permitted the sending of family remittances to the PRC.

In 1971 relations between the PRC and Malaysia greatly improved. This change began with friendly overtures by the PRC, including the sending of a PRC-sponsored dance troupe from Hong Kong to Malaysia to raise money for flood victims there. In addition, the Chinese Red Cross sent blankets for these victims. Another indication of increased friendliness was that PRC radio broadcasts from Peking began for the first time in 1971 to refer to the country occasionally as Malaysia, instead of Malaya.

In May an unofficial Malaysian trade mission was cordially received in Peking, and its ethnic Chinese members were exhorted by Premier Chou to be loyal to the country in which they now lived and not to regard China as the motherland anymore. In July Malaysian Premier Tun Abdul Razak in an address before parliament stated that the establishment of diplomatic relations with the PRC was a matter for future consideration but that at present bilateral relations would remain unofficial and the main emphasis would be on trade. In August 1971 a trade agreement was reached covering various commodities, shipping, banking, and travel facilities. Of greatest importance to Malaysia—the world's leading producer of natural rubber—was that the PRC agreed to buy all the rubber stockpile of the Malayan Rubber Fund Board and also agreed to consider making additional purchases annually.

Singapore, independent since August 1965, recognized the PRC but as of mid-1971 did not have diplomatic relations with it. It is the only independent state, aside from the PRC and Nationalist China, to contain an ethnic Chinese majority. There has been no insurgency in Singapore, and the People's Action Party, led by Prime Minister Lee Kuan Yew, has faced little competition from the opposition. The PRC did not recognize the emergence of Singapore in 1965 as an independent state and has directed propaganda broadcasts against the "Lee Kuan Yew clique."

Trade between the PRC and Singapore has been extensive, however, since 1966, when the PRC reentered the Singapore rubber market. By 1968 the PRC had become the third most important supplier of goods to Singapore and an important customer. The Bank of China has maintained a branch there although, in conformity to Singapore regulations, none of the staff of the bank in 1971 were PRC citizens. In October 1971 there were indications that relations between the PRC and Singapore were improving, the most important being the sending to the PRC of an unofficial Singapore trade mission.

Thailand

There are strong historical ties between the peoples of Thailand and those of the PRC; the Thai originated in China, where there is still a substantial Thai-speaking minority population. In addition, it was estimated in the mid-1960s that ethnic Chinese constituted approximately 10 percent of Thailand's population. There have also always been many persons of part-Chinese ancestry, including some within the Thai royal family. There have been, nonetheless, periodic outbreaks of domestic anti-Chinese sentiment among the Thai since the early twentieth century, during which public attention has focused upon Chinese secret society activity and upon the Chinese dominance of domestic trade, commerce, and industry. A tendency to suspect the ethnic Chinese community of disloyalty and, after 1949, of harboring Communists has been characteristic of the various military regimes that have ruled Thailand virtually continuously since 1948.

The Thai became conscious of a threat from the PRC in 1950, when the Chinese Communist regime occupied Tibet and intervened in the Korean conflict. Thailand, which contributed troops to the UN force in Korea, was thus engaged in hostilities against the PRC forces. The Thai government viewed the 1953 PRC announcement of the creation of an autonomous local government for the Thai minority in Yunnan Province as a preparatory step toward the subverting of Thailand. This belief was reinforced in 1954 when Former Thai Prime Minister Pridi, who had fled his country, broadcast from mainland China appeals to the Thai people to overthrow their government. In the early 1960s the Thai government blamed both the PRC and North Vietnam for the intensified communist activity in South Vietnam, and its anti-PRC attitude was further stiffened in January 1965 when the PRC hinted that Thailand would be the next target of a so-called war of national liberation and that a guerrilla war would begin in Thailand before the end of 1965.

In the late 1960s, however, the possibility of improved relations was being explored by the Thai government. In February 1969 Thai Foreign Minister Thanat Khoman revealed in Bangkok that some Thai officials in Geneva had attempted to contact Communist Chinese officials there to probe the possibility of opening a dialogue with the PRC.

In May 1971 Thanat noted that "our differences have narrowed. ... The situation has improved. Peking leaders have begun to understand us. It may well lead to a real dialogue." A Thai official also observed that his government's radio commentaries on communist countries had moderated their tone and that a corresponding softening could be discerned in the broadcasts of the so-called Voice of Free Thailand, a clandestine station that purports to originate inside Thailand but broadcasts from a South China transmitter. The official further indicated that there had been a recent reduction in activity by the Communist Chinese-sponsored insurgent groups that had been operating since the mid-1960s in northeast and northern Thailand.

Laos

The PRC participated in the Geneva Conference of 1954, which established Laos as an independent nation under neutralist leadership. The PRC was concerned to prevent its encirclement by United States military bases and to assure the continuation of "liberation" group activities in Indochina. At the Bandung Conference of 1955 Premier Chou extended an invitation to the Laotian prime minister to visit Peking. This invitation was taken up in 1956 by Prince Souvanna Phouma when he became prime minister. He is believed to have been offered aid by the Communist Chinese, which he refused. From late 1958 to mid-1960, during which time Souvanna Phouma was not in power and an anticommunist prime minister was installed, the PRC waged a propaganda campaign against the Laotian government.

Souvanna Phouma returned to power briefly in the latter half of 1960 but was ousted by a rightist coup in December of that year. With Souvanna Phouma's ouster, the PRC endorsed North Vietnam's proposal to reconvene the Geneva Conference and declared Souvanna Phouma's government-in-exile to be the legal government of Laos.

Ch'en I led the PRC delegation to the fourteen-nation Geneva Conference convened in May 1961. As a result of the conference, a provisional government headed by Souvanna Phouma was agreed upon, although it did not take office until June 1962. Meanwhile, in October 1961, consulates general were exchanged with the PRC in Phong Saly, Laos, and in K'un-ming, Communist China. In November a Communist Chinese economic and cultural mission was set up in Khang Khay, the headquarters of the Pathet Lao. This mission became a center for PRC propaganda and the headquarters of Pathet Lao radio (reported to have been operated with the help of Communist Chinese technicians). Also, before the Souvanna Phouma provisional government took charge, an agreement was signed between the PRC and Laos in January 1962 on air transport and roadbuilding. By this agreement the PRC was given permission to build a road from Yunnan to Phong Saly.

In June 1962 Souvanna Phouma's provisional government took office, and the following month the PRC signed a declaration respecting the sovereignty, independence, and neutrality of Laos. In September diplomatic relations were established, and the PRC sent an ambassador. In March 1963 the king of Laos visited the PRC, and in the same month Souvanna Phouma visited Peking to ask the PRC's aid in inducing North Vietnamese troops to withdraw from Laos. There were, after that, reports of increasing military activity by Communist Chinese in Laos and evidence that the PRC was building more roads than the one into Phong Saly.

Since the mid-1960s the PRC propaganda media have consistently attacked the right-wing faction in Laos and have supported the Pathet Lao in its protracted war against the Laotian government. (Military support for the Pathet Lao continued to come chiefly from the North Vietnamese, however.) From early 1967 to early 1969 the Communist Chinese chargé d'affaires to the Royal Laotian Government in Vientiane was absent, but he returned in February 1969, and relations since then between the two countries have been polite but restrained. Diplomatic missions in Peking and in Vientiane in 1971 were headed by chargés d'affaires. The PRC roadbuilding project continued in the early 1970s, and by February 1971 the road from Yunnan extended 100 miles into Laos, reaching Mong Houn, thirty miles from the Pathet Lao town of Pak Beng. Should the road be completed as far as Pak Beng, the PRC would then have a two-lane artery from Yunnan to the insurgents on the Mekong River. In February 1971 Souvanna Phouma voiced his fear that Communist Chinese "volunteers" might enter Laos and join with the Pathet Lao forces against the Vientiane government.

Cambodia

While attending the Bandung Conference in 1955, Prince (formerly, King) Norodom Sihanouk sought to establish friendly relations with the PRC, and in February 1956 the prince, then prime minister, paid a visit to Peking. In April 1956 agreements on trade and aid were signed. This represented the first aid given by the PRC to a noncommunist country. Premier Chou visited Cambodia in November 1956, at which time he spoke in favor of peaceful coexistence. Finally, in July 1958, Cambodia recognized the PRC, and ambassadors were exchanged between the two countries. A friendship and nonaggression treaty between the two was signed in December 1960. Friendly visits and aid by the PRC continued into the early 1960s, although the amount of aid given at this time was less than formerly because of the economic problems in the PRC resulting from the failure of the Great Leap Forward. In 1964, after Cambodia cut itself off from United States aid, more Communist Chinese aid was received, and in October 1964 it was announced that the PRC would build two factories in Cambodia and an international airport at Siam Reap, near the great tourist attraction the Angkor temple complex.

Various agreements for economic, scientific, cultural, and military cooperation were signed in 1965 and 1966, but relations cooled in 1967 when the PRC, in consonance with the Cultural Revolution, backed Maoist activity among Cambodia's resident Chinese and supported subversive activity in certain areas of the country. Despite Chou's official apology for publicly supporting a subversive group, the NCNA was banned in Cambodia in mid-1967, and Sihanouk's government began keeping a close watch on PRC diplomats and aid officials.

In 1968 relations improved again, and the PRC gave more military, medical, and education aid and equipment to Cambodia. In October 1969 Prime Minister Prince Sihanouk and two other ministers led a delegation to Peking to attend the PRC's twentieth anniversary celebrations.

In March 1970 situations changed. Prince Sihanouk was unseated through a parliamentary maneuver, and General Lon Nol assumed government leadership. In August 1970 the PRC signed an agreement to give free aid to the government-in-exile of Prince Sihanouk and to support the Cambodian people in their "just war against United States imperialism and its lackey." Prince Sihanouk's government-in-exile had its headquarters in Peking in 1971.

Other Countries

Relations with other Asian countries—Afghanistan, Burma, Ceylon, Nepal, and the Philippines—in 1971 were warm except with the last. All but Ceylon and the Philippines share borders with the PRC. In 1971 Ceylon and Nepal, along with Pakistan, served as cosponsors of the Albanian resolution in the United Nations General Assembly on the question of Chinese representation.

The PRC maintains no diplomatic ties with the Philippines and has been critical of the latter's membership in the Southeast Asia Treaty Organization, the Association of Southeast Asian Nations (see Glossary), and the Asia and Pacific Council (see Glossary); these regional organizations are attacked in Communist Chinese propaganda as being anti-PRC. The PRC also continues to support the communist rebels (called "local Maoists" in Manila) operating in the Philippines. Its critical attitude toward the government in Manila remained essentially unchanged in 1971 despite the efforts, since the mid-1960s, of the Philippines to establish a friendly dialogue with the PRC. In January 1969, for example, President Ferdinand Marcos indicated that his country would be prepared to coexist with the PRC but without abandoning its firm anticommunist measures against indigenous rebels. A similar statement was repeated in early August 1971 amid growing evidence of stepped-up local Maoist terrorist activities in both urban and rural areas. Later in August, when he proclaimed a state of communist rebellion, the president declared that this rebellion was aided by the "active moral and material support of a foreign power."

Relations with Afghanistan have been generally cordial since the opening of diplomatic relations in 1955. The PRC has respected Afghanistan's nonalignment policy and has not interfered with its internal affairs, although the latter maintains friendly relations with both the Soviet Union and the United States. Between 1960 and 1965 Afghanistan and the PRC signed three major agreements: a treaty of friendship and nonaggression in 1960; a treaty on border demarcation in 1963; and an agreement on cultural, scientific, and technical cooperation in 1965. Under the 1965 accord, the PRC pledged a long-term, interest-free loan equivalent to US$28 million for projects to be agreed on later. It also aided the country on a number of projects dealing with irrigation, land reclamation, and hydroelectric plant construction.

Burma was the first noncommunist nation to recognize the PRC, in December 1949, but its relations with the northern neighbor were tense until 1954 because of the presence on Burmese soil of Nationalist Chinese irregulars who conducted occasional forays into the Communist Chinese territory. Many of these irregulars were evacuated to Taiwan in 1954, and border talks began in 1956. Four years of intermittent negotiations resulted in the Sino-Burmese border agreement of 1960. In 1960 a treaty of friendship and mutual nonaggression was concluded, this pact to remain in force "without any specified time limit" if it survived the first ten years (in 1971 it was still in effect). Under this treaty the PRC pledged not to interfere in Burma's internal affairs, and Burma in turn agreed not to join any alliance directed against the PRC.

In 1961 the PRC agreed to give a six-year, interest-free loan equivalent to US$84 million, to be utilized by the end of September 1967. Sino-Burmese relations were strained considerably during the Cultural Revolution, especially in 1967 when anti-Chinese riots erupted in Rangoon over a dispute involving Mao badges to be worn by local Chinese residents. The PRC reacted by suspending its aid program, which at that time represented the single largest Communist Chinese foreign aid activity in the noncommunist world. In addition, beginning in August 1967, the CCP for the first time publicly declared its support of the so-called people's revolutionary armed struggle led by the pro-PRC Burmese communist rebels.

Since late 1969 the PRC has substantially toned down its anti-Burmese propaganda attacks. While General Ne Win, Burma's chief of state, was in Peking in August 1971, Premier Chou was reported to have stated, "We are happy to see that over the past two years the relations between our two countries have returned to normal." In October 1971 the PRC agreed to resume its aid program in Burma. There were indications, however, that the PRC's support to the

Burmese communist rebels continued, although the level of support appeared to be much lower than it was during the Cultural Revolution.

Ceylon recognized the PRC in 1950 and signed a five-year Ceylonese-rubber-for-PRC-rice agreement in 1952, but it was not until 1957 that diplomatic exchanges took place. In 1971 Sino-Ceylonese relations were cordial, despite the suspicion in Ceylon that the antigovernment student uprisings, which occurred earlier in the year, had been instigated by the Communist Chinese as well as by North Korean diplomats stationed in Colombo. The North Korean embassy officials were all expelled from the country in April, but no action was taken against the Communist Chinese mission, presumably because of the continuing importance of the rubber-for-rice transactions. In June 1971 the PRC signed an economic aid agreement with Ceylon.

As in the past, Nepal in 1971 was subject to conflicting pressures from the PRC to the north and from India to the south. This landlocked Himalayan country traditionally maintained close links with both countries and, in fact, until 1953 Nepal was the recipient of annual tribute payments from Tibet, which it defeated in a war in the mid-nineteenth century. The PRC's efforts to promote its interest, in competition with India, began in 1954, when it initiated an effort to establish diplomatic relations with Nepal; this was achieved the following year. In 1956 the PRC announced an unconditional grant of aid.

Communist Chinese encroachment on the Nepalese territory in 1959 led to border talks, and a frontier demarcation agreement was reached two years later. Meanwhile, in 1960 the PRC offered Nepal a grant equivalent to US$21 million and signed a treaty of peace and friendship with that country. Among various projects to be financed by the Communist Chinese aid was the construction of a road from the Tibetan border to Katmandu; this road, linking Lhasa with the Nepalese capital, was opened in May 1967. In the latter half of 1967, increasingly virulent Maoist propaganda against Nepal caused anti-Chinese riots in Katmandu. Cordiality had been restored by mid-1969, and in May 1971 the official NCNA quoted the Nepalese prime minister Kirti Nidhi Bista as saying, "China's behavior towards its neighbors and friends is very friendly and cordial."

MIDDLE EAST AND NORTH AFRICA

The PRC's interest in the Middle East and North Africa has been to reduce the influence of the United States and the Soviet Union in the region, to enhance its own influence through a variety of formal and informal contacts, and to gain access to the area's oil.

The PRC has consistently supported the Arab cause in the Arab-Israeli conflict, has sought to gain a political foothold by forming rival factions among the predominantly pro-Soviet Arab communist organizations, and has aided not only the Palestinian liberation movement but also insurgent activities in other parts of the area. Its ability to penetrate the Arab world has been hampered by its limited capabilities to project military and economic power.

The PRC gained entry into the Middle East by befriending Egypt, which it had come to regard, by 1955, as the key to its policy of seeking recognition from the countries of this region. In 1955 Premier Chou had contacts with Egypt's Abdul Nasser at Rangoon and Bandung, these contacts resulting in exchange of diplomatic recognitions the following year. During the Suez crisis of 1956, the PRC supported Egypt and offered volunteers to fight against Israel. It began radio broadcasts to this area in Arabic, Turkish, and Persian in 1957 and also participated in the Afro-Asian People's Solidarity Conference, which held its first meeting at Cairo in the same year.

The PRC's relations with the United Arab Republic (UAR) between 1958 and 1971 cooled somewhat for reasons having to do with the UAR's domestic priorities and with the intensification of Sino-Soviet competition for influence in the Afro-Asian world. The PRC was apparently disturbed by President Nasser's strident anticommunist domestic policy, his close ties with the Soviet Union and Yugoslavia, and his sympathy with India during the Sino-Indian border fighting; nevertheless, it refrained from aggravating the situation. Instead, it sought to cultivate close ties with the UAR by identifying with President Nasser's aspirations. In December 1963 Premier Chou ended a week-long visit to Cairo with a joint communiqué in which he gave full support to UAR foreign policy objectives and also reaffirmed the Chinese support of "the people of Palestine in their struggle for national sovereignty and regaining their lost homeland." In another gesture of friendship, the PRC signed an economic and technical agreement with the UAR in December 1964, which included a loan equivalent to US$80 million.

The two countries shared a similar outlook toward many international problems but differed over others. In 1965, for example, they took opposing stands on the question of convening the second Afro-Asian People's Solidarity Conference, the UAR resisting the PRC attempt to exclude the Soviet Union from the conference. At the end of 1965, after uncovering a Communist Chinese attempt to establish a pro-PRC communist organization in the UAR, Nasser's government asked the PRC ambassador to leave the country. His replacement, Huang Hua, arrived in January 1966 and stayed until mid-1969, the only Communist Chinese chief of mission who was not called home for "reeducation" during the Cultural Revolution. The

PRC's apparent purpose was to give the UAR its continued assurance of support for Nasser's stand against Israel.

When the Arab-Israeli War began in June 1967, the PRC supported the Arab side, offered unconditional economic aid, and later opposed the ceasefire which, it asserted, was brought about "under pressure from United States imperialism and Soviet revisionism." Sensing the UAR's disillusionment with the Soviet Union's measured restraint during the crisis, the Communist Chinese accused the Soviet leadership of "betrayal" of the Arab people and of seeking to use its "military and economic aid" to "the Arab and other Asian, African, and Latin American countries" as a lever for interfering in the internal affairs of recipient states.

The PRC and the UAR were at odds again in 1968; early in the year the UAR refused to return a Communist Chinese defector and later complained that the Communist Chinese mission supported the leftist student riots at Alexandria. In order to smooth the situation, the PRC in January 1969 renewed the 1964 economic and technical cooperation agreement; however, as of January 1971, only about the equivalent of US$10 million of the US$80 million offered had been used to buy industrial spare parts from the PRC. In January 1971 the first official UAR delegation to visit mainland China since before the 1967 war arrived in Peking and signed a protocol for increased trade between the two countries.

Relations with Algeria, Iraq, Libya, Morocco, Sudan, Syria, Tunisia, the Arab Republic of Yemen, and the People's Democratic Republic of Yemen were generally free of differences. The PRC has offered varying amounts of economic and technical assistance to Algeria, the two Yemens, and Syria. It has been also quick to exploit any situation to advantage in its competition with the Soviet Union for influence in this region. Thus, after the short-lived coup in July 1971, which the Sudanese government charged was aided by the Soviet Union, it pledged full support for Sudan's independence "against all pressures" and the following month extended economic aid totalling the equivalent of US$35 million.

Communist Chinese support of Palestinian guerrilla activities has been steadily rising. In 1965 the PRC became the first major power to back the Palestine Liberation Organization by permitting it to open a permanent mission in Peking. It has also given training and arms to other movements, such as the Al-Fatah (Palestine National Liberation Movement), the Democratic Front for the Liberation of Palestine, and the Popular Front for the Liberation of the Occupied Arabian Gulf. The last of these organizations is an insurgent movement that has been waging an armed struggle for the past seven years in Dhofar, the southeastern province of Oman.

AFRICA SOUTH OF THE SAHARA

Mainland China's interest in Africa, as in the Middle East, began at Bandung in 1955, when most African territories were not yet independent. When an African colony became independent, the PRC was quick to extend diplomatic recognition and a helping hand, playing up the theme that it too had been oppressed by the "imperialists" and had gained self-respect by revolutionary struggle. Hundreds of African leaders were invited to Peking, and Mao and Chou made a point of meeting them. In their discourses, they accused the Western powers, particularly the United States, of racism. The Communist Chinese leaders invariably emphasized that the Chinese people are also nonwhite and that their land is poor and called for African-Asian solidarity in a common struggle against the white man, Soviet and Western alike. Many Communist Chinese missions visited African states in order to develop friendly relations and plan for political, cultural, and economic cooperation. By October 1971 the PRC had been recognized by roughly half of the forty-odd independent African states.

The PRC was interested in gaining access to Africa's raw materials, in seeking recognition as the only lawful government of the Chinese people, in countering both United States and Soviet influences by organizing the broadest possible united front of African peoples against these superpowers, and in exalting its status as the most revolutionary and reliable ally of the people in underdeveloped and emerging nations.

The PRC's African policy has operated on many levels: conventional diplomacy; the "people's diplomacy"; economic and technical aid; and ideological and material support of insurgent movements. Its diplomatic approach swung into high gear in the early 1960s after the PRC realized that Nationalist China's campaign for diplomatic exchanges, opened in 1959, had begun to pay dividends. During the December 1963–January 1964 period Premier Chou visited a number of African states, reaffirming the five principles of peaceful coexistence as a basis for Sino-African relations, underscoring the importance of self-reliance as the key to ensuring both political and economic independence, and extolling the principle of equality of all nations, large and small. Formal relations were supplemented by exchanges of student, cultural, and friendship groups and extensive information and propaganda activities through Radio Peking, NCNA correspondents, and locally organized pro-PRC front organizations.

Political penetration was facilitated by the extension of foreign aid. During 1964 alone the PRC offered to the Central African Republic, Congo (Brazzaville), Ghana, and Tanzania the equivalent of more than US$113 million in interest-free loans and grants; about 40

339

percent of this total went to Tanzania, 24 percent to the People's Republic of the Congo (Brazzaville), and 20 percent to Ghana.

The PRC's attempts to penetrate and control leftist and insurgent movements apparently were greatly stepped up during 1964; it used its embassies as command posts and broadened contacts with local antigovernment groups. Communist Chinese diplomats in Africa were said to have spent most of their time fomenting rebellion, organizing and training local rebels, and giving them arms and money.

Meanwhile, African leaders grew increasingly suspicious of Communist Chinese motives; they were amenable to receiving what the PRC called "disinterested aid" but became disenchanted with the PRC's call for continued struggle and revolution against "colonialism, United States imperialism, and Soviet revisionism." Preoccupied with their own domestic problems, many African countries were reluctant to be drawn into the crossfire of the Sino-Soviet dispute or of the East-West ideological conflict. They also became wary of PRC interference—often clandestine—in local affairs, such as playing faction against faction.

A period of hostile reaction against the Communist Chinese began in 1965; in February the Communist Chinese embassy staff was expelled by Burundi for subversive activities. Four months later, many African leaders, led by the UAR, thwarted the PRC's maneuvers aimed at exploiting the proposed second Afro-Asian People's Solidarity Conference as a rallying point for the formation of a broad united front of Afro-Asian countries against the superpowers. About the same time, Kenya expelled an NCNA correspondent for subversive activities. In 1966 Dahomey suspended diplomatic relations and expelled the Communist Chinese. The Central African Republic broke off relations after the discovery of a "people's army" with suspected Communist Chinese backing and expelled Communist Chinese diplomats, technicians, and NCNA correspondents. In March two Communist Chinese diplomats were asked to leave Kenya on suspicion of subversive activities, but diplomatic relations were not suspended. Relations with Ghana were informally suspended when the military government that replaced Kwame Nkrumah announced the discovery of Communist Chinese involvement with a Nkrumah-sponsored secret training camp used for subversion in other African countries; later in the year the PRC withdrew its diplomats and NCNA correspondents. The PRC also antagonized Nigeria by supporting the unsuccessful Biafran secessionist movement. Among the countries affected by Communist Chinese activities, Burundi, Kenya, and Nigeria supported, in October 1971, the resolution to seat the PRC in the United Nations, whereas the Central African Republic, Dahomey, and Ghana supported another measure amounting to a two-China policy.

The PRC's troubles with some countries were offset by friendly relationships with others. Between 1960 and 1971 the Communist Chinese government signed many agreements with (among others) Congo (Brazzaville), Ethiopia, Guinea, Mali, Mauritania, Somalia, Tanzania, Uganda, and Zambia. In 1968 it signed with Guinea and Mali an agreement for the construction of the Guinea-Mali railroad that would give Mali an outlet to the sea; little was heard of this project after a military coup in Mali in November 1968 (the new military regime disbanded the Communist Chinese-trained "people's militia") until 1971, when the PRC showed interest in reviving the project.

The PRC acquired considerable influence in Guinea through its aid program; in 1967, for example, about 3,000 Chinese technicians were present in the country working on a number of PRC-sponsored air projects. In 1971 the PRC was also involved militarily in Congo (Brazzaville), to which it agreed to supply military advisors and arms. In October 1971, while Emperor Haile Selassie of Ethiopia was in mainland China, Premier Chou and the emperor signed trade and aid agreements. The aid portions of these accords provided for a long-term Communist Chinese loan equivalent to US$84 million, an amount surpassed only by similar loans the PRC extended to Pakistan and Tanzania.

By any standard, the PRC's closest African friend in 1971 was Tanzania; the PRC was Tanzania's largest communist trading partner and supplier of arms. The PRC's largest single aid project was agreed on, in September 1967, with Tanzania and Zambia for the construction of the Tanzania-Zambia Railroad, which would provide an outlet to the sea for Zambia's copper belt. It pledged an interest-free loan equivalent to US$280 million for this 1,200-mile railroad project; work was started in October 1970, and in mid-1971 the Zambian government reported that construction was "already a year ahead of schedule." According to Western reports, at least several thousand Chinese technicians were working on the project in 1971; some of these technicians were members of the railroad, engineering, and signal corps of the People's Liberation Army (PLA). PRC military aid includes the training of Tanzanian technicians and the provision of tanks, guns, ground equipment, coastal patrol boats, and reportedly also a limited number of MIG–17 fighters.

The PRC is also providing money, training, and arms for insurgent groups based in Tanzania and Zambia, the aim of these organizations being to overthrow the white-ruled minority governments in southern Africa (South Africa, Mozambique, Angola, Rhodesia, and South-West Africa). These groups are composed of black refugees who seek to foment unrest inside their homelands and to conduct guerrilla warfare from bases inside black African countries. The PRC has regarded their efforts as in line with its own concepts of "people's war" and has sought their support in its dispute with the Soviet Union on the question of national liberation movements.

WESTERN AND EASTERN EUROPE

By mid-1971 the PRC's relations with European countries (except for the Soviet Union) had, by and large, improved after having deteriorated considerably during the Cultural Revolution. Relations with these countries have been uneven since the PRC was founded in 1949. In 1949 and 1950 the communist countries of Eastern Europe recognized the PRC government, as did the United Kingdom, the four Scandinavian countries, Switzerland, and the Netherlands. There were no further recognitions by noncommunist European countries after this period until 1964, largely because of the PRC's intervention against the UN forces in the Korean conflict.

Relations with Eastern European countries were cordial through the mid-1950s, except with Yugoslavia. Then relations with Eastern Europe began to deteriorate as the dispute with the Soviet Union sharpened. Only Albania sided promptly and unequivocally with the PRC. In the early 1960s, however, as part of an effort to consolidate its independence of the Soviet Union, Romania also showed signs of friendship with the PRC; it signed agreements on scientific, technical, and cultural cooperation with the PRC and, in April 1964, declared its neutrality in the Sino-Soviet dispute.

Relations with Yugoslavia have been on the whole very poor, but they were not affected significantly, favorably or unfavorably, by the Sino-Soviet dispute. Yugoslavia was regarded by the Communist Chinese as the arch "revisionist" (until the 1960s, when the Soviet Union became the chief target of such charges by the PRC) for having defected in 1948 from the Soviet bloc. In 1955 PRC relations with Yugoslavia temporarily improved, as did the latter's relations with other communist countries, including the Soviet Union. By December 1956, however, the PRC renewed its charges of revisionism, and in mid-1958 the ambassadors in Peking and Belgrade were recalled. After 1960, although the PRC, too, had by then left the Soviet sphere of influence, the Chinese Communists intensified their propaganda attacks on Yugoslavia, especially its foreign policies of peaceful coexistence and nonalignment and its domestic economic policies.

Observers have suggested that one factor that has contributed to unfriendly relations between the two countries has been competition for influence in the third world. Tito's pretensions to leadership of the nonaligned nations have been deprecated by the PRC, which has regarded itself as the prime model for Afro-Asian countries to emulate; since the dispute with the Soviet Union, Premier Chou has publicly referred to the PRC's international role as that of "standing together with oppressed countries and peoples in firmly opposing power politics of superpowers."

The Sino-Soviet rift affected the PRC's relations with communist parties in Western Europe as well. With the exception of the Dutch party, which remained neutral, all the communist parties of Western Europe sided with the Soviet Union and only gradually, in the mid-1960s, did some splinter communist groups and parties emerge that supported the PRC.

Trade between the PRC and Western Europe has been important to both sides since the early 1950s (see ch. 18, Trade and Transportation). It increased substantially after the Sino-Soviet split became public in 1960. The increase in trade with Western Europe, chiefly with the Federal Republic of Germany (West Germany) Great Britain, and France but also with Sweden, Finland, the Netherlands, Denmark, and Norway, came at a time of great reductions in Communist Chinese trade with Eastern Europe.

By 1964 relations with the countries of Western Europe were growing more cordial. For example, in January of that year, France announced its decision to establish diplomatic relations with the PRC. As a result, Nationalist China severed relations with France in February. A number of cultural exchanges occurred in the next two years, with the French minister of culture, Andre Malraux, visiting Peking in 1965. An agreement on the exchange of trade missions with Italy was signed in November 1964, and trade missions were exchanged in 1965.

In Eastern Europe, Communist Chinese relations with Albania remained close, the PRC providing Albania with substantial amounts of aid since 1962. This aid compensated for the withdrawal of assistance to Albania from the Soviet Union in February 1961. The Romanian prime minister led a party delegation to the PRC in 1964, and Chou went to Romania afterwards, eschewing any oral attacks on the Soviet Union during his visit. Trade with Poland, which had been substantial up to 1960 and then declined sharply, experienced an upward turn in 1965, and in 1966 a Polish industrial exhibition was held in Peking. Poland also continued to serve, as it had since 1958, as the site for meetings between the representatives of the PRC and United States governments. Relations with the German Democratic Republic (East Germany) showed some improvement with the signing in 1965 of an agreement on exchange of students between the two countries. Relations with Czechoslovakia, Hungary, and Bulgaria, however, remained distant, as they had been since the Sino-Soviet rift.

From late 1966 to mid-1969, the strident propaganda and subversive activities of Maoist radicals and their supporters serving in embassies, consulates, and trade offices and as news correspondents abroad hurt the PRC's relations with many European countries. The

1967 recall of diplomatic chiefs of posts, most trade mission heads, and many other PRC representatives had the effect of partially isolating the PRC from the outside world. The manhandling of diplomats, expulsion of foreign press representatives, and demonstrations and attacks upon foreign missions in the PRC brought many official protests and reprisals from countries all over Europe. The Finnish mission in Peking was the only Western European one to come through the Red Guard phase of the Cultural Revolution completely unscathed. The British were subject to some of the harshest treatment meted out during the Cultural Revolution. The existence of the British colony Hong Kong and also of Portuguese Macao, although extremely important for the PRC's foreign exchange earnings, was resented by the Red Guards, who provoked incidents in both territories.

In connection with the Cultural Revolution, relations with Eastern Europe deteriorated as well, except in the cases of Albania, Romania, and Poland. In Albania, the press began praising the Red Guards in late 1966, and in February 1967 Albania was launched on a "cultural revolution" of its own. In June 1967 Albania was host to the first Red Guard unit to go abroad.

In August 1968 came the invasion, by the Soviet Union and its Eastern European allies, of Czechoslovakia. The PRC and Albania denounced this invasion in similar terms, and the following month Albania formally withdrew from the Warsaw Pact, an action hailed by the PRC as contributing to the international communist movement.

At the Romanian National Day reception in Peking in August 1968, immediately after the invasion of Czechoslovakia, Premier Chou stated that Romania was "now facing the danger of foreign intervention and aggression" and pledged the Chinese people's support. Romania, for its part, opposed the Soviet-sponsored move in June 1969 to excommunicate the PRC from the "socialist commonwealth." Romania was the first Eastern European country, after Albania, to regain a PRC ambassador, returned after recall during the Cultural Revolution.

Although Poland had never denied its primary loyalty to the Soviet Union, it had avoided statements or actions that would deepen the quarrel between the Soviet Union and the PRC. The PRC's propaganda through 1967 was comparatively mild concerning Poland, although it asserted that Poland was revisionist. Relations worsened, however, after the invasion of Czechoslovakia, toward which Poland had contributed troops. In September 1968 Radio Peking began to broadcast in Polish, and the following month it announced the existence of a rival "Communist Party of Poland" that had allegedly charged the "Gomulka clique" with having launched "a bandit-like invasion."

Beginning in 1969 PRC ambassadors and chargés d'affaires began returning to their European posts, or new ones were appointed. Relations began to improve from their Cultural Revolution slump. In January 1969 the Italian government announced its decision to recognize the PRC, and subsequently diplomatic relations were established. Also in January 1969, Belgium announced that it was considering recognizing the PRC. During 1970 delegations of various types—parliamentary, commercial, and military—were exchanged with Eastern European countries. Albania, Romania, Czechoslovakia, East Germany, Poland, and Hungary either received Communist Chinese visits, sent delegations to the PRC, or both in that year.

Relations with Western Europe after the Cultural Revolution were concerned primarily with trade, in many instances with countries that did not recognize, or were not recognized by, the PRC, such as West Germany and Greece. By 1970 roughly 20 percent of the PRC's total trade was with Western Europe, as against 12 percent with the communist countries of Eastern Europe.

One indication of improving relations with Western Europe was the voting in the UN General Assembly in October 1971 on the admission of the PRC. In previous years most Western European delegations had voted in favor of requiring the Albanian resolution to be treated as an "important question" (that is, they had voted against the wishes of the PRC's sponsors), with only the Scandinavian countries and France opposing and Portugal and Austria abstaining. By 1971, however, only four European countries voted in favor of the "important question" resolution: Greece, Spain, Portugal, and Luxembourg. The first three had diplomatic relations with Nationalist China. The remainder of Europe opposed or abstained on that resolution.

In the 1971 voting Malta was the only one of the Western European countries opposed to the Albanian resolution to seat the PRC and expel Nationalist China. Of the three Western European countries that had voted against the Albanian resolution in 1970, Spain and Greece chose to abstain, and Turkey joined the majority in passing the resolution.

LATIN AMERICA

In January 1971 Chile became only the second Latin American nation to extend diplomatic recognition to the PRC, Cuba having maintained official ties since 1960. In October 1971 the PRC gained the political support of Cuba, Chile, Ecuador, Guyana, Peru, and Tobago in the crucial "important question" vote in the UN General Assembly; these countries were then joined by Mexico in their affirmative vote on the seating of PRC representatives in the UN.

Communist Chinese interest in this region was largely commercial but, although the first trade contact was established with Brazil in 1956, it was not until the early 1960s that the Communist Chinese government stepped up its efforts to increase its influence in Latin America. During the 1960s the PRC's political objectives were to counter the ideological influence of the Soviet Union and to organize a broad united front of Latin American "peoples" against the United States "imperialism." The CCP therefore set up anti-Soviet factions within the communist parties in at least ten countries; called on leftist intellectuals and Maoist activists to reject the Soviet concept of peaceful transition to socialism and to fight against "revisionist cliques" within their respective countries or communist movements; promoted "revolutionary violence"; and actively supported the activities of the Three People's Solidarity Organization (also known as the Tri-Continents Solidarity Conference). A conference of this organization, which both Communist Chinese and Soviet representatives attended, met at Havana in January 1966 and decided "to oppose the worldwide enterprises of imperialism with a global revolutionary strategy." (The next meeting of this organization, scheduled to be held in Peking in May 1967, was aborted because of the Cultural Revolution.)

Pro-Maoist organizations generally failed in the 1960s to establish bases in either the rural or the urban areas. They had to contend not only with the pro-Soviet communist parties in Latin American countries but also with anticommunist authorities in most of these countries. Occasional guerrilla activities carried out by elements variously labeled as Maoists, Castroites, or Che Guevarists usually ended in disaster. Although as recently as January 1970 the NCNA continued to comment favorably on "revolutionary struggle" and "revolutionary mass movement" in a number of countries in this region, it became increasingly clear that the Communist Chinese strategy was not proving successful.

Later in 1970 a new Latin American policy was adopted by the PRC. In essence the new strategy sought to capitalize on what the PRC suspected was the surging tide of anti-United States economic nationalism in many Latin American countries. It was designed to drive a wedge between the United States and Latin America by sharpening the so-called antagonistic contradictions between the two sides. Thus in 1970 and 1971 the principal focus of Communist Chinese propaganda and activities in Latin America was on struggles against alleged United States political domination and economic exploitation. This struggle was to be carried out by both the peoples of Latin American countries and their "reactionary" but nationalistic leaders who themselves were supposed to be victims of "superpower hegemonism." In an obvious effort to make common cause with Latin American peoples and their governments, the PRC supported the "ocean rights" of these governments (such as Ecuadorean and Peruvian demands for 200-mile territorial waters) and their "principled stand against the plunder of their water resources by the two superpowers." Among other issues that the PRC sought to exploit were the future status of the Panama Canal, the United States-Chilean dispute over the nationalization of United States-owned enterprises, and the alleged United States domination of the Organization of American States.

Meanwhile, the PRC began to tone down in 1970 its previously inflexible stand on class struggle and revolutionary violence against "reactionary ruling circles." This moderate line was not to be applied to all Latin American countries, however. The PRC's support for "the broad masses of peasants and farm workers of some Latin American countries" in their fight "to recover their land and for the right to live" continued unabated in early 1971. Brazil, Bolivia, Colombia, and Venezuela were frequently mentioned in connection with these peasants' struggles.

By 1971 the PRC's relations with Cuba had been restored to cordiality. In earlier years, especially during the early 1960s, these relations had been frigid as a result of Cuba's policy of noninvolvement in the Sino-Soviet dispute. In those years the Soviet Union was the principal donor of military and economic aid to Cuba. The PRC applied considerable pressures on the Cuban government in order to enlist its political and ideological support. When this effort failed, it defaulted, according to Premier Fidel Castro's charges made in early 1966, on a sugar-for-rice agreement signed in 1964. The Cuban premier also accused the PRC of having "betrayed the good faith of the Cuban people" and of having carried out an "economic reprisal for purely political reasons." Nevertheless, in 1970 the PRC tended to emphasize areas of common agreement in Sino-Cuban relations and sought to play down its differences with the Cuban government.

As of mid-October 1971 Chile had yet to post its ambassador in Peking. The PRC embassy, however, had been opened in Santiago.

CHAPTER 12

PUBLIC INFORMATION AND PROPAGANDA

The 1954 State Constitution of the People's Republic of China (PRC) guaranteed both a free press and freedom of speech, and these "fundamental rights" were reiterated in the draft state constitution of 1970. Nevertheless, even in the brief period during the Hundred Flowers Campaign (see Glossary) when criticism of the Party was officially encouraged, such criticism was only permitted within limits imposed by the regime (see ch. 10, Political Dynamics).

In the Communist Chinese view, public information should be neither objective nor disinterested: the dissemination of information is not considered as an opportunity for business enterprise, as an instrument solely to enlighten the people, or as a means to express or reflect private or public opinion. It is, rather, regarded as a political tool to "serve the interest of proletarian politics," in the words of Chinese Communist Party (CCP) theoreticians. Thus, what has constituted information to the leadership of the PRC has been the correct interpretation of the data or events that would lead to the fulfillment of the government's political, social, and economic programs. Moreover, timeliness of subject matter is considered far less important than ideological correctness.

To carry out this policy, the CCP has maintained total control over both the media of mass communications and the substance that they disseminate. This control includes measures intended to exclude foreign sources of information. The result is the output of rigidly controlled reporting and commentary that makes information and propaganda virtually synonymous.

Innovation comes only when a change in direction of Party policy necessitates new statements in the various media to conform with the new line. Such changes can result in great upheavals, such as occurred during the Great Proletarian Cultural Revolution, when virtually every newspaper was purged and reoriented. Some were closed permanently; others changed their names or frequency of publication, or both; still others had their entire editorial staffs removed and replaced by more politically reliable cadres (see Glossary).

In order for the CCP to maintain its monopoly of sources of information, it limits and controls news entering the country from abroad. Only such materials as are approved by the regime's top media control mechanism and are released through official or

349

government-approved agencies may be employed in any internal medium. Any incoming foreign radio broadcasts that are considered undesirable are jammed. Foreign news releases and publications, communist and noncommunist alike, are censored. Visiting groups, missions, or individuals are under governmental guidance during their sojourn to ensure that they see primarily those places and things compatible with Communist Chinese interests.

The PRC makes effective use of its monopoly of the various media. Materials are disseminated through a far-flung distribution and control system that permeates all levels of society, reaching the grassroots level of the remotest parts of the country. Substance is constantly repeated in all media in every possible thematic variation. Slogans and mnemonic devices are an integral part of this procedure, used to ensure that the message is thoroughly understood and remembered. The result is a general monotony, although the use of such new media as television and motion pictures provides some novelty, and there is presumably a certain excitement for the millions of newly literate in being able to read.

The most attentive audience of the public information media reportedly is composed of persons with political and social ambitions. Such people study the media seeking to learn of the sometimes unpredictable shifts in official policies and attitudes, since such changes can vitally affect careers (see ch. 5, Social System and Values).

The most important technique used by the PRC to mobilize public support of propaganda themes presented is the mass mobilization campaign. Such campaigns provide novelty, excitement, and periodic shifts in emphasis in the content of official propaganda.

The character of these mass mobilization campaigns has changed periodically since 1949. The campaigns of the early 1950s involved ruthless physical persecution of "enemies of the people" and were characterized by a high emotional pitch. They were followed by the campaigns of the mid-1950s, which relied primarily on techniques of persuasion. During this time mass organizations were established that encompassed virtually all of the people. These structures facilitated the efforts of cadres in enforcing a high level of participation in the massive Great Leap Forward campaign of 1958 to 1960 (see ch. 3, Historical Setting).

The mass campaigns of the early 1960s emphasized education and persuasion and were more moderate than the violent class struggle campaigns of the previous decade. In the case of the 1963–66 socialist education campaign, internal dissension within the national political leadership after 1959 resulted in reduced responsiveness both of the Party and mass organizational apparatus to Mao Tse-tung's efforts at arousing a high level of enthusiasm (see ch. 10, Political Dynamics).

The Great Proletarian Cultural Revolution (1966–69) brought a revival of the high emotional pitch of the early 1950s. The violence did not, however, reach the same level as that of the early 1950s period. In this campaign Mao called on support from outside the Party and from mass oganizational structures. The disruption of these established organizations during the Cultural Revolution left the regime, as of 1971, at least temporarily with less effective channels for the implementation of mass mobilization campaigns than formerly. There were indications that campaigns in the early 1970s would derive from People's Liberation Army (PLA) sources and would depend largely on PLA cadres for implementation.

HISTORICAL DEVELOPMENT OF MASS MEDIA

Chinese historians take pride in pointing out that newspapers were published in China as early as the seventh century A.D., roughly 800 years before they appeared in Europe. These early efforts, however, were little more than gazettes that distributed government news to officials and were never intended as facilities for expressing or influencing public opinion. It was not until the end of the nineteenth century that newspapers and publications in the modern sense came into existence.

The treaty ports were established after China's defeat by Great Britain near the middle of the nineteenth century; their foreign concessions, concentrations of population, and modern facilities provided an ideal milieu for the growth and development of information channels in which initially the press and, later, all media proliferated (see ch. 3, Historical Setting). These facilities were used by the revolutionary movement that brought the last imperial dynasty to an end in 1911. The new republican government in 1912 inherited a fairly well established, printed-media public information system.

After attaining control of most of the country in the late 1920s, the Nationalist government of Chiang Kai-shek moved to expand the public information system and place it under control. A first press law governing newspapers, magazines, and other publications was promulgated in 1930. Both government and private radio broadcasting stations were set up in major political and commercial centers. The principal effort was concentrated in urban areas until the outbreak of the Sino-Japanese War in 1937; the mass media paid only minimal attention during this time to rural communities in Nationalist-controlled areas.

The Communists, on the other hand, who until after 1945 held few urban centers, concentrated their public information efforts upon the masses in the rural areas. All means of dissemination, ranging from conventional newspapers and radio broadcasts to billboards and handbills, were employed to win support from the peasantry.

In the war with Japan (1937–45), the Japanese occupied most of the coastal regions and drove the Nationalist Chinese government inland. Chungking, in Szechwan Province, became the wartime capital and emerged as the center of public information. Many newspapers and periodicals, as well as government-operated radio stations, publishing houses, and other communications facilities, were reestablished there or at other cities in the interior; in many of these cities no such facilities had existed before.

After the defeat of the Japanese in 1945, Nationalist information media exhibited a short-lived resurgence of vitality; freedom of expression was greater than formerly and was restricted only by laws against treason, espionage, and libel. Then, however, increasing demands of the civil war with the communist forces brought a concerted effort on the part of the Nationalists to regulate and supervise the dissemination of public information. A system of registration was instituted for all publications and radio stations, many of the more influential of which were either subsidized or directly controlled by the government.

The press of Nationalist China in the post-World War II period retained considerable independence of outlook and policy, however. Although the Central News Agency, first as a Nationalist Party organ and later as a government enterprise, had a virtual monopoly on domestic news dissemination in the areas the Nationalists controlled, other agencies, such as the Associated Press and Reuters, were available to provide the public with some balance in the presentation of news.

ORGANIZATION OF INFORMATION AND PROPAGANDA

After the communist takeover of the mainland in 1949, the direction and control of information activities until the Cultural Revolution were reserved primarily for the CCP. Within the Party structure, policy responsibility for these was centralized in the Politburo (Political Bureau—see Glossary), while day-to-day operations were discharged through a separate Department of Propaganda in the Secretariat of the Party Central Committee (see ch. 9, Political System and Values).

From 1945 to 1966 the Department of Propaganda was headed by Lu Ting-i, who had been associated with Party propaganda activities since the 1920s. Lu was ousted in the early part of the Cultural Revolution and was succeeded briefly by T'ao Chu. T'ao, then fourth in rank in the Politburo, was in turn purged by the beginning of 1967.

Direction of information and propaganda at the center was, from all indications, then taken over by the leaders of the Cultural Revolution Group (see ch. 10, Political Dynamics). After early 1967—in the absence of effective Party machinery—information and propaganda direction was assumed by revolutionary committees that functioned generally under the direction of the provincial military commands. Little was known about the specific organization of the Party's Department of Propaganda after the Cultural Revolution, and its director had not yet been identified as of late 1971.

Also substantially involved in the information field until the Cultural Revolution was the Ministry of Culture and Education, which had coordinated all film, drama, and artistic activities with Party policies; had incorporated the Party line into the curricula of the schools; and had developed, published, and distributed books and lesser publications. The ministry owned and operated the studios that produced the nation's feature, documentary, and news films and, in conjunction with the Broadcasting Administrative Bureau (BAB), was responsible for the school programs carried over radio and television stations. After the minister, Lu Ting-i (who held this post concurrently with that of director of the Party's Department of Propaganda) was purged in 1966, there was much disruption of the ministry's functions. In mid-1971 it was not yet known to what extent the ministry had resumed its former activities.

The Ministry of Posts and Telecommunications also has played a small role in public information. This ministry has responsibility for obtaining subscriptions and distributing newspapers and periodicals to regular subscribers.

Propagandists have been a permanent part of the Party structure at every echelon down to branch committee level (see ch. 10, Political Dynamics). Below branch organization, as in cells where membership is very small, a single Party member or activist is usually designated to act as propagandist. The mission of propagandists at every level has been to ensure the widest possible dissemination of the regime's informational materials. Each propagandist interviews people in his area and relays Party directives to them. He also organizes newspaper-reading, film-reviewing, and book-reading groups; monitors radio broadcasts and other media and reproduces their substance in handwritten wall newspapers throughout his neighborhood; displays posters, documents, and other printed and pictorial matter received from higher echelons; organizes and presents amateur talent shows dramatizing Party themes; marshals people for mass demonstrations and parades or to listen to speakers supporting approved movements and campaigns; organizes and conducts political study classes and self-criticism and accusation meetings; and visits families or simply talks to people in their homes or at work. In short, he does everything possible to ensure that Party information saturates his neighborhood and that every individual in it not only is aware of what the Party wants him to hear but also understands and does something about it.

Through the efforts of such persons, the information and propaganda that emanates from the highest level in Peking flows essentially unaltered and unimpeded to every corner of the land. Additionally, it is transmitted to all continents of the world by the many powerful radio transmitters of the BAB. Some of the overseas broadcasts are in Chinese, and part are in the appropriate foreign languages. The purpose of the broadcasts appears to be both to inform expatriates and to guide propagandists stationed abroad in carrying out their assigned missions.

METHODS AND TECHNIQUES

Information and propaganda efforts consist primarily of carefully planned and formulated programs that are based on general principles developed by the national leadership. These programs are developed in accordance with established and empirically proven guidelines that govern their substance and conduct: the recognition that different social groupings in a society respond differently and require separately designed forms of mental and physical stimulation; the employment of organized mass movements involving the active participation of great segments of the population; and the intensive employment of specific thematic campaigns. Efforts are made to coordinate the functioning of media to create the effect of a single voice and to gain maximum impact.

Overall Principles and Guidelines

In the conduct of any information or propaganda campaign little is left to chance or to the discretion of individual local propagandists. Policies and tactics are determined at the very top national level, and it is incumbent on all subordinate leaders to follow them exactly as directed. The foundation of this system is based on operating tenets laid down as early as 1943 by the Party's Central Committee in its "Resolutions on Methods of Leadership." In general, this document contained directives to all propagandists, instructing them to investigate the attitudes and receptiveness of the people before attempting to inform or propagandize them; to make it appear that Party policies originated in the people; to incorporate general slogans into local operations; and to discover and employ aggressive activists in the community to stimulate and agitate more backward elements in the same locality. Efforts were to be concentrated on only one campaign at a given time, supporting this when necessary with closely related secondary drives. Each action was to be reviewed carefully after it had been completed in order to benefit from the experience and to improve future efforts. All cadres were to be thoroughly educated before being sent on information or propaganda missions among the masses.

Each effort was supported by a specific, detailed outline of objectives, methods, tactics, and priorities. As a result, even in remote areas where close and direct supervision by the top leadership has not been possible, there has been a remarkably high degree of consistency. Thus phrases, slogans, and themes—devised in Peking—are repeated verbatim throughout the entire country.

Mass Mobilization Campaigns

Propaganda campaigns to incite the masses to behave in certain ways and to participate in certain activities have been carried out by the regime since the inception of communist rule. The propaganda material usually presents each new campaign as the result of initiatives spontaneously arrived at on the local scene that have come to the attention of the nation's leaders, rather than having originated at the top.

Mass campaigns may be either national in scope or restricted to a particular sector of society. Depending upon the success of a movement in one sector or region, it may then be utilized for a national campaign. The beginning of such a campaign is often indicated by publicity in the press and radio given to a particular person, institution, or situation; this is accompanied by editorial comment citing the subject of the report as being characteristic of what the masses should extol or expunge. A subsequent speech or voicing of approval by Mao, or some other authoritative figure, signals that the campaign should start. By this time, cadres and activists from the Party and mass organizations charged with implementing it at the local level have usually been thoroughly geared up for the campaign.

Throughout the campaign, mass communications media disseminate stories of successful experiences from various parts of the country, focus attention on practices to be condemned or followed, and single out heroes to be emulated. Local authorities and leaders and activists of mass organizations at the local level work to mobilize active popular participation in the campaign. Masses of people are directed to parade, sing, and shout slogans; put up wall posters; hold public meetings; or otherwise demonstrate in support of an objective announced by the regime. After the movement has been in progress for a time, its accomplishments and failures are evaluated by the leadership, and a decision is made either to intensify the campaign, allow it to taper off, or terminate it.

Mass campaigns have differed from time to time since 1949 in the emotional intensity of their propaganda and in the degree of support given them by the people, elements of the Party leadership, and the mass organization hierarchies. In the campaigns of the early 1950s, the hatreds and resentments of the so-called oppressed classes were roused by Party agitators against selected targets. These campaigns included the 1950–52 land reform campaign, the 1950–51 movement against counterrevolutionaries, the 1951–54 "resist-America, aid-Korea" campaign, the 1951–52 ideological reform of intellectuals movement, and the "three-antis" and "five-antis" campaigns of 1952 against evildoers in the government and private enterprise (see ch. 3, Historical Setting). The targets of these campaigns were alleged by the Party to be in a state of "antagonistic contradiction" against the people and were therefore to be ruthlessly crushed. Summary execution at the end of mass trials and suicide after public humiliation brought death to hundreds of thousands—some report a million or more—of targets of campaigns during this period.

Beginning in the mid-1950s, the campaign techniques became less harsh than formerly; most campaign targets of the period—for example, middle peasants—were regarded as being chiefly in a state of "non-antagonistic contradiction," which could be peacefully resolved through persuasion, reeducation, and other reformative, rather than solely punitive, measures. In mid-1956 the most liberal campaign ever launched by the regime—the Hundred Flowers Campaign began—and, for a year, encouraged more free expression in arts and letters than had been permitted previously. Then, in early May 1957 the Hundred Flowers movement was directed toward encouraging criticism of the Party, and of the regime, by intellectuals. Some frank and harsh criticism quickly ensued. Within less than a month the movement was abruptly terminated, and the critics came under attack in an "anti-rightist" campaign carried out by the Party.

From 1958 to 1960 the Great Leap Forward (see Glossary) campaign was carried out, chiefly in rural areas. As part of the campaign, there was an attempt to organize society into communal units of greater size than had been traditional while at the same time reducing familial allegiances (see ch. 5, Social System and Values; ch. 14, Agriculture). The propaganda that accompanied the Great Leap Forward was designed to elicit a high level of enthusiasm and optimism. Slogans of the campaign were "Twenty years in a day" and "Hard work for a few years, happiness for a thousand." The propaganda stressed the importance of mass enthusiasm, inspired by proletarian political ideology, in the achievement of economic and social goals. Expertise and experience were alleged to be less important than enthusiasm and political correctness. The nation was exhorted to put "politics in command." Largely as the result of the work of mass organizational cadres, a high level of actual participation in the Great Leap campaign was achieved in 1959. By 1961, however, largely because of the Great Leap's adverse impact on the economy, the campaign had begun to taper off (see ch. 13, Character and Structure of the Economy).

The next national mass campaign was the 1963-66 socialist education campaign. Propaganda cadres and activists were charged with reviving revolutionary morale, chiefly of the rural people, and with reactivating their concern with "class struggle" by reminding the peasants of the bitterness of their life under the old regime.

A series of campaigns confined to the PLA began in 1960. These were regarded by the Party leadership as quite successful, and starting in 1964 a new national campaign was initiated exhorting people to "learn from the PLA" on how to become worthy successors of the revolutionary generation (see ch. 21, The Armed Forces). The masses were urged to emulate various soldier heroes who had, under peacetime circumstances, given their lives for the public good. In mid-1965 an intensive drive began to establish the primacy of Mao Tse-tung Thought in the national ideology. The study of Mao's thought was officially stated to be "the most basic guarantee for the success of the socialist education movement." Not only did the Party propaganda apparatus engage in the campaign, but the PLA also figured prominently; its General Political Department published the authoritative "little red book," *Quotations from Chairman Mao*, which quickly became the omnipresent symbol of Maoist orthodoxy (see ch. 9, Political System and Values).

Because of differences of opinion among the leaders over the correct policies to be pursued during the middle and late 1960s, the socialist education campaign was not carried out as thoroughly as had been the Great Leap Forward. Within the Party and the governmental and mass organizational bureaucracies, there were many who agreed with the then chairman of the PRC, Liu Shao-ch'i, that the time was not ripe for another revolutionary upheaval of the Great Leap type that had brought such disruption to the economy and society in the late 1950s and early 1960s. Many cadres, therefore, failed to give the socialist education campaign their full support, and the Party and mass organizations—which had functioned up to that time as the major channels through which mass mobilization was brought about—did not fulfill their duties during this campaign to Mao's satisfaction.

Partly as a result, the Great Proletarian Cultural Revolution campaign of 1966 to 1969 was launched and largely controlled outside the existing Party and mass organizational structures. Initiated by Mao, it utilized instead propagandists and activists recruited from among PLA cadres, anti-Liu and pro-Mao factions in the Party and civilian bureaucracies and, in particular, millions of teenaged students who in 1966 were organized as Red Guards to be the vanguard of a new revolutionary movement and were given the mission of weeding out all persons, ideas, and activities that Mao and his supporters regarded as not sufficiently progressive in character (see ch. 10, Political Dynamics).

Resort to use of the generally undisciplined Red Guards, and other Maoist rebel groups, resulted by 1967 in the entire country's being thrown into confusion. In 1967 the PLA was called upon to restore order, and the Red Guards and some other rebel mass organizations were disbanded in 1968. The damage done at this time to established mass organizational and Party machinery is regarded by experienced observers, as having had, at least temporarily, a debilitating effect upon the regime's power to mobilize the masses.

It appeared in 1971 that mass mobilization, as with all other national leadership functions, was receiving its chief ideological inspiration and support from the PLA. For example, the most prominent propaganda campaign in the early 1970s was one exhorting the people to "three supports, two militaries' work." This phrase was the official abbreviation for the campaign to support industry, agriculture, and the broad masses of the Left as well as the work of military control and political and military training. This campaign had been launched first within the PLA in the late 1960s and by early 1971 had begun to spread to propaganda directed at the civilian population, along with the PLA-inspired Four Good Movement (see ch. 21, The Armed Forces).

MASS COMMUNICATION MEDIA

The PRC in 1971 operated a widespread communications system that included both formal and informal channels. The formalized media included newspapers, periodicals, books, and other publications; radio and television; and drama, art, and motion picture production and exhibition facilities. Other media included handwritten wall newspapers, handbills, posters, and street corner skits. Neighborhood meeting and discussion assemblies and large numbers of clubs were organized to read and discuss newspapers and books, listen to the radio, watch television, or discuss political and current affairs.

The Press

On the eve of the Cultural Revolution approximately 400 daily newspapers were being published, as well as nearly 1,200 nondaily newspapers and nearly 2,000 specialized periodicals. Several newspapers and a few periodicals were directed to the national audience, others were directed primarily toward specific provincial and subprovincial audiences; a host were specialized publications for Party members, government officials, military personnel, educators, scientists, workers in industry, rural residents, women, young people, or other special groups. A few were published in indigenous minority languages, such as Kazakh, Korean, Mongolian, Tibetan, Uighur, Chuang, and Yi. There were also some publications produced especially for overseas readers that were published in more than a dozen foreign languages.

Domestic

During the Cultural Revolution all but a few newspapers and periodicals suspended publication. During the early 1970s some of the suspended publications were revived, and as of mid-1971 it was known that at least one daily newspaper was being published in every province and autonomous region, and there were also several being published in each of the three municipalities—Peking, Tientsin, and Shanghai.

The most important national newspapers in 1971 were *People's Daily* (*Jen Min Jih Pao*), the official newspaper of the CCP, and *Liberation Army Daily* (*Chieh Fang Chun Pao*), the official organ of the PLA; both were published in Peking and were known to Western scholars by their English titles. Both newspapers were regarded as authoritative, as was the Party's theoretical journal, the monthly, *Red Flag* (*Hung Ch'i*), which was also known in the West by its English title. Articles first published in these periodicals were picked up and reprinted widely in provincial and municipal newspapers. The two aforementioned daily newspapers, *Red Flag*, and the news releases of the New China News Agency (NCNA) constituted the authoritative public information sources of the PRC.

The Department of Propaganda of the Party Central Committee was reportedly responsible in 1971 for supervising the publication of *People's Daily* and *Red Flag*, while the NCNA along with the other principal government agency involved in public information—the Broadcasting Administration Bureau (BAB)—were reportedly under the direct supervision of the State Council.

Before the Cultural Revolution, the PLA's *Liberation Army Daily* was of consequence chiefly to military personnel. After the purge of longtime director of the Party's Department of Propaganda, Lu Ting-i, in 1966, however, and the subsequent increase in political influence of the PLA under Lin Piao's leadership, the *Liberation Army Daily* became, during the latter 1960s, the most authoritative journal from which the two Party publications took their cues. Indications were, however, that *People's Daily* was, by the early 1970s, on approximately equal footing with the PLA newspaper.

It has been common since the mid-1960s for occasional editorials to be published jointly by the *Liberation Army Daily* and by either or both Party journals, to commemorate certain anniversaries and to reinforce the authoritative character of certain policy statements.

Another technique for calling the reader's attention to a particularly important policy statement or authoritative message is the use of articles by-lined "Commentator." Articles under this by-line, appearing chiefly in the Party publications, *People's Daily* and *Red Flag*, are perused with more than usual care by the politically aware reader. This is also true for articles that are called "investigative reports." Such a report of a particular situation in a specific place, purportedly by an on-the-spot observer, provides indications of the manner in which the leadership wants a particular subject or situation handled. Occasionally—as, for example, during the public debate of the late 1960s and early 1970s concerning the proper way to reform the educational system—several varying "investigation reports" are published (see ch. 8, Education, Intellectual Expression, and the Arts). This signals the fact that the subject is still open for debate while, at the same time, delimiting the boundaries within which debate is permissible.

The NCNA (known also as Hsinhua News Agency) is the chief source of domestic news and the sole source of international news for the PRC domestic press. Its function is to make official announcements of programs, documents, meetings, policy statements, and the like, as well as to release material that newspapers, radio, and television may use if they wish. Before the Cultural Revolution, it had been under the control of the Ministry of Information. Up to that time, NCNA had had approximately 1,500 subordinate offices and 70,000 part-time reporters working for it throughout the country. Although its releases continued to be broadcast daily (probably still, as before the Cultural Revolution, in twelve indigenous languages and dialects and eleven foreign languages), information was lacking in mid-1971 concerning the number and location of its offices and staff.

The press at the subnational level has been more severely disrupted by, and slower to recover from, the Cultural Revolution than has the national press. Nonetheless, by 1971 all of the provinces and autonomous regions and probably all the major cities had local newspapers. Circulation figures were lacking, except for occasional scattered reports, such as, for example, for the *Hsi-an Jih Pao*, published in the capital city of Shensi Province, which had in 1971 a daily circulation of 180,000. Circulation figures on newspapers are not, in any case, adequate indicators of the influence and exposure given the daily press in the PRC since an individual copy is often circulated among a sizable number of readers, and copies are publicly posted as well.

Another technique commonly used to disseminate news is the use of a so-called wall newspaper. One man is chosen as a newspaper disseminator in each village or street. His job is to maintain a wall bulletin board or slate in a public place, on which he records news and information according to instructions passed on to him by the local

NCNA office or by radio or other means. In rural areas the news disseminator is obliged to read aloud from the wall bulletin regularly for the benefit of illiterates in his community.

At times of severe ideological rigidity, the newspapers and other periodicals in the provinces have tended to depend almost exclusively on national news releases, but at other times appreciable local material is generated. In the early 1970s there was generally widespread homogeneity of content in the press, local and national, with the exception of two newspapers published in Shanghai, *Wen Hui Pao* and *Chieh Fang Jih Pao*. In 1971, both of these Shanghai newspapers had a substantial nationwide readership among the politically active.

The *Wen Hui Pao* was a local newspaper of the Shanghai Municipality until the Cultural Revolution. In 1967 it was accused of having degenerated into a capitalist weapon that refused to further Mao Tse-tung Thought; it was taken over by intimates of Mao. Since then *Wen Hui Pao* and another Shanghai newspaper, *Chieh Fang Jih Pao*, have sometimes supported more radical positions than have other journals. Foreign observers have suggested that these two newspapers have occasionally served as platforms for Mao's wife, Chiang Ch'ing, and others of her faction to enunciate positions of the Maoist vanguard.

All newspapers and periodicals for the domestic audience on various special subjects—such as medicine, history, or science—or those directed toward a particular sector of society—such as an ethnic minority, Buddhists, women, youth, or factory workers—were believed to have been suspended during the Cultural Revolution. As of 1971 foreign observers had no information as to which of these, if any, had resumed publication. A *Red Flag* editorial in early 1971 led foreign observers to predict, however, that some increase in the number of periodicals published was being contemplated.

Foreign

The principal source of PRC news for foreign audiences is the NCNA international service, which releases daily English-language bulletins as well as news releases in some other languages. It maintains a number of branches in foreign countries; some of its correspondents have been expelled from several African and other countries for alleged subversive activities (see ch. 11, Foreign Relations). The China News Agency, a subsidiary of the NCNA, provides news to Overseas Chinese periodicals and newspapers.

Many PRC periodicals intended for distribution outside the country were also suspended or curtailed during the height of the Cultural Revolution. All underwent extensive reorganization and staff replacements before resuming their normal publication schedules in about 1969. In 1971 periodicals of major importance for external distribution were the monthlies *China Pictorial* and *China Reconstructs* and the weekly *Peking Review*. *China Pictorial*, published in Chinese and in fifteen foreign languages including English, somewhat resembles in appearance and format the United States magazine *Life*. (*China Pictorial* formerly was published in Mongolian, Tibetan, Uighur, and Chuang. These editions were suspended in 1967.) The magazine has high-quality color illustrations and photographs depicting various aspects of current life and development in the PRC.

China Reconstructs is an illustrated monthly devoted to articles depicting economic, social, and cultural progress of the PRC under the communist regime. In 1971 it was being issued in English, Spanish, French, Russian, and Arabic editions. *Peking Review* is an English-language weekly summary and digest of important news and commentary originating in the domestic press. One other periodical known to be still published in 1971 was *Chinese Literature*, an English-language monthly (with a quarterly edition in French) devoted to translations of contemporary Chinese-language short stories, poems, plays, folksongs, and other miscellaneous literature of the popular variety.

Books

Between 1950 and 1960 the number of books in print rose from about 275 million to over 2.5 billion. In 1962 the Party leadership called for a new emphasis in publishing, namely on books that recalled the revolutionary struggle and works on science and technology. This emphasis on the political and the practical at the expense of other fields was intensified during the Cultural Revolution, when various works of Mao Tse-tung virtually dominated the publishing scene. For example, 150 million four-volume sets of the *Selected Works of Mao Tse-tung*, 40 million copies of selected readings from those works, and 740 million copies of the PLA publication *Quotations from Chairman Mao* (the little red book) were reported to have been issued, mostly in small pocket-sized editions.

Reportedly, everyone carried a copy of the little red book at all times as a sign of loyalty to Mao and as an authoritative reference work to be consulted continually. Judging from pictures and reports of foreigners in 1971, the degree of concern with overt display of the little red book that characterized the late 1960s appeared to have diminished somewhat. Mao's works continued to be popular, however, as were books of plays and operas that had been written under the supervision of Mao's wife, Chiang Ch'ing, and accounts of communist heroes, exemplary workers, and heroic soldiers, many of which have been published by the General Political Department of the PLA (see ch. 8, Education, Intellectual Expression, and the Arts).

The actual production of books has been accomplished by a number of publishing houses that are concentrated in Peking and, to a lesser extent, in Shanghai. Their precise number is not known, but it is estimated that before the Cultural Revolution there were as many as 400.

By mid-1971 most had not published anything for about five years. There were indications, however, that a revival in publishing of books, as well as of periodicals, was about to start. A *Red Flag* editorial early in that year entitled "Publish More and Better Reading Material" decried the fact that:

> Some comrades hold that "publishing more or less popular reading material does not matter much" and hence may be "assigned a lower priority and even delayed". ... Such thinking is obviously incorrect. Not only do China's people need a great deal of political literature [but also writings] on literature and art, science and technology, history, geography, international affairs and so forth.

A widely publicized event in the autumn of 1971 was the appearance of the first novel to be published since the start of the Cultural Revolution.

Wall Posters

Wall posters known as *tatzupao* (big character papers) have constituted an important mass communications medium since the late 1950s. Usually handwritten, they appear to have been used to a limited extent during the revolutionary struggle before 1949, and a few were evident in the early days of the communist regime. They first became a major propaganda device during the Hundred Flowers Campaign in 1957 and 1958, when they proved so effective that the government officially adopted the technique and directed every department and bureau to establish a special unit to produce and mount *tatzupao* of its own.

During the Great Proletarian Cultural Revolution *tatzupao* reached a peak as major instruments for dissemination of public information and propaganda. According to Ch'en Po-ta, a leading interpreter of Mao Tse-tung Thought, a *tatzupao* provided the spark that ignited the movement into one of its most intense phases. This occurred in early 1966, when Mao supporters affixed a *tatzupao* to the walls of Peking University attacking the school's administration and its president, Lu P'ing, in particular, for a lack of revolutionary zeal. When Mao Tse-tung was informed of the poster he applauded it as constituting the "first Marxist-Leninist poster in the whole country" and directed that its contents be broadcast over the Central People's Broadcasting Station in Peking. With this approbation, *tatzupao* rapidly developed into a major instrument for organizing the masses in support of the Cultural Revolution.

Red Guards (see Glossary) quickly adopted the use of *tatzupao* to spread their charges against suspected Party cadre, private and government officials, institutions, and practices. Party propagandists; mass organizations; worker, peasant, and labor groups; and student bodies also followed this practice. Even private individuals, angry over a seeming injustice, put up simple posters to make charges against or to pass along insinuating messages about their neighbors. Soon the nation was swamped with *tatzupao*. In some areas every inch of space on the sides and fronts of government buildings, schools, factories, stores, shops, and apartment houses were covered with posters. Sometimes persons who had been attacked wrote *tatzupao* of their own and hung them up beside the originals to answer their charges or to thank their accusers for pointing out their errors. In a short time the PRC was turned into a battleground of contending *tatzupao*.

By 1971 most of the vehemence incorporated in the *tatzupao* during the Cultural Revolution had disappeared, and their content seemed to be largely exhortatory or instructive. They appeared still to be ubiquitous and to have firmly established themselves as a major medium for disseminating information and Party propaganda among the masses.

Electronic Media

Electronic media are fully exploited and are regarded as second only to newspapers in linking the Party leadership to the people. An extensive system of government mediumwave and shortwave facilities provides domestic service to every area of the country, and a number of powerful transmitters are engaged in transmitting information and propaganda to audiences all over the world. Television service is available in the major urban areas, and it was reported in operation in several parts of Outer China (see Glossary) in late 1970. It was also beginning to reach country areas outside some urban centers.

Radio

Communist radio broadcasting formally began in Shensi Province, when the New China Broadcasting Station was established in Yenan in September 1945. The Red Army's military successes against the Japanese throughout World War II and in the civil war that followed brought additional facilities under communist control, and by the time the communist regime assumed control over all of China in 1949, the original station at Yenan had been expanded to forty-nine. These stations were reorganized into a single system known as the Central People's Broadcasting Station (CPBS), which had its headquarters and key station at Peking.

Party leaders fully recognized the value of radio as an instrument of public information and propaganda and the necessity for the state to have complete control over its operations. Accordingly, they set up a special organ, called the Broadcasting Administrative Bureau, under the State Council to establish, improve, and expand the network throughout the country. In 1971 the Broadcasting Administrative Bureau and the CPBS were still operating under their original titles.

According to the latest available listing, valid at the beginning of 1970, there were 1,021 radio broadcasting transmitters in the country: 713 mediumwave, 307 shortwave, and one in the ultra high frequency (UHF) radio band. The single UHF transmitter, except for the audio portion of television stations, was as of early 1970 the only frequency modulation (FM) facility in the country.

These transmitters were assigned variously to separate radio stations located in every province, autonomous region, and municipality. Some stations had one or more mediumwave transmitters; some had one or more shortwave transmitters; and others had both types in irregular combinations. None of the stations was assigned an individual call letter but simply identified itself as a unit of the CPBS or other government agency, usually adding the name of the city or the province in which it was located. Stations were reportedly located in over 150 cities scattered throughout the nation.

A majority of the broadcasting facilities were concentrated in or around Peking. These facilities included a country headquarters and a total of some 480 shortwave and mediumwave transmitters, as well as the single FM station. The headquarters setup—composed of network control facilities, modern studios, and four mediumwave and nineteen shortwave stations—formed the nucleus of the entire national network. It developed and directed all activities in both the domestic and the international broadcast services. All national programs originated here and were broadcast over the four mediumwave stations for audiences in the Peking area. These programs were simultaneously fed into the nineteen shortwave transmitters for dissemination to, and rebroadcast from, the many regional and local stations throughout the country. All other mediumwave transmitters in Peking were grouped into four stations operated by the Peking Municipality for local radio broadcasts. The single FM station was operated by the Ministry of Culture and Education as an outlet for educational programs for citizens of the capital and its environs.

Forty-six of the shortwave stations in Peking were assigned to the China Press Agency, a subsidiary of NCNA, for transmitting NCNA's daily news file to both domestic and international listeners. Much of this was broadcast at dictation speed. The other shortwave facilities in the capital area were organized into sixty-two stations known collectively as Radio Peking that carried on the PRC's international radio service beamed to every corner of the world. This service in late 1970 was broadcasting in thirty-three languages and five Chinese dialects for a total of over 1,500 hours a week.

Most stations outside Peking were employed in the regular domestic service, but there were five significant groups of other facilities that offered specialized types of service. One group of thirteen mediumwave and four shortwave transmitters, located along the eastern coast opposite Taiwan, was used for propaganda service to Nationalist government officials, forces, and residents of that island. A second group of ten shortwave and eight mediumwave stations, scattered about Fukien Province and operated by the PLA as the Fukien Front Station, broadcast to the Nationalist-held offshore islands and was also used for relaying portions of the Taiwan service. The third group of about forty mixed mediumwave and shortwave stations located in Inner Mongolia, Sinkiang, Tibet, and South China were organized into separate networks broadcasting appropriate non-Chinese-language programs to minority nationalities in those areas. The fourth group, of a varying number of stations strategically located in northern China, specialized in Russian-language programs directed at the Soviet Union. The fifth group, believed to be situated in Yunnan Province, consisted of at least three so-called clandestine stations that identified themselves on the air as the Voice of Free Thailand, the Voice of the People of Burma, and the Voice of the Malayan Revolution. They were used to support communist insurgent forces in Southeast Asia.

There was no way in 1971 to determine the total number of radio receivers in use in China. The development of small, inexpensive, battery-operated transistor sets broadened opportunities for individual listening, but the cost factor appeared to preclude widespread individual ownership. Most receivers, therefore, were believed to be owned by Communes or cooperatives and installed in communal halls. The government has frequently donated or sold sets at a loss to groups and organizations to encourage group, rather than individual, listening.

Wired Broadcasting

Great emphasis has been placed on the development of wired broadcasting, in part presumably to compensate for the lack of radio receivers but largely because of its apparent value to the regime for the dissemination of propaganda and the Party mass line. An NCNA domestic broadcast in September 1971, for instance, pointed out that the installation of wired broadcasting had promoted widespread development of the mass movement to study and apply Mao Tse-tung Thought in a living way everywhere.

According to this same NCNA statement, the extension of wire broadcasting was given great impetus by the Cultural Revolution; its spread was particularly marked after the establishment of the revolutionary committees (see ch. 10, Political Dynamics). It was also claimed that the number of loudspeakers in the countryside by 1971 was eight times that before the Cultural Revolution and that wired broadcasting had been installed in more than 96 percent of the nation's production brigades and more than 87 percent of the production teams. In a number of places, especially in urban and adjacent areas, wired broadcasting reportedly had been installed in individual dwellings.

The program to increase the number of the wire broadcast Commune stations, which pick up programs from local and regional transmitters and feed them into the loudspeaker net; the laying of new wire connections; and the installation of additional speakers were slated to be carried out chiefly through collectively raised funds. Substantial use of local materials for manufacturing wire poles and speakers also was reported.

The substance of radio broadcasts is generally identical to that carried in newspapers and other media, except that it is edited for the greatest appeal to the domestic, international, or specialized audience to which it is addressed. It is also augmented by radio's unique capability of increasing interest and impact through the use of music; drama; personalized speeches and commentaries by recognized individuals; and on-the-scene coverage of parades, celebrations, demonstrations, mass meetings, official functions, and sports activities.

Television

The PRC's first television station, constructed with Soviet technical assistance, went into regular operation in September 1958 in Peking. That year other stations were also established in Harbin and Shanghai. Development was steady thereafter. In 1971 the country reportedly had perhaps forty to fifty stations. Service remained limited, however—stations telecasting only on certain days and programs generally lasting only a few hours. There were indications that in addition to major urban centers most, if not all, of the provincial capitals had stations. By the end of 1970 stations were also known to be operating in the Inner Mongolian and Sinkiang Uighur autonomous regions, and a station was expected to be in operation soon in the Tibetan Autonomous Region as part of a government effort to establish television stations in minority areas.

Television stations produce pictures that are exceptionally clear and of fine definition. The system uses a 625-line scan (as compared to the United States standard of 510) and very high frequency (VHF). Most telecasts were live camera or films. Live coverage of events within the station area was provided by both Peking Television and other stations. There was no evidence in early 1971 of the use of videotape. About a dozen factories were reported to be engaged in the manufacture of television sets.

At the start of the Cultural Revolution in 1966 probably 100,000 or more television receivers were in use. The number presumably has increased; a Japanese source in early 1971 estimated that there were up to 200,000 sets. Most of these are found in factories, urban and suburban communal meeting halls, dormitories, government office recreation rooms, army recreation facilities, and other places where group viewing can take place. Apparently some wired television service has also been extended to rural Communes outside certain of the large urban centers. Private sets could be purchased without a license in 1971, but ownership was limited, at least in part, by the comparatively high price, which was reported to be about 200 yuan (2.46 yuan equal US$1—see Glossary) for an eight-inch black and white set and 440 yuan for a fourteen-inch set.

Telecasting was disrupted during the Cultural Revolution throughout most of the country. Peking Television ceased transmitting in January 1967 with the announcement that television was not needed while the Cultural Revolution was underway. "Revolutionary" groups also took over stations in Shanghai and Canton. Resumption of transmission appears to have occurred about the beginning of 1968.

During the Cultural Revolution, also, Red Guards attacked private ownership of television sets as a "bourgeois luxury" and demanded their confiscation. Popular attitudes toward this question since the Cultural Revolution were not known.

Television programming, like that of other media, is used to promote those movements, campaigns, and ideas desired by the Party leadership. Programs consisted primarily of live drama or feature propaganda films. They included documentaries, largely on agriculture and industry, and scientific, literary, sports, and educational films. News concentrated on domestic events, such as overcompletion of a quota, and little time was devoted to international affairs. There were also lectures on Maoist thought. "Revolutionary" operas, presented in part for entertainment, were accorded considerable transmission time. The Ping-Pong matches with the team from the United States in April 1971 received wide coverage.

Before the Cultural Revolution the PRC had television exchange programs with Poland, the German Democratic Republic (East Germany), Romania, Czechoslovakia, Bulgaria, Japan, Cuba, and the Soviet Union. The status of these agreements was not known in 1971. In mid-1971, however, Peking Television reportedly signed an agreement with an international group jointly owned by British interests for an exchange of news films.

Of particular interest in television programming was the development of the Television University in 1960, through which viewers in the Peking area who, having registered and passed an entrance examination, could earn credits in numerous subjects equivalent to residence study at secondary schools and colleges. The program was subsequently expanded to several other urban centers. The effect of the Cultural Revolution on this program was not known, and its status in 1971 remained unclear.

Films and Lantern Slides

Films and lantern slides are considered of great importance by the regime, partially because such media reach and influence the large number of illiterates among the population. Their display also requires the assembly of people in fairly close quarters where Party cadre can accompany the showing by a running commentary and where discussion meetings can be held at the end of the showing. Consequently, films and slides are subject to as strict Party control and direction as other media.

Overall policy determination on film and slide activities was exercised by the CCP's Department of Propaganda until the Cultural Revolution, although actual operations were carried out under a special Film Administration Bureau in the Ministry of Culture and Education. Whether this arrangement still held in 1971 was unknown. The Film Administration Bureau had two major divisions: one was concerned with production in film studios and associated processing plants; the other had responsibility for the distribution and showing of the finished products. This headquarters structure was repeated at each provincial and municipal level, where it was augmented by three basic operating sections designed to cover the widest possible audiences. Each lower echelon has one section that operated, supervised, and serviced permanent motion picture theaters in its area. A second section organized, directed, and recruited motion picture-viewing clubs and audiences for film showings. The third section organized and dispatched mobile projection teams throughout the countryside. The mobile projection teams were equipped with vans fitted with large folding screens and projectors for both motion pictures and slides. They moved from village to village, parked at places where people naturally gathered or where they had been assembled by Party activists, and presented their shows. In rural areas, particularly where educational levels are low, slide showings were used as much as, or more than, motion picture films.

Reliable statistics on production and distribution facilities for 1971 were not available, but before the Cultural Revolution there were reported in operation seven major film studios that produced feature films, cartoons, newsreels, and documentaries on a national basis and numerous smaller studios in the provinces and municipalities that turned out lesser local documentaries and newsreels. At that time also, at least eight major slide studios and perhaps a number of

369

smaller ones were in production. In the area of distribution in the same period, 4,000 motion picture-viewing clubs, over 2,000 permanent motion picture theaters, and approximately 12,000 mobile projection teams were said to be operating.

Feature films and slides shows are not meant merely to entertain. Their main purpose is propaganda and, in all productions, the forces of good, always represented by communist heroes and ideas, inevitably triumph over their formidable capitalistic and reactionary enemies. All glorify the revolutionary struggle, Mao Tse-tung's invincible thought, and people's war. Their basic purpose, outlined by an article in the *People's Daily*, has been to "create the heroic images of workers, peasants, and soldiers, eulogize their great struggle, express the certain law of the development of the revolution, and indicate the path to seize the inevitable victory."

The number of feature films, some of which are produced in excellent color, is not large. Many films were purged during the Cultural Revolution. Among feature color films still being shown in mid-1971 were *The Red Lantern* and *Taking Tiger Mountain by Strategy*—both of which were film versions of Peking "revolutionary opera" presentations—and *The Red Detachment of Women*, a ballet. *The Red Lantern* is the story of the downfall of a supposedly loyal Communist who actually proved to be a traitor; *Taking Tiger Mountain by Strategy* depicts victory by Communists over bandits who retarded establishment of the revolution in their area; *The Red Detachment of Women* highlights the revolutionary exploits of Chinese women. Other films, in black and white only, included the opera *Shachiapang*, the ballet *The White Haired Girl*, and two films, *Tunnel Warfare* and *Mine Warfare*, about ingenious methods used by villagers against Japanese invaders during the 1937–45 period. Another film, *Heroic Son and Daughter*, showed Chinese troops in action during the Korean conflict. *The Invisible Frontline*, a Korean-made film of espionage featuring caricatures of United States and South Korean agents, was also being shown.

In addition to these major features, there were shorter films. Among these was a popular, cleverly drawn, cartoon in color about two little girls who saved their Commune's herd of sheep in Inner Mongolia, and a great variety of newsreels and documentaries. The documentaries featured such subjects as Vietnamese insurgent fighters, shipbuilding in Shanghai, rice planting, and the happy life of young people who had been transplanted from urban to rural areas.

Although the photography in all pictures is excellent from a professional point of view, production methods and techniques were often crude and makeshift. Most productions were filmed in the studio against painted backdrops that make mountains, for example, appear unreal. As had always been the case with traditional Chinese stagecraft, film techniques were concerned chiefly with indicating character, at the expense of maintaining an illusion of reality. For example, camera angles and lighting blatantly played up heroes and denigrated villains. Heroes were always placed upstage and photographed from a low angle to make them seem tall and strong. They were also always placed in good strong light, giving them the appearance of openness, confidence, and warmth. Villains, on the other hand, were photographed from above to make them appear small and cringing and were kept in shadow where they assumed a sickly hue.

SECTION III. ECONOMIC

CHAPTER 13

CHARACTER AND STRUCTURE OF THE ECONOMY

In 1971 the economy of the People's Republic of China (PRC) was a loosely planned and highly decentralized socialist one with goals of steady economic development and self-sufficiency. Major emphasis was on increasing the output of the vital agricultural sector to provide the raw materials for processing in consumer goods industries and the savings for a sustained—and steadily rising rate of—investment in capital goods industries. The country remained in 1971 basically agricultural and underdeveloped. Western economists estimated that the gross national product (GNP) in 1971 was the equivalent of US$80 billion. Assuming a population of about 800 million, the per capita income was equivalent to US$100 (see ch. 2, Physical Environment and Population).

The country has published no general national economic indicators since 1961, and, with only limited exceptions, estimates of agricultural and industrial growth and of economic growth were subject to considerable error. General trends could be indicated, on the basis of the fragmentary economic information revealed through public sources, with greater confidence than specific levels of output could be assessed.

One highly regarded Western economist had calculated an index of economic growth for the country, taking 1950 as the base year (1950 equals 100). This estimate set a figure of 180 for 1966, the country's peak year before the Great Proletarian Cultural Revolution (see Glossary), with a drop to 175 for 1968, and a recovery and slightly further increase to 190 for 1970. These estimates implied an average annual growth of 4 percent in GNP in the 1950–70 period and, on the generally accepted assumption of an average annual rate of growth in population of 2 percent in the same period, would mean a 2-percent annual average increase in per capita income. Reports of several experienced Western and Asian observers on personal surveys of the PRC in 1971, including those of many who had visited and studied the country on several other occasions between 1950 and 1970, seemed to bear out this calculation.

Whereas Western and Asian analysts might differ among themselves on the importance of specific developments, they were in general agreement on broad trends. They agreed that the outstanding fact about economic performance in the PRC was the sharp contrast in the character of economic development during the first decade of its history as compared with the second decade. The economy had been rapidly moving forward between 1949 and 1959 but faltered and stagnated between 1960 and 1970.

The impressive advance of the economy in the 1950s could in part be attributed to contributions made by certain onetime factors: economic recovery from wartime disruption; the psychological momentum and political stability growing out of the victory of the Chinese Communist Party (CCP); reorganization of economic institutions; and Soviet aid. The force of these factors was largely, though not completely, dissipated by the end of 1955. At that time the constraints of the country's resources began to appear, and basic strategic decisions had to be made concerning the future directions of economic development.

The model of Soviet economic development had been more or less taken for granted in the PRC up to 1955. Because of the impact of the onetime factors, however, the applicability of the Soviet model to conditions in the PRC had never been thoroughly reviewed before 1955 nor had there been much concern on the part of the CCP leadership in general and Mao Tse-tung in particular about the ideological or societal validity of the Soviet economic model. By 1955, the economic planners and analysts of the PRC had begun to realize that the Soviet model was not applicable to conditions in the PRC—that a strategy of economic development built on industrialization at the expense of agriculture was not viable in the light of the availability of natural resources in the PRC.

During the mid-1950s two somewhat different approaches to economic development gradually took form in the leadership of the PRC. These approaches not only referred to technical problems but also were at the core of national policymaking. They were therefore necessarily political (see ch. 9, Political System and Values; ch. 10, Political Dynamics). The issues that appeared to have divided the policymakers for the PRC revolved around the pace of development, the rate of investment, the pattern of investment among sectors, the structure of incentives, and the importance of technical skills and technical modernization in the process of economic development. Positions assumed by members of the leadership on specific issues of policy were closely related to their attitudes on these broader problems.

The preferences of Mao Tse-tung appeared to have tended consistently in the direction of raising the pace of collectivization and communization; minimizing material incentives and stressing the importance of ideological appeals; restricting the scope of the private sector, particularly in agriculture; stressing the need for frugality and self-denial and raising the rate of saving and investment; urging the mobilization of all resources, including labor, as a means of accelerating economic development; and placing great emphasis on zeal and commitment to communist values as an essential prerequisite of industrialization under socialism.

In reaction against the fragmentation of the country during the decades prior to the formation of the PRC in 1949, and with the Soviet model before them and Soviet advisers to guide them, the regime during the First Five Year Plan (1953–57) (see Glossary) attempted an extremely high concentration of economic power in the central government in Peking. The incompatability of this type of economic organization with conditions in the PRC was recognized in the economic decentralization ordered by a series of governmental decrees in 1957 and 1958. The problem that the economic decentralization had been designed to solve was the evident administrative impossibility of far-reaching, direct economic control throughout the country from Peking. The decentralization ultimately led to a considerable increase in provincial economic autonomy. This basic shift in the locus of the bulk of economic policymaking and administration was, however, temporarily concealed by the direct executive control of economic activities by the CCP during the Great Leap Forward (see Glossary), officially proclaimed in May 1958 (see ch. 3, Historical Setting; ch. 9, Political System and Values; ch. 10, Political Dynamics).

The first experiment with an original CCP strategy, embodied in the Great Leap Forward, ended in a near disaster for the economy that was constantly in the memory of the CCP leaders through 1971. The Great Leap was a crucial dividing point for the economic system as a whole. It was a major defeat and setback for the regime, creating a spirit of uncertainty, groping, lack of self-confidence, and lack of consensus among the leaders. Mao's leadership was questioned, and he retired into the background in regard to domestic economic policy while other Party leaders sought economic recovery through new policies. These "revisionist" (see Glossary) policies were, however, unpalatable to Mao and contrary to his value system. In part because of this factor, he finally decided to recapture his influence, not only over broad policy issues but over day-to-day decisionmaking. This element was one of the central issues in the Cultural Revolution (see ch. 3, Historical Setting; ch. 10, Political Dynamics).

The Great Leap represented a maximum effort at mobilization that stretched the organizational, administrative, and bureaucratic capacities of the economic system as a whole beyond its capabilities. This was apparent in many ways, such as mistaken directives, mismanagement of projects, planning errors, and technical errors in the construction of projects. The planning, organizational, and management collapse ultimately produced the acute agricultural crisis, which affected the rest of the economy (see ch. 14, Agriculture). Poor weather conditions contributed to the decline in output, but were not the principal cause.

This overmobilization seriously damaged the whole system of economic, social, and political organization. In many ways the economy was brought to a state of prostration similar to that produced by the devastation of war. Some Western observers have compared the effect to that produced on the economies of the Western world and their then-dependencies by the Great Depression initiated by the stock market crash in the United States in 1929. Whereas in 1949 and 1950 the regime had been impelled by a wave of victory and forward momentum, in 1960 it was being pushed by a cumulative contraction and depression. The process of recovery from the Great Leap was a much more difficult and painful one than that of 1949. By means of the new economic policies adopted in 1961 and the ingenuity of the leadership, acting with Mao's acquiescence but not under his dominance, economic recovery was attained within a period of three years, between 1962 and 1965. Levels of economic activity had declined by over 20 percent between 1960 and 1962, and the economy required about three years to recover to former levels.

The economy had only barely recovered when the Cultural Revolution was launched. It inflicted serious damage on the economy, particularly on industry and transportation (see ch. 15, Industry; ch. 18, Trade and Transportation). By launching and pursuing the Cultural Revolution, Mao demonstrated that in his determination to combat the rise of revisionist tendencies in the economy and society he was willing to pay the price of lower economic growth.

After the Cultural Revolution the trend appeared to be toward a return to an economic rationality that was in some respects reminiscent of the country's first decade under communist rule. At the same time management of the economy appeared to be more decentralized, and considerable emphasis was placed on the development of small-scale industry.

The decentralized management of the economy seemed to be the result of a realization of the limitations imposed by the administrative capabilities of the regime. Aside from the growth of local economic autonomy stemming from the economic decentralization ordered in 1957 and 1958, other factors weakened the control, both of the central government and also of local authorities, over the functioning of the economy. Deficiencies in statistical and accounting work set stringent limits to the possible extent of any kind of economic control. The shortage of competent administrators and managers had the same result. These weaknesses made the ascertainment of national totals of production and revenue virtually impossible.

ROLE OF THE GOVERNMENT

The organization of the economy of the PRC continued in 1971 to be the subject of intensive study by Western and Asian scholars, despite the lack of national economic statistics and the fragmentary information made public on the subject. These scholars studied this topic with particular attention to two closely connected criteria: how firmly could the government of the PRC impose its will throughout the country in economic matters, and within what limits was the country's economy effectively subject to direction by any central government. Much of the available information on those topics in 1971 arose out of the government's 1957–58 economic decentralization measures. The limited information available in 1971 did not indicate any drastic change in the direction of economic policymaking and administration after 1958, either toward further decentralization or a return to the extent of centralization in practice before the 1957–58 changes.

The economic decentralization initiated by the decrees, however, had been temporarily diverted by the attempt in the second half of 1958 to enforce highly centralized policies during the Great Leap Forward (see ch. 3, Historical Setting; ch. 10, Political Dynamics). The attempt failed; the period of the Great Leap witnessed an increase in provincial economic self-sufficiency and independence. In 1958 interprovincial transfers of grain declined, despite the good harvests in that year. Chaotic conditions in the system of allocation of raw materials and producers' goods (machinery and equipment) and in the transportation network made it more necessary for each administrative unit to seek the highest possible degree of self-sufficiency.

The government had intended that, after the economic decentralization of 1957–58, control by the CCP should ensure enforcement of central economic policy throughout the country. The role of the CCP, as the chief instrument at that time of the central government's control of the economy, dictated the presence of its branches in all parts of the country, extending into all administrative and economic units (see ch. 9, Political System and Values; ch. 10, Political Dynamics).

From 1958 on, the involvement of the CCP in administration and management of the economy at all levels expanded greatly. The CCP in this period, especially in urban areas, was in the process of being transformed from a purely ideology-oriented group to a functional bureaucratic and managerial elite, a club of technocrats. Western observers at this time commented on the emergence in the PRC of a "new class" of CCP administrators and managers. The Party's provincial branches could not be relied upon as a dependable means for enforcing central policies that might conflict with the interests of the provinces and lower level authorities and of enterprises.

From the 1957–58 period until the Cultural Revolution, almost all economic activities occurring within a province, except those concerning the People's Liberation Army (PLA) and the most important economic enterprises, were under the surveillance of the CCP provincial committee and particularly its secretariat. Below the provincial level, the Party committees and secretaries of lower level authorities had similar authority.

Western analysts have pointed out that because the main duty of CCP organs in economic sectors was to produce certain economic results, the leading elements in these CCP organs had to concentrate their energies on economic matters. Furthermore, even if the tasks of the CCP were expressed in political terms, performance in these may have been measured by the degree of subsequent economic success, that is, the attainment of economic objectives was the most easily ascertainable proof of ideological zeal. One official source stated: "Whether or not an enterprise is able to fulfill the whole of the plan laid down by the state is the chief way of determining if theoretical political work in the enterprise has been done well or badly."

The decentralization of the 1957–58 period provided the framework for greater autonomy of the provincial level authorities. This situation meant increased authority for the CCP secretaries at the provincial level. Once a provincial CCP secretary had become in fact responsible for the government of a province, he had necessarily become identified with the provincial administration, with its particular interests and problems. He had also become the representative of the province in negotiations with the central government. These considerations meant that the provincial CCP committees were no longer, in fact, reliable economic agents of the central authorities.

The overwhelming advantage of the provincial authorities in relation to the central government in the work of economic control and development was that of familiarity with local conditions. Administering an average population of 20 to 30 million persons, the provincial administrations were better situated than the central government ministries for decisions on the policies and priorities of most kinds of industrial growth and agricultural improvement. The provinces were the major unit for policymaking and implementation in the domain of agricultural mechanization (see ch. 14, Agriculture). The advancement of electrically powered irrigation and electrically powered processing industries had been based on electric transmission lines radiating mainly from the provincial capitals. The provinces were in the late 1960s and early 1970s the most significant level for the development of industry except in cases of the very largest and the very smallest industries. In some areas, however, municipalities under provinces and special municipalities were important centers of industrial growth (see ch. 15, Industry).

Once the provincial Party cadres had acquired economic power, they began to act in a manner similar to that of the central government during the First Five Year Plan. There was also in 1958 a new element in the economic reasoning of the regime that called for the development of economic cooperation regions, a policy that favored the increase of provincial economic power. Although there was much discussion in the press and economic periodicals as to what geographical expanse should constitute an economic cooperation region, there was general agreement in these analyses that national economic self-sufficiency and independence required some degree of autonomy at the level of the economic cooperation regions. Some articles discussed the division of the PRC into seven large economic zones.

Insofar as the range of political authority was a determining factor in economic decisions, economic cooperation tended to develop at the provincial level. The provinces, and not the larger economic cooperation regions or the smaller Communes, began to develop as autarkic entities. The result was that many provinces began to act like underdeveloped nations, desiring to create integrated complexes of industry, agriculture, commerce, and education within their borders. The implementation of decentralization had a profound effect on the economic role of the government in the PRC. Provincial government emerged as a powerful level of administration, with great control over the economic system, specifically over supply, production, and sales.

The most important consequence of the economic decentralization of the 1957–58 period was to make the provincial Party committees supreme decisionmaking bodies for all provincial economic activities. Because the scope of provincial economic activity had greatly expanded, this meant great economic power.

Until the Cultural Revolution was launched in 1966, the provincial Party committees had the power to set economic targets and to determine wage policy and plans, and they enjoyed considerable freedom in fixing these control figures in accordance with local conditions. This pattern of management was disrupted by the Cultural Revolution. Revolutionary committees (a new form of local and provincial governments) began to be formed at the provincial level beginning in January 1967, and a large number of such committees were organized, primarily under the determining influence of the PLA, in late 1967 and up to September 1968 (see ch. 9, Political System and Values; ch. 10, Political Dynamics). The provincial revolutionary committees took over the economic administrative functions previously performed by the Party provincial committees. Revolutionary committees were in 1971 functioning in all provinces, special municipalities, autonomous regions, and lower level authorities and were also operating in economic units, such as factories and production brigades.

The provincial revolutionary committees were in 1971 formally responsible for the administration of economic affairs in the provinces and for the conduct of economic relations between the provinces and the central government. Western observers had noted, however, that whereas the time periods of the published provincial economic plans varied from three to six years, the time periods of the economic plans of the provinces within a given military region were identical. This suggests that the commanders of the military regions were playing a very important, if undetermined, role in the conduct of economic affairs. The assumption of military influence was strengthened by the pattern of leadership of the provincial revolutionary committees in which the commanders of the military districts, the boundaries of which are coterminous with the provinces, or the first political commissars of the military districts, were in almost all cases the chairmen of the provincial revolutionary committees (see ch. 21, The Armed Forces).

The data available in 1971 indicated that fundamental changes in the formal system of administration of the economy had not been made by the Cultural Revolution. The main formal change appeared to be that instead of the pre-Cultural Revolution practice of factory managers' consulting with the provincial CCP committees, factory revolutionary committees were in the late 1960s and early 1970s sent from the factory to consult with the revolutionary committees of provinces, special municipalities, autonomous regions, and lower level authorities.

Transition to State Control

In 1949 the country's economic and industrial base was smaller than that possessed by Russia in 1914 and smaller than that of India at independence in 1947. With the exception of the foreign-controlled trading ports, the country in 1949 did not have a long history of a market society and therefore lacked the network of economic institutions and relationships on which a market society is usually built (see ch. 3, Historical Setting).

At the time of the founding of the PRC in 1949 it was inhabited by roughly 540 million persons, who resided in about 120 million households (see ch. 2, Physical Environment and Population). Of this total, about 100 million units were peasant households, whose members engaged primarily in agricultural production, largely for their own consumption. Some of the peasant, and most of the economically active nonpeasant, population was occupied in a large number of primarily small enterprises in various branches of the economy. About 7 million persons, most of whom were self-employed, were occupied in 4 million commercial establishments. The numbers of handicraft establishments and of handicraftsmen were in the same range.

There were in 1949 more than 126,000 industrial establishments with more than 3 million employees; most of these enterprises were small. In addition, there were great numbers of small transport enterprises, as well as the state-operated railroads, plus a few large shipping companies. (In this context, "large" means fifteen or more employed persons without mechanical power and thirty or more employed persons with mechanical power.) The average size of enterprise was extraordinarily small not only in transportation but in all branches of the economy. The management of most economic activities was highly decentralized.

Before 1949 the governmental apparatus had been used to manage a small fraction of all the economic activities and lacked the ability in 1949 to intervene effectively on a larger scale. In the beginning it was thus necessary for the new regime to use the existing forms of economic organization.

Following this policy, the government in the main collected the established taxes through the established channels. In addition, however, the government raised, as well as rearranged, the rates of taxation and enforced the tax laws much more vigorously.

The initial changes in other forms of government intervention in economic activities were limited. The government nationalized few existing enterprises in the beginning. In 1949 the government owned 2,677 industrial establishments, most of which had been nationalized in 1945 by the Nationalist government (see ch. 3, Historical Setting). The government also owned 109 enterprises jointly with the Soviet Union and 193 enterprises jointly with private partners. Most of these enterprises were relatively large, however, and together they represented close to 50 percent of total industrial employment.

Large-scale nationalization was at first limited to the industrial assets belonging to supporters of the former government; these were labeled "bureaucrat capitalist" as contrasted to "national capitalists," whom the new government tolerated for the moment. The "national capitalists" were smaller businessmen who had attempted to build independent industry. They were considered as a progressive force, and they possessed valuable skills that the regime required. The government's policy was not to expropriate them but gradually to assimilate them into the state-managed sector. They continued to receive interest on their investments and were paid relatively high salaries to continue managing their enterprises. Many produced under contract to the government, and by 1952 about one-quarter of the value of industrial production originated from this group of enterprises. The government was during this period simultaneously creating joint state-private enterprises plus completely state-owned industry in the capital goods sector (factory buildings, machinery, locomotives, trucks and tractors, and others).

In 1949 the entire economy was dependent on agriculture for food and for most of the raw materials entering into other consumer goods. About three-fourths of the product of the agricultural sector was consumed within that sector, and the remaining one-fourth was sold to the nonagricultural sector. The government believed that control over this sale was necessary and therefore developed state commerce, initially under the Ministry of Commerce, to compete with private commerce (see ch. 18, Trade and Transportation). Ministries, state companies, and marketing cooperatives proliferated during the 1949–52 period. In the domestic sale of final products, state wholesalers supplied a great number of private retailers, in addition to increasing numbers of state and cooperative retailers—state stores, rural marketing cooperatives, and urban consumer cooperatives. In the case of intermediate products, state commerce increasingly contracted with capitalist industrial enterprises for their processing. By 1952 more than 50 percent of the production of capitalist industry was accounted for by capitalists who worked exclusively for the state.

The growing dependence of private farms and businesses on state trade was supported by the credit policy of the state banking system, headed by the People's Bank of China, which had been created in 1948 (see ch. 19, Fiscal and Monetary System). The banking system provided credit through the various economic affairs ministries, including the Ministry of Commerce, to peasants and state agents in advance payments on sales contracts or in delayed payments on purchasing contracts.

Simultaneously as the government consolidated its control over markets, it developed additionally a more comprehensive set of economic affairs ministries for specific types of production, particularly in the industrial sector. Ministries that dealt with the newly developing branches, and particularly with the manufacture of producers' goods (machine tools, generators, blast furnaces, freight cars, and the like), became numerous and important.

The development of new industries required government investment. From the beginning capital formation was provided for in the state budget (the consolidated central and local government budget of the PRC) under the heading "Economic Construction." These increases in expenditures were matched by revenues chiefly from state-owned enterprises and undertakings that increased greatly in absolute, as well as relative, terms in this period and sufficed to finance most of the state expenditures under the "Economic Construction" heading in the state budget (see ch. 19, Fiscal and Monetary System). The development of new industrial sectors was therefore within the limits set by the productivity of labor, or, in other words, finance was not a constraint.

By 1952 the new regime had nationalized a broad range of industry. All industries regarded as necessary for the industrialization program were put under direct central ministerial rule. These comprised not only heavy industrial plants, but many falling into the light industry category. What the PRC defines as heavy industries consists of industries strategically important for the developmental goals of the regime; whatever remains is considered light industry.

Centralized Economic Planning

The period of highly centralized economic planning in the PRC began and ended with the First Five Year Plan (1953-57). The decentralization of industrial management and of economic planning introduced by the government in 1957 and 1958 reduced the country's subsequent national economic planning to little more than the setting of broad goals and to the drafting of lists of resolutions. Annual national plans were published up to, and including, 1960. As of September 1971, no national economic plans, whether annual or longer term, had been published since 1960.

An official source reported in September 1971 the existence of a Ministry of Economic Affairs. The exact functions and responsibilities of this body were unknown to external observers as of October 1971, but some analysts speculated that the new ministry might have been created from the former State Economic Commission, which had been responsible for preparation of annual and short-term national economic plans but apparently had ceased functioning during the Cultural Revolution.

The First Five Year Plan was drafted by the large number of Soviet nationals working in the State Planning Commission, the body created in November 1952 to prepare long-term economic plans. The period of the plan was one of growth, during which heavy industry was given priority in government investment.

In that period national economic planning included the allocation of resources, production, distribution of the product, financial administration, and use of technology. In scope the completed First Five Year Plan covered in detail industrial production; agricultural production; transportation; labor and employment; allocation of materials; commodity flow; projects of capital construction; social, cultural, and welfare undertakings; foreign trade; technological development; production costs; and commodity prices. Plans at provincial levels were also formulated.

The formulation and implementation of the First Five Year Plan involved a great number of governmental agencies. Twenty-five different ministries were involved in providing information for the plan and in carrying out industrial production within the limits of decisions reached. Other ministries controlled trade and financial administration. In the final plan, goals were established for production, costs, and profits.

The major aim of the First Five Year Plan was to lay the foundations for a comprehensive industrial structure as quickly as possible. Over 50 percent of the government's investment funds were given to the capital goods industries. By the end of the plan period gross fixed investment had reached an annual level of almost 25 percent of the gross national product. Most of the plan's industrial objectives were achieved, and some were surpassed; by 1957 heavy industry, the favored sector under the plan, constituted 48 percent of industrial output.

What the government described as "socialist transformation" took place in the First Five Year Plan period. As one result, the numbers of organization units in production and distribution decreased drastically. By May 1956, 110 million peasant households had been organized into 1 million agricultural producer cooperatives (see ch. 14, Agriculture). In handicraft production, more than 5 million craftsmen had become members of handicraft production cooperatives by the end of 1956, and more than 3 million establishments had been combined into nearly 100,000 units with an average number of fifty-one craftsmen per cooperative.

In industry, employment increased from more than 3 million persons in 1949 to nearly 8 million persons in 1956, while the number of establishments fell from more than 126,000 to 60,000 during the same period. Average employment per establishment therefore rose from twenty-four persons to 132 persons. Most of this growth in average size took place during the 1955–56 period, when the large number of small capitalist enterprises were consolidated into a much smaller number of correspondingly larger, joint state-private enterprises.

In commerce the number of employed persons declined somewhat during "socialist transformation," but the number of commercial establishments decreased much more. In 1955, whereas private commerce typically employed less than two persons per establishment, state commerce employed eleven persons per organizational unit. In the case of marketing cooperatives a staff of about five persons per store was reported (see ch. 18, Trade and Transportation).

The transformation of established enterprises constituted only one part of the government's strategy for the development of socialism in this period. The other part consisted of the creation of new enterprises and undertakings, most of which were organized, owned, and operated by the state. An official source concluded that the state sector grew in this period primarily by investment of state revenues and only secondarily by the expropriation of private enterprise.

Decentralization of Economic Policymaking and Administration

The economic decentralization of the 1957–58 period was carried out by decrees relating to two major areas of economic policymaking and administration. One area was that of industrial management; this was reformed by governmental decrees in November and December 1957. The other area was that of economic planning; this area was reorganized by another governmental decree in September 1958. These two reforms represented together the most far-reaching change in economic policymaking and administration that occurred in the first twenty-two years of the history of the PRC. The abolition of the Ministry of Control on April 29, 1959, by the Second National People's Congress was a belated recognition of the impossibility of using Soviet-style central planning in the PRC.

Two concepts were basic to the economic decentralization. The first concept was that of transfer balances. The second was that of economic control figures.

The balancing process is a method of reconciling the resource requirements called for by the production and investment programs during a given period with anticipated supply availabilities and of distributing the final product. The material balances are set primarily in physical terms, that is, in volume of coal and rice and numbers of machines and pigs. Corollary financial plans serve mainly as a means of control through the banking system. In the PRC the material balances controlled by the central government are the balances transferred from one province to another or the balances transferred out of or into the country. They are therefore referred to as transfer balances.

Economic control figures are quantitative measurements of the performance of certain vital segments of the PRC's economic system. They can be expressed as either quotas, indices, totals, or averages.

The central government announced at the time of the decentralization that it intended only a limited number of economic control figures to remain within its jurisdiction. Credit policy remained more centralized than most other economic matters, although from the mid-1960s control in this field had been somewhat diffused by the establishment of the Agricultural Bank of China on a level equal to that of the People's Bank of China (see ch. 9, Fiscal and Monetary System).

According to the information available in September 1971, the economic control figures under the jurisdiction of the central government were the following: first, output and transfer balances to and from provinces of major industrial products; second, output and transfer balances to and from provinces of major agricultural products; third, total exports and imports and the volume of important export and import commodities; fourth, volume of freight of railroads and of transportation undertakings directly under the Ministry of Communications; fifth, total investment, new productive capacity, and major investment projects; sixth, total wages and the average number of staff employees and workers; and seventh, enrollment in higher educational institutions and the allocation of graduates. To provide flexibility, the centrally fixed economic control figures could be adjusted by the local authorities provided that the national economic objectives concerning construction projects, productive capacity, and revenue were reached.

Economic control figures not fixed by the central government included the total value of industrial output, irrigated acreage, arable acreage, total distribution of commodities, total retail sales, local transportation, and the volume of construction and maintenance work. These goals were determined by the local authorities and the ministries among themselves.

In the allocation of raw materials, the central government concentrated on attempting to control interprovincial transfers of certain major commodities, both agricultural and industrial. For example, in the procurement of grain, the main concern of the central government was not with what happened within any province but instead whether the province delivered its required quota for interprovincial transfer or for export from the country or, in the case of a grain-deficient province, whether the province demanded more than its stipulated inward transfer of grain.

All other controls on allocation of raw materials were delegated to the provinces. Provincial control over allocation of raw materials included the requirement that even central government enterprises had to apply for supplies to the planning organizations of the provincial level authorities. In special cases—such as materials for the armed forces, armament industries, and the railroads, fuel for civil aviation, and goods for export—exceptions to this rule were authorized; in these cases requisitions for raw materials continued to be submitted to the appropriate central authorities.

Among the items specified as continuing under central government control had been amounts of transfers of revenue between the central government and the provincial level authorities. The figure approved by the central government for the budgetary expenditure of a provincial level authority was compared with the amount of the total revenue the authority was responsible for raising, that is, all the revenue from its area except for customs duties and the net income of state enterprises under direct central government control. Approved deficits were financed by the central government; if the estimated revenue of the provincial level authority exceeded its estimated expenditures, a proportion of the estimated excess revenue was required to be transferred to the central government. Figures for these balances were the only financial targets at the provincial level still directly controlled by the central government after the economic decentralization of 1958 (see ch. 19, Fiscal and Monetary System).

The economic decentralization also applied to the control of prices. The appropriate ministries of the central government continued to control the procurement prices of major agricultural products: grain, raw cotton, vegetable oils, jute, ramie, tea, tobacco, timber, and live pigs. At important commercial centers they also continued to control the selling prices of grain, edible oil, pork, timber, cotton yarn and cloth, woolen cloth, edible salt, sugar, coal, petroleum, chemical fertilizers, and wristwatches. Both kinds of centrally fixed prices, procurement and selling, applied to standard types of the goods under price control, whereas prices of other types of these goods and of the standard types when sold at places other than the main commercial centers were determined by the local authorities. Prices of all other goods, both agricultural and manufactured, were also under local control.

The central government's control of investment had been closely connected with another centrally controlled economic maximum— that of total wages—which had to be kept in alignment with the supply of consumer goods if inflation was to be avoided. The ceiling for total wages was linked with that set for the average number of employees. These two indices together constituted control of the wage levels in the country and, with the system of urban residence permits, control of the movement of the population into towns and cities. The central government's control over the disposition of the country's foreign exchange reserves, by means of its control over foreign trade and over the banking system, had also strengthened its control of investment, as well as control over the allocation of certain key commodities, particularly grain and machinery. Central control of the volume of freight carried by the railroads and the major modern transportation enterprises had helped to reinforce central controls over other economic indices.

Another important item determined by the central authorities was the annual budgetary allotment of funds to the state banks to be used together with the banks' retained profits and net increases in deposits for the expansion of credit. The estimated loanable funds of the state banks were allocated in the 1960s among the provincial branches of the banks (see ch. 19, Fiscal and Monetary System).

The fragmentary evidence available in mid-1971 suggested that in the 1960s relaxation of central control took place even in some items, such as the procurement prices of grain, which earlier had been reserved for the jurisdiction of the central government. Western analysts reasoned that the turmoil of the central government during the Cultural Revolution had probably strengthened the tendency of the provinces to expand the large powers devolved to them by the economic decentralization of 1958.

The only revenues directly controlled by the central government after economic decentralization were import duties, profits accruing from foreign trade, and profits of those state enterprises under direct management of the central government. The financial dependence of the central government upon the provincial authorities was therefore marked (see ch. 19, Fiscal and Monetary System).

The great bulk of production, consumption, and domestic trade was intraprovincial and, sometimes, intracounty (see ch. 18, Trade and Transportation). The economic relations between the central government and the provinces were concerned only with transfers at the minimal level, that is, with shipments of food or raw materials above the level required for internal consumption by one province to meet the deficiency of food or raw materials that another province was unable to supply from within its area. The production, consumption, and domestic trade that took place within a province was of little direct concern to the central government, provided that the province met its extraprovincial obligations.

The vital economic matters for negotiation between the provinces and the central government were, in the 1960s and early 1970s, the net transfers of major agricultural and industrial commodities out of, or into, a province; net payments of revenue; and the allocation of loanable funds by the state banks to their provincial branches.

That a large part of the central government's revenues was collected by provincial authorities and forwarded by them to the central Ministry of Finance strengthened their position in negotiations with the central government or at least the position of those provinces that had a net outward payment of revenue. Those provincial-level areas, such as the Sinkiang Uighur Autonomous Region, which were subsidized by the central government, were in a weaker position.

Central Enterprises and State Farms

The extent of economic decentralization in the PRC in 1971 was substantial. Certain parts of the economic system were considered by the central government as particularly vital, however, and were therefore retained under its direct control. For example, most important undertakings in heavy industry remained under direct control of ministries of the central government. These undertakings included large metallurgical and chemical enterprises; major coalfields; large electric power stations and electricity grids; oil refineries; factories manufacturing large and precision machines, electric motors, and instruments; the military equipment industry;

and other technically complex branches of industry, together with experimental factories and special cases.

In transportation, the main railroad system, other than small local railroads and lines built to serve individual coalfields, factories, or lumber areas, were under direct central control, together with the major civil aviation services. Road transportation was mainly under local control, but the central government has been responsible for building, and presumably for maintaining, certain major highways. The main coastal shipping services were directly under the central government. A central government organization, the Yangtze Navigation Administrative Bureau, exercised general supervision of shipping on the Yangtze River. In addition to the bureau's own vessels, local authorities and joint state-private companies also operated ships on the river. Transoceanic shipping under the flag of the PRC, whether owned or chartered, was presumed to be directly controlled by the central government, as was the China Ocean Steamship Agency, which handled the clearing of foreign ships and ships' agency work at all ports at which foreign ships were accustomed to call (see ch. 18, Trade and Transportation).

The central government had direct control of the river conservancy commissions. These commissions extended across several provinces and were charged with the multipurpose development of the respective rivers. The commission established to improve the Grand Canal for purposes of both navigation and water conservancy was placed under the chairmanship of the minister of communications.

The banking system, operating under the direct control of the central government, and particularly the omnipresent network of the People's Bank of China, was an extremely important instrument of supervision and control by the central government over the entire economy (see ch. 19, Fiscal and Monetary System). The national foreign trade corporations also were under direct central control, but the provincial foreign trade corporations, together with those established by local authorities below the provincial level and those established at ports, were under the joint supervision of the Ministry of Foreign Trade and of the local authorities concerned (see ch. 18, Trade and Transportation).

The chief institutions of scientific research had been maintained as national, rather than as provincial, organizations, and their subordination to the central government was believed by Western observers to have promoted the control by the central government of both the economy and the armed forces (see ch. 16, Science and Technology). Telecommunications had been directly controlled by the central authorities (see ch. 18, Trade and Transportation).

Among the economic undertakings subject to the direct control of the central government were the group of state farms, factories, mines, and other enterprises of the PLA's Production and

Construction Corps (see ch. 21, The Armed Forces). These were significantly expanded in the late 1960s. Several provinces, in addition to the Sinkiang Uighur and Inner Mongolian autonomous regions, were known in 1971 to have such a corps. The total personnel strength of the expanded Production and Construction Corps was believed to equal or exceed that of the regular PLA.

In the early 1960s large numbers of students, many of them from Shanghai, had been sent to Sinkiang to join the Production and Construction Corps. Before the Cultural Revolution a few provinces had rudimentary organizations similar to the Production and Construction Corps in Sinkiang, but they were small and loosely organized. After the Cultural Revolution, however, production and construction corps were established in numerous other provinces. This activity first became known to Western observers in 1968; it accelerated in 1969 and 1970. The evidence available in 1971 indicated that the largest and most advanced corps were located in the border areas of Heilungkiang and Kwangtung provinces and the Inner Mongolian Autonomous Region (Inner Mongolia).

With the elevation of the corps to national status, there was reported an emphasis on economizing, production, and self-reliance. As new corps were formed, previously existing production units were absorbed into the corps with the result that these new corps were functioning economic undertakings from the beginning.

Other important groups of state farms were those in Heilungkiang Province and in a frontier district of Inner Mongolia. The direct control by the central government of these state farms and of the undertakings operated by the PLA Production and Construction Corps had given the central government a close hold over certain strategic areas, as well as providing sources of grain supplies under its immediate control (see ch. 14, Agriculture).

ECONOMIC PERFORMANCE

Governmental Claims

In September 1971 the government of the PRC, in a series of articles issued by its press agency, claimed a steadily rising standard of living for the people of the PRC as a result of state policies and of rising agricultural and industrial production.

The articles contained no figures for the output of the country as a whole. The reports coincided generally with the observations of Western visitors to the country in the spring and summer of 1971 and stressed the progress made in agriculture, which had been given major emphasis in economic management in the 1960s. One article claimed that the PRC was self-sufficient in grain and had a surplus; the PRC continued to import grain mainly to increase varieties and help other countries, the statement asserted. Western economic analysts believed that the imports of grain facilitated the supply of coastal cities and thereby avoided shipments of grain on the country's overloaded transport systems.

The press agency articles depicted the country's industry as progressively supplying the nation not only with more consumer goods but also with capital equipment for steady industrial expansion and for the mechanization of agriculture. Industrial wages were claimed to have risen steadily, particularly for those in lower grades, and were asserted to provide a much better income than they otherwise might because of full employment, low rents, cheap prices for necessities, and the absence of income taxes (see ch. 7, Living Conditions; ch. 17, Labor; ch. 19, Fiscal and Monetary System).

Monthly rent and charges for water and electricity in cities were claimed to absorb from 4 to 5 percent of family income. In addition, workers receive free medical treatment and other welfare benefits; and the aged, infirm, injured, and disabled were given care (see ch. 7, Living Conditions). Industrial wages were set low to reduce the disparity in living conditions between urban and rural areas and between industrial and agricultural workers (see ch. 17, Labor). Both types of workers, according to the articles, had enough income for savings, which were reported to be 28 percent higher in 1970 than in 1965; the base figure for 1965 was unknown (see ch. 19, Fiscal and Monetary System).

The articles indicated that a considerable part of the claimed rise in standards of living was a result of governmental adjustments of prices and of payment of higher prices for agricultural products by the government. It was claimed that the prices of general consumer goods had been stable during the 1959–70 period. Another good agricultural year was predicted for 1971, claimed to be the tenth good year in succession. Considerable credit was allotted to large-scale water conservation projects that provided irrigation, prevented floods, and made possible a large increase in double-cropping (see ch. 14, Agriculture).

Sector Growth Patterns

The claims of a steadily rising standard of living were difficult to evaluate because the State Statistical Bureau had been shattered in 1958 by administrative decentralization, by political pressure leading to false reporting of output figures, and by the hostility toward professional competence that characterized the Great Leap. Since 1960 few statistics about the economy have been published.

Agriculture had been perhaps the simplest sector to monitor. Western observers calculated that the growth in output of grain during the 1958–70 period had approximately matched the estimated growth in the population in that period (see ch. 2, Physical Environment and Population; ch. 14, Agriculture). Rice provided the major proportion of the country's grain output, and the country was in 1971 the world's largest producer of this crop. The caloric intake was estimated to have risen slightly in 1970 to a daily average of 2,150 calories, slightly above the estimated average of 2,000 to 2,100 calories in the mid-1960s and late 1960s.

The policy of the PRC during the post-Cultural Revolution period had been to subordinate industrial production to agricultural needs, to establish local industries, and to improve small plants. The establishment of a decentralized industrial system, with factories all over the country, was intended to reduce transportation costs and also was devised as a precaution against the PRC fear of invasion (see ch. 11, Foreign Relations; ch. 18, Trade and Transportation; ch. 21, The Armed Forces).

Strengths and Weaknesses

The chief economic forces welding the PRC together since 1949 have been modern transport and telecommunications, the banking system, regional power grids and multipurpose river valley commissions, national trading corporations for domestic and for international trade, the various technical institutes of the central government ministries, the frequent national conferences on economic and other matters, the directed mobility over the country of professional and skilled manpower and the forced migration of the less skilled.

The resources and the efficiency of the provincial authorities varied greatly. The latitude given to the provinces by the economic decentralization of the 1957–58 period had been found, in practice, to be more extensive than the formal regulations would indicate. This factor, together with the natural differences between the provinces, resulted in a growing differentiation of local policies. After 1958 a greater degree of economic decentralization existed in the PRC than in most other developing countries.

One major example of the limitations placed on attempts on economic control by the country's weaknesses in administration and in accountancy had been the inability of the central government to prevent the illicit use of extrabudgetary funds (see ch. 19, Fiscal and Monetary System). Large amounts from these sources had been diverted to unplanned investment and thereby made state investment plans meaningless. This unplanned investment had also often led to the diversion of state-allocated raw materials from their planned uses.

During its first twenty-two years the PRC had borrowed liberally from the Soviet Union both in forms of economic organization and in methods of operation, as well as in technical matters. Examples were: in agriculture, the formal organization of agricultural producer cooperatives, state farms, and agricultural machinery stations, and the compulsory sales of grain; in industry, its general organization (the 1957–58 decentralization measures following shortly after similar steps in the Soviet Union), the economic accounting system, and the definition of costs and concepts; in labor, the role of the trade unions and the grading and bonus system of workers in state enterprises; in foreign trade, its conduct through special corporations; in finance, the close similarity between the PRC industrial and commercial tax and the Soviet turnover tax, many budgetary practices, and the supervisory role of the banks.

The Great Leap of 1958 had represented a revulsion against the adoption of Soviet methods. This had been demonstrated most obviously by the formation of the Communes and by the continuing prominence given to economic development through labor-intensive small-scale industry. Another divergence from the Soviet pattern was the practice of sending CCP and government functionaries, professional people, and the managerial and administrative staff of industrial enterprises to the rural areas for periods of manual labor. Other differences from the Soviet Union in economic organization in 1971 included the use of an agricultural tax in kind, the greater powers of local authorities in fixing prices, the function of the semiannual Canton International Trade Fair in the country's foreign trade, and the existence of joint state-private enterprises (see ch. 18, Trade and Transportation).

After the initial period of Soviet-type strategy emphasizing heavy industry, the policy of the PRC had shifted to one of getting the quickest returns to the most people. This included an emphasis on developing agriculture first, then light industry (as defined by the PRC). It also included an overriding importance given to efficient organization. Western observers in the late 1960s and early 1970s were particularly impressed by the resilience of the country's economy and the ability of the country's manufacturing sector to respond to changing orders for new designs and models. The country's industries could meet unexpected demand quickly by subcontracting with small-scale factories, households, and Communes to produce large quantities of light industrial goods. These observers reported that in deciding on construction of a new factory—if calculations of cost, availabilities of supplies, and the period of recovery of investment proved satisfactory—people at every level were brought in to see how they would contribute. The result of this flexibility and efficient organization, they asserted, was that there was a smaller gap between plans and realization in the PRC than in most other developing countries.

As of September 1971 the PRC had managed to develop an appropriate system for the supply of raw materials to producing units and a marketing and distribution network for end-products. The country's major economic weakness continued to be the relatively small size of the transportation network; in practice, this meant the railroad system because extensive introduction of automobiles had been judged to be too expensive at the stage of the country's economic development. An obstacle limiting the availability of resources to the country was the constriction of foreign exchange in attempting to finance imports of component parts (see ch. 18, Trade and Transportation).

CHAPTER 14

AGRICULTURE

The People's Republic of China (PRC) published few meaningful statistics on the agricultural sector in the decade ending in mid-1971. Figures for acreage, crops, and yields appeared relatively reliable until the beginning of the Great Leap Forward (see Glossary) in 1958. They became progressively more problematical from 1958, when substantial inflation of production totals occurred. The dislocations of agricultural labor and output caused by the Great Leap were followed by disastrously poor crops from 1959 through 1961 and the suspension of issuance of statistical detail (figures given out since then are generally in percentages only).

Agriculture was of fundamental importance in the economy in 1971. More than four-fifths of the population was engaged in agriculture, although only about 11 percent of the country's total land area was arable. Estimates of its contribution to the economy varied. One estimate stated that it provided nearly half of the gross national product (GNP); another, that the value of the agricultural product in 1970 was about 25 percent of the total combined output value of industry, transportation, and agriculture. Moreover, exports of agricultural products furnished the major part of the PRC's foreign exchange earnings.

The estimated grain crop in 1970 ranged between 215 and 240 million metric tons; this was about equal, on a per capita basis, to that produced in 1957, the latest year for which reasonably acceptable detailed statistics were released (see table 7). The total, plus grain imports and less stored reserves, probably provided nutrition about or very slightly above the minimum subsistence requirement of the population.

Chinese agriculture has been traditionally labor intensive, resulting in fairly high yields per land unit but relatively low productivity per man. Such intensive cultivation over centuries required the use of fertilizers to maintain soil fertility. In 1971 fertilizers consisted of animal manure, human excrement, and compost, but chemical fertilizers were increasingly being used.

Irrigation and water conservancy were highly developed early in the country's history. These were an essential function of government and were carried out in part because of the danger of floods and droughts, especially in the Yellow and Huai rivers areas. The communist

Table 7. People's Republic of China, Estimated Major Crop Output and Yields, Selected Years, 1952–65

Crop	1952	1957	1961	1965 [1]
Output [2]				
Food Grains				
Rice _____	78.6	86.8	75.0	97.8
Wheat _____	20.0	23.7	15.4	20.4
Miscellaneous grain _____	51.3	52.7	47.0	55.0
Tubers _____	20.0	21.9	24.5	26.7
Total [3] _____	170.0	185.0	162.0	200.0
Other Crops				
Soybeans _____	9.5	10.1	5.5	7.5
Oilseeds _____	3.7	3.8	2.3	3.4
Cotton _____	1.3	1.6	0.9	1.4
Yields [4]				
Rice _____	2,332	2,396	2,225	2,634
Wheat _____	712	761	623	757
Miscellaneous grain _____	890	927	774	890
Tubers _____	1,780	1,856	1,558	1,825
Soybeans _____	730	703	703	739
Oilseeds _____	703	579	579	668
Cotton _____	208	253	229	260

[1] The latest year for which a detailed estimate is available.
[2] In million metric tons.
[3] Totals do not add because of rounding.
[4] In pounds per acre. Yields converted from metric tons per hectare.

Source: Adapted from Joint Economic Committee of the United States Congress, *An Economic Profile of Mainland China* (Praeger Special Studies in International Economics and Development Series), New York, 1968.

government has pushed the further expansion of irrigation throughout the country and has also undertaken a major water conservancy program in the potential disaster areas in North China.

Increasing population pressures have resulted in continuing emphasis on crops that are edible by humans—mainly those providing carbohydrates but also some protein in the case of soybeans. Use of byproducts for fuel, fertilizer, and building material are also maximized in the deforested areas of population concentration. Among the industrial crops, cotton and tobacco are the most important, with cultivation centered largely in China Proper (see Glossary).

The collectivized organization of agriculture in 1971 differed markedly from the pattern that existed before the communist takeover. In place of the earlier large number of small, fragmented landholdings, there were an estimated 74,000 People's Communes that were organized into production brigades and production teams. The Communes corresponded generally to previous political entities and local market areas. The production teams, consisting generally of twenty to thirty households each, are the basic collective landownership and accounting unit for purposes of tax payment and grain delivery to the state. The Communes and the much less important state farms, which were believed to number some 2,000 in the late 1960s, administer the political, technical, and financial policies of the government in rural areas. In this they shared some functions with the formal administrative subdivisions and sometimes also acted in conjunction with the People's Liberation Army (PLA).

The Chinese agricultural community, which is predominant in China's population, has played a vital part in the history of the Chinese communist movement. Dissension within the Chinese Communist Party (CCP) over agricultural policies was an element in the split between Mao Tse-tung and Liu Shao-ch'i in the late 1950s. Agriculture was disastrously affected by the Great Leap Forward; however, it appears to have been little affected, directly at least, by the Great Proletarian Cultural Revolution. Since assuming power, the party has conducted numerous ideological campaigns aimed at, among other things, increasing agricultural production. Great successes have been attributed to these campaigns by the press and other mass communications media. The reports, however, are uncoordinated, and the actual overall results achieved as of 1971 could not be ascertained.

Since 1962 the economic policy of the PRC has given priority to agriculture over industry, with the goal of increasing agricultural output, thus reversing earlier priorities (see ch. 13, Character and Structure of the Economy). Efforts to reach this objective by modernization of agricultural techniques continued in mid-1971 but were largely dependent on the investment by farmers of their own labor to create capital necessary for the purchase of equipment and materials and for improvement and some expansion of cultivable land. Mechanization of irrigation by use of pumps, the somewhat greater use of chemical fertilizers (with preference given to industrial crops), and land reclamation contributed to the increase during the decade to 1971 of overall agricultural output (see fig. 12). None of these measures, however, nor the series of intense ideological campaigns to maintain collectivized agriculture that accompanied them had, up to 1971, solved the basic problem of Chinese agriculture —too little land for the number of persons engaged in farming. Overall, however, there was greater stability in the agricultural sector in the second decade of the PRC than in the first.

AGRICULTURAL REGIONS

The major agricultural land-use regions in the PRC are determined by temperature, precipitation, terrain, soils, availability of water for

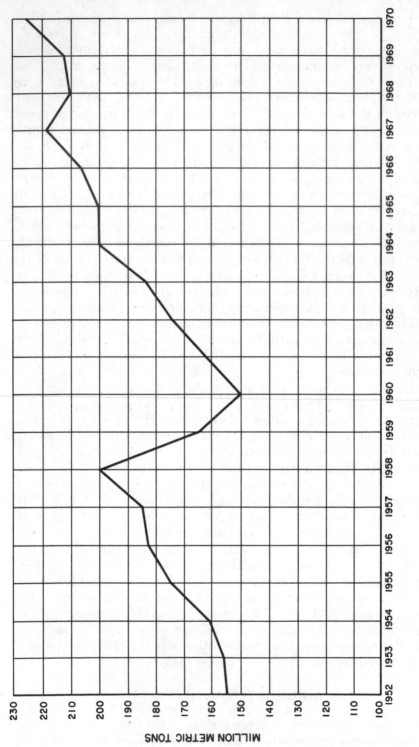

Figure 12. People's Republic of China, Food Grain Output, 1952–70.

irrigation, and population pressures. In areas of China Proper that have been settled and farmed for many centuries, crops and cropping systems have evolved into a pattern of wheat, with kaoliang (see Glossary) and millet in North China, rice in South China, and a mixture of the two in central China (see fig. 13). Besides these major food grains, a broad range of edible and industrial crops is grown in the arable lands, concomitantly with livestock raising, pisciculture, and fishing. Grazing is virtually unknown in this area but is important in Outer China, which is also the principal area where forestry is carried on.

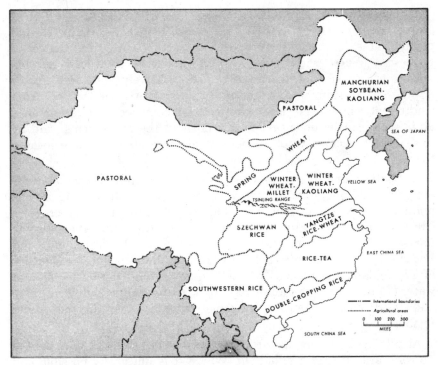

Figure 13. People's Republic of China, Agricultural Areas, 1971.

Precipitation is the critical factor to the farmers in the "subhumid" area north of the Yangtze River. The average annual precipitation for the several crop regions north of the Tsinling range is less than 40 inches, with a heavy concentration in the summer rainy season; for example, about three-fifths of Peking's average annual total rainfall of 24.7 inches falls during that season (see ch. 2, Physical Environment and Population). The sensitivity of the government to this vital factor in agriculture in these regions is illustrated by front-page treatment in the *People's Daily* to late-winter snow in North China (see ch. 12, Public Information and Propaganda).

North China is vulnerable not only to drought but also to floods that cause frequent, widespread crop loss. This flooding results in part from the concentration of rainfall in the summertime. Historically, when his main crop was lost because of drought or flood, or pests or frost, the Chinese farmer turned, where possible, to alternative crops as a survival measure, particularly if there were no grain reserves available and he had no money to buy food. Reports indicate that this practice still persisted to 1971 in afflicted areas, even though grain storage and transportation have been improved by the PRC. In general, however, barring widespread disaster the favorable and unfavorable factors affecting crops among the many subdivisions of each region tend to offset one another.

Temperature and precipitation make the north a region of low-yield crops, usually one per year. The region shades off to forest and pastoral areas in the extreme north and, farther away from the coast, to desert. Where agriculture is possible in the shortened growing season of the far northern part, the relatively flat and lightly populated terrain makes possible a dramatic departure from traditional Chinese farming practices. Mechanized cultivation on a large scale can be undertaken, and most of the state farms, said by mid-1971 to occupy about 10 percent of the arable land, are located there.

In South China, where water supply is adequate and temperatures are generally favorable for high-yield crops, terrain and soils are the main determinants of land use. The almost vertical rocky crags in Chinese landscape painting are features of the landscape of some parts of South China (see ch. 2, Physical Environment and Population). Temperature helps to redress the imbalance of shortage of arable land (38 percent of the country's total) and adequacy of water (75 percent of the water resources) and permits double cropping and much more extensive multiple cropping than in the colder regions.

Altitude is a limiting factor for agriculture in much of China; half of its total area is over a mile high. Where it is physically possible and water is available for irrigation, Chinese farmers have constructed elaborate terraces for rice and other crops. Unimproved slopes are utilized for miscellaneous crops, such as vines and tubers.

In the 1970s arable land was estimated to be, as it has been for the past several decades, about 267 million acres, or 11 percent of the total area of China. This is equivalent to about one-third of an acre per capita; however, multiple and double cropping adds roughly 100 million acres in figuring the estimated sown area. Efforts to increase the area of cultivation have historically been in the form of extension of traditional agriculture to the marginal lands to the north and west and were usually only transitory; the settlement of Manchuria, largely in the twentieth century, is the conspicuous exception (see ch. 2, Physical Environment and Population). The PRC has continued to follow this practice in addition to carrying out reclamation projects and to expanding double-cropped acreage to increase rice production.

MAJOR CROPS AND PRODUCTS

Food Crops

Rice

Rice maintained in the beginning of the 1970s its traditional position as the most important crop in the PRC. Its cultivation occupies less than 25 percent of the sown area, mainly in the regions south of the Yangtze River. In addition, it is grown throughout the country whenever conditions permit, with differences in kinds of rice grown and of cropping systems depending on types of soil and availability of water.

The wet-rice cultivation in the southern region exploits the acid, leached soils prevailing there. On slopes, terracing of plots, generally small, allows flooding and emptying by gravity. The initial water supply is trapped from rainfall at the highest level or raised by available animal, human, or mechanical means. Years of such use of the soils tend to build up a clay pan in each terrace, helping to retain the water for the period required.

For the farm population in 1971 this kind of cultivation remained almost as demanding as ever of individual labor. Some mechanical substitutes have been introduced, but nonetheless ricegrowing continued to be labor intensive; this is especially true during the transplanting of seedlings, when long hours of hard work must be put in. Mechanical devices for this chore have been invented, and some are reported effective, but the extent of their use in 1971 was not clear. Many additional man-hours are required when the grain ripens and is cut and the grain heads are removed and collected. At this stage it is commonly referred to as paddy or unhulled rice, which will be milled for food use.

The Yangtze River valley, with some exceptions, produces one crop of rice a year, whereas the southernmost provinces are able to grow two and sometimes three crops annually in most places. The area between tends largely to produce three crops in two years, although double cropping has increasingly been tried, with mixed results, since 1960. Szechwan Province is the single largest rice producer in the country. Some rice has always been grown north of the Yangtze and, in recent years, even in Manchuria. As a rule, the farther north that the rice is grown, the poorer the harvest and the greater the risk of crop failure because of lack of moisture. Furthermore, the attempts to produce rice on a large scale in traditionally wheat-producing areas have almost invariably lowered the fertility of the soil.

Rice is of some importance as the raw material for rice wine, which is produced almost everywhere. The center of industrial production has been in Shaohsing, Chekiang Province, which has become synonymous with the best grades. Local use is also found for all parts of the plant, mostly for fodder and thatching and as fuel, commonly by pulling up the roots to dry and burn.

Rice has attained through centuries of production and consumption a symbolic value among the Chinese, who consider it a preferred food even where it is not grown; they generally prefer the less glutinous varieties. Rice is unlikely to be supplanted as one of the two major food crops of the country.

Wheat

Wheat, a lower yield grain, is grown on a little less than 20 percent of the sown land. The transition from ricegrowing to the growing of wheat north of the Tsinling range is a function of a change in soil as well as of the more temperate climate, lower precipitation, and generally less broken terrain. In the northern agricultural regions generally, the soils are typically lime-bearing loess that is little leached. The original cover may have been grassland, wooded steppe, or forest, but any forestation has long since been destroyed in the millennia of habitation and cultivation in the Yellow River valley. Very early in China's history, flood control and water conservancy works were undertaken in this region; they are still vital to this area and, as of 1971, were the responsibility of the Ministry of Water Conservancy and Electrical Power (see ch. 9, Political System and Values).

There are two main varieties of wheat grown in the northern regions: winter wheat in the southern growing range and spring wheat farther north. The winter wheat grown in the Yangtze rice-wheat region is sown in September or October and is harvested in May or June so that it does not compete with rice or other crops sown in the same fields as summer crops. Spring wheat is planted during March and April and is reaped in July and August. Intensive hand cultivation and the longer growing season have resulted in much greater productivity per acre in the traditional wheat areas than in the newly opened and mechanized wheat farms farther north and west.

Variations of crop interplantings also occur throughout these wheat regions, decreasing as the growing season shortens. In general, the combination of growing conditions and major reliance on a low-yield crop results in a greater diversification of crops than in the primarily rice-growing regions. Another factor present in the north is that, without any grain production during the winter, farmers must depend for survival on stored or preserved food, for which they have developed suitable crops and processes.

402

Cultivation of wheat is less demanding of human energy than is that of rice, depending more on use of animal power or on machinery where it is available. Precipitation, however, is always a critical factor. When river water is not available, extensive use is made of shallow wells for irrigation in the North China Plain. In this case, effective utilization of either source introduces a power requirement, either human, animal, or mechanical, for pumping, distribution, and sometimes discharge.

Other Food Crops

Millet is grown only in the northern crop areas. It is a dietary staple in these areas, though somewhat less esteemed than wheat, which is more versatile in food use. In cultivation, harvesting, and processing it is much like wheat. It is sometimes eaten as a porridge made of the hulled or cracked seeds that are unmilled.

Barley is grown in the northern wheat-growing regions, including the Yangtze rice-wheat area. In addition to normal plantings, barley has traditionally been used as an emergency famine-relief crop in the north because it is the first to mature in the spring—the time when food supplies are most likely to be critically short.

Corn is grown throughout most of the arable areas of China Proper and Manchuria. It has been held in poor esteem as a food, and in South China corn has been considered the poorer peasant's subsistence crop. Whether this attitude has been changed under the communist regime was not known, but production of corn has increased substantially since 1949.

Kaoliang is a northern crop. It is a sorghum, the grain of which is considered by the Chinese to be low-quality human food, but it is extensively grown for its other uses as animal food and silage, green manure, fuel, and building material and because it is drought resistant. The grain is used to some extent as the raw material for the potent colorless alcoholic drink known as *pai-kar*.

White and sweet potatoes are cultivated in the southern rice areas, and white potatoes are also grown in the wheat regions. Sweet potatoes are an especially common secondary crop in the south, where they are an important supplement to rice. Production and consumption of potatoes are significant enough to include them in the consolidated grain crop totals at the ratio of four units of potatoes equaling one of rice. Some use of sweet potatoes presumably was being made as of 1971 as a raw material for alcohol and starch, but no statistics were available.

Soybeans, a legume, are grown throughout the country, with the exception of the far south; Manchuria is the major producer. This crop is extremely important in a country where there has always been a shortage of animal fat and protein in the human diet. The residue left after oil extraction is used as animal feed and fertilizer. Peanuts are also widely grown in China for their contribution to edible oil resources, as are rapeseed and sesame.

Sugarcane is grown for supplementary food usage in the extreme south, and sugar beets are grown in the extreme north. Despite a fourfold increase of sugar-producing crops since 1950, the sugar output reportedly remains insufficient for domestic requirements. The PRC in the latter 1960s was a net importer of sugar.

Tea is produced throughout most of South China, but major production centers in the south-central part of the country. Much tea is consumed locally. The United Nations Food and Agriculture Organization (FAO) has estimated the 1969 crop as 160,000 metric tons.

Silk is a quasi-agricultural product in that mulberry leaves are used as food for the silkworms. This activity is principally carried on in the provinces of Chekiang, Kiangsu, and Kwangtung and in the Kwangsi Chuang Autonomous Region. In many places sericulture is combined with pisciculture. The waste products from the silkworms provide fish food, whereas the mud from the bottom of the fishponds provides fertilizer for the mulberry bushes. This is another illustration of the effective utilization of all resources in the agricultural economy. It is probable that the PRC had by 1970 exceeded the pre-World War II level of annual silk production, though exact figures were lacking.

Industrial Crops

Cotton was the PRC's most important industrial crop in 1970, as it had been for many years, in terms of acreage and production and as a source of foreign exchange earnings. The acreage was estimated at about 12 million acres, and production, at 1.4 million metric tons. Cotton is raised mainly in the lower Yangtze River valley and the North China Plain, and it therefore competes with wheat for land utilization. In this competition cotton has been aided by strong government support. The cotton byproducts of seed, oil and oil meal, and cake are important, both for human consumption and as animal fodder.

Tobacco is grown to some extent nearly everywhere, with the 1969 crop estimated by FAO at over 770,000 metric tons. Production for industrial processing is centered in the lower Yangtze River valley and the North China Plain. It therefore also competes with wheat and cotton.

Ramie, hemp, and jute are also important industrial crops. Data on acreages and production were not available in mid-1971; however, estimated production in the mid-1960s was about 75,000 metric tons for ramie (a textile fiber, the cultivation of which is referred to in China as early as 2200 B.C.), 250,000 metric tons for hemp, and 300,000 metric tons for jute. The acreage devoted to such crops is considerable. Ramie is grown in the provinces along the Yangtze River, Hupeh Province being the largest producer; jute is produced in the same general area, mostly to the east, with Chekiang having the largest crop. Hemp is grown farther north, in Manchuria and East China, where Shantung and Shansi provinces are the largest growers.

Livestock

Small farm animals are found everywhere in the PRC, existing generally as scavengers and thus not competing with their owners for food. Chickens and ducks raised on private plots furnish some cash income as well as food. Many pigs are raised by individual farm households either for sale to the state or for their own use. Their major local value is their contribution of organic fertilizer. They also provide a small addition to the Chinese diet and are an element of foreign exchange earnings in the export of live animals, pork, and hog bristles. The number of small animals is difficult to estimate; however, in the aggregate, on the basis of several per acre of cultivated land, the number is very large. One Western study has estimated the number of hogs at 166 million in 1967.

Among the large animals, water buffalo are found exclusively in the southern rice regions where they are used for cultivation of the small paddy fields. Oxen and horses are used in the northern areas for cultivation, and horses, mules and donkeys, for transportation—either as pack animals or for pulling carts and wagons. Large farm animals were estimated at 97 million head in 1967. On the basis of the continued requirement for animal labor in cultivation, they probably exceeded that total in 1970. Sheep and goats, estimated to number about 127 million in 1967, are kept principally in Outer China (see Glossary) in large flocks. Bactrian camels are of minor importance in the same area and in North China for transportation and, like sheep, for production of wool.

Fisheries

The catch of fish in the PRC is variously estimated, depending upon the figures given for the large proportion derived from numerous ponds used for fish culture; estimates of the total were on the order of 5 million metric tons for 1969. The marine catch is produced from an area estimated to be about a quarter of the total fishing grounds of the world. The area includes both tropical and temperate-zone marine resources. Even though the yield of all fisheries in the PRC was estimated in 1969 to be fourth in size in the world and was about one-seventh of the world total, it contributed only a small proportion of the total protein dietary requirements of the population. Fisheries furnish some aquatic products for export (see ch. 18, Trade and Transportation).

Forestry

The area of forest cover is about 9 percent, or slightly less than the 11 percent comprising the arable area. The arable area supporting 98 percent of the population is an essentially deforested area, where timber is in chronically short supply. The major uses of the estimated annual production of 30 million cubic meters of wood and wood products are for construction—which takes about half of the timber production—in mining, and for railroad ties; use for pulp, paper, boxes, and furniture is small.

Timber production is mainly in Northeast China (Manchuria) and Inner Mongolia—which together account for about half of the total— and in the mountainous areas of Szechwan, and Yunnan provinces, the Sinkiang Uighur Autonomous Region, and South China. A wide variety of deciduous and coniferous trees grows in the several climatic regions of the country. Bamboo is an important component of timber production, although it is classified botanically as a grass. In 1955 the regime estimated that existing resources would last about thirty-five years without afforestation. This was based on a forest resource estimate of 5,400 million cubic meters (actually a pre-World War II estimate of the Nationalist government) and annual requirements of 150 million cubic meters. A program was adopted that projected reforestation of 235.6 million acres over a twelve-year period. The ultimate objective was forest cover over 20 percent of the country's land area.

Government policy on forestry appears to have shifted since 1955 from its original emphasis on mass planting, in which there apparently were very low survival rates—on the order of 10 percent— to one of conservation of the remaining natural forest resource. During the earlier stage of the program there were many ambitious projects for shelter belts, protective forests, soil stabilization, and erosion control. They were generally in locations adverse for planting, and their success has been rated low.

Most of the forest land in 1971 was in state forests, of which about 20 percent was controlled by Communes and other administrative subdivisions. South of the Yangtze River climatic conditions permit rapid forest growth, which offers an incentive for short-term returns. The state is reported to finance through contracts or loans longer range forestry projects undertaken by Communes, such as protective forests or the initial afforestation on land reclamation projects. In some cases, state forests are used for experimentation and research, on cash crops as well as on forestry.

The industrial crop element of Chinese forestry produces tung oil, camphor, tallow, nuts, and fruits as well as paper and fiber products, some of which are foreign exchange earners. Reportedly government policy has been to allocate half of the yearly tree planting to "industrial" trees. China in 1971 was generally self-supporting in forestry products, but the prospects for continued self-sufficiency appeared very poor, considering planned increases in timber-using mining and railroad construction and pulp and paper use and the virtual lack of replenishment of most forest resources except for fast-growing softwoods in the south.

It is apparent that the Chinese population has a tremendous total requirement for fuel. Satisfying this demand contributes to the low survival rate of trees due to the scarcity of other resources. No estimate of firewood consumption was available but, based on an estimate of consumption in India, the use of wood for fuel in China might be about five times that of commercial timber production. Scraps, dead limbs and trees, and permissible pruning of collectively owned trees supply most of the firewood.

Forestry as of 1971 was combined with agriculture in a single ministry (see ch. 9, Political System and Values). The forest service in the ministry is concerned with exploitation, management, reforestation, and research. In 1963 it reported 3,215 forestry centers throughout the country with an average manning of somewhat over 100 persons each. At that time there were nine forestry colleges and forestry departments in eleven universities. Their objective was to train about 5,000 students a year.

Chinese afforestation techniques were influenced by the adoption during the period of Soviet technical assistance of practices derived from the Soviet "new biology" associated with the name of Trofim Lysenko until his fall. Continuation of the Soviet practices has not provoked, apparently, charges of ideological deviationism; in forestry, the overall Soviet scientific impact has been small (see ch. 11, Foreign Relations).

AVAILABILITY OF FOOD

Western analysts generally conclude that the Chinese diet of the late 1960s was slightly less, on a per capita basis, than that of the smaller population of the 1930s. The country was producing food at no more than a subsistence level. Annual importation of grains constituted perhaps the margin necessary to maintain the population in reasonably good physical condition (see ch. 7, Living Conditions).

Rationing of grain products and cooking oil continued in mid-1971. Food grains were rationed on a sliding scale, based on the individual's physical labor, from about thirty to forty-five pounds per month (see ch. 7, Living Conditions). Descriptions of life in Peking in 1971 stated that rations were more than adequate and that other foods were abundant; prices also appeared moderate; one account concluded that, in Peking, "our man is well-fed."

Imports of grain, mostly wheat, were begun by the PRC in 1961, and similar imports still continued in 1971 to be a factor in food supplies. Some was held in reserve, and some was used to supplement the wheat produced in the northern agricultural regions where cotton is grown. Even during periods of barely adequate food supplies the government has maintained its support of cotton production as the raw material base to develop the textile industry to earn foreign exchange (see ch. 13, Character and Structure of the Economy).

TECHNOLOGICAL ASPECTS OF AGRICULTURE

Modernizing techniques of Chinese agriculture to increase production involves four main aspects: chemical fertilizers, mechanization, irrigation and water conservancy, and breeding of both crops and animals. Chemical fertilizers, however, promise the only long-range solution to the problem of raising yields, in combination with the other basic factors of water supply and mechanization.

Fertilizers

Fertilizers in traditional Chinese agriculture were entirely organic materials—animal, human, and vegetable. Inorganic chemical fertilizers, a fairly recent introduction, were first manufactured in the 1930s by the Japanese in Manchuria. The Chinese did not adopt their use at that time because of the lack of capital in the economy, both for the construction of manufacturing plants and for purchase of fertilizers by the farmer. The individual farmer instead invested labor, his only available resource, in the making, collection, and transportation of organic fertilizers; an estimated 30 to 40 percent of farm labor was used for this purpose. This was a high price for a low-yield product (especially in the most needed element of nitrogen), but the results were consistent with his other farming practices and enabled him to maintain the delicate natural balance that had developed over generations. This resulted in pre-World War II yields in China that compared favorably with those elsewhere in the world.

Given the level of fertilizer imports the economy could support at the time of the communist takeover, intensification of existing practices was the only feasible means of increasing fertilizer supplies during the leadtime required to build domestic chemical fertilizer plants. In the early and mid-1950s the planting of legumes for green manure increased, and the area devoted to them was expanded northwards. The raising of hogs for animal manure also increased. Both domestic production and imports of chemical fertilizer steadily increased during the 1950s, with production overtaking imports by the end of the decade. Production totals in the 1960s were issued only in percentages. Based on these percentages, a Western authority has estimated domestic output at over 10 million metric tons in 1967. In 1970 production was reportedly approximately 14 million metric tons; import figures were estimated to be about 7 million metric tons in 1970, half of the total coming from Japan (see ch. 18, Trade and Transportation). The government's goal is a total supply of from 30 million to 45 million metric tons from all sources by 1975.

The use of organic and chemical fertilizers in the latter 1960s was estimated at 60 and 40 percent, respectively. Average application of chemical fertilizers in China may still be below the world average, but overall use of fertilizers very likely would compare favorably. Chemical fertilizer distribution, however, discriminates in favor of cotton production, which contributes to China's leadership in cotton cloth output and consequent foreign exchange earnings; high-yield strategic grain production areas also have priority. There also may be greater use of organic fertilizers by individuals on private plots rather than on Commune lands. The type and quality of domestically produced fertilizers are said to be good in large plants but probably poor in small local factories. The location in different parts of the country of both large and small producing units appears appropriate for efficient distribution (see ch. 15, Industry).

The dearth of detailed information in 1971 did not permit any conclusions on the effectiveness of the application of chemical fertilizers in raising agricultural productivity. Supplies were clearly inadequate, nevertheless, for general application at an optimum rate.

Mechanization

The labor of the farmer generally in 1971 was, as in the past, little supplemented by energy other than that of animals. Construction of paddy fields and embankments, digging of wells, plowing, transplanting, cultivation, harvesting, and threshing continued to be accomplished on the Communes by the farmers, their families, and communal animals. Their farming implements and equipment were usually locally made and simple in design and construction.

The PRC has estimated that farming practices on some 190 million acres of farmland could be mechanized in various ways. Farming on reclaimed land, projected to be about another 45 million acres, could be mechanized also. One authority estimates that about 30 million acres of existing land with their present crops would be suitable for such mechanization, mostly in North and Northeast China.

Although the use of machinery in cultivation would be relatively minor, irrigation and drainage throughout the cultivated area could be mechanized, and this may be the only practicable way of applying machinery to wet-rice growing. In the pasture regions of the northeast and Outer China wells could be constructed by machine. The PRC's eventual goal for mechanization of agriculture would require an estimated 100 million to 150 million horsepower in tractors, harvesters, trucks, and pumps. This would be equivalent to one tractor per 247 acres, a combine and a truck for each 741 acres, and a five-horsepower pump per thirty-three acres. By 1971 this pattern of the use and distribution of agricultural machinery was starting to develop.

Since 1949 the PRC, through imports and domestic manufacture, has significantly increased the number of tractors. Units of fifteen horsepower, reported to be 400 in 1949, increased to 135,000 in 1965 and to an estimated 150,000 in 1967; however, this was far short of the 1.2 million tractors estimated by the PRC to be needed for full mechanization. As tractors became more numerous, production brigades and Communes were designated as the units to implement mechanization through the purchase of their own equipment. It appears that rates of progress toward the goals of mechanization have been very uneven. Prospective improvement in production has been important in the publicizing of tractors by the mass communications media, but as of 1971 there was little direct evidence of the actual results of their use. In any case, the area under mechanical cultivation was by mid-1971 still small in percentage terms, probably well under 10 percent.

Mechanized irrigation and drainage, using both electric and nonelectric power, such as diesel engines, are employed in the cultivated area generally. With an increase in the production and transmission of electricity, electric pumps were more widely used and became more important than nonelectric pumps in the mid-1960s. One estimate is that some 60 million acres were mechanically irrigated in 1967—36 million by electricity and 24 million by nonelectrical means.

Production of the major items for mechanization of cultivation has been reported as far below requirements, and in addition some resistance to this innovation has been reported. Improved handtools, more efficient animal-drawn implements, and small engine-driven machines apparently were the principal mechanical contributors to the increase of agricultural production. There have been reports of ingenious modifications and adaptations of equipment, some using hand or pedal power. Perhaps the most important have been attempts to mechanize the transplantation of rice seedlings—a major labor requirement of rice cultivation; none as yet has been fully successful.

Irrigation and Water Conservancy

Water conservancy, or water resource management, has historic as well as practical importance as a government function, especially in the flood-prone areas of central and northern China. The building of levees and dikes to prevent flooding, carried out over centuries, has resulted in riverbeds that are above the level of the surrounding countryside; these must be continuously maintained to prevent breeching. The undependability of precipitation in North China creates a drought problem, compounded by the impossibility of building reservoirs in the area's porous loess soils. In the 1950s a start was made in combining construction of hydroelectric generators with water conservancy projects; in North China this has not been very successful because of great seasonal variations in flow and because of the high silting rate.

Irrigation works in the north, canals, and wells are necessary to utilize the scarce rainfall and, alternatively, to provide drainage for the seasonally concentrated precipitation which, if left undrained, will result in waterlogged fields or excessive salinity or alkalinity. In the south, where rainfall is abundant, irrigation is used as a means of distributing the supply, in often difficult terrain, to meet the demands of the cycle of cultivation. As part of the Great Leap Forward beginning in the late 1950s, the government attempted a solution to the problem in the north in the Yellow and Huai river basins by applying mass human labor. It was still doing so in 1971, twenty years after a 1951 statement by Mao that the Huai must be harnessed. The early attempts were largely unsuccessful because of deficiencies in planning of size, location, and coordination. One result was loss of land from cultivation both directly because of use of the land itself for the projects and because of failure to provide adequate drainage. The government claims, however, that the large projects of 1971 were producing cultivable land that was of high grade and unaffected by seasonal variation of precipitation, thus having a stable yield.

Reports indicate that thousands of small-scale projects had been carried out throughout the country in the latter 1960s that were designed to extend cultivated areas and to reclaim waterlogged land or land uncultivable because of excessive salinity or alkalinity. Although neither scale nor pace was as great as that reported during the Great Leap Forward, the projects represent in the aggregate millions of man-years of labor. Incomplete descriptions do not permit calculation of any net increase in arable land from this widespread activity, reported to be improving in coordination and effectiveness.

Breeding of Crops and Animals

Western authorities estimate that crop yields could be increased by 10 to 20 percent through seed improvement. Annual seed requirements in the early 1970s were on the order of 2 million metric tons, divided into a large number of genera, species, and varieties. Scientific breeding and selection were able to supply only a very small part—the supply was estimated in 1963 to have been about 1.15 percent. In 1965 most *hsien* (county) agricultural services had propagation centers, providing another 2 percent of seed. The details of the situation in 1971 were not known; however, it seemed probable that the overwhelming part of seed requirements continued to be met through field selection by the producing unit or by selection or retention by the state companies. Complaints of seed impurities have been constant.

Some progress appears to have been made in certain crops; for example, there have been reports of development of longer staple cotton with greater unit yields. New and improved sugarcane, soybean, and rapeseed varieties have been reported. New varieties have been reported in the critical rice and wheat crops, but the results are unclear. Only minimal results have been reported from experiments on rice and wheat varieties designed for use in the extensive areas of cold, drought, and saline soils. The tendency of the new varieties has been to degenerate, probably because of extension to areas of nonsuitability. Accordingly, initial claims by PRC sources for new varieties must be treated with some reserve.

There appeared by 1971 to be a greater recognition by the government of the various factors involved in the introduction of new crop varieties. There were occasional reports of proposed changes in agriculture which, if carried out, would mean complete alteration of the farming system, but they did not seem to be statements of official policy. In the late 1950s the government had failed to recognize the consequences of changing to new varieties to get immediate increases in yield; their unsuitability was a principal cause of the decline of crop yields at that time. In extreme cases the central government's policy of change to new varieties left farmers without even seed to revert to their former crops. There was still reference in 1971 to Mao's "Eight Character Charter" of 1956, a list of eight general principles for agricultural practice included in his National Agricultural Development Program for 1956–67. Two of these, which came to have the meaning of close planting and deep plowing, have long since been quietly abandoned as unsuitable. They were no longer thought of as technical instructions to be followed literally.

The increase in animal population during the 1960s was accompanied by government support for the breeding of large animals. The principal objective was quantity, both for fertilizer and

412

draft work, while chemical fertilizers and mechanization were being developed. The means used during the 1960s included state ranches for large-scale animal raising, improvement of grazing areas in Outer China, and the setting up of breeding stations and veterinary centers in some areas. Efforts have also been made to improve the quality of the wool clip through sheep breeding, with results unclear.

Minor Agricultural Technology

Annual losses of food crops from plant diseases and pests are estimated to be about 10 percent, and that of fruits, about 30 per cent. Such losses may be much greater locally, for example, in cases of locust plague. Losses of animals from disease have been heavy in the past. Considerable success in overcoming these problems has been attributed to the efforts during the 1960s to improve the methods and treatment of plant and animal disease, especially through increased production of agricultural chemicals. One report states that the use of pesticides has increased rapidly and is an important element in increased crop yields. Nationwide networks have been set up to provide information on pests and infestations; however, there was no indication of their adequacy or efficiency.

Agricultural Research and Education

Agricultural research activity, which in 1971 was reportedly limited to applied research, is under the jurisdiction of the Academy of Agricultural Sciences, established in 1957. Some additional agricultural research is also carried on by the Chinese Academy of Sciences, where several outstanding agricultural scientists were reported to be working. Qualified scientists, many of whom have had training in the West, had by the mid-1960s been given responsibilities and facilities to develop the technology to increase agricultural production. This objective was explicit and emphatic in the major agricultural research tasks set forth by the Conference of Agricultural Science and Technology in 1963, which included the investigation of natural resources, combination of traditional and scientific technology, better utilization of land and water areas, and strengthening of theoretical, experimental, and research work (see ch. 16, Science and Technology).

Many provinces and autonomous regions have agricultural academies and research institutes. Research institutes are also located in some counties for specialized activities. Details of numbers, location, personnel, and projects were not available in mid-1971. The constant reference in the mass media to "consolidating the farmers' experience and techniques" implies an emphasis on practical agricultural practice, essentially short-term improvements that can be accomplished on the farms themselves but which do not constitute systematic research and experimentation.

The training given in agriculture for the personnel assigned to extension and demonstration facilities, other than scientists who are under constant pressure to undertake practical work among the farmers, generally appears to be relatively on a low level. The number of trained personnel is very small for the overall requirement, although some improvement in quality of personnel was reported during the late 1960s as the training system expanded. Demonstration farms, or plots, which were intended to give farmers the opportunity of seeing and learning the usefulness of scientific knowledge in agriculture, were an innovation during the same period. Planning for them was on a scale that would require a very large number of technical and scientific personnel. In the official terminology, those in charge of these demonstration farms have the functions of consolidating the farmers' experiences and techniques, setting a consistent pattern for agricultural production, and conducting experiments to assist local farmers (see ch. 8, Education, Intellectual Expression, and the Arts).

During the period of Soviet technical assistance to the PRC in the 1950s, Soviet experts participated in state planning for agriculture but were not directly involved in technical aid to agriculture in the sense of supplying new plant materials or species. There was, however, an echo of Lysenko theory in the inclusion in Mao's "Eight Character Charter" of close planting and deep plowing. These practices, along with other efforts to transform agriculture by fiat, contributed to the failure of the Great Leap Forward (see ch. 11, Foreign Relations; ch. 16, Science and Technology).

EVOLUTION OF COLLECTIVIZED AGRICULTURE

The long history of the agricultural population endowed it with clearly defined traditional values and attitudes toward government (see ch. 3, Historical Setting). Having only indirect contact with the civilian administrative apparatus, farmers for centuries thought government something to be endured but not participated in. The farmer's overriding concern was with his land, and his allegiance was to local institutions, within a strong cultural community.

Land Tenure and Reform to 1949

The interrelated aspects of the problem of farm ownership—by the farmers themselves, by absentee landlords, partial ownership, rents, and tenancy—were long debated on political and economic grounds in China before World War II. Sun Yat-sen included "land to the tillers" as a key economic policy in his political program. This was not based upon a specific economic justification but rather or a vague egalitarian notion.

Studies of the problem in the 1930s produced more dependable information on the extent of tenancy, which was the main focus of debate. Both government and foreign investigations showed that tenancy was less widespread than had been thought, in a range of from 17 to 30 percent, with owners actually constituting the largest group of farmers. There was found to be no discernible distinction in the sizes of farms held by owners and tenants. Tenants were apt to be better farmers than owners. The majority of tenant farmers were under a fixed-rent arrangement rather than a sharecropping system, which operated as a production incentive. One conclusion was that land reform, which would remove the tenancy system, would not solve the economic problems of agricultural production. It would neither enlarge the average size of farms nor affect the total amount of land available for farming. From this point of view, the fundamental difficulties were overpopulation—that is, the man-land ratio—and the lack of modernization.

Local variations of tenancy occurred, such as so-called "permanent tenancy"; in another form, ownership was separated from the right to use the land. In general, landlords, especially absentee owners, tended to buy more land rather than to improve what they had. In the 1920s and 1930s there was some shift of interest away from rural to urban investments.

The Nationalist government did not implement Sun Yat-sen's "land to the tiller" policy, but it did advocate a movement for reduction of rents, which had been found high in the surveys of the 1930s. The government also made some effort to carry out certain small-scale, tenant land purchase projects. In the immediate post-World War II period a comprehensive survey was made by the Republic of China-United States Agricultural Mission, and a number of projects were approved, but these had only just been started when the Communists took over.

Before coming to nationwide power in 1949 the Chinese Communist Party (CCP) attitude toward land reform was complex, though in theory the existing system was regarded as exploitation. A basic element of their mass line concept was to seek maximum political advantage from the "contradiction between the landlords and the peasantry," and in the late 1920s they experimented with various policies to do so. In the 1920s and early 1930s the Red Army practiced confiscation from all landowners, redistributing the land to the landless. After the Japanese attack in 1937 the united front was formed with the Nationalist government and, as one element in that agreement, the Communists shifted to a moderate rent-reduction policy.

Land Redistribution, 1950–52

In one Communist's view, "Chinese farmers in general were hampered by certain common characteristics, such as conservatism, narrowmindedness and backwardness; moreover, they evinced a traditional reverence for private ownership." In view of this, the Communists maintained, at the time they took over the mainland, that changing or uprooting a traditional concept like private property required time and education, and they skillfully utilized the genuine grievances of the Chinese peasants in their struggle for political power. Before the consolidation of the newly "liberated" areas in central and South China in mid-1950, their agrarian policy for these areas was the reduction of rent and interest, whereas in the old "liberated" areas land redistribution had already been carried out by 1949. By mid-1950 they proclaimed land redistribution for the whole of China in order to establish a monopoly of political and economic power and to serve as a first step toward the gradual socialization of the rural economy.

The new Agrarian Reform Law of June 28, 1950, adopted by the State Council, significantly modified the earlier agrarian law adopted by the CCP in September 1947. The old law called for the requisition of the surplus rural properties of rich peasants. The new law stipulated that land owned by rich peasants and worked by them or their hired laborers was not to be touched. Rich peasants could also retain small portions of land rented out by them. In addition, people engaged in nonagrarian occupations, such as workers or professional people, who owned and rented out small parcels of land were not to be classified as landlords and were allowed to keep and to rent out such parcels of land. The dual purpose of these changes was to encourage the early restoration of stability and agricultural production and to isolate the landlords.

For the effective execution of the land redistribution policies in central and South China, the areas that had the majority of the rural population, an elaborate official definition of the class status of the rural populations was adopted by the State Council on August 4, 1950. Cadres (see Glossary) were sent there to organize "village peasant meetings, peasant representative conferences, and committees of peasant associations." These meetings and conferences, under the leadership of the village people's government, then determined through "self-assessment and public discussion" each individual's class status according to the official definition, that is, whether he belonged to the landlord, rich peasant, middle-class peasant, poor peasant, or farm laborer class.

In the case of landlords their land, draft animals, farm implements, surplus grain, and surplus houses in the countryside were confiscated. In the case of rich peasants, land that they cultivated by themselves or was cultivated by hired labor and small portions of land rented out, as well as their other properties, were protected from infringement. In the case of middle-class peasants, who constituted 20 percent of the rural population according to official reports, their land and other properties were also protected. A portion of the confiscated or requisitioned land was divided among the poor peasants and farm laborers, who reportedly constituted 70 percent of the rural population. The approximately 5 percent of rural lands belonging to ancestral shrines, temples, monasteries, churches, schools, institutions, and other public lands was also requisitioned. There were specific provisions for the treatment of special cases of landownership. For instance, land and houses owned by Overseas Chinese were handled separately, in accordance with the decisions of the respective provincial governments instead of under the 1950 land law.

In general, the Communists adopted a practical approach in adjustment to changing conditions and worked out different timetables for land reforms to fit different areas in China. The tactics in 1950 acknowledged a reliance upon the poor peasants and the farm laborers and sought the cooperation of the middle-class peasants and the neutrality of the rich peasants. Although peasants nominally had a voice in the peasant meetings and conferences, the CCP guided and controlled the direction and execution of this agrarian reform through Party directives and by providing Party cadres to initiate and supervise the reforms. To mobilize peasants and encourage them to reveal their grievances, land reform teams were organized in large numbers.

Land redistribution went on for more than three years, usually accompanied by violence and bloodshed (see ch. 10, Political Dynamics). By the summer of 1950 land redistribution was nearly completed in North China and Manchuria, where the rural population totaled about 145 million. The amount of land acquired through this redistribution was small—from 0.15 to 0.45 of an acre per capita. Toward the end of 1952 the land reform movement was reported to have been practically completed throughout the country. According to Liao Lu-yen, deputy secretary general of the State Council and then minister of agriculture, about 300 million peasants, or between 60 or 70 percent of the rural population, had received by September 1952 some 110 million acres. This amount was roughly 45 percent of the total land under cultivation at that time, from which landlords had annually collected more than 30 million metric tons of grain as rent before the land reform.

The Communists' land redistribution helped to extend and consolidate their power at the village level. The transfer of ownership of rural properties to the poor peasants and farm laborers was meant not only to elevate their economic status but also to influence them to replace the old system of social values with an entirely new pattern.

The Communists also asserted that land reform would release a part of the productive forces that were not fully and efficiently used under the old system and that increased productivity in rural areas would provide a basis for improving the living standard of the peasants. The result of equal redistribution of farmholdings among the large numbers of poor peasants, however, was that the size of the average farm became even smaller than before and forced a still more uneconomic use of agricultural resources.

Initial Stages of Communist Agricultural Collectivization, 1949–54

By 1952 the immediate political objective—that of gaining the support of "poor farmers" (an expression by no means synonymous with tenant farmers)—had been reached. The economic gains, however, were limited. This type of land reform was not investment or improvement of incentives in the agricultural system. It was an initial institutional change that would lead, in the prevailing communist theory of the time, to technical advance and thus to the goal of increased production; collectivization was to be reached later.

The preliminary organizational phase adopted in the strategy to transform agricultural productive institutions to collectives was utilization of so-called mutual-aid teams. This type of rural organization was already well-known to Chinese farmers, who were accustomed to neighborhood cooperation, especially at times of seedling transplanting and harvesting, as a means of meeting temporary demands for labor, implements, or animals that were beyond the capability of a single household. Mutual-aid teams, which were temporary in nature, were organized by Party cadres simultaneously with land reform. They were kept in the simplest form. Compensation to the teams was made in cash or kind on the basis of contributions of work and materials, but the productive activity was that of the individual household (see table 8).

The next step in socialization was an advanced mutual-aid team, formed on a more permanent basis of from six to ten households for continuous activity. These teams sometimes combined private ownership of individual property with common ownership of productive implements, such as tools and animals, for year-round use. Withdrawal was permitted. Compensation for work was figured on a workday basis.

The advanced mutual-aid teams were then consolidated into the succeeding step, the lower stage agricultural producers' cooperatives, which consisted of from thirty to forty households. Households in a lower stage cooperative still held their land in private ownership, and the land was farmed in common, in accordance with the plans made by a central management. The private property aspect was eliminated

Year	Mutual-aid Teams (in thousands)	Lower Stage Agricultural Producers' Cooperatives	Higher Stage Agricultural Producers' Cooperatives (collectives)
1950	2,700	19	1
1951	4,760	300	n.a.
1952	8,030	3,640	10
1953	7,450	15,000	15
1954	9,930	114,000	201
1955	7,150	633,000	529
1956	n.a.	681,697	311,935
1957	n.a.	n.a.	700,000
1958	0	0	740,000

n.a.—not available.

Source: Adapted from Marion R. Larsen, "China's Agriculture Under Communism," in U.S. Congress, 90th, 1st Session, Joint Economic Committee, *An Economic Profile of Mainland China*, I, Washington, 1967, p. 217.

with the next step, that of higher stage producers' cooperatives, which were in many cases synonymous with collectives. The speed of transition during this period was such that not all farmers' organizations went through all of the steps; some lower stage cooperatives were consolidated with others immediately into collective farms. Compensation for collectivized land, animals, and large tools was to be made over a three- to five-year period. Compensation for labor was on the basis of work performed and was distributed from the income of the collective after payment of state and collective requirements. Collectives, for their part, consisted of a number of permanent field production brigades of about twenty households each. Families also kept private plots. It was at this period that there was a large-scale slaughter of hogs, as the farmers lost their ownership and chose to take some profit from them rather than give them up.

Differences of view within the CCP may have existed as early as 1949 on the theory and tactics of the "socialist transformation of agriculture." They became important once the initial step of land redistribution had been completed. These Party debates were the precursors, and one cause, of the open dissension of the 1960s (see ch. 10, Political Dynamics). The central issue was timing. One point of view, later associated with Liu Shao-ch'i and Teng Tzu-hui, who was in charge of agrarian affairs in the Party's Central Committee, was advocacy of a gradual process. It opposed rapid collectivization on two main grounds: first, under their new, favorable circumstances, individual farmers would increase production and, when 70 to 80 percent of them had reached the income status of "rich farmer," they would be ready for collectivization; second, mechanization was an essential prerequisite for collectivization, both as an incentive for farmers to join and to provide the only economic advantage considered realizable from large collective farms.

Mao held the opposing view that, once land reform had achieved its political purpose, the farm economy should be immediately replaced by socialized agriculture. The "socialist transformation" should be completed in the shortest possible time. Reasons cited for this view were that immediate collectivization was easier since land reform had eliminated the landed class and had reduced the influence of the old "rich peasants"; the new rich and middle farmers had not yet appeared; and therefore, the sooner collectivization was carried out, the less resistance there would be to it. Mao's statement of 1953 that "With regard to the battle position in the rural areas, if socialism does not take it, capitalism will definitely occupy it" was based, according to one explanation, on his opinion that a backward peasant economy of small farms could hardly survive; the small farms would eventually be transformed into either large socialist farms or large capitalist farms.

The opposing views clashed directly in late 1953. The occasion was a top-level Party meeting at which Mao threatened with possible purge those officials (presumably the most important was Teng Tzu-hui) who were responsible for ordering the dissolution of cooperatives that had emerged in considerable numbers earlier that year, after the public announcement of a Party resolution originally adopted in 1951. This resolution, which had emphasized mutual-aid teams for the time being and had discouraged the premature organization of cooperatives, had apparently been misinterpreted by overly enthusiastic cadres. The outcome of the meeting was a new Party resolution, promulgated in December 1953; it was a compromise, raising the scheduled pace of collectivization but iterating gradualism. It stressed voluntary participation and persuasion in its implementation through the establishment of one or more model cooperatives in each locality to demonstrate the superiority of cooperative farming.

Acceleration of Collectivization, 1955–57

Events in rapid sequence in mid-1955 resulted in the escalation of "socialist transformation." They followed publication of the First Five Year Plan (1953–57) in July 1955, which revealed that completion of the whole process of collectivization was visualized in fifteen years and that collectivization was seen as the means of raising farm production without state investment. The plan embodied the 1953 compromises. Just before it was made public, however, there had been a repetition of the 1953 incident of dissolution of cooperatives; this time some 200,000 "unstable" cooperatives, as seen by Liu, Teng, and others who thought that the movement had gone faster than scheduled, were dissolved in May and June 1955 by a government order of "drastic compression."

Mao's reaction was to give a speech on July 31, 1955, entitled "The Question of Agricultural Cooperation" to regional Party leaders. This was the first complete expression of his theory on collective farming to be made public. In it he cited all his reasons for a "new upsurge in the socialist mass movement" and repudiated the so-called empiricism that was based on the analogy of the experience in the Soviet Union. Mao contended that it underestimated the socialist tendency of Chinese farmers and the ability of the Party to lead them. He held, as before, that collectivization must precede mechanization, not vice versa.

Mao's tactics were successful, culminating in the adoption in October 1955 of the "Decision on Agricultural Cooperation" along the lines of his July speech by an "enlarged meeting" of regional Party secretaries. The immediate change brought about by the decision was a moderate increase in goals for early collectivization: lower stage cooperatives would be formed in a majority of localities by spring of 1958, with 70 to 80 percent of all farmers in such cooperatives by 1960.

Collectivization was further accelerated by two more publications by Mao, one in December 1955 and one in January 1956. The first estimated that basic completion of the lower stage cooperatives could be done in a year. The second was Mao's National Agricultural Development Program for 1956-67. Mao called a central government meeting on January 25, 1956, which adopted the agricultural program he had proposed. The targets set were: in some areas with favorable conditions, all peasants should be brought into higher stage cooperatives (collectives) by 1957; in the rest of the country, each district should organize one or more higher stage cooperatives as models; the conversion of the whole countryside into higher stage cooperatives should be accomplished by 1958. The change in tempo within three months was striking; what was originally to be completed in fifteen years was now to be done within three years. Given the absence of economic incentives and technological transformation, this program actually constituted a massive assault on the traditional rural institutions and agricultural organization and also a challenge to the Soviet Union's position that mechanization should precede the collectivization of agriculture (see ch. 11, Foreign Relations).

Problems in state procurement in the 1953-55 period were also a factor in official support of faster collectivization; it was felt that the resulting smaller number of those responsible for grain deliveries would facilitate the government's task. After land reform, crops were good, but farmers were consuming more, deliveries were reduced, and there were food shortages in the cities. In 1953, therefore, the government had started a program of compulsory procurement and rationing of grain. Urban food shortages worsened, and by 1955 some saw in collectives a means of alleviating them.

The agricultural transformation envisioned in the First Five Year Plan had been nullified by these successive events. The Second Five Year Plan, adopted on September 27, 1956, by the Eighth Party Congress, contained a provision calling for completion of agricultural collectivization by 1962, compared to 1958 in Mao's program adopted by the government eight months before. Mao's opposition thus had momentary success in 1956 and early 1957, but they were largely silenced by two nationwide "rectification campaigns" in 1957. One was directed at "rightist deviation," primarily against noncommunist intellectuals but also easily applied to Party opponents; the second tried by political indoctrination to counter the disincentive effects of collectivization.

The result of the two campaigns was a renewal of the "high tide" of socialist agricultural transformation. The concluding event was a revision of Mao's National Agricultural Development Program for 1956–67, promulgated on October 25, 1957, by which collectivization was to be completed by the end of the year. During the fall a great debate on the choice between the two roads of capitalism and socialism was reported to have taken place countrywide.

People's Communes

The origin of the People's Communes is not exactly known. It appears that they were a local innovation, the early ones conceived and effected by cadres to solve labor shortages in 1958, within the context of the Great Leap Forward. They were, in essence, the response to pressures from above to meet production and construction goals by "walking on two legs"—simultaneous increase in both agricultural output and industrial growth—for which the capability of even the normally labor-surplus farming community was inadequate.

The new Communes were highly publicized in the press. Government attitudes toward this innovation appeared uncertain, however. In August 1958 Mao visited several and gave his approval. An enlarged Political Bureau (Politburo—see Glossary) meeting that month endorsed them—although some top Party members seemed to have doubts of their merits—and they were hailed as the "logical march of events," the release of the initiative of the masses, and the mass mobilization of labor and of the total energies of the people as a whole.

Organization of Communes was accelerated by the adoption of the August Party resolution—which approved them but did not provide regulations. By the end of 1958 there were more than 26,000

Communes, the result of amalgamating 750,000 collectives consisting of over 123 million households, or 98 percent of all peasant households. On an average, a Commune was made up of about 5,000 households in thirty collectives.

The 1958-59 Communes were highly centralized control and decision units. They controlled land use, production planning, and labor use and became the local government—merging with one or more former *hsiang* (township) administrative units (with the administrative head of the *hsiang* becoming the Commune chief). In cases where the Commune was set up for a whole *hsien* (county), the *hsien* administrative chief became the chief Commune officer. They also combined the usual administrative functions incident to trade, finance, taxation, and education, as well as military and security responsibilities. They took over remaining private property, composed of the small plots farmers had kept in collectives, and household farm production. Communal messhalls were usually established, but communal living quarters were less common. Everyone who was able was expected to work, to be paid for it partly in kind, and to receive communal services free.

Communes in this period were typically subdivided into production brigades, which represented roughly the former collectives. The brigades were the intermediary link to the basic unit, the production team, which was essentially the earlier producers' cooperative. The lower levels were also linked to their respective superior bodies by appropriate elected Party organizations.

This radical organizational change did achieve its primary goal of easy mobilization of labor, though whether it was effectively used remains problematical. There was much shifting of labor within the Communes and their constituent units, as production efforts were diversified. Labor productivity in general, including agricultural production, was adversely affected by the pattern of rewards ("to each according to his need"), which became a disastrous disincentive.

In 1959, as the results of the irrationality of agricultural practices, as well as other aspects of the Great Leap Forward, became apparent in reduced crop yields, criticism of the Communes increased among Party leaders (see ch. 13, Character and Structure of the Economy; ch. 3, Historical Setting). A retreat occurred under the added pressure of successive years of bad weather and poor crops, but it took three years to affect functional decentralization, restore private plots, and reopen free markets in the countryside. By 1961 agricultural production, consumption, and distribution had returned essentially to the 1955-56 collectivized stage. The Commune structure remained, however. The Communes retained many governmental administrative functions, including tax collecting and receipt of grain deliveries, transmitted plans to the lower units, and retained control of relatively large industries and irrigation facilities.

The production brigade continued as a link between the Commune and the production teams, but the brigades lost, in November 1961, their position as the basic unit to own most common property and for taxation, accounting and, consequently, income distribution. The production team then assumed these functions.

AGRICULTURAL POLICY AND ORGANIZATION IN 1971

The period of the evolution of collectivization of agriculture was one in which the major emphasis was actually on heavy industry (see ch. 13, Character and Structure of the Economy). Investment in the agricultural sector was principally in the form of labor within the sector, not in modernizing technological influence from outside. It was a period of experimentation and constant shifts in policy with the unavoidable effects of creating uncertainty among the people involved. Unfavorable weather at the end of this initial period further compounded difficulties and, far from accumulating a surplus from agriculture, China became a net importer of grain (see ch. 18, Trade and Transportation).

Basic Policy

The basic economic policy of the PRC was changed in early 1962; since then, agriculture has taken first priority. This is sometimes expressed as "let industry serve agriculture," and in practice it has meant a drastic change in investment, with more to agriculture, to consumer goods industries, and to industries directly related to agriculture, such as fertilizers (see ch. 13, Character and Structure of the Economy). It has resulted in a changed approach to incentives in the material aspects of lower taxes, price adjustments, and lower grain deliveries to the state and in the psychological aspect of more autonomy at the production level.

The underlying philosophy of the communist government has not changed, however, as illustrated by such campaigns as the "Socialist Education Campaign" of 1963, which was designed, among other objectives, to erase in the Communes the "spontaneous desire to become a capitalist." It has been stated that these campaigns had, before the start of the Cultural Revolution, largely eliminated rural supporters of the Liu Shao-ch'i line (see ch. 10, Political Dynamics). This is given as one reason why the agricultural economy was less affected, directly, by the later upheavals than was industry; yet the indirect effects on agriculture of the Cultural Revolution, through disruption of industrial production and transportation, were probably considerable though undocumented.

The Ninth Party Congress of April 1969 made only passing mention of agriculture, with no specific prescriptions to indicate any change of

424

policy or organization within the context of Mao Tse-tung Thought that dominated the meeting. Such mention as there was of Communes and their units was directed more at the Party apparatus and its purification than it was to the substance of Commune responsibilities (see ch. 10, Political Dynamics). The 1970 draft state constitution specifies continuance of private plot operation and the status of the production team as the basic accounting unit.

The predominantly agricultural population of China has apparently not been seriously diverted since 1960 from the fundamental government aims of increase of production and stabilization of the agricultural economy, judging from estimates of crop yields. Campaigns and "movements" have continued in the countryside, and some shifts in emphasis and local variations have undoubtedly occurred; overall, the second decade of agriculture under the PRC was stable in contrast with the first. The organization of agriculture remained in 1971 essentially in the compromise form of "socialist transformation," which emerged from the adjustments after the 1959–61 period.

The Communes in 1971 covered close to 90 percent of the arable land; the balance was in state farms. About 5 percent of the land in Communes was privately operated, and the remainder, collectively. The number of farm Communes remained at about 74,000—approximately the same as ten years before. They had some 750,000 production brigades subordinate to them. The several production teams (each of from twenty to thirty households) that comprised a brigade were usually coextensive with villages or hamlets. There appeared to be little correlation of Commune units with previous administrative units. Instead, the production teams were more apt to be the former market areas. In some cases in South China they were also lineage units (see ch. 6, Family). In traditional Chinese government organization, the hsien (county), of which there were over 2,200 in 1971, was the lowest formal administrative unit. The Commune system, in its administrative aspects, is therefore a penetration of government far deeper into the population than ever before. Party organization also penetrates deeper, although the presence of Party cells in production teams is reported to be exceptional (see ch. 9, Political System and Values).

Communes have evolved from the original concept of an instrument for collective living to a point in 1971 where their main function was to act as a level of local administration and Party organization. They did not, for practical reasons of size or specialized function or overlapping responsibilities, carry out direct control of all rural economic, political, and social operations. Initiation of local industry appears to be one area where the Communes' economic role has continued. Rural schools and health services, however, were generally a responsibility shared by Communes, their units, and the hsien. The larger and more prosperous Communes may have had their own hospitals, but clinics and health centers were a more usual adjunct. The Communes and their components also shared the building and maintenance of local roads.

One important divergence in character between the *hsien* and Commune was apparent in 1971. The Commune in the collective sector constituted basically an economic unit, and its budget was not included in the state budget for which the lowest level is the *hsien*. Rural labor was, and is, the only capital available for agricultural development. This was the original motivation for collectivization, which culminated in the Commune. Nonetheless, like the *hsien*, it was responsible for certain tax payments, for a share in some social services, and for the control and receipt of profits for the enterprises it managed. A Western authority has succinctly described the objective that the state sees for the people in the Commune system:

> ... produce a surplus ... sufficient to bring a profit to themselves and government purchasing monopolies, *and* accumulate capital savings to finance their own modernization, with minimal help from the state. *On the steady growth of wealth under intelligent management and zealous labor of the communes depends the whole future and success or failure of socialism in China.*

The decentralization of control that occurred in the early 1960s from the Commune to its constituent parts was an important element of the compromise structure in 1971. The production team, lowest of the three officially sanctioned layers of the Commune and composed of from twenty to thirty households, was the basic collective landownership and accounting unit. The accounting responsibilities included payment of state taxes and deliveries of grain to the state, as well as the expenses of production and administration and public accumulation and welfare funds. Wide variations have been reported in accounting practice in these categories, depending in part on circumstances and prosperity. The public accumulation fund (sometimes reserve fund) is especially important as the chief source of investment funds for the team. It appears that 20 percent of the gross income is the commonly recognized maximum allocation; in some cases, it might be nil. Apparently depreciation allowances are not common in team accounting practice (see ch. 19, Fiscal and Monetary System).

Payment for labor has been both a theoretical and a practical problem in collectivized agriculture. In 1971 agricultural "wages" were paid according to labor. This arrangement developed during the agricultural producers' cooperative stage in the 1950s but was abandoned in the early stages of the Communes, when payment was based on the individual's need, in the form of "free supply." The government gradually changed its concept of the basis for payment in the years of agricultural disaster and organizational compromise (1959–61). By 1961 those incapable of work were permitted free or subsidized rations, but all others were supplied on the basis of labor.

426

In 1971 payment to the individual production team member was figured on work points (see Glossary), which were an assessment, in effect, of both the quantity and quality of his work on collectively operated land and projects. The monetary value at a given time of one unit of the team's work points was calculated at the close of the accounting period by dividing the team's net income available for distribution to its members by the total of their work points.

Full details of the system used in 1971 were not known. They probably followed in general outline those reported during the 1960s, in which the individual was graded for skill, strength, and attitude— usually in one of four grades. This determined the number of work points he received for satisfactory completion of assigned tasks. The highest grade was reported to be worth four times that of the lowest. A common norm for a day's work was ten points and, on the basis of twenty-five to twenty-eight days per month spent on the team's collective activities, the individual member might average 250 points monthly. Bonuses might be added for performance above average, whether of skill or ideology. The system is cumbersome for farmwork with its variety of daily chores. One way to cut down the clerical burden and to lessen the frequency of inspection has been to give contracts for seasonal jobs to groups or to individuals, though the details of handling work points under such arrangements are not known.

It is impossible to generalize on individual or household income under the Commune system. There is great variation because of regional disparities in activities and their profitability; differences in assessment for such reasons as shortcuts of method to make it easier to handle; maintenance of incentives for the highly variegated types of farm labor; compensation of artisans and handicraftsmen in the team; work point credits for labor on projects not necessarily income producing, such as roads and water conservancy; and team social responsibilities, such as credits for disabled exservicemen and their dependents. One report gives a range of individual net income for 1969 of about 80 to 250 yuan (2.46 yuan equal US$1—see Glossary); for household, from about 200 to 700 yuan. Time of payment may vary, depending on the major activity; for most teams it appears to be effected after the harvest, or the second harvest in a double-cropping region, and is mostly or all in kind at the compulsory grain purchase price.

Farmers derive other income from private plots, livestock, and handicrafts. Some income is in cash in market sales; some, in barter; some, in work points based, for example, on the supply of manure to collectively farmed lands; and some, in consumption of their own produce. There have been severe shifts in official policy from the extreme of abolition and confiscation of private property at the height of the rush to collectivization in the 1950s, followed by overcompensation in some areas in the restoration of private property and production in the early 1960s and the limited permissiveness in this respect in 1971. These wide variations in policy illustrate the difficulties of providing incentives in a collectivized system under pressure to expand production, when all its productive resources except labor are scarce and difficult, expensive, or impossible to increase.

As technological modernization has gradually influenced collectivized farming, traditional practices have tended to be perpetuated on the 5 percent or so of privately operated land. The combination has produced some conflict; that most commonly reported is the use of organic fertilizer on private plots rather than supplying it to collective lands. Recent reports of the amount of time spent by individual farmers on private plots and in production team farming activities show a preponderance of team work, on the order of 250 to 300 days per year. Private plot farming, which is frequently small-animal raising as well as vegetable growing, appears to have become a part-time activity for the farmer himself.

The importance of the private plots for food and income was shown by an investigation made in 1956 that concluded that farmers obtained from them, on an average, 14 percent of their caloric intake and derived from them 9 to 60 percent of total farm income. This calculation was based on 2.5 to 3 percent of the land being devoted to private operation rather than the 1971 average of 5 percent. An estimate of 1967 stated that up to 20 percent of farmers' food requirements came from private plots. Later data were not available, but descriptions of rural communities indicate that the same general pattern probably prevailed in 1971.

State Farms

State farms (including for organization purposes agricultural machinery stations) in 1971 accounted for about 10 percent of the use of cultivable land. Their importance has been more in their functions of land reclamation, technological innovation, and occasionally of minor population absorption than in contribution to crop yield totals, which may be about 1 percent. State farms also serve an ideological purpose, being "owned by the whole people" rather than collectively, as is the case in the Commune, and are thus the highest form of agricultural organization. Their workers constitute a kind of rural proletariat, and their technological level is a model for the collectives. They have accordingly had a high priority in obtaining tractors and other machinery and chemical fertilizers and have had the benefit of considerable government investment. The state profits from the higher output per man in the receipt of a larger percentage in taxes from state farms than from the output of collectives.

428

The organization of state farms has resembled that of Communes, consisting typically of three layers, and, like the Communes, the state farms have gone through a period of decentralization of authority. The payment for labor has evolved from wages, originally higher on the state farms than on collectives, to a system of work points similar to those in Communes. The earlier differential presumably was reduced in the process, although the higher skills required for much greater mechanization on state farms enter into the calculation of the grades and points of individuals so employed.

In the absence of specific figures, the purely economic functioning of the state farms cannot be accurately estimated. Probably, however, their long-term economic benefit is more important than their current contribution to agricultural production, if their reclamation activities, in fact, add arable and pastoral land to China's limited supply. Strategic as well as economic interests are served by extensive farms and associated enterprises reported to be run by the PLA in parts of Manchuria and Sinkiang (see ch. 21, The Armed Forces). The government has established other state farms for specialized purposes, such as those in South China for returning Overseas Chinese. Most have been for land reclamation, and thus most have been located in the northern and northwestern areas and in the south, such as Hainan Island.

Agricultural Taxes and Compulsory Grain Sales

An agricultural tax is collected—mainly in kind—through the Commune system on output of the Commune production units. The amounts levied are based on the previously calculated expected yield of given land, not the actual crop; the calculation remains in effect for three years. In theory, this should act as an incentive to increase production, since any yield in excess of the figure calculated is not subject to tax. Tax exemption and differential rates have been used at times to encourage cultivation of certain crops, for example, cotton in the mid-1950s. Tax reductions may also be decreed for areas affected by calamities; this follows an imperial practice of many centuries.

There was no information in 1971 on the total revenue to the state accruing from the agricultural tax. The Second Five Year Plan set a nationwide average tax rate of 15.5 percent. One investigator concludes that, irrespective of rate, the total quantity levied has been fairly stable. It appears that in the 1950s the agricultural tax accounted for about 20 percent of the state's tax revenues; however, no comparable later figures were available (see ch. 19, Fiscal and Monetary System).

Local taxes in kind may be added to the central government's levy, perhaps on the order of 15 percent of the original calculation. Other taxes paid directly to the state by the rural community are those on fish production and on sideline production; it is unclear whether private individual sales at rural free markets are subject to the tax on commerce. In lieu of the usual agricultural tax, pastoral areas pay a pastoral tax, reported to be a capital levy expressed in terms of the total number of livestock, but whether the tax is in kind or cash is not reported. Exemption in pastoral areas from the agricultural tax on fodder is reported, and in areas devoted to agriculture an exemption from the pastoral tax is noted.

Compulsory sales of grain to the state (and of other crops and agricultural products) were introduced in 1953. They are not taxes, since they are paid for at a fixed price, but the quotas set by the state remove a further substantial proportion of crop outputs from local control. The basis for calculating these sales was set in 1955 on the "normal yield" concept already utilized for the agricultural tax. The result was an increase of about a third in the volume of grain available for domestic distribution. This was adequate for the 1950s, when crops were good, to feed the growing urban population and food deficit areas.

The statistical data of the 1950s showed compulsory grain deliveries somewhat larger than the amounts collected as agricultural tax; together they accounted for about half of the grain outputs at that time. In the 1950s purchasing prices were below free market prices. No more recent data are available for policies, prices, amounts, or incentive or disincentive effects on agricultural production. The state was said to have paid premium prices for over-quota deliveries in 1971, as had been the practice in the early 1960s as a means of encouraging production.

Agricultural Finance

Direct state investment in the agricultural sector of the economy increased during the decade ending in 1971, consistent with the priority given agriculture over industry in the policy announced in 1962. Planning figures for the 1953–57 period show a total state allocation of investment in agriculture of 6.1 billion yuan, or 8 percent of the total investment, most of which went into water conservancy projects aimed at increasing yields. The comparable figure for industry at that time was then 45.5 percent (see ch. 13, Character and Structure of the Economy). By including other elements of investment, agriculture's share of the total invested by the state at that time has been calculated at around 20 percent, with most of the balance attributable to the exertions of the farmers themselves in their traditional labor-intensive activities.

The investment pattern seems to have changed significantly after the 1962 policy announcement, with a greater share going to agriculture and to consumer goods. Moreover, within the industrial sector there was more emphasis on raising output directly related to agriculture, such as chemicals (fertilizer and insecticides), machinery, electricity, petroleum, and others (see ch. 15, Industry).

By 1968 agricultural financing policies were emphasizing greater self-reliance by the Communes, implying a correspondingly lesser dependence on the state. Data are lacking on capital and investment policy and practices in the Commune system as of 1971; however, policy may be inferred from general descriptive statements in the PRC mass media of the necessity that Communes accumulate funds to finance their own modernization with minimal help from the state. The government's policy of moving large numbers of people to the countryside, for example, during the Cultural Revolution, introduced a new source of labor for capital improvements in many areas, such as irrigation and other water conservancy projects and land reclamation (see ch. 17, Labor). Details of their nature and extent are, however, not known.

The PRC has established a system of credit institutions to serve the agricultural community. Capital investments and loans to institutions are handled by the Agricultural Bank of China. Short-term loans are made by rural credit cooperatives to Communes and to individuals. The credit cooperatives are responsible also for checking on the financial aspects of communal organizations (see ch. 19, Fiscal and Monetary System).

Grain Storage

The central government is responsible for interprovincial transfers of grain, a process involving investment in facilities for grain storage, as do wheat imports also (see ch. 18, Trade and Transportation). The locations of these facilities and their capacities are not known, nor are those of locally built and administered facilities for temporary storage. Traditionally, Chinese governments assumed this function as a means of balancing food supplies between surplus and deficit areas and of maintaining reserve stocks as insurance against short crops. The system had deteriorated with the general decline of the imperial government and was not effectively restored after it fell in 1911 (see ch. 3, Historical Setting). The PRC, in the construction of grain elevators and other food-storage facilities, has simply repeated the steps of successive strong Chinese governments over two millennia in their control and famine relief measures.

CHAPTER 15

INDUSTRY

Industry, understood to include manufacturing, mining, power, and construction, was estimated to have provided one-half of the gross national product (GNP) of the People's Republic of China (PRC) in 1970 (see ch. 13, Character and Structure of the Economy). One index of the country's industrial production, using 1957 as the base year, calculated that such output in 1970 was 1.2 times industrial output in the base period. On this assumption the average annual increase in industrial production during the 1957–70 period would be 6.2 percent.

The increase in industrial production between 1957 and 1970 was attributed primarily to the growing number of factory buildings, machinery, locomotives, trucks, and tractors available for the country's industrial sector. The nonagricultural labor force was estimated for 1971 to be in the range of 45 million to 85 million persons, of which from 14 million to 23 million persons were occupied in industry (see ch. 17, Labor).

Economically significant categories of manufacturing included the metallurgical industries; machine building; transportation equipment; electronics; textiles; chemicals, particularly fertilizers; and construction materials. Armament was an important segment of the country's manufacturing sector, but its economic significance was difficult to evaluate.

The relatively high proportion of the country's imports devoted to industrial raw materials, machinery, and equipment implied a considerable dependence of the country's industry on foreign suppliers (see ch. 18, Trade and Transportation). Technological advance in industry was to a considerable extent accomplished by importing prototypes of advanced machinery, which were later copied for domestic use (see ch. 16, Science and Technology).

Industrial organization in the early 1970s was characterized by both large installations using modern methods and small installations employing traditional ones. The production system consisted of state-owned industries, jointly operated state-private enterprises, and collectively owned projects. The direction of industry and its rate of development were dictated by the state in accordance with political goals (see ch. 9, Political System and Values). Development of basic large-scale industries was directed by ministries of the central government with state investment, whereas smaller industries were directed by government agencies at a provincial or lower level and financed by other sources (see ch. 19, Fiscal and Monetary System).

The PRC was in 1971 one of the world's major mineral-producing nations. Of the essential industrial metals, copper was scarce. Lead and zinc, which were scheduled for expanded production, also had only moderate known reserves. Of the energy-producing minerals, coal was abundant. New oilfields that had been discovered and exploited in the 1960s and early 1970s had added to the known oil reserves, and Premier Chou En-lai claimed in 1971 that the PRC was capable of providing for its own current needs for crude oil and refined oil products. The petroleum industry remained small in 1971, however, and by world standards the country was neither a major producer nor an important consumer of petroleum.

Informed analysts of the country's economy agreed that the PRC in the early 1970s had the potential for the development of a fully modern and diversified manufacturing complex on a scale equal to that of the United States or the Soviet Union. These resources included raw materials, power, labor force, capital, and technical knowledge, but they were not all of equal quantity, quality, or state of development. Analysts pointed out that given certain inferior or scarce resources the PRC had found it necessary to emphasize a search for substitute materials and new production methods and the full use of the country's most ample resource, manpower (see ch. 17, Labor). The principal industrial constrictions were the small number of modern plants and the shortage of skilled managers, engineers, and scientists (see ch. 16, Science and Technology). The PRC continued to rely heavily on foreign technology for the design and manufacture of complex processing, refining, and finishing equipment.

Despite the existence of resources, the significant progress that has been made in manufacturing, and the growing level of technical expertise—best illustrated by the production of nuclear and thermonuclear bombs—the PRC has not attained first rank as an industrialized nation. Based on the consumption of steel and the generation of electric power, which are major indicators of a modern industrial economy, the PRC still lagged developed nations in 1971.

TRENDS IN INDUSTRIAL PRODUCTION: 1949-71

By 1971 industry had expanded impressively from the small base inherited by the PRC in 1949. Industrial development before 1949 had been localized in the southern part of what was formerly known as Manchuria and elsewhere in leased and treaty port areas, including Tientsin, Tsingtao, Shanghai, Foochow, Canton, several Yangtze River port cities, and a number of other smaller centers. Manchuria had been developed as a base for heavy industry by the Japanese during the 1930s (see ch. 3, Historical Setting). The period of war and civil conflict that followed severely inhibited industrial growth, and many industrial enterprises were disrupted or destroyed. By 1949 industrial production had declined to one-half the peak pre-World War II level attained in 1936.

By the end of 1952 most branches of industry had recovered or surpassed pre-World War II production levels. The industrial economy then experienced a rapid rise in output during the First Five Year Plan (1953–57), a frenzied increase in tempo during the Great Leap Forward (1958–60), an abrupt decline of production in 1961 and 1962 after the cutoff of aid from the Soviet Union and the collapse of the Great Leap, and a period of gradual recovery (1963–66).

By 1966 industrial production was about 70 percent greater than it was in 1957. The year 1967 was the second of the Great Proletarian Cultural Revolution, with political chaos adversely affecting industrial production. Numerous and widespread armed clashes and open conflicts took place between industrial workers and technocrats (technologists and technicians), peasants, soldiers, and Red Guards (see ch. 10, Political Dynamics).

The decline in industrial activity in 1967 was accentuated by the breakdown of the delivery systems for the supply of raw materials and the shipment of finished products. The railroad system was disrupted, and there was considerable borrowing of trucks for demonstrations and other activities (see ch. 18, Trade and Transportation). The construction of factories, which had accelerated sharply in 1966, came to a standstill in 1967. Technical personnel and industrial workers found it hard to recover from the harassment of the Red Guards.

Industrial production in 1968 showed considerable improvement over 1967. During the first half of 1968 national efforts were still being directed toward ending violence and disorder but, by the second half of the year, most of the large mines and plants were again operating at pre-Cultural Revolution levels, and the delivery systems had been brought under control.

In 1969 the setback to industrial production created by the Cultural Revolution was reversed, although many problems remained unsolved and the programs for factory construction and development of mines still lagged. Some factionalism and anarchy persisted during the first half of the year, and this somewhat retarded industrial progress.

Industry was, from early 1969 and throughout 1971, focused toward the needs of agriculture. Large industrial enterprises stressed the production of fertilizers, farm equipment, and special metal products. Many small mines and local industries were established throughout the country; these included coal mines, fertilizer plants, hydroelectric power units, metal and machine shops, and cement plants. The leaders of the PRC generally emphasized industry together with agriculture and small industries together with large mines and plants.

Early in 1969 there had been considerable fear of a confrontation with the Soviet Union (see ch. 11, Foreign Relations; ch. 21, The Armed Forces). The government's program of stockpiling materials, which had caused exports of minerals to dwindle and imports of minerals to expand greatly, could be related to this apprehension (see ch. 18, Trade and Transportation). Decentralization of industries, particularly construction of new and medium-sized mines and factories, was stressed. Not much could be done with the existing large mines and factories, however, except to proceed cautiously, complete unfinished facilities, and maximize production.

There were in 1969 many published reports of industrial achievements in specific provinces and cities. Almost all the reports asserted great increases in the value of industrial output over the 1968 level at those locations. Large parts of the added value were related to greater sophistication of industry and a wider variety of products, but there were also claimed sizable increases in absolute tonnage of basic materials.

In 1970 the serious check to industrial progress created by the Cultural Revolution was fully overcome, and by the end of the year the PRC was again making significant headway in construction of factories and in industrial development. The program of stockpiling materials and decentralizing industries was also continued, and it was evident by the end of 1970 that the schedule for decentralization and industrialization of the interior of the country would be accelerated.

GEOGRAPHICAL LOCATION OF MAJOR INDUSTRIAL CATEGORIES

In 1971 the problem of the location of industries, which had troubled the country's leadership for twenty-two years, remained unsolved. The government of the PRC had, from its formation, been dissatisfied with the concentration of the country's industrial plants in the coastal area. In this context, the coastal area comprises the provinces of Liaoning, Hopeh, Shantung, Kiangsu, Chekiang, Fukien, and Kwangtung and the municipalities of Peking, Tientsin, and Shanghai. The remaining provinces and autonomous regions constitute the inland area (see fig. 2).

In 1952, 70 percent of the country's industrial production was located in the coastal area. To lessen the concentration of industry along the coast, the First Five Year Plan specified that two-thirds of the approximately 700 major new industrial projects would be located in the inland provinces. Inland cities, such as Pao-t'ou, T'ai-yuan, Wu-han, Sian, Lan-chou, and Ch'eng-tu, therefore greatly expanded in size and population. An estimated two-thirds of the industrial projects for which the Soviet Union agreed to supply material and technical assistance also were part of the inland development program (see ch. 11, Foreign Relations).

By 1956 the country's economic planners realized the importance of improving and increasing production in traditional industrial areas while at the same time constructing plants away from the old centers. A new policy was adopted in that year, aiming at a "balanced development" between the coastal and inland areas. This new policy was of short duration; beginning in 1958 development of the inland areas was reemphasized.

During the period of readjustment following the collapse of the Great Leap and the subsequent denial of Soviet aid, regional industrial development was seriously affected. Many of the small factories that had proliferated from 1958 through 1960 were closed. Perhaps one-third of the large factories that had been scheduled for completion on the basis of Soviet aid were dropped in this period or were left in various stages of construction.

Nevertheless, by 1970 the PRC appeared to have made considerable progress in building industrial centers in the country's interior. Factories and mines, however, were still concentrated in the eastern third of the country.

Northeast China, which comprises the provinces of Heilungkiang, Kirin, and Liaoning, continued in 1970 to rank as the area of largest industrial concentration and as the foremost center of heavy industry. It was the largest producer of electric power, iron and steel, gold, petroleum, timber, paper, trucks, and a variety of machinery and equipment. Although heavy industry continues to be concentrated in the southern part of Northeast China, perhaps one-fifth of the projects that were completed with Soviet aid are located to the north in Kirin and Heilungkiang, and nearly all of these are large heavy industrial facilities. Soviet assistance thus was instrumental in extending northward this geographic region's industrialized area.

East China, comprising the provinces of Shantung, Kiangsu, Anhwei, Chekiang, Kiangsi, and Fukien and Shanghai Municipality, had nearly one-third of the country's population, a factor that helped to explain the ranking position of this geographic region in the manufacture of textiles and other consumer goods. It was second in total industrial production, and the production of chemicals, electric power, machinery and equipment, and iron and steel was also large. Much of the region's productive capacity was located in Shanghai, the country's largest industrial and commercial metropolis.

North China, which comprises Hopeh and Shansi provinces, the Inner Mongolian Autonomous Region (Inner Mongolia), and Peking and Tientsin municipalities, ranked third in industrial production. Its major industrialized area was located in a triangle formed by the cities of Peking, T'ang-shan, and Tientsin. The region led the nation in coal output and ranked high in the production of iron and steel, chemicals, electric power, textiles, and paper. Except in the Tientsin-T'ang-shan coastal zone, most of this development had occurred since 1949. Industrial development of the region had been aided by plentiful supplies of local coal and a relatively good railroad network.

South-Central China, comprising the provinces of Honan, Hupeh, Hunan, and Kwangtung and the Kwangsi Chuang Autonomous Region and ranking second after East China in population, was the country's largest producer of refined sugar and ranked second in textiles and paper. Light industry was centered in the Canton area, which specialized in sugar, paper, silk textiles, and various handicrafts. Heavy industry was concentrated in the middle Yangtze River valley at Wu-han and Hsiang-t'an and at Lo-yang in northern Honan Province. The region continued to be an important producer of raw materials, particularly nonferrous metals, such as tungsten, manganese, and antimony.

The predominantly mountainous and formerly isolated area of Southwest China, which comprises the provinces of Szechwan, Kweichow, and Yunnan and the Tibetan Autonomous Region (Tibet), received a modest and diversified industrial enlargement under the PRC. Mining was important; the region probably led the nation in the production of tin, and it also was responsible for sizable outputs of copper and lead. Using the modest industrial base started during World War II, new heavy industrial facilities specializing in electronic equipment and chemicals have been constructed in the Szechwan Red River Basin.

Northwest China comprised the provinces of Tsinghai, Kansu, and Shensi and the Sinkiang Uighur and Ninghsia Hui autonomous regions. Although by far the largest geographic region, it was the least industrialized. Almost all industry in this geographic region had been developed after 1949. Apart from the petroleum industry, which was widespread and ranked second to that of Northeast China, important industrial facilities were concentrated around the cities of Lan-chou and Sian. Soviet assistance in the industrial development of the geographic region had been considerable, but a substantial part of the growing petrochemical industry at Lan-chou was being constructed with equipment and complete plants imported from Western nations (see ch. 18, Trade and Transportation).

MANUFACTURING

Iron and Steel

It was estimated that steel output in 1970 reached 17 million metric tons, 1 million metric tons greater than the levels reached in the previous top years of 1966 and 1969. In addition to the gain in output in 1970, there were significant advances during the year in the sophistication and variety of products, such as more complicated shapes and alloy steels. The PRC also improved the manufacture of steelmaking equipment. For some years the nation had been able to construct blast furnaces and open hearths. By 1970 it could build oxygen converters, simpler types of rolling mills, galvanizing plants, and automatically controlled electric furnaces. Greater use of sophisticated equipment could explain to some extent the rise in consumption of steel scrap in 1970.

The iron and steel industry is organized around eight major centers, which produced about 60 percent of the pig iron and 90 percent of the crude steel output in 1970. The PRC is reported to have some 300 medium and small plants that contribute significantly to the industry, especially in the production of pig iron. Plants of moderate size have been established in the Sinkiang Uighur Autonomous Region (Sinkiang) and Kansu Province in Northwest China.

The An-shan Iron and Steel Works in Liaoning Province is one of the ten largest steel centers in the world. It is a completely integrated complex and in 1970 consisted of fifty mines, ten blast furnaces, twenty-five open hearth furnaces, and finishing facilities for rolled steel sheet, steel plate, seamless steel pipe, steel rods, and other products. The An-shan works reportedly fulfilled the 1970 output targets for pig iron, steel ingots, rolled steel, iron ore, and coke. Production of steel ingots may have been as high as 6.8 million metric tons.

The An-shan works has long been considered a leader in the improvement of facilities and techniques, production of new products, and training of personnel. A corps of specialists from among the 200,000 claimed workers has been used to train technicians and managers for employment in other industrial centers. In the late 1960s many technical advances were reported for An-shan. Various methods of fuel injection into blast furnaces were introduced to reduce coke consumption and improve smelting efficiency. Many new products, including various kinds of large structural shapes, were manufactured at the An-shan works in the late 1960s. Production of the seamless steel pipe mill was good in 1970, especially in output of large-diameter pipes and special pipes for oil-refinery stills. Smelting operations were also improved in 1970, with significant savings in coal, coke, electricity, and other raw materials. Overall progress was made in iron recoveries and quality of concentrates, with the installation of new magnetic separation equipment at various mines.

The Pen-ch'i complex in Liaoning Province, comprising several dozen mines and plants, became fairly well integrated in the late 1960s with the addition of rolling mills and steel furnaces to complement the iron, coal, and refractory mines and the coke ovens and blast furnaces. Nearby iron ore and coking coal deposits are extensive and high grade. There are two blast furnace plants. The

Pen-ch'i complex is therefore able to produce annually about 1.5 million metric tons of pig iron. Output of steel ingots in 1970 was estimated at about 1 million metric tons.

Before 1970 the Wu-han steelworks in Hupeh Province had three blast furnaces, six open hearths, three byproduct coke plants, and various rolling mills, including a blooming mill and a heavy mill for making rails, girders, and beams. A new open hearth furnace went into production near the beginning of 1970. In May 1970 ground-breaking ceremonies were held to start construction work on a fourth blast furnace. Annual capacity for production of steel ingots by the Wu-han works was raised to approximately 2.5 million metric tons in 1970; output of steel ingots in 1970 was estimated at 2 million metric tons. Basic construction underway at the Wu-han works in 1970 indicated planned development into a major integrated center of steel production.

The Peking steelworks, a merger of the Shih-ching-shan and other plants in Peking Municipality, reached levels of output in 1969 and 1970 reported to be considerably higher than in earlier years. With the completion of a new blooming mill in September 1969, the Peking steelworks became more integrated, although some ingots and semimanufactured products were still sent to Tientsin and T'ang-shan. The facilities at the Shih-ching-shan plant included three blast furnaces, three coke units, sintering plants, top-blown oxygen converters, and rolling mills. Annual capacity for production of steel ingots was estimated at about 1 million metric tons.

The Shanghai steelworks, which in 1970 consisted of two large and eight small steel plants, produced an estimated 1.5 million metric tons of steel ingots in 1970. The Shanghai Steel Plant (Number 1) was the most important plant, with two blast furnaces, two open hearths, five small converters, three domestically manufactured oxygen top-blown converters, a slabbing mill, a medium plate mill, and a forging mill.

After the completion of a second rolling mill shop, the Ma-an-shan steelworks in Anhwei Province became almost fully integrated. In addition to this new facility, the Ma-an-shan works had fifteen blast furnaces, two open hearths, coke plants, a sintering plant, a number of top-blown oxygen converters, electric furnaces, and a heavy rolling mill. Many technical improvements had been made in the late 1960s, especially in open hearth and converter steel techniques, by means of which output had been raised very substantially. Production of rolled steel products had also increased greatly. The Ma-an-shan steelworks was in 1971 being enlarged into an industrial complex, with the completion of various manufacturing plants in addition to the steelworks. During 1970 production of pig iron and steel at the Ma-an-shan works was estimated to have reached 1 million metric tons.

Development of the T'ai-yuan plant in Shansi Province into an integrated steelworks moved ahead during 1970. Existing facilities included two fifty-five-ton Austrian basic-oxygen furnaces, five blast furnaces, two coke oven plants, an electric furnace shop, and two rolling mill plants. In 1970 the following facilities were brought into production: a sintering plant, a domestically manufactured top-blown oxygen converter, and an additional blast furnace. The T'ai-yuan steelworks were estimated to have produced more than 1 million metric tons of steel ingots in 1970.

Construction of the Pao-t'ou plant in Inner Mongolia into an integrated steelworks continued in 1970. Existing facilities before 1970 included a blast furnace, two byproduct coke plants, two open hearths, and supporting iron, coal, and refractory mines. Three significant developments occurred in 1970. Around the middle of the year a top-blown oxygen converter was brought into use. Preparation of iron ore for smelting was improved by making higher grade concentrates. A large, modern coal mine was completed to support the Pao-t'ou steelworks. In 1970 the annual capacity of this center for production of steel ingots was estimated at 800,000 metric tons. If raw materials were available, it was estimated that the capacity of the Pao-t'ou steelworks could ultimately be doubled.

The Chungking steelworks in Szechwan Province, with three blast furnaces and two open hearth workshops, is estimated to have a total capacity of 500,000 metric tons of steel ingots annually. There were reports of many improvements, modifications, and additions to several small iron and steel plants during 1970.

Machine Industry

Official sources claimed that the machine industry in the PRC was highly diversified and could produce machine tools, electric machinery and appliances, metallurgical and mining equipment, chemical and petroleum equipment, tractors and agricultural machinery, textile and other light industrial machinery, motor vehicles, aircraft, ships, instruments, and meters. Observers pointed out, however, that many of the new products thus advertised were not in sustained production in 1971.

In the late 1960s informed analysts still considered the machine industry to have many shortcomings in its general structure, management, and development. Its sectoral development was unbalanced; many modern products, such as precision instruments, automobiles, and electronics equipment, were evaluated as very weak. The industry as a whole lacked a base of feeder industries for the manufacture of parts and components. The majority of its labor force, recruited from handicraft workers and peasants, had still not overcome traditional habits that militated against the discipline necessary for operation of modern enterprises (see ch. 17, Labor).

Almost all provinces and autonomous regions had some machine-building industries. Development took place under the direction of seven machine-building ministries (see ch. 9, Political System and Values).

The expansion of the machine industry was stressed as a major goal of the 1970s after the buildup of basic industries and services that took place during the 1950s and 1960s. In the 1952–65 period the total growth of the machine industry was about 19 percent; by 1966 its share in total industrial output was estimated to be about 12 percent. There had been a constant evolution in the product mix; the composition of output in the machine industry in the 1960s differed significantly from that of the 1950s.

Shen-yang (an alternate name for Mukden), Harbin, T'ai-yuan, Lo-yang, Nanking, Peking, Shanghai, Tientsin, and K'un-ming are among the many centers of machine manufacturing. Machinery is produced for the export trade as well as for domestic use (see ch. 18, Trade and Transportation).

Unorganized small plants seemed common. Although more than 200 large modern machinery plants were built in the mid-1960s, most of the plants in the late 1960s were still small establishments with obsolete equipment and poor management. In the mid-1960s 60 percent of total machine output was produced by manual labor, and half of the equipment was thirty to fifty years old. Most of the small plants had no quality control, and a large portion of their final production was substandard or completely rejected. Because some of their products were supplied to the large plants, the quality of the products manufactured by the major plants was very unstable.

The vast majority of the machine plants built before the formation of the PRC in 1949 had adopted the varying standards of the foreign countries from which their equipment came. There was virtually no standardization in most of their products; parts were therefore not interchangeable among plants, and there were great difficulties in repair and maintenance. The absence of standardization also hampered specialization by plant, because many machine factories were forced to engage in a wide range of activities, producing almost everything from their own screws to the final machines. There was a tremendous loss of time in starting, stopping, and switching from operation to operation, and the rate of utilization of the machines and equipment was very low in most of the plants.

In 1970 complete sets of domestically built machinery were in service in coal mines, iron ore mines, iron and steel plants, electric-generating stations, chemical fertilizer plants, chemical industrial works, tractor plants, machine-manufacturing plants, and textile mills. The machine-building industry was reported to be able to produce complete sets of equipment for all phases of the petroleum industry—exploration, drilling, extraction, and refinement.

A wide variety of machinery is produced for agriculture. The main center for the tractor industry is the Lo-yang Tractor Plant. Six different types of tractors were being mass produced. They ranged from bulldozers suitable for land reclamation, caterpillar tractors, and models designed for cropping, cultivation, and fertilizer spreading to a small model designed for use in truck gardens. Tractors are also produced in Tientsin, Shen-yang, An-shan, Nan-ch'ang, and Wu-han. The exact annual output of tractors has not been announced, but observers estimate the annual output of the Lo-yang plant at 15,000 to 20,000 fifteen-horsepower units. About 150,000 tractors of the same size are thought to be in use. In addition to major agricultural machines, 25,000 farm tool workshops with a total employment of 810,000 have made more than 100 different varieties of semimechanized farm tools.

In Liaoning Province the Shen-yang Heavy Machinery Plant produces metallurgical and rolling machinery, forging machinery of different kinds, mining machinery, and crushing and breaking machines. The Shen-yang Textile Machinery Plant produces machinery for cotton, wool, silk, linen, and synthetic fibers. The plant exports machinery to a number of countries.

Shanghai produces machinery for both light and heavy industry. In a report on Shanghai as a center for the production of machinery for light industry, it was claimed that more than 1,400 kinds of equipment were produced. The major fields were textiles, equipment for food processing, and plastics manufacturing. Shanghai is said to have equipped 180 plants for the production of plastics in twenty-five provinces, autonomous regions, and cities.

The quantity and variety of machine tools have increased to support the growing machinery industry and reduce the dependency of the PRC on imports. At the Canton autumn export fair in 1968, more than twenty new machine tools were exhibited, all regarded as conforming to advanced international standards; they included a curvature grinding machine for optical tools built by the Shanghai Machine Tool Plant (Number 3).

Chemicals

The chemical industry has concentrated on the production of fertilizers to assist the agricultural sector of the economy, of plastics for consumer goods, and of industrial raw materials. To increase the production of fertilizers the government had originally emphasized the building of modern nitrogen plants, some large and some medium sized. Beginning in the late 1960s considerable stress has been placed on small but reasonably efficient plants, and hundreds have been built. In 1971 small plants accounted for about two-fifths of the nation's capacity. Serious attempts have also been made to renovate and expand the older major plants.

In July 1971 the premier of the PRC stated that agriculture needed 30 million to 35 million metric tons of chemical fertilizer annually and gave the latter figure as the country's goal for 1975. He also reported production, presumably for 1970, as 14 million metric tons. Experienced and well-informed analysts were inclined, however, to estimate production for 1970 as about 10 million metric tons of processed fertilizer, all of which was nitrogenous except for possibly 2 million to 3 million tons of chemical and ground phosphates. Most of the country's output of chemical fertilizer was ammonium sulfate and urea, although superphosphates, ammonium bicarbonates, and mixed fertilizers were also produced.

Production of chemical fertilizers in 1969 had been reliably estimated at 7.5 million metric tons. Output from new small plants in 1970 had made a major contribution to the 30-percent increase above the 1969 total. In the case of plants of medium and large size, a concerted effort was made to utilize industrial waste and byproducts. Many chemical and fertilizer facilities were established at metallurgical, coal, and petroleum complexes.

In 1970 seventeen major nitrogen plants produced an estimated 80 percent of the output of nitrogenous fertilizer. These included the pre-1949 plants in Dairen, Kirin, Lan-chou, and T'ai-yuan and the Yung-li plant in Nanking with a combined annual capacity of several million metric tons. A new urea-producing complex, with a capacity of 350,000 metric tons, in Lu-chou, Szechwan Province, began production in the late 1960s, and there were new plants in Shanghai, Canton, Tsinan (Shantung Province), K'un-ming (Yunnan Province), Li-ling (Hunan Province), Ho-fei (Anhwei Province), K'ai-feng (Honan Province), Cheng-chou (Honan Province), and Kuei-yang (Kweichow Province), plus a shale oil installation in Fu-shun.

The plant in Nanking reported an increase in output in 1970 exceeding 20 percent. Technical developments at the Nanking plant included the construction of a synthetic ammonia tower, adoption of more automated practices, and introduction of new techniques for making urea in pellet form. The capacity of the Kirin plant for production of synthetic ammonia was increased by rebuilding an ammonia absorption tower to recover waste coal gas. The T'ai-yuan plant improved its operations through recovery of waste gases and raised its annual capacity by 20,000 metric tons.

In addition to the major installations, numerous phosphate plants with capacities ranging from 3,000 to 15,000 metric tons were established throughout the country, and reports in 1971 indicated plans for additional plants of similar size. New mines of phosphate rock and sulfur-bearing ores were opened in the mid-1960s to increase the raw materials base for the industry.

Production of phosphate rock in 1970 surpassed 1.2 million metric tons, coming mainly from Ching-hsiang in Hupeh Province, Liu-yang, Shih-men and Hua-ch'iao in Hunan Province, K'ai-yang in Kweichow Province, and Nan-t'ung in Kiangsu Province. An extensive deposit of high-grade phosphate rock reportedly had been discovered in Yunnan Province.

Seven major phosphate plants were estimated to have produced a minimum of 2 million metric tons of phosphate fertilizer in the late 1960s. These included the Nanking Phosphate Fertilizer Plant, with an annual capacity of 200,000 metric tons, and the T'ai-yuan Fertilizer Plant in Shansi Province, with an equal capacity. The other major phosphate-producing plants were located in Chu-chou (Hunan Province), Chin-ning (Yunnan Province), Chan-chiang (Kwangtung Province), Nan-ning (Kwangsi Chuang Autonomous Region), and Kuei-yang (Kweichow Province).

With imports of 5 million to 6 million metric tons of chemical fertilizers annually during the late 1960s, in addition to imports of phosphate rock, the country had become rather important in the world trade in fertilizers (see ch. 18, Trade and Transportation). Public information in mid-1971 on signed contracts for 1970 and 1971 showed that the country's worldwide purchases would exceed 1.7 million metric tons of contained nitrogen in the span of one year.

Production of pyrite was estimated to have increased to about 2 million metric tons in 1970 because of requirements for the manufacture of sulfuric acid and fertilizers. Most of the output is believed to have come from Hsiang-shan in Anhwei Province and Ying-te in Kwangtung Province. At Hsiang-shan, the residue of iron from the manufacture of sulfuric acid has been cleaned and utilized as raw material for steel. Pyrite was also produced in Szechwan and Shansi provinces, but output from these sources was not included in the usual estimates because this pyrite is converted to about 250,000 metric tons of raw sulfur annually.

The plastics industry was still in a beginning stage in 1971. Through domestic research and the study of foreign scientific journals, production has advanced in plants of domestic design and in those that were imported from Japan and Europe. Major plants were established in Shanghai, Lan-chou, T'ai-yuan, and Peking, where technicians for the industry were trained. Small plants reportedly were also established throughout the country.

Although polyvinyl chloride has been the main type of plastic manufactured because of the availability of the raw materials, polystyrene went into production at Lan-chou in the mid-1960s. Many products have been trial produced, but raincoats, handbags, suitcases, radio sets in plastic cases, toys, musical instruments, and sports equipment have been mass produced.

Through mid-1971 official PRC publications continued to claim that PRC scientists and technologists had succeeded in 1966 in the first known production of synthetic benzene. Benzene is a basic raw material used in the production of plastics and other synthetics. The PRC publications stated that the facilities for production of synthetic benzene required very little investment and could be constructed quickly and that synthetic benzene plants could be built in localities throughout the PRC wherever there was a demand for this industrial raw material. This factor was asserted to be significant in promoting the development of the country's plastics, synthetic fiber, dye, and drug industries.

Transportation Equipment

The Ch'ang-ch'un Tractor Works in Kirin Province has been the major center of automobile production. The plant was producing 60,000 vehicles annually in the late 1960s and early 1970s. The Ch'ang-ch'un plant reported the production of a new luxury limousine and three new models of trucks in the mid-1960s. The plant makes station wagons and three- to seven-ton trucks as well as sedans. A forty-seat bus has been trial produced. This plant has supplied half of the country's provinces and municipalities with complete sets of presses for vehicles. It also has sent more than 600 kinds of machine tools to forty-nine industrial enterprises and provided 60,000 cutting tools to motor vehicle or repair plants throughout the country. More than ten provinces, cities, and autonomous regions manufactured motor vehicles in 1971.

The Shanghai Truck Works in 1970 produced the country's first fifteen-ton heavy-duty dump truck for mining work, another truck with a 180-horsepower engine and a twelve-ton load capacity, and a twenty-ton trailer. In the late 1960s Tientsin produced a light truck, a van, and a nine-seat minibus. Chungking in the same period was producing a twenty-five-ton dump truck; and Tsinan, a seven-ton dump truck that could unload in three directions. Official sources claimed that an automobile repair plant in Canton had produced a rear-engine bus that reportedly had been used to transport foreign guests at an export trade fair held in that city.

Locomotives are produced at Dairen in Liaotung Province, Ta-t'ung in Shansi Province, and Ssu-fang in Shantung Province. In the mid-1960s the Dairen Locomotive and Rolling Stock Plant initiated the production of diesel locomotives. The Ta-t'ung Locomotive Plant in Shansi Province also put a new kind of high-power steam freight locomotive into production in the mid-1960s. The Ssu-fang Locomotive and Rolling Stock Plant built one 5,000-horsepower hydraulic drive locomotive. In February 1970 the PRC announced its first production of a gas-turbine locomotive. Official sources claimed in 1970 that the PRC was able to produce many types and models of advanced diesel engines, including an 8,800-horsepower engine that could be used on ships of 10,000 displacement tons or larger.

The government reported that 10,000- to 15,000-displacement ton vessels were being produced in the country's shipyards, and Japanese sources estimated that nine such vessels had been launched in the late 1960s and early 1970s. Construction of inland shipping was also reported to have developed from ordinary maintenance to construction of complete ships on the Yangtze River.

In the mid-1960s progress was reported in building a comprehensive aircraft industry, based on domestic design teams and research establishments. At the State Aircraft Factory in Shen-yang, jet fighters, jet trainers, and helicopters were produced. In 1970 the PRC produced its first strategic bomber, a version of the Soviet Tupolev 16, a subsonic, medium-range aircraft. Aircraft were being produced in the mid-1960s at Harbin, Peking, and Shanghai for use by the civil aviation service; however, later data on these plants were unavailable (see ch. 18, Trade and Transportation). In 1966 the PRC exported eighty domestically produced MIG-19 jet fighter aircraft to Pakistan.

Textiles

Cotton textiles, which are basic consumer goods, have also been exported to provide foreign exchange to purchase equipment needed for industrialization. To control domestic demand, cloth rationing was continued through 1971 (see ch. 7, Living Conditions; ch. 18, Trade and Transportation).

Sharply increased production of cotton textiles in 1969 and 1970 was reported, according to Premier Chou En-lai. The country was estimated to have had 12 million spindles in the mid-1960s, and the considerable expansion of capacity in the late 1960s and early 1970s would have increased this figure by some undetermined but substantial amount.

A Chinese-language monograph published in Hong Kong in July 1969 was entitled *New Achievements in China's Science and Technology*. In the section devoted to synthetic fibers, it was stated that the PRC could not rely on domestic production of cotton, natural silk, and wool to provide the industrial raw materials necessary to manufacture sufficient clothing for the country's enormous population (see ch. 2, Physical Environment and Population; ch. 7, Living Conditions).

Because the country's production of raw cotton seemed unable to meet the demand of its textiles industry, the regime intensified its efforts for the development of the synthetic fiber component of its textiles sector. In the late 1960s capital construction projects in the textiles industry were concentrated on building synthetic fiber plants. The Peking Vinylon Plant introduced a number of important technological innovations, which were claimed to have increased the potential production capacity of any of the country's vinylon factories by 50 percent. The basic raw materials for production of vinylon—coal and limestone—are relatively common in the PRC, and its production costs are comparatively low.

The production of silk was expanding in the late 1960s and early 1970s and was again important as an earner of foreign exchange (see ch. 14, Agriculture; ch. 18, Trade and Transportation). Production is largely centered near the source of raw materials. Nan-ch'ang in the province of Kiangsi is said to be the largest integrated silk complex. Four large mills have been created from the numerous small workshops in Sheng-tse in the province of Kiangsu, and another modern mill has been constructed in Tsung-i in Kweichow Province.

Electronics

In 1971 the PRC was continuing to place strong emphasis on the development of the electronics industry. In the late 1960s and early 1970s more than 100 factories in Shanghai were engaged in the manufacture of electronics components and products. The Shanghai Institute of Radio Research had reportedly trial-produced electronic equipment of advanced design for use in industrial automation. Official sources claimed in 1970 that the Peking Semi-Conductor Factory had been supplying about twenty provinces and autonomous regions with an automatic high-precision heat energy diffusion furnace, asserted to be an important piece of equipment in the electronics industry. Another report in 1970 stated that more than 200 factories in Kwangtung Province could manufacture electronics products, including monocrystal-silicon, primarily used in semiconductor devices, such as transistors. A number of factories in Kwangsi Chuang Autonomous Region were reportedly manufacturing transistorized receivers and amplifiers, broadcasting equipment, and radio parts. At Fu-t'an University in Shanghai, teachers and students in 1969 established a microelectronics factory; products of the factory included equipment for the fields of semiconductors, radios, electronics, physics, and optics.

Building Materials

Brick and tile factories exist in many places, and in 1971 most provinces had at least one cement plant. In 1970 it was estimated that some thirty cement plants, each having a capacity of more than 100,000 metric tons, were in production. The two largest plants, with capacities of more than 100,000 metric tons, were located in Hupeh and Shensi provinces. The northeastern provinces, because of surplus production, were able to export some cement, but scarcity existed in other areas. During the 1960s additions had been made to capacity; new quarries had been opened; and others had been enlarged to increase the supply of raw materials and reduce transportation costs. Reports in 1970 indicated that most provinces had taken steps to increase the output of cement and other building materials.

Brick and tile factories in Liaoning Province use waste ash and slag to economize on the use of raw materials, and cinder block plants have been built in Peking, Shanghai, and Tientsin. In 1969 the Ch'ang-ch'eng Brick Works at Tientsin put into use the country's first tunnel kiln for the manufacture of clay bricks in one firing.

Paper

The province of Liaoning with twenty one mills is the leading producer of machine-made paper for industrial and domestic use. Mills also operate in Shantung, Szechwan, and Anhwei provinces. Papermaking is largely a small-scale industry. Because of the scarcity of timber, local raw materials are used when possible. Mills in Liaoning Province use reeds, and Tsinan produces fine white paper from wheat straw. In Szechwan Province sugar refineries use bagasse to make coarse paper for general as well as local use.

Other Products

A vast number of other products are manufactured, many mainly for export use but others also enjoy a domestic market. At the semiannual trade fairs in Canton in the late 1960s and early 1970s, the manufactured articles exhibited included toys, bicycles, typewriters, electric refrigerators, stoves, musical instruments, fans, irons, movie projectors, light bulbs, grand and upright pianos, and electric sewing machines with modern attachments.

MINING

In 1970 the PRC qualified as tenth among the major mineral-producing nations of the world. The overall value of mineral output in 1970 surpassed that of any single year during the 1960s and was estimated to be 10 percent greater than that of 1969. At the end of 1970 the trend in output of minerals was upward, and officials of the regime were predicting an even better year for 1971. The country was one of the three foremost producers of bituminous and anthracite coal, tin, tungsten, antimony, salt, and magnetite, and it ranked fourth in output of iron ore. Large deposits of uranium existed in Northwest

China, particularly in Sinkiang, and bauxite deposits were found in many parts of the country. Deficiencies existed in copper, nickel, and chromite. Although copper deposits were known to exist, they were considered to occur too deep for profitable large-scale exploitation. Reserves of lead and zinc were reported to be moderate.

After 1960 the improvement of existing mines and of techniques of treating minerals was considered more important than the discovery of new reserves, although exploration continued through 1970. The extent of reserves of major minerals, which has been the subject of conflicting reports, was not accurately known.

Coal

Coal accounted for about 93 percent of all the primary energy available in the PRC in 1970. Total reserves were estimated to range from 1 trillion to 1.5 trillion metric tons; proved reserves probably amount to 50 billion metric tons, ranking the nation third in the world in reserves after the United States and the Soviet Union. Coal reserves are mostly located in Hopeh and Shansi provinces. Although by 1971 deposits were claimed to have been discovered in every province, informed observers doubted that the new discoveries were substantial in quality and quantity in all instances. Major coal deposits were reportedly discovered in 1968 south of the Yangtze River in Hunan Province; this was significant because all large coalfields previously found in the PRC had been in North China. Varieties of coal in the PRC range from lignite to anthracite, with bituminous predominating. Most of the deposits are poor to fair in quality, and they must be improved by preparation and cleaning before utilization. Reserves of good coking coal are considered ample, but in some areas they are far from the widely dispersed coke plants. In spite of the problems to overcome, known reserves of coal are considered adequate to support a more highly industrialized economy.

Nearly two-thirds of the nation's coal production is concentrated in North China and Northeast China. In North China numerous mines are located near T'ang-shan. In Northeast China several mining complexes located in Liaoning Province, including the open-pit mine at Fu-shun, serve the heavy industry base of the southern portion of Northeast China. More distant from the major industrial areas are large and important mining complexes located in Heilungkiang Province. Efforts have been made to increase production in coal-deficient areas of the south; considerable shipments from coal-surplus areas, however, still are required to satisfy such centers of heavy demand as Canton, Shanghai, and the Yangtze River port cities.

Output in 1970, authoritatively estimated at 360 million metric tons of mine-run coal, was more than in any year during the 1960s. On the basis of the many official claims regarding attainment of targets, a still higher production level could be anticipated for 1971, if political developments did not restrain progress. Dislocations of the Cultural Revolution appeared to have been substantially overcome. The People's Liberation Army (PLA) was still the stabilizing force within the various revolutionary committees formed to bring industrial operations back to normal. Two national coal conferences held in 1968 had helped to restore usual operations in the coal mines. Another drive to raise production occurred in 1969, using political slogans such as "Grasp revolution, promote production, and prepare against war." The national emulation campaign, which was started at the Peking steelworks, reached many coal mines by the latter part of 1969, with reportedly good results. The transportation problem created by the Cultural Revolution eased in 1969 and 1970, and local coal shortages lessened, although drives were still in progress in 1971 to economize on coal with a view to improving efficiency of utilization. Significant trends included development of small mines, construction of coal preparation plants, and emphasis on assuring adequate supplies of better quality coking coal for the steel industry.

According to PRC official sources, the coal mining sector was making steady progress in 1970, with output of many established mines stabilized at record levels. In the first half of 1970, national production of coal was reported to be substantially higher and costs somewhat lower than in the corresponding period of 1969, and as much new capacity was reportedly brought into production as in all of 1969. It was claimed that small- and medium-sized mines may be just as economical and rational to develop as large mines, and production from many small coal mines was reportedly high in 1970.

Coal is produced by such diverse installations as primitive mines, where men are lowered down a shaft by rope and the coal is mined by pick, raised to the surface in wicker baskets, and carried away by mules, to modern underground mines where descent is made by pit-cage into concrete-lined, well-ventilated corridors with at least partly mechanized mining, and to large open pits where coal is removed by power shovel. The contribution of primitive mines was small in the 1960s and early 1970s.

Mechanization of mines was proceeding in 1971. Manufacture of an array of mining machinery had begun in the early 1960s. In 1970 the Fu-shun mine in Liaoning Province and the Ta-t'ung mine in Shansi Province were described as being the most highly mechanized. Fu-shun was a very large and expanding industrial complex, with oil, cement, shale, aluminum, nonferrous, and chemical operations in addition to coal mining.

Much had been accomplished in the 1960s in improving the quality of coal and of extraction. Large coal processing capacities had been developed, and most coal bases, particularly the new shafts and pits, had such facilities. There was considerable emphasis on washing and blending of coking coals to meet the needs of the steel industry; local coals near the centers of steel production were used as much as possible. A drive to conserve quality coal for the most appropriate uses and to achieve economies in the consumption of coal was continuing in 1971. The exploitation of new mines had been hampered by the need to build railroads to transport coal to the centers of demand and by the lack of timber for pit props. In spite of the problems to be overcome, known reserves of coal were considered adequate to support a more highly industrialized economy.

Petroleum

The exploration and development of new petroleum resources has had high priority in the PRC. Production of crude oil has increased markedly to an estimated 24 million metric tons in 1970 (including approximately 4 million metric tons of crude oil from shale), thus ending the country's dependence on imports. During the 1960s the petroleum stores of the nation had been improved by the expansion of refining capabilities and by restrictions on consumption. By the end of 1966 the PRC had developed an integrated petroleum industry.

Potential petroleum production is derived from both crude oil and shale oil deposits. In 1970 natural petroleum reserves were estimated to be more than 2 billion metric tons, and shale oil reserves, to be 3.9 billion metric tons. Natural crude oil deposits, with the exception of the Ta-ch'ing field in Heilungkiang Province, are concentrated in Northwest China—in Sinkiang and in the provinces of Kansu, Shensi, and Tsinghai—and in Southwest China in the province of Szechwan. The largest oilfield was Ta-ch'ing, at which the output of crude oil in 1970 was conservatively estimated at 10 million metric tons. Other large oilfields are Karamai in Sinkiang and Yu-men in Kansu Province, each of which had an estimated annual production in 1970 of 3 million metric tons. Shale oil deposits are concentrated near centers of industry in the provinces of Liaoning in Northeast China and in Kwangtung in South-Central China.

Refineries are generally near traditional producing areas rather than major consumption centers. The Lan-chou refinery, estimated to have an annual capacity of 3 million metric tons and the largest and most modern in the PRC, was built to process the output from the western fields; as the hub of an expanding transportation network, the Lan-chou site thus was a compromise location between producing and consuming areas. The Lan-chou refinery reportedly includes all of the technical facilities necessary in the processing of crude oil. The industrial complex of which it is a part also has petrochemical, fertilizer, and machinery plants.

Smaller refineries are located at Tu-shan-tzu, Leng-hu, Yu-men, and Nan-ch'ung. Coastal refineries at Dairen, Chin-hsi, and Shanghai were constructed before 1949 and have subsequently been expanded. A large refinery, originally capable of producing somewhat over 2 million metric tons annually, was constructed at Ta-ch'ing to serve that major field; the refinery throughput capacity was subsequently expanded to possibly 4 million metric tons. Although petroleum refining capacity had increased in the 1960s and early 1970s, this increased capacity apparently had only matched the increase in the production of crude oil.

Iron Ore

The PRC has very extensive deposits of iron ore, but much of the ore is low grade. Production for 1970 was calculated at 44 million metric tons. Increasing industrialization will place heavier pressure on iron ore reserves and enhance the importance of developing improved techniques for using low-grade ores. In the late 1960s and early 1970s emphasis had been placed on strengthening the raw material base for the iron and steel industry through exploration for more iron ore and processing to improve the physical and chemical properties of what was available. There had also been some stress on building small and medium-sized mines to utilize local resources better. Significant additional reserves of iron ore were found for the large enterprises in 1970.

POWER RESOURCES

Installed electric power generating capacity at the end of 1968 was estimated at 15.9 million kilowatts, of which 11.7 million kilowatts were thermal and 4.2 million kilowatts were hydroelectric. Total production in 1968 was calculated at 42 billion kilowatt-hours, of which 29 billion kilowatt-hours were generated by thermal facilities and the balance by hydroelectric sources.

The PRC in 1968 was estimated to be in fifteenth place as a producer of electric power in the world, ranking just behind Australia. One estimate placed production of electric power in the PRC in 1970 at 60 billion kilowatt-hours, with the proportional distribution between thermal and hydroelectric sources assumed to be approximately the same as had prevailed in 1968.

One well-informed analyst of the PRC's industrial development carefully surveyed in 1967 the ability of the country's engineers and technicians to design large powerplants, the capability of the country's machine-building industry to manufacture generating equipment, the financial requirements of new projects, and the country's potential production of coal. On the assumption of a sufficiently strong demand for electric power, he concluded that the PRC would have no difficulty in raising its total generating capacity from the approximately 13 million to 14 million kilowatt level of the mid-1960s to 34 million kilowatts by 1975. On the basis of a moderate utilization rate, this generating capacity could yield approximately 160 billion kilowatt-hours of electric power annually.

The country's electric power sector in the late 1960s was considered by informed analysts to be adequate to meet the country's demands, although the breadth of development and the level of technology employed were low by Western standards. The general level of technology in the country's electric power sector was evaluated by one Western industrial analyst who visited the country in the mid-1960s as being equal to that achieved by the United States in the 1920s. The total consumption of electric energy per industrial worker in the mid-1960s was about the level reached in the United States before World War I.

An official source claimed that in the 1960s there were about 200 thermal and hydroelectric powerplants under construction. These projects included the construction of new units and the expansion of existing plants. Information from scattered Chinese sources, reporting the progress of individual construction projects, identified 100 major thermal and hydroelectric plants under construction in the 1960s. These were relatively large projects that had individual designed capacities of over 10,000 kilowatts. The approximately 100 projects not listed in these reports were smaller ones with individual designed capacities of under 10,000 kilowatts; the average size of the smaller plants was assumed to be about 5,000 kilowatts.

Consumption of electric power in the PRC in the 1960s was relatively very low—an annual average of fifty-six kilowatt-hours per person—for a country with such a large population, area, and resources. This low consumption was a reflection of the generally low level of development in industry, transportation, and urban amenities. Manufacturing and construction accounted for about 84 percent of the final consumption of electric energy in the mid-1960s.

The electric energy used by the transportation sector included both urban transportation—streetcars and trolley buses—and railroads, but there was no extensive railroad electrification in the PRC in 1971 (see ch. 18, Trade and Transportation). Consumption of electric energy by urban areas for residential and commercial use was low by Western standards (see ch. 7, Living Conditions). Annual average consumption in the mid-1960s was about twenty kilowatt-hours per urban inhabitant; most of it was used for street lighting and the lighting of public buildings. Home use was negligible or nonexistent in most areas.

Consumption of electric energy in agriculture was the only category of consumption that had shown consistent gains. Most of the increase had gone to networks of irrigation and pumping stations built for purposes of assuring water supply and draining farmland (see ch. 14, Agriculture). Eighty percent of the electric power consumed by the rural areas in the mid-1960s was used for irrigation. The remaining 20 percent was used for such activities as subsidiary production, grain processing, and lighting. The countryside was otherwise essentially unelectrified. Total consumption of electricity by the rural sector in the mid-1960s was reported to be about 3.2 billion kilowatt-hours. Of this amount, about 60 percent was supplied by the major electric networks, and 40 percent, or about 1.3 billion kilowatt-hours, was generated by the rural hydroelectric stations. Small hydroelectric plants of capacities below 500 kilowatts were preferred in the rural areas. These plants were generally operated for from eight to ten hours a day for a period of six to ten years.

Despite the enormous potential of the country's hydroelectric resources, estimated at 536 million kilowatts in the mid-1960s, 3 percent of which had been harnessed at the end of 1968, the nation's plans in 1971 continued to call for maintaining roughly the two-to-one ratio of thermal electric to hydroelectric installed capacity over the next two decades. The distribution of coal and hydroelectric resources in the country is complementary; North China and Northeast China are major coal producers, with large coal reserves and relatively limited waterpower resources; in contrast, South-Central China and areas in Southwest China apparently lack large coal reserves but possess immense hydroelectric resources. Many of the best potential hydroelectric sites are located in Yunnan, western Szechwan, and the eastern part of the Tibet.

Most of the country's electric power facilities are concentrated in three areas—in industrialized Northeast China in the vicinity of An-shan and Fu-shun, in North China around Peking, and in East China in the Shanghai-Nanking area. The principal powerplants as well as the three major transmission networks of the PRC serve these areas. Separate power systems, comprising a number of small plants with rudimentary interconnections, serve the main industrial and urban centers in the densely populated Yangtze River valley, Szechwan Red River Basin, and scattered areas extending from Chekiang Province on the coast to Yunnan Province in Southwest China. In other parts of the country small isolated plants are situated at important towns, mining centers, and manufacturing plants.

Many of the country's electric power facilities were developed by technicians from the Soviet Union, Czechoslovakia, and the German Democratic Republic (East Germany) on a base left by the Japanese. Since the termination of large-scale Soviet and East European assistance after the Sino-Soviet rift, the PRC has demonstrated a capacity to complete unfinished projects and, in a few cases, to design and construct new generating plants. The PRC also has a capability to manufacture small and medium-sized generating equipment modeled largely after Soviet designs.

The most important hydroelectric project in 1971 was the San-Men Gorge plant on the Yellow River in Honan Province. Plans for this station, with a designed capacity of 1.2 million kilowatts, were drawn up by specialists from the Soviet Union, which was to supply eight turbine electric generators, each with a capacity of 150,000 kilowatts, and technicians to install them. In 1960 one generator arrived, but it was not accompanied by the expected technicians. In mid-1971 the San-Men Gorge plant was not expected to be completed for several years.

CONSTRUCTION

A marked upward trend in construction activity was apparent during 1970. Much of the additional construction was concentrated in small factories, mines, and hydroelectric power stations. Most provinces reported the completion of hundreds or thousands of capital construction projects after the beginning of 1970. Most of these projects, however, were small factories, often employing no more than twenty persons, or small power stations with a capacity of a few kilowatts. Analysts estimated that, although the total amount of construction in 1970 had been relatively high, no more than a dozen major construction projects had been completed in that year.

CHAPTER 16

SCIENCE AND TECHNOLOGY

The first principle governing science and technology in the People's Republic of China (PRC) is to make a maximum contribution to the attainment of the nation's political goals. The result has been an emphasis on applied science and research projects that served national aims. Almost all the efforts and achievements of the country's science in mid-1971 were related to practical or technological advance. The specific objectives set for science and technology by the regime include both the promotion of national security and the country's military power and the furthering of economic development.

In 1971 the country was concentrating on research intended to meet the most urgent demands of the nation's defense and industrial establishments, with funds for research efforts apparently divided equally between these two sectors. The sense of urgency that has characterized the formulation and implementation of national policy on science and technology since the formation of the PRC in 1949 continued in 1971.

Reports by Western observers in 1971 indicated that the country's scientific research establishment had survived the turmoil of the Great Proletarian Cultural Revolution relatively intact (see ch. 8, Education, Intellectual Expression, and the Arts; ch. 10, Political Dynamics). Vigorous activity was reported to be underway in nuclear physics, electronics, and medicine. On May 1, 1971, a popular magazine entitled *Scientific Experiment* had begun publication in the PRC with the evident purpose of spreading information both internally and externally about the country's advances in scientific research. At about the same time the regime began to ease access to the country by Western scientists.

In 1971 the PRC had about 500,000 engineers and 100,000 scientists, including some 5,000 who had received training abroad. These Western-, Soviet-, and Japanese-trained scientists and engineers constituted the backbone of Chinese professional, scientific, and technical manpower. They formed much of the core of scientific personnel in the Chinese Academy of Sciences (also known as the Academy of Sciences) and other research organizations, and they had also become a leading force in institutions of higher learning. The senior scientists, many in their sixties and seventies, provided the driving force of the country's scientific enterprises in 1971. A number of the most prominent scientists held twenty or more jobs, and many noted scientists, even at an advanced age, were required to work at least fourteen hours daily.

Many of the foreign-trained scientists were in 1971 still influenced by foreign concepts and methods, but a new generation of scientists trained in the PRC was progressively assuming importance. Visible evidence of the results of the emphasis on self-reliance was appearing; Western scientists reported that almost all of the scientific equipment and supplies they saw in use in the PRC in 1971 had been made there.

Some of the most important advances in science in the PRC in the 1960s and early 1970s had occurred in the field of physics. The country had successfully launched two space satellites in the eighteen months ending in March 1971. An October 1970 detonation of a thermonuclear device was the latest in a series of at least eleven nuclear and thermonuclear devices detonated since 1964 (see ch. 21, The Armed Forces).

The effort in nuclear and space physics has stimulated research in electronics. In 1971 the country was operating a modern radiotelescope for ground-based observation. Among the new products being manufactured as a result of electronics research were digital computers and electron accelerators. Development in the computer field, however, was estimated by informed analysts to be about ten years behind that in the United States and Japan. The researchers had also developed a laser interferometer for measuring distance, and the Institute of Electronics and Optics claimed to have produced a 400,000-power electron microscope. Both instruments appeared comparable to United States models available in the late 1960s.

Important advances were made in chemistry. Emphasis was being placed on producing synthetic ammonia, a vital ingredient of fertilizer, and chemicals needed to build a solid industrial base for the country. The nation had constructed an ammonia plant using sea water to produce chemicals for the manufacture of paper, textiles, and leather goods.

Significant scientific advances were also reported in medicine, both in the laboratory and in the field (see ch. 7, Living Conditions). The synthesis of bovine insulin, a total protein, by PRC scientists was an event of world importance; it meant that the development of low-cost synthetic human insulin to treat diabetes might be possible in the 1970s. Research had also made the PRC self-sufficient in the manufacture of antibiotics and had developed a new antibiotic to treat infections of the human respiratory and urinary tracts.

By mid-1971 several of the PRC's objectives in science and technology appeared to have been substantially attained. The country had made notable advances in nuclear technology; it had exploded uranium-235 and hydrogen devices earlier than Western observers had expected. Planners possessed a more accurate knowledge of the country's resources than had been available to them in 1949. Important improvements had been made in the PRC's ability to make large and sophisticated equipment. Measured in expenditure, fields of science, scientific publications, and reported innovations, a rapid growth in scientific and technological institutions, manpower, and effort had occurred. The country had also achieved significant success in the popularization of science. Technical innovation was readily accepted in industry.

Western observers agreed, however, that all these developments appeared to have their negative aspects. Among the most significant were rigid subordination of science to political dogma and political interference with the work of researchers. These were presumed by Western analysts to have lowered the efficiency of the country's scientific effort below its real potential. The country's science administrators had admitted that coordination between research and production had not always been efficient. The lead time needed in planning the supply of manpower and scientific and technological tasks had not always been adequate. Overspecialization and the uneven quality of scientific and technological personnel had resulted, moreover, from the speed with which scientific projects were sometimes undertaken and from the frequent disruptions of work for political reasons. Faulty national economic planning had adversely affected scientific work and the implementation of its results, particularly in agricultural research (see ch. 14, Agriculture).

An elaborate administrative superstructure had been formed to organize scientific and technological functions. There was a clear chain of command from the Scientific and Technological Commission, the supreme decisionmaking body in the scientific structure under the State Council, to the performing research institute. Within the People's Liberation Army (PLA) the National Defense Scientific and Technological Commission had been established to oversee the militarily oriented science programs (see ch. 21, The Armed Forces). The Academy of Sciences, an organizationally autonomous body, controlled its five academic research departments. Central government ministries, the most important being those of national defense, culture and education, agriculture and forestry, and public health, had jurisdiction over their respective research institutions.

Party control of science had created many obstacles to scientific development: emphasis on the political reliability of experts and students at the expense of orderly advance under expert guidance; emergence of a new set of rituals, such as paying homage to the omnipresent, inspirational value of Mao Tse-tung Thought; emphasis on the virtue of self-criticism and stress on the potential of the "wisdom of the masses", frequent interruptions of training and research to participate in political movements; loss of the long-term benefits implicit in undirected basic research; and inability to seek external assistance in research.

Centralized decisionmaking, however, supported by the power to act, had facilitated several measures: channeling of available scientific and technological knowledge and manpower to priority uses; direction of manpower to specialized training and job assignments; consolidation of independent institutions; sharing of men and equipment among formerly separate research institutions; and establishment of research institutes to serve many enterprises simultaneously so as to make the most economical use of scarce scientific and technological resources. The regime had also made ample funds available for the nation's scientific effort; finance had not been a restraint on high-priority items in science and technology.

China's modern scientific and technological advance had begun well before the formal inauguration of the PRC in 1949. Technological development occurred throughout the country's earlier history (see ch. 3, Historical Setting). Until late medieval times China pioneered in technological inventiveness and systematic observation of nature. It led the world in the development of paper and printing, chemical explosives, mechanical clocks, seismography, and the beginnings of pharmacology and in discoveries in magnetism and in aspects of mathematics. Other technological inventions that came from China were the wheelbarrow, the barrow with a sail (sailing carriage), the crossbow, the kite, deep-drilling techniques, cast iron, the iron-chain suspension bridge, the canal lock, the fore-and-aft rig, the watertight compartment, and the sternpost rudder.

Successive influxes of foreign scientific influence have been experienced since the sixteenth century. Isolationist influences, however, led to resistance to adoption of Western learning and the scientific outlook until the 1850s, when the demonstration of Western military power and technological developments brought grudging acceptance of Western technological institutions by a fearful and resistant Chinese government.

Although the initial criterion of the worth of Western innovations to the Chinese was mainly their military defense value, the spread of scientific influence and concepts led to the establishment of many modern scientific research institutions from about 1900 until the mid-1930s. The second Sino-Japanese war (1937–45) and subsequent civil conflict had a deleterious effect on the development of science and technology. The scientific research institutions established before 1949, however, were significant beginnings for the expanded scientific establishment of the PRC; of thirty-eight Chinese science and technology organizations listed as of 1961 in a United States government study, eighteen had been founded before 1949.

Until the Cultural Revolution of the late 1960s, scientific information had been exchanged between the PRC and other countries, and the PRC had ready access to new scientific and technological advances in the rest of the world. The PRC had conducted an ambitious and impressive program of acquisition of scientific publications from abroad and had undertaken a substantial amount of translation of foreign scientific journals. Publishing in the natural and applied sciences had constituted a major portion of publishing in the PRC through the mid-1960s, when the Cultural Revolution forced approximately 200 Chinese scientific journals to cease publication. After the Cultural Revolution and before 1971 little information about scientific research and development had been available from the PRC, but in mid-1971 there were indications that the information blockade was being relaxed.

SCIENCE AND TECHNOLOGY TO 1949

The country's first sustained encounter with modern science began in the seventeenth century with the use of Jesuit missionaries as technical advisers and assistants. Some served in official capacities, particularly Father Ferdinand Verbiest (1623–88), who aided in the production of Western-style cannons and other armament. After the death of Emperor K'ang Hai in 1722, Western scholarship and ideas lapsed in prominence in China, although they persisted inconspicuously in some form and in some degree.

Western learning had to some extent been introduced into court circles in Peking. About seventy Western books on mathematics, astronomy, engineering, geography, and other subjects were translated and published. Mathematics along Western lines retained an influence but did not supplant Chinese mathematical practices. Books on geography and other subjects declined markedly. The cartographic survey of China made in 1707 by Jesuit fathers and Chinese students and other subsequent efforts are evaluated by historians of the subject as the best maps of China and adjacent territory then existing. These maps were little used, and some were not published in China, although they were widely known in Europe. The Chinese subsequently lost their interest in surveying and preparing maps and their ability to do so. This rejection of Western learning persisted until the pressures of modern Western power caused these subjects to be reintroduced and relearned.

The effort to introduce elements of Western culture, including science, had been barely tolerated, but Western knowledge of weaponry was utilized. One factor in the Chinese resistance to the adoption of Western learning and the scientific outlook was the Chinese sense of cultural preeminence. The traditional Chinese view was that science, like technology, was utilitarian but not an essential part of culture. This assessment gradually altered, but the opinion that science was associated with the foreigner and his offenses contributed to its unacceptability.

The second wave of Western scientific influence in China began about 1800. It was missionary in origin, began in South China, and was affected by considerations of military defense. It may be dated approximately from the introduction of smallpox vaccination in Canton in 1805 by a British doctor. The first Protestant missionary arrived in Canton in 1807, and during the following decades schools, clinics, and hospitals were founded as public service additions to evangelism. In later years medical education and the practice of modern medicine became the leading field of modern science in China and, therefore, a major route for professional advancement.

The Chinese reaction to Western military power, as demonstrated in the First Opium War and the Second Opium War, was the Self-Strengthening Movement, which concentrated on military technology. Some Chinese officials publicly championed the adoption of modern technology. The series of civil wars in the nineteenth century, including the Taiping Rebellion, were quelled by Western arms and with the help of Western army officers (see ch. 3, Historical Setting).

Incorporation of modern technological institutions into the Chinese government establishment was spurred by a clear demonstration of the need to adopt the technology of modern military and industrial power. Western forces took Peking in 1860 and burned the Summer Palace. When the Manchu emperor and the court returned to Peking, a strong incentive for the establishment of military academies, arsenals, and shipbuilding and other facilities had been created. Training schools that were adjuncts to these organizations started to translate and publish Western works on technology and science. Other schools were established, including a foreign-language school in Peking to train interpreters. These schools employed foreign teachers, who taught such subjects as geography, biology, mathematics, chemistry, physics, anatomy, and mechanics. These innovations heightened a continuing controversy regarding the consequences of exposure to foreign learning. Advocates of Western ideas, methods, and devices supported their attitude with the phrase "Chinese learning for the essentials; Western learning for utilitarian things."

In the second half of the nineteenth century military defense was the major motivation and the primary channel for the introduction of science into the country. China's first scientific journal was the *Chinese Scientific and Industrial Magazine*, founded in 1876 and published at the Kiangnan Arsenal, which had been established in Shanghai ten years earlier. In the span of about thirty-five years the arsenal translated and published almost 200 books, primarily basic and applied scientific works in English but also important German and French publications of the period.

Japan's defeat of China in the Sino-Japanese War of 1894–95 shocked the Chinese, who realized that changes beyond the acquisition of Western military equipment might be necessary. In 1898 the Chinese began, through a group of Chinese reformist advisers to the Manchu emperor, a period that came to be known as the Hundred Days of reform. From June to September 1898 the court issued a flood of reform edicts concerning the founding of agricultural schools, use of scientific methods in agriculture, opening of mines, building of railroads, and a crisis program to translate all books of Western knowledge. The wars of the nineteenth century had demonstrated the superiority of foreign weapons and gunboats, which made the Chinese ruler aware of the need for knowledge of modern sciences and technology to cope with Japan and the West. The crushing of the bitterly xenophobic Boxer Rebellion in 1900 by a combination of Western and Japanese military contingents further demonstrated the country's inadequacies (see ch. 3, Historical Setting).

Japanese educational institutions played a notable role in training Chinese students in modern subjects from the last years of the nineteenth century through the early years of the Republic of China. Chinese students had begun taking advanced training in Japan in 1896 in the aftermath of Japan's demonstration of military power. Peking National University—usually abbreviated as Peita, from its Chinese name—was founded in 1898 and was deliberately modeled after Japan's Tokyo Imperial University; the first name of the Chinese institution was also the Imperial University. Japan's successful acceptance of Western scientific technology, demonstrated in national economic and military strength, served as one of the sharpest stimulations to Chinese modernizers. The Research Institute of Oceanology at Amoy was an example of Japanese scientific influence. Japanese marine scientists and technical specialists were particularly interested in the Amoy Marine Biological Laboratory.

Chiaot'ung Polytechnic University, which became an important center for training engineering and technical personnel, was founded in Shanghai in 1896. Twelve years later Tung-ch'i Polytechnic University was established in the same city.

The imperial Manchu regime experimented with modernization during its waning years at the beginning of the twentieth century, assimilating Western science and technology into the vast complex of Chinese traditions. In the initial stages of modernization, Japanese influence predominated. There were 500 Chinese students in Japan in 1902. By 1904, the first year of the Russo-Japanese war, Chinese students were going to Japan at the rate of 100 a month. This number grew to over 750 a month during the next year, as Japan defeated

Russia, and reached a total of 13,000 students in 1906. In the subsequent years of the first decade of the twentieth century, the flow averaged about 15,000 students annually. The peak year was 1908, when 17,000 Chinese students were reported to be studying in Japan. Geographic proximity allowing low travel costs together with low living expenses encouraged this exchange. Of the 356 foreign teachers in Chinese schools in 1909, 311 were Japanese.

By 1910 there were 300 Chinese students in Europe, 500 in the United States, and 30,000 in Japan. In 1908 the United States Congress had authorized the return to China of the surplus from the Boxer Indemnity Fund, consisting of the excess of indemnity payments not allocated to claimants and amounting to US$10 million. The Chinese government decided to use this fund for the purpose of preparing and sending students to pursue higher education in the United States. The return of the Boxer Indemnity Fund to China for educational purposes was soon imitated by other Western powers, including Great Britain, France, Russia, Belgium, Holland, and Italy, and by Japan. Most of the Boxer Indemnity Fund was allocated for subsidies to science teachers in well-established Chinese institutions of higher learning or for scholarships enabling Chinese students to pursue advanced studies in the respective countries. In 1911 Tsinghua College was founded in Peking to prepare Chinese students for advanced work at educational institutions in the United States.

Modernization proceeded during the early years of the Republic of China. The Science Society of China, the first Chinese professional scientific association, was founded in 1914 by Chinese students studying in the United States and was dedicated to the "diffusion of the scientific spirit and knowledge among the Chinese people." In several respects the Science Society of China typified the commitment of an increasing number of Chinese scholars to the country's modernization through science. The society's journal, patterned after the journal of the American Association for the Advancement of Science, began publication in 1915. Membership of the society included the leading scientists and engineers of the time, although membership did not exceed 1,500 until the post-World War II period.

In 1922 the society established in Nanking a biological laboratory, which became the most important one in China and a research center for many Chinese botanists and zoologists. The society pioneered in the development and popularization of science through an active and diverse publication program, science information and library services, a biological laboratory, the improvement of science teaching, public lectures, and participation in international scientific meetings.

The National Geological Survey was the leading and earliest of the scientific research institutions established by the government of the

Republic of China. Founded in 1912 and formally inaugurated in 1916, the survey is credited with introducing systematic geology to the country. The survey undertook extensive geological mapping, petroleum exploration, soil surveys, and industrial research on coal and its byproducts. Associated with the survey was the Geological Society of China, founded in 1922, which during the subsequent two decades published several thousand monographs and articles and many books.

Harbin Polytechnic University was founded in 1920; its major task was the training of railroad technicians. In 1925 Tsinghua College, an important center for Sino-American scientific cooperation, was raised to university status.

The establishment of the Nationalist government at Nanking in 1927 was soon followed by the establishment of scientific institutions. The Academia Sinica was founded in 1928 and included a dozen institutes in major fields. The academy was the highest governmental research organization in the country; it conducted research and advised the government on scientific questions. Many research and training institutions were founded in rapid succession. Despite their limited resources and personnel, much of their work was of high quality, and they were very productive. The Fan Memorial Biological Institute, founded in Peking (known as Peiping from 1928 to 1948), in 1928 with Boxer Indemnity Fund financing, was one of the most well known research institutes in China before World War II. In 1929 the Peiping Research Laboratory, which ultimately had institutes in physics, biology, physiology, pharmacy, and other fields, was founded.

Until the 1930s almost all Chinese who obtained advanced scientific degrees devoted their professional careers to education and administration. By 1930 enough trained persons began to return from universities abroad to provide a large enough supply of modern scientists so that scientific research began to emerge as part of Chinese intellectual life. The Academia Sinica, the Peiping Research Academy (later, the Peking Research Academy), and some of the leading universities provided support and facilities to perform basic research and published the results. The three main centers of scientific research were Peking, Nanking, and Shanghai, and most institutions had their headquarters in these cities. Nanking, as the capital of Nationalist China, tended to be the site of organizations that had the closest ties with the government. Various scientific societies provided means for publication and were important avenues of communications and stimulation for scientific and related professional work. The applied sciences of medicine and engineering accounted for a substantial portion of the technical literature. Chemistry, principally biochemical studies, was the leading field of research in the basic sciences. Several chemists, physicists, and mathematicians published regularly in both Chinese and foreign journals.

The number of learned organizations established from 1911 to 1936 was 270; forty-six were devoted to the natural sciences, and sixty-six were in the fields of applied sciences. The establishment of these organizations marked the beginning of the professionalization of science. In the 1930s there were biological research laboratories and zoological collections or herbaria in twenty-three universities or colleges. Entomology laboratories, agricultural experiment stations, marine and terrestrial flora and fauna observation and experiment stations, and many other facilities were created.

From 1937 until the end of World War II in 1945, the disruptions of war drove a large number of the country's educators, scientists, technical specialists, and students into inland areas. They established new institutions, some of which subsequently became permanent, either as independent entities or as branches of central organizations that moved back to Peking or Shanghai from their wartime bases. Some institutions in Nanking and Hankow took much of their equipment directly up the Yangtze River by boat. The Academia Sinica transported its Sinological library to a village on the Yangtze River in Szechwan Province. The faculties of Peita, Tsinghua, and Nanking universities cooperated to establish and operate the Southwest Associated University at K'un-ming. Five missionary institutions used the campus of West China Union University at Ch'eng-tu.

The Nationalist government considered science as a tool with which to develop the country's resources and national strength. A World War II directive from Generalissimo Chiang Kai-shek stated:

> To be able to shoulder the heavy responsibility of reviving and completing our revolution, we must have at all costs a clear idea of the content and meaning of science; we must propagate the spirit of science and we must utilize the methods of science; so that one man will be as efficient as ten, and in one day ten days' work will be done.

The number of scientists fully employed at research institutions in the 1930s and 1940s was extremely small compared to the number of institutions. By 1949 there were more than 170 research centers and programs: thirty-two in engineering and technology, 112 in agriculture, seventeen in geology, and eleven in medicine and pharmacology. In many cases the research institutes were a supplementary professional activity for scientists whose principal task was teaching, administration, or some applied professional task. The first Chinese contributions to modern basic science were made in the 1930s by about forty scientists, most of whom had undertaken graduate training in Western countries after the completion of their undergraduate education in China and who were working in the fields of mathematics and chemistry.

At the time of the formation of the PRC in October 1949, there were in science and technology an estimated 52,000 persons holding a college or equivalent degree. About 10,000 were in the natural sciences; about 25,000, in engineering; about 10,000, in agriculture; and about 7,000, in medicine.

SCIENCE AND TECHNOLOGY FROM 1949 TO 1965

Efforts to bring scientists within the network of mass organizations of the Chinese Communist Party (CCP) were begun several months before the PRC was formally proclaimed on October 1, 1949. Before that date, over 90 percent of the country's professors and scientists had been approached and urged to remain at their posts. In July 1949 the CCP made plans for a national conference of the country's scientists, and the delegates to the first plenary session of the Chinese People's Political Consultative Conference (CPPCC), held in Peking from September 21 to 30, 1949, included fifteen from the Preparatory Committee of the First All-China Natural Science Conference.

In the view of the CCP the first principle of Chinese science is its utilitarian nature. When the CPPCC adopted its Common Program on September 29, 1949, Article 43, Chapter 4 stipulated: "Efforts should be made to develop the natural sciences in order to serve construction of industry, agriculture, and national defense. Rewards should be given for scientific discoveries and inventions. Dissemination of scientific knowledge should be greatly strengthened." Article 42 of the Common Program proclaimed "love of science" to be a basic virtue, as one of the "five loves" to be taught to all students, starting with primary school.

Immediately after the establishment of the new regime, Ch'en Pota, vice director of the CCP Propaganda Department, consulted S.I. Vavilov, president of the Soviet Academy of Sciences, on the role and organization of the Soviet Academy of Sciences, the Russian system for planning scientific research, and the link between science and technology. After Ch'en's return to China, the government ordered the establishment of the Chinese Academy of Sciences directly under the jurisdiction of the central government "to direct and promote the development of science in China."

On November 1, 1949, the Chinese Academy of Sciences was formed through the reorganization of the twelve institutes of the Academia Sinica, located in Peking, Nanking, and Shanghai, and the eight institutes of the Peking (formerly Peiping) Research Academy. The purpose of the reorganization was to concentrate the available scientific manpower in institutions that could best serve the requirements of national development in industry, agriculture, and defense.

Kuo Mo-jo, a literary and cultural figure and one of the four vice premiers in the new administration, was made president of the Chinese Academy of Sciences upon its establishment and was still holding this position in mid-1971. He went to the Soviet Union in

November 1949 for further information and discussions with leading Soviet science administrators concerning scientific organization. Upon his return, Vavilov's book *Thirty Years of Soviet Science* was translated into Chinese to serve as a guide for the organization of natural sciences in the PRC.

The initial tasks of the Academy of Sciences were to reorganize and consolidate the research institutes of the country; to provide for the continuation of research activities and plans and to relate them to requirements in industry, education, and national construction; to compile a national roster of scientists and determine assignments for them on a planned basis; to develop plans to increase the country's scientific manpower in cooperation with the universities, through training programs, foreign education, and recruitment of Chinese scientists abroad; and to educate research workers in Marxism-Leninism.

Research institutes in the physical sciences were organized or maintained for research in geology or geophysics, earth sciences, modern physics, applied physics, physical chemistry, organic chemistry, physiology, biophysics, experimental biology, marine biology, botany, paleontology, and archaeology. In addition to these research institutes, educational institutions and government departments under which individual productive enterprises were operated had their research institutes.

One of the functions of the Academy of Sciences was to coordinate the work of the educational institutions and other research organizations with the academy's own work. This coordination could involve joint appointments, research subsidies, allocation of research materials, and training of researchers. The main purpose was to establish communications between the specialists and educators, on the one hand, and those engaged in practical and technological work, on the other. The academy was to provide the facilities and other means for cooperation in research.

Coordination of the work of researchers in different sectors of the economy was to be matched by the careful integration of production and research goals. In regard to research goals, express emphasis was given to natural science. National policy was to expand and enrich the existing research institutions and their work on the basis of the requirements of the economy, integrating research workers that were previously unknown to each other and research projects that were previously unconnected.

The first step was to establish a roster of Chinese scientists, undertaken by the Academy of Sciences in December 1949 on the basis of the membership list of the Academia Sinica and other scientific organizations and societies. The result was a roster of 233 persons, ranked in the order of their accomplishments in their respective fields. In March 1950 the academy conducted a second survey, which established a roster of 865 persons. Of this group, 160 were appointed as specialist consultants to the academy.

The All-China Natural Science Conference held in August 1950 in Peking, with about 470 participants, formally established the All-China Federation of Natural Science Societies with "the aim of rallying all the scientific societies and organizing all the scientific workers so as to carry out scientific research work for the improvement of production technique and thus to promote New Democratic economic and cultural construction." Also established was the All-China Association for the Dissemination of Scientific and Technical Knowledge, designed to assist the government in popularizing science.

Surveys undertaken during 1950 by the All-China Federation of Natural Science Societies and by the Academy of Sciences were designed to determine the magnitude of scientific manpower available for research and development. Of the 865 natural scientists on the March 1950 roster, 174 persons, or 20 percent, were not then in the PRC. One of the country's major tasks, therefore, was to increase its available scientific manpower by accelerating training and by inducing the return of Chinese scientists from abroad. Many letters and telegrams were sent to Chinese scientists residing abroad, urging them to return to serve the country. These communications were a combination of persuasion and implied threats. Concurrent with the dispatch of these messages, a group of ten students were sent abroad for advanced work. These students were all young, promising scientific workers recommended by specific consultants of the Academy of Sciences.

The Academy of Sciences was instructed by the government in March 1951 to make a systematic determination of the requirements of the production sectors of the economy and to adjust scientific research to the indicated specific objectives. The entire national scientific effort was to be planned to satisfy these production needs. The academy was given the responsibility for convening conferences of the nation's science workers, of delineating the research tasks of the science community, and of demanding the cooperation of all concerned government departments.

The setting of goals for Chinese science was also to be determined partly by requirements in the various fields as indicated by the professional societies. Coordination of research and development was to be implemented in two areas: coordination of means with ends and coordination of the separate research and development efforts of many individual institutions. The direction of the national research effort was, therefore, determined by the production tasks assigned by national economic policy, and the activities of all science workers were fitted to the ends selected by the government.

The First Five Year Plan for development of the national economy covered the years from 1953 to 1957; it included only brief objectives for the Academy of Sciences. The plan provided few details on scientific or technological advancement but did acknowledge the need for scientific research:

> Efforts must be made in this 5-year period to lay a firmer foundation for scientific research, to improve the work of rallying together all scientists, to establish closer contacts between scientific research organizations and related departments, to improve scientific research and experimental work, to constantly sum up new scientific and technical experience, to master the latest achievements in scientific service and techniques, to improve step by step the investigation and study of the national conditions of our country, its natural resources and social conditions, and to raise stage by stage the level of research work in the fundamental branches of the natural sciences and social sciences.

In addition to these general tasks, the plan specified eleven important fields that should constitute the principal work of the Academy of Sciences: peaceful use of atomic energy; construction of new iron and steel facilities; petroleum production; seismology; multipurpose exploitation of river valleys; tropical plants in South China; natural and economic divisions of the PRC; antibiotics; polymers; theoretical problems relating to national construction during the transition to socialism; and contemporary Chinese philosophy and history.

In an effort to consolidate the expanding facilities of the Academy of Sciences, four departments of the academy were established in a preparatory status in April 1954. After the adoption on September 20 of the 1954 State Constitution, the Academy of Sciences was nominally made an independent organization; it was no longer under the jurisdiction of the newly formed State Council, as it had been under the counterpart predecessor organization. The academy, however, did receive guidance from the State Council.

Mutual scientific and technical cooperation between the PRC and the Soviet Union formally dates from an agreement of October 12, 1954; the agreement specified that both parties would share technical specifications and would exchange information and specialists. Under the terms of the agreement, it could be extended after fifteen years by mutual consent. Scientific and technical experience and achievements were to be exchanged without compensation through sharing licenses, various documents, and drawings of projects. Payment was to be made only for the expenses of preparing copies of the documents. To implement the agreement, the Soviet-Chinese Scientific and Technical Cooperation Commission, composed of nine representatives from each country, was created. The semiannual meetings of the commission alternated between Peking and Moscow; the first meeting was held in Peking in April 1955.

Sino-Soviet scientific cooperation entered a new phase in April 1955 when an agreement was concluded in Moscow for the construction in mainland China of an atomic reactor with a 7,000- to 10,000-kilowatt capacity and a cyclotron capable of accelerating alpha particles to 25 million electron volts and the construction of several betatrons (accelerators in which electrons are propelled by the inductive action of a rapidly varying magnetic field). In June 1955 a delegation sent by the Soviet Academy of Sciences met members of the Chinese Academy of Sciences to discuss cooperation between the two institutions. Six points of cooperation were decided: cooperative exchange of research by members of the two academies; exchange of material between the two academies; reciprocal invitations to conferences sponsored by the two organizations; short-term lecture and study tours by academy members in the two countries; cooperative training programs in research for students sent from one academy to the other; and cooperative editing and publication of scientific works.

In June 1955 the four departments of the Academy of Sciences, organized on a preparatory basis fifteen months earlier, were given permanent status, and the department of biology and earth sciences was separated into two independent departments, raising the total to five. The departments after this change were the departments of physics, chemistry, and mathematics; biology; earth sciences; technical sciences; and philosophy and social sciences. The departments were expanded by the appointment of 233 new members. The academy's research institutes were strengthened; its control over scientific personnel was increased; and it was empowered to encourage science through a system of national science awards.

The position of the social scientists within the Academy of Sciences has differed markedly from that of the natural scientists. According to the latest data available in mid-1971, of the more than 100 research institutes of the Academy of Sciences, only thirteen came under the department of philosophy and social sciences, and only four of these specialized in the social sciences. Among the sixty-three members of the academic department committees, eight were in the fields of the social sciences or humanities. Within the department of philosophy and social sciences, most of the department members were Marxist-Leninist economists or philosophers who had been connected with the CCP since the 1930s; many held important offices in the government or in the Party.

The reorganization of the academy in June 1955 had been intended, among other goals, to improve coordination of research and development policy with economic and political policies because this had been found to be difficult to achieve. The president of the Academy of Sciences commented in July 1955 on the difficulties of coordination:

Our liaison with the government ministries has been very deficient; we do not know clearly the requirements of the government agencies that affect scientific research. We do not have a clear knowledge of the present conditions and development of certain branches of modern science or the potential of China's science workers. ... We have not been able to propose on the basis of the requirements of national construction the specific fields of science that would be explored and the specific research institutions that should be established.

On September 15, 1955, the Academy of Sciences approved a directive for formulating a fifteen-year, long-term development plan for the academy. The fifteen-year period was intended to coincide with the term of the three five-year plan periods from 1953 to 1967 as projected in 1955. The science planning, however, was not begun until 1955, and it could therefore cover only the period from 1956 to 1967. The long-term development plan for the academy was consequently known as the Twelve-Year Science Plan (1956–67).

In January 1956 the compelling scientific needs of national economic construction led the Central Committee of the CCP to call for "a march on science." In March 1956 the presidium of the Soviet Academy of Sciences, at the invitation of the PRC, sent a delegation of eighteen top scientists to aid in the preparation of the Twelve-Year Science Plan. On March 14, 1956, the Scientific Planning Commission was formed under the State Council for the purpose of "strengthening the state's guidance of scientific planning work." In its initial stages, under the chairmanship of Marshal Ch'en I, the commission was intended as a temporary organization to prepare a comprehensive plan for scientific research and development.

Two months after the creation of the Scientific Planning Commission, the State Technological Commission was established. Its functions were not made public, but they were believed by Western analysts to have been similar to those of the Scientific Planning Commission but concerned with technological fields, including the design and installation of pilot plants and machine prototypes.

In the course of seven months 200 Chinese scientists, assisted for two months by Soviet scientists, prepared the draft Twelve-Year Science Plan, which was presented to the first session of the Eighth Party Congress of the CCP, held from September 15 to 27, 1956, and was endorsed by the Party congress on the last day of the session. The draft plan was then sent to the Soviet Union, where it was reviewed by Soviet scientists.

The Scientific Planning Commission, at its inception, was more concerned with coordination than with administration. Of the four vice chairmen of the commission, two were scientists and two were CCP officials. The commission, as first organized, had thirty-five members, of which eighteen were scientists.

In early 1957, with the regime's consent to hold free public discussion of public issues during the short-lived Hundred Flowers Campaign, the scientists responded by advocating abolition of the Scientific Planning Commission and restoration of the primacy of the Academy of Sciences (see ch. 8, Education, Intellectual Expression, and the Arts).

In mid-May 1957 the Scientific Planning Commission was changed from a temporary to a permanent agency and made into a standing commission of the State Council; its membership was increased from thirty-five to 106 to accommodate more scientists. Marshal Nieh Jung-chen was named chairman. The commission replaced the Academy of Sciences as the "national organ for policy making" in scientific matters. The commission's assigned functions were: supervising the execution of the Twelve-Year Science Plan, particularly major research projects; preparing long-term and annual plans of scientific research; coordinating the work of the various sectors of scientific research; establishing working standards and pay scales for scientists; controlling the use of research funds for major projects; conducting international cooperation in scientific research; and planning and controlling the training, assignment, and employment of senior specialists, including the recruitment of Overseas Chinese scientists and their employment after their return.

On June 9, 1957, a group of scientists published a proposal pleading for more favorable conditions for scientific study and research. They proposed that scientists be freed from political and administrative duties in order to devote more time to study and research, that they be excused from extraneous activities such as entertaining foreign visitors, that they be provided with more assistants and adequate equipment, and that each be permitted to pursue the line of study in which he was most proficient. The scientists emphasized the importance of encouraging and fostering young talent and proposed that, instead of giving major consideration to political qualifications in the selection and promotion of students, equal weight should be given to academic achievement and that the scientists should have more influence in such matters.

In the "anti-rightist" campaign after the brief period of free criticism in 1957, this proposal of the scientists was labeled the anti-Party, anti-socialist scientific program. The attack on the program was led by the president of the Academy of Sciences. Speaking to the fourth session of the first National People's Congress, held from June 26 to July 15, 1957, he described the proposal as "a wanton attack on the Party and the government and an attempt to seize the leadership for scientific work and to lure scientists away from the socialist road."

The Twelve-Year Science Plan was formally approved at the June–July 1957 session of the People's Congress. The guiding principle of the plan was that:

> In accordance with the requirements of national construction, to introduce the world's most advanced scientific achievements to China and to build up the weakest links of China's scientific branches, so that by the end of 1967 ... China can catch up approximately with the world's advanced levels.

The plan contained specific provisions for pursuit of the most urgently needed fields of science. It also attempted to project a rate of growth for various scientific branches, to determine geographic distribution of research organizations, and to clarify the division of labor between the Academy of Sciences, production enterprises, and the institutions of higher learning. More than 580 problems relating to science and technology had been selected for the plan and then assigned under fifty-seven aspects of research. These in turn had been grouped under twelve major categories: peaceful uses of atomic energy; new electronics techniques; jet propulsion; automation in production and precision equipment; surveying and prospecting for petroleum and other scarce materials; exploration of mineral resources; metallurgical studies; development of fuels and heavy machines; technical problems associated with exploitation of the Yellow and Yangtze rivers; agriculture, with emphasis on mechanization, electrification, and use of chemicals; prevalent diseases; and basic natural sciences. Every research organization adopted its own twelve-year plan based on the list of crucial assignments.

The extent of Sino-Soviet scientific cooperation up to 1957 had been considerable, but the emphasis on this relationship was increased after the formal adoption of the Twelve-Year Science Plan. By 1957 the Soviet Union had given the PRC 751 blueprints for industrial enterprises, transportation plans, and cultural projects; 2,200 sets of technical documents covering the production and assembly of equipment; and 688 memorandums on productive technology.

In late October 1957 the president of the Academy of Sciences headed the largest group of high-level scientific talent that mainland China had ever sent abroad at one time. It was a component of the Chinese delegation led by Mao Tse-tung that went to Moscow ostensibly to participate in the celebrations commemorating the fortieth anniversary of the Russian revolution of November 7, 1917. The Chinese scientists conferred about their country's Twelve-Year Science Plan with Soviet scientists and negotiated for increased scientific and technical cooperation. After Mao Tse-tung returned to Peking in November, the president of the Chinese Academy of Sciences and the Chinese scientists remained in Moscow for extended negotiations. The subdelegation of Chinese scientists requested Soviet cooperation on 100 of the 582 research projects outlined in the Twelve-Year Science Plan. On December 11, 1957, the president of the Chinese Academy of Sciences signed a protocol for cooperation between the Chinese and Soviet academies of sciences during the 1958 –62 period as well as a 1958 plan for cooperation.

On January 18, 1958, the president of the Academy of Sciences signed an agreement of joint research on important problems of science and technology and assistance from the Soviet Union to mainland China in this work. The two countries were to cooperate on 122 major scientific and engineering problems during the 1958–62 period.

474

The formal approval of the Twelve-Year Science Plan, the agreements with the Soviet Union covering assistance for the science plan, and the inauguration by the government in February 1958 of the Great Leap Forward quickened the tempo of research and development activity (see ch. 3, Historical Setting). In the first quarter of 1958 the Scientific Planning Commission decided to establish regional scientific supply centers in Tientsin, Peking, Shenyang (an alternate name for Mukden), Shanghai, Canton, and Wu-han (see Glossary).

In September 1958 the All-China Federation of Natural Science Societies and the All-China Association for the Dissemination of Scientific and Technical Knowledge were combined into a single body named the China Association for Science and Technology under the control of the Scientific Planning Commission. The effort to popularize and disseminate results of research and development and to exert control over scientists and technical workers on behalf of the CCP was thereby unified. One week later the University of Science and Technology was established in Peking under the joint supervision of the Academy of Sciences and the Ministry of Education (subsequently absorbed into the Ministry of Culture and Education). The president of the Academy of Sciences was appointed president of the university. The first group of 1,500 students was admitted in September 1958. This university was intended to educate the country's best scientific talent, which would be engaged in the study of such advanced subjects as atomic energy and jet propulsion. The following year, a branch of the university was established in Shanghai with 300 entrants.

In 1958 the PRC independent nuclear development program was also launched. Western analysts reasoned that the graduates of the University of Science and Technology were probably prepared and trained for eventual work in that program. They noted, however, that the five-year term of study at the University of Science and Technology would not permit the first students to graduate until 1963 and concluded that it was highly unlikely that these first graduates had played a significant role in the nuclear explosions in 1964 and 1965 but might have contributed to subsequent nuclear development.

The university had a full-time teaching staff and, in addition, was able to invite scientists of the research institutes of the Academy of Sciences to lecture. Students were expected to learn contemporary scientific theories essential for scientific research, to understand modern techniques for scientific experimentation, and to design engineering projects. A year before graduation students were required to participate in research at the relevant units of the Academy of Sciences.

In the fourth quarter of 1958 the country's political planners and policymakers took firmer control of the direction and administration of scientific policy and operations. The Scientific Planning Commission was replaced by a more powerful body, under the State Council, with jurisdiction over both scientific and technological activities. The Scientific and Technological Commission was established on November 23, 1958, through a merger of the Scientific Planning Commission and the State Technological Commission. Marshal Nieh Jung-chen retained the chairmanship, but all scientists, including the president of the Academy of Sciences, were dropped from membership. All six of the vice chairmen and twelve members of the commission in the 1960s were members of the CCP; the commission became, in fact, an arm of the CCP.

The functions of the Scientific and Technological Commission with respect to science are similar to those of the Scientific Planning Commission, but its jurisdiction is wider. It supervises not only research activities but also the associations of scientists and the organizations disseminating scientific information. As of mid-1971 the Scientific and Technological Commission, a ministerial-level agency, remained the supreme decisionmaking organ in science in the PRC.

During the time that the Great Leap lasted, a dichotomy of approaches to research and development existed. The orthodox and orderly approach to research and development was continued and elaborated during this period. Simultaneously, however, a wide-ranging "drive for science" to expand scientific and technological activity by multiplying the number of projects and institutions engaged in research and development was also adopted as a parallel approach. This second approach was a concerted drive to begin a technological revolution by mass activity.

In contrast to the sustained advance of research and development in the conventional manner, the mass-movement approach attempted to increase the number of projects and persons in scientific activity under several slogans. One slogan called for combining the modern scientific approach with the use of traditional methods of production and with traditional ways of solving problems. Both the central and local governments were exhorted to increase their research and development efforts; this was equivalent to calling for a multiplication of the levels at which scientific and technological institutions and personnel were to be employed. Another slogan urged coordination of teaching with production and research; although this particular slogan was in accord with the conventional approach, actual application proved to be cruder than could be inferred from the stated general principle.

The conventional approach was exemplified by a statement in the May 1959 issue of the official journal of the Academy of Sciences that the new science drive of the Great Leap was to be concentrated in fields that were important because of their pivotal significance in certain economic tasks or because they constituted basic research important to the advancement of all other sciences or could act as leading elements in generating important advances in a number of scientific and technological areas. This attitude had been stated by the president of the Academy of Sciences in a speech on April 7, 1959, in which he called attention to the importance of maintaining quality in research, despite the drive for quantity in research and the demand for important contributions by scientists to the massive industrialization effort.

Overambition and inadequate preparation of persons not trained in the basic scientific disciplines diverted the interests and energies of scientists and diluted the results of research. Because the political leadership of the CCP controlled the mass movement in research and development, the fanatic enthusiasm of these dedicated CCP members, stimulated by the heedless adulation and obedience of the individuals constituting the body of the CCP, destroyed the sense of proportion and of perspective in the development of science and technology. The number of research institutes multiplied, as did the number of local branches of the Academy of Sciences and of the China Association for Science and Technology. During this period agreements for scientific cooperation were signed between the PRC and Czechoslovakia, Romania, Poland, and Hungary.

The intensity of Sino-Soviet scientific cooperation began to decline in the fourth quarter of 1959. On June 1, 1959, the president of the Chinese Academy of Sciences signed with his Soviet counterpart a one-year supplementary agreement covering the 1959 portion of the 1958–64 Sino-Soviet master agreement on scientific cooperation. Through mid-1971 no information regarding any subsequent subsidiary agreements was publicly available. On December 1, 1959, a three-year survey of the Amur river basin, in which 300 Chinese scientific workers and 130 Soviet scientists from the Soviet Academy of Sciences had taken part, was completed.

The Great Leap proved by 1960 to be largely an illusion. During the Great Leap the government established hundreds of research institutes throughout the country and sponsored thousands of research projects. Because standards were necessarily lowered, research became chaotic. In mid-1960 the president of the Academy of Sciences told a conference of academy workers that the Scientific and Technological Commission was engaged in formulating new three-year and five-year plans.

By 1960 the country had begun to accumulate a supply of scientific manpower that had benefited from education abroad after 1949; over 1,300 science students had returned from the Soviet Union and other socialist countries after completing from two to five years of study. By February 1960 the Soviet Union had sent to the PRC 10,000 sets of specifications, including more than 1,250 designs for capital construction, about 4,000 blueprints for the manufacture of machinery and equipment, and more than 4,000 sets of technological and departmental specifications. In return the Soviet Union had received from the PRC 800 sets of scientific and technical specifications, including 215 sets of blueprints for the manufacture of machinery and other equipment, and more than 500 sets of technological and departmental specifications.

According to an editorial published in 1963 in the *People's Daily* newspaper, the Soviet authorities in July 1960 "suddenly and unilaterally decided to withdraw all their experts, totaling 1,390, who assisted China in its work, tore up 343 contracts and supplementary agreements concerning the experts, and annulled 257 items of scientific and technical cooperation. After that they heavily slashed the supply of whole sets of equipment and crucial parts of installations." According to information published in a United States periodical, when the Soviet experts left they took with them their blueprints and everything movable. The number of PRC students receiving advanced training in the Soviet Union also declined substantially.

The ninth session of the CCP Eighth Central Committee, meeting in Peking from January 14 to 18, 1961, suspended the Great Leap and established guidelines for adjustment, consolidation, and retrenchment. Science and technology were included among the affected sectors. Increased emphasis was placed on adjusting scientific effort to realities and on improving its quality. To concentrate scientific manpower in those branches of the Academy of Sciences that had better facilities, many provincial and local branches of the academy were merged, and several were abolished. Research projects were also adjusted in the interests of efficiency.

The withdrawal of Soviet scientific and technical assistance and the formal suspension of the Great Leap shortly thereafter induced a reorientation of national policy regarding science and technology. In previous years, particularly during the Great Leap, research and development programs had been simultaneously initiated in many fields, some for practical reasons and some for considerations of prestige. During the 1960–65 period scientific efforts were focused on a few strategic fields, particularly agriculture and nuclear development. Other less urgent fields were temporarily abandoned.

This reorientation of science and technology conserved the limited supply of trained scientific personnel. After the departure of Soviet scientific and technical personnel, all responsibility for science and technology had to be delegated to the country's own scientists and technicians. Because they were ordered to perform many tasks previously handled by the Soviet personnel, many scientists were shifted from their original projects, and much less research and development could be undertaken. The retrenchment in the scope of research and development projects was largely caused by the shortage of trained personnel; finance was not a major factor.

During this period particular interest was taken by the regime in the quality of research and development. In April 1962 PRC Premier Chou En-lai spoke of the necessity for the government to "adjust cultural, educational, scientific research, and public health undertakings and improve the quality of work in these areas."

The PRC at that time increased its efforts to collect scientific and technological information from abroad. The acquisition of foreign information frequently was carried out by the exchange of journals between domestic and foreign learned societies and libraries. The PRC made the most skillful use of its limited number of scientific journals to effect as large a number of exchanges as possible. On many occasions the PRC sent the same journal to the different societies of a foreign country and, in return, received a vast assortment of scientific publications.

The reoriented research and development program emphasized the technological transformation of agriculture as an economic objective and the development of an independent nuclear deterrent as a political and military objective (see ch. 14, Agriculture; ch. 21, The Armed Forces). In an exhortation to the workers in October 1962, PRC Premier Chou En-lai stated:

> We must grasp the technological transformation of agriculture as the central link and mobilize and organize all forces in every quarter and department for the task. There are ample opportunities in this respect for scientists. They should go all out and closely integrate scientific research with the technical transformation of agriculture.

On September 27, 1963, the Peking Science Center for the World Federation of Scientific Workers was formally inaugurated. The PRC officially declared that "the Center will devote itself to the promotion of international scientific interchanges for the advancement of science in Asia, Africa, and Latin America." An editorial in the *People's Daily* on this occasion urged that the PRC rely entirely on its own scientific and technical workers. Self-reliance, the editorial added, did not mean a policy of isolationism.

The shift in emphasis in national policy regarding science and technology was reflected in a new science plan. In January 1964 the existence of the new Ten-Year Science Plan (1963–72) was disclosed. The Ten-Year Science Plan did not appear to be as comprehensive as the previous Twelve-Year Science Plan; the ten-year plan consisted primarily of isolated individual plans for various fields. In many aspects it was composed of adaptations of parts of the original Twelve-Year Science Plan, with the completion date extended to 1972. Knowledgeable observers interpreted this announcement as an indication that the PRC had lost five years in its overall schedule of scientific development but believed that the reduction in scope of scientific effort after the failure of the Great Leap did not prevent the attainment of significant success in selected high-priority areas.

The leaders of the PRC, in addition to stressing self-reliance, advanced a new effort to compete with the Soviet Union on international scientific and technical fronts. The first major activity of the Peking Science Center was the convention of the International Scientific Symposium, held in Peking in August 1964. A reported 367 delegates representing forty-three countries attended, excluding the Soviet Union and the communist countries that accept the Soviet Union as the leader of the world communist movement. During the ten-day conference, 247 papers were submitted, and 194 were read, among them forty from Japan, thirty-three from the PRC, seventy-one from other Asian countries, three from Australia, two from New Zealand, thirty-six from Africa and the Middle East, and nine from Latin America. The subjects included basic science, engineering, agricultural science, and medicine.

EFFECTS OF THE GREAT PROLETARIAN CULTURAL REVOLUTION

One of the first statements about science and the Cultural Revolution came in the decision of the eleventh session of the Eighth Central Committee of the CCP, adopted on August 8, 1966. Point twelve of the sixteen-point decision referred specifically to the treatment of scientists and technologists and was headed "Policy Towards Scientists, Technicians and Ordinary Members of Working Staffs":

> As regards scientists, technicians and ordinary members of working staffs, as long as they are patriotic, work energetically, are not against the Party and socialism, and maintain no illicit relations with any foreign country, we should in the present movement continue to apply the policy of "unity, criticism, unity." Special care should be taken of those scientists and scientific and technical personnel who have made contributions. Efforts should be made to help them gradually transform their world outlook and their style of work.

Western analysts inferred that the issuance of a special ruling for scientists and technologists suggested that by 1966 many of them still did not accept the ideas of Mao Tse-tung. The analysts also believed that the statement confirmed that the CCP considered scientific work of national importance and considered that the reference to illicit contact with foreign countries meant that all communications between Chinese and foreign scientists must be funneled through official channels.

Both before and after the decision was announced, there were a number of overt conflicts between supporters of Mao Tse-tung and alleged supporters of Liu Shao-ch'i over the control of the research institutes of the Academy of Sciences. In the process the pro-Mao faction split into rival groups, and for twenty days a "civil war" waged between the two pro-Mao groups.

The Cultural Revolution also affected overseas study. More than 300 Chinese students and researchers were recalled from Europe. Sino-Soviet student exchanges had been sharply reduced before the Cultural Revolution. They were completely halted by a PRC directive of September 20, 1966, issued by the Ministry of Education, instructing all foreign students to leave China within fifteen days. About fifteen Soviet students in China were sent to their home country, and the Soviet Union returned sixty-five Chinese students.

More than 1,000 other foreign students were affected by this order. Other scholarly relationships were affected at all levels. Visiting scholars reported that they were prevented from making trips to institutions of special interest to them or of seeing Chinese specialists in their field. By the autumn of 1966 the exchange of practically all scientific and technological publications from the PRC had halted; over 200 scientific journals had ceased publication.

At the time of the August 8, 1966, decision, most of the leaders in the Academy of Sciences appeared to have been loyal to Liu Shao-ch'i. During much of the autumn of 1966 and the following spring of 1967, there were attempts on the part of the pro-Mao scientists to seize power from the pro-Liu group. Fighting occasionally erupted in some of the research institutes, particularly those in Peking, but most of the serious quarreling appears to have been among rival groups, all of which claimed to be supporters of Mao Tse-tung.

The main scientific crimes of Liu Shao-ch'i and his supporters were announced at a rally in Peking in April 1967. Representatives of the "revolutionary rebels" of the Academy of Sciences accused the supporters of Liu Shao-ch'i of promoting research that was aimed at restoring the ancient and worshiping the foreign and that was theoretical and divorced from the needs of the country. His followers were also accused of supporting the use of titles, such as "professor," and of having called for high salaries for scientists and awards for those who had made special contributions.

In late July 1967 a rally of all the "proletarian revolutionaries" of the Academy of Sciences was held in the Great Hall of the People in Peking. The rally reportedly marked the seizure of power from the supporters of Liu Shao-ch'i and the formation of a new revolutionary committee, which was to be the organ of power in the academy. Representatives of the PLA were included in the revolutionary committee, and the military authorities were therefore in a position to exercise some control over civilian science. Two of the revolutionary committee members were Ch'en Po-ta and Wu Yu-hsun, both of whom had been vice presidents of the Academy of Sciences for many years. Together with Kuo Mo-jo, the president of the academy, they retained their former positions of leadership.

Some scientific projects that had allegedly been put aside by the scientific supporters of Liu Shao-ch'i were restored when the pro-Mao group gained authority. For example, work on a large radio telescope had begun in 1958 but was stopped when the pro-Liu group gained control; subsequently, the radio telescope was rushed to completion in time for the period of intense solar activity in 1968. Another notable achievement of the Academy of Sciences was a major scientific expedition to Mount Everest; 100 scientists from thirty scientific fields participated in a comprehensive survey covering a large area. The expedition gathered, for the first time, geomagnetic data and information on solar radiation at an altitude of 6,500 to 7,700 feet. Other accomplishments of the research institutes of the Academy of Sciences reported in the Chinese press in late 1967 or early 1968 included the discovery of a new fossil skullcap of the Peking man at Chou-k'ou-tien and the construction of a new, all-purpose transistorized digital computer.

In mid-1971 the latest available published statement of Party and PRC policy toward science and technology was contained in an instruction of Mao Tse-tung, reported in the *People's Daily* of July 21, 1968. This instruction had been described by the Chinese press as the July 21 Directive. It contained a statement in reference to a study of the model Shanghai Machine Tool Plant:

> It is still necessary to have universities; here I refer mainly to colleges of science and engineering. However, it is essential to shorten the length of schooling, revolutionize education, put proletarian politics in command and take the road of the Shanghai Machine Tool Plant in training technicians from the workers. Students should be selected from among workers and peasants with practical experience, and they should return to production after a few years' study.

STRUCTURE OF THE SCIENTIFIC SECTOR

Political Supervision

In mid-1971 a combination of the PLA and the CCP apparatus exercised all political power (see ch. 9, Political System and Values; ch. 10, Political Dynamics). All aspects of science and technology and all scientific and technological organizations were subject to control by this combination. Whether the research organizations being supervised were operated by the Ministry of National Defense appeared to be the main criterion for the choice of the means employed to exercise this control.

The function and status of the National Defense Scientific and Technological Commission of the PLA in mid-1971 could not be determined on the basis of available data. Organization and administration of research institutes not under the Ministry of National Defense were controlled and supervised by CCP cadres to ensure the compliance of these institutions with the demands of the regime.

At the beginning of the Cultural Revolution the highest Party organization specializing in scientific affairs was the science division of the department of propaganda of the Central Committee of the CCP. Of the president and six vice presidents of the Academy of Sciences in the mid-1960s, five were members of the Party and, of these, two were members of the Central Committee of the CCP. A Party committee within the Academy of Sciences was its real governing body; the dominant Party functionary at the academy was the secretary of the Party committee.

In the mid-1960s the CCP ensured control over the academy by dominating its secretariat and its research institutes. All five secretaries of the academy in the mid-1960s were CCP members. Each research institute had a branch Party committee. The CCP usually placed trusted Party officials as deputy directors to supervise research institute affairs; their function has been completely political, requiring no scientific background or training. In the provincial branches of the Academy of Sciences many of the presidents and vice presidents served concurrently as secretaries of the provincial Party committees. The CCP also exercised jurisdiction over the China Association for Science and Technology.

Scientific and Technological Commission

As of mid-1971 the Scientific and Technological Commission supervised implementation of major research projects, drafted both annual and long-term research plans, coordinated scientific research sectors, provided reference materials and equipment needed for scientific research, conducted international cooperation in scientific research, controlled funds of the country's pivotal research projects, and directed training and assignment of senior specialists. The commission was also responsible for supervision of the associations of scientists and of the China Association for Science and Technology. The commission had also extended its direct control, through local commissions, over scientific research in all parts of the country. These commissions, under the leadership of the local CCP units, organized and administered the activities of branches and institutes of the Academy of Sciences, industries, and higher educational institutions. The commission's responsibilities included delineating local plans for science and technology, assigning parts of the local plans to various institutions, and ensuring the inclusion of all projects in the national plan of scientific and technological development.

Chinese Academy of Sciences

According to the latest information available in mid-1971, the Chinese Academy of Sciences was, under the guidance of the

Scientific and Technological Commission, the highest organ for science and technology in the PRC. It included more than 100 research institutes, employed about 8,000 scientists, and was the most important single center for scientific research in the PRC.

The academy was in mid-1971 an organizationally independent body within the government. It received guidance from, but was not under the direct jurisdiction of, the State Council. The Scientific and Technological Commission, as an arm of the State Council, supervised matters of organization and personnel in the Academy of Sciences.

The Academy of Sciences was divided into three levels. At the top was the Council of the Academy of Sciences. Under its jurisdiction were five academic departments directing research activities. At the base of the academy were the more than 100 participating research institutes of the academy.

The academy also controlled the branch academies in the provinces and municipalities. These branch academies were responsible for the control of research institutes located within their jurisdiction that were part of the Academy of Sciences and were also responsible for the establishment and operation of new local institutes. They were charged with correlating research and development activities with requirements of industrial production enterprises.

The branch academies exercised two forms of jurisdiction according to two categories of institutes. One form applied to the research institutes that were delegated to their control by the Academy of Sciences itself; the other covered those research institutes that fell geographically under their administration. This distinction defined the source of funds for their operation; the delegated research institutes derived their support from the Academy of Sciences, and the others were presumably financed from the branch academies' own budgets.

Information on the exact nature of the Council of the Academy of Sciences was not available in mid-1971. In the mid-1960s the council elected its standing committee, which consisted of the president, six vice presidents, and the secretary general. This standing committee was the top decisionmaking body and supervised the entire Academy of Sciences.

The secretariat had originally been established to assist the Council of the Academy of Sciences in all matters pertaining to academic leadership. In the mid-1960s the secretaries were veteran Party personnel, and the secretariat had been transformed into a Party control mechanism. Twelve bureaus and committees under the secretariat were in charge of administrative and scientific work.

The most important components of the academy consisted of the academic departments. The five departments have historically been served by the country's outstanding scientists. The number of members appointed to the academic departments ranged around 250 in the mid-1960s.

The academic department committees supervising the work of the research institutes were in 1971 the working organizations of the academy. Each research institute was an academic unit, with a director, usually a leading scientist in a particular field, and several deputy directors. Most of the research institutes employed from several dozen to several hundred persons. Senior scientists composed only a small fraction of these workers, the balance being technicians, assistants, and trainees.

Each research institute had its own scientific or academic committee, whose members were experts in a particular field. These persons were drawn from within and outside the institute, and many of the members were university professors. The number of scientific members varied depending on the scope of the institute and the available manpower.

A scientific committee for a research institute was not an administrative organization. Its functions were limited to discussing and examining the orientation, tasks, plans, and working reports of the institute; appraising important scientific papers and work contributed by the institute's research personnel; monitoring the application and dissemination of scientific results and making recommendations to the appropriate authorities; hearing defenses of dissertations submitted by research students and approving the awarding of academic titles or degrees; and organizing scientific workers to study the advanced experience of other countries.

Within each institute several laboratories or divisions engaged in research in the specific field. Most of the institutes had from six to eight laboratories, each with a senior scientist and several assistants and trainees.

Research Institutes Under Government Ministries

In addition to the research institutes operated by the Academy of Sciences, the ministries of the national government also operate more than 400 research institutes under their respective jurisdictions. Four of the ministries are particularly important in this respect: national defense, culture and education, agriculture and forestry, and public health. Each of these ministries controls an independent system of research activities. Other ministries also have many research institutes attached directly to them.

The research institutes under the Ministry of National Defense are separated into five divisions, the largest of which is the Academy of Military Sciences, with over forty institutes. Among the other research divisions is the Academy of Military Medicine. The research institutes under the defense establishment enjoy autonomy in decisionmaking on scientific matters. All nondefense discoveries or innovations are evaluated by the Scientific and Technological Commission for possible awards, but defense-oriented discoveries and innovations are reported to the Ministry of National Defense for evaluation.

The Ministry of Culture and Education has jurisdiction over all institutions of higher learning in the PRC and through them the dependent or component research institutes. As of mid-1971 very few institutions of higher learning had reopened since the Cultural Revolution (see ch. 8, Education, Intellectual Expression, and the Arts).

The Ministry of Agriculture and Forestry controls and directs its research institutes through the Chinese Academy of Agricultural Sciences. This organization had been established in Peking in 1957 as the leading national center for agricultural research. Officially, its purpose was "to meet the requirement for national plans of development, for agricultural production practices, and for the development of agricultural sciences within and outside the country; thus it was to organize and lead the agroscientists in basic as well as in applied research in agrotechnology." By the late 1950s the Chinese Academy of Agricultural Sciences controlled thirty-one research institutes and laboratories and 107 rural research stations.

Before 1966 the Ministry of Public Health had operated its research institutes through the Chinese Academy of Medical Sciences; the academy had been closed during the Cultural Revolution, and whether or not it had resumed operation by mid-1971 was unclear. Before the Cultural Revolution the Chinese Academy of Medical Sciences had operated twenty research institutes and maintained twelve research departments, which employed over 4,300 members, of whom 629 were scientific workers and 102 were senior scientists holding the rank of professor or associate professor.

Apart from these four ministries, before the Cultural Revolution other ministries also had research institutes under their own jurisdiction. The provincial and municipal governments also had their own systems of research organization.

The China Association for Science and Technology in the mid-1960s directed all the professional societies, 143 of which were active. The association was theoretically an independent organization consisting of scientists and technicians. In practice, it has become a CCP-controlled organ for the supervision and mobilization of scientists in the PRC.

NUCLEAR DEVELOPMENT

During the period from the explosion of the first atomic bomb in 1945 to 1954, the official attitude of the CCP toward nuclear weapons was one of constant disparagement. After the establishment of the PRC on October 1, 1949, the CCP also stressed that the PRC would not engage in the exploitation of atomic energy for military purposes.

The evidence available in mid-1971 indicated that, although the PRC did not definitely decide before 1958 to undertake an independent nuclear weaponry program, it had taken preliminary steps as early as March 1950. Uranium was reported to have been discovered about 1944 in Sinkiang (to become Sinkiang Uighur Autonomous Region in 1955). On March 27, 1950, the Sino-Soviet Non-ferrous and Rare Metals Company was established in Sinkiang to prospect for and mine radioactive minerals. In communist idiom "non-ferrous metal" is frequently used as a euphemism for uranium or thorium. Also in 1950 the PRC and the Soviet Union signed an agreement concerning the working conditions of Soviet specialists in China. A second agreement, signed on October 25, 1950, offered technical assistance for the installation and operation of Soviet equipment. Chinese assistants were assigned to Soviet scientists in Sinkiang, where atomic test reactors were reported in 1951.

The first of the eleven tasks slated for the scientific and technological sector in the First Five Year Plan (1953–57) was the study of the peaceful uses of atomic energy. In February 1953 Ch'ien San-ch'iang, director of the Institute of Atomic Energy of the Academy of Sciences, led a delegation of twenty-six scientists to the Soviet Union to discuss mutual assistance in atomic energy research. One month later the Soviet Union provided an atomic accelerator to the PRC and helped it organize several nuclear laboratories. In July 1953 the Soviet Union supplied the Chinese Academy of Sciences with 10,000 metric tons of machinery and material needed in the study of atomic energy. In March 1954 the president of the Academy of Sciences reported that the foundation for research in atomic energy had been laid by the academy. In August 1954 the PRC and the Soviet Union reportedly signed an agreement establishing a joint atomic energy research organization for military purposes.

The Sino-Soviet agreement of October 12, 1954, on scientific and technical cooperation provided for the transfer to the PRC of the Soviet shares in the Sino-Soviet Non-ferrous and Rare Metals Company, to be accomplished by January 1, 1955. The PRC thus regained control of all its uranium ores in Sinkiang, which it was later to employ for the development of an indigenous nuclear weapons program. Some atomic equipment was reported to have been given to the PRC at the time of the transfer of the Soviet shares.

Two other Sino-Soviet agreements for scientific and technical cooperation were signed on January 17, 1955, and April 30, 1955. On January 18, 1955, the Soviet Union issued a statement on limited peaceful nuclear sharing; the announcement indicated that, in return for their contribution of raw materials to the Soviet atomic program, the Soviet Union had offered to help the PRC, Poland, Czechoslovakia, Romania, and the German Democratic Republic (East Germany) develop programs of research in the peaceful application of atomic energy. In February 1955 a chemical separation plant, vital to the production of weapons grade uranium-235 and plutonium, was established with Soviet aid in Sinkiang.

Under the implementing Sino-Soviet agreement of April 30, 1955, the Soviet Union undertook to supply the PRC with Soviet-made, isotope-producing experimental atomic reactors and primary particle accelerators; to send Soviet specialists to assist in assembling these machines and in putting them into operation; to deliver unspecified amounts of radioisotopes until the supplied reactors began to produce isotopes; to furnish free of charge necessary scientific and technical documents relating to these reactors and accelerators; and to train specialists from the PRC at Soviet scientific research institutes and universities.

In July 1955 plans were made for the construction of atomic reactors at Lan-chou in Kansu Province and at Pao-t'ou in the Inner Mongolian Autonomous Region (Inner Mongolia), with completion scheduled for 1960. A Japanese source reported that the PRC planned in 1955 ultimately to enlarge the facility at Lan-chou to include a gaseous diffusion plant. Uranium deposits were reported to have been discovered in the provinces of Kansu and Tsinghai in the mid-1950s.

On March 26, 1956, the PRC sent twenty-one scientists to participate in research with other communist nations at the Joint Institute of Nuclear Research at Dubna near Moscow in the Soviet Union. The PRC was the second largest contributor to the expenditures of the institute, accounting for 20 percent of the total, compared with 47 percent for the Soviet Union.

In 1956 the PRC had ambitious plans to establish nuclear research facilities. Small atomic reactors, to be supplied by the Soviet Union, were planned for locations near Harbin and in Shen-yang. In September 1956 the Soviet Union announced that it would provide assistance for thirty-nine centers for atomic research in the PRC during the 1956–60 period. The first five fields of importance in the PRC Twelve-Year Science Plan, made public in September 1956, were relevant to either nuclear or missile development.

During 1957 the number of trained scientists and technicians increased greatly as hundreds of new graduates left the Institute of Atomic Energy of the Academy of Sciences in Peking. Enrollment in the institute at that time has been estimated at 10,000. The immediate facilities at the institute employed about 100 scientists and engineers.

On October 15, 1957, the PRC and the Soviet Union concluded an agreement on new technology for the national defense of the PRC. In this agreement the Soviet Union pledged to provide the PRC with a prototype atom bomb and technical data concerning its manufacture. On November 6, 1957, a high-level PRC military delegation arrived in Moscow for the fortieth anniversary of the Russian revolution. The deputy leader of the mission was Marshal Yeh Chien-ying, a vice chairman of the National Defense Council (see ch. 9, Political System and Values).

A protocol signed on December 11, 1957, between the Chinese and Soviet academies of science provided for the construction of atomic reactors in Chungking, Mukden, Peking, and Sian. A supplementary agreement of January 18, 1958, between the two academies provided for joint research by the two countries in the 1958–62 period; key fields in this joint research effort were to be physics and the peaceful uses of atomic energy. In February 1958 another institute for research in atomic energy was established at Shanghai with Soviet aid. On March 6, 1958, construction of the Soviet-supplied atomic reactor at Peking was completed.

In March 1958 the Academy of Military Sciences was established in Peking. This academy was to sponsor, coordinate, and direct research of military organizations; it is believed to have played a major role in weapons development. The publicly stated mission of the academy was to "guide the army's study of military sciences." Speaking at the inaugural ceremony, Marshal Yeh Chien-ying, the academy's president and political commissar, said that "the Academy should make full use of the latest scientific and technical developments and carry out research in a planned way, combining the advanced Soviet military sciences with the concrete situation in China, so as to accelerate the modernization of the Army."

An article in the May 9, 1958, issue of an official periodical stressed the need to develop chemical and aeronautical industries, for "in the future the principal weapons for national defense would be rockets and missiles of all types." The article went on to point out that mainland China's "needs with respect to peaceful uses of atomic energy, rocket manufacturing, radio, radiation chemistry, biophysics, high-temperature alloys, air mechanics, chemical fuel, and other such new scientific lines, which constitute the essential aspects of science in the present world, still remain unanswered up to the present." On the following day Ch'en I, then minister of foreign affairs, told German correspondents in Peking that the PRC would manufacture atomic bombs. Two weeks later the commander of the PLA air force wrote:

> China's working class and scientists will certainly be able to make the most up-to-date aircraft and atomic bombs in the not too distant future. By that time, in addition to the political factor in which we always occupy an absolutely predominant position, we can use atomic weapons and rockets in coping with the enemies who dare to invade our country and undermine world peace. By that time, another new turning point will probably be reached in the international situation.

On June 13, 1958, the first chain reaction occurred in Peking. The 7,000- to 10,000-kilowatt atomic reactor was fueled with 2 percent enriched uranium and moderated with heavy water. On September 27 the reactor went into full operation.

The *Peking Review* magazine revealed in 1963 that the PRC had in 1958 rejected an offer from the Soviet Union for the possible placement of Soviet strategic missiles on the territory of the PRC, with control of the nuclear warheads retained by the Soviet Union. A Western analyst has suggested that this event may have actuated the intensified efforts of the PRC.

On October 1, 1958, the chairman of the Scientific Planning Commission, speaking at the first national congress of the China Association for Science and Technology, urged maximum speed in acquiring the important techniques of the "spearhead" sciences, by which he was understood to have meant electronics and the applications of atomic energy. According to charges made by the PRC in 1963, on June 20, 1959, the Soviet Union unilaterally abrogated the 1957 agreement to supply the PRC with an atom bomb and with technical data concerning its manufacture.

Soon after this act the PRC embarked on a program of acquiring complete self-sufficiency in achieving a nuclear weapons capability. The first PRC supplies of weapons grade uranium-235 came from the continuous operations of the Soviet-supplied Peking reactor and Soviet-supplied reactor fuel. In 1959 the Institute of Atomic Energy created branch institutes or research organizations in every province, major city, and autonomous region. A smaller research reactor, the first all-Chinese built model constructed from Soviet blueprints, was erected at Peking. It was fueled with enriched uranium supplied by the Soviet Union before June 20, 1959.

Western observers recorded that the Soviet refusal of assistance did not diminish the determination of the PRC to proceed with its indigenous program. In early 1960 construction of the gaseous diffusion plant at Lan-chou was in progress. In November 1960 Liu Shao-ch'i declared that there were at least four atomic reactors in the PRC. At a conference of communist parties in Moscow in that month, the CCP reportedly circulated a document stating that the PRC had four nuclear reactors in operation and that it intended to turn these over to other than peaceful applications if its security needs were not met.

From 1959 through 1961 small atomic reactors for experimental purposes were established at Wu-han in Hupeh Province and in Shensi and Kirin provinces, and the installation of an entirely Chinese designed and manufactured three-kilowatt research reactor was completed at Nan-k'ai University. During the 1961–62 period progress of the PRC toward the fabrication of an atomic bomb was nearing a climax. Reactors significantly larger than previously existing models were established at Sian and Chungking; they were capable of producing sufficient quantities of weapons-grade uranium in a relatively short time. An outstanding nuclear research team, composed of the best scientists and engineers in North and Northeast China, was transferred to Sinkiang to produce the prototype weapon and engage in research on suitable missile delivery systems for future use. During the 1959–63 period more than forty chemical separation plants were built in the PRC for the extraction of uranium and thorium from the country's abundant deposits of uranium ore and monazite sands and for the chemical exchange of radioactive substances such as weapons-grade plutonium from the spent uranium fuel left in the reactor rods.

Throughout the 1959–63 period a gaseous diffusion plant utilizing a large 300-megawatt reactor was under construction at Lan-chou. It was estimated that the PRC invested over 3.7 billion yuan (2.46 yuan equal US$1) in the construction of the plant. In the spring of 1963 it was reported that the gaseous diffusion plant had begun operating. With adequate separation facilities, the Lan-chou plant could produce in a little over one month enough weapons-grade uranium-235 for a twenty-kiloton atomic bomb.

On July 31, 1963, the PRC issued a vigorous denunciation of the partial nuclear test ban treaty, of which the United States and the Soviet Union were signatories. Western analysts saw as one implication of this step an indication that the PRC would continue to develop its nuclear program. On October 28, 1963, Ch'en I, then minister of foreign affairs, told a group of Japanese newspapermen visiting Peking that Soviet Premier Nikita Khrushchev had once said that the manufacture of atomic weapons cost so much money that China might not have any money left to make trousers. Ch'en I stated that the PRC would have to manufacture atomic weapons with or without trousers.

The first successful test explosion of a Chinese-made atom bomb occurred near Lop Nor in Sinkiang on October 16, 1964. The bomb used uranium-235 as fissionable material. The bomb was detonated on a seventy-seven-foot tower. The static explosion yielded power equivalent to 20,000 metric tons of TNT (trinitrotoluene), or twenty kilotons. The second test explosion was also held at Lop Nor and took place on May 14, 1965; this bomb was dropped from a Soviet-built TU-4 aircraft. The yield of the second explosion was in the low intermediate range (twenty to 200 kilotons) and has been evaluated at fifty kilotons.

The first two Chinese detonations utilized uranium-235 (enriched uranium) as the primary fissionable material. Uranium-238 was also present in the tests. The detonation of any device that also contains uranium-238 results in some fissioning of the uranium-238.

Western analysts considered that the first Chinese atomic explosion on October 16, 1964, raised some puzzling questions. Preparations for the test had been under surveillance by other nations for some time before the detonation occurred. Analysis of the fallout from the first Chinese test revealed that the fissionable material was uranium-235 instead of plutonium. The four nations that had previously detonated atomic devices—the United States, the Soviet Union, Great Britain, and France—had begun by exploding plutonium devices, and Western analysts had expected that the PRC would do the same.

The Western analysts pointed out that any nation with a nuclear reactor could produce plutonium, though perhaps only slowly and in small quantities; when natural uranium is treated in a reactor, some of the relatively abundant uranium-238 isotope is converted into fissionable plutonium. Production of uranium-235 for weapons, however, requires technologically demanding processes for concentrating the fissionable uranium-235 isotope. Western analysts had been aware of the gaseous diffusion plant at Lan-chou. The nature of the gaseous diffusion process imposes certain requirements of plant size, however, and, by comparison with gaseous diffusion complexes in the Western world, the Lan-chou plant did not appear to be adequate for the production of substantial quantities of uranium-235 in the concentration required for nuclear explosions.

With gaseous diffusion, the engineering problems are most severe at the high-concentration end of the process. Using gaseous diffusion to enrich uranium from 0.7 percent uranium-235 to 8 or 10 percent uranium-235 is a difficult process, but a much higher order of technology and a much larger plant are required to obtain the degree of enrichment required for uranium-235 weapons. With electromagnetic separation, by contrast, the very large costs occur at the low-concentration end of the process. If the separating began with natural uranium, use of a large amount would be necessary to get a small amount of uranium-235. This could be done by a rich nation with great industrial resources, but it would be a method requiring a very large installation and use of immense quantities of electrical energy. The electromagnetic process is much simpler and much less costly, however, if it can begin with enriched uranium; for example, 8 percent uranium-235 instead of natural uranium. If both processes are available, therefore, they may expediently be combined: enrich uranium to an intermediate percentage of uranium-235 by gaseous diffusion and then continue with electromagnetic separation. The United States used such a combination of processes in the production of uranium-235 for the first atom bomb.

The known facts suggested to Western analysts that the PRC had used a similar sequence of processes to produce uranium-235 for its nuclear devices: first, enrichment of natural uranium to an intermediate percentage of uranium-235 by gaseous diffusion at the

Lan-chou gaseous diffusion plant, then further enrichment to weapons-grade uranium-235 by some other process that was probably electromagnetic separation. Western analysts considered that construction and operation of an electromagnetic plant to process enriched uranium would have been within the technical and industrial capabilities of the PRC. They noted that abundant information on the design of the electromagnetic separation process was readily obtainable by the scientists of the PRC. The electromagnetic enrichment techniques had been completely declassified by the United States in 1955, and the Soviet Union had in 1958 revealed a considerable amount of data about its own electromagnetic separation technology. The technology of the process had therefore been available in full descriptive detail to any nation, including the PRC. It appeared to Western analysts, consequently, that in producing weapons-grade uranium-235 the PRC had employed, not a new technology, but the old technology that the United States had used to produce uranium-235 for the first atom bomb.

Western analysts also speculated about how the PRC had managed to build a gaseous diffusion plant. They concluded that the PRC had obtained abundant indirect assistance from the Soviet Union provided, not under the October 15, 1957, Sino-Soviet defense technology treaty, but under an atoms-for-peace program. These analysts pointed out that nuclear reactors intended for the peaceful production of electric power can produce plutonium, which in turn can be used either as fuel for nuclear reactors or as material for nuclear weapons. They also noted that uranium enriched in a gaseous diffusion plant can be upgraded into uranium-235 for atom bombs or it can be used as an atomic reactor fuel for the production of power or plutonium.

These analysts reasoned that the PRC could credibly have asked the Soviet Union for assistance in building a gaseous diffusion plant as a facility for peace rather than war; that is, as a way around the potential industrial difficulties involved for the PRC in producing the large quantities of pure aluminum, graphite, and other materials needed for a nuclear reactor. These analysts believed that the Soviet Union had felt compelled to continue helping the PRC in peaceful uses of atomic energy, even after the abrogation of the defense technology agreement in 1959. They noted that there were many indications of continued Sino-Soviet atomic cooperation after 1959 and that, in particular, a large contingent of PRC scientists had remained at the Joint Institute for Nuclear Research at Dubna until June 1965.

The third PRC nuclear weapons test occurred on May 9, 1966. It employed lithium-six, a thermonuclear material, and produced a yield of over 200 kilotons. The device was dropped from a TU-16 aircraft at the Lop Nor site.

The fourth test, on October 27, 1966, was a guided missile-nuclear weapons test. The nuclear warhead had a yield of around twenty kilotons. The delivery system was a medium-range ballistic missile, believed to be a copy of the Soviet SS-4 medium-range missile. The missile was fired from the missile test range at Shuang-ch'eng-tzu in Inner Mongolia and was carried a distance of about 600 miles, with the impact area at Lop Nor. The missile-delivered fourth test demonstrated that the PRC had the capability to design a low-yield fission warhead compatible in size and weight with a missile.

The fifth bomb was detonated on a tower at the Lop Nor test site on December 28, 1966. The fallout contained thermonuclear material, as in the third test. The yield was between 300 and 500 kilotons. The fifth test indicated that the PRC had taken a major step toward a thermonuclear weapon.

The sixth PRC nuclear test occurred in the atmosphere on June 17, 1967, at the Lop Nor test site. The sixth test device was a thermonuclear bomb, dropped from a TU-16 aircraft, and had a three-megaton yield (explosive force equivalent to that of 3 million metric tons of TNT). Analysis of the debris indicated the use of uranium-235, uranium-238, and thermonuclear material. Western analysts concluded after this test that the PRC had developed a capability to design a multimegaton thermonuclear device suitable for delivery by aircraft.

The seventh PRC nuclear test, which occurred on December 24, 1967, was assessed by Western analysts as a probable failure. The seventh test was a thermonuclear bomb, which was dropped from a TU-16 aircraft at the Lop Nor test site and had a yield of about twenty kilotons. For the first time there was no public announcement from the PRC about a nuclear test.

The eighth nuclear test occurred approximately one year later, on December 27, 1968. The device was again thermonuclear and dropped from a TU-16 aircraft at the Lop Nor site, but the yield was in the three-megaton range.

The ninth and tenth tests occurred almost simultaneously. The ninth test was announced by the PRC as having occurred on September 22, 1969, and as being the first successful underground test the country had undertaken. The yield was assessed as in the range of twenty to 200 kilotons. One week later, on September 29, 1969, a thermonuclear bomb was detonated in the atmosphere, with a three-megaton yield. The bomb had been dropped from a TU-16 aircraft over the Lop Nor site.

The eleventh test was conducted on October 14, 1970, when a thermonuclear device was exploded in the atmosphere with a yield of from three to four megatons. The device released very little radioactivity into the atmosphere. No public announcement was made by the PRC.

CHAPTER 17

LABOR

No official statistical data on labor have been published by the People's Republic of China (PRC) since 1960, and no detailed employment data have been released since 1959. Media accounts have contained a few isolated figures since then, but there is not enough detail for a comprehensive description of the labor force, employment, union organization, and working conditions.

The labor force in 1970 was estimated to have been about 350 million persons, or about 44 percent of the population; probably somewhat more than three-quarters of them were in the agricultural sector, and less than one-quarter were in nonagricultural employment. Industrial workers and employees were estimated to compose roughly half of the nonagricultural labor force. The entire labor force was collectivized, including handicraft workers, who still constituted an important productive group in 1971.

The outstanding characteristic of the labor force continued to be the surplus of unskilled labor, manifested not so much in unemployment (officially nonexistent) as in underemployment, primarily in agriculture. Government policies toward labor have had as their basic goal its maximum utilization for increased productivity, channeling as much as possible of the value created into capital for further economic development. The first major effort to do so was by mass mobilization in the unsuccessful Great Leap Forward (see Glossary) from 1958 through 1960. During the 1960s the PRC used less extreme and slower means to carry out labor policies, but the basic goal still had not been attained by the early 1970s.

The PRC modeled its original labor organization, laws, regulations, and most practices, including wage scales for nonagricultural labor, on the Soviet Union pattern. The Chinese Communist Party (CCP), however, has had serious ideological problems with labor unions. The most important incident occurred in 1966, when activists of the Great Proletarian Cultural Revolution destroyed the national labor union organization, the All-China Federation of Trade Unions (ACFTU). By mid-1971 no successor to this central labor union federation had appeared, and no minister of labor had been publicly identified since 1966. Apparently the administration of activities delegated to unions by law, such as handling retirement and medical benefits, continued, but press accounts did not describe the details.

Reports of the effect of the Cultural Revolution on local labor union organization are fragmentary. Party regional union committees, generally conservative in attitude, apparently maintained their control over local unions at the enterprise level during the Cultural Revolution, despite the efforts of the former ACFTU leadership to carry out new, pro-Mao policies. One interpretation is that the turmoil divided industrial labor generally into competing groups based on different material interests. Irregular workers, such as contract, seasonal, and casual laborers, who were ineligible for the advantages of union membership and benefits but wanted them, tried unsuccessfully to take over local unions. From this analysis it appears that the motivation of each group was material self-interest, not their ideological allegiance, even though the aggressors might be labeled pro-Mao and radical, and the apparent victors, pro-Liu Shao-ch'i and conservative.

The official New China News Agency stated in September 1971 that the average annual income for a worker or employee was around 650 yuan (2.46 yuan equal US$1—see Glossary), adding that, because of a low and stable price level, no income tax, low rentals, and free medical and other benefits, workers' livelihood was gradually improving "since their full wages are at their disposal." The statement made it clear that the PRC was still following in the early 1970s the "rational low wage" policy intended both to narrow the disparity between agricultural and higher nonagricultural incomes and to achieve capital accumulation from labor, which had been initiated in the mid-1950s.

Appeals to the entire labor force to increase production through cooperative endeavor and emulation of those who have "grasped the revolution" were unremitting in 1971. Emphasis on nonmaterial incentives has been pushed much farther in the PRC than in the Soviet Union. A prominent feature of this barrage since the Cultural Revolution was the exhortation to low wage grade industrial workers to disdain and to shame others into refusing pay for overtime and overquota production, although the wage payment system was constructed to emphasize additional payment for overfulfillment. No indices were available for the productivity of the labor force. One Western analyst, basing his estimates on the approximately equal contributions made by the agricultural and industrial sectors to the estimated gross national product (GNP), concluded that the productivity of the one-sixth of the labor force employed in industry was about five or six times that of the labor force engaged in agriculture.

By 1971 Chinese industrial labor was somewhat more widely distributed throughout the country than it had been before World War II, but the coastal and riverine cities of East and North China and Manchuria continued to be the major centers of industrial employment (see ch. 15, Industry). There was not enough information available, however, to describe educational qualifications, training, and mobility in the industrial labor force. Gradual modernization of agriculture had required some modification of farmers' skills in the use of improved implements, the utilization of machinery for irrigation, and the application of chemical fertilizers. Forced labor remained legally sanctioned in 1971, though no information beyond reports of refugees in Hong Kong from labor assignments in Kwangtung Province had become available; the operation of the system and the numbers of people involved were unknown.

The PRC has not participated in international labor organizations since December 1966 when, as a consequence of the Sino-Soviet ideological divergence, the PRC representatives were excluded from a committee meeting of the communist-dominated World Federation of Trade Unions (WFTU) at Sofia, Bulgaria. The WFTU has, however, reserved an executive council seat for the PRC since 1968.

SIZE AND COMPOSITION OF THE LABOR FORCE

The PRC has never published an official figure for the size of the labor force. An estimate of about 300 million in the mid-1960s is generally concurred in by Western analysts, and one analyst has suggested a figure of 350 million for 1970. In some PRC sources the age range of the labor force is given as sixteen to sixty years for men and sixteen to fifty-five years for women; students over sixteen years of age have usually been excluded. These age brackets, however, are irrelevant in the predominant, traditional sectors of the economy where many start to work very young and most individuals do not retire until they are physically incapable of working.

Agricultural Labor

The agricultural population according to PRC definition has included both persons solely engaged in agriculture and those individuals engaged concurrently in agriculture and subsidiary occupations. This total is not the same statistically as that for the rural population, which has included also the farming population residents in the "urban areas" as well as the residents of nonurban areas. Nonurban areas included certain small towns and villages, the majority of whose population was engaged in agriculture.

In the absence of any data for 1971, an estimate of the agricultural labor force has been derived from the estimate of the total labor force, using the 80 to 85 percent figure thought to represent rural population, though some Western analysts prefer 75 percent in order to distinguish between agricultural and nonagricultural labor in the rural population (see ch. 2, Physical Environment and Population).

The agricultural labor force would thus be between 260 million and 295 million in 1971, using 75 to 85 percent of the total labor force. The farming population was for the most part concentrated in the eastern part of the country, in South China, and in the Red Basin in Szechwan Province. Some of this labor force was engaged in fishing and forestry; others, chiefly non-Han peoples, were engaged in grazing, mainly in Outer China (see ch. 14, Agriculture). All members of the labor force were in 1971 nominally in the collective sector of the economy.

A relatively comprehensive survey of farm households in the 1930s showed that men did about 80 percent of the farmwork; women, 13 percent; and children, 7 percent. There are no comparable data for any later dates. Observers, however, have generally concluded that the collectivized farming system has brought a considerable increase in female farm labor; this was one of the original motivations for the agricultural commune system.

Industrial Labor

The nonagricultural labor force was estimated in the mid-1960s to be 15 to 25 percent of the total; thus, for 1971 it would be in the range of 45 million to 85 million. This labor force, which was not necessarily urban, was about 80 percent male.

PRC statistics issued during the 1950s divided the nonagricultural labor force into two parts: the material production branch and the nonproductive branch (see table 9). The material production group included—in addition to industrial workers, handicraft workers, and workers in traditional transportation services—workers in salt extraction; fishing; water conservancy; capital construction; modern transport and communication; and the trade, food, and drink industries. The nonproductive branches covered finance, banking, and insurance; services; traditional medicine; state education, medicine and public health, and cultural affairs; government administration; mass organizations; urban public utilities; and meteorology.

In the labor statistics published in 1957, individuals in both the material production and the nonproductive divisions of nonagricultural employment were classified as workers and employees (sometimes translated as workers and staff members). The term was used for both white- and blue-collar employment in the production of material goods or services, in organizations "owned by all the people," such as factories and state farms, where the individual was completely or chiefly dependent on wage income. Government personnel were included in the category, as well as wage earners and salaried employees of cooperatives. The term was not applied to nonsalaried members of cooperatives and People's Communes (see Glossary) who were distinguished from the worker and employee category both by

Table 9. People's Republic of China, Nonagricultural Employment by Branch of the Economy, 1957

Branch of Economy	Number [1]	Percent Distribution
Material Production		
Handicrafts and carrier services	6,560	16.5
Salt extraction	500	1.3
Fishing	1,500	3.8
Industry	7,907	19.9
Water conservancy	340	0.9
Capital construction	1,910	4.8
Transport, posts, and telecommunications		
Modern	1,878	4.7
Traditional	2,539	6.4
Subtotal	4,417	11.1
Trade and food and drink industry		
Trade	6,719	16.9
Food and drink industry	1,100	2.8
Subtotal	7,819	19.7
Total material production	30,953	78.0
Nonproductive		
Finance, banking, and insurance		
State	400	1.0
Rural credit	221	0.6
Subtotal	621	1.6
Services	489	1.2
Traditional medicine	1,363	3.4
State education, medicine and public health, and cultural affairs		
Education	2,542	6.4
Medicine and public health	545	1.4
Cultural affairs	124	0.3
Subtotal	3,211	8.1
Government administration	1,698	4.3
Mass organizations	1,184	3.0
Urban public utilities	133	--[2]
Meteorology	15	--[2]
Total nonproductive	8,714	22.0
GRAND TOTAL	39,667	100.0

[1] Figures in thousands at end of year.
[2] Less than 0.5 percent.

Source: Adapted from John Philip Emerson, *Nonagricultural Employment in Mainland China, 1949–1958* (International Population Statistics Reports, Series P–90, No. 21), Washington, 1965, p. 128.

their "collective ownership" of the means of production and by the remuneration of members from their own communal production.

Workers and employees as presented in the latest reasonably reliable, comprehensive official data for 1957 totaled 39,667,000. Data for 1958 were distorted by inaccuracies introduced in connection with overly optimistic reporting on the Great Leap, and no data have been published by the PRC since then. Western estimates for the worker and employee category for the late 1960s were in the range of 40 million to 64 million. The proportion of women in the category was only about 20 percent and for the most part was in two major branches of light industry—textiles and food processing—in which women constituted as much as 70 percent of the work force.

Both the geographic distribution of labor and the kinds of industry employing it at the time of communist takeover in 1949 had been somewhat changed by 1971 as the result of government economic policy. The First Five Year Plan (1953–57) included plans for new industrial and communications centers in the interior. Significant centers of industrial, mining, and petroleum activity have been established in Kansu, Szechwan, and Sinkiang, and transportation facilities have been expanded throughout the country. Nonetheless, in 1971, the nonagricultural work force was still concentrated in the two dozen or so major cities of East and North China and Manchuria, where modern commerce and industry were first developed by Europeans and Japanese. The switch in 1962 of basic economic policy to priority for agriculture and, within industry, to emphasis on light industries and to those supporting agriculture also had an effect (see ch. 15, Industry). Changes in the labor force these developments brought about could not be precisely determined, but the known existence of wage differentials both by geographic location and by branch of industry implies that the government was obliged to adjust wage incentives as a means of redistributing labor.

Handicraft Labor

Handicraft workers, both individual and those in cooperatives, were thought to be about one-third of the numbers of workers and employees shown in the 1957 statistics. The figures for 1958 showed a decrease of about 5 million handicraftsmen, leaving about 3 million persons in that category. In the absence of an official explanation, it is thought that the change reflected a transfer from the handicraft labor category to that of worker and employee, probably in industrial employment for which acquaintance with and experience in mechanical techniques might qualify them. A single mention in the early 1960s of 6 million handicraftsmen appears to be the only available later figure, and it does not provide the basis for a comparison with previous data. Observers nonetheless considered handicraft labor a significant element of employment in 1971, both as a principal source of income and as a sideline occupation.

LABOR MOBILITY

The labor pool in the PRC in 1971 was presumably under the same theoretically complete state control as that described in the mid-1960s. There was very little freedom to change jobs. In industry a change required permission of both the employer and the local Party organization and, in addition, that of an unidentified authority above the enterprise that the individual sought to leave. Information was lacking on any step in the process and on the extent of labor mobility under these circumstances.

The government has been reported to practice a directed horizontal mobility by transferring individuals or groups of workers and employees from established enterprises to newly opened ones. Group transfers appeared to be largely temporary and designed to provide initial training of the newly hired. The length of time of transfer probably varied with the kind of enterprise and the level of skills. It seemed likely, though it was not documented, that some individual transfers may have been longer, perhaps permanent. Not all such transfers were welcomed; carrying them out sometimes involved the use of coercion, extreme pressure, or even penalties, to the point where there was little difference between this kind of mobility and forced labor.

The shortage of skilled labor was such that restrictions on the individual's mobility were to some extent balanced by opportunities for upward mobility within a given enterprise. An account by a Western observer before the Cultural Revolution noted a number of instances of promotions obtained through completion of educational requirements by spare-time study; in most but not all instances, this was accompanied by acquisition of Party membership to provide an acceptable mixture of "redness" (see Glossary) with expertise.

LABOR REQUIREMENTS, SKILLS, TRAINING, AND ALLOCATION

Indirect evidence from scattered information on wages, demography, educational standards, trade data, and official publicity and exhortations permits some inferences as to effective employment, rates of unemployment, proportions of various skills, training, and allocation.

Unemployment

The PRC up to mid-1971 had never published any national figures for total unemployment. In 1971 the New China News Agency stated in a release that "unemployment was eliminated in China over ten years ago"; however, this statement contrasts with the suggestion in the First Five Year Plan that the problem of unemployment might not be entirely solved until the second or third five-year plan, or about 1966.

In the agricultural sector the density of population in the major farming regions, even those engaging in traditional labor-intensive practices, has resulted in a general underemployment of labor. The surplus in this sense consistently changed to a labor shortage at times of planting and harvest and less often during periods of greatest requirement for irrigation. Seasonal idleness, especially for farmers in the one-crop regions of the north, was, however, a problem only partially solved by subsidiary work on the farm or in the cities (see ch. 14, Agriculture).

Unemployment rates among male and female nonagricultural workers were unknown. Estimates during the 1950s showed an average of 25 percent among males. This appears to have been largely the result of large-scale migration of the unskilled from the countryside to the cities at a time when government policy favored capital-intensive industrial projects that provided initial employment for at least some of the migrants. Government statistics showed that the urban population grew at a faster rate than that of the increase in nonagricultural employment at that time. The regime took steps in the early 1960s to stem this movement and, with the exception of a period during the Cultural Revolution, sent large numbers of individuals to rural areas. The continuation in 1971 of such labor practices as assignment of college and school graduates to work in the countryside for extended periods, rather than for "exchanging experiences," suggested that job opportunities in the cities probably remained limited.

Labor Skills

Some of the traditional practices of Chinese farmers had been affected by the limited, gradual modernization of agriculture that had taken place by 1971. Some modification of their skills was required by semimechanization of cultivation, greater use of chemical fertilizers, mechanized irrigation, improvement of crops and breeds, and expansion of double-cropped acreage. There have been reports of some resistance to such innovations, though less to new crops, in a rural technology that had remained stagnant for some 500 years.

Accounts in the PRC press and other media describing the productive skills of workers and employees in nonagricultural employment concentrate almost exclusively on the ideological factors that should motivate them rather than on their technical proficiency. An example of this was the much-publicized achievements of workers

502

at the Ta-ch'ing petroleum complex in Northeast China, which was the model for raising industrial production by "grasping the revolution," that is, emphasis on political rather than technical factors in labor performance (see ch. 15, Industry). Such accounts are generally exhortations to increase production and serve as indirect evidence of the continued need to raise the level of skills to achieve it, but since the people to whom the appeals for emulation are addressed are the low-wage grade workers, they are not necessarily representative of the labor force as a whole. Somewhat similarly, the recurring accounts of ingenious adaptations, inventions, and production by improved processes are more indicative of the political objectives of the propaganda than they are either of skills among ordinary laborers credited with success or of the lack of skill in managerial and technical personnel who fail to be mentioned. The growth of industry and the increasing sophistication of production have undoubtedly been accompanied by a rise in the level of skills in the industrial labor force, but there have been no data published for measurement or comparison. A comparison would be possible on the basis of the numbers of workers and employees in each wage grade scale; when this was done in a 1955 census, the results showed that average wage grades were low. This was officially interpreted at the time as a reflection of shortages of highly skilled workers and the youthfulness and inexperience of the work force.

The data in the 1955 census showed differences in average wage grade levels by branches of industry. These were not officially explained; presumably they arose from a combination of factors, such as the length of time each branch had been established, its rate of employment growth, and the level of technology each required. Wage grades were on an average higher in the coal and textile industries, which were the oldest and most developed and exhibited the slowest growth in the size of the work force. The lowest wage grades were in the chemical and building materials industries; the chemical industry was then new, and the building materials industry needed only a low level of technology.

The regime's information and propaganda media have regularly reported on increases claimed in the number of higher level personnel in the worker and employee category, although detailed official data have not been issued since 1957. The numbers of engineers and technicians in 1957 was nearly half a million, or 2.7 percent of workers and employees. Probably no more than one-tenth were actually engineers, and a very large but unknown proportion of those in engineering and technical positions lacked adequate educational qualifications. The low average level of professional educational qualifications was probably further reduced by the practice of assigning top-level managerial and administrative positions solely on the basis of Party records.

503

There appears to be no way of measuring the level of 1971 handicraft skills. Such skills usually are low by the productivity standards of industrial technology; however, some of China's handicrafts have traditionally had a cultural and aesthetic value that required a different standard of judgment. Accounts of the PRC in 1971 did not indicate whether this kind of skill had survived or whether existing skills constituted only a residue left after the absorption of most handicraft workers into industry in the late 1950s.

Training and Allocation

In the agricultural sector the type of training presumably remained in 1971 what it had been for generations: on-the-job for both farming and subsidiary occupations, including handicrafts. It may have been somewhat modified by the degree of modernization in a given locality and also supplemented by government demonstration plots (see ch. 14, Agriculture). The basic means of training used in these plots was literally a demonstration of methods to a farming population that had adopted new crop varieties fairly quickly but had not otherwise changed its technology in several centuries. A low literacy level was an important reason for this demonstration approach, as well as the consideration of the farmers' memory of the agricultural disaster in the late 1950s occasioned in part by government efforts to transform agriculture by fiat.

The nonagricultural labor force in industry presumably continued in 1971 to benefit from on-going state policies and regulations abetting on-the-job training, though the effects of the Cultural Revolution on the system were not ascertainable. In the mid-1960s, before the Cultural Revolution, many employees were reported to be training in union-supervised programs. This favorable worker attitude toward training and education was said to be spurred by the existence of many opportunities for advancement in industrial and other enterprises; betterment of qualifications and skills often made possible such advancement. Programs to enable workers and employees to raise their levels of skill were reported in operation throughout Chinese industry at that time. Reports of the detailed contents of such programs or of their effectiveness were unavailable in 1971.

It appears likely that government practices on labor allocation in 1971 continued to discourage migration to the cities, preventing it if possible, and to force migration from the cities to the countryside; for example, the assignment of country jobs to school graduates continued in 1971. This general policy was related to the continuing overall surplus of unskilled labor in the PRC's predominantly agricultural subsistence economy and the lure of higher income in the cities. This situation, still resistant in 1971 to the regime's efforts to transform it, had led some Western observers to conclude that, without another major drive in the line of the Great Leap, the development of a modernized industrial economy would occur only very gradually.

LABOR UNION ORGANIZATION AND MOTIVATIONS TO 1966

The PRC's known labor union organization has followed the original Leninist view that unions were "transmission belts" from the Party vanguard, or elite, down through the advanced class of the proletariat, to the peasant masses. Acting on Lenin's views, the CCP founded its first labor union in 1921, the same year in which the Party was established. In 1922 it gained firm control of the national labor union movement at the First National Labor Congress in Canton. The ACFTU was established at the second meeting of the congress in 1925, also held in Canton; it then claimed a membership of 2.8 million workers. The CCP unions participated in two more national congresses before the CCP's break with the Kuomintang (Nationalist Party, often abbreviated as KMT) in 1927.

Political exploitation of labor unions took place during this period of KMT–CCP collaboration and was instrumental in the success of the Northern Expedition of 1926–27 (see ch. 3, Historical Setting). One reason for the political effectiveness of the relatively small numbers in organized labor groups was their strategic location and consequent capability of immobilizing transportation centers.

In 1927 the CCP and its labor movement went underground. The membership claimed for unions under communist control in 1927 was about 2.7 million, of whom 1.5 million were in industrial unions. From 1928 to 1948 the CCP organization was far removed physically from the country's industrial establishments and the urban proletariat and concerned itself with union matters chiefly in theoretical terms (see ch. 3, Historical Setting). The CCP resumed its practical interest and activity in urban affairs in 1948, when the ACFTU was established, with headquarters in Harbin, Manchuria.

After the communist takeover in 1949, labor unions in the PRC were regulated by the Labor Union Law, promulgated in June 1950. Labor unions were defined as "voluntary popular organizations of the working class." All skilled and unskilled workers living wholly or largely on wages were eligible for union membership, whether or not they were in the service of a permanent employer. Only industrial unions could be organized under this law, and all labor unions had to be approved by the proper governmental authorities.

Until the Cultural Revolution the various unions were grouped under the ACFTU, which apparently was headed by an Executive

Committee elected by the National Labor Congress. Under the Executive Committee were a number of departments, and directly under its supervision were also the Workers' Press, the newspaper office of *Kung Jen Jih Pao*, the Cadres Training School of the ACFTU, the Bureau of Labor-Insurance Collective Projects, the Policy Research Institute, and the Private Enterprises Working Committee.

The lowest organizational level of labor in the federation was the basic-level union. According to regulations issued by the ACFTU in August 1950, a basic-level union could be an organization in a factory, mine, shop, farm, government department, or school where twenty-five or more persons were employed. Organizations in which 500 or more persons were employed could establish separate basic-level union committees in various departments and workshops of a single organization. Under a basic-level union committee, subcommittees and work groups could be established in accordance with the needs of the work assigned to the basic-level labor union.

The structure of labor unions above the basic level was set forth in the ACFTU Charter. All basic-level organizations in one industry or type of employment were grouped together in an "industrial labor-union organization," consisting of an overall national union plus one in each town, county, city, and province. Each union had a council as its organ of power and a committee as its executive organ. They were organized along territorial lines, in a manner corresponding to the local government system, in each province, city, county, and town. A town federation of labor had jurisdiction over all basic-level organizations, or local unions, in the town through their membership meetings. The council of a county was elected by the councils of federations of the several towns within the county; councils for cities were probably elected in the same way. The councils of all the county and city federations within a province elected the provincial federation council, and the councils of federations of all the provinces and those cities independent of provincial control elected the National Labor Congress. National congresses usually met once every four years.

The ACFTU Charter listed as sources of income the registration fees of new members; income from cultural, athletic, and other activities of the labor unions; and any subsidies from the government. All expenditures of the labor unions had to be properly budgeted and audited, the procedures for which were prescribed in special regulations.

Before 1949 Chinese labor unions were generally weak and tended to side with employers rather than with the mass of workers. In the industrial confusion and the strikes that accompanied and followed the communist takeover in October 1949, existing labor organizations —in line with Party policy aimed at economic stabilization—often advocated compromise with employers. This occurred not only in private industry but also in state enterprises. In the process "class struggle" was ignored.

In June 1950 Mao called for a rectification campaign in labor leadership. Union leaders, themselves Party members, were accused of "commandism" (siding with management), "bureaucraticism," and alienating the workers. A reaction, stimulated by the campaign, set in; by the end of 1950 the action had carried union leadership to the other extreme of "economism" (actively siding with the mass of workers). This position was given further support during 1951 editorially by the *Chung-kuo Kung-jen*, monthly organ of the ACFTU; the editorial committee of this periodical was headed by Li Li-san, officially first vice chairman of the ACFTU and de facto head of that organization.

From the ideological standpoint, siding with the mass of the workers was no more justifiable than siding with employers, since in theory the Party was concerned with the national interest as a whole. At the end of 1951 the Party moved to halt a developing independence of action by ACFTU leadership; leading comrades were accused of ignoring the Party and of anti-Party actions. This matter was first made fully public, however, at the Second Plenum of the ACFTU Executive Committee meeting of February 1953, when Li was ousted from his de facto ACFTU leadership and replaced by Lai Jo-yu, who was elected chairman of the ACFTU (see ch. 10, Political Dynamics).

A second ACFTU leadership-Party crisis came to a head in late 1957 over essentially the same question of union independence. In the interim Lai had fought against the growing dominance of local CCP committees over the basic union organizations, which reduced the ACFTU's control downward through its industrial union structure. Within the local unions the increased tempo of modernization and the growing strength of the industrial union structure had brought about a professionalism in union attitudes and activities and had increased a desire for local autonomy. Wage reform measures in 1956, union responsibilities for spare time technical and cultural education in factories, and the establishment of new industrial unions were among the factors that made national union direction more important and led to efforts by the ACFTU leadership to strengthen its position.

Lai's position was that a union must "unfold its own independent activities" while submitting to Party policy and ideological leadership. His basic argument was that the unions must have autonomy of operation in order to be an effective transmission belt. The argument lost out at an ACFTU meeting in September 1957. The Eighth Trade Union Congress held in December 1957 amended the Trade Union Constitution, which had been adopted in 1953 and had stressed vertical control, to read "The trade unions of China are formed on the principle of coordinating organization on industrial lines on a local area basis." In effect this meant that actual control of the unions was in the hands of the local Party committee.

Lai died in May 1958, and his faction in the ACFTU was purged in August. Provincial labor union organizations also appeared to have been purged in 1958. Liu Ning-yi, later an avowed Maoist, was elected chairman to succeed Lai. Although no marked change was made in the industrial union structure, the operation of the union transmission belt had apparently been adjusted to the satisfaction of the CCP, and the unions were usually not heard from between 1958 and the Cultural Revolution. There was a continuing growth of professionalism among union cadres generally during that time.

LABOR AND THE GREAT PROLETARIAN CULTURAL REVOLUTION

There was no official information on any labor organization in the PRC in mid-1971. By one account ACFTU headquarters was dismantled by the Red Guards (see Glossary) on December 27, 1966. The ACFTU newspaper, *Kung Jen Jih Pao*, survived until an apparently final issue was printed on March 9, 1967. Since the Great Proletarian Cultural Revolution official silence appears to have been maintained on the question of continued ACFTU existence. In early 1971, however, Peking radio reported, without further detail, that ACFTU cadres were running a May 7 cadre school (see ch. 8, Education, Intellectual Expression, and the Arts).

There were reports, both during and after the Cultural Revolution, of workers' groups, such as workers' congresses, economic supervisory groups, and workers' investigation groups, all of unspecified membership, responsibilities, and duration. Whatever their orientation and allegiance, they have not appeared to constitute the base for a mass labor organization of the orthodox communist kind.

During the Cultural Revolution factories, mines, and state enterprises generally were invaded by Red Guard units. Targets included all kinds of cadres in the industrial system. Presumably the union cadres so attacked were considered to have become more "expert than red," in spite of the strong Maoist position of ACFTU Chairman Liu. Liu was reportedly in the Cultural Revolution guiding group until he disappeared from public life in January 1968.

Since the Cultural Revolution there has been a general narrowing of the gap between the lowest and highest wages of nonagricultural workers and a heavy emphasis on nonmaterial incentives. Such measures implied that the unions were being attacked once more for siding with the mass of the workers. Western analysts have also interpreted the Red Guard activities directed against labor unions as a possible attack on an institution considered as elitist and

508

nonegalitarian, which produced too much professionalism and reduced labor mobility, thereby diminishing the prospect of the development of the Maoist's ideal, all-purpose Chinese Communist man. Still another interpretation has been that Red Guard activities may have been a preparatory step to executing the policy, later announced by Mao in October 1968 and then by Lin Piao in April 1969, of giving preeminence to industrial workers in the CCP's plans for building the Party (see ch. 10, Political Dynamics).

Reports indicate that local worker groups resisted attempts to lower wages and opposed with physical force many Red Guard incursions into industrial plants. It is not clear in what way physical opposition was organized and carried out, nor is it reported whether the leadership of the major strikes in Shanghai in 1967 protesting a downward revision of wages came from the cadres associated with union groups. Within enterprises, participation in pro-Red Guard mass organizations consisted apparently of contract workers, day laborers, seasonal employees from rural areas, and members of handicraft cooperatives who, ineligible for union membership, did not enjoy the benefits of the regular workers and employees. In reality, these irregular workers evidenced more "economism," about which they complained, than did the regular employees, because the objective of the casual workers was higher wages rather than ideological purity.

Events involving local labor groups during the Cultural Revolution were perhaps illustrated in the attitudes of many older, more experienced workers at the large and long-established K'ai-lan coal mines in T'ang-shan, Hopeh Province. The veteran miners at K'ai-lan allied themselves with the local, conservative administrative and agricultural Commune leaders in a counterattack on the Red Guards. It appears that veteran workers managed to keep their own organization intact and formed their own committee after labor union cadres had been purged. They competed successfully with the short-lived groups of irregular workers known as the National Rebel General Corps of Red Laborers, which was ordered dissolved in February 1967. The conservative worker groups subsequently had the cooperation of the People's Liberation Army (PLA) in the formation of the local revolutionary committee.

Workers, Party cadres, and managers formed tripartite committees in the later stages of the Cultural Revolution; PLA initiative and representation was usual in these groups. Accounts of their formation did not, however, give details of the manner of selecting worker representatives or of the nature of their participation in the committees. Regular labor, however organized, appeared in the early 1970s to have maintained its position and perhaps to have improved it.

Heavy emphasis on ideological incentives was a prominent feature of Cultural Revolution activities in the labor field; this has continued. The lowest level industrial workers were the most frequent target of these unremitting media exhortations. It was not possible to estimate the results of this stimulus to productive endeavor; however, numerous PRC accounts report inventions, adaptations, and new techniques of the use of production machinery, all contributing to increased production by grasping the revolution (see ch. 12, Public Information and Propaganda).

During and after the Cultural Revolution the PRC media featured prominently two practices affecting labor designed to further Maoist ideological objectives. One practice was the worker-peasant system of transferring labor between the agricultural and the nonagricultural sectors, a scheme started in 1964 and reported to be resented by regular workers who lost their relatively favorable employment (see ch. 5, Social System and Values). The second practice was the expansion of a program for temporary assignment of intellectuals to agricultural Communes for productive labor, an experience that was intended to heighten their revolutionary consciousness.

WORKING CONDITIONS

The Ministry of Labor is charged with all matters concerning labor, including recruitment, systems of remuneration, technical training, and safety measures. The ministry was reported in December 1970 to be one of the eleven ministries coordinated by the General Office for Industry and Communications of the PRC State Council. Its administrative framework was complemented by legislation providing for labor union organization and activities and, as in all other elements of the PRC administrative apparatus, by interlocking ties with the Party organization (see ch. 9, Political System and Values).

Wages

The question of wages, bonuses, and other material incentives for labor remained an ideological problem for the regime in 1971, as it had been since 1949. Perhaps more important, however, were the practical considerations related to the disparity between the lower income of the country's very large agricultural labor force and the higher income of the much smaller nonagricultural labor force. The New China News Agency in September 1971, for instance, noting that industrial wages had risen steadily, commented that industrial wage levels were actually set quite low "in order to strengthen worker-peasant unity."

In designing income systems throughout the economy, the state has attempted to tie rewards directly to quality and quantity of performance—as in any industrial society—consistent with its overriding economic objective of a high rate of capital accumulation. Its incentive system was modeled originally on the advanced experience of the Soviet Union, and the similarity in wage payments, or material incentives, remained striking in 1971. The principal dissimilarity was in the greater use of nonmaterial incentives in the PRC system.

Agricultural Wages

In 1971 farmers got their income from the distribution of the net income of the production teams to which they belonged, mostly in kind, with a much smaller amount in cash. An individual's share of the distribution was calculated on his total work points (see Glossary) resulting from a complicated time and piece rate pay scale and on an assessment of his strength, skill, and ideological attitude. This was generally formalized into grades, which might be as many as seven; bonuses might also be added. The system provided penalties for failure to meet work quotas, but they reportedly were seldom invoked. Men and women received equal points for similar work (see ch. 14, Agriculture).

The work point system evolved in communist-held areas before 1949 after some experimentation with schemes to transform farmers into wage earners. This objective, however, had not been attained by the early 1970s. A major incentive to increase agricultural production lay in government prices of agricultural commodities paid as taxes or sold as compulsory grain deliveries. Raising such prices would increase the value of work points, other factors being equal (see ch. 18, Trade and Transportation). The PRC claimed in September 1971 that prices had been raised by 90 percent since 1950, citing this as a cause of reported improvement in living standards.

Wages in Industry

There was no detailed information on the structure and level of industrial wages in 1971. In the mid-1960s the basic wage mechanism in industry was a multiple wage grade pattern that emphasized overfulfillment of work quotas. In general, 80 percent of the established wage was base pay, and the balance of 20 percent was used as remuneration for overquota production; payment for such production was calculated on a piecework basis or given as a straight bonus. Wage scales were commonly set up in eight grades, with variations by industry or region; intergrade differences usually varied from 9 to 18 percent, with workers in the highest grades paid about 2.5 to 3.2 times those in the lowest. Wages were the same for both women and men in a given wage grade classification.

Differentials in wage grade structures have been used primarily as a spur to production by providing a direct reward; the wage range had also been increased in industries for which government policies were seeking the most rapid growth. The wage structure during the First Five Year Plan illustrates this use of wages; at a time when the established rough standard for industry generally was a highest wage grade three times that of the lowest, the favored industries (coal mining, steel, machinery, electric power, and petroleum) were given a maximum variation above three to one. Others for which less speedy growth was scheduled (flour milling, construction, textile weaving, and other consumer goods) were held at ratios below three to one. Wage differentials have been used to attract workers or to keep them in new or remote locations by setting wages a certain percentage above the standard scale.

Production over the quota set for the wage grade was paid for on a piece rate basis, either to an individual or to a production group, or as a bonus where piece rate measurement was not practicable. Overquota production was paid for, however, only if it met quality standards. In general, the PRC's implementation of policies on wages for overquota production has been reported as less liberal than the provisions of wage regulations, an example being the limitation of bonuses to 15 percent of the standard wage in question, irrespective of the output, quality, or cost savings basis for the additional payments. Although below-quota output has resulted in the reduction of wages, there have been reports that lower grade workers have not been penalized more than 25 percent of their standard wage scale figure even if their output had fallen below that percentage. This, in effect, established a minimum wage.

Among the few figures on wage scales and levels made public since the late 1950s were those in a statement contained in a New China News Agency release in September 1971 that "the average yearly wage of Chinese workers and staff members is around 650 yuan." The news agency declared that the state had on several occasions readjusted wages, resulting in a gradual rise in incomes, especially for those in the low grades. The 650 yuan average earned wage was said to be over 50 percent higher than the average wage in 1952. It permitted workers to accumulate savings, which for both workers and peasants were reported to be 28 percent higher in 1970 than in 1965. Urban income was said to be higher than rural income but to have increased proportionately less, though the highest wage grade was said to be five times the lowest. The news agency declared that this was a "small wage gap between top and bottom" and implied that workers' income was actually better in real wage terms than it appeared because of "universal employment, low rent for housing, cheap prices for goods, and no personal income tax." In addition, the worker had free medical treatment, labor protection, and other benefits. In fact, the average wage is almost the same as that of 1957 on the basis of official PRC data for that year.

512

The effects of the Cultural Revolution on industrial wages had not become clear by late 1971. It was reported that wage demands were among the first problems raised by workers when they started to participate in the Cultural Revolution; however, in mid-1969, after the formal end of the Cultural Revolution, the regime apparently had still done little to reform the old wage structure and conditions of employment, although it had made occasional promises to do so. Ideological campaigns directed at industrial workers, in full operation in 1971, strongly implied official opposition to overquota payments in any form.

Wages in Nonindustrial Occupations

Wages for workers in handicraft cooperatives have been reported to be based on a combination of wage grade and piecework schemes. The grade was determined, presumably within the cooperative, by level of technique and skill, and a quota was fixed in day's labor units for specified quality standards. For overquota production in a given month, the worker received an additional amount, of which 70 percent was turned over to him and the remaining 30 percent was put into the welfare fund of the cooperative.

The pay of the relatively small percentage of professionals and semiprofessionals in industry has been reported to be graduated on the same kind of wage scale as that of the workers. The number of grades was reportedly much greater because the scale was intended to cover all kinds of positions up to the top government levels. No monetary equivalents for the grades were reported (see ch. 5, Social System and Values).

Nonmaterial Incentives

The different material rewards of the wage system have consistently been accompanied by other incentives aimed at increasing labor productivity and at other targets as well, especially ideological ones. The PRC adopted many of the forms of nonmaterial incentives evolved in the Soviet Union, including competitive, both individual and group, and cooperative kinds.

PRC practice in the use of nonmaterial incentives for labor has aimed chiefly at increasing quantitative performance and encouraging improvement of techniques and learning of new skills. There has been a succession of slogans, campaigns, movements, and mass participation activities generally. The CCP has played the central role in all such activities through cadres, mass organizations, and propaganda.

Competitive contests for both groups and individuals have been widely used. The wide range of objectives of such competition has included the decreasing of accidents and reducing costs, as well as raising productivity. Rewards include titles, such as Red Standard-Bearers, in an impressive hierarchy, promotions, tours, and conferences.

Cooperative incentives differ from the competitive form largely in that an appeal is made to a wider group—for example, to the entire community. The change in emphasis has an ideological significance in the substitution of an ideal labor performance by everyone in a socialized economy in place of material motivation for the individual. Such appeals do, however, have competitive features. The major use of this form of incentive has been in the mobilization of mass labor, and it affects the rural population more than the urban. The practice continued in 1971, though on a smaller scale than in the Great Leap period, in which everyone was supposed to work for the common benefit. Other uses of the cooperative technique have been in mass decisionmaking and in involving workers in self-criticism and evaluation, another form of large group activity not directly related to the income of the individual worker.

Social Benefits

Some regulations providing insurance benefits for sickness, injury, disablement, maternity, old age, and death were promulgated in 1951. The legal provisions of the PRC social insurance system stem from the first PRC State Constitution of 1954, which in Article 3 stipulated the right of working people to material assistance in old age and in cases of illness or disability. Article 27 of the draft state constitution of 1970 contained the same provision. Coverage included workers and employees and their families in government agencies as well as in state-operated enterprises. Those in transportation, in rural Communes, and in handicraft cooperatives were excluded from this system, but they had recourse to other assistance, such as communal welfare funds.

The social insurance element of the Communist Chinese labor system was generally similar to its Soviet model in varying benefits with working conditions, duration of employment, and quality of performance. Like the Soviet model, it was all-inclusive regarding workers' chief risks of sickness and accident. The system required no contributions from the workers but provided benefits proportionate to wages or salaries and higher payments to labor union members than to nonmembers.

The operation of the social insurance benefits was in 1971 unclear because the ACFTU, responsible for their administration, had disappeared in 1966. Press accounts made reference to free medical treatment and other welfare benefits in 1971, without providing any details on their administration.

514

No statistics on the number of workers covered under this system have been published. In an early estimate in 1958 the government stated that nearly 14 million of the 45 million then at work were covered.

A Western observer in 1966 noted the generally high quality of the medical services provided by large enterprises and in workers' sanatoriums that he visited. The generally liberal benefits prescribed by regulations, however, were not made available to all on an equal basis. Workers who were not labor union members were eligible for only half the benefits prescribed, and a labor union recommendation for model workers and army combat heroes made such workers eligible for an increase in benefits.

Safety Measures

Safety measures in industry and mining were the subject of voluminous regulations, with responsibility for checking delegated to the local union. One account of visits to a number of factories in 1966 found unsafe and unhealthful working conditions at some plants and concluded that ineffective enforcement of safety regulations undoubtedly hindered managerial effectiveness and productive efficiency at many factories.

Forced Labor

Forced labor has consisted of two main categories: corrective labor in penal institutions and various forms of labor assignments under Party control and supervision. *Hsia fang* (send down campaigns) and assignment of students and intellectuals to manual labor have been the most prominent of these labor assignments. According to reports both categories of forced labor existed in the PRC in 1971.

Corrective labor for those deprived of political rights was stipulated in Article 19 of the 1954 State Constitution of the PRC and in Article 14 of the draft state constitution of 1970. In both cases those subject to corrective labor were sentenced in order to transform themselves into self-supporting citizens. Corrective labor was a prominent feature of the PRC's "socialist transformation" during the 1950s and 1960s, when large numbers of persons were forced to undertake it. In 1955 the secretary general of the United Nations (UN) and the International Labor Organization (ILO) published a report on corrective labor in the PRC, which stated that there had been from 20 million to 25 million in regular permanent camps in the PRC from 1949 through 1954. The 25 million figure was estimated to include 12.5 million people in corrective labor institutions at that time; they included individuals classified as class enemies and counterrevolutionaries. In 1954 the great majority of these persons

515

were reported to be participating in some form of productive activity, such as agriculture, forestry, and the construction of roads, railroads, or water conservancy work projects, under conditions described by former inmates as poor. It is not known how many were released, and there is no information available on the operation and numbers of people involved in corrective labor, although clearly it has remained a system of reformation and punishment for political nonconformists and nonpolitical criminals (see ch. 20, Public Order and Internal Security).

The *hsia fang* of large numbers of city people to the countryside and assignments of school graduates to rural Communes still continuing in the 1970s was a form of forced labor through the exercise of degrees and combinations of ideological motivation, persuasion, and coercion (see ch. 8, Education, Intellectual Expression, and the Arts). Students especially were reported to have been moved in considerable numbers. In 1971 there was continuing evidence of their dissatisfaction in the accounts given by refugees reaching Hong Kong from Kwangtung Province. Dislike of the work assigned appeared to be the main motivation for escape. Kwangtung authorities were said to have issued a warning that the death penalty would be invoked for leaving a work post. Nonetheless, the number of refugees, who were mostly from seventeen to twenty-five years old and had a primary or secondary education, had become greater by September 1971 than at any time since 1962. No information was available for other regions, but observers suggested that similar conditions existed elsewhere.

PRODUCTIVITY

The PRC has claimed officially that industrial labor productivity increased by 61 percent during the First Five Year Plan. Using the government's data, a Western analyst concluded that the value added per worker increased 40.2 percent during the First Five Year Plan and that the increase in productivity accounted for 45.6 percent of the growth in industrial output. There were, however, extreme differences from year to year and within the various branches of industry. This analysis noted that capacity was probably not fully utilized before the First Five Year Plan and that its more intensive utilization was possibly an important element of the increase in productivity reported during the plan period.

A decline in industrial labor productivity almost certainly occurred in the Great Leap period of 1958–60; however, it is probable that by the mid-1960s it had recovered to a level equal to or slightly above that of 1957. More exact measurement has not been possible because data for 1958 included employment and the output of the handicraft and Commune industry, and since then none has been reported.

A qualified Canadian observer noted a number of factors affecting labor productivity during visits to Chinese industrial establishments of various kinds in 1966. On the positive side, he concluded that the general health and physical condition of workers were factors in an apparently lower absenteeism and labor turnover rate in China compared with that in India. He also indicated that motivation, dedication, resourcefulness, and hard work were elements in the apparently significant progress of industry and noted the stress on preventive maintenance, though this was not necessarily efficiently handled. As negative factors, he cited overstaffing and the resultant use of inefficient techniques to utilize excess labor; the use of oppressive tactics to secure unpaid overtime; and ineffective enforcement of safety regulations. This observer estimated labor productivity to be higher in 1965, just before the outbreak of the Cultural Revolution, than it had been in 1957. The effects of the Cultural Revolution on productivity cannot be determined.

A chief cause of higher productivity may be the length of time the establishment has been in operation and the consequent length of experience of its labor force and effectiveness of its management. Overall, general estimates of Chinese economic development tend to confirm the assumption that labor productivity has risen with the provision of capital equipment, in the PRC as elsewhere, although specific data on Chinese industrial and labor performance to corroborate this assumption have been lacking.

In comparing productivity of industrial labor with that of the agricultural labor force, another Western analyst concludes that, although employment figures are not known, one-sixth of the total working population is likely to produce the one-third of the national product defined as manufactured products. In industry, therefore, the productivity of labor may be said to be five to six times that of the farms.

PARTICIPATION IN INTERNATIONAL LABOR ACTIVITIES

The ACFTU was a member of the Soviet-dominated WFTU until the Sino-Soviet divergence, which resulted in the exclusion of the PRC delegation from a meeting of the WFTU general council in early December 1966. During its earlier membership PRC representatives held prominent positions in the communist body. An ACFTU vice president was a member of the WFTU executive bureau, and he and another ACFTU officer were full members of the WFTU executive committee. The listing for 1971 of the WFTU executive bureau includes one place reserved for the PRC. There has been no indication of the attitude of the PRC about membership in the ILO, a specialized agency of the UN, after the UN vote on October 25, 1971, to seat the PRC.

CHAPTER 18

TRADE AND TRANSPORTATION

Trade and transportation in the People's Republic of China (PRC) are essentially under the control of the state and conducted through governmental channels. During the Nationalist regime they had to a large extent been conducted through state organizations. After the assumption of power by the Communists in 1949 these were taken over by the new regime, and the remaining private institutions were brought under the control of the state as rapidly as possible. Both foreign and domestic trade have been planned by the central government and used as instruments to achieve national goals, both economic and political, on a domestic and international plane.

Domestic trade is carried on according to official plans by organizations of the central government and by commercial organs at the province, People's Commune (see Glossary), and local levels. The degree of centralization of control of trade has varied from time to time. Major objectives of the state have been the direction of distribution toward political and social, as well as economic, goals and the assurance of an adequate supply of goods at stable prices. The private sector has played a small part in domestic trade through the rural free market and private traders, such as peddlers. In 1971 these institutions continued to exist on a small scale.

Information concerning the value, composition, and direction of foreign trade has been derived from the records of trading partners, as no official data have been made public by the PRC since 1960 and figures for the previous two years were uncertain. The need to make multiple currency conversions in arriving at trade values and the different methods of calculating import and export values used by participating countries also have made it difficult to achieve accurate figures.

Quantitatively, the foreign trade of the PRC has been of little importance, domestically and internationally. In 1970 it was the source of about 4 percent of total domestic income. Per capita income from export trade was only the equivalent of about US$2.60. In contrast, the foreign trade of India, which is also an agricultural country, accounted for about 8 percent of total income, and the per capita income of exports was the equivalent of about US$3.60. Internationally, the foreign trade of the PRC accounted for less than 1 percent of the value of total world trade. Qualitatively, however, it had an importance out of proportion to its relative value.

Foreign trade has contributed to rapid economic development in accord with the central plan through providing a source for the acquisition of capital goods and complete plants for the increase and diversification of industrial production. Exports have been an important source of payment for imports, both as earners of foreign exchange and as commodities to be bartered for imports. Trade has also provided a connection with the more highly industrialized nations, thus serving as a source of new ideas and new technology.

Although the overall value of trade has been inconsequential, some categories of commodities have been significant on the world market. The large-scale wheat imports since 1960 have been important outlets for the surplus grain of Canada and Australia, and a continuing demand for wheat on a somewhat comparable scale could be an object for competition among world grain producers. A population of the size of the PRC provides a potential market of international consequence, although in 1971 the low per capita income and the desire to be self-sufficient indicated that foreign trade would not soon rise rapidly in absolute or relative value (see ch. 13, Character and Structure of the Economy).

Foreign trade has been of considerable significance as an instrument for the pursuit of foreign policy ideological goals through the selection of trading partners. The direction of trade has changed importantly from 1949 to 1971. For at least the first ten years trade was conducted almost entirely with other communist countries, partly because of ideological sympathies and partly because of embargoes instituted by Western nations against trade with the PRC. After the rupture with the Soviet Union in the early 1960s, trade relations expanded to include Western countries that had lowered their prohibitions against trade with the PRC, including many that had no diplomatic relations with it. Trade and foreign aid also were turned toward the underdeveloped nations and those that were ideologically uncommitted.

At the beginning of the 1970s almost all barriers to trade with the world community had disappeared, and diplomatic recognition was accelerating. The United States began to drop limitations on relations with the PRC in 1969. Restrictions were further eased in 1970, and on April 14, 1971, the United States overall embargo on direct trade in nonstrategic commodities was removed.

No direct trade had been conducted between the two countries as of the beginning of October 1971, however, and no businessmen from the United States had been invited to attend the October Canton International Trade Fair. Some American products had been purchased through non-American suppliers, and Chinese products worth several million dollars had reached the United States through third countries, but China had not permitted direct shipments. The awarding of trade contracts at this time seemed to depend to some extent on political relations, but it was too early to assess to what degree direction of trade would be determined by political conditions and to what degree it would be determined by the supply, demand, and prices of the international market.

The transportation system has been inadequate for the needs of both domestic and foreign trade. To deal with this problem at the beginning of the 1970s, a plan was proposed to initiate a national integrated system.

DOMESTIC TRADE

Until the twentieth century trade was more or less local in character, and areas were largely self-sufficient in the production and distribution of goods. Foreign merchants, who were active in the supply of capital for the conduct of external trade, participated also in domestic trade by the provision of externally produced commodities that were sold in the interior, such as petroleum products, cigarettes, some textiles, and oils and dyes.

The war with Japan, the Japanese occupation, World War II, and the civil war combined to change the pattern of domestic trade. The country was cut off from overseas commerce, and foreign merchants no longer were able to supply the limited number of commodities distributed throughout the country or to pick up domestic products for sale. In an attempt to fill the gap caused by the resultant disorganization, the Nationalist government established trading companies to buy and sell certain commodities, mainly food, fuel, and cotton. The Communists also established supply and marketing cooperatives to carry on trade in the territory that they controlled.

When the Communists came to power in 1949, they were confronted with disorganization and fragmentation in the economic and political sectors. Production had declined and transportation was disrupted. As a consequence, internal trade had ceased to function adequately, although organizations for carrying on trade were inherited from the Nationalist regime and from the areas already under communist control. In keeping with the policy of centralizing the economic system as well as the political system, early in the regime, action was taken to bring trade under government control.

Organization of Trade

As a beginning step the Ministry of Trade was established to control both domestic and foreign trade. Corporations were formed to deal with specialized categories of goods for internal and external trade and functioned under the ministry. In 1952 domestic trade was placed under the Ministry of Commerce, and foreign trade was placed under the Ministry of Foreign Trade, both located in the General Office for Finance and Trade of the State Council; specialized corporations were placed in relevant divisions. The ministries created at this time continued to function in mid-1971 (see ch. 9, Political System and Values).

The duties of the Ministry of Commerce were: the drafting and carrying out of general plans for state and cooperative trade in accordance with the economic and financial plans of the State Council; the approval of the business and financial plans of the trading companies and the supervision of their execution; and the management and regulation of state commercial capital and stocks (investment and inventory) throughout the country. In addition, the ministry was charged with the responsibility for fixing wholesale prices of state trading corporations at major markets; the provision of guidance for private trade and for market control at all levels; and the establishment of regulations for commercial accounting. The functions of the Ministry of Commerce remained essentially the same at the beginning of the 1970s as they were when originally established.

In the transformation of commerce, trading companies were created in numerous categories, including grain, cotton and textiles, salt, general merchandise, coal and building materials, native products, tea, minerals, hog bristles, edible oil, industrial equipment, silk, petroleum, metals and machinery, industrial chemicals, communications and electrical equipment, medicine, and consumer goods not elsewhere classified. The six most important national companies, all established in 1950, were the China Grain Company, the China Cotton and Textile Company, the China Coal and Building Material Company, the China Salt Company, the China General Merchandise Company, and the China Native Products Company. Under these national organizations, trading companies were organized at lower levels. Through these means the state controlled 60 percent of wholesale sales and 18 percent of retail sales by 1951. The sales and purchasing offices of state trading corporations increased from 8,000 in 1950 to 97,405 in 1955. Employment in state trading corporations also increased from 216,000 to 1.1 million during the period.

Another instrument of trade was the supply and marketing cooperative, which was not new, having been tried by the Communists before 1949. Supply and marketing cooperatives were most important in rural areas, where they engaged in both buying and selling. In 1950 they accounted for 44,000 retail outlets and purchasing points; in 1955 the number had risen to 236,000. In 1954 a central agency, the All-China Federation of Supply and Marketing Cooperatives, was initiated for supervision and regulation.

Conduct of Trade

Commerce was conducted through several channels, including state trading organs, supply and marketing cooperatives, private enterprises, and joint state-private enterprises known as "state-capitalist and cooperativized commerce." Although information concerning the absolute value was not available after 1950, when total sales through these channels were estimated at 18.2 million yuan (2.46 yuan equal US$1—see Glossary), examination of the published relative share of each sector of the marketing mechanism was illustrative of the trend toward transformation of the system away from private ownership and of the rapidity with which it was consummated.

In 1950 the bulk of domestic trade was conducted by private enterprises, which accounted for 76.1 percent of the value of wholesale sales and 83.5 percent of the value of retail sales. State commerce accounted for 23.2 percent of the value of wholesale trade and 9.7 percent of the value of retail trade. Supply and marketing cooperatives and state-capitalist and cooperativized enterprises, which were joint state-private enterprises, together accounted for less than 1 percent of wholesale trade and about 6.8 percent of retail sales.

From 1950 to 1955 the share of private commerce dropped sharply in both wholesale and retail sales. The share in trade of state trading companies, which operated through a system of wholesale depots established at various administrative levels, rapidly rose to 60.5 percent of sales value in 1952 and to 82.2 percent in 1955. In retail trade, because of the importance of private expertise and capital, private enterprises retained a larger share, accounting for 17.5 percent of total retail sales value in 1955, while that of state companies increased to only 31.6 percent of the total in the same year. In 1957, however, it was claimed that private outlets accounted for only 2.7 percent of retail sales, and domestic trade was essentially out of the hands of private owners.

From 1950 to 1955 supply and marketing cooperatives gained in number, membership, and share of trade. Their growth was a goal of government and was encouraged by preferential treatment in taxes and loans and in obtaining commodities from state trading companies. In 1954 there were 156 million members, in contrast to 25 million in 1950. The number of outlets had increased from 44,000 in 1950 to 236,000 in 1955. Supply and marketing cooperatives in 1955 accounted for 12.6 percent of the value of wholesale and 35.7 percent of the value of retail trade.

Supply and marketing cooperatives, mostly rural in location, engaged in both buying and selling. Their functions were not always readily distinguishable from those of state commercial organs. The cooperatives sold consumer goods and agricultural supplies and equipment, most of which were supplied by state trading companies. They purchased commodities from the peasants on behalf of the state, and in 1953 it was estimated that they were responsible for about 75 percent of total state purchases.

Another important step in the socialization of commerce from 1950 to 1955 was the transformation of private trading units already in existence. Large enterprises, after undergoing what was known as socialist transformation, became joint state-private or state-capitalist organizations. Private enterprises that were unable to continue in operation because of the problems of obtaining supplies and financing accepted state capital and state assistance in management. Private owners frequently received interest on their invested capital.

Small enterprises, traders, and peddlers were gradually drawn into socialized commerce by being organized into cooperative groups that served as retail distributors, commission agents, or purchasing agents for state commerce. A further step was the organization of cooperative stores in which profits and losses were shared by members. By the end of 1956 about 800,000 small retail enterprises had been merged into cooperative stores.

Control of Trade

A number of measures were adopted to control trade for the achievement of a reasonable balance of supply and demand and to ensure the allocation of materials in accord with state planning and the implementation of plans. Changes in the marketing mechanism were first applied to the production of cotton, a vital industrial crop that was in short supply for the production of textiles, which had been unobtainable as imports since the 1930s. As a guideline for the supply of cotton, a system of advance-purchase contracts was initiated in 1950. Under this system a contract was signed between the state and the farmer in the spring, setting forth the amount of cotton the farmer was to deliver to the state at harvesttime and the price (which was increased) to be paid by the state. At this time, the farmer also received a certain percentage of the amount due in the fall to pay his expenses in the interim. Manipulated prices and advance-purchase contracts were also applied to other commodities of lesser importance, including edible oils, tea leaves, jute, green hemp, tobacco, silkworms, local silk, and wool. The system was inaugurated later for these commodities than for cotton and did not affect to any great extent the supply brought to market.

The goals of matching supply and demand and allocating commodities in keeping with state plans were further aided by conferring a monopoly position on state commercial organs and supply and marketing cooperatives in dealing with commodities important to the economic plan. In 1951 the purchase of cotton yarn was limited to state trading agencies, and in 1953 the practice of planned purchase and planned supply was initiated. Planned purchases were tried as an answer to the deficit in the grain supply existing at that time. Peasants were required to deliver to the state, at official prices, quotas of grain based on the requirements of urban areas and on the peasant's own needs. Any surplus grain could be sold through state commercial agencies at slightly higher prices. In 1954 the system of planned purchase was extended to other commodities.

The demand for goods was brought under control by rationing the planned supply to consumers. The articles rationed included food grains, edible oils, raw cotton, cotton yarn, and cotton cloth. Distribution of rationed commodities was conducted by the State Council through the State Economic Commission. After 1958 the State Planning Commission assumed responsibility for distribution.

In 1953 the state added another system of commercial control known as unified purchase, which fixed quotas for delivery to the state of a number of commodities not included in the planned purchase system. This system, which covered ramie, hemp, sugarcane, tea leaves, draught animals, and live pigs, differed from planned purchase and planned supply in that peasants were permitted to dispose of the surplus as they wished and the products were not rationed.

Commodities centrally controlled through planned purchase and planned supply were known as first-category commodities; those controlled through unified purchase were known as second-category commodities. The composition of these changed from time to time. Subsidiary production of such commodities as vegetables, hogs, and poultry, produced by farmers on their own plots in their spare time, were known as third-category commodities. These also were brought under the control of the government, and by 1955 all commodities had to be exchanged through state commercial organizations. The rural free markets were closed at this point. They were reopened later, however, to meet new commercial needs.

The Decree on the Reform of the Commercial Management System, promulgated in 1957, introduced an element of decentralization in the control of commerce. Changes proposed were based on experiments that had been tried on a limited basis.

Under the new system authority over commerce that had been lodged in the central government was moved to, or shared with, provincial and lower level local authorities. Although the State Council retained the function of promulgating major plans, the number of details involved was reduced, and a greater degree of responsibility for implementation was transferred to provincial and local authorities. The Ministry of Commerce lost part of the control over trade when local specialized trading corporations that had formerly been controlled by national corporations were merged with local commercial departments.

Large wholesale depots, refrigerator plants, and granaries, which are essential to the smooth functioning of the distribution system, had been controlled by central authorities. After decentralization plans were effected, they were placed under the joint control of central and provincial authorities. Responsibility for smaller wholesale depots was shared by provincial and lower level authorities.

The initiation of Communes in 1958 affected the organization of trade in both rural and urban areas and carried still further the trend away from sole control by state commercial agencies. In urban Communes municipal departments of commerce assumed functions ranging far from a narrow interpretation of trade. In 1960 commercial organs in urban Communes were expected to establish messhalls, nurseries, and service and welfare facilities as well as conduct the distribution of commodities and operate the rationing system for nonstaple consumer goods; they also worked with street factories in obtaining materials needed for production (see ch. 15, Industry).

The importance of commercial organizations in urban Communes varied. In Chungking they organized and operated comprehensive stores in each street area. In many other urban Communes they were less active.

The initiation of the rural Commune brought a number of changes to the pattern of trading and to institutions conducting trade. One important change was the transformation of supply and marketing cooperatives into supply and marketing departments of the rural Communes. Although the supply and marketing cooperatives were placed under local Communes, commercial organs of the central government continued to have some control, and the exact relationship between Commune-level departments and state commercial organs was unclear.

The scope and character of retail trade was changed by the Commune way of living. Food, which was locally produced, for the most part was delivered to messhalls and other public institutions. The changed way of living in the rural Commune also altered the categories of goods demanded. Because of employment outside the home, women no longer had time to produce goods that had formerly been produced domestically, thus increasing the demand for readymade clothing and shoes.

Just before the initiation of the Communes, a measure of decentralization was introduced into the system of grain procurement and sales. Although the central government continued to set the targets for grain procurement and sales, the guidelines of the central government were simplified in detail, and the responsibility for grain collection and supply to fill established state targets was transferred to the level of the agricultural producers' cooperatives. Targets for grain procurement were fixed by contracts. The same system was also applied to other commodities.

Rural Free Markets

Rural free markets, much like fairs, had been the traditional outlet for surplus agricultural production and peasant handicrafts. They had been held at regular intervals at market towns. Peasants brought their surplus goods for sale and purchased needed commodities that they were unable to fill by their own efforts. The existence and character of markets after 1949 varied with the policies applied to commerce and the results obtained from these policies. Rural markets filled a social as well as an economic function (see ch. 5, Social System and Values).

As a result of the increased control of trade by the central government through planned purchase, planned supply, and unified purchase agreements, rural markets had almost ceased to exist by the end of 1953. Their decline reduced the supply available to consumers, and by 1956 the reopening of rural markets was encouraged. Restrictions were imposed on the operation of the markets, and in October 1956 a decree was pronounced excluding from the markets first- and second-category commodities and others for which the supply was inadequate to the demand; this edict was soon relaxed, and it was permissible to sell second-category commodities after compulsory sales had been filled. By November 1956 nine provinces had reopened rural free markets.

The relaxation of regulations concerning products that could be offered at the free market was found to have adverse effects on the supply of commodities to the state. Peasants spent more time on commodities that could be sold at the free market than on those to be delivered to the state; furthermore, some excluded articles found their way to the free market. Because of this situation, by mid-1957 the government imposed further regulations on the operation of the market, and in early 1958, as a result of the increasing time demands made on the peasants during the Great Leap Forward (see Glossary) and the market changes brought about by the inauguration of the Commune system, the rural free market was abolished, as was the peasant's private plot.

Conduct of Domestic Trade, 1959 to 1969

In 1959, toward the end of the Great Leap Forward, new regulations for domestic trade were propounded with the purpose of encouraging production of agricultural commodities, increasing knowledge of their actual supply and demand (knowledge that had been distorted during the height of the Great Leap Forward) and reestablishing avenues of control by the central government.

In mid-1959 the Ministry of Commerce called for a gradual opening of rural free markets, and in September 1959 the Central Committee of the Chinese Communist Party (CCP) and the State Council issued Regulations on the Organization of Rural Markets. This directive set forth the commodities that could be sold and the conditions of sale and designated eligible participants.

Surplus first- and second-category commodities could be sold at rural markets, but they had to be sold at state purchasing prices, which lessened the possibility of their being sold on the market instead of to state agencies. Sideline and handicraft goods of Commune members could also be sold at rural markets. The main participants included Communes, production brigades (see Glossary), individual Commune members, and local state commercial departments. Outside potential traders were required to obtain official permission. Peddlers and small tradesmen had to be licensed to operate in the area. The regulations also provided for the organization of market management committees, including representatives of commerce, food, banking, revenue, industry, and agriculture. Each such committee was under the authority of the local Party committee.

Although there was a trend toward the reestablishment of rural free markets soon after the pronouncement in 1959, many markets did not reopen until 1961 or 1962. It was estimated that there were 40,000 rural markets in existence in 1961. At this time the right of peasants to have private plots was restored.

In mid-1961 a further measure was taken to strengthen the control of the central government over trading institutions and patterns. At this time the rural supply and marketing cooperatives, which had been merged with the supply and marketing departments of rural Communes in 1958, were separated from the Commune department and made separate entities under state supervision.

The organizational framework for trade that was outlined in 1959 and the early 1960s continued to function with reasonable smoothness through 1962. Farmers were urged to sell what they produced on their private plots to supply and marketing cooperatives, which would then sell the goods at a small profit at rural free markets. Production of private plots was important in providing food for city dwellers (see ch. 14, Agriculture). The rural free markets continued to function, but in early 1963 changes were made in the organization of larger markets, and free markets became state-run markets, which were said to charge higher prices.

According to the draft of the economic plan for 1965, the basic framework for the conduct of commerce was expected to continue in the same pattern, with some improvement in functioning. The plan called for an improvement of markets, an increase in the supply of basic goods, and establishment of better lines of commodity exchange between country and city. The plan encouraged the continuance of sideline production, which had been important in the economic recovery after the Great Leap Forward. It also envisaged the continuance of rural free markets, which were under the supervision of state supply and marketing cooperatives.

The emergence of the Great Proletarian Cultural Revolution in 1966, which was scheduled to coincide with the first year of the Third Five Year Plan (1966–70), disrupted the organization and conduct of commerce, as it did other sectors of the economy (see ch. 10, Political Dynamics). Although no official changes in organization were announced in the early part of the Cultural Revolution, turbulence of the time was responsible for a breakdown of the accepted marketing mechanisms in both rural and urban areas.

The functioning of the marketing mechanism suffered from conflicting political ideologies during the Cultural Revolution. It was reported that some persons in power urged that more foodstuffs be retained by the Communes and less be given over to the state to fulfill agreed upon contracts. It was also reported that some cadres in Communes encouraged the withholding of foodstuffs. Farm produce was not surrendered, and government quotas were not filled. To meet the situation in 1967, troops were mobilized to enforce military control over rural areas, assist in requisition and purchase of agricultural products, and suppress reactionary forces. Despite these efforts, collection goals were not met.

In urban areas the reduced production of consumer goods for the market, the desertion of trade personnel for other fields, the strain on transportation facilities for moving goods, and the withholding of commodities from the market in hope of receiving higher pries resulted in short supplies, particularly of goods basic to everyday needs. In some cities, especially Canton, it became necessary to reinstitute meat rationing in early 1967. By the spring of 1968 consumer goods had become even more scarce, and customers stood in line at markets to make even simple purchases. Speculation and black markets flourished.

Near the end of the Cultural Revolution, reforms were undertaken in the organization and conduct of trade to strengthen the socialist commercial network in rural areas. In 1965 the rural commercial network was made up of federal cooperatives at the *hsien* (county) level, supply and marketing cooperatives at the Commune level, and purchasing and selling agencies and stores at the production brigade level. This system was administratively independent from the Communes, production brigades, production teams, and profit seeking within the rural commercial framework in part accounted for the breakdown of the marketing system during the Cultural Revolution.

By 1968 reform of the supply and marketing cooperatives had been undertaken in some Communes. Poor and lower-middle peasants had reorganized the commercial mechanism by establishing supply and marketing service cooperatives at the Commune level and service stations at the production brigade level (see ch. 5, Social System and Values). Former staff members who were considered undesirable were expelled. Control was exercised by management teams consisting of representatives from poor and lower-middle peasants and members of revolutionary committees at the Commune and brigade levels. They were responsible for administrative and personnel matters. The state was responsible for control over finance, pricing, purchase and sales plans, and the allocation of merchandise and its disposal.

The object of the reorganization was the elimination of the element that had placed "profit before politics," the improvement in services for the peasants, and the organization of markets to ensure the fulfillment of state purchase quotas. In January 1968 the Party, the Military Commission, and the Cultural Revolution Group jointly promulgated a directive laying down policies for the elimination of black market speculation and profiteering, which plagued urban as well as rural commerce. The policies set forth strengthened the role of the state.

In addition to a reform in management, a reform in the organization of rural commerce was proposed, and it was planned to initiate an integrated large, medium, and small commercial network. The goal was to provide better service for the countryside.

Before the Cultural Revolution all city stores were supervised by specialized corporations, which were under the control of the head office of the corporation in Peking and the appropriate provincial or municipal bureaus. The Ministry of Commerce stood at the head of the trading structure. Because of the turmoil caused by the Cultural Revolution, city trade at all levels—stores, bureaus, and specialized corporations—essentially came to a standstill, and it was considered necessary for the People's Liberation Army (PLA) to take over the Ministry of Commerce in an effort to renew the functioning of trade channels. In this period specialized corporations were no longer important, and the office of military representatives for commerce established within the ministry dealt directly with financial and commercial groups of various revolutionary committees at the provincial, municipal, and district levels in matters pertaining to purchases, storage, and distribution of merchandise, regulation of working capital, and allocation of raw materials.

By 1969 city trade had been reopened, but the exact manner of operation was not clear. Military personnel had not been withdrawn from the Ministry of Commerce. Local specialized corporations were again in operation, and Party committees had been set up within the specialized corporations to launch political and ideological movements among the workers and staff members of all their subordinate stores. Revolutionary committees had also been set up in large and medium-sized retail stores in cities and were assisting in the management of business. Further information concerning specialized corporations was not available in 1971.

Retail Trade in the Early 1970s

In early 1971 a number of foreign visitors had the opportunity to observe retail markets in a number of large cities and, to a lesser degree, in some smaller communities. Almost all observers agreed that stores seemed to have ample stocks of basic necessities at least, although there was some difference of opinion as to the variety of goods available and the character of retail outlets.

Department stores were government owned. There was no advertising, but stores bore signs announcing that they were government department stores; many displayed large pictures of Chairman Mao Tse-tung. Large city stores operated under the administration of the municipal commerce department with supervision from the revolutionary committee within the municipality. In 1971 it was reported that department stores in Shanghai exhibited a greater variety and quantity of goods than had been available since 1949. The Shanghai General Department Store (Number 1), which occupied a modern five-story building, was said to compare favorably with modern Western department stores in its facilities as did the largest department store in Peking. In Canton, department stores were smaller in size and plain, with less modern facilities.

All the city department stores visited catered to the needs and convenience of the working people. Transistor radios and small television sets were available, but little was displayed that could be called luxury goods. Clothing mostly consisted of work clothes in blue, gray, or khaki, but children's clothes were obtainable in bright colors. Of the specialty shops, bicycle shops were the busiest, since bicycles were becoming an increasingly important means of transportation.

Foodshops had ample stocks of food at prices low enough to make a reasonably diversified diet available to low-income groups. Because of rulings of the Ministry of Commerce, prices were essentially the same throughout the country, only a small difference reflecting relative transportation costs.

In 1971 cereals, cooking oil, and inexpensive cotton goods were rationed. Wool, silk, rayon, and synthetic materials, which were more expensive, were not rationed. Certain articles made of cotton cloth required ration coupons. Special arrangements were made for foreigners to obtain in "friendship shops" commodities that required ration coupons or were available only in government stores.

Retail trading was organized for the benefit of workers. In Shanghai the General Department Store (Number 1) was open seven days a week from 8:00 A.M. to 9:00 P.M., and a special department was open from 6:00 P.M. to 8:00 A.M. for the benefit of late-shift factory workers and peasants who brought produce from their Communes and private plots to the city for the early-morning market. The store reportedly employed 1,921 persons who worked eight-hour shifts.

The buying plan for the store was constructed semiannually by the store supervisor and state commerce officials. Demand for each category of commodities, which was based partly on the reports of survey teams, was estimated; unsold goods, however, were to be returned to the central state distribution agency. The store obtained goods directly from factories and wholesale houses, as well as from the state distribution center.

Stores in rural areas carried a more limited supply of merchandise than did urban stores. All stores carried basic necessities, and it was reported that a village store in a Commune south of Peking carried cotton, synthetic, and rayon cloth in a wide variety of patterns, as well as sandals, thermos jugs, and other items that could be obtained in city stores; furthermore, other goods could be ordered from city department stores.

FOREIGN TRADE

Foreign trade has been a means of working toward modernization and industrialization by the acquisition of new techniques, materials, and equipment that were not available domestically. Trade was planned to fit the development programs of the state, and exports were planned for the purpose of paying for needed imports rather than for disposing of excess production. The ultimate goal, which had not been achieved in 1971, was self-sufficiency.

In 1971 foreign trade was conducted through eight ports: Lu-ta (Dairen), Ch'in-huang-tao, Tientsin, Tsingtao, Lien-yun-chiang, Shanghai, Chan-chiang, and Canton. The China Ocean Steamship Agency handled the clearing of foreign ships and agency work at all ports. In 1970 the merchant fleet consisted of 248 ships with a total tonnage of 867,994 deadweight tons, compared with a registered tonnage of 402,000 tons in 1960. In addition to the registered fleet, there was an unspecified number of foreign ships under charter.

Organization of Trade

Foreign trade is a monopoly of the state. Early trade had been initiated by foreign private enterprise. In 1949, however, it was in a state of grave disorganization after the years of internal strife, the war with Japan, and the disruption of trade in World War II. After the

Communists took power, the state began the reorganization of trade to bring it into control and channel it toward official objectives.

The Ministry of Foreign Trade, which was separated from the Ministry of Trade in 1952, controls the conduct of foreign trade, implementing the goals of the central planning agency. It enters into trade agreements, supervises trading corporations, and oversees trade promotion.

Trade, for the most part, is carried on through a network of corporations established to deal with specific categories of industrial goods and commercial services. State trading companies were established early in the economic reorganization period of the 1950s. Although the goal of trading companies is to buy in a market with the lowest prices and sell in one with the highest prices, they follow the dictates of economic plans that are sometimes determined by noneconomic considerations. If trading companies suffer a net loss they are reimbursed from the budget; if they make a profit it accrues to the state budget.

The number and categories of trading companies have varied at times since the system was initiated. A report published in early 1971 listed the following eleven trading corporations—China National Chemicals Import and Export Corporation; China National Native Produce and Animal By-Products Import and Export Corporation; National Light Industrial Products Import and Export Corporation; China National Textiles Import and Export Corporation; China National Cereals, Oils, and Foodstuffs Import and Export Corporation; China National Machinery Import and Export Corporation; China National Metals and Minerals Import and Export Corporation; Sinofreight Chartering and Shipbreaking Corporation; Complete Plant and Export Corporation; Publications Center; and Foreign Trade Transportation Corporation. The head office of each of these companies was in Peking, and they had branch offices in major cities. They also had representation in Hong Kong and Macao through the China Resources Company.

The China Committee for the Promotion of International Trade is a quasi-governmental agency for the promotion of trade with noncommunist countries. It functions primarily to establish trade with countries not having diplomatic relations with Communist China.

Trading Procedures and Promotions

Foreign trade is carried on by negotiation with a variety of entities, including individuals interested in doing business with the PRC and groups of businessmen representing large foreign firms, and through various means, such as unofficial agreements with representatives of foreign countries and official agreements between governments. In all instances, state trading companies rather than end users or suppliers conduct negotiations for the PRC.

The establishment of contact with the appropriate trading corporation through its head office in Peking is the initial step for the foreign businessman desiring to enter into trade relations with the PRC for the first time. The trading corporation requires full information about products so that it may make a decision as to its interest. Samples may be sent only after permission to do so is received. All trading corporations are equipped to conduct correspondence in English; in some instances, the interested trader is invited to visit Communist China.

For groups representing large foreign firms accustomed to concluding contracts and for semiofficial delegations from other countries, the procedure is essentially the same as for the individual who is a novice. In all instances, the conclusion of a contract requires great care and considerable time, as the Chinese strictly observe all provisions of the contract and expect reciprocal compliance.

The best known and probably the most effective channel for promoting trade is the Chinese Export Commodities Fair, generally known as the Canton International Trade Fair. This fair was instituted in 1957 and is held in Canton from April 15 to May 15 and from October 15 to November 15 each year.

Since the Canton International Trade Fair was first initiated, the number of exhibits, visitors, and countries represented and the proportion of foreign trade that results from the fair have grown rapidly. Representatives of PRC trading corporations attend. Foreign countries send trade delegations, trade officials, and representatives of state-operated companies. Representatives of major foreign industrial and commercial firms that have previously established trading relations also attend but only upon invitation.

It has been estimated that about 30 to 50 percent of the total value of trade arises from negotiations that start at the trade fair. Contracts, however, are signed in Peking after the fair has ended and are the result of careful bargaining. About 4,500 businessmen representing sixty countries attended the spring fair in 1971. Overseas traders considered that business was disappointing, perhaps because some of the major transactions had already taken place and others had begun before the fair opened.

Trade is also promoted by the participation of the PRC in foreign trade fairs and exhibits and by governmental missions sent abroad for trade discussions. In September 1971 a delegation of nine, headed by the minister of foreign trade, visited France to discuss trade prospects between the two countries. The visit was in return for a visit to Peking by a French governmental official in 1970.

In Canada the embassy of the PRC was planning to build a pavilion at the Canadian National Exhibition in Toronto in 1972 and to construct a display at the permanent exposition in Montreal. It was also reported that the opening of consulates in Montreal and Vancouver to promote trade was under consideration. Denmark was given permission to hold a trade fair in the PRC in 1972, the first trade fair to be held by a Western country since the Cultural Revolution.

In mid-1971 it was reported that trading relations existed with more than 100 countries on the basis of both formal intergovernmental agreements and informal agreements with so-called friendly firms. The China Committee for the Promotion of International Trade usually dealt with these friendly firms. For the most part formal agreements were bilateral. They were made on an annual basis and included a list of the specific commodities to be exchanged, the terms of delivery, the currency of payment, and the determination of prices. Trade agreements culminated in specific contracts. Among other agreements, a number of trade agreements representing small amounts were signed with a number of communist countries in 1969. In March 1971 the annual trade accord was reached with Japan. Later in the year a new trade and payments agreement was signed with the Soviet Union in Moscow.

Composition of Trade

From 1950 to 1969 the total value of trade fluctuated from time to time, mostly in response to periods of economic activity, but the general direction was upward. The value of trade in 1969, which was the equivalent of US$3,875 million, was well over twice the value in 1950 of about US$1,573 million (see table 10). From 1950 to 1954 imports exceeded exports in value, and the trade balance was unfavorable. From 1955 to 1969 exports exceeded imports in value, and the trade balance was favorable except in 1967, when the value of exports dropped. Preliminary figures for 1970 indicated that the value of imports rose, leaving an unfavorable balance in that year.

Imports

The composition of imports has responded to the priorities of state economic planning and to needs arising from events beyond the control of the state. From 1950 to 1960 imports consisted mostly of producer goods for the development of heavy industry. These included chemicals, metals, ores, and other industrial materials, as well as machinery and equipment. During this period complete plants, most of which came from the Soviet Union, were an important component of imports. In 1957 they represented about 20 percent of total value.

Year	Exports	Imports	Total
1950	697	876	1,573
1951	977	1,025	2,002
1952	922	984	1,906
1953	1,056	1,179	2,235
1954	1,197	1,307	2,504
1955	1,431	1,310	2,741
1956	1,684	1,449	3,133
1957	1,697	1,398	3,095
1958	1,985	1,777	3,762
1959	2,248	2,026	4,274
1960	2,017	1,953	3,970
1961	1,556	1,382	2,938
1962	1,562	1,085	2,647
1963	1,595	1,165	2,760
1964	1,788	1,390	3,178
1965	1,958	1,801	3,759
1966	2,170	2,035	4,205
1967	1,915	1,945	3,860
1968	1,890	1,820	3,710
1969	2,050	1,825	3,875

Source: Adapted from Alexander Eckstein (ed.), *China Trade Prospects and U.S. Policy* (Praeger Library of Chinese Affairs Series), New York, 1971, pp. 276–277; and "China's Foreign Trade in 1969," *Current Scene: Developments in Mainland China* [Hong Kong], VIII, No. 16, October 7, 1970, pp. 4, 8.

Military equipment also constituted a large, but unspecified, item in imports.

In 1961 there was a change in the structure of imports. Because of the agricultural crisis arising from poor crops in 1959 and 1960, the import of foodstuffs, of which wheat was the principal component, was increased. At the same time, however, that wheat was imported, rice, which brought a higher price in the world market, was exported to nearby countries. Imports of producer goods also declined in relative importance because of the decrease in industrial investment during the recession years after the Great Leap Forward. Because of the new emphasis on agriculture in the 1960s, commodities for the use of agriculture became important and continued to rank high until the end of the decade.

From 1966, when the Cultural Revolution was beginning, to 1969, when it had passed the height of its activity, the value of imports declined from the equivalent of US$2,035 million to about US$1,825 million. The relative share of industrial sectors also was rearranged to some extent (see table 11). Imported foodstuffs dropped absolutely, as did manufactures. Iron and steel imports increased in value, whereas those of machinery and equipment decreased, indicating that investment in plants was decreasing and that there was need for more raw and intermediate materials by plants already constructed. Chemicals increased in total value absolutely and relatively. During this period fertilizers remained the most valuable chemical import in accord with the policy of emphasizing agriculture; but other chemicals, such as dyes, pesticides, pharmaceuticals, and medicines, increased in value, and it was anticipated that the demand for pharmaceuticals and medicines would grow in the 1970s. Crude materials, fuels, and edible oils (which included rubber) decreased in absolute value but increased in share of the total.

Table 11. People's Republic of China, Value of Imports, by Industrial Sector, 1966 and 1969

(in million US$)

Sector	1966	Percent	1969	Percent
Foodstuffs	510	25.0	360	19.7
Chemicals	250	12.3	295	16.2
Manufactures	910	44.7	810	44.4
Crude materials, fuels, and edible oils	340	16.7	330	18.1
Miscellaneous	25	1.3	30	1.6
TOTAL	2,035	100.0	1,825	100.0

Source: Adapted from "China's Foreign Trade in 1969," Current Scene: Developments in Mainland China [Hong Kong], VIII, No. 16, October 7, 1970, p. 4.

Exports

In 1969 manufactured goods were the most valuable category of exports, followed in order by foodstuffs; crude materials, fuels, and edible oils; chemicals; and miscellaneous articles. This followed the pattern of industrial categories in 1966, with some small change in value, and in share of the total (see table 12).

The most valuable single export item in 1969 was textile yarn and fabrics, which consisted of cotton and a small amount of silk, which had been a prized export by tradition. Cotton work clothing also was a valuable export. For the most part, foodstuffs, including meat and fish, fruit and vegetables, and rice, were exported within the area. The amount of rice exported varied according to the surplus that could be spared domestically and the demand from nearby countries.

Crude materials accounted for about 23 percent of the value of exports in 1969, a slightly larger share than in 1966. This category included a wide variety of commodities, such as textile fibers, soybeans, ores and minerals, oilseeds, hides and skins, hog bristles,

Table 12. People's Republic of China, Value of Exports, by Industrial Sector, 1966 and 1969

(in million US$)

Sector	1966	Percent	1969	Percent
Foodstuffs	595	27.4	580	28.3
Chemicals	90	4.2	90	4.4
Manufactures	900	41.5	835	40.7
Crude materials, fuels, and edible oils	480	22.1	470	22.9
Miscellaneous	105	4.8	75	3.7
TOTAL	2,170	100.0	2,050	100.0

Source: Adapted from "China's Foreign Trade in 1969," *Current Scene: Developments in Mainland China* [Hong Kong], VIII, No. 16, October 7, 1970, p. 8.

wool and cashmere, feathers, and human hair. The country had long been a source of most of these commodities in international trade.

Prices of exported manufactured goods in some instances were fixed by appropriate import-export corporations. They were usually fixed at competitive levels and were included in contracts.

Direction of Trade

The direction of foreign trade has been influenced by political policies and by controls and limitations imposed by other countries, as well as by geographical location, favorable prices, and the supply and demand of world markets. The availability of credit also has been instrumental in directing trade.

Before 1949 trade was carried on mostly with Great Britain, the United States, Japan, Hong Kong, France, and Germany. After 1949 the composition of trading countries was influenced by the policy of alignment with other communist countries known as "leaning to one side." Under this policy, trade with the Soviet Union and with countries of Eastern Europe, which had formerly accounted for a minimal share, began to assume new importance. This trend was augmented by controls instituted by the United States at the time the Communists assumed control of the government and was reinforced when a total embargo was invoked and export licenses were revoked after the beginning of the Korean conflict. Participation in trade controls was broadened to include the other Western nations and member countries of the United Nations.

The trade embargo closed Western nations as sources of supply and as markets for commodities earning foreign exchange. The value of trade with communist countries rose rapidly, increasing from the equivalent of US$604 million in 1950 to US$1,034 million in 1951 (see table 13). From 1952 through 1960 trade with communist nations constituted more than 60 percent of total value, rising to slightly more than 75 percent in 1954.

Table 13. People's Republic of China, Trade with Communist and
Noncommunist Countries, 1950–65

(in million US$)

Year	Noncommunist Countries	Percent	Communist Countries	Percent	Total Trade
1950 _____	969	61.6	604	38.4	1,573
1951 _____	968	48.4	1,034	51.6	2,002
1952 _____	588	30.9	1,318	69.1	1,906
1953 _____	672	30.1	1,563	69.9	2,235
1954 _____	622	24.9	1,882	75.1	2,504
1955 _____	761	27.4	1,990	72.6	2,751
1956 _____	1,008	32.2	2,125	67.8	3,133
1957 _____	1,145	37.0	1,950	63.0	3,095
1958 _____	1,453	38.6	2,309	61.4	3,762
1959 _____	1,301	30.4	2,973	69.6	4,274
1960 _____	1,351	34.0	2,619	66.0	3,970
1961 _____	1,245	42.4	1,693	57.6	2,938
1962 _____	1,228	46.4	1,419	53.6	2,647
1963 _____	1,504	54.5	1,256	45.5	2,760
1964 _____	2,067	65.0	1,111	35.0	3,178
1965 _____	2,609	69.4	1,150	30.6	3,759

Source: Adapted from Alexander Eckstein (ed.), *China Trade Prospects and U.S. Policy* (Praeger Library of Chinese Affairs Series), New York, 1971, pp. 276–277.

The 1960s ushered in a new trend in direction of trade and a new policy aimed at diversification of partners (see ch. 11, Foreign Relations). In 1961 trade with communist countries declined sharply. Total trade value also declined in this year, but the share conducted with communist countries dropped from 66 percent to about 58 percent of total value. This trend continued throughout the 1960s. In 1963, for the first time, trade with noncommunist nations constituted more than 50 percent of total value, and in 1969 the share was estimated at about 70 percent of the total. A significant feature in the changed direction of trade was the purchase and installation of complete plants from Western European countries and from Japan, thus replacing the Soviet Union as a source of industrial installations.

A combination of factors entered into the changing direction of trade. It was initiated by deteriorating relations with the Soviet Union; Soviet technicians withdrew at the beginning of the 1960s, and construction projects underway or planned were brought to a halt. The trend away from communist countries was also influenced by the need for large-scale grain imports beginning in 1961 and by the desire of the PRC to expand trade and economic relations with some of the underdeveloped countries of Asia and Africa.

The most important factor in the change in trading relations was the lifting of embargoes and trade controls by Western nations in the 1960s. The United States, which was the last major nation to liberalize trading policies, instituted a series of modifications beginning in July 1969. At that time the policy of the United States was modified to permit tourists to bring back a limited amount of goods from the PRC. At the end of 1969 the policy was expanded to remove the limitation of value on noncommercial goods that might be brought into the country by individuals and nonprofit institutions and to permit foreign subsidiaries of United States firms to carry on nonstrategic trade with the PRC. An announcement was made in April 1971 of changes broadening trading relations in several aspects and permitting limited direct trade. In June 1971 an export-control bulletin that made clear the implications of the April pronouncement was published by the United States Department of Commerce. No further information was available, however, in September 1971.

Japan, Hong Kong, and the Federal Republic of Germany (West Germany) ranked as the three most valuable trading partners in 1970, maintaining the same positions as in 1969. Below this level there were some changes in the composition of the twelve most valuable noncommunist trading partners. In 1970 Malaysia was included in the top twelve, and the Netherlands, which was included in 1969, was dropped from the list. There was also a change in rank of other partners.

In 1970 the PRC enjoyed a favorable balance of trade with Hong Kong, Singapore, Italy, Malaysia, and Ceylon. Hong Kong was the outstanding source of foreign exchange. Singapore also was an important market for exports. An unfavorable balance existed with Japan, West Germany, Australia, the United Kingdom, Canada, France, and Pakistan.

Trade with Japan, which began in 1949, has fluctuated according to political relations between the two countries. In 1951, during the Korean conflict, it declined sharply, but trade agreement on a nongovernmental basis was concluded in 1952, and trade began to increase in value. In 1960 transactions were begun with so-called friendly firms, which were firms recommended by Japanese political parties and organizations sympathetic to the PRC. In 1962 the Liao-Takasaki Agreement authorized long-term private trading in a number of categories in addition to trade with friendly firms. When the original five-year period of the Liao-Takasaki Agreement expired in 1967, the agreement was renamed the Japan-China Memorandum Trade. Memorandum trade was planned on an annual basis and usually consisted of large-scale transactions in manufactured goods.

Trade with friendly firms increased in value absolutely and relatively from 1964 to 1969, when it accounted for 90 percent of the total.

Imports from Japan included iron and steel, chemicals, machinery, textile goods, and nonferrous metals. Fertilizers constituted the largest component of chemicals, but the category also included synthetic fibers and plastics. Exports to Japan included foodstuffs, marine products, and raw silk. In 1969, because of surplus production in Japan, rice was not included in the export list.

Hong Kong has been an important market for exports, as the PRC has daily provided crops and livestock to feed the population. Imports from Hong Kong are minimal; in 1970 it was estimated that exports to Hong Kong, excluding reexports, were valued at the equivalent of US$353.6 million, but imports were valued at only US$5 million. In addition to the foreign exchange earned through trade, Hong Kong has also provided exchange through remittances and business earnings.

In 1970 West Germany was the most important trading partner in Western Europe, a position it had held in 1969 and also in 1968. It has been an important source of supply of finished and semifinished metal products (mainly steel), chemicals, metals and ores, and machinery. In mid-1970 an agreement was concluded for the delivery of thirty large locomotives in 1972. West Germany has provided a market for animal byproducts, hides and skins, wool, and other textile fibers.

The United Kingdom has provided a source of copper, platinum, and diamonds for industrial use and a market for wool, cashmere, chemicals, foodstuffs, and raw silk. Malaysia has provided raw rubber. Singapore, indirectly, had been a source of natural rubber, but in 1970 more direct trade was carried on with Malaysia. Singapore provided a market for textiles, yarn, clothing, and processed foods.

Trade with Canada and Australia, the two major sources of needed wheat imports, has fluctuated according to contracts and delivery schedules of the grain. In 1970 and 1971 it also had political implications. In 1970, shortly after the establishment of diplomatic relations, a new agreement was signed with Canada for the delivery of 2.7 million metric tons of wheat valued at the equivalent of US$160 million, and in mid-1971 it was indicated that Canada would be considered as the first source of wheat. Although in 1970 and early 1971 Australia delivered wheat contracted for in 1969, no further contract was signed at the time, and no further information was available in mid-1971.

Balance of Payments

In 1971 no comprehensive information concerning the balance of international payments was available. Estimates for the 1950–64 period were largely based on data reported by trading partners.

From 1951 through 1955 there was a favorable balance of payments. Despite the fact that the value of imports exceeded that of exports from 1950 to 1954, exports were expanding rapidly and provided an important source of international payments. The deficits on the merchandise and service account, which also included payments for freight and insurance, were met by large-scale, long-term credits, mostly from the Soviet Union, and by remittances from Overseas Chinese. Expropriation of foreign exchange and gold from private individuals also added to governmental reserves of foreign exchange during this period.

The trend of international payments changed in 1956 when a small deficit developed. Despite the fact that exports had expanded rapidly in value and there was a surplus of the equivalent of US$235 million in merchandise trade in 1956, the decrease in credits from the Soviet Union and the beginning of debt repayments and of foreign aid payments more than absorbed the surplus achieved.

The demand for imports during the intense activity of the Great Leap Forward in 1958 and 1959 placed a strain on the international payments situation. The decrease in agricultural exports in 1960 and heavy wheat purchases beginning in 1961 also added to the strain. The burden of large-scale wheat purchases was partially alleviated by cutting nongrain imports to a minimum. The increase in imports during 1958 and 1959 and the transportation of wheat after 1960 also called for higher payments for freight and insurance during the period, since the PRC did not have an adequate fleet and it was necessary to charter ships.

During 1963 and 1964, in the recovery after the devastation of the Great Leap Forward and the agricultural failures, the international payments situation improved somewhat. The merchandise trade balance increased, and the country was able to repay its debt to the Soviet Union and other countries of Eastern Europe. Growing trade with the West, however, increased indebtedness to the rest of the world, and the reserve of Western currencies and gold declined from the equivalent of US$645 million in 1957 to US$400 million in 1964.

Since 1965 there has been little comprehensive quantified information summarizing the international balance of payments. From 1966 to 1969 there was a favorable trade balance except in 1967. Payments for foreign aid have continued; the shipping fleet has continued to be inadequate to needs; and there was no foreign investment. After the break in economic relations with the Soviet Union, there had been no long-term credits, and credits from the Western nations were short term.

TRANSPORTATION

The transportation system has been the victim of invasion, civil war, and internal political and economic movements, such as the Great Leap Forward and the Cultural Revolution. Reorganization into a system adequate to fill economic and military needs has been a goal of the government since the accession of the Party; fulfillment of plans, however, has been interrupted from time to time by various crises.

In 1949 the transportation system was made up of two sectors, modern and traditional. The modern sector included railroads, highways, and civil aviation routes, not all of which were in operation at that time. The traditional sector included junks and sampans plying the waterways, a variety of vehicles using animal or human power for hauling, and human beings serving as cargo carriers. In the mid-1960s the traditional sector continued to operate along with modern facilities, and traditional forms were especially important for short distances. Bicycle-propelled rickshaws provided transportation for people; freight was conveyed by junks and sampans, and in 1971 men, women, and children pulled carts laden with goods. Nevertheless all categories, of modern transportation had increased in services rendered since 1949.

When the CCP assumed control of the government, transportation facilities, which were basically inadequate and underdeveloped, were in a state of chaos. During the civil war the transportation system, because of its strategic function in communication and in the movement of men and goods, had been a target for control or destruction by opposing forces. Railroads, which were the most important segment of the system, had been severely damaged. Roadbeds had deteriorated, lines had been cut, bridges had been destroyed, and rolling stock was in a state of disrepair. In other transportation sectors, some ships and civil aircraft had been removed to Taiwan by the Nationalists.

From 1949 to 1952, with the efforts of PLA members, prison labor, and conscripted peasant labor, the system was repaired and enlarged. Railroads and highways were extended, and civil air routes were instituted during the period; the amount of freight and the number of passengers carried also increased. The socialist transformation of the system required less change than some sectors of the economy because almost 90 percent of the modern sector already was state owned by 1949. By 1957 it was estimated that 99.7 percent of the system was state owned, and the remainder was under joint state-private ownership.

The First Five Year Plan (1953–57) recognized the need for the integration of transportation into the development program. In September 1954 Chou En-lai stated that transportation policy should be planned for the benefit of industrialization and defense programs. The policy was twofold, embracing the use of existing facilities and envisioning the construction of new ones. It proposed a more efficient use of waterways and highways to relieve the strain on railroads and an improvement in operation of existing railroads. The plan called for construction of new highways in Southwest China and in border and coastal areas. It was proposed that waterways should be used for shipping grain from Szechwan Province and for shipping coal and other materials to the lower Yangtze River valley.

In the five-year plan railroads were given priority in transportation investment. Of the total, almost 60 percent, or 5.67 billion yuan, was allocated to railroads; of this amount, 41.7 percent was planned for new construction, mostly in less developed areas.

The Transportation System from 1958 to 1971

The transportation system was disorganized and disrupted by two great upheavals—the Great Leap Forward, which began in 1958 and lasted until 1960, and the Cultural Revolution, from 1966 to 1968. Each movement left the system with the need for reconstructing and reorganizing facilities and services.

The Great Leap Forward created pressure on the transportation system by the burden of increased production activity in numerous fields. Coal production was increased faster than local transport systems could carry it away. Increased industrial production required machinery and supplies beyond the ability of the system to handle.

To fill the need for increased facilities, small local railroads were constructed to connect mines and factories with established railroads and navigable waterways. From 1958 to 1959 more than 400 such railroads were built. Teams of local laborers laid railroad tracks made of "backyard" steel, pig iron, or sometimes timber; and cars were hauled by locomotives with gas, diesel, electric, or small steam engines. In an effort to relieve pressure on the transportation system, enterprises were expected to use local supplies whenever possible, but planning had not been well coordinated, and the provision of materials often posed an added burden on the already inadequate system. The few years after the Great Leap Forward were spent in improving already existing facilities, weeding out those that were unsuccessful and adding new facilities at an orderly pace.

Almost from the beginning of the Cultural Revolution, the transportation system, especially the railroads, suffered disorganization. Railroad facilities were monopolized by members of the Red Guards (see Glossary) and students traveling from Peking to various provinces and by others coming to Peking from provinces and municipalities (see ch. 10, Political Dynamics). It was estimated that about 20 million Red Guards and students, exchanging revolutionary experiences, crowded the railroads during the first year of the Cultural Revolution. The great passenger load resulted in freight piling up at stations and seriously interfered with the flow of supplies. The Red Guards also crowded buses and trucks. Additional pressure was placed on the transportation system by the number of workers, including transportation workers, who left their jobs and traveled to Peking to present petitions. At the end of 1966 Red Guards and students were ordered to return to their homes, and this pressure was mitigated in 1967.

The railroad system also suffered from conflicts between those in power in bureaus and subbureaus and those promoting the Cultural Revolution. In many instances there seemed to be a deliberate attempt to paralyze the railroads by damaging equipment and failing either to run trains on time or to load freight cars as scheduled. A period of armed struggle emerged in which workers went on strike, and the system almost ceased to function.

In 1967 military forces were placed in charge of the transportation system. Members were stationed on trains, and service was gradually improved. The height of the period of upheaval was followed by a period in which the various transport sectors, under the control of the PLA, gradually began rebuilding services and planning for the future.

An important phase of transportation improvement was the introduction in 1969 of the plan for an integrated system, including all sectors of transportation—rail, highway, and water—to facilitate an efficient flow of freight and people. An integration of sectors was accomplished in several provinces by 1970, but there was no report on the progress of the national plan.

Government Regulation of Transportation and Communications

Since the reorganization of the government beginning in 1949, a number of ministries and agencies have become involved in the regulation and operation of the transportation and communications systems. The framework evolved over a period of time, and comprehensive information as to the exact date of the initiation of various ministries and agencies was not available in 1971.

At the national level the General Office for Industry and Communications of the State Council controlled the ministries involved in transport and communications activities. In 1966 there was also the Industry and Communications Political Department within the Central Committee. In the government framework the Ministry of Communications dealt with water and road transportation through two bureaus, the General Bureau of Highways and the General Bureau of Sea and River Navigation. Since April 1962 civil aviation has been controlled by the China Civil Aviation General

Administration, which is a special agency under the State Council (see ch. 9, Political System and Values).

The Ministry of Posts and Telecommunications and the Ministry of Railroads, which was closely connected with the PLA, also performed functions in overseeing activities of relevant sectors of transportation. The Ministry of Railroads, which was established early in the communist regime, administered the railroad system through a number of administrative bureaus that were set up in 1950. Activities of the national network were coordinated within the ministry. During the upheaval of the Cultural Revolution, military control was established over the railroads, and by 1971 the Ministry of Railroads had been absorbed into the Ministry of Communications.

Composition of the Transportation System

Both before and after 1949 railroads provided the backbone of the country's transportation system. According to a 1959 source issued by the PRC government, railroads accounted for 78.5 percent of the country's total freight transported during 1958. By comparison, inland water transports carried 18.6 percent, and motor vehicles, 2.9 percent. Also during 1958 railroads carried 71.7 percent of all passenger traffic. During the 1960s both inland vessels and motor vehicles apparently increased their share of transportation but, according to fragmentary indications, the railroad system remained dominant for economic as well as military transportation purposes.

Railroads

Railroads, which have been the most important form of modern transportation, began to function when a line was opened from Shanghai to Peking in 1876. Foreign countries, through concessions and financial support, were instrumental in the early construction and operation of railroads, which developed as separate lines rather than as an integrated network. Attempts to create a national system before 1949 were thwarted by civil war and foreign invasion.

Before the communist regime, the total length of railroad trunklines, branches, and spurs was reported to be 16,675 miles. At the end of 1949, 13,750 miles were in operation. Railroads were concentrated in the coastal provinces, which were the most highly industrialized areas. Six coastal provinces—Liaoning, Hopeh, Shantung, Kiangsu, Chekiang, and Kwangtung—accounted for 42 percent of the total length of operating trunklines. Inland provinces accounted for 58 percent of total trackage; it was not, however, evenly distributed. The less developed provinces in the northwest and southwest—Sinkiang, Tsinghai, Kansu, and Szechwan—and the regions of Ninghsia Hui and Tibet had no railroads in operation in 1949. Fukien, a coastal province, also lacked railroads.

In the railroad construction of post-1949 years, the greatest expansion took place in the strategically important northwest region, particularly in the Sinkiang Uighur Autonomous Region (Sinkiang), where a line was built to Urumchi. Lines had also been constructed in Kansu and Tsinghai provinces and in the Ninghsia Hui Autonomous Region, and trackage had been added in Shensi Province. Railroads were also constructed in the southwest in the provinces of Szechwan, Yunnan, and Kweichow; in 1966 a railroad was planned for the Tibetan Autonomous Region (Tibet), but no further information was available in 1971. Lines had been built or planned to move raw materials to the more highly industrialized areas eastward, to open up the western and northwestern part of the country to development and settlement, and to move troops to border areas in emergencies (see fig. 14).

In the increase of route length after 1949 the northwest region ranked first, followed in order by Northeast China, North China, the Inner Mongolian Autonomous Region (Inner Mongolia), Southwest China, South China, Central China, and East China. In 1949 the railroad system had been most highly developed in the northeastern provinces because of the concentration of heavy industry there. Information concerning the development of railroads from 1966 to 1971 was fragmentary, and no comprehensive official report was available, but in 1970 it was reported that route length was about 24,000 miles.

In 1969 railroads were classified into three major systems. The north-south trunklines included lines from Peking to Canton, from Tientsin to Shanghai, and from Pao-chi to Chan-Chiang by way of Ch'eng-tu and Chungking. The east-west trunklines included lines from Lan-chou to Urumchi, from Peking to Lan-chou, and from Shanghai to the border of North Vietnam. The third group of lines formed the Manchurian system of the northeast.

Mainland China is connected internationally by rail with the Soviet Union, Mongolia, the Democratic People's Republic of Korea (North Korea), the Democratic Republic of Vietnam (North Vietnam), and Hong Kong. Because of differences in gauge, however, transloading facilities are required at the Soviet and Mongolian connections.

Waterways

Waterways also were opened up for transportation in the mid-nineteenth century by foreign powers. During the 1930s, however, the Nationalist government prohibited foreign shipping on inland waterways, and the communist government continued the prohibition after it assumed power. For the most part water transportation is more abundant in undeveloped than in developed areas. In the mid-1960s the Yangtze River was the most important inland waterway.

In 1949 it was estimated that there was 46,000 miles of navigable inland waterways. Of the total, 15,125 miles were navigable by steam vessels, and 30,875 miles, by nonmotorized vessels. By 1957 the length of navigable inland waterways had been increased to 90,000 miles, of which 25,000 miles were open to steam vessels. The increase in length was the result of such improvements as the dredging of waterways already in use and of smaller ones that had formerly been of marginal service. Navigable stretches of the Sungari River and the Yellow River were lengthened; waterways were opened up in Szechwan Province, and part but not all of the upper Yangtze River was made navigable by night.

Inland waterways are under the control of navigation bureaus of the central government and provincial communications departments. Central bureaus own and operate ships on rivers; local authorities and joint state-private shipping companies also operate river vessels. The development of waterways is in accord with classification of rivers. Rivers essential to whole provinces are the responsibility of the provinces for development. For rivers that benefit several counties, there is joint responsibility for the development of water facilities; for shorter streams, the Commune has responsibility.

Highways

Reports on the length, character, and condition of highways vary considerably, as there has been no generally accepted basis for the classification of roads and their use. In 1949, according to official statistics made public in 1959, there were 50,625 miles of highways open to traffic. By 1959, when roads had been repaired and new ones built or begun, usable highways had increased in length to 125,000 miles. An official report for 1969 fixed total highway mileage at 500,000 miles, of which 187,500 miles were all-weather roads and 312,500 miles were secondary roads.

New highways had been constructed in less developed regions rather than in developed ones, similar to the policy of railroad extensions. New roads, not always intended to be permanent, often preceded the building of railroads, since they were necessary to transport supplies to building locations.

Roads are divided into classes for administration and control. Trunk roads are those that were considered to be of major importance for economic or strategic reasons; they are administered by national or provincial authorities. Local roads of lesser importance are administered by *hsien* or Communes. Specialized roads also have been built to serve mines, factories, and forest enterprises and, in general, are built and maintained by the enterprises they serve. Major highways are built and maintained by the central government. In Tibet and Sinkiang strategic new roads have been built with the assistance of the PLA Railroad Engineering Corps and the PLA

Production and Construction Corps. Other highways are frequently built by local labor or by provincial, county, or local agencies, and small rural roads are built and cared for by Communes.

Highways serve trucks for the hauling of freight and buses for the transportation of passengers. For short distances, they also serve a variety of nonmotorized vehicles and human beings carrying loads. There are some passenger cars in use, but they are not used by private individuals. Trucks are owned and operated by departments of communications at various levels or by government organs and enterprises for their own use. For the most part motorbus services are operated by authorities at the province or lower level.

Air Transportation

About 10,560 miles of domestic air routes were serving passengers and mail before the communist period. Civil aviation was in the hands of the China National Aviation Corporation, which was owned by the Nationalist government and Pan American Airways. When the Nationalist government removed to Taiwan, it took with it a large part of the air fleet; and the communist government, after its accession to power, began the organization of a civil aviation bureau, which in 1970 was known as the China Civil Aviation General Administration. It was subject directly to the State Council.

By the end of 1966 fifty domestic air routes were in service. The national network, which covered 25,000 miles, touched seventy cities internally and linked the country with cities of the Soviet Union, Mongolia, North Korea, North Vietnam, and Burma. Most air routes radiated from Peking, but Shanghai and Canton were lesser centers. In 1966 airlines from the Soviet Union, Pakistan, France, North Korea, and Cambodia maintained regularly scheduled flights into the PRC.

In 1971 international flights remained essentially as they had been since 1966. The PRC, however, expressed some interest in extending flights of the China Civil Aviation General Administration to cities in Western Europe, Africa, Latin America, and Canada.

In addition to carrying passengers and freight, civil aircraft performed a number of other services, such as spraying insecticides, sowing seeds, and distributing fertilizer. They also made surveys for mining, the location of roads and railroads, and water conservation projects.

In 1966 it was estimated that there were about 500 civil aircraft, but not all of these were in usable condition. In August 1971 the PRC ordered six British jetliners, capable of improving domestic service and extending international service. As of late October 1971 Shanghai, Canton, and Peking were the only civil airports with runways adequate to service aircraft of this type.

In January 1967 in the midst of the Cultural Revolution, by joint order of the State Council and the Central Military Commission, civil aviation bureaus at all levels, ground service and maintenance units, airports, and flying schools were placed under the control of military forces. The air force was the branch placed in control. In 1969 the air force continued to control the complete air transport system, and in 1971 there was no indication that the system had changed.

TELECOMMUNICATIONS

In 1971 little quantitative information was available concerning the prevalence of telephone, telegraph, and postal services. In 1951, shortly after the establishment of the PRC, it was estimated that 255,000 telephones were in use. No official figures had been made public since that time.

In 1968 in urban areas most enterprises had telephones, and the service was reported to be reasonably efficient. In rural areas all Communes were linked by telephone. Long-distance service was available. The existence of a telephone network had been of benefit to the government in connecting all sections of the country and implementing national policies. Countrywide telephone conferences were often held for announcing new programs and working out problems connected with them. The telephone network also was an aid in maintaining control of the country by conveying information of conditions in outlying provinces. Business enterprises used the telephone in planning production, obtaining supplies, and planning sales.

The telegraph service was fairly well developed. It connected all the principal cities in the country, and lines were established to neighboring areas. The postal service was reported to be dependable, but no details were available at the end of the 1960s. When quick communication was needed, there was a tendency to use the telegraph system instead of postal service both between cities and within the city. Messages within the city were delivered by messenger, either on foot or on bicycle.

In early 1971 there was a trend toward the resumption of international telephone communications, which had been discontinued for some time. In March 1971 it was announced that service with the United States would be reestablished through a Japanese link. Service was to be available from 9 A.M. to 9 P.M. (New York time). In April a direct connection was reopened with Great Britain after a cessation of twenty-two years. The connection was to operate by high-frequency radio between London and Shanghai. Service was available for only three hours daily, from 9 A.M. to noon (British standard time). The connection was first established in 1948 and closed in 1949.

CHAPTER 19

FISCAL AND MONETARY SYSTEM

The essential function of the fiscal and monetary system of the People's Republic of China (PRC) is to ensure that the regime has sufficient financial resources to undertake planned capital investment and to pay normal government current expenses. The Ministry of Finance and the banking network, headed by the People's Bank of China, are the major instruments of financial supervision and control of the economy. The nation's financial resources are obtained primarily by means of the state budget and from the state enterprises, institutions, and organizations. Deposits in the state banks, extrabudgetary funds, and rural credit cooperatives are additional sources of capital.

As of mid-1971 no comprehensive budget document had ever been made public by the PRC. The annual budget report by the minister of finance to the National People's Congress contained only summary figures on receipts and expenditures. The available data, however, indicated that the scope of the budget was much greater than that of budgets of noncommunist countries. It allocated the greater part of the national output among investment, consumption and defense and distributed investment among economic sectors and regions. Over 90 percent of budgetary revenue was derived from profits and taxes generated by state enterprises.

The Ministry of Finance is responsible for the preparation of the annual state budget in consultation with all relevant government agencies. The state budget includes the receipts and expenditures of both the central and local governments. A department, or bureau, of finance and taxation that corresponds to the Ministry of Finance of the central government is established in the local governments. The budgets of the local governments are prepared by their finance departments in accordance with regulations issued by the central government Ministry of Finance. In the financial system of the PRC, therefore, the functions of a budget office are assumed by the Ministry of Finance and the financial departments of the local governments.

All banks are under complete state control. The national bank, the People's Bank, is a combination central bank, commercial bank, and settlement bank. It is directly subordinate to the State Council and is independent of the Ministry of Finance. The banking network is a mechanism for directing the flow of monies between enterprises, institutions, and organizations as desired by the state financial authorities. Receipts and payments among state enterprises are made entirely through bank accounts. The People's Bank has over 34,000 branches throughout the country and is used by the government to monitor the performance of the state enterprises. Rigid requirements for speedy deposit of all receipts by all types of economic entities and heavy pressure on the population to place cash holdings in savings accounts have served to restrain the demand for goods and services.

PUBLIC FINANCE

The State Budget

The state budget, which is the consolidated central and local government budget of the PRC, is a major financial control mechanism for implementing national economic policy (see ch. 13, Character and Structure of the Economy). According to the latest data available in mid-1971, about three-fourths of investment in the country was financed through the state budget. A substantial part of industrial investment is undertaken with funds allocated by the state budget, and the budget also includes large sums for investment in the agricultural sector (see ch. 14, Agriculture; ch. 16, Science and Technology; ch. 15, Industry). The remaining approximate one-fourth of investment is financed by other sources, including extrabudgetary receipts and expenditures of local government units and individual enterprises, receipts and payments of ministries in charge of industrial enterprises, and the budgets of units of collective agriculture. There is not, therefore, an absolute correspondence between the sums allocated in the state budget for investment and the investment projects that are actually undertaken. The state budget, nonetheless, is a basic instrument for the implementation of economic plans and social goals through the centralization of control over public revenues and expenditures.

The Budget Bureau of the Ministry of Finance coordinates the compilation of the state budget. The state budget is composed of both the central budget and the budgets of the local authorities. The state budget is, therefore, the total of budgetary expenditures at all levels of government. The state budget includes, under each item of revenue and expenditure, those sums of each item that are attributable to local authorities. It does not show transfers between different levels of administration.

The central budget takes into consideration the needs of the various ministries and agencies that are part of the system of national government. The local budgets are divided into three levels: provincial, municipal, or autonomous regional; county and county-municipal; and town and market town. Certain items of revenue accruing to local authorities or to state enterprises, and the expenditures made from these revenues, are excluded from the local budgets and from the central budget. These items are known as extrabudgetary expenditures and receipts.

The fiscal year extends from January 1 to December 31. The budget is compiled on the basis of draft budgets submitted to the Ministry of Finance from both the central government ministries and the provincial and equivalent local authorities. These draft budgets are to be prepared in accordance with national economic policies. After consolidation of unit estimates, the draft budget for the current year and the final accounts for the previous year are presented annually by the minister of finance to the National People's Congress for approval, which is required by the Constitution of 1954. The Standing Committee of the People's Congress has the power to enact the budget if the People's Congress is not in session. Administration is under the direction of the Ministry of Finance.

A series of conferences is held at various levels in the process of compiling the state budget. There are usually two annual conferences at the national level on the budget. These are attended by officials from the Ministry of Finance and by the chief financial officials of the provincial-level authorities. The first of the national conferences is held before the compilation of the budget. Although by regulation it should meet toward the end of the previous fiscal year, in November or December, it usually meets in February or March. This conference lasts for up to ten days. After an opening report from one of the vice ministers of finance, the conference divides into two groups based on area and on function. Each provincial-level authority is represented at the appropriate area group and at all the functional groups. After three or four days of meetings of the small groups, the results are sent back to the Ministry of Finance. The final budgetary figures for each province are agreed to after bargaining between the provincial department of finance and a senior official of the central government's Ministry of Finance. After the national conference, each province holds conferences in a similar way for its subordinate local authorities.

The second national-level conference is usually held three or four months after the budget has gone into operation. At this time any revisions that are considered necessary in the current budget are discussed, and preliminary consideration is given to the budget for the following year. The budget is usually not compiled sufficiently early to become operative at the beginning of the fiscal year to which it applies.

The budget for the coming year is supposed to be approved by the People's Congress by November 15 and announced by the end of that month, but these dates have not always been observed. In July 1963 the minister of finance reported to the Standing Committee of the

People's Congress on the final accounts for 1961 and 1962. In December 1963 the People's Congress approved the budget for 1963 and the preliminary plan for 1964. In July 1964 the final accounts for 1963 and the draft budget for 1964 were approved and, similarly, in July 1965, the final accounts for 1964 and the budget estimates for 1965 were approved. As of mid-1971 no information was available on examination of the annual budgets subsequent to 1965 by governmental bodies superior to the Ministry of Finance.

The economic authorities of the PRC favor balanced national and local budgets; budgetary revenue goals are determined by requirements for expenditure. They desire, further, that a budgetary surplus should accrue in the course of implementation of the national and local budgets. This surplus should ideally be in the range of from 3 to 5 percent of total revenues.

Expenditures

The heading, Economic Construction, accounted for over 60 percent of total budgetary expenditures for the last several years for which figures were available in mid-1971. Economic construction consists of allocations to state enterprises for acquisition of fixed assets, supplementary working capital, and certain miscellaneous business expenses. Working capital is authorized and made available by the government to the enterprises and consists of the excess of current assets over current liabilities; these excess current assets are available to carry on business operations.

The category, Social Services, Culture and Education, and Science, covered both capital and current budgetary expenditure of the sectors concerned and amounted to over 12 percent of total budgetary expenditures. The same proportion was devoted to the category of expenditures for National Defense. Expenditures under the category of Administration, comprising 5 percent of the total, covered the expenses of governmental, public security, and legal organs and of the police, foreign relations, and mass organizations. The 11-percent balance of total budgetary expenditures comprised various miscellaneous items, including allotments of credit funds to the People's Bank and a revolving fund for local authorities.

Undertakings eligible for appropriations are identified as budgetary units. They include three major types: enterprises, institutions, and administrative units. Enterprises receive budgetary appropriations for fixed assets and working capital and are also eligible for bank loans for additional working capital. Institutions and administrative organs are ineligible for bank loans.

Various methods are used for granting appropriations and exercising financial management in regard to institutions, which include schools, hospitals, and cultural organs. The first method is the expenditure budget method, under which all expenditure is met from the budget and all receipts are paid in as budgetary revenue. This method is used for institutions, such as schools and research institutes, that have only a small income of their own.

The economic accounting system, as used by enterprises, is the second method of making budgetary grants and controlling the financial affairs of institutions. Under this system, institutions may receive subsidies and budgetary appropriations for fixed and working capital; they generally have the same degree of independent operation and similar duties as enterprises. Similar to enterprises, institutions practicing this system pay taxes and remit profits to the state. Because only enterprises can have profits, according to the economic terminology used in the PRC, the profits of these institutions are described as surpluses. Institutions operating under this accounting system are those earning a substantial income from their own activities, such as motion picture studios, motion picture theaters, printing plants, and publishing firms. The classification of such concerns as institutions rather than as enterprises originates in the opinion that cultural organs should not be considered on the same basis as ordinary economic undertakings.

The third budgetary method of granting appropriations and exercising financial management of institutions is one of total sum management and fixed sum subsidy. This method is employed for institutions that have a certain income of their own but which is insufficient to satisfy all their requirements. The institution is permitted to keep its own income and receives a budgetary subsidy equal to the predetermined amount allowed for its deficit. This method, like the expenditure budget and economic accounting methods, is consonant with the desire of the financial authorities of the PRC that groups and corporate bodies be assigned definite responsibilities and that fixed limits be set to the financial obligations of the state.

Revenues

Revenue from state enterprises has been the largest single item of budgetary revenue in the PRC; according to the latest data available in mid-1971, this source has provided about 65 percent of the state's budgetary income. Among the factors that have made revenue from state enterprises the major proportion of the state's budgetary receipts have been the construction of new state enterprises, the expansion of existing industries, and the state policy of maintaining prices sufficiently high to assure a large volume of profits.

The revenue from state enterprises consists of profits, depreciation reserves for amortization of fixed assets, return of surplus working capital, receipts from sale of fixed assets, and income from other business activities. The financial authorities of the PRC have defined profit as "the net income of sales proceeds obtained according to state-regulated prices after the deduction of production cost and tax payments." Profits and depreciation reserves have been remitted to the state either directly by the enterprise concerned or through the central government ministry that administered the enterprise. The planned annual profit of an enterprise was divided into monthly quotas, and from 60 to 80 percent of the planned profit for a particular month was transmitted to the government on the twenty-fifth day of the month. The balance has been submitted on the eighth day of the following month, with adjustments made when necessary to the actual amount of profit earned.

Monthly depreciation charges have been forwarded to the Ministry of Finance or to the government ministry that supervises the enterprise on the fifteenth day of the following month. The actual amount of the depreciation charge has been determined by the enterprise according to recommended amortization schedules. Funds for major repairs of capital assets, however, are retained in special bank accounts by individual enterprises.

Revenue from taxes has provided about 35 percent of budgetary income. All taxes are collected through a revenue system that has branches at all levels from the central government through the provinces, special districts, counties, and municipalities and, in some instances, tax collectors are permanently stationed in production plants. The only exceptions are the salt taxes and customs duties, which are separately administered. Money taxes are deposited in the branches of the People's Bank or are received by local tax offices for immediate deposit in the People's Bank. Agricultural taxes in kind are collected at harvesttime in summer and autumn and stored in government granaries. Money taxes are collected according to a fixed schedule. Tax receipts are credited by the People's Bank to the accounts of various governmental units according to predetermined ratios.

Tax offices and administrators have a wide variety of functions, in addition to the collection of current revenue. Tax administrators, in the course of their general collection activities, are directed to provide assistance to industrial and commercial enterprises in the improvement of their financial and accounting systems. The assignment of accounting responsibilities to the tax offices has been based partly on the need to establish business records that will be adequate for tax collection efforts, such as completion of returns and postauditing, and partly on the desire to introduce more effective accounting techniques throughout the country's industry and commerce. It was reported that revenue collections increased in the mid-1960s through the assistance of better trained fieldworkers. Fieldworkers also, because of a wide knowledge of areas, have been able to assist enterprises in the procurement of needed materials and in marketing products.

There are four major sources of tax revenue: consolidated industrial and commercial taxes, agricultural taxes, salt taxes, and customs receipts. The largest source of tax revenue is the consolidated industrial and commercial tax. This tax is payable, with certain exceptions, by all enterprises and other units in state, private, joint state-private, or collective ownership and by individuals engaged in industrial production, the purchase of certain types of agricultural output, the importation of goods, retail trade, transportation, and services.

The consolidated industrial and commercial tax is assessed as a percentage, which varies according to the types of goods or services provided. In the case of industrial enterprises and retailers, the tax is assessed as a percentage of total sales proceeds. For importers and purchasers of agricultural output, the tax is imposed as a percentage of total payments made. In the case of transportation, communications, and service enterprises, the tax is assessed as a percentage of business income. For industrial producers, importers of nonagricultural goods, and retailers, the tax rate is commonly set as the difference between the retail and wholesale price, after allowing for a markup for distribution costs.

State banks, insurance concerns, agricultural machinery stations, medical and health institutions, and scientific research bodies were exempt from the industrial and commercial tax. Provincial and equivalent authorities were allowed to grant exemptions or otherwise make changes in the tax within limits set by the national authorities.

The tax is not payable on intermediate products manufactured by an industrial enterprise and used in its own production; this exemption, however, does not apply in the cases of cotton yarn, hides and skins, and wines and spirits. Except for these three groups of commodities, each commodity is taxed only once during the production process and again at retail, if it reaches that stage of distribution.

The tax is levied on prices received by producers and distributors for the commodities concerned. Tax payments are due at the time that sales proceeds are received; the regulations require that the tax be paid on the day that the proceeds of the sale are deposited in the seller's bank. The major part of the total tax collections from industrial enterprises, therefore, represents a bank transfer from the taxpayer to the tax office at the time that sales proceeds are received. In the case of retail trade and service activities, the taxes are due on the day that the proceeds of the sale are received, but actual payments can be made at intervals ranging from one to thirty days, according to individual circumstances.

Rural markets are used for collecting the consolidated industrial and commercial tax on commodities sold at retail. Press reports have indicated that the government has attached great importance to these markets as sources of revenue but that the task of collecting the tax has been complicated by the large number of small sellers involved. Peddlers are subjected to a complex system of financial surveillance. Trade warehouses have been employed to monitor payments of taxes at rural markets.

The agricultural tax, the second largest source of tax revenue, is not a tax on the value of land, as is true of the agricultural tax in most Western countries. The authorities have not placed a value on land for tax purposes but instead have used as the tax base the harvest or income obtained from the land during the course of a normal farming year. The tax rate has then been applied to the tax base—income from the land—to determine the amount of tax payment.

The agricultural tax is levied on the normal yield of the land rather than on the actual yield or harvest obtained each year. Allowance is made for local differences in taxable capacity by adjusting the proportionate rate from one province to another and also within provinces. The tax is levied on income-yielding land regardless of whether the actual farms were producing food grains, industrial crops, orchard products, vegetables, or other crops. The normal yield is calculated on the basis of the major crop in each locality. About 90 percent of the agricultural tax is paid in farm products, primarily grain, and the remainder is paid in cash.

On a national average, according to the data available in mid-1971, the rate of agricultural tax was 15.5 percent of the normal yield. The tax level for each province was fixed by the State Council—the rates ranging from 13 percent for Sinkiang Uighur Autonomous Region to 19 percent for Heilungkiang Province. For purposes of the agricultural tax the provinces were ranked in a general order of the relative wealth or poverty of their rural population. Within each province the provincial authorities were authorized to vary rates of tax from one area to another, provided the total fixed for the province was paid. Similar discretion was given to the lower governmental units. The local supplementary tax, which is additional to the agricultural tax and which is collected on the same basis as the agricultural tax, was .not to exceed 15 percent of the agricultural tax, according to the national government's instructions. Reliable reports, however, indicated that in practice the local supplementary tax sometimes exceeded this maximum.

Exemptions or reductions of the agricultural tax are authorized for newly cultivated land, for areas damaged by natural disaster or that were backward or distressed, and also for other worthy cases. The collection of the agricultural tax usually occurs at two seasons, summer and autumn; in cases in which the summer crops are relatively insignificant, the whole tax can be collected in the autumn. Taxpayers are obliged to deliver the tax commodities to the specified collecting centers and to pay the cost of transportation up to a distance generally equivalent to one day's round trip.

The collection of the agricultural tax requires close cooperation between the Ministry of Finance, operating through its Agricultural Tax Bureau, the Ministry of Agriculture and Forestry, and the Ministry of Commerce. The Ministry of Finance and the equivalent local bodies do not themselves establish collecting points for the agricultural tax paid in kind. This operation is done by the local food and commercial departments, according to the products involved.

The salt tax is levied at different rates according to the use of the product. Taxes are applied to table salt and fishery salt, but fishery salt is assessed at only 30 percent of the tax on table salt. No taxes are levied on salt used by industry and agriculture, and exports are exempt.

Customs duties have been retained for bargaining purposes in foreign trade negotiations and additionally as a source of revenue controlled directly by the central government. Although taxes other than the four major categories have been levied from time to time, they have not been important sources of revenue. In addition, a number of fees and licenses have been collected by local governments for local use.

No national bonds have been issued since June 1958, and by the end of 1968 all the national government's internal public debt should have been paid, according to the information available in mid-1971. Through 1959 loans from the Soviet Union annually averaged about 2 percent of total budgetary revenue; repayment of the Soviet loans was completed in 1965. So far as is publicly known, the country has not subsequently incurred any external debt. In mid-1971, therefore, the country appeared to be in the unusual situation of a nation without internal or external public debt.

Extrabudgetary Revenues and Expenditures

Extrabudgetary funds are those sources of revenue that are not entered into the budget and that are under the control of local authorities of different levels, or of enterprises and of institutions of various types, and of their supervisory ministries. These funds include major regular revenues. The largest single item has been profits retained by enterprises and their supervisory ministries. Other items include the local surtaxes on the industrial and commercial tax, on the agricultural tax, and on urban public utility charges. Miscellaneous sources are local budgetary surpluses, major repair funds of enterprises, labor welfare funds, irrigation charges, fees for the certification of weights and measures, rentals of halls and of vehicles, income from water supplies, income from the labor of students and employees of schools and other organizations, and fees for admittance to parks, museums, and sports fields.

Some extrabudgetary funds are tied to specific expenditures because of their origin. Others are not as restricted, particularly retained profits, and these have occasionally been employed by local authorities for a wide range of investments. Although capital investment has been reported to be the largest single type of expenditure from extrabudgetary funds, the funds have been used for other varied and miscellaneous purposes. The less restricted types of extrabudgetary funds on occasion have not been used as soon as they were collected and in the interim have been employed to liquidate immediate debts of local authorities. In the mid-1960s a new system of budgetary management provided that certain local supplementary taxes that had previously been treated as extrabudgetary funds were to be calculated as part of the national financial plan.

BANKING AND CURRENCY

The People's Bank of China

The People's Bank of China is a state bank—a national bank under the direct control of the central government. The People's Bank is subordinate directly to the State Council and has always been independent of the Ministry of Finance. Despite the separation of the People's Bank from the Ministry of Finance, however, the two institutions operate in close liaison in many areas of common concern. The People's Bank has subordinate to it two banks with special functions that operate as its agents— the Bank of China and the Joint State-Private Bank. The People's Bank was founded on December 1, 1948; in the late 1960s it was reported to be the largest and most extensive economic organization in the country.

The People's Bank is known as the national bank, despite the existence of other banks completely owned by the state. It receives appropriations from the state budget, and these funds, along with the bank's retained profits and net increases in its deposits, are used to finance the expansion of credit. These funds are distributed throughout the country among the provincial branches of the bank, then by the provicinal branches to their subordinate branches, and ultimately to the enterprise that is authorized a loan. The People's Bank is the only channel for the distribution of these funds, which move through its hierarchical structure.

The People's Bank is the sole currency-issuing organization in the PRC, and its notes and coins are the sole legal tender. It keeps the government accounts. Every government organization or enterprise, every military unit, and every cooperative is required to have an account with the People's Bank and to deposit with it all cash above three days' normal expenditure or, in the case of enterprises at locations at which the bank does not have a branch, above normal expenditure for one month. In a separate account, an enterprise must deposit stipulated sums for its major repairs fund. Individuals are also under strong pressure to keep money in savings deposits with the bank. All settlements between state organizations and enterprises are made through book transfers on the bank's deposit accounts. The People's Bank is the central source of credit for nonagricultural sectors of the economy and has direct deposit and lending relations with economic units rather than with financial organizations. State enterprises, institutions, organizations, military units, and rural credit cooperatives are prohibited from extending short-term commercial credit in their mutual dealings. The People's Bank oversees and supervises all payments of wages and payments of monies in the nature of wages, such as bonuses and allowances, by state enterprises, state organizations, and all economic units operating under the system of collective ownership. It is the bank's duty to guarantee that an enterprises does not pay wages exceeding the planned total amount authorized for the enterprise.

The People's Bank buys, sells, and has central control of dealings in gold and silver; sales of gold and silver are restricted to pharmaceutical, industrial, and other legitimate uses. The People's Bank is also responsible for handling receipts and payments in foreign currency, foreign exchange control, and the effecting of international settlements; these functions are performed primarily through its subordinate institution, the Bank of China.

The head office of the People's Bank is in Peking. Branch banks are located in provincial capitals, in cities under the direct jurisdiction of the central government, and in autonomous regions. Subbranches are located in county seats and fairly prosperous towns. Branch offices are established in street districts in towns. Other subordinate organs are stationary and mobile savings and business offices in urban and rural areas. In the mid-1960s it was estimated that 34,000 branches of various types were in existence.

The chain of command among the branches of the bank is parallel to the civil administrative system. Provincial-level branches of the bank control the branches at county and equivalent levels, which have small local offices subordinate to them. The bank also has its own offices or representatives attached to large factories and mines. The bank's savings offices, in addition, are located in all types of enterprises and institutions. The urban population is constantly urged, and at times has been subjected to strong pressure, to deposit money with the People's Bank either in demand deposits or, preferably, time deposits. The bank has opened many special offices to handle savings, and at times street associations have acted as agents of the People's Bank in savings matters.

Communication between the head offices and branches of the bank is maintained by regular reports, by periodic meetings of the managers of provincial-level branches to consider current matters, and by special meetings to discuss specific problems. Aside from such meetings held in Peking, conferences are called from time to time at other locations.

The Bank of China

The Bank of China is subordinate to the People's Bank and acts as its agent in handling foreign exchange and international settlements. The Bank of China is important in the matter of remittances from Overseas Chinese. The head office of the Bank of China is in Peking, and it has branches at the chief ports of mainland China and in the main home districts of Overseas Chinese. There are also a number of branches abroad, particularly in Southeast Asia and in Western Europe. The Bank of China carries on deposit, loan, and general banking business abroad, but in mainland China it confines its activities to banking business connected with foreign trade and foreign exchange.

The Joint State-Private Bank

The Joint State-Private Bank was established in December 1952 as a consequence of a series of mergers between over eighty private banks in Shanghai that commenced in mid-1949. Since its formation it has been completely subordinate to the People's Bank, for which its only function is to accept savings deposits.

The Agricultural Bank of China

In November 1963 the Agricultural Bank of China was established, under the direct jurisdiction of the State Council. This move placed it on a level equal to the People's Bank, to which previous agricultural banks, organized in the 1950s but subsequently abolished, had been subordinate. The new bank was staffed by transferring personnel familiar with the relevant operations from both the People's Bank and from the ministries that had been engaged in rural appropriations. The work of the Agricultural Bank and that of the People's Bank were to be closely coordinated. The head office of the Agricultural Bank was established in Peking, with branch banks in provinces, cities, and autonomous regions, subbranch banks in counties, and business offices in districts. The Agricultural Bank was gradually to assume the supervision, previously divided among several ministries, of both investment grants and of loans to state-owned enterprises and institutions in the agricultural sector.

The main functions of the Agricultural Bank are making payments and loans on behalf of the state in accordance with state plans, budgets, policies, and institutions and exercising unified supervision over these transactions. In exercising these functions, the Agricultural Bank is guided by the policies of the Chinese Communist Party (CCP) and the state regarding payments of state funds for capital investments in the fields of agriculture, forestry, pastoral industries, and water conservation; state grants and loans to state farms, state forests, state fishing grounds, tractor stations, and drainage and irrigation stations; and state grants and loans to People's Communes (see Glossary), production brigades, and production teams.

Rural Credit Cooperatives

One of the aims of the Agricultural Bank, like its predecessors, is to guide and help the rural credit cooperatives. The rural credit cooperatives obtain their funds from bank loans and from rural deposits. They act essentially as rural auxiliaries to the banks, conducting a substantial proportion of the lower level banking functions in the countryside. In the mid-1960s press reports indicated that about 60 percent of the banks' credit operations with the Communes was transacted through the rural credit cooperatives. All personal loans to members of the Communes were also made through these organizations. The rural credit cooperatives, similar to the banks, have supervisory responsibilities, such as checking the financial affairs of units of collective agriculture.

The credit cooperatives derive the main portion of their funds from peasants, who have simultaneous seasonal demands for cash. The cooperatives are therefore restrained to making loans for periods not longer than one year. On the basis of the information publicly available in mid-1971, there was apparently no source other than private persons from which individual peasants could get long-term loans.

The authorities have reportedly urged that the higher positions in the rural credit cooperatives should be occupied by poor and lower middle class peasants. Credit workers have frequently been instructed to emphasize assistance to poor and lower middle class peasants and not make ability to repay the only criterion for the approval of loans. This evidence indicated that in the late 1960s the former landlords and the rich and upper middle class peasants were still the most credit-worthy groups in the rural community.

Other Financial Institutions

Subordinate Units of the Ministry of Finance

According to the latest information available in mid-1971, the Ministry of Finance, since the late 1950s, had been supervising the People's Construction Bank of China and the People's Insurance Company of China. These organizations had a separate legal status, but were considered to be part of the administrative system of the Ministry of Finance.

The People's Construction Bank was established in October 1954 as a medium for paying to enterprises and institutions the funds provided by the state budget for investment. The Construction Bank was also given the responsibility for supervising the use by enterprises and organizations of their extrabudgetary funds retained for purposes of capital investment. In addition to making nonrepayable investment grants, the bank issued short-term loans to construction units and enterprises fulfilling contracts for capital investment projects, and supervised the use of these funds. In the mid-1960s the bank started making loans to finance technical changes in small- and medium-range industrial enterprises. The Construction Bank has been responsible for investment funds for all sectors of the economy except agriculture. The main task of the bank has been to act as an instrument of the Ministry of Finance for distributing nonreimbursable budgetary grants for capital investment and for supervising the use of these grants.

The head office of the Construction Bank is in Peking, and branches have been established throughout mainland China. The bank is a part of the Ministry of Finance, and the local branches are subject to the control of the local departments of finance to the same extent as are other units of the administrative system of the Ministry of Finance.

The People's Insurance Company of China was established as a state company in October 1949. It has been authorized to issue all types of insurance: agricultural insurance; fire insurance, including industrial, commercial, and personal; personal insurance, including accident and life insurance, both individual and group; transportation insurance covering all means of transportation; and shipping insurance. Insurance with the People's Insurance Company against certain specified risks had been made compulsory in 1951 for all state enterprises and institutions and for cooperative organizations at the county level and higher. In 1958 most types of insurance were transferred to provincial-level authorities to conduct through local companies. The exceptions were insurance related to foreign trade and the compulsory insurance of rail, air, or ship passengers.

Effective in 1959, central government enterprises were no longer required to insure their property. Local enterprises were to be governed on this matter by the directives of local authorities. The local authorities were also to determine whether local insurance activities were to be put under the control of the local branch of the People's Bank or of the local department of finance. The local insurance companies were directed to establish funds to meet claims; the core of these local funds would be provided by the distribution of part of the reserve funds of the People's Insurance Company and its subordinate state companies, the Insurance Company of China and the Pacific Ocean Insurance Company.

The Insurance Company of China is a subordinate organization of the People's Insurance Company. The relationship between these two insurance companies has been described as similar to that between the People's Bank and the Bank of China. Abroad, the Insurance Company of China undertakes some of the insurance business connected with foreign trade and transportation, and it also has domestic branches through which it carries on international transportation insurance and general insurance business. The head of the company is in Peking, and it has branches at Hong Kong, Macao, Singapore, Penang, Kuala Lumpur, Djakarta, Surabaya, and London.

The Pacific Ocean Insurance Company was formed by the amalgamation of a number of private insurance companies. It operates under the guidance of the People's Insurance Company and concentrates on overseas business.

The insurance companies are administrative rather than commercial organizations. The collection of premiums and the payment of claims are questions of governmental accounting rather than commercial transactions. The insurance companies provide a means for increasing the proportion of the revenues of enterprises that is transferred to the state in the form of taxes and other fixed charges rather than in the form of profits.

Overseas Chinese Investment Corporations

The Overseas Chinese investment corporations are state companies in which Overseas Chinese, including Chinese residents of Hong Kong and Macao, have been encouraged to invest. Interest of 8 percent yearly is paid, free of taxation by the PRC, and half of the interest payments may be converted into foreign exchange. After twelve years invested capital may be withdrawn in the currency of the PRC, or the capital may be reinvested on a variety of terms. By the mid-1960s Overseas Chinese investment corporations had established or expanded over 100 enterprises, including sugar refineries, textile and paper factories, rubber factories, and hydroelectric plants; most of these firms had been organized in areas from which Overseas Chinese had emigrated.

Private Banks

Two Western banks, the Hong Kong and Shanghai Banking Corporation and the Chartered Bank, were operating branches in Shanghai, according to the latest data available in mid-1971. These branches engaged solely in the financing of foreign trade and in foreign exchange transactions; they did not offer either deposit or savings facilities and did not make individual loans.

There are three banks associated with the Overseas Chinese—the Chi-Yu Banking Corporation, the Bank of East Asia, and the Overseas Chinese Banking Corporation. These banks have their head offices outside the PRC and engage in the business of remittances from Overseas Chinese.

Currency and Coinage

The People's Bank issues and controls the currency. The ban on any other source of currency has been vigorously maintained; the currency regulations are extremely strict, and nonobservance often entails heavy jail sentences. The unit of currency is generally known as the yuan, although its formal name is the Jen Min-pi, or People's Currency. The yuan was fist issued by the People's Bank on December 1, 1948, the same date as the formation of the People's Bank and some months before the establishment of the PRC.

A major reform of the currency occurred on March 1, 1955, at the time of a new issue of the currency; 1 yuan was exchanged for 10,000 yuan of the old currency. At the same time the government decreed an official exchange rate of 1 United States dollar to 2.46 yuan. The official doctrine is that the acceptability and value of the yuan are supported by the political and economic power controlled by the state. Despite the severe penalties imposed for illegal dealings in foreign currency, recurring reports have indicated that a black market in trading yuan for United States dollars has persisted. At one point in mid-1962 the black market rate had reached 21.25 yuan for 1 United States dollar, but by the first half of 1970 the rate had fallen to 3.46 yuan for United States dollar and had not exceeded 5 yuan to 1 United States dollar since June 1963.

The yuan is divided into 10 chiao and 100 fen. In the late 1960s the following kinds of currency were in circulation; 10-yuan, 5-yuan, 2-yuan, and 11-yuan notes; 5-chiao, 2-chiao, and 1-chiao notes; and 5-fen and 2-fen notes. Aluminum coins of 5-fen, 2-fen, and 1-fen denominations were also in circulation.

There is no legal limitation to the issuance of currency. The general policy of the PRC has been stated to be that "the volume of currency issued in the market should be designed to increase from year to year along with the development of production and the enlargement of the sphere of commerce." Almost all means of production are paid for through bank transfers. Cash—meaning currency and coins—is used by enterprises and organizations for wage payments, for purchasing agricultural products from individual peasants, and for certain miscellaneous purposes. The restriction of cash payments to these purposes, in which after-harvest wage payments to peasants and the purchase of agricultural products are the major uses, has caused marked seasonal fluctuations in the issuance of currency. The peak period in December and January occurs after payments have been made for state agricultural purchases and immediately before the Spring Festival, the most important festival of the year, before which extra consumer goods are purchased (see ch. 7, Living Conditions). During this period the issuance of currency averages about 50 percent above the lowest point, which takes place in May and June.

There is no official gold exchange rate for the yuan. In mid-1971 the most recent official purchase prices for gold and silver published by the People's Bank were 3.04 yuan for one gram of gold and 0.40 yuan for 1 gram of silver. Private persons are allowed to hold gold and silver, although the amount authorized to be held has been rigorously restricted and cases of confiscation have been reported. The state gold and silver jewelry shops sell ornamental articles in gold and silver, fulfill orders for badges and medals, and do processing work on provided materials. These shops are authorized to sell but not to buy.

Data on the total amount of currency in circulation had not been published until mid-1969, when official speeches gave a figure of 16.1 billion yuan. A calculation made ten years earlier by a respected professional analyst of the country's economy had placed the average volume of currency in circulation in 1956 at 12.8 billion yuan. On this basis, the average annual growth rate of the currency in circulation for the 1956–69 period would be about 1.8 percent. Observers had commented on the marked increase in hoarding of cash by peasants, which had begun in the mid-1950s and was reportedly still taking place in the late 1960s. These analysts noted that, after the collectivization of agriculture in the mid-1950s, individual peasant families were unable to hold stocks of grain, cotton, and other crops and believed that this situation had stimulated the peasants to maintain their savings in cash.

Monetary Policy

The obligation of state enterprises, institutions, and organizations to deposit their cash with the People's Bank and to conduct all financial transactions with other concerns through the bank gives the bank the power to exercise strict control over business dealings. This control is reinforced by the bank's domination as the major source of short-term credit, although the rural credit cooperatives and the Agricultural Bank are other sources.

There is no formal ban on private moneylending. The resurgence of moneylending in rural areas in the md-1960s, nevertheless, has been a source of concern to the government. Rural credit cooperatives were advocated by the government as the major means of countering any tendency toward the revival of private moneylending and lowering the interest rates charged by those engaged in the practice. In the case of urban workers, mutual aid savings associations are similarly prescribed by the government as the authorized sources of personal credit; trade unions have actively organized such associations (see ch. 17, Labor).

The sources of the funds from which the banks can make loans comprise budgetary grants; the fiscal surpluses of the national government and subordinate governmental units; the original capital of each bank as supplemented by retained profits; deposits of state organizations, enterprises, and other entities and deposits of individuals; and the expansion of the money supply. Budgetary grants for capital investment purposes are nonreimbursable and interest free; depreciation reserves for amortization of fixed assets, however, must be returned to the government. Fiscal surpluses of governmental units have been used to finance the expansion of credit through bank loans. The requirement that all enterprises and undertakings keep their spare cash on deposit in the People's Bank has provided considerable funds available for loans.

Interest is paid on bank deposits, including deposits of state enterprises. Part of the deposits of departments of finance and other state agencies, however, do not earn interest. In 1966 interest rates of one-third of 1 percent per month on one-year deposits were reported. Schemes combining savings deposits with lottery tickets have also been used occasionally.

The major portion of bank loans is made to enterprises. Institutions, administrative organizations, and individuals are not eligible for loans from banks. Except for the investment grants made by the Construction Bank, funds from the banks are generally intended to be used only for short-term purposes. In the case of agriculture, medium-term loans for up to five years' duration have been provided by the Agricultural Bank and the People's Bank.

The efficiency of the government's control over the working capital of enterprises has been a constant source of concern to the financial authorities. There have been frequent reports of the wrongful conversion to investment purposes of funds provided by the banks to enterprises for working capital. Such conversions, it has been noted by the financial authorities, result in unplanned investment projects that add to the strain on scarce supplies of equipment and raw materials and, in addition, the unauthorized conversions create a shortage of working capital.

Enforcement of the prohibition on using bank loans made for working capital to obtain fixed assets has been proved continuously difficult. Publicity was given in the mid-1960s to the tendency of enterprises to use working capital bank loans for fixed investment. Managers of enterprises were reportedly chided for asserting that maintaining production by, if necessary, emergency use of working capital to acquire fixed assets was more important than possible criticism for ignoring the regulations on use of bank loans.

Changes in the method of supplying working capital to enterprises have been introduced with the intent of imposing more stringent controls. The method in effect in the 1960s was a division of the working capital requirements of enterprises into two types. The first was described as fixed-quota working capital, by which was meant the minimum permanent requirements of the enterprise. The second was called above-quota working capital and was intended to cover seasonal and other temporary requirements. In regard to industry and transportation, 80 percent of fixed-quota working capital was to be supplied by the Ministry of Finance or its local departments to the enterprises; the remaining 20 percent was to come from the People's Bank. All above-quota working capital, however, was to be channeled through the People's Bank.

Interest is payable on loans for working capital; in contrast, the budgetary grants for capital investment are interest free. The interest rates charged in the 1960s were reportedly six-tenths of 1 percent per month on above-quota working capital and one-fifth of 1 percent per month on fixed-quota working capital. The function of the rates of interest charged has been the encouragement of prudence in the use of loans. The rationing of credit has been carried out by direct means. Interest rates, therefore, do not play a regulatory role in the economy.

The responsibility for enforcing the limits set by the national government on the total loans and wage payments authorized for any province rests with the provincial branch of the People's Bank and, in the case of agricultural operations, with the provincial branch of the Agricultural Bank. Numerous press references suggest difficulties in preventing the overspending of the wage fund.

Considerable publicity was given in the mid-1960s to the supervisory role of the state banks. Their control of credit and the requirement that all payments between enterprises must be made through the banking system should, it was argued, provide the banks with information on the operations of all enterprises. The banks were expected to monitor the fulfillment of the production plans of enterprises and discover any divergencies from plans. Some large enterprises often had bank personnel assigned to them for site auditing. Banks have reportedly searched the warehouses of enterprises to discover derelictions, such as unauthorized inventories. Banks also were ordered to refuse to release funds from an enterprise's account for purposes not in conformity with the enterprise's plan and to reject loan requests from the enterprises in such circumstances.

The allocations of loans received by an industrial enterprise were theoretically expected to be sufficient, but not more than sufficient, to enable the enterprise to finance its production plan. The provision of working funds, in other words, should occur simultaneously with the provision of the noncapital factors of production (that is, raw materials and labor), all according to the schedules in the enterprise's production plan. This result was supposed to be determined by the "first principle of socialist credit policy"—that there must be material resources as security for loans.

Before 1965 agricultural loan funds had been centralized under the control of the Agricultural Bank; the bank allotted funds between provinces, and the funds remained under the bank's control after the decision had been made. After 1965 this method was replaced by a system of dividing the total amount available for agricultural loans among the provincial authorities to provide separate revolving funds for rural credit in each province. These funds were then under the control of the local departments of finance. Provinces temporarily needing extra funds for agricultural loans could borrow from the head office of the Agricultural Bank, which also reserved the authority to transfer funds from provincial-level units when required.

Two types of production loans are made to the agricultural sector. Short-term loans, described as "loans for production expenses," are generally made for one year and pay low interest; these funds are to be used for purchasing chemical fertilizers, agricultural chemicals, seed, and small agricultural implements. Medium-term loans are labeled "loans for production equipment," are from three to five years, and are interest free; they are to be used to purchase work animals, water wheels, wheelbarrows, fishing nets, drainage and irrigation machinery, plus plows, harrows, and other middle-sized agricultural implements.

It has been the regime's policy that loans to the agricultural sector are intended only for productive purposes, and that seasonal consumption needs of agriculturists must be covered by peripheral production, such as pigs, poultry, and handicrafts. There are some exceptions, however, to the general prohibition of state credit for peasant consumption. Loans are made to disaster areas and to individuals for medical expenses. Rural credit cooperatives lend their

574

own funds to individuals for both consumption and production. The survival of private lending at high rates of interest through the late 1960s indicated that an acute shortage of credit for consumption purposes still existed up to that period.

SECTION IV. NATIONAL SECURITY

CHAPTER 20

PUBLIC ORDER AND INTERNAL SECURITY

The public order and internal security system in 1971 was still in a state of confusion because much of it had been rendered inoperative by the chaotic developments of the Great Proletarian Cultural Revolution. Apparently, disruptions in the system were greatest in urban areas where the formal agencies lost their power to control people, and the informal committees and groups continued more as vigilantes than as constituted agencies. In rural areas the operation of the system was less affected.

During and after the Cultural Revolution the People's Liberation Army (PLA) played a major role not only in restoring tranquillity to the nation but also in attempting to revive the security system. The rebuilding process was still underway in 1971.

In maintaining internal peace the policies of the People's Republic of China (PRC) have undergone significant change since the assumption of power in 1949. At that time, the loyalty of the people was in question, organized resistance remained in various sectors of the country, the government of the Republic of China on Taiwan maintained a hostile and threatening posture, and the possibility of counterrevolution was real. Accordingly, force and coercion were used relentlessly until all significant internal opposition was suppressed, and strong countermeasures against the infiltration of agents from Taiwan into coastal areas were instituted. The result has been that, in 1971, there was no overt evidence of subversion capable of seriously threatening the regime.

The existence of various non-Chinese minorities in outer regions and some parts of China Proper (see Glossary) was of considerable concern to the regime after 1949. Traditionally, these groups opposed any central government efforts to assimilate them into Han culture and continued to do so even under communist rule (see ch. 4, Ethnic Groups and Languages; ch. 10, Political Dynamics). Tibetans, for example, challenged the central authority of Peking in armed uprisings during the 1950s, and similar uprisings occurred among Muslim tribesmen of north-central China and in various parts of Sinkiang Uighur Autonomous Region and Tsinghai Province. In these areas internal security measures that worked effectively among the Han Chinese had to be substantially liberalized in order to minimize the possibility of unrest and border infiltration by subversive elements from adjoining countries. During the Cultural Revolution tensions were heightened in many areas inhabited by minority peoples because of Red Guard violence, but these were not serious enough to pose a major internal security problem to the government.

In the meantime, as the power and authority of the new regime became consolidated in the mainland, naked force gave way to milder forms of persuasion. Coercive control measures have been replaced by indoctrination coupled with manual labor.

China was governed for thousands of years more by custom than by statutory law. The rule of law, as the term is understood in the West, never developed strong roots. Likewise, under the Communists, the official concept of law and order is predicated less on abstract legal principles than on political considerations. They are in line with the ideological conviction that the fight for internal stability is an aspect of class struggle rather than one of due process of law. Chinese Communist ideology teaches that legal codes, courts, and police, in the past, were instruments employed by the capitalist class to ensure its dominant place in society, whereas in the new communist state these institutions are weapons used by the broad masses of working peoples to eliminate all forms of exploitation and exploiters. From this point of view public order is defined as that state of affairs resulting from the full comprehension of Marxism-Leninism-Maoism by every citizen, the total eradication of bourgeois class consciousness and distinctions, the final solution of all social contradictions, and the establishment of an egalitarian society in which there is neither incentive nor opportunity for anyone to seek personal advantage (see ch. 5, Social System and Values).

The creation of this ideal society demands that legal processes and actions be flexible enough to change with the situation at any given time or place, and the regime has avoided casting such standards in a rigid pattern that might hinder the revolutionary struggle. Movements and campaigns to indoctrinate the people in proper behavior patterns have been launched from time to time. All of these drives have been accompanied by great strife and turmoil, continuing until the authorities felt a point of diminishing return had been reached and halted their rigorous implementation (see ch. 12, Public Information and Propaganda).

At no time in the indoctrination process, however, has an understanding of the doctrine been considered sufficient to bring the desired society into being. In addition, every individual has been expected to do something about what he has learned by subordinating his personal desires to the good of society as a whole and by carrying out prescribed programs established for that purpose. Those who failed to demonstrate a willingness to participate in the program, or who could even be accused of an indisposition to do so, have been denounced as reactionaries, guilty not only of disorderly conduct but also of counterrevolutionary (subversive) activity.

Ordinary criminal cases, such as theft, are treated differently than they are in the West. Theft is a crime not so much because it is a violation of property rights, which is an anathema to the regime anyway, but because it bespeaks a residual parasitic class consciousness that the regime seeks to eradicate. Consequently, rectification does not involve punishment as much as it does the thief's comprehension of the counterrevolutionary implications of his act and his stated determination to study the doctrine further and to behave more correctly in the future.

The conception of public order generally centers on a sociopolitical conformity as defined by the Chinese Communist Party (CCP). The Party is the sole repository of ideological truth, and the Party way, as defined by Chairman Mao Tse-tung, is the correct way; all other ways are fraudulent, corrupt the process of revolution, and engender class divisions and conflicts that render the maintenance of order impossible.

The role of the state in this scheme of law and order is one of mere agency. Under normal circumstances the armed forces, the police system, the judicial system, and various informal control mechanisms are administrative arms that prescribe only what the Party directs and prosecute everything that the Party declares to be unorthodox. All deviations from Party-directed correct behavior may be judged disorderly or treasonable, depending on political priorities in force at the time of commission and the social class antecedents of the accused.

The extent to which the application of justice is regulated and fashioned by these political considerations is nowhere more evident than in the common practice of ascribing the term counterrevolutionary to any accused who in thought, word, or deed exhibits something less than total dedication to the fulfillment of Party policies and programs. It is discernible in the severity of punishments for identical crimes imposed upon individuals of different class origins. A poor peasant or worker, for example, is dealt with less harshly because as a member of a formerly exploited class he is believed to have no genuine desire to oppose the revolution that brought him freedom. He is looked upon simply as an individual who is politically immature and still unable to comprehend his new role in communist society. Corrective measures for him consist primarily, if not wholly, of further indoctrination without other punishment.

A former landlord, capitalist, or intellectual, however, is viewed in a totally different light. An offense committed by one of these individuals has tended to be judged as evidence of inherent, ineradicable hostility and opposition to the communist order. Rehabilitation has been believed unlikely in many cases no matter how intensely additional indoctrination was scheduled. Accordingly, the punishment has usually approached the maximum limits authorized by law.

The PRC does not publish statistics on the incidence of crime, and the only figures available are those gleaned from occasional speeches and reports of Party officials or isolated listings that appear from time to time in mainland newspapers. It is difficult, moreover, to separate offenses into civil and criminal categories. Many civil cases of a social or economic nature have often been treated as criminal depending on political circumstances bearing on them.

LEGAL BASES FOR PUBLIC ORDER AND SECURITY

In 1949 the incoming communist regime abolished all existing civil and criminal codes. In the absence of these formal authorities the government has since relied on various directives and administrative regulations derived from the Common Program, which served as a constitution for the first five years of communist rule.

With reference to public order and security this document merely declared that it was a fundamental duty of government to suppress all counterrevolutionary activities and individuals who opposed the cause of revolution. The adoption of a new state constitution in 1954 did nothing to alter the situation. Moreover, the 1970 draft state constitution makes no reference to any basic changes in the system of rule by decree (see ch. 9, Political System and Values).

Among major decrees, those bearing on counterrevolutionary activities issued in 1951 during the drive for agrarian reform, have served as basic guides in handling virtually every subsequent form of disorder. Under them the prosecution of landlords proved effective in gaining popular support and in eliminating sources of political opposition (see ch. 10, Political Dynamics). Thus subsequent decrees, such as those for the protection of state secrets, for the registration of social groups, against corruption, waste, and theft of state property, and against forgery, counterfeiting, and listening to foreign broadcasts, were worded in such a way that any aberration could be, and was, interpreted and prosecuted as counterrevolutionary.

This system of administering justice has often led to confusion between what is legal and what is illegal at any particular time. Mao Tse-tung holds that the development of a true communist society involves a process of continuing revolution in which control measures must change with the evolving situation. Under this concept, decrees are subjected to overriding imperatives of revolutionary necessity and may be changed to meet every new contingency. Thus, Chinese citizens can be brought to account for acts that occurred before the decree governing their alleged offenses was issued.

THE PUBLIC SECURITY SYSTEM

During the Cultural Revolution many of the personnel of the public security system, particularly those at leadership levels, were dismissed and replaced by those of unquestionable loyalty to Party Chairman Mao Tse-tung. The basic command structure, nevertheless, remained intact at the national level; it has apparently assumed some of its pre-Cultural Revolution functions, but it has been under the overall control and direction of the PLA since 1966.

Below the national level the situation was more complex, and the damage to the public security system was correspondingly greater. Most of the formal operating agencies collapsed under the weight of Red Guard attacks and were left in a position from which recovery has been slow.

In the vanguard of these disruptive developments were the Red Guards. The PLA was instructed to give Red Guard units logistical support but to avoid becoming embroiled in their activities; the established public security forces were ordered to cooperate, but not to interfere with them. Thus, aided and abetted by Chairman Mao and his faction within the Party, the Red Guards were permitted to run wild. Enthusiastic units of the organization attacked the security and judicial systems at every administrative level on the grounds that they were "bureaucratic" organs modeled on those of "bourgeois" countries and that they hindered the revolution. They arrested innumerable officials and subjected them to mass-accusation rallies and trials until they promised to reform. They overwhelmed police forces, forcing many to abandon their posts, and closed police stations in a number of areas. They invaded private homes, desecrated ancient temples, and destroyed priceless and irreplaceable art treasures to eradicate counterrevolutionaries, anti-Mao elements, and everything inherited from the former bourgeois society. They occupied and closed government offices, schools, factories, and enterprises, throttling the administrative and economic life of the country. They even criticized Minister of Public Security Hsieh Fu chih.

As the Cultural Revolution evolved, the Red Guards were split into wrangling factions, each attempting to carry out Mao's program of reforms and transformation in its own way, often vying with rival factions in an effort to demonstrate revolutionary zeal. All these groups, although mainly located in urban areas, roamed throughout the nation creating havoc wherever they went. Their tactics aroused much antagonism, but with the police absent or impotent there was little that could be done to halt their depredations. In many areas residents were forced to form their own informal groups, similar to vigilantes, in order to protect their lives and property. The result was that in 1967 China was thrown into a state of civil disorder bordering on anarchy.

Finally, in early 1967, in order to save the nation from the brink of total collapse, the PLA was called upon to restore order (see ch. 10, Political Dynamics; ch. 21, The Armed Forces). The army took over the ruling apparatus at every administrative level and assumed control of all public security services, occupying and operating the basic public security bureaus at every level and sending out military patrols to replace the impotent or defunct police forces. Police personnel and units that had survived were incorporated into the local military commands and continued to operate under army direction.

In the overall peace-keeping process, meanwhile, a variety of new local law and order groups composed of workers, militia, former police personnel, ex-servicemen, revolutionary cadre, and members of mass organizations were created to aid the army in restoring and maintaining order in the face of civil disturbances. By the end of 1969 most of the rioting had been stopped, and the PLA had become the nation's sole effective national agency for law and order.

In 1971 the PLA was still in firm control of all security services; but many of the emergency groups that had been created to assist the military had, or were being, dismantled, and the system appeared to be returning to a semblance of what it had been before 1966. At that time the people of mainland China were subject to the control of a multiplicity of formal and informal agencies within the structure of the civil government as well as the mass organizations to which everyone was required to belong. The formal agencies of the civil government originated at the highest national levels and were represented in all administrative units down to the lowest. The informal units penetrated deeply into society and functioned through popular mass organizations established on the basis of residence or place of employment. The entire system was, in turn, guided and directed by the ubiquitous authority of the Party (see ch. 9, Political System and Values; ch. 10, Political Dynamics).

Formal Control Structure

Formally, the apex of the public security system was, in 1971 as in the past, the General Office for Internal Affairs, which supervised the activities of two ministries: the Ministry of Internal Affairs and the Ministry of Public Security (see ch. 9, Political System and Values). Actually, the whole system was under the temporary supervision of the PLA; presumably the PLA's police role would be terminated as soon as the public security system was restored to the position it had before the Cultural Revolution. It is probable that, once the PLA is removed from its directing role, the actual, ultimate power of control over the public security system would revert to appropriate departments of the Party Central Committee, which, like other public organizations, were disrupted during the Cultural Revolution and in 1971 were only slowly resuming their former activities.

In addition to these agencies, various aspects of internal security functions fell within the purview of other top-level offices and ministries. The General Office for Industry and Communications and the General Office for Agriculture and Forestry also supervise subordinate ministries that have specialized units concerned with the control of economic sabotage (see ch. 9, Political System and Values). The extent to which these ministries were still used by the PLA and the degree to which their normal responsibilities had been returned to them in late 1971 were unknown. Presumably they were still operating, although not as autonomously in security matters as they had been before the PLA took over the entire system.

The Ministry of Internal Affairs was basically a support organization. It operated the nation's only crime laboratory, formulated police programs, and administered police schools and institutes throughout the provinces. Apart from these generalities, little is known of the ministry's organization or operation.

The Ministry of Public Security was the main operating element in the security system. It was the national headquarters for a hierarchy of subordinate organizations, called public security bureaus, established at each provincial, autonomous region, county, and municipal level. Details of the ministry's organization have never been released, but apparently it had an administrative office and several departments that acted as directorates for various types of security operations, such as political security, economic security, police operations, penal institutions, communications security, intelligence, personnel, and an unknown number of others. The ministry directly commanded the People's Police attached to the public security bureau at each administrative level. Since these lower bureaus were elements of the civil government, they were subject to the lateral control of CCP committees.

Below national level the security system before the Cultural Revolution consisted of descending levels of formal agencies, represented by public security bureaus and public security stations (or police stations) augmented by a variety of subordinate informal agencies, such as elements of mass organizations, security defense committees, street offices, residents committees, and residents groups. Information on the manner in which these formal and internal bodies actually functioned in 1971 was not readily available.

Provincial bureaus had separate subdivisions for general police activities, foreign nationals, population control, traffic regulation, and firefighting, as well as for the operation of police schools and hospitals established within their jurisdictions. County and municipal bureaus usually had units concerned with arrest and detention, administration of houses of detention, population registration, surveillance, health and welfare, and firefighting. The precise number and type of subdivisions varied with the size and nature of the territory within the responsibility of the bureau in question.

In rural and urban areas alike, public security bureaus regularly established one or more branches to bring their operations closer to the people wherever the size of the territory or the density of the population made it advisable to do so. In rural areas these branches might consist of a security staff officer, a census officer, and a public security officer in charge of a force of uniformed and plainclothes policemen, or they might involve only an area public security officer and a small police force. In urban areas branches were necessarily larger and more complex. Most Chinese cities were divided into districts, and usually a branch containing sizable sections for political and economic security and for public order was established in each.

Every public security bureau and branch in both rural and urban areas also had one or more public security stations associated with and subordinate to it. The size and capability of these stations were dependent on the magnitude of the security tasks it had to perform. In rural areas some counties were so sparsely settled and undeveloped that a single public security station directly under the county bureau might be sufficient. In others, where branches were required, there might be one central station under the county bureau and one or more as needed under each branch. Such stations were usually small, operating under a chief, perhaps a deputy-chief, a minimal administrative staff, and a small force of police.

In urban areas public security stations were usually established on the basis of one for every tenth street. They were commanded by a chief who was assisted by one or more deputy chiefs, a security secretary, a sizable administrative staff, a small force of plainclothes policemen, and from seven to eighteen patrolmen on the beat.

Common to all public security bureaus, public security branches, and public security stations—regardless of size or area—was a section of the staff known as the household office. Its task was to check on travelers, overnight guests, hotel patrons, births and deaths, and marriages and divorces. The ultimate aim was to develop dossiers on members of each household, including detailed information on the source of income, education, class category, family background for at least three generations, personal history from childhood, and the number of relatives inside and outside China.

Informal Control Agencies

Below the formal civil government security organizations, order and security were maintained through other agencies that reinforced police

584

operations. Many were mass organizations created to support indoctrination and propaganda drives, mass movements, and campaigns directed by the authorities. Others, such as labor unions, professional societies, and cultural groups, served the same objectives. More pertinent, however, were the urban street offices and residents' committees and groups in large cities and the security defense committees in both urban and rural areas.

Urban Areas

These agencies were first established by the Act for the Organization of Urban Street Offices of 1954. The act specified that it was mandatory for every city having a population of 100,000 or more to set up an urban street office. It further stated that such offices were optional in cities with populations between 50,000 and 100,000. Cities and districts with less than 50,000 residents generally had no urban street office.

Each urban street office was headed by a director, who was aided by a staff of varying size, according to needs. The director usually had from three to seven deputy directors, one of whom was required to be a woman to carry out work among females. All personnel were drawn from residents of the area served by the office. They were appointed as full-time, salaried employees of the municipal civil government.

The mission of the urban street offices was to forge closer ties between the government and the people, to facilitate the development of mass organizations, and to supervise a wide variety of civil tasks, such as welfare, relief, sanitation, and the maintenance of household records. In the area of law and order, each office entered the system by guiding subordinate street agencies and by reporting people's attitudes and opinions to the appropriate public security bureau.

In each city area served by an urban street office, residents' committees were set up on the basis of one for each neighborhood of from 100 to 600 households. The functions of the committee were to manage public welfare, to report the political attitudes of the people within its jursidiction, to mobilize the masses for meetings, assemblies, speeches, and other public functions, to lead the people in security defense work, and to mediate disputes among the residents of its areas. Thus, like the urban street offices, residents' committees were largely concerned with civil administration but also had important responsibilities for law and order that were carried out through specialized sections known as mediation committees and security defense committees.

Both mediation committees and security defense committees were originally established in neighborhoods, factories, schools, enterprises, and mass organizations. Gradually, however, most of them merged and became an integral part of residents' committees, although a few may have remained in factories that employ large labor forces and in some schools and other organs. In rural areas the security defense committees retained their original structure and functions.

Mediation committees consisted of from three to eleven members under a chief and one or two deputies. Their mission was to take advantage of the traditional Chinese preference for dealing with disputes and antisocial conduct informally by persuasion rather than by recourse to the police. In practice, they settled ordinary disputes and minor criminal cases by mediation only and were not authorized to punish disputants or to take them into custody.

Security defense committees had about the same size and organizational structure as mediation committees but sometimes were further subdivided into groups of from three to five activists under a group chief. They were employed to carry out propaganda and political education activities and to organize and lead the masses in denouncing, supervising, and combating counterrevolutionary and "bad" elements in their communities. They could arrest counterrevolutionaries and criminals but were required to turn them over to the public security bureaus immediately. They had no authority to interrogate or detain those whom they arrested or to supervise the labor and production of those already under control. They did, however, aid the police otherwise in maintaining public order and in performing guard duty.

In neighborhoods where the area was large and activities were complex, residents' groups were often established under the residents' committee for each unit of from fifteen to forty households. These groups each had from seven to seventeen members, and their chairmen were ex officio members of the larger residents' committee. The chairman usually had a deputy, and the group was organized into specialized work committees for social welfare, culture, education and health, mediation, and women's activities.

The missions of each group were identical to those of the residents' committee to which it was subordinate. The restriction of its responsibility to a few families, however, enabled controls to be extended downward until they embraced individual residents on every street.

Rural Areas

In rural areas formal public security bureaus and public security stations usually did not exist below county seat level and, although sometimes a public security branch might be established, control areas were so large that the system could not maintain the degree of omniscience demanded by the central authorities without help. The rural patterns of living, however, made the development of informal auxiliary agencies based on street residence impossible, so a different form of control organization was adopted.

In the rural system one member of the county public security bureau or branch was assigned to supervise all security functions in each People's Commune or cluster of three or four villages. If the functions were beyond the capability of one man, a member of a Commune or a village administrative staff was assigned full-time security duty. This individual, working directly under the public security bureau through its assigned member, organized and worked through a number of security defense committees in his Commune or village.

The rural security defense committees differed only in one respect from their urban counterparts. They were not considered part' of the government structure but were described as organizations of the masses that were simply directed and controlled by the basic-level governments and the public security bureaus in their areas.

POLICE FORCES

The police forces, like so many of the nation's public institutions, had not yet fully recovered in 1971 from the effects of the Cultural Revolution. Before 1966 primary responsibility for maintaining public order and security was vested in the People's Police, a national military-type organization of the Ministry of Public Security.

When the security structure collapsed in 1966 and 1967, the PLA was called upon to provide essential police protection for the nation. The PLA occupied the public security bureaus, manned public security stations with military units, and employed military patrols to replace patrolmen on the beat. Overburdened PLA units were then augmented and assisted by an assortment of new mass organizations of workers, militia, ex-servicemen, remnants of the People's Police, students, representatives from mass organizations, and various activists formed under the direction of the new revolutionary committees (see ch. 9, Political System and Values).

In the aftermath of the Cultural Revolution, the PLA continued to serve as the ultimate police authority, but since about 1969 it has been endeavoring to reconstitute the People's Police and to restore the force to its former size and capability. In late 1971 the process was far from complete, and many of the emergency mass organizations were still in operation although, as the situation began to stabilize, they seemed to be taking a more subordinate role.

The People's Police

The People's Police was formally established by the Police Act of 1954, although it had been operating in substantially the same form for several years before that. Under the act the police were subject to the overall policy guidance and supervision of the Ministry of Public

Security but were placed under the operational and administrative control of the local public security bureaus.

Police operations and activities have always been classified as state secrets so that details of the organization and strength of the People's Police are extremely limited. The last figure on their strength, for example, was made public in 1960, when the minister of public security told an American journalist that the security forces totaled about 1.7 million officers and men. This figure, however, is believed to have included members of border guard units, which have since been absorbed into the PLA.

The regular police were organized into an indeterminate number of uniformed and plainclothes sections assigned to every public security station. The urban units and, to a lesser degree, the rural elements operated through highly compartmentalized sections concerned with economic security; vital statistics; traffic control; criminal investigation; arrest and detention; railroad, port, and river activity control; intelligence and counterintelligence collection; and firefighting. In addition, the People's Police in all areas were responsible for many duties that, as stated in the Police Act of 1954, were civil in character. Among them were household registration and population control; registration of births, deaths, marriages, and changes of residence and jobs; licensing of firearms, explosives, and radio, engraving, printing, and communications equipment; control of listening to foreign broadcasts; issuance and authentication of travel permits; and other activities classified as threats to the public order.

In carrying out these missions the People's Police controlled and directed the security defense committees in rural areas, the committees and groups in cities, and other mass organizations in both areas that made the police presence felt down to the lowest levels of society. Formal and informal agencies alike were used extensively by the People's Police to mobilize the people behind state-directed programs and movements, to organize mass meetings for indoctrination, to denounce individuals suspected of counterrevolutionary tendencies, or to ensure compliance with Party directives.

These official missions and activities were so stringently applied and enforced that the police came to be heartily disliked and hated by the people, which was one of the reasons why they were so bitterly attacked and finally rendered impotent in the early stages of the Cultural Revolution. Although the police were under the aegis of the PLA in 1971, visitors to Peking report that the police had not yet been able to establish rapport with the people, who tend to ignore their authority and services.

Personnel for the police were drawn from every segment of the population without restriction as to sex or ethnic origin. All candidates, however, had to pass close Party scrutiny for loyalty. As a result, most recruits came from communist youth organizations or were discharged members of the PLA who had served their required tours of duty.

Police schools were operated by some municipalities, and there was at least one in every province. Attendance at these institutions was usually restricted to those in leadership positions who required specialized knowledge to pass on to their subordinates. Beginning about 1967 there was also a critical need for police authorities to be better grounded in Mao's version of how a communist society must be operated; so many public security officials were removed from their bureaus and stations when the PLA took over the security system, and the officials were sent to institutions for concentrated study of Mao Tse-tung Thought. Courses at the regular schools meanwhile included training in economic security; the use of firearms; propaganda; fire control; and techniques of surveillance, search, and mail interception; interrogation; population control; and intensified indoctrination in Mao's concepts. From time to time these courses were augmented by short courses or lectures on specialized and technical subjects conducted by visiting senior security officials from Peking.

There was also a national school, called the Central Public Security Institute located in the national capital, that presumably offered advanced courses in investigation and surveillance as well as police administration. Its student body was restricted to senior officers of high provincial rank and to chiefs of staff sections in the Ministry of Public Security. No mention of this institution has appeared in the late 1960s and early 1970s, but it was presumed to have been still in operation.

Under a 1954 regulation, police at all levels were given the right to investigate, search, and detain suspected criminals. These powers were officially limited by regulations that required a court warrant before an arrest could be made and that placed a forty-eight-hour limitation on the time an individual could be held without a formal charge. The same regulations, however, provided for so many exceptions that the regulations were more flouted than observed. No warrant was required, for example, if an offender was caught in the act or if he could not identify himself or prove that he was employed. Of even greater significance, none was necessary if his act had, or could be broadly interpreted to have, overtones of counterrevolutionary behavior.

In practice, therefore, the People's Police handled a number of violators without recourse to formal legal process, except in some important cases where public prosecution was considered to have desirable potential for indoctrinating the masses. Police investigated, apprehended, detained, and sentenced offenders sometimes on their own, imposing sanctions that ranged from the simplest admonitions and warnings to live more cautiously through private and public sessions of criticism. These sanctions could be culminated in mandatory written statements of repentance and a determination to avoid repeating past aberrations; exposure to one's peers at public assemblies to criticism, vituperation, and intimidation; fines; short periods of detention, often involving forced labor on public works projects; longer periods of confinement at a labor camp; and finally summary and immediate execution. The degree of punishment imposed for identical violations varied according to local interpretations of policy, the social background of the offender, and his political motivation.

The People's Police were aided by the militia in maintaining public order, especially in rural areas. In this connection the militia usually were assigned to guard public buildings and property and to protect factories, railroads, enterprises, warehouses, bridges, and forests (see ch. 21, The Armed Forces).

Post-1969 Mass Security Organizations

The Cultural Revolution created a vacuum that was only partially filled by the PLA when it took over the security system. Military units were able to suppress rioting, control major disturbances, and provide general protection everywhere, but most routine police activities were beyond their capabilities. Consequently, crime and hooliganism increased, particularly in the cities; bands of thugs brawled in the streets, often engaging in gun battles with one another; and begging, burglary, and theft became widespread. Adding to the disorder were thousands of young people and former Red Guards who had been sent to the countryside for manual labor and secretly slipped back into the cities where, lacking jobs or even permits to be there, they caused trouble.

The situation demanded the formation of new organizations to aid the PLA, and great emphasis was placed on mass participation. At the lowest levels some of these agencies were developed by residential committees and groups in cities and by security defense committees in rural areas to perform routine police duties in their neighborhoods; others consisted of security enforcement teams of surviving police, revolutionary cadre, and concerned residents—often with the participation of militiamen—to take over similar tasks. At higher levels larger, paramilitary organizations of soldiers and civilians were established by recently formed revolutionary committees with the aid and support of the PLA.

The bulk of the personnel for the larger organizations were drawn from the tens of thousands of idle industrial workers whose factories had been closed down in the turmoil. Their numbers were increased by other hundreds of PLA veterans, former members of the People's Police, militiamen, students, interested members of various mass organizations, and Party activists. There was no standard organization for these units although most were formed along military lines into divisions, brigades, regiments, battalions, and companies and all were operationally controlled by the local army commander.

The new organizations also were known by different names in various areas. Some were called Workers' Provost Corps because of the predominance of workers in their memberships; others took the name of People's Provost Corps to indicate the broader mass representation among their personnel; still others adapted a phrase coined by Ch'iang Ching (Madame Mao Tse-tung) in a speech and designated themselves as "Attack by Violence-Defend by Force Commands." Relations among these groups, some of which operated in the same localities, were acrimonious, and much factional infighting broke out among them, accompanied by charges of ideological deviation, corruption, and abuse of powers. Generally, however, they were praised for their dedicated work in house searches, travel document checks, street patrols, general security duty, organization of Mao study sessions, firefighting, apprehension of youth missing from rural areas, and overall preservation of order.

Gradually, as the nation became more tranquil, these emergency security organizations began to give way to the reconstituted People's Police. As factories were reopened and the workers were called back to their jobs, some retained their basic organization and continued to police the plant or their home neighborhoods during off-duty hours. Some members were recruited into the People's Police or into the PLA. In 1971, however, many apparently continued to perform security duties, showing no signs of disbanding. Whether they will ultimately give way to the regular police or will continue as a new, separate law enforcement agency appears likely to depend on the effectiveness of the reconstituted People's Police.

THE JUDICIAL SYSTEM

As authorized by the 1954 State Constitution and pertinent laws, the judicial system consists of two theoretically independent organs answerable to the National People's Congress: the Supreme People's Court and the Supreme People's Procuratorate. The highest judicial body in the land, the Supreme People's Court, in theory supervises three levels of subordinate people's courts; the Supreme People's Procuratorate, the highest prosecuting authority in the land, directs a hierarchy of procurators, or public prosecutors, that parallels the court system (see ch. 9, Political System and Values).

The PRC has neither a penal code nor codes of criminal and judicial procedure, making it impossible to talk of justice in isolation from Party principles. Under those principles, the work of judges and procurators, like that of the police, must serve the political mission of the state. That which is beneficial to the mission is just; that which hinders or impedes it is unjust; and on this basis all crime and criminal acts are adjudicated and punished.

The Supreme People's Court is headed by a president, elected by the People's Congress and assisted by several vice presidents, divisional presidents, and judges appointed by the Standing Committee of the People's Congress. This court has primary and original jurisdiction over all serious cases involving national security and violations by a high government or Party official or by a lesser individual whose prosecution can be useful in educating or propagandizing the masses. The Supreme People's Court may exercise an appellate or review function on its own initiative, but this has occurred only rarely—and then only when it was requested to do so by the Supreme People's Procuratorate.

The Supreme People's Court has the power to rule on matters that involve the application of specific laws or decrees but not on their legality or interpretation. This function is reserved exclusively to the Standing Committee. Decisions of this tribunal are usually considered to be final but, when grounds for challenge seem to warrant it, the Standing Committee can order a retrial.

The higher people's courts, which operate in the special municipalities of Peking, Tientsin, and Shanghai as well as at the provincial level, are courts of first instance for serious cases developed in their areas or referred to them by lower courts. They also hear appeals from decisions of the same lower tribunals.

The intermediate people's courts, usually located in large cities, try cases that have political implications, including those involving foreign nationals or organizations. The basic people's courts, at the county level, have original jurisdiction over most routine criminal and civil cases.

The Supreme People's Procuratorate is the apex of the procuratorial system. Procurators and their staffs are organized in a single, rigid hierarchy with an unbroken command line from top to bottom and are charged with the mission of safeguarding the interests of the Party and the state and of serving as a check on the whole court system.

In general, the Supreme People's Procuratorate has authority over all departments of the State Council, all local organs of the state, persons working in these organs, and the citizenry in general. It is headed by a chief procurator under whom are a varying number of deputy chiefs and procurators. At each administrative level, the people's procuratorate is assisted by a committee consisting of the chief procurator, his deputies, a secretary general, and representatives of the central government, the public security bureau, and certain other organizations. This committee advises the procuratorate on Party policies and their implementation.

Procurators at all levels are authorized to prosecute any person suspected of criminal and counterrevolutionary activities. They also are empowered to supervise decisions, orders, and measures of state organs to ensure their conformity with law; to inquire into criminal cases and prosecute them; to supervise the adjudication of the courts; to act as watchdogs over the execution of judgments and reform activities; and to exercise the right to join in the prosecution of important cases involving the state and the people.

In accordance with the official Chinese Communist principle of encouraging maximum mass participation in the development of society, courts at every level are provided with a system of assessors (sometimes called people's jurors). There is no set form or number of assessors named for any court, but their membership is composed of laymen drawn from labor unions, from PLA personnel, and from Party organizations as needed.

Originally, assessors shared in adjudicating civil and criminal cases, in examining the accused and all witnesses during trials, and in having the same powers as judges. They sat with the judge, examined and decided not only points of fact but also points of law, and shared in handing down decisions. During the 1960s, however, their role may have been reduced to one that is largely advisory, because official reference to assessors has almost disappeared.

About 1957 the leadership of the regime decided that, since the Party represented the vanguard and chief agent of the proletariat, its authority over the judicial system, including the handling of individual cases, must be made absolute. Among the measures adopted to establish this supremacy was the creation of judicial committees at every court level. These committees were units of Party, government, and court officials that exercised political control over the courts. They reviewed judgments and decisions in cases of high importance to determine whether or not they were in consonance with Party policy and summarized judicial experience as a guide to historical development but not as precedents for courts to follow.

Under the 1954 Organic Law of Procuratorates, procuratorates were not to be subject to interference by state organs on the same administrative level. A procurator at any level had the right to pass on to the next higher court any objection to decisions returned by the court on his level. The chief procurator in Peking might do the same with decisions of the Supreme People's Court by referring the matter to the Standing Committee of the People's Congress.

Procurators conducting examinations or investigations had the right to send representatives to attend meetings of relevant organs and to gain access to their files, orders, decisions, and other records. Organs involved in these actions were required to supply all necessary explanations and information requested by the procurators.

Before the Cultural Revolution procurators were among the most powerful officials in the entire judicial system, but during the violence and chaos of that movement they were bitterly attacked, their prestige dropped, and their importance waned substantially. Since the late 1960s the importance of these procurators in the judicial system seems to have decreased. At all administrative levels, their main mission has become one of acting as clearinghouses to exchange and coordinate experience and to render legal advice. Whether this new pattern will continue under the yet-to-be fully restored judicial system remained unclear in 1971.

Mass Trials

Historically, formal action taken by the courts against criminals and social misfits has sporadically been replaced by so-called trials conducted informally before great masses of the people. This form of dealing with nonconformists has been commonly followed during major propaganda campaigns and mass movements in which the regime has attempted to give the implementation of its revolutionary program the appearance of legality and of carrying out the will of the people. Thus mass trials were the major means by which landlords and bourgeois elements were destroyed during the agrarian reform movement in the 1950–52 period. The technique was revived and given priority in the campaign against counterrevolutionaries in 1955 and had been employed irregularly during similar movements up to 1971. The latest manifestation occurred during the Cultural Revolution, when both the courts and the procuratorates were criticized and overwhelmed by the ebullient Red Guards and other radical supporters of Mao Tse-tung.

Mass trials are held not so much for the administration of justice as for the political education of the people—to indoctrinate, agitate, and rally them behind Party policies and to intensify their hatred of anyone or anything the regime considers to be a threat to its revolutionary program. Contrary to their outward appearance of spontaneity, mass trials are not conducted in a hit-or-miss fashion but are well prepared, organized, and contrived to terminate in predetermined convictions. A regular judge usually presides, and associated procurators are there to give the event dignity and a semblance of legality. The meetings are highly publicized before they take place, and the masses are mobilized by residents' committees or some other mass organization to provide a crowd.

The trail begins when the people are assembled, and the procurator, or anyone present, rises and makes accusations against the defendant

594

or defendants. As the proceedings unfold, inflammatory speeches are delivered by Party officials, activist leaders, trained agitators scattered among the crowd, or anyone present who has been sufficiently aroused to speak up. Theoretically, the accused may speak in his own defense, or he may be represented and defended by a lawyer. Actual defense, however, is rare because the charge is consistently one of counterrevolutionary activity, and anyone daring to oppose it is afraid of being deemed guilty by association.

When the emotions of the assemblage appear to have reached a climax, the judge rises, summarizes the proceedings, and asks the crowd for its verdict. The people invariably shout back their condemnation, usually calling for imposition of the maximum penalty. Punishment is then immediately enforced in the presence of the agitated crowd.

Judicial Procedures

In normal times, the judicial procedures for handling criminals begin when the People's Police on their own or as a result of tips from some individual or group among the masses uncover a possible violation of law or Party policy. An investigation is then launched and usually results in the arrest of the individual or individuals involved.

Both the 1954 State Constitution and the draft state constitution of 1970 guarantee every citizen freedom of person and specifies that arrests can be made only by a court decision or with the sanction of a procurator. Police authority is further limited by Regulations on Arrest and Detention promulgated in 1954, but in practice little heed is paid to any of these restrictions. Furthermore, those who are arrested are not treated as suspects but as criminals and are thus presumed to be guilty. While under detention, which may be for months, they are treated in the same way as those convicted. Protestations of innocence are futile.

Persons arrested are taken to the police station, where they are subjected to intensive interrogation in order to extract a confesssion to the charges. Physical coercion is sometimes used in the process, but the more common form of interrogation is the application of psychological pressure. The suspect is relentlessly reminded, for example, that it is his duty to the revolution to admit his aberrations and that those who confess are treated leniently while those who remain obstinate are enemies of the people who must be punished severely. In time, a confession of some sort is nearly always obtained.

Once a confession has been obtained, the police may impose punishment directly if the offense is a relatively minor one or turn the case over to the local procurator for more formal disposition if the offense is serious. The local procurator may, however, upon further investigation, remand it to the police for disposition.

Procedures for both trials and appeals are highly flexible and, in the absence of a formal code of procedures, judges have to rely on their own common sense as well as decrees of the government and Party policies. On the county level, trials are usually held before a one-judge tribunal but, when the case is difficult or important, a panel of three judges may sit. On the provincial and national levels, three-man tribunals have been the rule. In both instances the judges may or may not be advised by assessors.

The law stipulates that trials must be open and that the accused has the right to counsel and of defense. He may defend his case personally or designate advocates (close relatives or citizens recommended by a mass organization) to speak for him. The position of defense is difficult, however, since the accused is practically convicted once he is arraigned—it being unthinkable that the Party-controlled organization could make a wrong accusation. Moreover, the defender must act both for the accused and for the state. Although he must defend the accused, he must also defend the state and the revolution and, should he be too successful and gain an acquittal, he may render himself liable to later charges of incorrect revolutionary behavior.

The conduct of a criminal trial is divided into a preparatory session and the main session. In the preparatory phase the judge, the procurator, and the assessors (if any) examine the reports of the investigation to see whether or not there is sufficient justification for prosecution and conviction. After this, a date for the main session is fixed.

The main session is divided into four parts: preparation, investigation, discussion, and sentence. The preparation is similar to original action taken by the police in collecting evidence against the accused. Much attention in this phase is placed on getting evidence from every conceivable source. Included among admissable sources is the prisoner's past history, whether it bears directly on the act for which he was arrested or not.

Procedures in the investigation phase are quite informal. The accused is brought into the court office where the judge reads the act of accusation and then questions the defendant and all witnesses and experts called in for testimony. This is followed by the discussion phase in which the procurator and the defending counsel (if there is any) make their speeches and propose the sanction to be adjudicated by the court. After these have been concluded, the accused may speak if he chooses to do so.

At the conclusion of the discussion phase the judge or the panel of judges, the procurators, and the assessors retire and arrive at a decision by majority, not unanimous, vote. The judge prepares a proposed judgment and submits it to the judicial committee and to the local Party branch for approval. After this had been done, the approved judgment and sentence are announced.

After the trial the procurators have the right to appeal the verdict, or a higher procuratorate may object to the sentence as being too lenient and call for sterner punishment. In any case, the trial moves to a higher court for rehearing.

In the case of appeal by the defendant, both judges and procurators take a hostile attitude toward those who wish to appeal, regarding the act as resistance to the will of the state. Appeals, therefore, are seldom made because both the appealing individual and those who make the appeal for him are likely to be designated resistors. Appeal may be filed from the verdict of a lower court but, after the appeal has been heard by the next higher tribunal, decisions are considered final.

THE PENAL SYSTEM

Reform Through Labor

The *Regulations Concerning Reform Through Labor*, a document published in 1954, stipulates that all those who are spared the death penalty must be reformed through labor and that only after this has failed is serious punishment in order. Reform through labor is a combination of punishment and education. On the one hand, counterrevolutionary attitudes are eradicated; on the other, violators are trained in production techniques so as to become skilled workmen who can contribute to the economic progress of the nation.

Convicted persons whom the authorities regard as safe enough to work outside are assigned to reform-through-labor teams established by provincial and municipal public security bureaus. The teams are then organized into brigades of various sizes. A supervisory committee, consisting of the head of the labor brigade, one or two members of the public security bureau, and one or two representatives of the court, is put in charge of every 3,000 convicts. Since the productive work done by the convicts is an integral part of the state plan of economic construction, they are taught technical skills according to government needs (see ch. 17, Labor).

Penal Institutions

There are three main types of penal institutions: detention houses, prisons, and houses of correction. Figures on their number, population, and capacities have never been released. It is known, however, that the communist regime inherited about 121 prisons and over 1,800 houses of detention from the Nationalist government—all of which may still be in use. It is unlikely that their number has been increased significantly because of the government's preference for assigning most prisoners to work teams in the newer form of corrective institution called labor reform camps.

Detention houses are established at the national, provincial, special administrative district, and county levels under the jurisdiction of the public security bureaus at each corresponding level. They are meant primarily for the confinement of those awaiting trial, those whose cases are pending, and those condemned to less than two years' imprisonment. The inmates in them are required to undergo reform through labor.

On the basis of the scant information available, it appears that prisoners usually work nine to ten hours a day, with seasonal work often as high as twelve hours. They have a minimum of one hour daily for indoctrination and about eight hours for sleep. Two days a month are set aside for rest. Relatives may visit an inmate twice a month, for periods not to exceed thirty minutes each time. All letters, incoming and outgoing, are censored.

Very little is known of actual conditions within prisons but, according to the report of one Western observer who was permitted to visit a prison in Peking during the mid-1950s, the prison was similar to a great textile factory, starkly and almost aseptically clean though badly in need of repair. The resident population was about 2,000, including 130 women; approximately two-thirds of the prisoners were classified as counterrevolutionaries. Among the inmates the report stated there were some sentenced to life imprisonment, although most were serving terms of ten years or less. Rations consisted of one pound of vegetables, one-third ounce of oil, one-half ounce of salt, and a variable amount of rice and flour per day. Once a week each prisoner received four ounces of meat.

The prison reform program consisted of four stages. In the first stage all prisoners were required to explain the nature of their crime and acknowledge the improper thinking that caused them to commit it. They then underwent labor education, since only a few of them had ever held a job of any kind. This was followed by training in labor techniques, which at this particular prison consisted of learning how to operate the textile machines. Finally all prisoners attended current events classes to develop correct ideological thinking and an understanding of the simpler Marxist principles. Illiterate prisoners also received training to master at least 2,000 characters.

Commutation, Clemency, and Release

The only valid basis for commutation and clemency is a demonstrated change of heart. Evidence of this change may be developed in a number of ways. In every case there must be an apparently sincere admission of previous failure to understand revolutionary principles and Mao Tse-tung Thought. This admission must be accompanied by an unblemished record of hard and dedicated effort to excel in assigned productive labor; a selflessness in helping one's fellows to develop proper political attitudes, including denunciation of their aberrations; and a declaration of intention to accept Party leadership and to participate voluntarily in approved revolutionary programs and movements.

When this evidence is forthcoming, a prisoner may receive preferential treatment in the form of extra rations and privileges, may be assigned a position of leadership among his fellow inmates, may be awarded a reduction in his sentence, or may be granted a parole or outright release from custody. When it is not forthcoming, a prisoner's sentence may be extended indefinitely until he does show signs of reformation.

When release from custody is warranted, whether or not his full sentence has been completed, a prisoner is usually given some form of employment. In most cases this involves a grant of land in some uninhabited area upon which the exconvict and his family may settle. Released prisoners may also be retained and may continue their employment in the labor brigades if they so choose. Such retention is usually followed if the prisoner volunteers and his work is needed for production, if he has no home to which he may return, if he is unable to find work elsewhere, or if his labor is needed for the settlement of uninhabited lands. In the early 1960s it was estimated that as a rule about 20 percent of all released prisoners elected to remain in their labor brigades.

CHAPTER 21

THE ARMED FORCES

The People's Liberation Army (PLA), as the Chinese Communists have called their armed forces since 1946, was in 1971 one of the world's largest military establishments. The PLA grew out of a small force of volunteers that ultimately defeated the powerful Nationalist forces of Chiang Kai-shek by a strategy of protracted armed struggle, aimed at gradually increasing its own strength while weakening the capability of its adversary. The PLA is heir to a unique tradition in which its soldiers not only had to fight but also to carry out propaganda work among the masses, organize Chinese Communist Party (CCP) units, indoctrinate Party members, and engage in a wide range of production work. It has become so deeply embedded in the civilian life of the country that the history of the PLA is in a real sense also the history of the Party. The centrality of the PLA to the Chinese Communist movement was aptly described by Mao Tse-tung in 1945 when he declared, "Without a people's army, the people have nothing."

Until his triumph in 1949 Mao was obliged to fight almost always from the position of weakness against Chiang's superior Nationalist forces. He was painfully aware of the situation in which, although "political power," as he put it in 1939, "grows out of the barrel of a gun," he did not have enough guns to overwhelm the Nationalists. By force of circumstances, Mao was left with no choice but to rely on factors other than the purely military. Thus, although conceding that "weapons are an important factor in war," he said that they were by no means "the decisive factor." Instead, Mao asserted: "It is people, not things, that are decisive. The contest of strength is not only a contest of military and economic power, but also a contest of human power and morale. Military and economic power is necessarily wielded by people."

The argument that "man is superior to weapons" was heard much less frequently in the first half of the 1950s, during which time the Chinese Communists concentrated their efforts on modernizing the PLA's organization and equipment, based almost exclusively on the "advanced experiences" of the Soviet Union's Red Army. The argument was revived, however, about 1958 when, in the context of deteriorating Sino-Soviet relations, the People's Republic of China (PRC) decided to embark on a policy of military self reliance. Efforts to restore its own "revolutionary traditions" have been stepped up since 1960, when the Soviet Union abruptly terminated its military assistance to the Chinese government, compelling it to rely on its already limited internal resources to maintain its massive defense establishment.

As of early 1971 the PLA, which encompasses the Army, the Air Force, and the Navy, had an estimated total strength of 2.88 million men, of which the ground forces accounted for 2.55 million (2.85 million if some 300,000 border security troops are included), or more than 90 percent of the total strength. The Air Force had about 3,500 combat aircraft, mostly of obsolete Soviet types, and a personnel strength of 180,000. The Navy had about 150,000 men manning a surface fleet of approximately 900 vessels, many in various stages of obsolescence. The PLA was backed up by a massive reserve force of more than 200 million enrolled in the militia, but of this huge number approximately 7 million men were estimated to be combat worthy. Annually an estimated 6.5 million to 7.5 million youths were reaching the military age of eighteen, but less than 10 percent of these draft-age youths were actually inducted.

In 1970 the government's defense expenditure was estimated to be the equivalent of US$8 billion, or about 10 percent of the country's gross national product (GNP). Although this sum was the world's third largest in absolute terms after the United States and the Soviet Union, it probably was among the lowest in terms of per capita defense spending. The level of 1970 spending, as during much of the 1960s, appeared to impose heavy burdens on a national economy that was barely able to satisfy the basic needs of the nation's population, estimated at about 800 million in 1971.

In 1971 the PLA posed no strategic threat to any power outside Asia. As far as was ascertainable, it deployed fewer than twenty nuclear-tipped medium-range ballistic missiles but had no operational intermediate or intercontinental missiles. The primary means of delivery for its nuclear devices was about thirty Soviet-model TU-16 jet bombers, which had a combat radius of 1,650 nautical miles. According to most observers, the PRC might, by the middle or late 1970s, be able to deploy up to 100 medium-range ballistic missiles and between ten and twenty-five intercontinental ballistic missiles. These observers also agreed that the PRC appeared to be striving for regional, not intercontinental, capability in its nuclear strategy, at least in the 1970s.

In conventional warfare, however, the PRC was capable of posing a major threat to its immediate neighbors, a threat that would become more formidable when it acquired full nuclear capability to strike any major target in Asia. Nonetheless, the Chinese Communist capacity to wage major offensive operations was restricted in 1971 because of its limited logistical resources and limited sea and airlift capabilities.

Moreover, according to qualified sources, the country could commit its forces in a conventional war on no more than one front and then only if there were no interdiction of its lines of communications.

In 1971 the PRC had yet to recover fully from the massive convulsions of the Great Proletarian Cultural Revolution. The Party apparatus still remained weak, and the PLA was playing a major extramilitary role as the de facto leader and administrator in both Party and governmental affairs and also as the guiding force in the economic domain. A PLA representative could be found directing and supervising operations in nearly every center of power and responsibility. These ranged from factories, farms, schools, and universities to county and provincial governments, all branches of central government departments, state enterprises, and even such places as hospitals and film studios. Thus, according to Edgar Snow, a frequent visitor to the PRC, if the entire country could be considered "a great school of Mao Tse-tung thought," then the PLA could be described as "its headmaster."

The PRC in 1971 was allied militarily with the Soviet Union under a Sino-Soviet mutual assistance treaty signed in February 1950, a treaty concluded while the two countries maintained warm relationships and which was to be valid for thirty years. For all practical purposes, however, this pact has been moribund since 1960 because of ruptured ideological and interparty relations between the two countries (see ch. 11, Foreign Relations). Since the border conflict of 1969 the PRC has come to see the Soviet Union as the primary threat to its territorial integrity. Both countries have since continued to exchange accusations that the other was plotting a war of aggression.

EVOLUTION OF THE PEOPLE'S LIBERATION ARMY

The birthplace of the People's Liberation Army (called the Red Army until 1946) is officially considered to be Nan-ch'ang, the capital of Kiangsi Province, where on August 1, 1927, some 30,000 Communists and other dissidents of Chiang's National Revolutionary Army revolted against the central government at Nanking. The insurrection was quickly quashed, but its leaders—Chu Te, Chou En-lai, Ho Lung, Yeh Ting, and Nieh Jung-chen—and most of their combat units survived to form the nucleus of what was to become the Red Army. Lin Piao, still a junior officer only twenty years old at the time, also participated in the uprising in a minor role.

The Nan-ch'ang uprising marked the beginning of the Communist Chinese armed struggle for power as an independent political force. It was in fact the culmination of a process of alienation and competition for power between the Kuomintang (Nationalist Party, often known as the KMT) and communist elements that had begun several years before. This process had started with an agreement signed in January 1923 between Sun Yat-sen and Adolph Joffe, a representative of the Soviet foreign ministry, that pledged to support Sun's efforts to subdue self-seeking provincial warlords and unify the country (see ch. 3, Historical Setting). Several months later Soviet advisers arrived in order to create a party-controlled army patterned after the Soviet model.

In the following year a modern military academy was established at Whampoa, near Canton, for the training of future officers and political cadres. Chiang was named its first commandant; and Chou, the head of its political department. The faculty of the Whampoa Military Academy was drawn from three major sources: Russian officers, graduates of the Chinese military academies at Yunnan and Paoting, and those trained in Japan.

The Soviet advisers encouraged the induction of young, radical Chinese revolutionaries into the ranks and the commissioning of Communists and leftists in the officer corps. Infiltrating the administrative echelon as far down as the regimental level, they also facilitated the assignment of such officers to top combat command posts, policymaking positions on the general staff, and important political posts at schools and training centers.

The Soviet effort, however, was so obvious and so blatant as to arouse suspicion and antagonism among many Chinese and especially among the KMT's right-wing leaders. The growing Soviet and Chinese Communist influence in both military and political spheres thus led to the progressive widening of the Communist-KMT rift. In March 1926 Chiang, who had been named commanding general of the KMT's National Revolutionary Army the previous summer, struck a blow at the local communist leadership at Canton, arresting a number of Soviet advisers at the Whampoa academy. When the Soviet military mission to China threatened to withhold arms and equipment, the KMT's Central Executive Committee countered in the following month by adopting Chiang's proposals for limiting Soviet authority in political and administrative matters. Nonetheless, the Communist-KMT entente continued, albeit on a less cordial note.

The successful Northern Expedition launched by Chiang in July 1926 brought under his control the southeastern provinces with their numerous arsenals and thus had the effect of reducing his dependence on the Soviet officials and their Chinese collaborators at Wu-han (see Glossary). Meanwhile, riots and disorders fomented by Communists in newly liberated territories revolted many Chinese and frightened commercial interests in the treaty ports. Consequently, many previously uncommitted warlords decided to support Chiang, and

Shanghai banking circles, which had been apathetic to the Nationalist cause, made substantial financial aid available to Chiang.

These developments so strengthened Chiang that he decided to break with the Communists. In April 1927 his army decimated the Communists in Shanghai, and he established his own government at Nanking. The rupture of the KMT-Communist united front had been completed by the end of July, when the Soviet advisers were forced to leave the country.

When the Nan-ch'ang revolt failed in August 1927, the rebel force fled southward and made another attempt at Swatow. Here, too, they were routed but regrouped under Chu Te and spent the next year moving about Fukien, Kiangsi, and Hunan provinces and fending off efforts by Nationalist forces to exterminate them.

Meanwhile, in eastern Hunan, Mao Tse-tung was organizing peasants and an assortment of workers, deserters from the KMT Left, and stragglers from the abortive Nan-ch'ang and Swatow revolts into a patchwork armed force called the First Division of the First Peasants and Workers Army. With it, he incited and led in Hunan what became known as the Autumn Harvest Uprising (also known as Autumn Harvest Insurrection). Nationalist forces quelled the insurrection and forced Mao and his surviving elements to seek refuge in the inaccessible Chingkang Mountains on the Hunan-Kiangsi border, which for centuries had served as a haven for bandits and fugitives. Chu Te, also pressed for a hideout, joined Mao in May 1928, and the two merged their forces into the new Fourth Peasants and Workers Red Army of roughly 10,000 men. Chu Te became its military commander, and Mao, its political commissar.

If Nan-ch'ang was the birthplace of the Red Army, the Chingkang Mountains, officially described as "the first revolutionary base," might well be called the cradle of this army. It was at this mountain base with its limited economic resources where Chu Te (often referred to in Western publications as "the Father of the Red Army") and Mao Tse-tung mapped out their tactics of survival in the form of guerrilla warfare, disciplined the troops, and introduced a semblance of organization.

After a brief stay the Red Army was obliged to abandon the base because of logistical difficulties as well as Nationalist harassment. It fought its way through the Nationalist blockade to a more secure base at Jui-chin in southern Kiangsi which, with the addition of many Party leaders driven out of Shanghai, soon became the actual center of the Party.

Beginning in late 1931, the Nationalists attempted to dislodge the Communists in Kiangsi, but it was not until late 1933 that Chiang's forces, ably assisted by German military advisers, could exert serious pressures on the Kiangsi base. In October 1934, before a decisive battle could be joined, the Communists broke through the Nationalist siege and embarked on the Long March, an epic of trials and physical endurance unparalleled in military annals.

The Long March

A Party history places the number of marchers leaving Jui-chin at about 100,000. The route taken by the columns, which when scaled on a map measures less than 2,000 miles, is actually around 6,000 miles (8,300 miles according to the Party source) when its serpentine nature and all side marches and retracing of steps are taken into account. According to Snow's account in *The Red Star Over China*, en route to its final destination the force crossed eighteen mountain ranges (at least five of them are snow covered the year round), forded twenty-four rivers, passed through twelve provinces, took sixty-two cities, and fought its way through the areas of ten hostile warlords. Throughout most of the journey it was pursued by Nationalist forces and had to fight innumerable rearguard actions to avoid extermination. Communist losses because of hunger, privation, and the elements were even heavier than combat losses, and much of the tuberculosis prevalent among Party members in later days is attributed to the hardships endured during the Long March.

The marchers, initially led by Chu Te, meandered westward through Hunan, Kwangsi, and Kweichow into Yunnan, sometimes splitting into several columns for easier passage and better forage, at other times regrouping to gain greater strength in penetrating well-defended areas. The main force made a bitterly contested crossing of the Yangtze River north of K'un-ming and continued westward toward Tibet. It turned north along the eastern edge of the Tibetan Plateau and traversed Szechwan, where Chu Te stayed behind to pacify hostile elements in the area. Now under the command of P'eng Te-huai, the march continued far to the west of the Red Basin and reached Kansu before turning eastward again; it ended at Pao-an, in northern Shensi in October 1935. Less than 20,000 are said to have survived the ordeal.

It was during the Long March that Mao gained control of the Party's central apparatus, at the Tsun-i Conference of January 1935. It was also during this "strategic retreat," as the Communists call it, that Mao crystallized his four rules of guerrilla operations: when the enemy advances—we retreat; when the enemy halts—we harass; when the enemy avoids battle—we attack; and when the enemy retreats—we attack. The very fact that the marchers completed the retreat appeared to give unimpeachable authority to his basic contention that a small, poorly equipped force can ultimately prevail over vastly superior opposition, provided it is wisely organized, directed, and motivated. In other words, man rather than material assets is the decisive element in any struggle, and the collective strength of a properly organized and indoctrinated society will more than compensate for the individual weaknesses of its members. Mao, by this epic feat, proved "the practicality of the impossible," as Western military leaders have learned. His strategic and tactical doctrines proved themselves again in the 1940s in the successful campaigns against the Nationalists. In 1950 the Communists moved large field armies through the impenetrable mountains of the Democratic People's Republic of Korea (North Korea), an achievement that was at the time considered to be "impossible." They also attacked Indian forces through the impassable Himalayas in 1962, a feat of major magnitude.

In time Mao's military doctrines provided a basis for the ideological dispute between Communist China and the Soviet Union and remained as the dynamic force behind the drive for the glorification of Mao Tse-tung Thought and the Communist Chinese strategy of fomenting the world revolution in Mao's own image (see ch. 9, Political System and Values; ch. 11, Foreign Relations).

The Yenan Years, 1936–47

Relatively unopposed in remote Shensi, the hardened Red Army quickly brought under its control parts of Shensi, Kansu, and Ninghsia provinces, an area of more than 60,000 square miles. In the fall of 1936 Chu Te rejoined the group from Szechwan and once again was named commander of the armed forces. As the stability of the new Chinese Soviet regime became known throughout the land, some stay-behind units from South China and elsewhere, as well as dissident guerrilla and bandit units from various areas, made their way northward and were incorporated into the Red Army, which had grown from about 20,000 to 90,000 regulars.

The control of the Red Army remained in the hands of the Party's Revolutionary Military Council (first set up in 1931 at Jui chin), chaired by Mao. Chu Te maintained a rudimentary staff headquarters organization, devoted mainly to the issuing of orders to individual unit commanders. At operating levels the organization retained its guerrilla characteristics.

Military and political academies were set up at Yenan and other places in northern provinces in order to provide four to six months of schooling in political indoctrination and in Mao's guerrilla tactics. The best known of these academies was the Anti-Japanese Red Army University, opened at Yenan in 1936. Trainees, as well as soldiers on combat assignments, were exhorted to work in the fields wherever possible in order to enhance the solidarity between the army and the people. Peasants were mobilized with the troops every morning before leaving for the fields and also underwent physical training in the form of gymnastics and were given some instruction in guerrilla operations.

While tending the fields, they were expected to be ready whenever necessary to drop their hoes and rakes at a moment's notice and rally to the defense of the communist-controlled area. As trained militiamen, these peasants played an important role during the 1937–45 anti-Japanese war and provided the manpower during the rapid Red Army expansion from 1946 to 1949.

During the early Yenan years Mao also expended considerable energy on organizing Party activities throughout rural areas of northern, central, and eastern China. Dedicated cadres, trained at the rate of about 10,000 annually at various academies, mobilized restless young people in the villages, trained them in guerrilla warfare, and used them to gain political control of the countryside. They then attracted adherents by seizing large landholdings and distributing them among the peasants who worked them. At the same time they intensified propaganda against the Nationalist government for its dilatory tactics against Japanese aggression.

The war with the Nationalist forces continued in 1936 and 1937 but seldom involved more than desultory skirmishes. Mao's main concern was to build the Red Army strength, to conserve it for the future revolution, and to expand his political base by capitalizing on the mounting anti-Japanese sentiments in the land. In May 1936 Mao renewed his appeal to the Nationalists for the creation of a new united front against the Japanese (the first appeal was made in August 1935); in doing so he softened his hitherto anti-Nationalist propaganda (see ch. 3, Historical Setting).

Nevertheless, Chiang was resolved to eradicate the Communists, who in October 1936 were declared his main enemy. He began preparing for another major extermination campaign (the sixth) to be directed from his temporary headquarters at Sian, Shensi. There was, however, countrywide pressure on the Nanking government to halt military opposition to the Yenan Communists and instead to accept the Red Army's offer to aid against the Japanese invaders. In December 1936 this pressure culminated in a bizarre circumstance at Sian, where Chiang was arrested by a group of concerned nationalistic officers and agreed in principle before his release two weeks later to resist the Japanese first and cease his extermination campaign. Nationalist attitudes toward the Communists softened noticeably after Sian, but the military blockade of the "Chinese People's Soviet Republic" was not called off. Meanwhile, the Communists took advantage of temporary peace to extend surreptitiously their influence to the countryside of Shensi and parts of nearby provinces.

The Anti-Japanese United Front, 1937–45

The Nationalist-Communist relationship entered a new phase with the outbreak of the Sino-Japanese War in July 1937. Almost immediately Chiang, as did Mao, called on the whole nation for armed resistance. Mao pledged Red Army support and sent Chou to Nanking to work out terms of a new united front with the KMT.

In late September the united front came into being, the Communists pledging, among other things, to place their armed forces, now renamed the Eighth Route Army, under the unified command of the Nanking government although actually commanded by Chu Te; to redesignate the Chinese People's Soviet Republic as the Shensi-Kansu-Ninghsia Border Region of the Republic of China; and to abandon their policy of insurrection and sovietization. For their part, the Nationalists agreed to cease their anti-Red suppression campaign and to subsidize the Eighth Route Army in the north on the basis of an agreed upon strength of 45,000 men (the actual strength was about 100,000 at the time, including those not integrated into the Nationalist command). In Central China along the Yangtze River, Mao also had the 11,000-man Fourth Route Army.

Events following the September entente would show, however, that the two sides regarded the united front at best as a "marriage of convenience" to be broken at an opportune time. Deeply mistrustful of each other, both sides worked toward their own ends wherever opportunities presented themselves.

Mao's forces contributed to the war effort considerably by guerrilla operations behind Japanese lines, avoiding head-on battles, destroying communications lines, and seizing arms and ammunition to strengthen their own fighting capability. At the same time they lost little time in expanding their political control in the countryside by confiscating and redistributing lands and organizing Red bases, although they had agreed not to engage in such activities under the 1937 agreement. Soviets sprang up in the rural areas across most of North China.

In the latter half of 1938 unremitting mutual suspicion and antagonism caused the deterioration of the united front. The Communists not only refused to give up their military and political control over the so-called liberated areas to the Nationalists but also pressed their demand that Chiang's one-party dictatorship be abandoned. Chiang sought to check the steady expansion of his adversary by outlawing communist-sponsored mass organizations in Hankow and ordering a military blockade of the Red bases in the north. In late 1939 one of his division commanders actually attacked the communist forces in an area where the Japanese forces were conducting, at about the same time, their own anti-Red operations. Whether the Nationalist-Japanese operations were coincidental or prearranged, as one source suggested, remains unclear.

For all practical purposes, the united front became a fiction after January 1941, when the two sides clashed in an episode known as the Fourth Route Army Incident (see ch. 3, Historical Setting). From then on both sides tended to concern themselves more with internal struggles than fighting the Japanese.

By April 1945, when the Party held its seventh congress at Yenan, the Red Army had grown to about 910,000 regulars (800,000 in the Eighth Route Army and 110,000 in the Fourth Route Army); the communist forces were scattered about in nineteen large soviets, with major concentrations in the north, which had a combined population of about 96 million, or one out of every five Chinese then on the mainland. The Red Army was at the time less than a quarter of the Nationalist forces in size and, although it had adequate small arms, it lacked heavy equipment. The Nationalist advantage in manpower and firepower was offset in part by the Red Army's superior leadership training and experience in guerrilla warfare and by its ability to command extensive peasant support.

The Strategic Offensive, 1947–49

Mao's chances for a successful revolution appeared to be as remote as ever in early 1945, but events immediately after the Japanese surrender caused a decisive shift in the balance of power. To begin with, through Soviet subterfuge, the Red Army came into possession of vast Japanese stockpiles of weapons and munitions, including some heavy equipment in Manchuria. Since the Communists were the first Chinese to arrive in the northeast, they were hailed by local residents as the true liberators of China. Thousands of Manchurians and some Nationalist units stationed in the region flocked to the Red Army banner.

In the subsequent civil war with the Nationalists the People's Liberation Army (formerly, the Red Army, renamed in 1946) was cautious at first, attacking only small, isolated outposts against which it could concentrate overwhelming strength. Not infrequently, these outposts surrendered with little resistance, so that by judicious treatment of prisoners and defectors and much indoctrination, the PLA was able to incorporate KMT soldiers. As the civil war progressed, communist military strength multiplied, and larger positions could be reduced. When only major key points remained, the PLA attacked the communications lines linking them, isolated them from sources of supply, and let them wither. Nationalist forces sent to relieve these garrisons were ambushed by swift hit-and-run strikes or, in some instances, defected en masse to the PLA. By mid-1947 the PLA had grown to more than 1 million battle-seasoned and disciplined regulars, as against the KMT's 2.7 million men.

Heartened by these developments and sure of popular support, Mao decided the time was now propitious for the long-awaited showdown with Chiang. In July 1947 the PLA opened large-scale offensives or "switched from the strategic defensive to the strategic offensive," as a

Party history described the shift. In quick succession it scored impressive victories by a combined guerrilla and positional warfare, reducing the Nationalist strength to about 1 million regulars and 500,000 service troops by February 1949. Nationalist resistance collapsed almost everywhere after the fall of Peking in January 1949, by which time the Communists had, for the first time, achieved decisive advantages in size and combat effectiveness as well.

The communist victory is attributable to no single cause. Militarily, the PLA commanders effectively applied Mao's theories of "avoiding strength and striking at weakness"; they seldom permitted themselves to be forced into a head-on clash with superior forces and avoided the temptation to occupy fixed positions, relax discipline, or be satisfied with maintaining the status quo. Wherever possible they lost no opportunities in courting the peasantry, hardening themselves by constant training in forced marches, and acquiring skill in operating and employing captured Japanese, as well as American, weapons.

The PLA's mobile warfare also proved highly successful against the Nationalist strategy of positional warfare. The Nationalists failed to exploit their early successes against the Communists; they did not pursue the forces they routed, nor did they maintain contact and employ their superiority in firepower to destroy them. Instead they adopted a strategy of occupying urban centers and key points, garrisoning them heavily, and digging in to defend them to the last ditch. They then lost aggressiveness in a wait-and-see policy, and the troops, for whom life was easy, lost the will to fight.

The PLA was aided also by military blunders of the Nationalist government. The Nationalist High Command alienated many of its most able field commanders. Many top Nationalist commanders who had distinguished war records were replaced in the field by Whampoa Military Academy graduates who were considered to be more politically reliable. Displaced leaders and the units they commanded were disgruntled at the cavalier manner in which they had been treated; they suffered a crippling drop in morale and were thus vulnerable to communist blandishments. New field commanders, frequently of mediocre or untested ability, were shuffled and switched so often that there was no continuity in combat activities. Nationalist headquarters were fraught with dissension as leaders vied for favor.

Mao's position was strengthened no less by the KMT's misrule and corruption and rapidly deteriorating economic situation. The Nationalists also unwittingly aided the communist tactics of the united front by outlawing the urban-intellectual-oriented Democratic League in late 1947 because of its alleged subservience to the Communist Party. Although politically weak, the league had enjoyed considerable prestige, having as its members many prominent intellectual leaders. The KMT, already unpopular in urban areas because of rampant inflation, lost whatever sympathy it could garner from urban dwellers in general and the youth and student groups in particular.

THE PEOPLE'S LIBERATION ARMY SINCE 1949

By late 1949 the PLA had mushroomed into a huge, decentralized body of 5 million men, skillfully led by officers of demonstrated ability in civil and military tasks; but it was a completely unbalanced force of infantry elements with no air and naval arms. It was equipped with a motley assortment of obsolete captured Japanese- and American-manufactured weapons. The PLA was essentially a sprawling guerrilla force organized and trained for operations in which conventional military science and technology played no significant part.

Soviet Influence and Modernization

The need for military reform and modernization was clearly recognized in the Common Program, or the provisional constitution, adopted in September 1949 but, because of more pressing priorities, it was not until after the outbreak of the Korean conflict that the process of modernization was speeded up. For the immediate purpose of defense against foreign attack China, in February 1950, became allied militarily with the Soviet Union under the Treaty of Friendship, Alliance, and Mutual Assistance. Still in force in 1971, the treaty states:

> In the event of one of the Contracting Parties being attacked by Japan or any other state allied with her and thus becoming involved in a state of war, the other Contracting Party shall immediately render military and other assistance by all means at its disposal.

The Sino-Soviet treaty contains no explicit clause for the provision of Soviet materiel and training, but within a month after the pact was signed a Soviet military mission was established in Peking and a small number of military experts arrived in China to assist in reorganization and to prepare plans for reequipping the PLA. Meanwhile, the communist regime began initiating measures for partial demobilization in an attempt to divert more resources to the economic sector.

The modernization program had barely gotten underway when in late October 1950 the PLA entered the Korean conflict under the name of the Chinese People's Volunteers (CPVs). It was a new and unfamiliar type of regular warfare for the Chinese, who were commanded by P'eng; nonetheless, the CPVs, some of whom were drawn from the best units in the entire PLA, overwhelmed the extended United Nations forces in North Korea and drove them back to south of the 38th parallel.

612

Once the initial shock of the Chinese thrust had been absorbed and its impetus checked, however, the Communists (still equipped largely with obsolete weapons) discovered that masses and sheer determination alone were no match for a professionally trained, well-equipped and technologically superior enemy. By mid-1951, as the United Nations forces were able to assemble and apply greater firepower, the Chinese and North Koreans were thrown back, badly battered. The conflict continued, but despite their augmented strength the CPVs were never able to regain the offensive; the lack of air support for the ground troops and the overextended logistical system were also contributing factors.

The Korean experience proved to be a blessing in disguise for the PLA. Although the Chinese forces had been mauled, they had at least given a good account of themselves against the most powerful "imperialist enemy." The Korean intervention greatly enhanced the prestige of the PLA and strengthened the position of senior officers who advocated urgent professionalization of the armed forces.

It was actually in the course of the Korean conflict that the PLA's modernization program swung into high gear, especially after late 1951 when the Chinese, aided by Soviet military advisers, began using large numbers of new weapons supplied by the Soviet Union. The PLA undertook to reorganize and standardize its defense organization, stressing the need to "learn from the advanced experiences of the Great Soviet Red Army" and the importance of mastering "modern techniques of military science and the skillful use of modern weapons and equipment." The result was an influx of newer and more sophisticated Soviet equipment of all types and increased attention to specialized and technical military training. Firepower was increased at all levels. By the end of 1951 the Chinese had received a substantial number of Soviet MIG fighters and twin-jet bombers. Impressed by this conversion process, the *People's Daily* editorially commented in July 1954 that "The future People's Liberation Army would resemble the Soviet army of today."

By mid-1955 the campaign to rid the PLA of its old guerrilla structure had been for the most part completed, assisted by at least several thousand Soviet instructors and hundreds of Chinese officers and men who had returned after varying periods of training in Soviet military academies. The PLA came to have most of the trappings of a typical modern army.

The nation's first centralized Ministry of National Defense was created in June 1954, and three months later the People's Revolutionary Military Council, the top-level policy advisory body, was replaced by the more broadly constituted National Defense Council (see ch. 9, Political System and Values). The six military regions, which overlapped with the same number of administrative regions, were abolished and, for military purposes, the country was parceled into thirteen military regions; at the same time, the five field or regional armies that existed more or less autonomously, each with its own headquarter and staff departments, were broken up and placed under the unified direction and control of the General Staff Department of the PLA in Peking. (In 1970 the number of military regions was reduced to eleven, both Tibet and Inner Mongolia having been downgraded to military districts.) Personal and professional loyalty growing out of the field army system, nevertheless, endured in later years, and its impact on the military and political scene was still evident in 1971.

These changes notwithstanding, the ultimate power of control remained in the hands of politico-military leaders holding membership in the Party's Military Affairs Committee, which apparently had come into being as a separate entity in 1949. Whether this committee functioned before 1949 independently, or as part of the People's Revolutionary Military Council, remains obscure.

Also in 1955 a system of grades and ranks, identical to that of the Soviet Red Army, was introduced for the first time in Chinese Communist history. A schedule of insignia was adopted to denote command responsibility or position; a gradation of cash pay scaled according to rank or position replaced the old one of simply providing funds for military personnel regardless of job responsibility. Additionally, a system of military orders and honors was instituted to stimulate morale and a desire to excel in the military arts. The pace of establishing various military academies and specialized training centers was greatly speeded up. Almost forgotten during the conversion process was Mao's principle of putting human factors before weapons and technical factors.

No less important for the modernization drive was the introduction of conscription in late 1954. Up to this time military service had been voluntary, there being no legal requirement for compulsory service. The conscription law adopted and promulgated in that year made it possible for the regime to recruit annually about 500,000 qualified men over the age of eighteen. The new system also facilitated demobilization, contributing to the diversion of manpower and financial resources for agricultural and industrial production. Demobilized veterans joined the militia, giving among other things, military as well as political training to the men and women of the militia.

Professionalism Versus Party Control

Professionalization, coupled with the traumatic experiences of the Korean conflict, induced a number of high-ranking Communist Chinese officers on the general staff to display stronger attitudes toward the relative merits of professional versus political competence in military matters. These officers, or "modernizers" as they are sometimes called in the West, did not deprecate the decisive role of man in combat, so central to the Maoist tradition, but neither could they discount the importance of weapons and technology. They did not underestimate the value of ideological fervor, which Mao held to be decisive, but neither were they willing to accept the principle that professionalism must always be subordinate to politics.

This critical attitude developed into a subdued, but very real, doctrinal dispute in Peking. Although the discord was never permitted to get out of hand, it soon became apparent after the mid-1950s that the Sino-Soviet military relationships would be affected by the growing political estrangement between Moscow and Peking. The Communist Chinese desire to manage their own domestic and external matters independently of, and at times in competition with, the Soviets did not gain Moscow's favor. Frustrated in its efforts to bring Communist China into a unified Communist-bloc scheme of economic and military collaboration, the Soviet leadership toughened its attitude toward the Communist Chinese (see ch. 11, Foreign Relations).

To a group of senior military officers in Peking the deterioration of Sino-Soviet relations was especially disturbing because of its potentially adverse impact on the Chinese nuclear program, which was almost totally dependent on Soviet goodwill (see ch. 16, Science and Technology). In their advocacy of accelerated modernization, these officers stressed the importance of nuclear and other advanced weapons and of greater professional autonomy and training; at the same time, they sought to downgrade the need of political indoctrination and PLA participation in agriculture and industry.

This group was opposed by a combination of Party and military leaders, including Chu Te, Lin Piao, Ch'en I, and Ho Lung, who insisted that professionalism in its extreme form would have the unfortunate consequence of bringing overdependence on the Soviet Union, and thus, with certainty the erosion of Chinese political and military independence. Moreover, these leaders argued that the professionalism-first line would cause the downgrading of Mao's "people's army" concept, a concept that extols the virtue of the everyone-being-a-soldier tradition.

Not surprisingly, Mao and the Party adopted a policy of self-reliance in national defense, that is, the policy of making at home "the most up-to-date aircraft and atomic bombs in the not too distant future" without relying on the Soviet Union. Mao and others criticized the dissenters for their "exclusive military viewpoint" and reliance on "outside aid." In later years these dissenters, said to have been led by Liu Shao-ch'i, were accused of having advocated "the dependence of China's national defense on Soviet atomic bombs" and also of having hampered the domestic development of "up-to-date science and technology."

By early 1958 the Party opened a campaign for an intensified study of Mao's military theories, and the PLA launched in August 1958 the so-called "Everyone a Soldier" movement, which was aimed at mobilizing the entire adult population into militia, a movement said to be "a new development of Comrade Mao Tse-tung's strategic thinking on the people's war." The emphasis on the militia was part of the People's Commune scheme inaugurated at the same time. These developments, whose ideological implications were at the heart of the emerging Sino-Soviet dispute, and the Communist Chinese-provoked Formosa Strait crisis of 1958 proved, according to a Chinese accusation leveled in 1963, to be sufficiently disturbing to Premier Nikita Khrushchev that in June 1959 he tore up the Sino-Soviet agreement of October 1957. Under this accord the Soviets were to have provided a sample of an atomic bomb and related technical information to the Chinese (see ch. 11, Foreign Relations; ch. 16, Science and Technology).

In September 1959 Minister of National Defense P'eng and his chief of staff, Huang K'o-ch'eng were dismissed. Marshal P'eng is generally known to have countenanced, if not instigated, the rise of professional influence and to have personally communicated to Khrushchev his dissenting views on Mao's military, as well as Great Leap Forward policies (see ch. 10, Political Dynamics). By August 1960 about 1,400 Soviet technicians and advisers had been withdrawn from China.

THE PEOPLE'S LIBERATION ARMY UNDER LIN PIAO

The new defense minister was Lin Piao, who also became the de facto head of the Party's Military Affairs Committee (the nominal chairman being Mao Tse-tung). The most urgent need faced by Lin Piao was to reestablish Party control over the armed forces, to restore the PLA's morale (affected by the severe economic aftereffects of the Great Leap), and to raise the PLA's political loyalty and ideological standards. In his first important policy speech made at the end of September 1959, Lin stated:

> Some comrades take the view that modern warfare differs from warfare in the past, that since the weapons and equipment available to our army in the past were inferior we had to emphasize dependence on man, on his bravery and wisdom. ... They say that modern warfare is a war of technique, of steel and machinery, and that in the face of these things, man's role has to be relegated to a secondary place. ... Contrary to these people, we believe that while equipment and technique are important, the human factor is even more so.

The campaign for the politicization of the PLA went into high gear after a special session of the Military Affairs Committee (MAC) in September–October 1960. At the session Lin Piao exalted "human and politico-ideological factors" as the primary force determining the outcome of a war and extolled politics as "the soul and the supreme command"; these exhortations in effect became the basis of the "four firsts" principle that Lin Piao put forward at the MAC conference. This principle as enunciated stands for: human factor first; political work first; ideological work first; and living thought first.

The "four firsts" were inspired by Mao's code of conduct for all PLA men called "the three-eight work style," which is expressed in three phrases and eight characters. The three-phrase portion stands for: a correct political orientation, a simple and industrious work habit; and a flexibility in strategy and tactics. The eight-character part (two characters forming a single thought-unit) urges: unity, alertness, seriousness, and liveliness.

Several more or less annual political work conferences were held in succeeding years under the auspices of the General Political Department (the PLA's political control center) in order to underscore the centrality of the "four firsts" principle, the need to energize the movement for the creative study and application of Mao's thought, and the urgency of restoring Party control over the armed forces. These conferences brought together political commissars of various headquarters and major combat units, representatives of political sections of division-size units, political chiefs of service academies and research organizations, and ranking Party officials. These sessions also sought to highlight the danger of tendencies "unilaterally pursuing a purely military viewpoint."

The PLA's political work was focused especially on the company-level Party committees, which were revived and made the basic unit for purposes of political control and education. The company level campaign took the form of the "Four Good" emulation movement, which stressed the importance of being good in political and ideological work, in military training, in the "three-eight work style," and in management of living. For the political enlightenment of the ordinary soldier, a "Five Good" drive was also launched in early 1961 (as was the "Four Good" movement); the "five good" soldier was supposed to be good in political thought, in military training, in the "three-eight work style," in accomplishing assigned tasks, and in physical training.

By 1964 the PLA had become the shining example, the showcase of correct communist behavior. Beginning in February 1964, the masses were then urged to participate in a popular campaign called Learn from the People's Liberation Army. They were enjoined to emulate the PLA's acceptance of new ideas, to adopt its demonstration of true revolutionary fervor, and to unite with it in creating a new China. The movement spread quickly to government agencies, economic and commercial enterprises, and mass organizations, where political departments had been newly established. Experienced PLA political cadres were lent to these departments to direct political education in them, thus accelerating the trend already begun in the previous year. PLA units also provided training or get-acquainted facilities for Party and government cadres and specialists working in the economic sector.

Highlighting the reaction against professionalism was a change of considerable symbolic importance in May 1965, when the system of ranks—a conspicuous sign of Soviet influence that was introduced in 1955—was abolished altogether. This change was explained as a step to carry forward the PLA's glorious tradition of "close relations between the officers and men, between the higher and lower levels, and between the army and the people." This abolition was aimed not only at "those whose heads are crammed full of foreign doctrines" but also at the creeping "rank consciousness" that was alleged to be poisoning Mao's "proletarian military line." One advantage of this abolition of rank was to reduce the power of those senior PLA officers who were not actually in command of troops and to facilitate Mao's attempts to regain the political control that he had partly lost earlier to Liu Shao-ch'i.

The PLA reverted to the pre-1955 practices of calling an officer by job title, such as Company Commander Wang; an ordinary soldier had been called Fighter Lin or simply as comrade fighter. Members of the three services, officers and the rank and file alike, were required to wear the same simple Chinese-style uniform, the same red star on their "liberation cap," and the red badge on their collars. Branch insignia or shoulder patches were dispensed with, as was the Western-style uniform worn by officers of field grade and above.

Lin Piao pressed his drive toward perfecting the PLA as a model to be emulated by the whole nation and to reinforce the indomitable spirit of the Long March and the Yenan years. His efforts were rewarded during the Cultural Revolution, especially after January 1967, when the PLA was called upon to intervene on Mao's behalf and quickly emerged as "the main force" in the Mao-instigated revolution. In 1969 Lin Piao was officially designated as Mao's "successor" (see ch. 10, Political Dynamics).

CHARACTER AND MISSION OF THE ARMED FORCES

The character and mission of the PLA are shaped as much by tradition as by the categorical imperative of an independent, sovereign nation to defend itself in any war situation—guerrilla, conventional, or nuclear. In 1971, as in the years after its founding in 1927, the PLA was more than a conventional military establishment: it was also a sociopolitical institution performing varied roles according to internal exigencies. As visualized in official literature, the PLA was a "people's army," an army made up of sons of the workers and peasants, an "army of the people, [which] must regularly maintain close relations with the masses, and nourish itself with what is required from the struggles waged by the masses."

The mass character and the multiple role of the PLA derive from the early years of the Red Army's experience as the Party's fighting machine, political organizer, and producer. During the period of the anti-Japanese war (1937–45) and especially after 1941, the army had to combine labor with fighting in an effort to alleviate the mounting burden of taxation on the civilian population. Soldiers raised their own food crops, ran factories, and operated shops and food processing plants. Every soldier was a peasant or worker as the occasion demanded. The army's economic activities were necessary not only for its own survival but also for enlisting broad popular support. The slogan of "Support the Red Army and care for the People" has been an essential feature in the evolution of the PLA.

It was against this background that in 1949 the Common Program stipulated: "The armed forces of the People's Republic of China shall, during peacetime, systematically take part in agricultural and industrial production in order to assist in national construction work, provided such work does not interfere with their military duties." This stipulation was in addition to the primary mission of the PLA, that is, "to defend the independence, territorial integrity and sovereignty of China, and to defend the revolutionary gains and all legitimate rights and interests of the Chinese people." The Common Program also required the PLA to set up a system of political work and educate the commanders and rank and file of the defense and public security forces "in a revolutionary and patriotic spirit."

The 1954 State Constitution, which was framed at a time when the Soviet-influenced military modernization drive was gathering momentum, made no mention of the PLA's economic or political duties. Instead, the Constitution stated: "The armed forces of the People's Republic of China belong to the people; their duty is to safeguard the gains of the people's revolution and the achievements of national construction, and to defend the sovereignty, territorial integrity and security of the country."

The pre-1954 tradition of the army mission was again restored in the 1970 draft state constitution, which stated: "The Chinese People's Liberation Army is forever a combat troop, a work troop, and a production troop." The 1970 document also called for "guard against subversion from imperialism, social-imperialism [euphemism for the Soviet Union], and their running dogs."

For purposes of discharging its primary mission, the PLA has defined the United States as the main enemy, as much because of its being the principal "imperialist power" as because of its role in the Korean conflict and its intervention in the Communist Chinese-provoked Formosa Strait crises of 1954 and 1958. India has been added to the hostile nation list since the Sino-Indian border conflict of 1962 but only as a minor adversary. Since the mid-1960s Japan has loomed large in the minds of Chinese defense planners for its continued close relationships with the United States. Other contributing factors have been Japan's establishment of state relations with South Korea in 1965 and Japan's steady, but low-keyed, efforts in developing its defense capability (see ch. 11, Foreign Relations).

Meanwhile, the Soviet Union has become a source of heightened tensions in Peking. The Communist Chinese government is known to have been disturbed by the Soviet Union's lukewarm fraternal posture on the Formosa Strait crisis of 1958, by its refusal to aid the Communist Chinese in the development of nuclear capability, and by its neutrality toward the Sino-Indian border conflict of 1962. The Communist Chinese perception of the Soviet threat—against the background of deteriorating relations between the two communist giants—surfaced clearly after the Soviet military intervention in Czechoslovakia in August 1968. At the time, the Communist Chinese leadership began voicing growing concern over the buildup of Soviet forces along the Sino-Soviet border regions, and a top military leader in Sinkiang warned, "Should the Soviet revisionists dare to attack us, we would wipe them out resolutely, thoroughly, wholly, and completely."

These developments, coupled with border tensions that culminated in open clashes in the Amur-Ussuri border area (in Manchuria) between March and August 1969, have reinforced the Communist Chinese strategic thinking that now defines the Soviet Union and the United States as the twin-enemy to be dealt with. Such charges as "social imperialism is colluding with the United States imperialism to launch a war of aggression against our country," were not infrequently heard in 1970 and 1971. Communist China's fear of the Soviets is reflected in the heavy concentrations of troops in military regions bordering the Soviet Union; in 1970 the PLA had at least forty-seven divisions out of its total of an estimated 120 divisions deployed in the border regions. In addition, the bulk of the PLA's air force units was assigned to the defense of Peking and Shen-yang (Mukden) military regions (see fig. 15).

In 1971 the PLA's involvement in nonmilitary activities was expected to continue in the near future. The immediate basis for this involvement was to be found in Mao's letter to Lin Piao dated May 7, 1966, or the "May 7 Directive," as the Party calls it, which stated:

> The People's Liberation Army should be a great school. In this great school, our army men should learn politics, military affairs, and culture. They can engage in agricultural production and its side occupations, run some medium-sized or small factories and produce a number of products to meet their own needs or for exchange with the state at equal values. They can also do mass work and take part in the socialist education movement in factories and villages.

In another directive, issued in March 1967, Mao also called on the PLA to "give military and political training in the universities, middle schools and the higher classes of primary schools ... help in reopening school classes, strengthening organization, setting up the leading bodies on the principle of the 'three-in-one' combination." (The three-in-one combination refers to the three-way alliance at the local level consisting of representatives of revolutionary mass organizations, of the PLA units, and of Party and government cadres) (see ch. 9, Political System and Values).

The PLA's full-scale intervention in politics and government actually began in January 1967, when it was called on to "take the side of the proletarian revolutionaries and resolutely support and help the proletarian Leftists." In ordering this action, the Mao-Lin Piao group reversed "all past directives concerning the army's non-involvement" in the Cultural Revolution. The PLA was also ordered to seize power "from the handful of persons in the Party who are in authority and taking the capitalist road" wherever necessary, be it in factories and rural areas; in financial, trading, cultural, and educational departments; in Party or government departments; or in mass organizations.

During the Cultural Revolution the army was pressed into action also as policemen charged with restoring order and discipline in schools. Given the extensive disruption of the regular public order system, the PLA has since 1967 emerged as the single most effective agency for law enforcement in the country. In 1971 it was responsible not only for much of police functions formerly carried out by the Ministry of Public Security but also for control and supervision of activities aimed at restoring the police functions to civil law enforcement bodies (see ch. 20, Public Order and Internal Security).

Red Guard rampages virtually paralyzed the school system in March 1967, and the PLA soldiers were brought in to give political and military training to the students and help reopen classes. Most returned to their barracks as soon as calm was restored; however, in colleges and middle schools some remained to set up revolutionary committees that took over administration of these schools (see ch. 8, Education, Intellectual Expression, and the Arts).

The PLA's economic participation has been quite extensive. With the civil war over in 1949, the PLA was called on to initiate a production movement, as from the spring of 1950, and to assist in the rehabilitation of the war-torn economy by providing manpower and technical expertise. It was not until after the Korean conflict, however, that the movement started gathering momentum. Although some high-ranking military officers apparently had serious reservations, soldiers were detached from combat duties or demobilized to be assigned to a multitude of projects dealing with water conservancy, construction of factories, repairing plants, reopening mines, repairing bridges, guarding railroads, building irrigation dams, reclaiming wasteland, and other matters.

The Great Leap Forward witnessed the deepening of PLA involvement in production work; officers and men were obligated to contribute one to two months a year in uncompensated labor to the army projects as well as civilian projects. This production movement was relaxed somewhat in 1962 and 1963 so as to allocate more time for military training and political indoctrination. To what extent the PLA contributed to the national economy through its "free labor" campaign remains obscure, but the Party has made no secret of its conviction that the army's labor assignment was a principal means of fostering a "proletarian mass outlook," combating bourgeois attitudes, and solidifying comradely relationships between the PLA and the people.

The army's economic role expanded considerably during the Cultural Revolution. Apart from providing the usual manpower, it had to assume powers to supervise and indoctrinate civilian managerial and technical personnel, especially in those factories disrupted by Red Guard activities. In many cases the PLA soldiers served as substitutes for civilian managers and also took over the communications and transportation systems in strategic areas in order to ensure their uninterrupted operation. Their contribution to agriculture was no less significant, providing heavy equipment for irrigation projects and performing relief work in areas affected by natural calamities. By and large, the army intervention had the effect of restoring a semblance of economic calm. In 1970 PLA officers continued to hold supervisory and managerial powers, especially at the provincial level. Whether they would remain in that capacity in the future was problematical because of their limited knowledge and experience in economic matters.

POSITION IN THE POLITICAL SYSTEM

The PLA was born as an organization subordinate to the Communist Party and remained so until 1967, when it emerged as the dominant political power group in the country. Although in 1971 the standard official rhetoric continued to extol Mao's saying that "the Party commands the gun, and the gun must never be allowed to command the Party," the military position changed considerably after late 1967 and particularly after the Ninth Party Congress in April 1969. The emerging picture was that, despite the standard trappings designed to show the Party's absolute control, the army actually was in control of power unparalleled anywhere in communist nations. Prominent in this ascendancy was the rise to the inner council of power of those senior military and Party figures closely identified with

Lin Piao. There was growing evidence in 1971 that unless the Party apparatus, shattered during the Cultural Revolution, was rebuilt and could effectively reassert its former preeminence, Communist China might well become the first communist state in which the gun would command the Party (see ch. 10. Political Dynamics).

The dramatic indication of military influence was reflected in the composition of the most powerful Party organ, the Politburo (Political Bureau—see Glossary), in which military membership was roughly 60 percent. Moreover, nearly half of the 279 Central Committee members "elected" by the Ninth Party Congress in 1969 were military officers. Military membership on the provincial revolutionary committees, aptly described in a August 27, 1971, *New York Times* dispatch from Shanghai as "the effective governing apparatus right down to the rice roots of the countryside," was much higher. One qualified analyst estimated, in 1970, that military membership on the Central Committee, the Politburo, and the revolutionary committees would amount to roughly 65 percent. The situation in 1970 differed substantially from that at the time of the Eighth Party Congress in 1956 when, according to a perceptive Western observer, the PLA influence had not extended to the innermost Party ranks.

Under the 1954 State Constitution the formal authority to make war or declare peace and to direct and maintain the armed forces was vested in the National People's Congress or its Standing Committee. This authority was delegated to the chairman of the People's Republic (Mao, 1949 to 1959; Liu, 1959 to 1968; Mao, de facto from 1968), the constitutional commander in chief of the PLA. The chairman's power was exercised through the Ministry of National Defense with the nominal advice of the National Defense Council and the State Council (see ch. 9, Political System and Values).

The 1970 draft state constitution, which did not provide for the office of chairman of the People's Republic as such, was silent on the national defense responsibility of the National People's Congress or its Standing Committee. Instead, it declared: "Chairman [Party Chairman] Mao Tse-tung is ... the supreme commander of the armed forces of the whole country." It also named Lin Piao as "Chairman Mao's close comrade in arms and successor and the deputy supreme commander of the armed forces."

The political loyalty of the PLA to both the high command and the Party was ensured through a parallel, but interlocking, chain of command, which extended downward from the Party's Military Commission to the company-level units in the field. At the core of this dual command structure was a hierarchy of Party committees and political commissars or officers (who were concurrently secretaries of these committees and of local civilian Party committees), subordinate to the General Political Department.

This inner structure had its own command channels, which were inviolate and functioned independently of military commanders. The military commander could neither interfere with their operations nor question either the advisability or the authority of the substance passed through them. Command of units was in fact held jointly with the political commissar, and the latter's decisions were final in political matters. Although the military commander was responsible for any military decision and the political officer was not supposed to interfere with its execution, the prior endorsement of all military operational orders by the political officer was almost mandatory.

Supporting the political officer at each unit level were Party committees of rank-and-file members, who met periodically to decide the type and quantity of political or economic work their unit would undertake and to pass judgment on the political efficiency and reliability of their military commanders and others. The political work was most intense at the company level, the basic unit having a Party committee; below this level was the Party cell. The Party committees were usually subject to the control and decisions of those local civilian Party committees in their respective areas.

This control system was not without problems. The military commander frequently resented the political officers, whose interference he regarded as an obstacle to organizational efficiency. Unless the two could get together on a give-and-take basis, the military commander could do little to relieve his frustrations because whatever grievances he might have had were referred usually to the Party committee located in his unit, which was headed by the same political commissar with whom he disagreed.

After 1967 the military-political friction appeared to be somewhat less evident because in many cases professional officers replaced the previously all-civilian political commissars. This step was necessary because the regular local party organization had ceased to function effectively (see ch. 10, Political Dynamics).

SOURCE AND QUALITY OF MANPOWER

The conscription law of 1955 (believed to be still in force in 1971 except for clauses relating to reserve service) specifies that all males, regardless of ethnic, social, educational, or religious distinctions, are obliged to serve in the armed forces when they reach eighteen years of age. Under this law youths under eighteen might enroll in military academies, but there was no legal requirement that they do so against their will. A regulation issued in 1961, however, empowers the PLA to induct youths under eighteen and to train them to meet the defense need for "special technical personnel." The total number of military age (eighteen to forty) males subject to drafting was estimated as of mid-1970 to be about 150 million out of China's total population of nearly 800 million. Exempt from military service are only a few hardship cases; "counterrevolutionaries" and others disqualified by law for criminal convictions are not eligible.

Except for leaders or officers (there being technically no commissioned officers in the PLA), manpower is procured almost solely through conscription. The estimated total of 6.5 million to 7.5 million youths who reach military age annually provides a continuing and abundant flow of manpower. Estimates of the inductees range from 500,000 to 700,000 each year. Although the specific requirements are unknown, this suggests that recruitment is highly selective. The youths who are not drafted are enrolled in the reserve service, which in 1957 was merged with the militia.

Under the conscription law, as revised in January 1965, conscripts and noncommissioned officers, or squad leaders, must serve terms that vary with the element to which they are assigned. Terms are set at four years for infantry duty; five years for the Air Force, shore-based Navy, and certain specialized ground force units, such as the engineers, artillery, or armored corps; and six years for sea duty in the Navy.

The service period may be extended for soldiers and squad leaders (limited to four months under the 1955 law) on the basis of both need and personal willingness. Those qualifying for extended active service must be "outstanding ones who are politically pure, ideologically progressive, technically trained, and physically strong, and have the capacity for further training." The need for this extended service ranged (in 1961) from 20 to 25 percent for the ground forces, the Air Force, and the Navy in terms of required numbers relative to the total number of active servicemen; the extension was usually from one to three years but in some instances ran to eight years and more.

As far as is known, there are three channels through which leader status may be achieved. Most commonly, young men who show aptitude and exceptional political awareness and loyalty are selected by their local Party branches for enrollment at one of the numerous military academies and advanced military technical institutes. Academy courses last for three years and, upon graduation, cadets are assigned to a combat unit as a common soldier for another six months before receiving a leader status comparable to that of a second lieutenant in other countries.

A second source is graduation from civilian colleges that conduct a reserve officer training program. An undetermined number of graduates from these institutions, after also serving for six months in the ranks, are given leader status. The final source is selection from the ranks. Veteran soldiers who have been serving as squad leaders, or performing similar duties that are usually the responsibility of noncommissioned officers, may apply for periodically scheduled promotion examinations. Those who score the highest enter an appropriate service academy and, upon graduation, are given leader assignments without having to serve in the ranks again.

There seems to be only one source for personnel to fill assignments usually discharged by noncommissioned officers. Promising soldiers, whose zeal, political reliability, and demonstrated ability attract the attention of both their local military commanders and political commissars, are appointed to special battalions in selected divisions for advanced training. Actual training time is unspecified and is usually determined by need but, when completed, qualifies a man to return to his unit as a squad leader.

Although untrained manpower is no problem for the armed forces, the lack of skills among troops appeared in 1970 to be a major deterrent to efficiency. Beginning in 1955 a strenuous effort was made to raise the educational level of officers and men, but this effort was interrupted in the years after 1960 when the Party began stressing the study of Mao's political and military thought or Mao's "living thought" as distinguished from "book learning." Nonetheless, most officers apparently completed advanced schooling, both civilian and military, but for some the average educational level was roughly the equivalent of high school. As a rule, company grade officers probably have been graduated from colleges.

Most of the men in the ranks are from rural areas where the schools are less than adequate as compared with those in the cities. Precise figures on illiteracy are not available, but it may be assumed that a 20- to 40-percent illiteracy rate applies among the troops. When this is coupled with the large amounts of time devoted to literacy training, political indoctrination, and nonmilitary labor in agriculture, industry, and public works projects, there is little time left for professional development of military aptitude.

The typical Communist Chinese soldier is a fine physical specimen. Years of hard, unrelieved labor have made him strong and durable. He is inured to hardship and is capable of withstanding extremes of cold, dampness, or dryness. He undergoes sustained periods of physical exertion without flagging and can make forced marches over unusually long distances in a single day. An excellent diet, good quarters when in garrison, and well-designed seasonal clothing of good quality sustain these attributes and add to a physical fitness generally greater than that found in most Western armies.

Morale within the armed forces is high, especially among the lower ranks where the troops fare much better than they would in civilian life. Moreover, the constant indoctrination to which they are subject is effective; it has instilled a conviction that their leadership is correct and has bred a deep hatred of everything foreign. Consequently, the Communist Chinese soldier is tough, tenacious, noncomplaining, obedient, and ready to fight. He is a difficult, if unskilled, opponent who will face overwhelming odds without flinching, in the firm belief that even though he may die his cause inevitably will prevail.

ORGANIZATION AND STRENGTH

The Ministry of National Defense directs and administers the unified military establishment through the General Staff Department (headed in late 1971 by Huang Yung-sheng, who had held the position since March 1968), which performs overall staff and operational functions. This department in effect serves as the army general staff headquarters, in addition to discharging staff duties for the Air Force and the Navy. The General Staff Department, assisted by the General Rear Services Department, provides logistical support and services to the PLA as a whole. The general staff level is rounded out by the General Political Department, the authoritative command center for matters relating to Party affairs within the armed forces (see fig. 16).

Specific operational functions are carried out, as directed by the General Staff Department, by the various staff directorates for the armored corps, engineer corps, railway corps, the Air Force, the Navy, the Public Security Force, artillery corps, second artillery corps (possibly missile associated), and signal corps. Territorially the country is divided into eleven military regions, the commander of each region being responsible for the air and naval forces assigned to him, the militia, and in some cases border troops.

The PLA is not a balanced force but is dominated by the ground forces, which account for more than 90 percent of the combined strength of 2.88 million men (as of late 1970), excluding the militia and border security troops. The ground forces are, themselves, overly weighted with light infantry units. Much of this imbalance can be attributed to Communist China's inability, given its limited internal resources, to equip and maintain a larger air force and naval establishment.

In 1970, as throughout the 1960s, it was estimated by many sources that Communist China probably spent 9 to 10 percent of its gross national product on national defense (including research and development for nuclear weapons programs). Defense spending in 1970 probably amounted to between the equivalent of US$7.2 billion and US$8 billion.

According to qualified sources, Communist China's logistic capabilities were generally adequate, in 1970, for conducting major conventional offensive operations beyond its borders against Southeast Asia and India, but a commitment of forces on more than one front was expected to impose serious burdens on their limited resources. Heavy equipment and communications facilities were in short supply. Adequate quantities of small arms and ammunition,

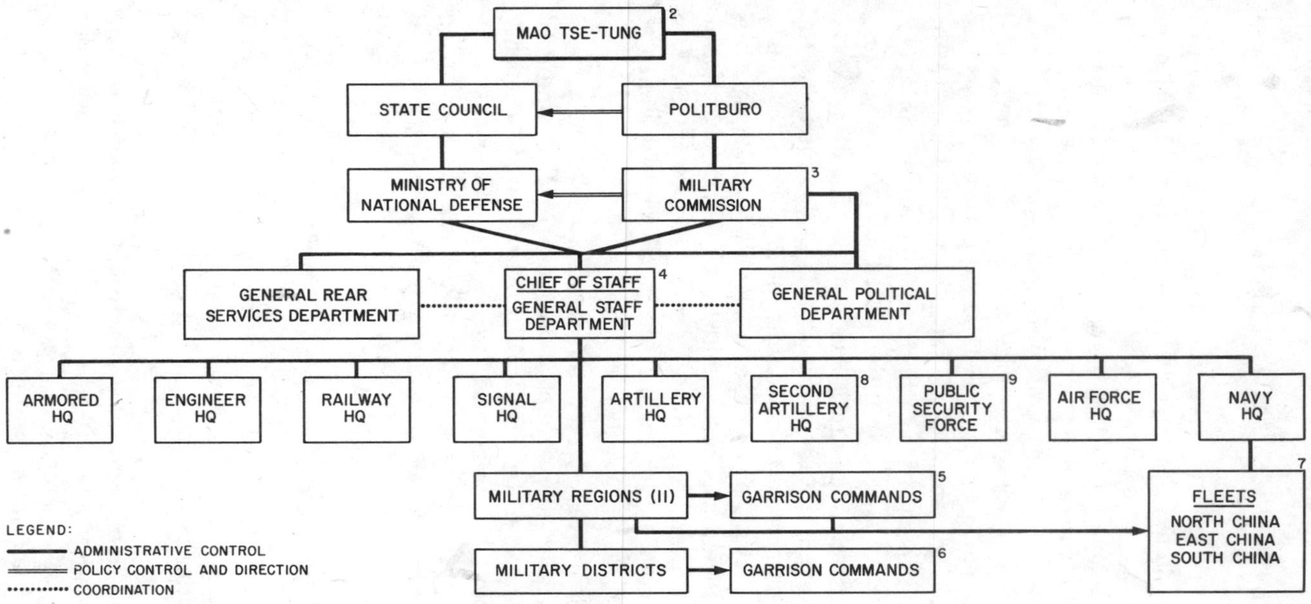

Figure 16. People's Republic of China, National Defense
Organization, Mid-1971.

LEGEND:
——— ADMINISTRATIVE CONTROL
═══ POLICY CONTROL AND DIRECTION
········· COORDINATION

1 BASED ON INCOMPLETE INFORMATION.
2 THE 1970 DRAFT STATE CONSTITUTION STATES MAO TO BE "THE HEAD OF STATE...AND THE SUPREME COMMANDER OF ...THE WHOLE ARMY."
3 ALSO KNOWN AS MILITARY AFFAIRS COMMITTEE;CHAIRED BY MAO.
4 CHIEF OF STAFF HUANG YUNG-SHENG -- ALSO SECRETARY GENERAL OF THE MILITARY COMMISSION AND A POLITBURO MEMBER.
5 INCLUDES ONLY THE LARGEST CITIES, SUCH AS PEKING, SHANGHAI, AND TIENTSIN; REPORT DIRECTLY TO THE MILITARY REGION.
6 LOCATED IN MOST PROVINCIAL CAPITALS; REPORT TO THE MILITARY DISTRICT.
7 DEPENDING ON CIRCUMSTANCES, REGIONAL OR GARRISON COMMANDERS MAY CONTROL AIR AND NAVAL UNITS STATIONED IN THEIR RESPECTIVE JURISDICTIONS.
8 EXISTENCE BECAME PUBLIC KNOWLEDGE IN JUNE 1967; POSSIBLY MISSILE-ASSOCIATED.
9 COMMANDS THE BORDER SECURITY FORCES.

rocket launchers, mortars, recoilless rifles, flamethrowers, and medium artillery pieces were produced, but they were Communist Chinese adaptations of largely obsolete Soviet prototypes.

In limited quantities local industry provided a version of the Soviet T-34 tank and a limited number of the heavier T-54 tank (produced in Communist China under the designation T-59); armored scout cars and vehicles; small torpedo boats; some short-range surface-to-air and surface-to-surface missiles; and motor torpedo boats, destroyers, and destroyer escorts.

By 1971 Communist China had apparently succeeded in producing a ground support jet fighter of its own design (designation: F-9) with a combat radius of 300 to 500 miles and capable of flying at about 1,400 miles per hour. Another achievement was in building a diesel-powered submarine designed by Communist Chinese engineers. In 1960 Premier Chou, while in Burma, was said to have stated that Communist China would have an atomic submarine within five years; as of the mid-1960s, there was no evidence that one had been produced, but in 1971 it was generally believed among Western analysts that at least one nuclear-powered submarine was under construction in Communist China.

The Communist Chinese have been producing their own copies over the years of the Soviet YAK-18 and MIG-15 trainers; MIG-17, MIG-19, and reportedly MIG-21 jet fighters; and MI-4 helicopters. They are also believed to be making about fifty TU-16 medium-range jet bombers a year, and they appeared to have the capacity to manufacture about 200 to 300 MIG-19s annually; some of these models were even sold to Pakistan in the late 1960s.

Ground Forces

Ground forces include the regular Army, the militia, and border security troops. The militia is a massive organization of lightly armed civilians of both sexes between sixteen and fifty years of age. It forms the basic reserve for the regular armed forces. The border security forces were estimated as of mid-1970 at about 300,000 men; very little was known about this organization.

The Army

The regular Army, including the railway corps and engineer corps, had in 1970 a total strength of 2.55 million, organized into armies and a descending echelon of operating units comparable to conventional ground forces everywhere. Military practice seems to follow task force, rather than rigid, formal, principles of organization. Where defense requirements are high, as in areas adjoining the Soviet border, combat units are larger and better equipped than in areas where such requirements are relatively low.

The basic operating unit is the company, which has a strength ranging from 100 to 200 men. Infantry companies usually have a triangular organization—that is, they are made up of three platoons, subdivided into three squads each. Usually three companies are organized into a battalion, and three battalions, into a regiment, although each of these units may have as few as two or as many as five components each. At echelons above regiment the triangular organization usually disappears. Two or more regiments may form a division; and generally three divisions, an army. As far as could be determined in 1970, the PLA had about 120 divisions.

Supporting units for an infantry division usually begin at the regimental level where engineer, reconnaissance, antitank, antiaircraft, artillery, and signal companies are found. At division level these elements are augmented to include special antigas, chemical, and truck-training companies, as well as artillery and tank battalions.

The basic weapon for the ordinary soldier is the submachinegun, the rifle, or the carbine. Appropriate elements are armed with locally produced mortars, rocket launchers, recoilless rifles, antitank guns, and field guns for antitank defense. Artillery batteries are equipped with guns and howitzers, some of which are self-propelled. Tank companies and battalions employ either the Soviet T-34 medium or the heavier T-54 tanks.

The Militia

The militia is not a centralized organization in that it has no general headquarters of its own but is trained, controlled, and administered locally by military commanders and the county-level Party committees. Theoretically, all able-bodied adults of both sexes between the ages of sixteen and fifty belong to this organization, but only those between sixteen and thirty are considered to be active members. Service in the militia is officially on a voluntary basis, but political pressures are known to be so great that it is almost impossible for the people to remain detached. Drawn from every segment of the population, members are unpaid and, except for monies used to provide them with weapons, the organization constitutes virtually no drain on the central government treasury.

Militia units are classified as either "basic" or "ordinary." Males between sixteen and thirty years of age and women between sixteen and twenty-five, plus demobilized veterans and Party cadres, are grouped into the basic unit; all others belong to the ordinary unit. Only the basic unit members are given arms—and then only when they are assigned to security duties.

In 1959 the Party claimed a total militia manpower of 200 million, of which 33 million were said to be basic members. At the start of the Cultural Revolution in 1966, most estimates placed the total at about

200 million, of which 125 million were men and 75 million were women. Of the 1966 total, only about 7 million were considered to be combat worthy. Militiamen are given military training, usually by demobilized veterans, in marksmanship, drilling, grenade throwing, and bayonet practice. Studying Mao's guerrilla warfare (or people's war) theories is a standard feature, in addition to studying various political writings of Mao.

Apart from providing auxiliary support for the armed forces, the militia forms a vast labor force in that it can be quickly mobilized for projects that need speedy execution. It is also a medium for the political indoctrination of its members and for disseminating Party and military lines to the general population. In peacetime the specific duties of the militia include assisting the local law enforcement forces; performing sentry duty in coastal or border areas; protecting harvest, factories, and railroad facilities; guarding state properties; suppressing counterrevolutionary activities; and making intelligence reports on public political attitudes. In time of war militia units maintain order in rear areas, perform security duties in coastal areas, provide logistic support to the fighting forces, and fight locally themselves. In the event the Army has to retreat, the militia is supposed to form the stay-behind element to harass enemy supply lines, conduct hit-and-run attacks on enemy outposts, and carry out sabotage and other guerrilla activities in the Maoist tradition of "people's war."

The Air Force

The Air Force, with considerable early help from the Soviet Union, is the third largest in the world. Its planes, however, are rapidly becoming obsolete in comparison with modern Western types and probably will remain so, at least in the 1970s. The operational readiness of planes that are available is further limited by a reported shortage of spare parts and by an insufficient supply of fuel.

The territorial organization of the Air Force consists of nine air defense regions (as of 1967, the latest year for which information was available in 1971), which had at least twenty-one major military airbases. These bases are jet capable and well equipped with ground control devices, radar, communications, fuel storage facilities, and maintenance shops. Most of them have long, paved runways capable of accommodating large transports and bombers in all kinds of weather. Eight of these bases are situated along the Soviet border; two are in the Peking area; five are along the east coast between Shanghai and Canton; five are in the south and southwest in the Chungking-K'un-ming-Hainan triangle; and one is in Lhasa, Tibet.

In 1970 the Air Force had an estimated total of 3,500 combat aircraft, including at least 500 for the Navy's air arm; most were jet fighters, such as MIG-15s, MIG-17s, MIG-19s, and advanced MIG-21s. There was no information as to the number of F-9s that Communist China was reportedly producing in 1970 and 1971. Also available to the Air Force were some 150 Soviet IL-28s, which are jet-powered light bombers capable of carrying a nuclear bomb of nominal yield about 500 miles. Communist China had also an undertermined number of Soviet TU-16 twin-jet medium bombers with a combat radius of 1,650 nautical miles, far enough to strike any major target in the Far East. There were no heavy bombers nor any long-range types except a few TU-4s, which were obsolete Soviet copies of the United States B–29. The rest of the aircraft consisted of old propellor-driven transports of various types, at least six jet-prop Viscounts purchased from Great Britain in 1964, and an assortment of light liaison planes of local design and production.

Communist Chinese pilots include some excellent flyers trained earlier in the Soviet and the satellite countries, but they find it difficult to fly often enough to keep their proficiency. There are an undetermined number of women pilots in the Air Force. Available evidence suggests that the Air Force has no significant offensive capability; it could offer spirited, but not sustained, opposition to invasion by a major foreign power. The insufficiency of transports seriously limits airlift capability; the maximum number of troops that can be airlifted at one time for offensive or reinforcement operations was estimated to be about 5,000 in 1970.

The Navy

The Navy is the smallest of the PLA components, having a strength of about 150,000 men (including 16,000 for its air force and 25,000 marines) and a surface fleet of about 900 vessels in various stages of obsolescence. It has neither heavy capital ships nor effective capability to support, as of 1970, a major amphibious operation. Its mission and orientation are geared essentially to coastal defense.

Major naval equipment in 1970 consisted of four Soviet-supplied destroyers of the Gorkyi class and nine Soviet destroyer escorts of the Riga class, none of which provided much of a threat to a hostile seaborne force. Other major vessels included more than forty attack submarines, most of them aging, Soviet-built, medium- and long-range types and some Communist Chinese copies of the Soviet models. There was one Soviet G-class submarine with surface missile-firing tubes. The remaining vessels were an assortment of submarine chasers, guided missile patrol boats, minesweepers, fast motor torpedo boats, motor gunboats, and landing ships. The Navy's 500 shore-based aircraft (including 100 IL-28 torpedo-carrying light bombers and 350 MIG-15 and MIG-17 fighters) were integrated into the unified air defense system and were subject to the operational command of various military regions or garrison commands to which they were assigned.

NUCLEAR CAPABILITY

Communist China began planning for the development of nuclear weapons as early as 1950, but it was not until after the mid-1950s that serious efforts were made to accelerate the pace of this program. Initially, the Communist Chinese were aided considerably by a series of Soviet technical and material assistance programs but, when confronted with the Soviet decision to withdraw such assistance for a number of reasons, they adopted a policy of nuclear self-reliance, just as they did in the economic sphere in the form of the Great Leap Forward (see ch. 11, Foreign Relations; ch. 13, Character and Structure of the Economy; ch. 16, Science and Technology).

Mao is quoted by Party journals as having stated in June 1958, "I think it is entirely possible for some atom bombs and hydrogen bombs to be made in ten years' time." Six years later, in October 1964, Communist China exploded its first atomic bomb, and two years and eight months thereafter, its first hydrogen bomb. Between 1964 and October 1971 it detonated eleven nuclear devices (the last in October 1970), seven of the last nine tests involving thermonuclear devices. Seven of the eleven devices were air dropped, two were tower exploded, one was delivered by a missile, and one was set off underground. As of mid-1971 various Western sources estimated that Communist China probably had stocks of fissionable material sufficient for at least 120 twenty-kiloton nuclear bombs.

There was a considerable body of evidence in 1970 that the Communist Chinese nuclear delivery program was lagging behind the impressive nuclear weapons program. Lacking operational ballistic missiles or any modern long-range bombers, the communist regime depended on its limited number of 1,650-mile-range TU-16s as the primary means of delivery. Also available for delivery was one G-class diesel-powered missile-launching submarine with three tubes for missiles of about 400-mile range, but as of mid-1971 there was no evidence that the Communist Chinese had any operational missiles for it.

The missile delivery system was apparently still undergoing extensive flight testing in 1971 at the Lop Nor nuclear center in Sinkiang Uighur Autonomous Region. In October 1966 the Communist Chinese first lobbed a ten- to twenty-kiloton atomic warhead using a Soviet-type SS-4 medium-range ballistic missile (MRBM); this missile has a range of between 400 and 600 miles. Based on this and other related developments, Western sources estimated in late 1966 that Communist China could launch its first intercontinental ballistic missile (ICBM) by the end of 1967. This launching never materialized; some analysts attributed the nonoccurrence to the disruptions of the Cultural Revolution or some unexplainable technical difficulties. Others have blamed faulty analysis. Whatever the case, testimony before the United States Senate in February 1970 indicated that Communist China could possibly have a strike force of from eighty to 100 MRBMs by the mid-1970s. Such a medium-range missile would have a range of up to 1,000 miles. Western sources in March 1971 suggested that the Communist Chinese had already deployed about twenty MRBMs.

In 1971 it was largely a matter of speculation as to whether the Communist Chinese nuclear missile efforts were focused on the ICBM or MRBM. What was ascertainable, based on fragmentary evidence, was that the ICBM program was behind schedule and that, as of late 1971, Communist China did not yet have available a thermonuclear warhead for flight-testing over an intercontinental range of 6,000 miles. There was also a report suggesting that in 1970 the emphasis in Communist Chinese research and development had apparently shifted from the MRBM to the development of an intermediate-range ballistic missile (IRBM). Experiences gained in the MRBM and IRBM programs were expected to accelerate the ICBM program considerably. A United States government source indicated in February 1970 that the Communist Chinese might have between ten and twenty-five ICBMs in 1975 if they could conduct an initial ICBM test by early 1973. It was suggested, however, that if this initial test took place later, achievement of such an ICBM force would be delayed accordingly.

A major technological breakthrough for the ICBM program was the successful orbiting of the first Communist Chinese earth satellite in April 1970, with a payload of 381 pounds; apparently, however, it lacked a sophisticated guidance system. Observers suggested that a two-stage booster, capable of delivering a payload to a range of 1,200 to 1,500 miles, was probably used in the orbit shot. A second satellite was placed in orbit in March 1971, but it was not determined whether Communist China was using the booster of its MRBM or was testing the booster stage of an ICBM. A week before the second space shot, a presidential message to the United States Congress noted: "China continues to work on strategic ballistic missiles and, by the late 1970s, can be expected to have operational ICBMs capable of reaching the United States."

According to many qualified observers, Communist China is not expected to pose a strategic nuclear threat to either the United States or the Soviet Union in the 1970s. Communist China may indeed be able to produce a limited number of ICBMs by the late 1970s, but the likelihood of these being launched against the heartland of either of the two nuclear superpowers is discounted by most observers as very remote. These observers generally agreed that, although appearing bold and full of rhetorical threats, Communist China would more likely be tactically cautious. Peking's immediate objective in nuclear strategy appeared to be directed toward acquiring a limited defensive second-strike capability as a minimal deterrent against the threat of attack by either the United States or the Soviet Union. Thus, at least until the middle or late 1970s, the Communist Chinese nuclear threat would seem to be regional, not intercontinental. In the likely event of achieving this regional capability by the mid-1970s at the latest, Communist China, according to most observers, would be able to deter the real or imagined United States or Soviet attacks on itself by the threat of retaliating against United States allies in the Far East or against selected targets in Soviet Central Asia or the Soviet maritime provinces.

BIBLIOGRAPHY

SOURCES USED

Section I. Social

Aberle, David F. *Chahar and Dagor-Mongol Bureaucratic Administration*. New Haven: Human Relations Area Files Press, 1962.

Adams, Ruth (ed.). *Contemporary China*. New York: Vintage Books, 1966.

Ajia Chosakai (ed.). *Chugoku Soran, 1971* (Survey of China, 1971). Tokyo: Ajia Chosakai, 1971.

Anderson, Dick. "Street Committees in China, 1968," *Eastern Horizon* [Hong Kong], VII, No. 6, November–December 1968, 27–30.

Andrew, Geoffrey. "China: An Academic Appraisal," *American Scholar*, XXXII, No. 3, Summer 1963, 377–386.

Barnett, A. Doak. "Social Stratification and Aspects of Personnel Management in the Chinese Communist Bureaucracy," *China Quarterly* [London], No. 28, October–December 1966, 8–39.

Benda, Harry J., and Larkin, John A. *The World of Southeast Asia: Selected Historical Readings*. New York: Harper and Row, 1967.

Bennett, Gordon A. "Political Labels and Popular Tension," *Current Scene: Developments in Mainland China* [Hong Kong], VII, No. 4, February 26, 1969, 1–16.

Bernal, Martin. "China: The Contemporary Scene." Pages 163–177 in Guy Wint (ed.), *Asia Handbook*. (Rev. ed.) Harmondsworth: Penguin, 1969.

Bowers, John Z. "Medicine in Mainland China: Red and Rural," *Current Scene: Developments in Mainland China* [Hong Kong], VIII, No. 12, June 15, 1970.

Buchanan, Keith. *The Transformation of the Chinese Earth*. New York: Praeger, 1970.

Busby, John. "Creating a Ruling Class." Pages 169–185 in Werner Klatt (ed.), *The Chinese Model*. Hong Kong: Hong Kong University Press, 1965.

Bush, Richard C., Jr. *Religion in Communist China*. Nashville: Abingdon Press, 1970.

Candlin, A. H. S. "China: The Army, the Party and the People," *Military Review*, LI, No. 2, February 1971, 24–32.

Carrasco, Pedro. *Land and Polity in Tibet*. Seattle: University of Washington Press, 1959.

Casella, Allesandro. "China Seeking New Education," *Washington Post*, May 2, 1971, A23, A26.

——. "Open-Ended Revolution," *Far Eastern Economic Review* [Hong Kong], LXXII, No. 26, June 26, 1971, 24–25.

"Chairman Mao on Revolution in Education," *Current Background* [Hong Kong], No. 888, August 22, 1969, 1–8.

"Changes in Chinese Society, 1949–1969," *China News Analysis* [Hong Kong], No. 774, September 19, 1969, 1–7.

Chang, Kwang-chih. *The Archaeology of Ancient China*. (Rev. ed.) New Haven: Yale University Press, 1971.

Chao, Kang. "Industrialization and Urban Housing in Communist China," *Journal of Asian Studies*, XXV, No. 3, May 1966, 381–396.

Cheng, Chu-yuan. "Peking's Minds of Tomorrow," *Current Scene: Developments in Mainland China* [Hong Kong], IV, No. 6, March 15, 1966.

——. *Scientific and Engineering Manpower in Communist China, 1949–1963*. (National Science Foundation Series, NSF 65–14.) Washington: GPO, 1965.

——. "Social Scientists in Communist China." Pages 246–267 in *Scientific and Engineering Manpower in Communist China, 1949–1963*. (National Science Foundation Series, NSF 65–14.) Washington: GPO, 1965.

Cheng, J. Chester (ed.). *The Politics of the Chinese Red Army*. Stanford: Hoover Institution on War, Revolution and Peace, 1966.

Chen, Jack. "Treason at the Top," *Far Eastern Economic Review* [Hong Kong], LXXIII, No. 29, July 17, 1971, 21–23.

Ch'en, Jerome, and Tarling, Nicholas (eds.). *Studies in the Social History of China and South-East Asia: Essays in Memory of Victor Purcell*. Cambridge: Cambridge University Press, 1970.

Chen, Pi-chao. "The Political Economics of Population Growth: The Case of China," *World Politics*, XXIII, No. 2, January 1971, 245–272.

Chen, S. C., and Ridley, Charles P. (eds.). *The Rural People's Communes in Lien-chiang*. Stanford: Hoover Institution Press, 1969.

Chen, Theodore Hsi-en. "Education in Communist China: Aims, Trends and Problems." Pages 257–280 in Ruth Adams (ed.), *Contemporary China*. New York: Vintage, 1966.

——. "Education in Communist China": Pages 175–198 in Frank N. Trager and William Henderson (eds.), *Communist China, 1949–1969: A Twenty-Year Appraisal*. New York: New York University Press for American-Asian Educational Exchange, 1970.

Chen, Theodore Hsi-en (ed.). *The Chinese Communist Regime: Documents and Commentary.* New York: Praeger, 1967.

Chen, Wen-hui C. *The Family Revolution in Communist China.* Lackland Air Force Base, Texas: Air Force Personnel and Training Research Center, 1955.

Chiang Ch'ing. *On the Revolution of Peking Opera.* Peking: Foreign Languages Press, 1968.

"China: Middle Men," *Far Eastern Economic Review* [Hong Kong], LXXII, No. 26, June 26, 1971, 14.

China News Summary [Hong Kong], No. 346, November 19, 1970.

"China." Pages 555–613 in *Encyclopaedia Britannica*, V. Chicago: William Benton, 1969.

"China's Feminist Movement," *Current Scene: Developments in Mainland China* [Hong Kong], IX, No. 1, January 7, 1971, 18–19.

"China's 'Reformed' Universities: The First Year," *Current Scene: Developments in Mainland China* [Hong Kong], IX, No. 6, June 7, 1971, 1–7.

China Survey. Cambridge: Americans for Reappraisal of Far Eastern Policy, May 1966. (Newspaper published just for one issue.)

"China the Wonderful," *China News Analysis* [Hong Kong], No. 498, January 3, 1964.

China Yearbook, 1966–67. Taipei: China Publishing, n.d.

Chinese Sociology and Anthropology, I, No. 4, Summer 1969, 1–48.

Chi, Pen-yu. *Patriotism in National Betrayal: On the Reactionary Film "Inside the Ching Court."* Peking: Foreign Languages Press, 1967.

Chou En-lai, et al. *The People's New Literature.* Peking: Cultural Press, 1950.

Chou Yung-tung. *Social Mobility in China.* New York: Atherton Press, 1966.

Chow, Yung-teh. *Social Mobility in China.* Chicago: Aldine, 1966.

Ch'u, Chung. "Buddhism and Chinese Art and Culture." Pages 116–117 in Ralph C. Croizier (ed.), *China's Cultural Legacy and Communism.* (Library of Chinese Affairs Series.) New York: Praeger, 1970.

Chugoku Kenkyujo (Chinese Research Institute). *Shin Chugoku Nenkan, 1970* (New China Yearbook, 1970). Tokyo: Taishukan Shoten, 1970.

Chu, Hao-jan. "Mao's Wife—Chiang Ch'ing," *China Quarterly* [London], No. 31, July–September 1967, 148–150.

Chu, Hung-ti. "Education in Mainland China," *Current History*, LIX, No. 249, September 1970, 165–169, 181–182.

Ch'u T'ung-tsu. *Law and Society in Traditional China.* The Hague: Mouton, 1961.

"Close-Up of Red China: Now a Real Leap Forward," *U.S. News & World Report*, LXX, No. 7, February 15, 1971, 68–70.

Commemorating Lu Hsun—Our Forerunner in the Cultural Revolution. Peking: Foreign Languages Press, 1967.

"Common Sense," *China News Analysis* [Hong Kong], No. 594, January 7, 1966.

"A Commune in Inner Mongolia," *China News Analysis* [Hong Kong], No. 599, February 11, 1966.

Communist China, 1964, II. (Communist China Problem Research Series, EC37.) Hong Kong: Union Research Institute, 1965.

Communist China, 1967. (Communist China Problem Research Series EC41.) Hong Kong: Union Research Institute, 1968.

Communist China, 1968. (Communist China Problem Research Series EC47.) Hong Kong: Union Research Institute, 1969.

Communist China, 1969. (Communist China Problem Research Series EC48.) Hong Kong: Union Research Institute, 1970.

"Communist Tibet (Part I)," *China News Analysis* [Hong Kong], No. 547, January 15, 1965.

"Communist Tibet (Part II)," *China News Analysis* [Hong Kong], No. 548, January 22, 1965.

Coon, Carleton S. *The Living Races of Man.* New York: Knopf, 1965.

Cressey, George B. *Land of the 500 Million: A Geography of China.* (McGraw-Hill Series in Geography.) New York: McGraw-Hill, 1955.

Croizier, Ralph C. *China's Cultural Legacy and Communism.* (Praeger Library of Chinese Affairs Series.) New York: Praeger, 1970.

_____. *Traditional Medicine in Modern China: Science, Nationalism and the Tensions of Cultural Change.* Cambridge: Harvard University Press, 1968.

deBary, William Theodore (ed.). *Sources of Chinese Tradition.* (Introduction to Oriental Civilizations Series.) New York: Columbia University Press, 1960.

deBaiv, William Theodore; Wing-tsit, Chan; and Watson, Burton (eds., *Sources of Chinese Tradition.* New York: Columbia Univei ;ty Press, 1960.

Diao, Richard K. "The Impact of the Cultural Revolution on China's Economic Elite," *China Quarterly* [London], No. 42, April–June 1970, 65–87.

Domes, Jurgen. "The Ninth CCP Central Committee in Statistical Perspective," *Current Scene: Developments in Mainland China* [Hong Kong], IX, No. 2, February 7, 1971, 5–13.

Donnithorne, Audrey. *China's Economic System.* New York: Praeger, 1967.

"Draft Constitution: Via Taiwan," *China News Analysis* [Hong Kong], No. 823, December 4, 1970, 1–7.

Durdin, Tillman. "Army Aides Gain in Chinese Shifts," *New York Times,* August 29, 1971, 18.

_____. "China's Changing Society Seems to Cut Birth Rate," *New York Times*, April 21, 1971, 1, 8.

_____. "China Transformed by Elimination of the Four Olds," *New York Times*, May 19, 1971, 14.

_____. "The Kilns Near Canton," *New York Times*, May 17, 1971, 38.

_____. "The New Face of Maoist China," *Problems of Communism*, XX, No. 5, September–October 1971, 1–13.

Dutt, Gargi. *The Rural Communes of China*. New York: Asia Publishing House, 1968.

"Economic Situation in Sinkiang," *China News Analysis* [Hong Kong], No. 591, December 3, 1965.

"Educational Reform and Rural Resettlement in Communist China," *Current Scene: Developments in Mainland China* [Hong Kong], VIII, No. 17, November 7, 1970, 1–8.

"Educational Reform in Rural China," *Current Scene: Developments in Mainland China* [Hong Kong], VII, No. 3, February 8, 1969, 1–17.

"Education, 'Bourgeois' or Proletarian?" *China News Analysis* [Hong Kong], No. 617, June 24, 1966.

Fairbank, John King. "China's World Order: The Tradition of Chinese Foreign Relations," *Encounter* [London], XXVII, No. 6, December 1966, 14–20.

_____. "How to Deal with the Chinese Revolution," *New York Review of Books*, February 17, 1966.

_____. *New Views of China's Tradition and Modernization*. (Service Center for Teachers of History Publications, No. 74.) Washington: American Historical Association, 1968.

_____. "The People's Middle Kingdom," *Foreign Affairs*, XLIV, No. 4, July 1966, 574–586.

_____. The United States and China. (Rev. ed.) New York: Viking Press, 1958.

Fairbank, John King; Reischauer, Edwin O.; and Craig, Albert M. *East Asia: The Modern Transformation*, II: A History of East Asia Civilization. Boston: Houghton Mifflin, 1965.

"The Family," China News Analysis [Hong Kong], No. 776, October 3, 1969, 1–7.

The Far East and Australasia, 1971: A Survey and Directory of Asia and the Pacific. London: Europa Publications, 1971.

Far Eastern Economic Review Yearbook, 1971. Hong Kong: Far Eastern Economic Review, 1971.

Feuerwerker, Albert (ed.). *History in Communist China*. Cambridge: Massachusetts Institute of Technology Press, 1968.

Field, Robert Michael. "A Note on the Population of Communist China," *China Quarterly* [London], No. 38, April–June 1969, 158–163.

"A Film," *China News Analysis* [Hong Kong], No. 552, February 19, 1965.

Fitzgerald, Charles P. *The Birth of Communist China*. New York: Praeger, 1964.

———. "Book Review: Chinese Intellectuals and the West, by Y. C. Wang," *Pacific Affairs* [Vancouver], XL, Nos. 1 and 2, Spring and Summer 1967, 139, 140.

———. "Notes and Comment: Religion and China's Cultural Revolution," *Pacific Affairs* [Vancouver], XL, Nos. 1 and 2, Spring and Summer 1967, 124–129.

Fokkema, D. W. "The Chinese Criticism of Humanism: Campaigns Against the Intellectuals, 1964–1965," *China Quarterly* [London], No. 26, April–June 1966, 68–81.

Fraser, Stewart (ed.). *Chinese Communist Education*. Nashville: Vanderbilt University Press, 1965.

Freedman, Maurice. "The Family in China, Past and Present." Pages 27–40 in Albert Feuerwerker (ed.), *Modern China*. Englewood Cliffs: Prentice-Hall, 1964.

Freedman, Maurice (ed.). *Family and Kinship in Chinese Society*. Stanford: Stanford University Press, 1970.

Friedman, Edward. "Cultural Limits of the Cultural Revolution," *Asian Survey*, IX, No. 3, March 1969, 188–201.

Fried, Morton H. *Fabric of Chinese Society*. New York: Octagon Books, 1969.

Funnell, Victor C. "Change of Social Values." Pages 3–18 in Werner Klatt (ed.), *The Chinese Model*. Hong Kong: Hong Kong University Press, 1965.

Gayn, Mark. "A Very Different Campus Scene in China," *Washington Evening Star*, May 18, 1971, A8.

Geddes, W. R. *Peasant Life in Communist China*. Ithaca: Society for Applied Anthropology, 1963.

Gentzler, J. Mason. *A Syllabus of Chinese Civilization*. (Companion to Asian Studies Series.) New York: Columbia University Press, 1968.

"The Geography of Mainland China: A Concise Sketch," *Current Scene: Developments in Mainland China* [Hong Kong], VII, No. 17, September 1969, 1–21.

"Ghosts and Spirits on the Stage," *China News Analysis* [Hong Kong], No. 502, January 31, 1964.

Goldman, Merle. "The Aftermath of China's Cultural Revolution," *Current History*, LXI, No. 361, September 1971, 165–170.

———. *Literary Dissent in Communist China*. (Harvard East Asia Series.) New York: Atheneum, 1967.

Goodrich, L. Carrington. *A Short History of the Chinese People*. (Harper Torchbooks Series.) (3d ed.) New York: Harper and Row, 1959.

Goodstadt, Leo. "Nationalizing the Communes," *Far Eastern Economic Review* [Hong Kong], LXXI, No. 9, February 27, 1971, 5–6.

Great Britain. Naval Intelligence Division. *China Proper,* I and II. (Geographical Handbook Series.) London: 1945.

The Great Socialist Cultural Revolution in China (6 pamphlets). Peking: Foreign Languages Press, 1966.

Griffith, Samuel B. "Communist China's Capacity to Make War," *Foreign Affairs,* XLIII, No. 2, January 1965, 217–236.

Halperin, Morton H. *China and the Bomb.* New York: Praeger, 1965.

Handbook on People's China. Peking: Foreign Languages Press, 1957.

Han Suyin. *Destination Chungking.* Harmondsworth: Penguin, 1959.

_____. "Social Transformation in China." Pages 93–104 in Ruth Adams (ed.), *Contemporary China.* New York: Vintage, 1966.

Hawkins, John N. (trans.) *Educational Theory in the People's Republic of China: The Report of Ch'ien Chun-jui.* (Asian Studies at Hawaii, No. 6.) Honolulu: University of Hawaii Press, 1971.

"Health for the Millions," *China New Analysis* [Hong Kong], No. 738, January 3, 1969, 1–7.

Herrmann, Albert. *An Historical Atlas of China.* Chicago: Aldine, 1966.

Heuvel, Emile van. "China's New Mood: Relaxation and Self-Confidence," *New York Times Magazine,* Section 6, July 25, 1971, 10–11, 47–51.

Hickrod, Lucy Jen Huang, and Hickrod, G. Alan. "Communist Chinese and American Adolescent Subcultures," *China Quarterly* [London], No. 22, April–June 1965, 171–180.

"Higher Education," *China News Analysis* [Hong Kong], No. 816, October 2, 1970, 1–7.

"Higher Education: Problems of a Revolution," *Current Scene: Developments in Mainland China* [Hong Kong], IX, No. 1, January 7, 1971, 16, 17.

Hightower, James Robert. *Topics in Chinese Literature: Outlines and Bibliographies.* (Rev. ed.) (Harvard-Yenching Institute Studies, III.) Cambridge: Harvard University Press, 1966 (reprint of 1958 book.)

Hinton, Harold C. *Communist China: Domestic Political Scene.* (Paper P-527.) Arlington: Institute for Defense Analyses, August 1969.

Hobbs, Lisa. *I Saw Red China.* New York: McGraw-Hill, 1966.

Hoeber, Francis P. *The Economy Behind the Bamboo Curtain.* Menlo Park: Stanford Research Institute, 1966.

Hoffman, Charles. *Work Incentive Practices and Policies in the People's Republic of China, 1953–1965.* Albany: State University of New York Press, 1967.

Hookham, Hilda. *A Short History of China.* London: Longmans, Green, 1969.

Ho, Ping-ti. "The Examination System and Social Mobility in China, 1368–1911." Pages 60–65 in Verne F. Ray (ed.), *Intermediate Societies, Social Mobility and Communications: Proceedings of the 1959 Annual Spring Meeting of the American Ethnological Society*. Seattle: American Ethnological Society, 1959.

Ho, Ping-ti, and Tsou, Tang (eds.). *China in Crisis*, I: China's Heritage and the Communist Political System. (Book One.) Chicago: University of Chicago Press, 1968.

Howe, Christopher. "The Supply and Administration of Urban Housing in Mainland China: The Case of Shanghai," *China Quarterly* [London], No. 33, January–March 1968, 73–97.

"How to Correctly Treat the Problem of Exploiting Class Family Origin," *Chinese Sociology and Anthropology*, I, No. 1, Fall, 1968, 7–11.

Hsia, C. T. "Literature and Art Under Mao Tse-tung." Pages 199–220 in Frank N. Trager and William Henderson (eds.), *Communist China, 1949–1969: A Twenty-Year Appraisal*. New York: New York University Press for American-Asian Educational Exchange, 1970.

Hsu, Francis L. K. "Chinese Kinship and Chinese Behavior." Pages 579–608 in Ping-ti Ho and Tang Tsou (eds.), *Chinese Heritage and the Communist Political System*, II: China Crisis. Chicago: University of Chicago Press, 1968.

———. *Under the Ancestor's Shadow*. New York: Anchor Books, 1967.

Hsu, Immanuel C. Y. *The Rise of Modern China*. New York: Oxford University Press, 1970.

Hsu, Kai-yu. *Twentieth Century Chinese Poetry: An Anthology*. Garden City: Anchor Books, 1964.

Hsu, William. *Buddhism in China*. Hong Kong: Dragonfly Books, 1964.

Huang, Joe C. "Villains, Victims and Morals in Contemporary Chinese Literature," *China Quarterly* [London], No. 46, April–June 1971, 331–349.

Huang, Lucy Jen. "A Re-evaluation of the Primary Role of the Communist Chinese Woman: The Homemaker or the Worker," *Marriage and Family Living*, XXV, No. 2, May 1963, 162–166.

———. "The Role of Religion in Communist Chinese Society," *Asian Survey*, XI, No. 7, July 1971, 693–708.

Huard, Pierre, and Wong, Ming. *Chinese Medicine*. (World University Library Series.) (Translated from French by Bernard Fielding.) London: Weidenfeld and Nicolson, 1968.

Hu, Chang-tu, et al. *China: Its People, Its Society, Its Culture*. (Survey of World Cultures Series.) New Haven: Human Relations Area Files Press, 1960.

Hucker, Charles O. *China: A Critical Bibliography*. Tucson: University of Arizona Press, 1962.

Hudson, Geoffrey. "China." Pages 133–162 in Guy Wint (ed.), *Asia Handbook*. (Rev. ed.) Harmondsworth: Penguin, 1969.

Huenemann, Ralph W. "Urban Rationing in Communist China," *China Quarterly* [London], No. 26, April–June 1966, 44–57.

Hunter, Deirdre, and Hunter, Neale. *We the Chinese*. New York: Praeger, 1971.

Hunter, Neale. *Shanghai Journal: An Eyewitness Account of the Cultural Revolution*. New York: Praeger, 1969.

"In the Universities," *China News Analysis* [Hong Kong], No. 772, September 5, 1969, 1–7.

"In Tune with Chairman Mao," *Current Scene: Developments in Mainland China* [Hong Kong], III, No. 29, October 15, 1965.

Jacobs, Norman. *The Origin of Modern Capitalism and Eastern Asia*. Hong Kong: Hong Kong University Press, 1958.

Jen-Min Shou-Ts'e (People's Handbook), 1965. Peking: Ta-Kung Pao She, 1965.

Jenner, W. J. F. (ed.) *Modern Chinese Stories*. (Trans., W. J. F. Jenner and Gladys Yang.) London: Oxford University Press, 1970.

Jones, Francis P. (ed.) *Documents of the Three-Self Movement: Source Materials for the Study of the Protestant Church in Communist China*. New York: Far Eastern Office, Division of Foreign Missions, National Council of the Churches of Christ in the USA, 1963.

Jones, P. H. M. "China's Muslim Region," *Far Eastern Economic Review* [Hong Kong], XXXIII, No. 11, September 14, 1961, 492–494.

_____. "Civilising Influence," *Far Eastern Economic Review* [Hong Kong], LV, No. 7, November 17, 1966, 394, 396–397.

_____. "Farm and Factory in Inner Mongolia," *Far Eastern Economic Review* [Hong Kong], XXXVI, No. 7, May 17, 1962, 321, 323–327.

_____. "Feeding Tibet," Far Eastern Economic Review [Hong Kong], XXXVIII, No. 7, November 15, 1962, 373–375.

_____. *Golden Guide to Hong Kong and Macao*. Hong Kong: Far Eastern Economic Review, 1969.

_____. "Inner Mongolia Modernized," *Far Eastern Economic Review* [Hong Kong], XXXIV, No. 4, October 26, 1961, 233, 235, 237, 238.

_____. "Inner Mongolia Sinicized," *Far Eastern Economic Review* [Hong Kong], XXXIV, No. 6, November 9, 1961, 299–301, 303.

_____. "Respite for Tibet," *Far Eastern Economic Review* [Hong Kong], XXXII, No. 8, May 25, 1961, 365, 367.

_____. "Scripts for Minorities," *Far Eastern Economic Review* [Hong Kong], XXXVI, No. 2, April 12, 1962, 62–64.

_____. "Sensitive Sinkiang," *Far Eastern Economic Review* [Hong Kong], LV, No. 6, February 8, 1967, 189–191.

_____. "Sinkiang—China's Last Frontier," *Far Eastern Economic Review* [Hong Kong], XXX, No. 5, November 3, 1960, 200, 204–205.

_____. "Sinkiang Gets to Work," *Far Eastern Economic Review* [Hong Kong], XXV, No. 12, March 22, 1962, 654–656.

_____. "Sinkiang—The Road to Communism," *Far Eastern Economic Review* [Hong Kong], XXX, No. 7, November 17, 1960, 280, 284–287.

_____. "Tibet and the New Order," Far Eastern Economic Review [Hong Kong], XXXI, No. 9, March 2, 1961, 356, 360–362.

_____. "Tibetan Occasion," *Far Eastern Economic Review* [Hong Kong], XLIX, No. 12, September 16, 1965, 532–534.

_____. "Tibet Comes into Line," *Far Eastern Economic Review* [Hong Kong], XXXIV, No. 13, December 28, 1961, 489, 491.

_____. "Tibet's Emerging Economy," *Far Eastern Economic Review* [Hong Kong], No. 7, February 16, 1961, 288–291.

Kan, David. *The Impact of the Cultural Revolution on Chinese Higher Education.* (Dissertations and Theses on Contemporary China Series.) Hong Kong: Union Research Institute, 1971.

Kaplan, Frederick. "China's Directed Drama," *Far Eastern Economic Review* [Hong Kong], XLIV, No. 13, June 25, 1964, 634–636.

Keatley, Robert. "Chinese Proverbs," *Wall Street Journal,* CLXXVIII, No. 6, July 9, 1971, 1, 16.

Klatt, Werner. "A Review of China's Economy in 1970," *China Quarterly* [London], No. 43, July–September 1970, 100–120.

Klatt, Werner (ed.). *The Chinese Model.* Hong Kong: Hong Kong University Press, 1965.

Klein, Donald W., and Clark, Anne B. *Biographic Dictionary of Chinese Communism, 1921–1965,* I and II. Cambridge: Harvard University Press, 1971.

Kolmas, Josef. "The Minority Nationalities." Pages 51–61 in Ruth Adams (ed.), *Contemporary China.* New York: Pantheon Books, 1966.

Lal, Amrit. "Sinification of Ethnic Minorities in China," *Current Scene: Developments in Mainland China* [Hong Kong], VIII, No. 4, February 15, 1970, 1–23.

Lattimore, Owen. *Pivot of Asia: Sinkiang.* Boston: Little, Brown, 1950.

Lazure, Denis. "From Generation to Generation." Pages 423–429 in William T. Liu (ed.), *Chinese Society Under Communism: A Reader.* New York: John Wiley and Sons, 1967.

Lee, Renesselaer W., III. "The *Hsia Fang* System: Marxism and Modernization," *China Quarterly* [London], No. 28, October–December 1966, 40–62.

Leijon, Per-Olon. "Preserving the Old," *Far Eastern Economic Review* [Hong Kong], XIV, No. 7, November 17, 1966, 374–376.

Lethbridge, Henry J. *China's Urban Communes*. Hong Kong: Dragonfly Books, 1961.

Lewis, John Wilson. *Leadership in Communist China*. Ithaca: Cornell University Press, 1963.

_____. "Revolutionary Struggle and the Second Generation in Communist China," *China Quarterly* [London], No. 21, January–March 1965, 126–147.

_____. "The Role of the Party." Pages 107–110 in William T. Liu (ed.), *Chinese Society Under Communism: A Reader*. New York: John Wiley and Sons, 1967.

Lewis, John Wilson (ed.). *The City in Communist China*. Stanford: Stanford University Press, 1971.

_____. *Party Leadership and Revolutionary Power in China*. Cambridge: Cambridge University Press, 1970.

Liang, Pin. *Keep the Red Flag Flying*. Peking: Foreign Languages Press, 1964.

"Life in the Countryside, I: The Administration," *China News Analysis* [Hong Kong], No. 818, October 16, 1970, 1–7.

"Life in the Countryside, II: The Economic Situation of the Peasants," *China News Analysis* [Hong Kong], No. 819, October 23, 1970, 1–7.

Lindbeck, John M. H. "Chinese Science: It's Not a Paper Atom," *New York Times Magazine*, January 8, 1967, 37–38, 60–64, 70.

Lindbeck, John M. H. (ed.). *China: Management of a Revolutionary Society*. Seattle: University of Washington Press, 1971.

Lindquist, Sven. *China in Crisis*. (Trans., Sylvia Clayton.) London: Faber and Faber, 1963.

Li, Tien-yi. *The History of Chinese Literature: A Selected Bibliography*. New Haven: Yale University Press, 1970.

Liu, William T. *Chinese Society Under Communism: A Reader*. New York: John Wiley and Sons, 1967.

Liu, Wu-chi. *An Introduction to Chinese Literature*. Bloomington: Indiana University Press, 1966.

Lu, Ting-yi. "Let All Flowers Bloom Together, Let Diverse Schools of Thought Contend," *Current Background* [Hong Kong], No. 406, August 15, 1956, 1–17.

MacDougall, Colina. "The Cultural Revolution and the Communes: Back to 1958?" *Current Scene: Developments in Mainland China* [Hong Kong], VII, No. 7, April 11, 1969, 1–10.

_____. "Keeping House in China," *Far Eastern Economic Review* [Hong Kong], L, No. 12, December 23, 1965, 550–551, 558.

Mah, Feng-hwa. "Why China Imports Wheat," *China Quarterly* [London], No. 45, January–March 1971, 116–128.

Malden, William. "A New Class Structure Emerging in China?," *China Quarterly* [London], No. 22, April–June 1965, 83–88.

"Mao's Revolution in Public Health," *Current Scene: Developments in Mainland China* [Hong Kong], VI, No. 7, May 1, 1968, 1–20.

Mao Tse-tung. *Analysis of the Classes in Chinese Society.* (2d ed.) Peking: Foreign Languages Press, 1960.

_____. *On Literature and Art.* Peking: Foreign Languages Press, 1967.

_____. *On the Correct Handling of Contradictions Among the People.* Peking: China Pictorial, 1967.

_____. *Selected Works of Mao Tse-tung.* 4 vols. Peking: Foreign Languages Press, 1961–65.

_____. *Selected Works*, III: 1939–41. New York: International Publishers, 1954.

"Marxism—Ready to Die—Loose Discipline," *China News Analysis* [Hong Kong], No. 768, August 8, 1969, 1–7.

"Medicine to the Villages," *China News Analysis* [Hong Kong], No. 602, March 4, 1966.

Meisner, Maurice. "Utopian Goals and Ascetic Values in Chinese Communist Ideology," *Journal of Asian Studies*, XXVIII, No. 1, November 1968, 101–110.

Meserve, Walter J., and Meserve, Ruth (eds.). *Modern Drama from Communist China.* New York: New York University Press, 1970.

_____. "Research Communications No. 3.: China's Persecuted Playwrights—The Theater in Communist China's Current Cultural Revolution," *Journal of Asian and Africa Studies* [Leiden], V, No. 3, July 1970, 209–215.

Michael, Franz H. "The Role of Law in Traditional, Nationalist and Communist China," *China Quarterly* [London], No. 9, 1962.

Moseley, George. "Tibet—Tibetan vs. Reform," *Far Eastern Economic Review* [Hong Kong], L, No. 1, October 7, 1965, 13–16.

Mu, Fu-sheng. *The Wilting of the 100 Flowers.* New York: Praeger, 1962.

Munro, Donald J. "Dissent in Communist China," *Current Scene: Developments in Mainland China* [Hong Kong], IV, No. 11, June 1, 1966.

Munthe-Kass, Harald. "Roads and Rails in China," *Far Eastern Economic Review* [Hong Kong], LI, No. 7, February 17, 1966, 275, 276, 325, 326.

Myrdal, Jan. *Report from a Chinese Village.* New York: Pantheon Books, 1965.

Nagel's Encyclopedia-Guide: China. Geneva: Nagel, 1968.

"National Minorities: The Policy," *China News Analysis* [Hong Kong], No. 563, May 7, 1965.

Needham, Joseph. "Chinese Medicine." Pages 255–314 in Frederick N. L. Poynter (ed.), *Symposium on Medicine and Culture.* London: Welcome Institute of History of Medicine, 1969.

North, Robert C. *Chinese Communism*. (World University Library Series.) New York: McGraw-Hill, 1966.

Oksenberg, Michel C. "China: The Convulsive Society," *Headline Series*, No. 203, December 1970, 3–78.

———. "What's Going On in China?," *Asia*, No. 13, Autumn 1968, 13–20.

Oksenberg, Michel C.; Bateman, Nancy; and Anderson, James B. *A Bibliography of Secondary English Language Literature on Contemporary Chinese Politics*. New York: East Asian Institute, Columbia University, 1970.

Oliphant, Mark. "*Over Pots of Tea: Excerpts from a Diary of a Visit to China*," *Bulletin of the Atomic Scientists*, XXII, May 1966.

On the Reeducation of Intellectuals. Peking: Foreign Languages Press, 1968.

"The Operation of 'Socialist Universities'," *Current Background* [Hong Kong], No. 933, June 4, 1971, 1–7.

Orleans, Leo A. "Medical Education and Manpower in Communist China," *Comparative Education Review*, January 1969, 20–42.

———. "A New Birth Control Campaign?," *China Quarterly* [London], No. 12, October–December 1962, 207–210.

———. *Professional Manpower and Education in Communist China*. (National Science Foundation Series, NSF 61-3.) Washington: GPO, 1961.

———. "Propheteering: The Population of Communist China," *Current Scene: Developments in Mainland China* [Hong Kong], VII, No. 24, December 15, 1969, 13–19.

Osgood, Cornelius. *Village Life in Old China*. New York: Ronald Press, 1963.

Patterson, George N. "New Crisis in Tibet," *Far Eastern Economic Review* [Hong Kong], XLVII, No. 4, January 28, 1965, 130–132.

Pearcy, G. Etzel. "Mainland China: Geographic Strengths and Weaknesses," *Department of State Bulletin*, LV, No. 1418, August 29, 1966.

"Peking's Program to Move Human and Material Resources to the Countryside," *Current Scene: Developments in Mainland China* [Hong Kong], VII, No. 18, September 15, 1969, 1–17.

Pelzel, John C. "Notes on the Chinese Bureaucracy." Pages 50–57 in Verne F. Ray (ed.), *Cultural Stability and Cultural Change: Proceedings of the 1957 Annual Spring Meeting of the American Ethnological Society*. Seattle: American Ethnological Society, 1957.

"P'eng Chen, Peking, and Peking University," *China News Analysis*, [Hong Kong], No. 615, June 10, 1966.

People's Republic of China. Laws, Statutes, etc.
   The Constitution of the Communist Party of China.
      (Adopted by the Ninth National Congress of the Communist

Party of China on April 14, 1969.) Peking: Foreign Languages Press, 1969.

The Marriage Law of the People's Republic of China. Peking: Foreign Languages Press, 1953.

Perkins, Dwight H. "Mao Tse-tung's Goals and China's Economic Performance," *Current Scene: Developments in Mainland China* [Hong Kong], IX, No. 1, January 7, 1971, 1–15.

Pfeffer, Richard M. "Contradictions and Social Change in Communist China," *Pacific Affairs* [Vancouver], XXXIX, Nos. 3 and 4, Fall and Winter 1966–1967, 349–360.

"Philosophy," *China News Analysis* [Hong Kong], No. 518, May 29, 1964.

Population and Family Planning in the People's Republic of China. Washington: Victor-Bostrom Fund Committee and the Population Crisis Committee, Spring 1971.

Population Reference Bureau. *World Population Data Sheet, 1970* Washington: April 1970.

Priestley, K. E. (ed.) *China's Men of Letters: Yesterday and Today*. Hong Kong: Dragonfly Books, 1962.

"Public Health Developments, Continued Focus on the Farms," *Current Scene: Developments in Mainland China* [Hong Kong], VII, No. 24, December 15, 1969, 1–12.

Pye, Lucian W. "Coming Dilemmas for China's Leaders," *Foreign Affairs*, XLIV, No. 3, April 1966, 387–402.

Pye, Lucian W., and Leites, Nathan. *Nuances in Chinese Political Culture*. (P-4504.) Santa Monica: Rand Corporation, November 1970.

"Railroads and Highways," *China News Analysis* [Hong Kong], December 4, 1964.

Ray, Dennis. "Red and Expert in China's Cultural Revolution," *Pacific Affairs* [Vancouver], XLII, No. 1, Spring 1970, 22–33.

Reischauer, Edwin O., and Fairbank, John King. *East Asia: The Great Tradition*, I: A History of East Asian Civilization. Boston: Houghton Mifflin, 1960.

Rent Collection Courtyard: Sculptures of Oppression and Revolt. Peking: Foreign Languages Press, 1968.

"The Revival of the Communist Youth League," *Current Scene: Developments in Mainland China* [Hong Kong], VIII, No. 5, March 1, 1970, 1–7.

Roderick, John. "China Visit Shows Change of 25 Years," *New York Times*, April 19, 1971.

Rupen, Robert A. "Mongolian Nationalism (Part II)," *Royal Central Asian Societies Journal* [London], XLV, July–October 1958.

Salaff, Janet. "The Urban Communes and the Anti-City Experiment," *China Quarterly* [London], No. 29, January–March 1967, 82–109.

Sargent, Clyde B. "Chinese National Culture," *Naval War College Review*, XXIII, No. 9, May 1971, 41–51.

"Schools: Curriculum and Textbooks," *China News Analysis* [Hong Kong], No. 792, February 20, 1970, 1–7.

Schurmann, Franz. *Ideology and Organization in Communist China.* Berkeley: University of California Press, 1966.

Schurmann, Franz, and Schell, Orville (eds.). *The China Reader*, I: Imperial China: The Decline of the Last Dynasty and the Origins of Modern China, the 18th and 19th Centuries. New York: Random House, 1967.

_____. *The China Reader*, II: Republican China: Nationalism, War, and the Rise of Communism, 1911–1949. New York: Random House, 1967.

_____. *The China Reader*, III: Communist China, Revolutionary Reconstruction, and International Confrontation. New York: Random House, 1967.

Schwartz, Benjamin I. *Chinese Communism and the Rise of Mao.* (3d ed.) Cambridge: Harvard University Press, 1958.

Schwartz, Harry. *China.* New York: Atheneum, 1965.

"Science and Research, Summer 1964," *China News Analysis* [Hong Kong], No. 536, October 9, 1964.

Scott, A. C. *An Introduction to the Chinese Theater.* Singapore: Donald Moore, 1958.

_____. *Literature and the Arts in Twentieth Century China.* Gloucester, Massachusetts: Peter Smith, 1968.

"Secondary Education," *China News Analysis* [Hong Kong], No. 554, March 5, 1965.

Shaplen, Robert. "A Reporter at Large: The China Watchers," *New Yorker*, February 12, 1966; 41–106.

Sharp, Ilsa. "No Ivory Towers," *Far Eastern Economic Review* [Hong Kong], LXXII, No. 23, June 5, 1971, 64–66.

Shih, Vincent Y. C. "The State of the Intellectuals." Pages 221–242 in Frank N. Trager and William Henderson, *Communist China, 1949–1969: A Twenty-Year Appraisal.* New York: New York University Press, for American-Asian Educational Exchange, 1970.

Sieh, Marie. "The School Teacher: A Link to China's Future," *Current Scene: Developments in Mainland China* [Hong Kong], III, No. 18, May 1, 1965.

Skinner, G. William. "Chinese Peasants and the Closed Community: An Open and Shut Case," *Comparative Studies in Society and History*, XIII, No. 3, July 1971, 270–281.

_____. "Marketing and Social Structure in Rural China, Part 3," *Journal of Asian Studies*, XXIV, No. 3, May 1965, 363–399.

Skinner, G. William, and Winckler, Edwin A. "Compliance Succession in Rural Communist China: A Cyclical Theory." Pages 410–438 in Amitai Etzioni (ed.), *A Sociological Reader on Complex*

Organization. (2d ed.) New York: Holt, Rinehart and Winston, 1969.

Snow, Edgar. "Mao Tse-tung—and the Cost of Living," *New Republic*, CLXIV, No. 15, Issue 2937. April 10, 1971, 18–21.

_____. "Population Care and Control," *New Republic*, CLXIV, No. 18, May 1, 1971, 20–23.

_____. "Success or Failure? China's 70,000 Communes," *New Republic*, XXIV, No. 26, June 26, 1971, 19–23.

_____. "Talks with Chou En-Lai: The Open Door," *New Republic*, CLXIV, No. 13, March 27, 1971, 20–23.

Snow, Helen Foster. *Women in Modern China.* The Hague: Mouton, 1967.

Socialist Upsurge in China's Countryside. Peking: Foreign Languages Press, 1957.

Solomon, Richard H. "Educational Themes in China's Changing Culture," *China Quarterly* [London], No. 22, April–June 1965, 154–170.

_____. "On Activism and Activists: Maoist Conceptions of Motivation and Political Role Linking State to Society," *China Quarterly* [London], No. 39, July–September 1969.

"Sources of Labor Discontent in China: The Worker-Peasant System," *Current Scene: Developments in Mainland China* [Hong Kong], VI, No. 5, March 15, 1968, 1–28.

Spitz, Allan. "Maoism and the People's Courts," *Asian Survey*, IX, No. 4, April 1969, 255–264.

Statistical Yearbook, 1969. New York: United Nations, 1970.

Stover, Leon E. *China: Last of the Agrarian States.* New York: Mentor Books.

Sullivan, Michael. *A Short History of Chinese Art.* Berkeley: University of California Press, 1967.

Summary of the Forum on the Work in Literature and Art in the Armed Forces with Which Comrade Lin Piao Entrusted Comrade Chiang Ching. Peking: Foreign Languages Press, 1968.

Su, Y. H. *Literature in China.* Hong Kong: China Viewpoints, 1959.

Swamy, Subramanian, and Burki, Shahidjaved. "Foodgrains Output in the People's Republic of China, 1958–1965," *China Quarterly* [London], No. 41, January–March 1970, 58–63.

"Tibet, 1965–1967," *China News Analysis* [Hong Kong], No. 657, April 28, 1967.

"Tools for Research," *China News Analysis* [Hong Kong], No. 504, February 12, 1964.

Topping, Audrey. "The Peking Factory," *New York Times*, May 17, 1971, 38.

Topping, Seymour. "China: Economic Policy Stresses Local Self-Help," *New York Times*, June 27, 1971, 1, 20.

———. "China: Mass Efforts Achieve Great Feats," *New York Times*, June 26, 1971, 1, 8.

———. "China: New Dogma, New 'Maoist Man'," *New York Times*, June 25, 1971, 1, 3.

———. "Chinese Welfare Plan Seeks to Assure Minimum Living Standards," *New York Times*, June 3, 1971, 16.

———. "Revolutionary Committees Insure Discipline in China," *New York Times*, June 2, 1971, 2.

———. "Rural China Revisited: Change and Continuity," *New York Times*, May 30, 1971, 1, 14.

Townsend, James R. "Democratic Management in the Rural Communes," *China Quarterly* [London], No. 16, October–December 1963, 137–150.

Trager, Frank N., and Henderson, William (eds.). *Communist China, 1949–1969: A Twenty-Year Appraisal.* New York University Press, 1970.

"Training in Medicine," *China News Analysis* [Hong Kong], No. 577, August 20, 1965.

Trumbull, Robert (ed.). *This Is Communist China.* New York: David McKay, 1968.

Tsang, Chiu-sam. *Society, Schools and Progress in China.* Oxford: Pergamon Press, 1968.

"The Two Ch'en Historians," *China News Analysis* [Hong Kong], No. 529, August 21, 1964.

"Two Essays by Fung Yu-lan," *China News Analysis* [Hong Kong], No. 582, September 24, 1965.

Union Research Institute. "Education Via TV," *Union Research Service Reports* [Hong Kong], XXIII, No. 12, May 12, 1961.

———. *Who's Who in Communist China.* Hong Kong: 1966.

U.S. Congress. 90th, 1st Session. Joint Economic Committee. *An Economic Profile of Mainland China.* 2 vols. Washington: GPO, 1967.

U.S. Congress. 91st, 2d Session. House of Representatives. Committee on Foreign Affairs. Subcommittee on Asian and Pacific Affairs. *United States-China Relations: A Strategy for the Future.* Washington: GPO, 1970.

U.S. Department of Commerce. Bureau of the Census. Foreign Demographic Analysis Division. *The Size, Composition and Growth of the Population of Mainland China*, by John S. Aird. (International Population Statistics Reports, Series P-90, No. 15.) Washington: GPO, 1968.

U.S. Department of Commerce. Office of Technical Services. Joint Publications Research Service (Washington). The following publications are JPRS translations from foreign sources:

"French Student's Views on Cultural Revolution in Communist China," by Romain Mathieu in *La Nouvelle Critique, Revue du*

Marxisme Militant, Paris, November 1966. (JPRS: 40,005, *Translations on Communist China: Political and Sociological*, No. 382, February 23, 1967.)

"Population and Food Problems in Mainland China," by Lin Ch'en, in *Fei-ch'ing Yen-chiu*, Taipei, October 10, 1968. (JPRS: 47,112, *Translations on Communist China*, No. 37, December 19, 1968.)

U.S. Department of Health, Education and Welfare. Office of Education. *The Education of National Minorities in Communist China*, by C. T. Hu. (OE 14146.) Washington: GPO, March 1970.

U.S. Department of State. Bureau of Public Affairs. Office of Media Services. *Background Notes: Communist China*. (Department of State Publication No. 7751.) Washington: GPO, November 1968.

——. *Issues*. (Department of State Publication No. 8499, East Asian and Pacific Series 173.) Washington: GPO, December 1969.

U.S. Department of the Army. Office of the Deputy Chief of Staff for Military Operations. *Communist China: A Bibliographic Survey*. Washington: GPO, 1971.

"U.S. Team Invited to Peking," *Washington Post*, April 18, 1971, 1.

Usher in the Great 1970s. Peking: Foreign Languages Press, 1970.

Van der Ploeg, Paule. "Liberée de ses chaines, la femme chinoise doit se cacher pour aimer," *Jeune Afrique* [Paris], No. 296, September 11, 1966.

Van der Valk, M. H. *Conservatism in Modern Chinese Family Law*. Leiden: Brill, 1956.

Vogel, Ezra F. *Canton Under Communism: Programs and Politics in a Provincial Capital, 1949–1968*. Cambridge: Harvard University Press, 1969.

——. "China's New Society," *Diplomat*, XVII, No. 196, September 1966, 76–88.

——. "Communist Chinese Society," *Asia*, No. 11, Spring 1968, 1–29.

——. "From Friendship to Comradeship: The Change in Personal Relations in Communist China," *China Quarterly* [London], No. 21, January–March 1965, 46–60.

——. "From Revolutionary to Semi-Bureaucrat: The 'Regularisation' of Cadres," *China Quarterly* [London], No. 29, January–March 1967, 36–60.

Vreeland, Herbert Harold, III. *Mongol Community and Kinship Structure*. New Haven: Human Relations Area Files Press, 1957.

Waller, Derek J. "Elite Recruitment and Societal Change: The Eighth Central Committee of the Chinese Communist Party, 1958." [Paper presented at the Symposium on the History of the Chinese Communist Movement (1921–1971).] Storrs: University of Connecticut, March 1971 (mimeo.).

Wang, Gung-wu. *A Short History of the Nanyang Chinese*. (Background to Malay Series, No. 13.) Singapore: Eastern Universities Press, 1959.

Wang, Shu-tang. *China: Land of Many Nationalities*. Peking: Foreign Languages Press, 1955.

Webster, Norman. "China's Schools: Practical—and Political," *Washington Post*, July 8, 1971, F1, F5.

_____. "Remolded Tsinghua University: Growing Something Useful," *Washington Post*, July 8, 1971, F4.

Welch, Holmes. "Buddhism Since the Cultural Revolution," *China Quarterly* [London], No. 40, October–December 1969, 127–136.

_____. "Facades of Religion in China," *Asian Survey*, X, No. 7, July 1970, 614–626.

"What They Saw—And Didn't See," *Time*, May 3, 1971, 27.

Wheelwright, Edward L., and McFarlane, Bruce. *The Chinese Road to Socialism: Economics of the Cultural Revolution*. New York: Monthly Review Press, 1970.

"White Russian Go," *Far Eastern Economic Review* [Hong Kong], XLIV, No. 6, May 7, 1964, 281–282.

Whitson, William W. *Organizational Perspectives and Decision Making in the Chinese Communist High Command*. (Rand Paper P–4593.) Santa Monica: Rand Corporation, March 1971.

Wilford, John Noble. "New China Clings to Ancient Medical Practices," *New York Times*, January 24, 1967.

Wilson, Dick. *Anatomy of China*. New York: Weybright and Talley, 1968.

World Communications: Press, Radio, Television, Film. (4th ed.) New York: United Nations Educational, Scientific and Cultural Organization, 1964.

Wu, Yuan-li. *The Economic Potential of Communist China*. Menlo Park: Stanford Research Institute, 1964.

Wu, Yuan-li, and Sheeks, Robert B. *The Organization and Support of Scientific Research and Development in Mainland China*. New York: Praeger, 1970.

Wylie, Margaret. *Children of China*. Hong Kong: Dragonfly Books, 1962.

Yang, Ch'ing-K'un. *Chinese Communist Society: The Family and the Village*. Cambridge: Massachusetts Institute of Technology Press, 1965.

_____. *Religion in Chinese Society: A Study of Contemporary Social Functions of Religion and Some of Their Historical Factors*. Berkeley: University of California Press, 1967.

"Youth and Party Leadership (China)," *Radio Free Europe Research: Communist Area*, January 20, 1971, 1–5.

"Youth to the Land," *China News Analysis* [Hong Kong], No. 521, June 19, 1964.

(Various issues of the following periodicals were also used in the preparation of this section: *China Quarterly* [London], January 1967–

March 1971; *China Reconstructs* [Peking], January–July 1971; *Chinese Literature* [Peking], No. 12, December 1970; *Current Scene: Developments in Mainland China* [Hong Kong], January 1968–April 1971; *Far Eastern Economic Review* [Hong Kong], January 1967–April 1971; *Newsweek*, November 1970–June 1, 1971; *New York Times*, November 1970–May 1971; and *Washington Post*, November 1970–June 1, 1971.)

Section II. Political

Abramowitz, Morton. *Moving the Glacier: The Two Koreas and the Powers*. (Adelphi Series, No. 80). London: International Institute for Strategic Studies, 1971.

"Administration: The Soldiers, the State, and the Rebels," *China News Analysis* [Hong Kong], No. 822, November 20, 1970, 1-7.

Ajia Chosakai (ed.). *Chugoku Soran, 1971* (Survey of China, 1971). Tokyo: Ajia Chosakai, 1971.

Ajia Seikei Gakkai. *Chugoku Seiji Keizai Soran, 1968* (General Survey of Chinese Politics and Economy). Tokyo: Minshushugi Kenkyukoi, 1968.

Bailey, Sydney D. "China and the United Nations," *World Today* [London], XXXII, No. 9, September 1971, 365-372.

Barnett, A. Doak. *Cadres, Bureaucracy, and Political Power in Communist China*. New York: Columbia University Press, 1967.

_____. *China After Mao*. Princeton: Princeton University Press, 1967.

_____. "China and U.S. Policy: A Time of Transition," *Current Scene: Developments in Mainland China* [Hong Kong], VIII, No. 10, May 15, 1970, 1-7.

_____. *Communist China and Asia: Challenge to American Policy*. New York: Vintage Books, 1961.

_____. *Communist China: The Early Years, 1949-1955*. New York: Praeger, 1964.

_____. "Mechanism for Party Control in the Government Bureaucracy in China," *Asian Survey*, VI, No. 12, December 1966, 659-674.

_____. *A New U.S. Policy Toward China*. Washington: Brookings Institution, 1971.

_____. "A Nuclear China and U.S. Arms Policy," *Foreign Affairs*, XXXXVIII, No. 3, April 1970, 427-442.

Barnett, A. Doak (ed.). *Chinese Communist Politics in Action*. Seattle: University of Washington Press, 1969.

Barnett, Robert W. "After Ping-Pong, What?: For Taiwan Final Return to Mainland," *Washington Post*, April 25, 1971, B1-B2.

Baum, Richard. "China: Year of the Mangoes," *Asian Survey*, IX, No. 1, January 1969, 1-17.

Baum, Richard, and Teiwes, Frederick C. *Ssu-Ch'ing: The Socialist Education Movement of 1962-1966*. Berkeley: University of California, Center for Chinese Studies, 1968.

Ben-Dak, Joseph D. "China in the Arab World," *Current History*, LIX, No. 349, September 1970, 147–152, 174.

Bennett, Gordon A. "Political Labels and Popular Tension," *Current Scene: Developments in Mainland China* [Hong Kong], VII, No. 4, February 26, 1969, 1–16.

Berger, Vergil. "Chou Sees 'Strong' China in 1985," *Washington Post*, October 1, 1965, A10.

Black, Cyril (ed.). *Communism and Revolution*. Princeton: Princeton University Press, 1964.

Bloomfield, Lincoln P. *The United Nations and U.S. Foreign Policy: A New Look at the National Interest.* (Rev. ed.) Boston: Little, Brown, 1970.

Blum, Robert. *The United States and China in World Affairs.* New York: McGraw-Hill, 1966.

Bobrow, David B. "Liberation Wars, National Environments, and American Decision-Making." Pages 311–332 in Tang Tsou (ed.), *China in Crisis*, II. Chicago: University of Chicago Press, 1968.

Boorman, Howard L. "Sources of Chinese Communist Conduct," *Virginia Quarterly Review*, XLII, No. 4, Autumn 1966, 512–526.

Bowie, Robert R., and Fairbank, John King (eds.) *Communist China, 1955–1959: Policy Documents with Analysis.* Cambridge: Harvard University Press, 1962.

Boyd, R. G. *Communist China's Foreign Policy.* New York: Praeger, 1962.

Bridgham, Philip. "Mao's Cultural Revolution in 1967: The Struggle to Seize Power," *China Quarterly* [London], No. 34, April–June 1968, 6–37.

_____. "Mao's 'Cultural Revolution': Origin and Development," *China Quarterly* [London], No. 29, January–March 1967, 1–35.

_____. "Mao's Cultural Revolution: The Struggle to Consolidate Power," *China Quarterly* [London], No. 41, January-March 1970, 1–25.

Broman, Barry M. "Tatzepao: Medium of Conflict in China's Cultural Revolution," *Journalism Quarterly*, Spring 1969, 100–104, 127.

Buchan, Alastair (ed.). *China and the Peace of Asia.* New York: Praeger, 1965.

Bueler, William M. "Taiwan: A Problem of International Law or Politics?", *World Today* [London], XXVII, No. 6, June 1971, 256–266.

Bull, Hedley. "The New Balance of Power in Asia and the Pacific," *Foreign Affairs*, XLIX, No. 4, July 1971, 669–681.

Burton, Barry. "The Cultural Revolution's Ultra-Left Conspiracy: The 'May 16 Group'," *Asian Survey*, XI, No. 11, November 1971, 1029–1053.

"Cardinal Points in Foreign Policy," *China News Analysis* [Hong Kong], No. 811, August 14, 1970, 1–7.

Chai, Winberg. "China and the United Nations: Problems of Representation and Alternatives," *Asian Survey*, X, No. 5, May 1970, 397–409.

Chang, Chih-i, and Moseley, George. *The Party and the National Question in China*. Cambridge: Massachusetts Institute of Technology Press, 1966.

"Changes in Chinese Society, 1949–1969," *China News Analysis* [Hong Kong], No. 774, September 19, 1969, 1–7.

Chang, Parris H. "China in Flux: The Second Decade of Maoist Rule," *Problems of Communism*, XVIII, November–December 1969, 1–11.

_____. "Research Notes on the Changing Loci of Decision in The CCP," *China Quarterly* [London], No. 44, October–December 1970, 169–194.

Charles, David A. "The Dismissal of Marshal P'eng Te-huai," *China Quarterly* [London], No. 8, October–December 1961, 63–76.

Chassin, Lionel Max. *The Communist Conquest of China*. Cambridge: Harvard University Press, 1965.

Cheng, Chu-yuan. "The Effects of the Cultural Revolution on China's Machine-Building Industry," *Current Scene: Developments in Mainland China* [Hong Kong], VIII, No. 1, January 1, 1970, 1–13.

Cheng, J. Chester (ed.). *The Politics of the Chinese Red Army: A Translation of the Bulletin of Activities of the People's Liberation Army*. Palo Alto: Stanford University Press, 1966.

Cheng, Peter. "Liu Shao-ch'i and the Cultural Revolution," *Asian Survey*, XI, No. 10, October 1971, 943–957.

Ch'en, Jerome. *Mao and the Chinese Revolution*. New York: Oxford University Press, 1965.

Chen, Lung-chu, and Lasswell, Harold D. *Formosa, China, and the United Nations: Formosa in the World Community*. New York: St. Martin's Press, 1967.

Chien, Yu-shen. *China's Fading Revolution: Army Dissent and Military Divisions, 1967–1968*. Hong Kong: Center of Contemporary Chinese Studies, 1969.

China After the Cultural Revolution. (Vintage Book Series.) New York: Random House, 1969.

"China and the World," *China News Analysis* [Hong Kong], No. 820, November 6, 1970, 1–7.

"China (is, is not) an Aggressive Power," *New York Times Magazine*, March 13, 1966, 28–29, 88–92.

"China, 1971," *Far Eastern Economic Review* [Hong Kong], LXXIV, No. 40, October 2, 1971, 19–44.

"China's New Diplomacy, a Symposium (I)," *Problems of Communism*, XX, November–December 1971, 1–32.

Chinese Communist Party. Central Committee. *Circular of the Central Committee of the Chinese Communist Party, May 16, 1966.* Peking: Foreign Languages Press, 1967.

Chi, Wen-shun. "The Great Proletarian Cultural Revolution in Ideological Perspective," *Asian Survey*, IX, No. 8, August 1969, 563–579.

Chow, Tse-tung. *The May Fourth Movement.* Boston: Harvard University Press, 1966.

Chugoku Kenkyujo (Chinese Research Institute). *Shin Chugoku Nenkan, 1970* (New China Yearbook, 1970). Tokyo: Taishukan Shoten, 1970.

"Close Up of Red China: Now a Real Leap Forward," *U.S. News & World Report*, LXX, No. 7, February 15, 1971, 68–70.

Clubb, O. Edmund. "China and the United States: Beyond Ping-Pong," *Current History*, LXI, No. 361, September 1971, 129–134, 180.

_____. "China and the United States: Collision Course?" *Current History*, LIX, No. 349, September 1970, 153–158, 179.

_____. *Communism in China as Reported from Hankow in 1932.* New York: Columbia University Press, 1968.

Cohen, Arthur A. *The Communism of Mao Tse-tung.* Chicago: University of Chicago Press, 1964.

_____. "How Original is 'Maoism'?" *Problems of Communism*, X, No. 6, November–December 1961, 34–42.

Cohen, Jerome Alan. "Recognizing China," *Foreign Affairs*, L, No. 1, October 1971, 30–43.

Cohen, Jerome Alan (ed.). *The Dynamics of China's Foreign Relations.* Cambridge: Harvard University Press, 1970.

"Commemorate the Fiftieth Anniversary of the Communist Party of China," *People's Daily, Red Flag, and Liberation Army Daily*, July 1, 1971.

Communist China, 1967. (Communist China Problem Research Series, EC41.) Hong Kong: Union Research Institute, 1968.

Communist China, 1968. (Communist China Problem Research Series, EC47.) Hong Kong: Union Research Institute, 1969.

Communist China, 1969. (Communist China Problem Research Series, EC48.) Hong Kong: Union Research Institute, 1970.

Congressional Quarterly Service. *China and U.S. Far East Policy, 1945–1966.* Washington: Congressional Quarterly Service, 1967.

Creel, H. G. *Chinese Thought from Confucius to Mao Tse-tung.* Chicago: University of Chicago Press, 1953.

Croizier, Ralph C. *China's Cultural Legacy and Communism.* (Praeger Library of Chinese Affairs Series.) New York: Praeger, 1970.

"Disarmament: From the Barrel of a Gun? Peking's Attitudes Towards Nuclear Weapons Control," *Current Scene: Developments in Mainland China* [Hong Kong], III, No. 16, April 1, 1965, 1–12.

Doolin, Dennis J. *Territorial Claims in the Sino-Soviet Conflict: Documents and Analysis.* (Hoover Institution Studies, No. 7.) Palo Alto: Hoover Institution on War, Revolution, and Peace, 1965.

Doolin, Dennis J., and Golas, Peter J. "On Contradiction in the Light of Mao Tse-tung's Essay on 'Dialectical Materialism'," *China Quarterly* [London], No. 19, July–September 1964, 38–46.

Doolin, Dennis J., and North, Robert C. *The Chinese People's Republic.* Palo Alto: Hoover Institution on War, Revolution, and Peace, 1966.

Dorrill, William F. *Power, Policy, and Ideology in the Making of China's "Cultural Revolution".* (RM 5731-PR.) Santa Monica: Rand Corporation, 1968.

_____. "Transfer of Legitimacy in the Chinese Communist Party: Origins of the Maoist Myth," *China Quarterly* [London], No. 36, October–December 1968, 45–60.

"The Draft Constitution: Via Taiwan," *China News Analysis* [Hong Kong], No. 823, December 4, 1970, 1–7.

Durdin, Tillman. "Army Aides Gain in Chinese Shifts," *New York Times*, August 29, 1971, 18.

_____. "Chinese Red Complete Rebuilding of Party at Provincial Level," *New York Times*, August 26, 1971, 5.

_____. "The New Face of Maoist China," *Problems of Communism*, XX, No. 5, September–October 1971, 1–13.

Dutt, Gargi. "Peking, the Indian Communists Movement and International Communism, 1962–1970," *Asian Survey*, XI, No. 10, October 1971, 984–991.

Dutt, V. P. *China and the World: An Analysis of Communist China's Foreign Policy.* New York: Praeger, 1966.

Eastman, Lloyd. "Mao, Marx, and the Future Society," *Problems of Communism*, XVIII, May–June 1969, 21–26.

Ebon, Martin. *Lin Piao: The Life and Writings of China's New Ruler.* New York: Stein and Day, 1970.

Eckstein, Alexander (ed.). *China Trade Prospects and U.S. Policy.* (Praeger Library of Chinese Affairs Series.) New York: Praeger, 1971.

Editor and Publisher International Yearbook, 1971. New York: Editor and Publisher, 1971.

Elegant, Robert S. "China's Next Phase," *Foreign Affairs*, XLVI, No. 1, October 1967, 137–150.

Europa Yearbook, 1970, II: Africa, the Americas, Asia, Australasia. London: Europa Publications, 1970.

Fairbank, John King. "The Chinese World Order," *Encounter* [London], XXVII, No. 6, December 1966, 14–20.

_____. "The People's Middle Kingdom," *Foreign Affairs*, XLIIII, No. 4, July 1966, 574–586.

_____. *The United States and China.* (3d ed.) Cambridge: Harvard University Press, 1971.

The Far East and Australasia, 1971: A Survey and Directory of Asia and the Pacific. London: Europa Publications, 1971.

Fessler, Loren. "The Long March of Lin Piao," *New York Times Magazine,* September 10, 1967, 64–65, 125–140.

"Fiftieth Anniversary of the Chinese Communist Party," *Trends and Highlights* [Bangkok], August 1, 1971, 32–36.

Fitzgerald, C. P. *The Chinese View of Their Place in the World.* London: Oxford University Press, 1967.

Fitzgerald, Stephen. "Overseas Chinese Affairs and the Cultural Revolution," *China Quarterly* [London], No. 40, October–December 1969, 103–126.

Floyd, David. *Mao Against Khrushchev.* New York: Praeger, 1964.

Freedman, Robert Owen. *Economic Warfare in the Communist Bloc: A Study of Soviet Economic Pressure Against Yugoslavia, Albania, and Communist China.* New York: Praeger, 1970.

Frolic, B. Michael. "A Visit to Peking University—What the Cultural Revolution Was All About," *New York Times Magazine,* October 24, 1971, 29, 115–123, 128–129.

Funnell, Victor C. "Bureaucracy and the Chinese Communist Party," *Current Scene: Developments in Mainland China* [Hong Kong], IX, No. 5, May 7, 1971, 1–14.

_____. "The New Revolution, IV: Social Stratification," *Problems of Communism,* XVII, March–April 1968, 14–20.

Garthoff, Raymond L. "Sino-Soviet Military Relations," *Annals of the American Academy of Political and Social Science,* CCCXLIX, September 1963, 81–93.

Gasster, Michael. *Chinese Radicalism and the Intelligentsia.* Seattle: University of Washington Press, 1969.

Gayn, Mark. "China Convulsed," *Foreign Affairs,* XLV, No. 2, January 1967, 246–259.

_____. "China Today: An Egalitarian Poverty," *New York Times,* June 7, 1965.

_____. "Red China Today: Art an Ideological Tool," *New York Times,* June 11, 1965.

_____. "Red China Today: Nation Obsessed by Industrialization," *New York Times,* June 9, 1965.

_____. "Red China Today: Old Men in Power Bar Younger Chiefs," *New York Times,* June 8, 1965.

_____. "Red China Today: World Outlook Starts with Belief That Tomorrow Belongs to Peking," *New York Times,* June 12, 1965.

Gelber, Harry G. "Nuclear Weapons in Chinese Strategy," *Problems of Communism,* XX, November–December 1971, 33–44.

_____. "Peking, Washington and the Pacific Balance of Power," *Pacific Community,* III, No. 1, October 1971, 53–67.

————. "The Sino-Soviet Relationship and the United States," *Orbis*, XV, No. 1, Spring 1971, 118–133.

————. "Strategic Arms Limitations and the Sino-Soviet Relationship," *Asian Survey*, X, No. 4, April 1970, 265–289.

George, Alexander L. *The Chinese Communist Army in Action: The Korean War and Its Aftermath.* New York: Columbia University Press, 1967.

Ginsburg, Norton. "On the Chinese Perception of a World Order." Pages 73–91 in Tang Tsou (ed.), *China in Crisis*, II. Chicago: University of Chicago Press, 1968.

Ginsburgs, George, and Stahnke, Arthur. "Communist China's Trade Relations with Latin America," *Asian Survey*, X, No. 9, September 1970, 803–819.

Gittings, John. "The PLA—in Trouble or on Top—," *Far Eastern Economic Review* [Hong Kong], LVIII, No. 4, July 28, 1966, 143–148.

————. *The Role of the Chinese Army.* London: Oxford University Press, 1967.

————. *Survey of the Sino-Soviet Dispute: A Commentary and Extracts from Recent Polemics.* New York: Oxford University Press, 1968.

Goldman, Marshall I. *Soviet Foreign Aid.* New York: Praeger, 1967.

Goldman, Rene. "Mao, Maoism and Mao-ology: Review Article," *Pacific Affairs* [Vancouver], XLI, No. 4, Winter 1968–1969, 560–574.

Gray, Jack, and Cavendish, Pat. *Chinese Communism in Crisis.* New York: Praeger, 1968.

Gray, Jack (ed.). *Modern China's Search for a Political Forum.* London: Oxford University Press, 1969.

Greene, Fred. *U.S. Policy and the Security of Asia.* New York: McGraw-Hill, 1968.

Green, Marcus. "The National People's Congress," *China Quarterly* [London], No. 17, January–March 1964, 241–250.

Griffith, Samuel B. *Peking and People's Wars.* New York: Praeger, 1966.

Grossman, Bernard. "International Economic Relations of the People's Republic of China," *Asian Survey*, X, No. 9, September 1970, 789–802.

Gurtov, Melvin. "The Foreign Ministry and Foreign Affairs in the Chinese Cultural Revolution." Pages 313–366 in Thomas W. Robinson (ed.), *The Cultural Revolution in China.* Berkeley: University of California Press, 1971.

Halperin, Morton H. "Chinese Attitudes Toward the Use and Control of Nuclear Weapons." (With comments by Vincent D. Taylor.) Pages 135–160 in Tang Tsou (ed.), *China in Crisis*, II. Chicago: University of Chicago Press, 1968.

Halperin, Morton H. (ed.) *Sino-Soviet Relations and Arms Control*. Cambridge: Massachusetts Institute of Technology Press, 1967.

Halpern, A. M. "China and Japan" (With comments by Marius B. Jansen.) Pages 441–463 in Tang Tsou (ed.), *China in Crisis*, II. Chicago: University of Chicago Press, 1968.

Halpern, A. M. (ed.) *Policies Toward China: Views from Six Continents*. New York: McGraw-Hill, 1966.

Han Suyin. *China in the Year 2001*. New York: Basic Books, 1967.

_____. "Family Planning in China," *Japan Quarterly* [Tokyo], XVII, No. 4, October–December 1970, 433–442.

Harding, Harry. "China: Toward Revolutionary Pragmatism," *Asian Survey*, XI, No. 1, January 1971, 51–68.

Harding, Harry, and Gurtov, Melvin. *The Purge of Lo Jui-ch'ing: The Politics of Chinese Strategic Planning*. (R–548–PR.) Santa Monica: Rand Corporation, February 1971.

Hilsman, Roger. "Two American Counterstrategies to Guerrilla Warfare: The Case of Vietnam." (With comments by Morton A. Kaplan.) Pages 269–309 in Tang Tsou (ed.), *China in Crisis*, II. Chicago: University of Chicago Press, 1968.

Hinton, Harold C. "China and Vietnam." (With comments by David Mozingo and George McTurnan Kahin.) Pages 201–236 in Tang Tsou (ed.), *China in Crisis*, II. Chicago: University of Chicago Press, 1968.

_____. *China's Turbulent Quest*. London: Macmillan, 1970.

_____. *Communist China: Domestic Political Scene*. (Paper P–527.) Arlington: Institute for Defense Analyses, August 1969.

_____. *Communist China in World Politics*. Boston: Houghton Mifflin, 1966.

_____. "Conflict on the Ussuri: A Clash of Nationalisms," *Problems of Communism*, XX, Nos. 1–2, January–April 1971, 45–61.

_____. "The 'Democratic Parties': End of an Experiment," *Problems of Communism*, VII, No. 3, May–June 1958, 39–46.

_____. "Sino-Soviet Relations in the Brezhnev Era," *Current History*, LXI, No. 361, September 1971, 135–141, 181.

_____. *Soviet Pressures as a Factor in Chinese Policy Making*. Palo Alto: Hoover Institution on War, Revolution, and Peace, 1971.

Ho, P'ing-ti, and Tsou, Tang (eds.). *China in Crisis*, I and II. Chicago: University of Chicago Press, 1968.

Hottelet, Richard C. "What New Role for the People's Republic of China?", *Saturday Review*, September 18, 1971, 27–30.

Howse, Hugh. "The Use of Radio in China," *China Quarterly* [London], April–June 1960, 59–68.

"How Things Stand Now: Political Situation," *China News Analysis* [Hong Kong], No. 833, March 5, 1971, 1–7.

Hsiao, Gene T. "The Background and Development of 'The Proletarian Cultural Revolution'," *Asian Survey*, VII, No. 6, June 1967, 389–404.

Hsieh, Alice Langley. "China's Nuclear-Missile Programme: Regional or Intercontinental?" *China Quarterly* [London], No. 45, January–March 1971, 85–99.

――――. "China's Secret Military Papers: Military Doctrine and Strategy," *China Quarterly* [London], No. 18, April–June 1964, 79–99.

――――. *Communist China: Evolving Military Strategy and Doctrine.* (Paper P-646.) Arlington: Institute for Defense Analyses, June 1970.

――――. *Communist China's Strategy in the Nuclear Era.* Englewood Cliffs: Prentice-Hall, 1962.

Hsiung, James Chieh. *Ideology and Practice.* New York: Praeger, 1970.

Hsu, Immanuel C. Y. *The Rise of Modern China.* New York: Oxford University Press, 1970.

Hsu, Kai-yu. *Chou En-lai: China's Gray Eminence.* New York: Doubleday, 1968.

Huck, Arthur. *The Security of China: Chinese Approaches to Problems of War and Strategy.* New York: Columbia University Press, for the Institute for Strategic Studies, 1970.

Hudson, G. F. *Fifty Years of Communism.* New York: Basic Books, 1968.

Hunter, Neale. *Shanghai Journal: An Eyewitness Account of the Cultural Revolution.* New York: Praeger, 1969.

Hyer, Paul. "The Re-Evaluation of Chinggis Khan: Its Role in the Sino-Soviet Dispute," *Asian Survey*, VI, No. 12, December 1966, 696–705.

Issacs, Harold R. *The Tragedy of the Chinese Revolution.* (Rev. ed.) Stanford: Stanford University Press, 1961.

Israel, John. "The Red Guards in Historical Perspective: Continuity and Change in the Chinese Youth Movement," *China Quarterly* [London], No. 30, April–June 1967, 1–32.

Jan, George P. "Japan's Trade with Communist China," *Asian Survey*, IX, No. 12, December 1969, 900–918.

――――. "Radio Propaganda in Chinese Villages," *Asian Survey*, VII, No. 5, May 1967, 305–315.

Joffe, Ellis. "The Chinese Army in the Cultural Revolution: The Politics of Intervention," *Current Scene: Developments in Mainland China* [Hong Kong], VIII, No. 18, December 7, 1970, 1–24.

――――. "The Chinese Army Under Lin Piao: Prelude to Political Intervention." Pages 343–374 in John M. H. Lindbeck (ed.), *China: Management of a Revolutionary Society.* Seattle: University of Washington Press, 1971.

Johnson, Cecil. *Communist China and Latin America, 1959–1967.* New York: Columbia University Press, 1970.

Johnson, Chalmers A. "Building a Communist Nation in China." Pages 47–81 in Robert A. Scalapino (ed.), *The Communist Revolution in Asia: Tactics, Goals and Achievements*. Englewood Cliffs: Prentice-Hall, 1965.

_____. "The Changing Nature and Focus of Authority in Communist China." Pages 34–76 in John M. H. Lindbeck (ed.), *China: Management of a Revolutionary Society*. Seattle: University of Washington Press, 1971.

_____. "China: The Cultural Revolution in Structural Perspective," *Asian Survey*, VIII, No. 1, January 1968, 1–15.

_____. "Lin Piao's Army and Its Role in Chinese Society," *Current Scene: Developments in Mainland China* [Hong Kong], IV, No. 13, July 1, 1966.

_____. *Peasant Nationalism and Communist Power: The Emergence of Revolutionary China, 1937–1945*. Stanford: Stanford University Press, 1962.

Johnston, Douglas M., and Chiu, Hungdah (eds.). *Agreements of the People's Republic of China, 1949–1967: A Calendar*. Cambridge: Harvard University Press, 1968.

Joint Economic Committee of the United States Congress. *An Economic Profile of Mainland China*. (Praeger Special Studies in International Economics and Development Series.) New York: Praeger, for the Joint Economic Committee of the U.S. Congress, 1968.

Kalicki, J. H. "Sino-American Relations After Cambodia," *World Today* [London], XXVI, No. 9, September 1970, 383–393.

Karnow, Stanley S. "A Confused Army Moving into China's Vacuum," *Washington Post*, July 2, 1967, B3.

_____. "Peking Puzzle: Beneath a Stable Surface Lie the Seeds of Upheaval," *Washington Post*, October 3, 1971, A3.

_____. "Terror Replaces Policy in China," *Washington Post*, September 11, 1966, E2.

_____. "U.S.-Trained Intellectuals Advise China," *Washington Post*, February 27, 1966, E5.

Keesing's Research Report. *The Cultural Revolution in China: Its Origins and Course*. New York: Charles Scribner's, 1967.

_____. *The Sino-Soviet Dispute*. New York: Charles Scribner's, 1969.

Khalili, Joseph E. "Sino-Arab Relations," *Asian Survey*, VIII, No. 8, August 1968, 678–690.

King, Vincent S. *Propaganda Campaigns in Communist China*. Cambridge: Center for International Studies, Massachusetts Institute of Technology, 1966.

Klein, Donald W. "The Management of Foreign Affairs in Communist China." Pages 305–342 in John M. H. Lindbeck (ed.),

China: Management of a Revolutionary Society, Seattle: University of Washington Press, 1971.

――――. "The State Council and the Cultural Revolution," *China Quarterly* [London], No. 35, July–September 1968, 78–95.

LaDany, L. "China: Period of Suspense," *Foreign Affairs*, XLVIII, No. 4, July 1970, 700–711.

――――. "Mao's China: The Decline of a Dynasty," *Foreign Affairs*, XLV, No. 4, July 1967, 610–623.

LaFeber, Walter. "China and Japan: Different Beds, Different Dreams," *Current History*, LIX, No. 349, September 1970, 142–146, 178–179.

Lall, Arthur. *How Communist China Negotiates*. New York: Columbia University Press, 1968.

Langer, Paul F. "China and Japan," *Current History*, XLV, No. 265, September 1963, 144–150, 181.

Lee, Chae-Jin. "Communist China and the Geneva Conference on Laos: A Reappraisal," *Asian Survey*, IX, No. 7, July 1969, 522–539.

Lescaze, Lee. "China Plans to 'Publish More and Better'," *Washington Post*, September 23, 1971, E1, E6.

Levenson, Joseph R. "Maoism: The Persistence of the Old," *Problems of Communism*, XV, No. 5, September–October 1966, 20–22.

――――. *Modern China and Its Confucian Past: The Problem of Intellectual Continuity*. New York: Doubleday, 1964.

Lewis, John Wilson. *Leadership in Communist China*. Ithaca: Cornell University Press, 1963.

――――. *Major Doctrine of Communist China*. New York: Norton, 1964.

Lewis, John Wilson (ed.). *Party Leadership and Revolutionary Power in China*. London: Cambridge University Press, 1970.

"Life in the Countryside, I: The Administration," *China News Analysis* [Hong Kong], No. 818, October 16, 1970, 1–7.

Lifton, Robert Jay. *Revolutionary Immortality: Mao Tse-tung and the Chinese Cultural Revolution*. New York: Vintage Books, 1968.

Lindsay, Michael. "Contradiction in a Totalitarian Society," *China Quarterly* [London], No. 39, July–September 1969, 30–40.

――――. *Is Peaceful Co-Existence Possible?* East Lansing: Michigan State University Press, 1960.

Lisann, Maury. "Moscow and the Chinese Power Struggle," *Problems of Communism*, XVIII, November–December 1969, 32–41.

Liu, Alan Ping-lin. *Book Publishing in Communist China*. Cambridge: Center for International Studies, Massachusetts Institute of Technology, 1965.

――――. *Film Industry in Communist China*. Cambridge: Center for International Studies, Massachusetts Institute of Technology, 1965.

――――. "Growth and Modernizing Function of Rural Radio in Communist China," *Journalism Quarterly*, XLI, No. 4, Autumn 1964.

———. "Mass Communications and Media in China's Cultural Revolution," *Journalism Quarterly*, Summer 1969, 314–319.

———. *Radio Broadcasting in Communist China*. Cambridge: Center for International Studies, Massachusetts Institute of Technology, 1964.

Low, Donald M. *The Function of China in Marx, Lenin and Mao*. Berkeley: University of California Press, 1968.

Lowenthal, Richard. "Communist China's Foreign Policy." (With comments by Roderick MacFarquhar.) Pages 1–21 in Tang Tsou (ed.), *China in Crisis*, II. Chicago: University of Chicago Press, 1968.

———. "Russia and China: Controlled Conflict," *Foreign Affairs*, XLIX, No. 3, April 1971, 507–518.

MacDougall, Colina. "The Cultural Revolution and the Communes: Back to 1958?" *Current Scene: Developments in Mainland China* [Hong Kong], VII, No. 7, April 11, 1969, 1–10.

MacFarquhar, Roderick (ed.). *China Under Mao*. Cambridge: Massachusetts Institute of Technology Press, 1966.

McVey, Ruth T. "Indonesia Communism and China." Pages 357–394 in Tang Tsou (ed.), *China in Crisis*, II. Chicago: University of Chicago Press, 1968.

"Mainland China, 1970: Old Problems and New Solutions," *Current Scene: Developments in Mainland China* [Hong Kong], IX, No. 2, February 7, 1971, 1–5.

"Marxism," *China News Analysis* [Hong Kong], No. 812, August 21, 1970, 1–7.

"Marxism—Ready to Die—Loose Discipline," *China News Analysis* [Hong Kong], No. 768, August 8, 1969, 1–7.

Maxwell, Neville. *India's China War*. New York: Pantheon, 1971.

———. "The Threat from China," *International Affairs* [London], XLVII, No. 1, January 1971, 31–44.

Mehnert, Klaus. "Mao and Maoism: Some Soviet Views," *Current Scene: Developments in Mainland China* [Hong Kong], VIII, No. 15, September 1, 1970.

Meisner, Maurice. "Leninism and Maoism: Some Populist Perspectives on Marxism-Leninism in China," *China Quarterly* [London], No. 45, January–March 1971, 2–36.

———. *Li Ta-chao and Origins of Chinese Marxism*. Cambridge: Harvard University Press, 1967.

Melby, John F. "The Origins of the Cold War in China," *Pacific Affairs* [Vancouver], XLI, No. 1, Spring 1968, 19–33.

Meley, John. *The Mandate of Heaven: Record of a Civil War, 1945–1949*. Toronto: University of Toronto Press, 1969.

Michael, Franz. "Is China Expansionist? A Design for Aggression," *Problems of Communism*, XX, Nos. 1–2, January–April 1971, 62–65.

"Military Imprint on the Nation," *China News Analysis* [Hong Kong], No. 732, November 8, 1968, 1-7.

Moorsteen, Richard, and Abramowitz, Morton. *Remaking China Policy: U.S.-China Relations and Governmental Decision-Making.* Cambridge: Harvard University Press, 1971.

Moseley, George. *Sino-Soviet Cultural Frontier: The Ili Kazakh Autonomous Chou.* (East Asian Monograph Series, No. 22.) Cambridge: Harvard University Press, 1966.

Mozingo, David P. "China's Policy Toward Indonesia." (With comments by George McTurnan Kahin.) Pages 333-356 in Tang Tsou (ed.), *China in Crisis*, II. Chicago: University of Chicago Press, 1968.

———. "Containment in Asia Reconsidered," *World Politics*, XIX, No. 3, April 1967, 361-377.

Mu, Fu-Sheng. *The Wilting of the 100 Flowers.* New York: Praeger, 1963.

Murphy, Rhoads. "China and the Dominoes," *Asian Survey*, VI, No. 9, September 1966, 510-515.

Myrdal, Jan, and Kessle, Yun. *China: The Revolution Continued.* (Translated from the Revised Swedish Edition by Paul Britten Austin.) New York: Pantheon, 1970.

National Studies on International Organization. *China and the United Nations.* (Report of a Study Group set up by the China Institute of International Affairs.) New York: Manhattan Publishing, for the Carnegie Endowment for International Peace, 1959.

Neuhauser, Charles. "The Chinese Communist Party in the 1960s: Prelude to the Cultural Revolution," *China Quarterly* [London], No. 32, October-December 1967, 3-36.

———. "The Impact of the Cultural Revolution on the Chinese Communist Party Machine," *Asian Survey*, VIII, No. 6, June 1968, 465-488.

"1969 Through Peking's Eyes—A Survey of Chinese Media," *Current Scene: Developments in Mainland China* [Hong Kong], VIII, No. 3, February 1, 1970, 1-10.

Nixon, Richard M. "Asia After Viet Nam," *Foreign Affairs*, XLVI, No. 1, October 1967, 111-125.

North, Robert C. *The Foreign Relations of China.* Belmont, California: Dickenson, 1969.

———. *Moscow and Chinese Communists.* (2d ed.) Stanford: Stanford University Press, 1963.

Ohja, Ishwer C. *Chinese Foreign Policy in an Age of Transition: The Diplomacy of Cultural Despair.* Boston: Beacon Press, 1969.

Oksenberg, Michel C. "China: The Convulsive Society," *Headline Series*, No. 203, December 1970, 3-78.

_____. "Policy Making under Mao Tse-tung, 1949–1968," *Comparative Politics*, III, No. 3, April 1971, 323–360.

_____. "The Strategies of Peking," *Foreign Affairs*, L, No. 1, October 1971, 15–29.

Oksenberg, Michel C.; Bateman, Nancy; and Anderson, James B. *A Bibliography of Secondary English Language Literature on Contemporary Chinese Politics*. New York: East Asian Institute, Columbia University, 1970.

Oksenberg, Michel C., et al. *The Cultural Revolution in Review*. (Michigan Papers in Chinese Studies, No. 2.) Ann Arbor: Center for Chinese Studies, University of Michigan, 1968.

Orleans, Leo A. "Evidence from Chinese Medical Journals on Current Population Policy," *China Quarterly* [London], No. 40, October–December 1969, 137–146.

Palmer, Norman D. "China's Relations with India and Pakistan," *Current History*, LXI, No. 361, September 1971, 148–153.

Pan, Stephen. "Peking Struggle Sharpens," *Christian Science Monitor*, July 30, 1968.

"Peking-Moscow Relations, I: The Precedents," *China News Analysis* [Hong Kong], No. 752, April 11, 1969, 1–7.

"Peking's Radio Diplomacy," *Current Scene: Developments in Mainland China* [Hong Kong], IX, No. 9, September 7, 1971, 16–17.

Pfeffer, Richard M. "The Pursuit of Purity: Mao's Cultural Revolution," *Problems of Communism*, XVIII, No. 6, November–December 1969, 12–25.

Polemic on the General Line of the International Communist Movement. Peking: Foreign Languages Press, 1965.

Pond, Elizabeth. "What's Afoot in Red China?" *Christian Science Monitor*, November 26, 1966.

Poole, Peter Andrews. "Communist China's Red Diplomacy," *Asian Survey*, VI, No. 11, November 1966, 622–629.

Powell, David E. "The New Revolution, IV: Mao and Stalin's Mantle," *Problems of Communism*, XVII, March–April 1968, 21–30.

Powell, Ralph L. "China's Bomb: Exploitation and Reactions," *Foreign Affairs*, XLIII, No. 4, July 1965, 616–625.

_____. "Communist China As a Military Power," *Current History*, XLIX, No. 289, September 1965, 136–141.

_____. "The Increasing Power of Lin Piao and the Party-Soldiers, 1959–1966," *China Quarterly* [London], No. 34, April-June 1968, 38–65.

_____. "The Party, the Government and the Gun," *Asian Survey*, X, No. 6, June 1970, 441–471.

_____. *The Rise of Chinese Military Power*. Princeton: Princeton University Press, 1955.

Program Schedules of Foreign Broadcasting Stations: Communist World. (Revisions 93 through 122.) Washington: Foreign Broadcast Information Service, 1971.

Prybyla, Jan S. "Communist China's Strategy of Economic Development: 1961-1966," *Asian Survey*, VI, No. 10, October 1966, 589-603.

————. "Foreign Aid: The Chinese are Coming," *Current History*, LXI, No. 361, September 1971, 142-147, 181.

————. "The New Revolution, IV: The Economic Cost," *Problems of Communism*, XVII, March-April 1968, 1-13.

Pusey, James R. *Wu Han: Attacking the Present Through the Past*. (Harvard East Asian Monographs, No. 33.) Cambridge: Harvard University Press, 1969.

Pye, Lucian W. "China: Hostility and Authority in Chinese Politics," *Problems of Communism*, XVII, May-June 1968, 10-22.

————. "China in Conflict," *Foreign Affairs*, XLV, No. 2, January 1967, 229-245.

————. "Mass Participation in Communist China: Its Limitations and the Continuity of Culture." Pages 3-33 in John M. H. Lindbeck (ed.), *China: Management of a Revolutionary Society*. Seattle: University of Washington Press, 1971.

————. *The Spirit of Chinese Politics*. Cambridge: Massachusetts Institute of Technology Press, 1968.

Pye, Lucian W. (ed.) *Cases in Comparative Politics: Asia*. Boston: Little, Brown, 1970.

Ra'anam, Uri. "Peking's Foreign Policy 'Debate', 1965-1966." Pages 23-71 in Tang Tsou (ed.), *China in Crisis*, II. Chicago: University of Chicago Press, 1968.

Ramachandran, K. N. "Peking and Indian Communism Since 1965," *Current Scene: Developments in Mainland China* [Hong Kong], VIII, No. 6, March 15, 1970.

Ravenal, Earl C. "Approaching China, Defending Taiwan," *Foreign Affairs*, L, No. 1, October 1971, 44-58.

————. "The Nixon Doctrine and Our Asian Commitments," *Foreign Affairs*, XLIX, No. 2, January 1971, 201-217.

Ray, Dennis. "China After Mao," *International Affairs* [London], XLVII, No. 1, January 1971, 45-62.

Reischauer, Edwin O. "Fateful Triangle: The United States, Japan, and China," *New York Times Magazine*, September 19, 1971, 12-13, 46-47, 55-58.

Rejai, Mostafa. "Maoism: The Need for a Redefinition," *Problems of Communism*, XV, No. 5, September-October 1966, 18-20.

"The Revolutionary Committee and the Party in the Aftermath of the Cultural Revolution," *Current Scene: Developments in Mainland China* [Hong Kong], VIII, No. 8, April 15, 1970, 1-10.

Rhee, T. C. "Sino-Soviet Military Conflict and the Global Balance of Power," *World Today* [London], XXVI, No. 1, January 1970, 29–39.

Roberts, Chalmers M. "After Ping-Pong What? U.S. Awaits Rebounds in U.N., Moscow," *Washington Post*, April 25, 1971, B1–B2.

Robinson, Thomas W. (ed.) *The Cultural Revolution in China*. Berkeley: University of California Press, 1971.

Rue, John E. *Mao Tse-tung in Opposition, 1927–1935*. Stanford: Stanford University Press, 1966.

Saikowski, Charlotte. "Unpredictable China, Wary Soviet Union," *Christian Science Monitor*, April 4, 1969.

Sawhny, R. "China's Control of Tibet and Its Implications for India's Defense," *International Studies* [New Delhi], X, No. 4, April 1969, 486–494.

Scalapino, Robert A. *The Communist Revolution in Asia*. (2d ed.) Englewood Cliffs: Prentice-Hall, 1969.

_____. "Patterns of Asian Communism," *Problems of Communism*, XX, Nos. 1–2, January–April 1971, 2–13.

_____. "The Question of 'Two Chinas'." Pages 109–134 in Tang Tsou (ed.), *China in Crisis*, II. Chicago: University of Chicago Press, 1968.

Schapiro, Leonard. "Maoism: Totalitarian Traditions," *Problems of Communism*, XV, No. 5, September–October 1966, 22–23.

Schram, Stuart R. *Mao Tse-tung*. Middlesex: Penguin Books, 1967.

_____. *The Political Thought of Mao Tse-tung*. New York: Praeger, 1963.

_____. *The Political Thought of Mao Tse-tung*. (Rev. ed.) New York: Praeger, 1969.

_____. *Quotations from Chairman Mao Tse-tung*. New York: Praeger, 1967.

Schulman, Irwin J. "Mao as Prophet," *Current Scene: Developments in Mainland China* [Hong Kong], XIII, No. 13, July 7, 1970, 1–13.

Schurmann, Franz. *Ideology and Organization in Communist China*. Berkeley: University of California Press, 1966.

_____. *Ideology and Organization in Communist China*. (2d ed.) Berkeley: University of California Press, 1968.

_____. "Peking's Recognition of Crisis," *Problems of Communism*, X, No. 5, September–October 1961, 5–14.

Schurmann, Franz, and Schell, Orville (eds.). *The China Reader*. 3 vols. New York: Random House, 1967.

Schwartz, Benjamin I. *Communism and China: Ideology in Flux*. Cambridge: Harvard University Press, 1968.

_____. "Maoism: Stalinism or 'Chineseness'," *Problems of Communism*, XV, No. 5, September–October 1966, 17–18.

_____. "The New Turn in Sino-U.S. Relations: Background and Significance," *Pacific Community* [Tokyo], III, No. 1, October 1971, 19–31.

_____. "On the 'Originality' of Mao Tse-tung," *Foreign Affairs*, XXXIV, No. 1, October 1955, 67–76.

Schwarz, Henry G. *Leadership Patterns in China's Frontier Regions*. (External Research Paper 149.) Washington: Bureau of Intelligence and Research, Department of State, 1964.

Scott, Sir Robert. "China, Russia and the United States," *Foreign Affairs*, XLVIII, No. 2, January 1970, 334–343.

Sen, Chanakya. "Tibet and the Sino-Indian Impasse," *International Studies* [New Delhi], X, No. 4, April 1969, 523–541.

Shaplen, Robert. "A Reporter at Large: The China Watchers," *New Yorker*, February 12, 1966, 41–106.

Simmonds, J. D. *China's World: The Foreign Policy of a Developing State*. New York: Columbia University Press, 1970.

_____. "P'eng Te-huai: A Chronological Re-Examination," *China Quarterly*, [London], No. 37, January–March 1969, 128–138.

Simmons, Robert R. "China's Cautious Relations with North Korea and Indochina," *Asian Survey*, XI, No. 7, July 1971, 629–644.

Simon, Sheldon W. "Some Aspects of China's Asian Policy in the Cultural Revolution and Its Aftermath," *Pacific Affairs* [Vancouver], XLIV, No. 1, Spring 1971, 18–38.

Sims, Stephens A. "The New Role of the Military," *Problems of Communism*, XVIII, November–December 1969, 26–32.

Snow, Edgar. "Aftermath of the Cultural Revolution: Mao Tse-tung— and the Cost of Living," *New Republic*, CLXIV, No. 15 (Issue No. 2937), April 10, 1971, 18–21.

_____. "A Conversation with Mao Tse-tung," *Life*, LXX, No. 16, April 30, 1971, 46–47.

_____. "Interview with Mao," *New Republic*, February 27, 1965, 17–25.

_____. "Mao and the New Mandate," *World Today* [London], XXV, No. 7, July 1969, 289–297.

_____. "Talks with Chou En-lai: The Open Door," *New Republic*, CLXIV, No. 13, March 27, 1971, 20–23.

Solomon, Richard H. "On Activism and Activists: Maoist Conceptions of Motivation and Political Role Linking State to Society," *China Quarterly* [London], No. 39, July–September 1969, 76–114.

_____. "Parochialism and Paradox in Sino-American Relations," *Asian Survey*, VII, No. 12, December 1967, 831–850.

Spitz, Allan. "Maoism and the People's Courts," *Asian Survey*, IX, No. 4, April 1969, 255–264.

Starr, John Bryan. "Conceptual Foundations of Mao Tse-tung's Theory of Continuous Revolution," *Asian Survey*, XI, No. 6, June 1961, 610–628.

Steele, A. T. *The American People and China*. New York: McGraw-Hill, 1966.

Stucki, Lorenz. *Behind the Great Wall.* New York: McGraw-Hill, 1966.

Tao, Jay. "Mao's World Outlook: Vietnam and the Revolution in China," *Asian Survey*, VIII, No. 5, May 1968, 416–432.

Taylor, John J. "The Maoist Revolutionary Model in Asia," *Current Scene: Developments in Mainland China* [Hong Kong], IX, No. 3, March 7, 1971, 1–19.

Teiwes, Frederick C. "Provincial Politics in China: Themes and Variations." Pages 116–189 in John M. H. Lindbeck (ed.), *China: Management of a Revolutionary Society.* Seattle: University of Washington Press, 1971.

"Television in China," *Current Scene: Developments in Mainland China* [Hong Kong], IX, No. 9, September 7, 1971, 18–20.

Terrill, Ross. "Chinese People Curious, Surprised by Nixon Trip," *Washington Post*, July 22, 1971, Section A.

––––––. "Peking Seeking a Tripolar World," *Washington Post*, July 22, 1971, A1, A2.

"A Theoretical Weapon for Making Revolution Under the Dictatorship of the Proletariat: In Commemoration of the Tenth Anniversary of the Publication of Chairman Mao's 'On the Correct Handling of Contradictions Among the People'," *Peking Review* [Peking], June 23, 1967, 27–32.

"The Tortuous History of the Cult of Mao: The East is Red," *China News Analysis* [Hong Kong], No. 743, February 7, 1971, 1–7.

Townsend, James R. *Political Participation in Communist China.* Berkeley: University of California Press, 1967.

Trager, Frank N., and Bordonaro, Robert F. "The Ninth CCP Congress and the World Communist Conference: Their Meaning for Asia," *Orbis*, XIII, No. 3, Fall 1969, 736–762.

Trager, Frank N., and Henderson, William (eds.). *Communist China, 1949–1969: A Twenty-Year Appraisal.* New York: New York University Press, for American-Asian Educational Exchange, 1970.

Treadgold, Donald W. (ed.) *Soviet and Chinese Communism: Similarities and Differences.* Seattle: University of Washington Press, 1967.

Tretiak, Daniel. "The Chinese Cultural Revolution and Foreign Policy," *Current Scene: Developments in Mainland China* [Hong Kong], VIII, No. 7, April 1, 1970.

––––––. *The Chinese Cultural Revolution and Foreign Policy: The Process of Conflict and Current Policy.* (ASG Monograph No. 2.) Waltham: Advanced Studies Group, Westinghouse Electric Corporation, February 1970.

Tsou, Tang. "The Cultural Revolution and the Chinese Political System," *China Quarterly* [London], No. 38, April–June 1969, 63–91.

Tsou, Tang (ed.). *China's Policies in Asia and America's Alternatives.* Chicago: University of Chicago Press, 1968.

Tung, William L. *The Political Institutions of Modern China.* The Hague: Martinus Nijhoff, 1964.

Union Research Institute. *CCP Documents of the Great Proletarian Cultural Revolution, 1966–1967.* Hong Kong: 1968.

_____. *Union Research Service Reports* [Hong Kong], XL, No. 23, September 17, 1965.

_____. *Union Research Service Reports* [Hong Kong], Special No. 2750, 1966.

_____. *Union Research Service Reports* [Hong Kong], XXXI, No. 9, April 30, 1963.

_____. *Union Research Service Reports* [Hong Kong], XXXVII, No. 13, November 13, 1964.

_____. *Who's Who in Communist China.* Hong Kong: 1966.

_____. *Who's Who in Communist China.* Hong Kong: 1969.

_____. *Who's Who in Communist China,* II. Hong Kong: 1970.

U.S. Congress. 86th, 1st Session. Senate. Subcommittee on National Policy Machinery. *National Policy Machinery in Communist China.* Washington: GPO, 1959.

U.S. Congress. 88th, 1st Session. Senate. Subcommittee on National Security and Operations. *Staffing Procedures and Problems in Communist China.* Washington: GPO, 1963.

U.S. Congress. 91st, 1st Session. Senate. Committee on Government Operations. Subcommittee on National Security and International Operations. *Peking's Approach to Negotiation: Selected Writings.* Washington: GPO, 1969.

U.S. Congress. 91st, 2d Session. House of Representatives. Committee on Foreign Affairs. Subcommittee on Asian and Pacific Affairs. *United States-China Relations: A Strategy for the Future.* Washington: GPO, 1970.

U.S. Department of Defense. *Toward a National Security Strategy of Realistic Deterrence: Statement of Secretary of Defense Melvin R. Laird on the Fiscal Year 1972–1976 Defense Program and the 1972 Defense Budget Before the Senate Armed Services Committee, March 15, 1971.* Washington: 1971.

U.S. Department of State. *Fact Book of the Countries of the World.* New York: Crown, 1970.

U.S. Department of the Army. Headquarters. 7th Psychological Operations Group. *Communist Propaganda: Trends and Highlights Analysis, Printed Media,* Issue No. 4–71, August 31, 1971, entire issue.

_____. *Communist Propaganda: Trends and Highlights Analysis, Radio and News Service,* Issue No. 10–71, March 12, 1971, entire issue.

U.S. United States Information Agency. General Far East Files. "Rural Wired Broadcasting Networks," *China Topics*, No. YB368, February 15, 1966.

"The Unspectacular Foreign Policy: Speeding on First Year," *China News Analysis* [Hong Kong], No. 791, February 13, 1970, 1–7.

Van Ness, Peter. "Is China Expansionist? Mao Tse-tung and Revolutionary 'Self-Reliance'," *Problems of Communism*, XX, Nos. 1–2, January–April 1971, 68–74.

_____. *Revolution and Chinese Foreign Policy: Peking's Support for Wars of National Liberation*. Berkeley: University of California Press, 1970.

Van Slyke, Lyman B. *Enemies and Friends: The United Front in China's Communist History*. Stanford: Stanford University Press, 1967.

Vogel, Ezra F. "From Revolutionary to Semi-Bureaucrat: The 'Regularization' of Cadres," *China Quarterly* [London], No. 29, January–March 1967, 36–60.

_____. "Red China: Transition Without a Coup," *Christian Science Monitor*, November 22, 1966.

Walker, Richard L. *China Under Communism: The First Five Years*. New Haven: Yale University Press, 1955.

Webster, Norman. "Propaganda: Thin Red Story Line," *Washington Post*, June 6, 1971, Section B.

_____. "Where a Toothless Chiang was Captured 35 Years Ago," *Washington Post*, September 13, 1971, A20.

Whetten, Lawrence L. "Moscow's Anti-China Pact," *World Today* [London], XXV, No. 9, September 1969, 385–393.

Whiting, Allen S. *China Crosses the Yalu: The Decision to Enter the Korean War*. Stanford: Stanford University Press, 1960.

_____. "Political Dynamics: The Communist Party of China." In Robert E. Ward and Roy C. Macridis (eds.), *Modern Political Systems: Asia*. Englewood Cliffs: Prentice-Hall, 1963.

Wilcox, Wayne. "China's Strategic Alternatives in South Asia." Pages 395–440 in Tang Tsou (ed.), *China in Crisis*, II. Chicago: University of Chicago Press, 1968.

Wittfogel, Karl A. "The Influence of Leninism-Stalinism on China," *Annals*, CCLXXVII, September 1951, 22–34.

Wong, Paul. "Coding and Analysis of Documentary Materials from Communist China," *Asian Survey*, VII, No. 3, March 1967, 198–211.

Wu, Yuan-li. "Economics, Ideology and Cultural Revolution," *Asian Survey*, VIII, No. 3, March 1968, 223–235.

Yahuda, Michael B. "Chinese Foreign Policy After 1963: The Maoist Phases," *China Quarterly* [London], October–December 1968, 93–113.

Young, Kenneth T. *Negotiating with the Chinese Communists*. New York: McGraw-Hill, 1968.

Yu, Frederick T. C. *Mass Persuasion in Communist China*. New York: Praeger, 1964.

_____. "Persuasive Communications During the Cultural Revolution," *Gazette* [Amsterdam], XIV, No. 2, 1970, 73–87; XIV, No. 3, 1970, 137–148.

_____. *The Propaganda Machine in Communist China*. Lackland Air Force Base: Human Resources Research Institute, 1955.

Yu, George T. "China's Failure in Africa," *Asian Survey*, VI, No. 8, August 1966, 461–468.

_____. "Dragon in the Bush: Peking's Presence in Africa," *Asian Survey*, VIII, No. 12, December 1968, 1018–1026.

Zablocki, Clement J. (ed.) *Sino-Soviet Rivalry: Implications for U.S. Policy*. New York: Praeger, 1966.

Zagoria, Donald S. *The Sino-Soviet Conflict, 1956–1961*. Princeton: Princeton University Press, 1962.

_____. "The Strategic Debate in Peking." Pages 237–268 in Tang Tsou (ed.), *China in Crisis*, II. Chicago: University of Chicago Press, 1968.

Zorga, Victor. "Asia: Collective Security," *Survival* [London], XI, No. 8, August 1969, 248–260.

(Various issues of the following periodicals were also used in the preparation of this section: *China News Analysis* [Hong Kong], January 1967 to September 1971; *Current Background* [Hong Kong], January 1967 to September 1971; *Current Scene: Developments in Mainland China* [Hong Kong], January 1967 to September 1971; and *New York Times*, October 26, 1971.)

Section III. Economic

Adams, Ruth (ed.). *Contemporary China*. New York: Vintage Books, 1966.

Alley, Rewi. "Some Memories of Sinkiang," *Eastern Horizon* [Hong Kong], No. 7, July 1966, 35–39.

Andrew, Geoffrey. "China: An Academic Appraisal," *American Scholar*, XXXII, No. 3, Summer 1963, 377–386.

Ashbrook, Arthur G., Jr. "Main Lines of Chinese Communist Economic Policy." Pages 15–45 in U.S. Congress, 90th, 1st Session, Joint Economic Committee, *An Economic Profile on Mainland China*, I. Washington: GPO, 1965.

Audette, Donald G. "Computer Technology in Communist China, 1956–1965," *Communications of the Association for Computing Machinery*, IX, No. 9, September 1966, 655–661.

Barnett, A. Doak. "Aspects of the Chinese Communist Bureaucracy," *China Quarterly* [London], No. 28, October–December 1966.

———. *Communist China: The Early Years 1949–1955*. New York: Praeger, 1964.

———. *Communist Economic Strategy: The Rise of Mainland China*. Washington: National Planning Association, 1959.

"Behind the Turmoil in Red China," *U.S. News & World Report*, LXXI, No. 16, October 18, 1971, 32–35.

Berberet, John A. *Science and Technology in Communist China*. (Research Memorandum RM 60TMP-72.) Santa Barbara: General Electric, 1960.

Bleecker, Theodore. "Industrial Labor Policies in Transition in Mainland China," *Labor Developments Abroad*, XV, No. 10, October 1970, 1–7.

Brandt, Conrad; Schwartz, Benjamin; and Fairbank, John F. *A Documentary History of Chinese Communism*. Cambridge: Harvard University Press, 1952.

Buck, John Lossing. "Chinese Agriculture." In Albert Feuerwerker (ed.), *Modern China*. Englewood Cliffs: Prentice-Hall, 1964.

Buck, John Lossing; Dawson, Owen L.; and Wu, Yuan-li. *Food and Agriculture in Communist China*. New York: Praeger, 1966.

Chao, Kang. *Agricultural Production in Communist China, 1949–1965*. Madison: University of Wisconsin Press, 1970.

———. *The Construction Industry in Communist China*. Chicago: Aldine, 1968.

_____. *The Electric Power Industry in Communist China.* (Research Paper P–348.) Arlington: Institute for Defense Analyses, 1967.

Chao, Kuo-chun. *Agrarian Policies of Mainland China (1949–1956).* Cambridge: Harvard University Press, 1957.

Cheng, Chu-yuan. "China's Industry: Advances and Dilemma," *Current History,* LXI, No. 361, September 1971, 154–159.

_____. *Economic Relations Between Peking and Moscow: 1949–63.* New York: Praeger, 1964.

_____. "The Effects of the Cultural Revolution on China's Machine-Building Industry," *Current Scene: Developments in Mainland China* [Hong Kong], VIII, No. 1, January 1, 1970, 1–13.

_____. "Machine-Building Industry in the Chinese Mainland, 1952–68." (Paper presented at the First Sino-American Conference on Mainland China, Taipei, Taiwan, December 1970.) Ann Arbor: Center for Chinese Studies, University of Michigan, 1971 (mimeo.).

_____. *Monetary Affairs of Communist China.* Hong Kong: Union Research Institute, 1954.

_____. "Peking's Mind on Tomorrow: Problems in Developing Scientific and Technological Talent in China," *Current Scene: Developments in Mainland China* [Hong Kong], IV, No. 6, March 15, 1966, 1–18.

_____. *Scientific and Engineering Manpower in Communist China, 1949–1963.* (National Science Foundation Series, NSF 65–14.) Washington: GPO, 1965.

Chen, Kuan-I, and Uppal, Jogindar S. *India and China: Studies in Comparative Development.* Riverside, New Jersey: Free Press, 1971.

Chen, Nai-Ruenn. *Chinese Economic Statistics: A Handbook for Mainland China.* Chicago: Aldine, 1967.

Chen, Nai-Ruenn, and Galenson, Walter. *The Chinese Economy Under Communism.* Chicago: Aldine, 1969.

Chen, S. C., and Ridley, Charles P. (eds.) *The Rural People's Communes in Lien-chiang.* Stanford: Hoover Institution Press, 1969.

"China." In *Quarterly Economic Review: China, Hong Kong, North Korea, Annual Supplement, 1970,* Nos. 1–2. Hong Kong: Far Eastern Economic Review, 1970.

"China." In *Quarterly Economic Review: China, Hong Kong, North Korea, Annual Supplement, 1971,* Nos. 3–4. Hong Kong: Far Eastern Economic Review, 1971.

"China's Foreign Trade in 1969," *Current Scene: Developments in Mainland China* [Hong Kong], VIII, No. 16, October 7, 1970, 1–18.

"China's Foreign Trade in 1970," *Current Scene: Developments in Mainland China* [Hong Kong], IX, No. 8, August 7, 1971, 2, 7.

China's Legal and Security Systems. London: Institute for Strategic Studies, 1969.

"China's Nitrogenous Fertilizer Industry Steps into Top World Ranks," *China Reconstructs* [Peking], XVIII, No. 5, May 1969, 11–15.

"The China Trade: Hog Big Hog Fast," *Newsweek*, May 3, 1971, 71–72.

The China White Paper: August 1949, I and II. Palo Alto: Stanford University Press, 1967.

"Chinese Railways: Twenty-Years of Vigorous Growth," *China Reconstructs* [Peking], XVIII, No. 12, December 1969, 28–31.

Ching, Yi-hung. "Mao's Nuclear Base and Prospects," *Free China Review* [Taipei], XVI, July 1966, 34–38.

Clubb, O. Edmund. *Twentieth Century China*. New York: Columbia University Press, 1964.

Communist China and Arms Control. (Hoover Institution Publications, No. 78.) Palo Alto: Hoover Institute on War, Revolution, and Peace, 1968.

Communist China, 1967. (Communist China Problem Research Series, EC41.) Hong Kong: Union Research Institute, 1968.

Communist China, 1968. (Communist China Problem Research Series, EC47.) Hong Kong: Union Research Institute, 1969.

Communist China, 1969. (Communist China Problem Research Series, EC48.) Hong Kong: Union Research Institute, 1970.

Cone, Frederick M. *Chinese Industrial Growth: Brief Studies of Selected Investment Areas*. (Memorandum RM–5625–PR/ISA.) Santa Monica: Rand Corporation, May 1969.

——. *Chinese Industrial Growth: Overall Level of Investment and Its Relation to General Growth Rate*. (Memorandum RM–5841–PR/ISA.) Santa Monica: Rand Corporation, May 1969.

The Constitution of the Communist Party of China. Peking: Foreign Languages Press, 1969.

Cressey, George B. *Land of the 500 Million: A Geography of China*. (McGraw-Hill Series in Geography.) New York: McGraw-Hill, 1955.

Dawson, Owen L. *Communist China's Agriculture*. (Praeger Special Studies in International Economics and Development Series.) New York: Praeger, 1970.

Dernberger, Robert F. "Economic Realities." In Ruth Adams (ed.), *Contemporary China*. New York: Vintage Books, 1966.

"Doing Business at the Canton Trade Fair," *Business Week*, No. 2199, October 23, 1971, 41–42.

Donnithorne, Audrey. *China's Economic System*. New York: Praeger, 1967.

——. "The Organization of Rural Trade in China Since 1958," *China Quarterly* [London], No. 8, October–December 1961, 77–91.

Duncan, James. *A Businessman Looks at Red China*. Princeton: Van Nostrand, 1965.

Durdin, Tillman. "China Claims Gain for the Economy," *New York Times*, September 21, 1971, 13.

_____ . "The New Face of Maoist China," *Problems of Communism*, XX, No. 5, September–October 1971, 1–13.

Durdin, Tillman; Reston, James; and Topping, Seymour. *The New York Times Report from Red China*. New York: Quadrangle Books, 1971.

Ecklund, George N. *Financing the Chinese Government Budget*. Chicago: Aldine, 1966.

_____ . *Taxation in Communist China, 1950–59*. Washington: Central Intelligence Agency, 1961.

Eckstein, Alexander. *Communist China's Economic Growth and Foreign Trade*. New York: McGraw-Hill, 1966.

_____ . *The National Income of Communist China*. Chicago: Free Press of Glencoe, 1961.

Eckstein, Alexander (ed.). *China Trade Prospects and U.S. Policy*. (Praeger Library of Chinese Affairs Series.) New York: Praeger, 1971.

Eckstein, Alexander; Galenson, Walter; and Liu, Ta-chung (eds.). *Economic Trends in Communist China*, Chicago: Aldine, 1968.

Economist Intelligence Unit. *Quarterly Economic Review: China, Hong Kong, North Korea, Annual Supplement, 1971*. London: 1971.

Elegant, Robert S. *Mao's Great Revolution*. New York: World Publishing, 1971.

Emerson, John Philip. "Employment in Mainland China: Problems and Prospects." Pages 403–469 in Joint Economic Committee of the United States Congress, *Economic Profile in Mainland China*. New York: Praeger, for the Joint Economic Committee of the U.S. Congress, 1968.

_____ . *Nonagricultural Employment in Mainland China, 1949–1958*. (International Population Statistics Reports, Series P–90, No. 21.) Washington: GPO, 1965.

Esposito, Bruce J. "The Cultural Revolution and Science Policy and Development in Mainland China." (Paper presented at the 28th International Congress of Orientalists, Canberra, Australia, January 1971.) Hartford: University of Hartford, Department of History, 1971 (Unpublished paper not available for public distribution).

Europa Yearbook, 1967, I. London: Europa Publications, 1967.

Europa Yearbook, 1971, I. London: Europa Publications, 1971.

Fairbank, John King. *The United States and China*. (Rev. ed.) New York: Viking Press, 1958.

_____ . *The United States and China*. (3d ed.) Cambridge: Harvard University Press, 1971.

The Far East and Australasia, 1971: A Survey and Directory of Asia and the Pacific. London: Europa Publications, 1971.

Federal Power Commission. *World Power Data, 1968.* (FPC P–40.) Washington: GPO, 1971.

Feld, Bernard T. "On the Chinese Separation Technology," *Bulletin of the Atomic Scientists*, XXII, No. 7, September 1966, 33–34.

Field, Robert Michael. "Industrial Production in Communist China, 1957–1968," *China Quarterly* [London], No. 42, April–June 1970, 46 –64.

Finney, John W. "Communist China Orbits 2d Satellite," *New York Times*, March 4, 1971, 1, 18.

"The Food and Population Balance: China's Modernization Dilemma," *Current Scene: Developments in Mainland China* [Hong Kong], IX, No. 6, June 7, 1971, 1–6.

Frank, Lewis A. "Nuclear Weapons Development in China," *Bulletin of the Atomic Scientists*, XXII, No. 1, January 1966, 12–15.

Frolic, B. Michael. "A Visit to Peking University—What the Cultural Revolution Was All About," *New York Times Magazine*, October 24, 1971, 29, 115–123, 128–129.

Geddes, W. R. *Peasant Life in Communist China.* Ithaca: Society for Applied Anthropology, 1963.

Goldman, Merle. "The Aftermath of China's Cultural Revolution," *Current History*, LXI, No. 361, September 1971, 165–170.

Gould, Sidney H. (ed.) *Sciences in Communist China.* (Publication No. 68.) Washington: American Association for the Advancement of Science, 1961.

Great Britain. Naval Intelligence Division. *China Proper*, III. (Geographical Handbook Series.) London: 1945.

Halperin, Morton H. *China and the Bomb.* New York: Praeger, 1965.

Harper, Paul. "The Party and the Unions in Communist China," *China Quarterly* [London], No. 37, January–March 1969, 84–119.

Harris, William R. "Chinese Nuclear Doctrine: The Decade Prior to Weapons Development," *China Quarterly* [London], No. 21, January–March 1965, 87–95.

Hinton, Harold C. *Communist China in World Politics.* Boston: Houghton Mifflin, 1966.

Hoffman, Charles. *Work Incentive Practices and Policies in the People's Republic of China, 1953–1965.* Albany: State University of New York Press, 1967.

_____. "Work Incentives in Chinese Industry and Agriculture." Pages 471–498 in *An Economic Profile in Mainland China.* New York: Praeger, for the Joint Committee of the United States Congress, 1968.

Hoffman, Paul. "Food Production Gains in Far East," *New York Times*, August 23, 1971, 5.

Horn, Joshua S. *Away with All Pests: An English Surgeon in People's China, 1954–1969.* New York: Monthly Review Press, 1969.

Howe, Christopher. *Employment and Economic Growth in Urban China, 1949–1957*. Cambridge: Cambridge University Press, 1971.

Hsiao Hsia (ed.). *China: Its People, Its Society, Its Culture*. (Survey of World Cultures Series.) New Haven: Human Relations Area Files Press, 1960.

Hsieh, Alice Langley. "China's Nuclear-Missile Programme: Regional or Intercontinental?" *China Quarterly* [London], No. 45, January–March 1971, 85–99.

———. *Communist China's Strategy in the Nuclear Era*. Englewood Cliffs: Prentice-Hall, 1962.

Hudson, Geoffrey. "Paper Tigers and Nuclear Teeth," *China Quarterly* [London], No. 39, July–September 1969, 64–75.

Hudson, Geoffrey; Sherman, A.V.; and Zauberman, A. *The Chinese Communes*. London: Soviet Survey.

Hughes, T. J., and Luard, D.E.T. *The Economic Development of Communist China, 1949–1960*. London: Oxford University Press, 1961.

Human Relations Area Files. *Area Handbook for China*. Washington: GPO, February 1958.

Important Labor Laws and Regulations of the People's Republic of China. Peking: Foreign Languages Press, 1961.

Inglis, David R. "The Chinese Bombshell," *Bulletin of the Atomic Scientists*, XXI, No. 2, February 1965, 19–21.

Jackson, W. A. Douglas (ed.) *Agrarian Policies and Problems in Communist and Non-Communist Countries*. Seattle: University of Washington Press, 1971.

Jane's World Railways, 1970–71. (Ed., Henry Sampson.) New York: McGraw-Hill, 1971.

Japan. Ministry of Foreign Affairs. China Affairs Division. Asian Affairs Bureau. "The Present State of Japan-China Trade," *Current Scene: Developments in Mainland China* [Hong Kong], VIII, No. 9, May 1, 1970, 1–7.

Joffe, Ellis. *Party and Army: Professionalism and Political Control in the Chinese Officer Corps, 1949–1964*. (Harvard East Asia Monographs Series.) Cambridge: East Asian Research Center, Harvard University Press, 1965.

Johnson, Chalmers A. "China's Manhattan Project," *New York Times Magazine*, October 25, 1964, 117–119.

Joint Economic Committee of the United States Congress. *An Economic Profile of Mainland China*. (Praeger Special Studies in International Economics and Development Series.) New York: Praeger, for the Joint Economic Committee of the U.S. Congress, 1968.

Jonas, Anne M. *The Soviet Union and the Atom: Peaceful Sharing, 1954–1958*. (Rand Memorandum RM 2290.) Santa Monica: Rand Corporation, November 1958.

Kahin, George McTurnan (ed.). *Major Governments of Asia*. Ithaca: Cornell University Press, 1963.

Keatley, Robert. "Calm in Peking: China Regains Stability, Its Economy Improves But It Faces Problems," *Wall Street Journal*, CLXXVII, No. 126, June 30, 1971, 1, 16.

——. "In China: Self-Reliance Is Industry Watchword," *Wall Street Journal*, CLXXVIII, No. 2, July 2, 1971, 1, 21.

——. "Mao's Military: Army Plays a Key Role in Chinese Agriculture, Industries and Schools," *Wall Street Journal*, July 20, 1971, 1, 18.

Klatt, Werner. "A Review of China's Economy in 1970," *China Quarterly* [London], XXXXIII, No. 43, July–September 1970, 100–120.

Klatt, Werner (ed.). *The Chinese Model*. Hong Kong: Hong Kong University Press, 1965.

Klein, Donald W., and Clark, Anne B. *Biographic Dictionary of Chinese Communism, 1921–1965*, I and II. Cambridge: Harvard University Press, 1971.

Klochko, Mikhail A. *Soviet Scientist in Red China*. (Trans., Andrew MacAndrew.) New York: Praeger, 1964.

Kovner, Milton. "Communist China's Foreign Aid to Less Developed Countries." Pages 609–620 in U.S. Congress, 90th, 1st Session, Joint Economic Committee, *An Economic Profile of Mainland China*, I. Washington: GPO, 1967.

Kramish, Arnold. "The Great Chinese Bomb Puzzle—and a Solution," *Fortune*, LXXIII, No. 6, June 1966, 156–158, 246, 248, 250.

Kuo, Leslie T. C. "Communist China: Restoration and Expansion," *Library Journal*, LXXXVII, No. 20, November 15, 1962, 4133.

Kuo, Ping-Chia. *China*, III. (3d ed., rev.) London: Oxford University Press, 1970.

Kwang, Ching-wen. *The Budgetary System of the People's Republic of China: A Preliminary Survey*. Berkeley: Committee on the Economy of China, 1964.

Lapp, Ralph E. "China's Mushroom Cloud Casts a Long Shadow," *New York Times Magazine*, July 14, 1968, 6–7, 38, 40–41, 48, 50.

Larsen, Marion R. "China's Agriculture Under Communism." Pages 197–268 in U.S. Congress, 90th, 1st Session, Joint Economic Committee, *An Economic Profile of Mainland China*, I. Washington: GPO, 1967.

——. "Home Needs Influence China's Pattern of Foreign Agricultural Trade," *Foreign Agriculture*, IX, No. 41, October 11, 1971, 4–7.

Latourette, Kenneth Scott. *The Chinese: Their History and Culture*, I and II. New York: Macmillan, 1946.

Levine, Laurence W. "The Prospects of U.S.-China Trade," *East Europe*, XX, No. 6, June 1971, 2–6.

Lewis, John Wilson (ed.). *The City in Communist China*. Stanford: Stanford University Press, 1971.

Li, Choh-ming (ed.). *Industrial Development in Communist China*. New York: Praeger, 1964.

Lindbeck, John M. H. "Chinese Science: It's Not a Paper Atom," *New York Times Magazine*, January 8, 1967, 37–38, 60–64, 70.

————. "An Isolationist Science Policy," *Bulletin of the Atomic Scientists*, XXV, No. 2, February 1969, 66–71.

————. "The Organization and Development of Science," *China Quarterly* [London], No. 6, April–June 1961, 98–132.

Lindbeck, John M. H. (ed.) *China: Management of a Revolutionary Society*. Seattle: University of Washington Press, 1971.

Lippit, Victor D. "Development of Transportation in Communist China," *China Quarterly* [London], No. 27, July–September 1966, 101–119.

Lynch, Charles. *China: One Fourth of the World*. Toronto: McClelland and Stewart, 1965.

McArthur, H. R. "Engineering Education in China," *Engineering Journal* [Montreal], XLIX, No. 7, July 1966, 23–25.

MacDougall, Colina. "Mao's Restless 'Mandarins'," *Atlas*, XVIII, No. 5, November 1969, 25–27.

————. "Off the Rails Again?" *Far Eastern Economic Review* [Hong Kong], LXIII, No. 8, February 20, 1969, 306–307.

Macioti, Manfredo. "Scientists Go Barefoot," *Survival* [London], XIII, No. 7, July 1971, 232–238.

"Mainland China, 1970: Old Problems and New Solutions," *Current Scene: Developments in Mainland China* [Hong Kong], IX, No. 2, February 7, 1971, 1–5.

"Mainland China Trade Pattern in 1960s Points to Sales Possibilities Ahead," *Commerce Today*, I, No. 15, May 3, 1971, 3–9.

Measuring the Mainland Chinese Market. (Management Monograph No. 50.) New York: Business International Corporation, 1971.

"Mixed Blessings," *Far Eastern Economic Review* [Hong Kong], LXIV, No. 15, April 10, 1969, 78.

Miyashita, Tadao. *The Currency and Financial System of Mainland China*. Seattle: University of Washington Press, 1966.

Nielsen, Robert B. (comp.) *Scientific, Academic, and Technical Research Organizations of Mainland China: A Selected Listing*. (Rev. ed.) Washington: GPO, 1966.

Niu, Sien-chong. "China's Petroleum Industry," *Military Review*, XLIX, No. 11, November 1969, 23–27.

————. "Red China's Nuclear Might," *Ordnance*, LIV, No. 298, January–February 1970, 399–401.

Nunn, G. Raymond. *Publishing in Mainland China.* (Massachusetts Institute of Technology Report No. 4.) Cambridge: Massachusetts Institute of Technology Press, 1966.

Oksenberg, Michel C. "China: The Convulsive Society," *Headline Series*, No. 203, December 1970, 3–78.

Oldham, C. H. G. "Earth Sciences in the People's Republic of China: Report of a Visit," *Proceedings of the Geologists' Association* [London], LXXVII, No. 1, January 1967, 157–164.

_____. "Science for the Masses?" *Far Eastern Economic Review* [Hong Kong], LX, No. 20, May 16, 1968, 353–355.

_____. "Science in China: A Tourist's Impressions," *Science*, CXLVII, No. 3659, February 14, 1965, 706–714.

_____. "Science Travels the Mao Road," *Bulletin of the Atomic Scientists*, XXV, No. 2, February 1969, 80–83.

Oliphant, Mark. "Over Pots of Tea: Excerpts from a Dairy of a Visit to China," *Bulletin of the Atomic Scientists*, XXII, No. 5, May 1966, 36–43.

Orleans, Leo A. *Professional Manpower and Education in Communist China.* (National Science Foundation Series, NSF 61-3.) Washington: GPO, 1961

_____. "Research and Development in Communist China," *Science*, CLVII, No. 3787, July 28, 1967, 1–9.

Pao, Chin-an. "Peiping's Capacity for Nuclear Weaponry," *Chinese Communist Affairs* [Taipei], V, No. 2, April 1968, 6–9.

"Peking's Fourth Five-Year Plan," *Current Scene: Developments in Mainland China* [Hong Kong], VIII, No. 17, November 7, 1970, 19.

"Peking's Program to Move Human and Material Resources to the Countryside," *Current Scene: Developments in Mainland China* [Hong Kong], VII, No. 18, September 15, 1969, 1–17.

Perkins, Dwight H. *Agricultural Development in China, 1368–1968.* Chicago: Aldine, 1969.

_____. "Mao Tse-tung's Goals and China's Economic Performance," *Current Scene: Developments in Mainland China* [Hong Kong], IX, No. 1, January 7, 1971, 1–15.

_____. *Market Control and Planning in Communist China.* Cambridge: Harvard University Press, 1968.

Pick's Currency Yearbook, 1970. New York: Pick, 1970.

Price, Robert L. "International Trade of Communist China, 1950–65." Pages 579–608 in U.S. Congress, 90th, 1st Session, Joint Economic Committee, *An Economic Profile of Mainland China*, I. Washington: GPO, 1967.

"Procedures in Trading with Mainland Chinese Detailed," *Commerce Today*, I, No. 18, June 14, 1971, 33–36.

Production Yearbook, 1969, XXIII. Rome: United Nations Food and Agriculture Organization, 1970.

Prybyla, Jan S. *The Political Economy of Communist China.* Scranton: International Textbook, 1970.

Pye, Lucian W. *The Communes: A Microcosm of Chinese Communism.* Cambridge: Center for International Studies, Massachusetts Institute of Technology, 1964.

Reischauer, Edwin O., and Fairbank, John King. *East Asia: The Great Tradition,* I: A History of East Asian Civilization. Boston: Houghton Mifflin, 1960.

"The Revolution in China's Laboratories," *Business Week,* No. 2190, August 21, 1971, 88–89.

Richardson, Stanley D. *Forestry in Communist China.* Baltimore: Johns Hopkins University Press, 1966.

Richman, Barry M. *A Firsthand Study of Industrial Management in Communist China.* Los Angeles: Graduate School of Business Administration, Division of Research, University of California, 1967.

_____. *Industrial Society in Communist China.* New York: Random House, 1969.

Riskin, Carl. "Small Industry and the Chinese Model of Development," *China Quarterly* [London], No. 46, April–June 1971, 245–273.

Robinson, Joan. *The Cultural Revolution in China.* New York: Penguin Books, 1967.

Roderick, John. "Chinese Proud of Farm," *Washington Post,* June 3, 1971, G1.

Ryan, William L., and Summerlin, Sam. *The China Cloud.* Boston: Little, Brown, 1968.

Schneider, Linda B. "Mainland China." Pages 32–40 in United States Department of Agriculture. Economic Research Service, *The Agricultural Situation in Communist Areas: Review of 1970 and Outlook for 1971.* (ERS-Foreign 314.) Washington: GPO, 1971.

Schran, Peter. *The Development of Chinese Agriculture, 1950–1959.* (Illinois Studies in the Social Sciences Series, No. 56.) Urbana: University of Illinois Press, 1969.

Schurmann, Franz. *Ideology and Organization in Communist China.* Berkeley: University of California Press, 1966.

_____. *Ideology and Organization in Communist China.* (2d ed.) Berkeley: University of California Press, 1968.

Schwartz, Harry. *China.* New York: Atheneum, 1965.

_____. *Tsars, Mandarins, and Commissars.* Philadelphia: Lippincott, 1964.

"Scientists, 1957–1967," *China News Analysis* [Hong Kong], No. 696, February 16, 1968, 1–7.

Selling the Mainland Chinese Market. (Management Monograph No. 51.) New York: Business International Corporation, 1971.

Shih, Ch'eng-chih. *The Status of Science and Education in Communist China and a Comparison with That in the U.S.S.R.* (Communist China Problem Research Series, EC-30.) Hong Kong: Union Research Institute, 1962.

Snow, Edgar. "Aftermath of the Cultural Revolution: Mao Tse-tung—and the Cost of Living," *New Republic*, CLXIV, No. 15, (Issue No. 2937), April 10, 1971, 18–21.

———. *Red China Today.* New York: Random House, 1971.

———. "Success or Failure? China's 70,000 Communes," *New Republic*, XXIV, No. 26, June 26, 1971, 19–23.

———. "Talks with Chou En-lai: The Open Door," *New Republic*, CLXIV, No. 13, March 27, 1971, 20–23.

Statesman's Yearbook, 1971–72. (Ed., John Paxton.) New York: St. Martin's Press, 1971.

"Steel and Jasmine Tea," *Fortune*, LXXIII, No. 6, June 1966, 73–74, 76–80.

Stewart, Rosemary. "Managers Under Mao," *Management Today* [London], April 1967, 66–71.

Timberlake, P. A. (ed.) *China Trade and Economic Newsletter* [London], Nos. 183–190, January–August 1971.

Topping, Seymour. "Rural China Revisited: Change and Continuity," *New York Times*, May 30, 1971, 1, 14.

Trumbull, Robert (ed.). *This Is Communist China.* New York: David McKay, 1968.

"Two Views of Japan-China Trade," *Oriental Economist* [Tokyo], XXXIX, No. 730, August 1971, 28–29.

Uchida, Genko. "Technology in China," *Scientific American*, CCXV, No. 5, November 1966, 37–45.

U.S. Central Intelligence Agency. Directorate of Intelligence. Office of Basic and Geographic Intelligence. *Communist China Map Folio.* N.pl.: CIA, October 1967.

U.S. Congress. 88th, 1st Session. Senate. Committee on Government Operations. *Professional Employment Categories in Communist China.* Washington: GPO, 1963.

U.S. Congress. 90th, 1st Session. Joint Committee on Atomic Energy. *Impact of Chinese Communist Nuclear Weapons on United States National Security.* Washington: GPO, 1967.

U.S. Congress. 90th, 1st Session. Joint Economic Committee. *Mainland China in the World Economy, Hearings: April 5, 10, 11, and 12, 1967.* Washington: GPO, 1967.

U.S. Congress. 91st, 1st Session. House of Representatives. Committee on Foreign Affairs. *United States-China Relations: A Strategy for the Future Hearings: September 15, 16, 22, 23, 24, 29, and 30; and October 6, 1970.* Washington: GPO, 1970.

U.S. Congress. 91st, 2d Session. Senate. *Fiscal Year 1971: Defense Program and Budget.* Washington: GPO, 1970.

691

U.S. Congress. 92d, 1st Session. Senate. Committee on the Judiciary. Subcommittee to Investigate Administration of the Internal Security Act and Other Internal Security Laws. *The Human Cost of Communism in China.* Washington: GPO, 1971.

U.S. Department of Commerce. *Export Control Bulletin.* (ECB–OEC--46.) Washington: GPO, June 11, 1971.

U.S. Department of Commerce. Bureau of the Census. *Nonagricultural Employment in Mainland China, 1949–1958,* by John Philip Emerson. (International Population Statistics Reports Series P–90, No. 21.) Washington: GPO, 1965.

U.S. Department of Commerce. National Technical Information Service. "Harnessing the Huai River System," *China Mainland Press: Current Background,* No. 935, June 29, 1971, 1–39.

U.S. Department of Commerce. Bureau of the Census. Foreign Demographic Analysis Division, *Estimates and Projections of the Population of Mainland China, 1953–1986,* by John S. Aird. (International Population Statistics Reports, Series P–91, No. 17.) Washington: GPO, 1968.

U.S. Department of Commerce. Office of Technical Services. Joint Publications Research Service (Washington). The following publications are JPRS translations from foreign sources:

"Communist China's Transportation and Communications," *Fei-ch'ing Yueh-pao,* Taipei, September 1, 1970. (JPRS: 52,653, *Translations on Communist China,* No. 139, March 18, 1971.)

"New Achievements in China's Science and Technology." (JPRS: 51,330, *Translations on Communist China,* No. 116, September 8, 1970.)

U.S. Department of Labor. Bureau of Labor Statistics and Bureau of International Labor Affairs. "Labor Conditions in China (Communist)," *Labor Digest,* No. 20, 1963.

U.S. Department of State. Bureau of Public Affairs. Office of Media Services. *Issues.* (Department of State Publication No. 8499, East Asian and Pacific Series 173.) Washington: GPO, December 1969.

U.S. Department of the Army. Office of the Deputy Chief of Staff for Military Operations. *Communist China: A Bibliographic Survey.* Washington: GPO, 1971.

U.S. Department of the Interior. "The Mineral Industry of Mainland China," by K. P. Wang. Pages 1279–1295 in *Minerals Yearbook, 1963: Area Reports International,* IV. Washington: GPO.

Vogel, Ezra F. *Canton Under Communism: Programs and Politics in a Provincial Capital, 1949–1968.* Cambridge: Harvard University Press, 1969.

———. "China's New Society," *Diplomat,* XVII, No. 196, September 1966, 76–81.

Wang, Chi. *Mainland China Organizations of Higher Learning in Science and Technology and Their Publications.* Washington: GPO, 1961.

_____. "Nuclear Research in Mainland China," *Nuclear News*, X, May 1967, 16–20.

_____. *Nuclear Science in Mainland China.* Washington: GPO, 1968.

Wang, K. P. "The Mineral Industry of Mainland China." (In 1967) *Bureau of Mines Minerals Yearbook.* Washington: GPO, 1968.

_____. "The Mineral Industry of Mainland China." (In 1968) *Bureau of Mines Minerals Yearbook.* Washington: GPO, 1969.

_____. "The Mineral Industry of Mainland China." (In 1969) *Bureau of Mines Minerals Yearbook.* Washington: GPO, 1970.

_____. "The Mineral Industry of Mainland China. (Preprint from the 1970 Bureau of Mines Minerals Yearbook.) Washington: GPO, 1971.

Washenko, Steve. "Better Harvests As People's Republic of China Strengthen Push for Economic Development," *Foreign Agriculture*, IX, No. 41, October 11, 1971, 2–4, 16.

Wen, Fang. "Rapid Growth in China's Textile Industry," *China Reconstructs* [Peking], XVIII, No. 11, November 1969, 7–9.

Wheelwright, Edward L., and McFarlane, Bruce. *The Chinese Road to Socialism: Economics of the Cultural Revolution.* New York: Monthly Review Press, 1970.

Wilson, Dick. *Anatomy of China.* New York: Weybright and Talley, 1968.

_____. "China's Economic Prospects." In Ruth Adams (ed.), *Contemporary China.* New York: Vintage, 1966.

_____. "Technology in China," *Far Eastern Economic Review* [Hong Kong], L, No. 6, November 11, 1965, 289–291.

Winfield, Gerald F. *China: The Land and the People.* (2d ed.) New York: William Sloane, 1950.

Wu, Yuan-li. *Economic Development and the Use of Energy Resources in Communist China.* New York: Praeger, 1963.

_____. "The Economic Realities," *Diplomat*, XVII, No. 196, September 1966, 82–88.

_____. *The Economy of Communist China.* New York: Praeger, 1965.

_____. "Food and Agriculture in Mainland China," *Current History*, LXI, No. 361, September 1971, 160–164.

_____. *The Spatial Economy of Communist China.* (Hoover Institution Publications Series.) New York: Praeger, 1967.

Wu, Yuan-li, and Sheeks, Robert B. *The Organization and Support of Scientific Research and Development in Mainland China.* New York: Praeger, 1970.

Wu, Yuan-li, et al. *The Economic Potential of Communist China: Reappraisal, 1962–1970.* Menlo Park: Stanford Research Institute, 1964.

Yahuda, Michael B. "China's Nuclear Option," *Bulletin of the Atomic Scientists*, XXV, No. 2, February 1969, 72–77.

Yang, Allency H. Y. "Red and Expert: Communist China's Educational Strategies of Manpower Development." Unpublished Ph.D. dissertation. Berkeley: Department of Education, University of California, 1965.

Yearbook of International Communist Affairs, 1966. Stanford: Hoover Institution on War, Revolution and Peace, Stanford University, 1967.

Yoshimura, Toshio. "All Eyes on China Market," *Far Eastern Economic Review* [Hong Kong], LXXI, No. 12, March 20, 1971, 3–34.

"You Have Opened a New Page," *Newsweek*, April 26, 1971, 16–22.

"Youth to the Land," *China News Analysis* [Hong Kong], No. 521, June 19, 1964.

Zagoria, Donald S. *The Sino-Soviet Conflict, 1956–1961*. Princeton: Princeton University Press, 1962.

(Various issues of the following periodicals were also used in the preparation of this section: *China Trade Report* [Hong Kong], January 1971 to August 1971; and *Far Eastern Economic Review Yearbook* [Hong Kong], 1962 to 1971.)

Section IV. National Security

"Administration: The Soldiers, the State, and the Rebels," *China News Analysis* [Hong Kong], No. 822, November 20, 1970, 1-7.

Ajia Chosakai (ed.). *Chugoku Soran 1971* (Survey of China, 1971). Tokyo: Ajia Chosakai, 1971.

Armbruster, Frank E. "China's Conventional Military Capability (with comments by Samuel B. Griffith), II," Pages 161-200 in Tang Tsou (ed.), *China in Crisis*, II. Chicago: University of Chicago Press, 1968.

Barnett, A. Doak. "A Nuclear China and U.S. Arms Policy," *Foreign Affairs*, XLVIII, No. 3, April 1970, 427-442.

Bobrow, David B. "The Good Officer: Definition and Training," *China Quarterly* [London], No. 3, April 1970, 427-442.

Bueschel, Richard M. *Communist Chinese Air Power*. New York: Praeger, 1968.

Carlson, Evans Fordyce. *The Chinese Army: Its Organization and Military Efficiency*. New York: Institute of Pacific Relations, 1940.

"Changes in Chinese Society, 1949-1969," *China News Analysis* [Hong Kong], No. 774, September 19, 1969, 1-7.

Charles, David A. "The Dismissal of Marshal P'eng Te-huai," *China Quarterly* [London], No. 8, October-December 1961, 63-76.

Cheng, J. Chester (ed.). *The Politics of the Chinese Red Army: A Translation of the Bulletin of Activities of the People's Liberation Army*. Palo Alto: Stanford University Press, 1966.

Ch'en, Theodore Hsi-en (ed.). *The Chinese Communist Regime: Documents and Commentary*. New York: Praeger, 1967.

"China Reshaping Police Forces Under New Provincial Regimes," *New York Times*, May 7, 1968.

"China's Security Organs," *China Notes*, No. 391, January 4, 1971.

"Chinese Military Affairs," *China Quarterly* [London], No. 18, April-June 1964, entire issue.

The Chinese People's Liberation Army. Peking: Foreign Languages Press, 1950.

Clubb, O. Edmund. *Twentieth Century China*. New York: Columbia University Press, 1964.

Cohen, Jerome Alan. *Contemporary Chinese Law: Research Problems and Perspectives*. Cambridge: Harvard University Press, 1970.

_____. "The Criminal Process in China." Pages 103-143 in Donald W. Treadgold (ed.), *Soviet and Chinese Communism*. Seattle: University of Washington Press, 1967.

_____. *The Criminal Process in the People's Republic of China 1949–1963: An Introduction*. Cambridge: Harvard University Press, 1968.

_____. "Drafting People's Mediation Rules." Pages 29–50 in John Wilson Lewis (ed.), *The City in Communist China*. Stanford: Stanford University Press, 1971.

Collier, Harry H., and Lai, Paul Chin-Chih. *Organizational Changes in the Chinese Army, 1890–1950*. Taipei: Office of the Military Historian, 1969.

"Disarmament: From the Barrel of a Gun? Peking's Attitudes Towards Nuclear Weapons Control," *Current Scene: Developments in Mainland China* [Hong Kong], III, No. 16, April 1, 1965, 1–12.

Domes, Jurgen. "The Cultural Revolution and the Army," *Asian Survey*, VIII, No. 5, May 1968, 349–363.

Elliot-Bateman, Michael. *Defeat in the East*. London: Oxford University Press, 1967.

Ellis, Gerald. "China's Military Strength," *Military Review*, LI, No. 4, April 1971, 71–76.

Garthoff, Raymond L. "China's Armed Forces," *Problems of Communism*, XVIII, No. 2, March–April 1969, 46–47.

_____. "Sino-Soviet Military Relations," *Annals of the American Academy of Political and Social Science*, CCCXLIX, September 1963, 81–93.

George, Alexander L. *The Chinese Communist Army in Action: The Korean War and Its Aftermath*. New York: Columbia University Press, 1967.

Ginsburgs, George, and Stahnke, Arthur. "The People's Procuratorate in Communist China: The Institution in the Ascendancy, 1954–1957," *China Quarterly* [London], No. 34, April–June 1968, 82–132.

Gittings, John. "China's Militia," *China Quarterly* [London], No. 18, April–June 1964, 100–117.

_____. "The Chinese Army." Pages 187–224 in Jack Gray (ed.), *Modern China's Search for a Political Forum*. London: Oxford University Press, 1969.

_____. "The Chinese Army's Role in the Cultural Revolution," *Pacific Affairs* [Vancouver], XXXIX, Nos. 3 and 4, Fall and Winter 1966–1967, 269–289.

_____. "The 'Learn from the Army' Campaign," *China Quarterly* [London], No. 18, April–June 1964, 153–159.

_____. "The PLA—in Trouble or on Top—," *Far Eastern Economic Review* [Hong Kong], LVIII, No. 4, July 28, 1966, 143–148.

_____. *The Role of the Chinese Army*. London: Oxford University Press, 1967.

Gray, Jack (ed.). *Modern China's Search for a Political Forum*. London: Oxford University Press, 1969.

Griffith, Samuel B. *The Chinese People's Liberation Army.* New York: McGraw-Hill, 1967.

_____. "Communist China's Capacity to Make War," *Foreign Affairs*, XLIII, No. 2, January 1965, 217–236.

_____. "The Military Potential of China." Pages 65–94 in Alastair Buchanan (ed.), *China and the Peace of Asia.* New York: Praeger, 1965.

_____. *Peking and People's Wars.* New York: Praeger, 1966.

Halperin, Morton H. *China and the Bomb.* New York: Praeger, 1965.

_____. "China's Strategic Outlook." Pages 95–108 in Alastair Buchanan (ed.), *China and the Peace of Asia.* New York: Praeger, 1965.

_____. *Defense Strategies for the Seventies.* Boston: Little, Brown, 1971.

Halperin, Morton H., and Lewis, John Wilson. "New Tensions in Army-Party Relations in China, 1965–1966," *China Quarterly* [London], No. 26, April–June 1966, 58–67.

Harding, Harry. "China" Toward Revolutionary Pragmatism," *Asian Survey*, XI, No. 1, January 1971, 51–68.

Hinton, Harold C. *Communist China in World Politics.* Boston: Houghton Mifflin, 1966.

Ho, Kan Chin. *A History of the Modern Chinese Revolution.* Peking: Foreign Languages Press, 1959.

Hsieh, Alice Langley, "China's Nuclear-Missile Programme: Regional or Intercontinental?" *China Quarterly* [London], No. 45, January–March 1971, 85–99.

_____. "China's Secret Military Papers: Military Doctrine and Strategy," *Chinu Quarterly* [London], No. 18, April–June 1964, 79–99.

_____. "Communist China's Evolving Military Strategy and Doctrine." (Paper P–646.) Arlington: Institute for Defense Analyses, June 1970.

_____. Communist China's Strategy in the Nuclear Era. Englewood Cliffs: Prentice-Hall, 1962.

Huck, Arthur. *The Security of China: Chinese Approaches to Problems of War and Strategy.* New York: Columbia University, for the Institute for Strategic Studies, 1970.

Institute for Strategic Studies. *The Military Balance, 1969–1970.* London: 1969.

_____. *The Military Balance, 1970–1971.* London: 1970.

_____. *Strategic Survey, 1969.* London: 1969.

_____. *Strategic Survey, 1970.* London: 1970.

Joffe, Ellis. "The Chinese Army in the Cultural Revolution: The Politics of Intervention," *Current Scene: Developments in Mainland China* [Hong Kong], VIII, No. 18, December 7, 1970, 1–24.

───── . "The Conflict Between Old and New in the Chinese Army," *China Quarterly* [London], No. 18, April–June 1964, 118–140.

───── . *Party and Army: Professionalism and Political Control in the Chinese Officer Corps, 1949–1964.* (Harvard East Asia Monographs Series.) Cambridge: East Asian Research Center, Harvard University, 1965.

Johnson, Chalmers A. "Building a Communist Nation in China." Pages 47–81 in Robert A. Scalapino (ed.), *The Communist Revolution in Asia: Tactics, Goals and Achievements.* Englewood Cliffs: Prentice-Hall, 1965.

───── . "Lin Piao's Army and Its Role in Chinese Society," *Current Scene: Developments in Mainland China* [Hong Kong], (Part I), IV, No. 13, July 1, 1966, 1–24; (Part II), IV, No. 14, July 15, 1966, 1–24.

───── . *Peasant Nationalism and Communist Power: The Emergence of Revolutionary China, 1937–1945.* Stanford: Stanford University Press, 1962.

Klein, Donald W., and Clark, Anne B. *Biographical Dictionary of Chinese Communism, 1921–1965,* I and II. Cambridge: Harvard University Press, 1971.

Klochko. Mikhail A. *Soviet Scientist in Red China.* (Trans., Andrew MacAndrew.) New York: Praeger, 1964.

LaDany, L. "China: Period of Suspense," *Foreign Affairs,* XLVIII, No. 4, July 1970, 700–711.

Leng, Shao-chuan. *Justice in Communist China.* Dobbs Ferry: Oceana, 1967.

───── . "Pre-1949 Development of the Communist Chinese System of Justice," *China Quarterly* [London], No. 30, April–June 1967, 92–114.

"Lessons from the Past," *China News Analysis* [Hong Kong], No. 638, November 25, 1966.

Lewis, John Wilson. "China's Secret Military Papers: 'Continuities' and 'Revelations'," *China Quarterly* [London], No. 18, April–June 1964, 68–78.

"Lin Piao and the Cultural Revolution," *Current Scene: Developments in Mainland China* [Hong Kong], VIII, No. 14, August 1, 1970, 1–14.

Liu, F. F. *A Military History of Modern China, 1924–1949.* Princeton: Princeton University Press, 1956.

Li, Victor H. "The Evolution and Development of the Chinese Legal System." Pages 221–255 in John M. H. Lindbeck (ed.), *China: Management of a Revolutionary Society.* Seattle: University of Washington Press, 1971.

───── . "The Public Security Bureau and Political-Legal Work in Hui-yang, 1952–1961." Pages 51–74 in John Wilson Lewis (ed.), *The City in Communist China.* Palo Alto: Stanford University Press, 1971.

Lowenthal, Richard. "Russia Imprint on the Nation," *China News Analysis* [Hong Kong], No. 732, November 8, 1968, 1–7.

Mao Tse-tung. *Basic Tactics*. (Trans., Stuart R. Schram.) New York: Praeger, 1966.

_____. *Selected Military Writings*. Peking: Foreign Languages Press, 1963.

"Military Imprint on the Nation," *China News Analysis* [Hong Kong], No. 732, November 8, 1968, 1–7.

O'Ballance, Edgar. *The Red Army of China: A Short History*. New York: Praeger, 1963.

Pfeffer, Richard M. "Crime and Punishment: China and the United States." Pages 110–142 in Jerome Alan Cohen (ed.), *Contemporary Chinese Law: Research Problems and Perspectives*. Cambridge: Harvard University Press, 1970.

"PLA Soldiers in Politics," *China News Analysis* [Hong Kong] No. 751, April 4, 1969, 1–6.

Powell, Ralph L. "China's Bomb: Exploitation and Reactions," *Foreign Affairs*, XLIII, No. 4, July 1965, 616–625.

_____. "Commissars in the Economy: 'Learn from the PLA' Movement in China," *Asian Survey*, V, No. 3, March 1965, 125–138.

_____. "Communist China as a Military Power," *Current History*, XLIX, No. 289, September 1965, 136–141.

_____. "Communist China's Mass Militia," (Part I), *Current Scene: Developments in Mainland China* [Hong Kong], III, No. 7, November 15, 1964, 1–14.

_____. "Communist China's Mass Militia," (Part II), *Current Scene: Developments in Mainland China* [Hong Kong], III, No. 8, December 1, 1965, 1–24.

_____. "Everyone a Soldier: The Communist Chinese Militia," *Foreign Affairs*, XXXIX, No. 1, October 1960, 100–111.

_____. "Great Powers and Atomic Bombs are 'Paper Tigers'," *China Quarterly* [London], No. 23, July–September 1965, 55–63.

_____. "The Increasing Power of Lin Piao and the Party-Soldiers, 1959–1966," *China Quarterly* [London], No. 34, April-June 1968, 38–65.

_____. "Maoist Military Doctrine," *Asian Survey*, VIII, No. 4, April 1968, 239–262.

_____. "The Military Affairs Committee and the Party Control of the Military in China," *Asian Survey*, III, No. 7, July 1963, 347–356.

_____. "The Party, the Government, and the Gun," *Asian Survey*, X, No. 6, June 1970, 441–471.

_____. "The Power of the Chinese Military," *Current History*, LIX, No. 349, September 1970, 129–133, 175–179.

——. *The Rise of Chinese Military Power*. Princeton: Princeton University Press, 1955.

——. "Soldiers in the Chinese Economy," *Asian Survey*, XI, No. 8, August 1971, 742–760.

"The Purge—An Interpretation," *China News Analysis* [Hong Kong], No. 618, July 1, 1966.

"The Revolutionary Committee and the Party in the Aftermath of the Cultural Revolution," *Current Scene: Developments in Mainland China* [Hong Kong], VIII, No. 8, April 15, 1970, 1–10.

Rigg, Robert B. *Red China's Fighting Hordes*. Harrisburg: Military Service Publishing, 1952.

Robinson, Thomas W. "Lin Piao as an Elite Type." (Rand Paper P-4639.) Santa Monica: Rand Corporation, July 1971.

Rolph, Hammond. "'People's War': Vision Vs. Reality," *Orbis*, XIV, No. 3, Fall 1970, 572–587.

Ryan, William L., and Summerlin, Sam. *The China Cloud*. Boston: Little, Brown, 1968.

Snow, Edgar. *The Other Side of the River: Red China Today*. New York: Random House, 1962.

——. *Red Star Over China*. New York: Random House, 1944.

Spitz, Allan. "Maoism and the People's Courts," *Asian Survey*, IX, No. 4, April 1969, 255–264.

Stewart, Ian. "The Purge Is Mao's Path to a People's Army in Communist China," *New York Times*, August 7, 1966, E3.

Ting, Li. *Militia of Communist China*. Hong Kong: Union Research Institute, 1954.

Topping, Seymour. "Reds in China Back Mao and Reaffirm National Policies," *New York Times*, August 14, 1966.

Union Research Institute. *Communist China: Ruthless Enemy or Paper Tiger?* Hong Kong: 1961.

U.S. Congress. 91st, 2d Session. House of Representatives. Committee on Foreign Affairs. Subcommittee on Asian and Pacific Affairs. *United States-China Relations: A Strategy for the Future*. Washington: GPO, 1970.

U.S. Department of Defense. *Toward a National Security Strategy of Realistic Deterrence: Statement of Secretary of Defense Melvin R. Laird on the Fiscal Year 1972–1976 Defense Program and the 1972 Defense Budget Before the Senate Armed Services Committee, March 15, 1971*. Washington: 1971.

U.S. Department of State. Bureau of Intelligence and Research. *Politico-Military Relationships in Communist China*, by Ralph L. Powell. Washington: GPO, 1963.

U.S. Department of State. Bureau of Public Affairs. Division of Publications. *United States Relations with China with Special Reference to the Period 1944–1949*. (Department of State

Publication No. 3573, Far Eastern Series 30.) Washington: Division of Publications, 1949.

Van Ness, Peter. *Revolution and Chinese Foreign Policy: Peking's Support for Wars of National Liberation.* Berkeley: University of California Press, 1970.

Vogel, Ezra F. "Preserving Order in the Cities." Pages 75–98 in John Wilson Lewis (ed.), *The City in Communist China.* Palo Alto: Stanford University Press, 1971.

"What Has Happened to The Youth Corps?" *China News Analysis* [Hong Kong], No. 633, October 21, 1966.

Whitson, William W. "The Concept of Military Generation: The Chinese Communist Case," *Asian Survey,* VIII, No. 11, November 1968, 921–947.

––––––. "The Field Army in Chinese Communist Military Politics," *China Quarterly* [London], No. 37, January–March 1969, 1–30.

––––––. "The Military: Their Roles in the Policy Powers." Pages 95–122 in Frank N. Trager, and William Henderson (eds.), *Communist China, 1949–1969: A Twenty-Year Appraisal.* New York: New York University Press, for the American-Asian Educational Exchange, 1970.

––––––. *Organizational Perspectives and Decision-Making in the Chinese Communist High Command.* (Rand Paper P–4593.) Santa Monica: Rand Corporation, March 1971.

Zagoria, Donald S. *The Sino-Soviet Conflict, 1956–1961.* Princeton: Princeton University Press, 1962.

GLOSSARY

ASEAN—*See* Association of Southeast Asian Nations.

Asia and Pacific Council (ASPAC)—Formed in June 1966 by nine noncommunist nations to promote cooperation and solidarity among them. Participants are Australia, Japan, Malaysia, Nationalist China, New Zealand, Philippines, South Korea, South Vietnam, and Thailand.

ASPAC—*See* Asia and Pacific Council.

Association of Southeast Asian Nations (ASEAN)—Regional organization established in August 1967 by Thailand, Malaysia, Philippines, Indonesia, and Singapore to cooperate in the fields of food production, commerce, industry, civil aviation, tourism, communications, meteorology, and shipping

Brezhnev Doctrine—Also known as the "theory of limited sovereignty." The Soviet Union sought to justify its invasion of Czechoslovakia in August 1968 on the theory that other socialist countries had the right to intervene when internal developments in a socialist country endangered "the Socialist community as a whole."

cadre—Person who holds any position in the Chinese Communist bureaucracy but most often denotes a person in administrative work and seldom is applied to a functionary of the lowest rank. Term is often used, in a more restricted sense, to denote a person who has been fully indoctrinated in Party ideology and methods and is employed in ways that make use of this training. Cadres often are, but need not be, Chinese Communist Party members.

China Proper—Area of China, south of Great Wall, included in eighteen ancient provinces. That territory in 1971 was occupied by seventeen modern provinces and two autonomous regions. These were: in the North—Hopeh, Honan, Shansi, and Shantung provinces and Ninghsia Hui Autonomous Region; in the Northwest —Shensi and Kansu provinces; in the Center—Anhwei, Kiangsi, Hupeh, and Hunan provinces; in the East—Kiangsu and Chekiang provinces; in the Southwest—Szechwan, Yunnan, and Kweichow provinces; and in the South—Fukien and Kwangtung provinces and Kwangsi Chuang Autonomous Region.

Chinese—(1) Language of the Han (*q.v.*); (2) synonym for Han; (3) citizen(s) of the Chinese state (*Chung-kuo jen-min*); (4) indigenous ethnic groups of China or member thereof (*Chung-hua min-tsu*).

Comintern—Best known name for the Communist International; also known as the Third International. An international organization to promote world communism sponsored by the Soviet Union; it held its first congress in 1919. Six other congresses met before World War II began. It was disbanded in 1943. A successor to the international socialist organizations, the First and Second Internationals, that were founded in 1864 and 1889, respectively.

Commune—Also known as People's Commune, successor institution to agricultural collective of mid-1950s, utilized to socialize agriculture. First Commune founded in 1958 as part of Great Leap Forward (q.v.) campaign and in succeeding years underwent structural, as well as functional, changes. In 1959 Commune broken down into production brigades, each encompassing a large village or cluster of small villages; brigades were divided into production teams based on neighborhoods or hamlets. In early 1970s Communes performed some administrative functions and were framework within which production brigades and production teams operated.

Cultural Revolution—See Great Proletarian Cultural Revolution.

democratic centralism—The basic organizational principle of the People's Republic of China under which the representative organs of both state and Party are elected by lower bodies and in turn elect their executive arms at corresponding levels. Within both the representative and executive bodies, the minority must abide by the decisions of the majority, and lower bodies must obey the orders of the higher level organs.

fen—Smallest monetary unit; one-hundredth of yuan (q.v.); the official exchange rate is one fen equals US$0.004.

First Five Year Plan (1953–57)—Initial economic development effort after 1949–52 recovery from wartime disruption; followed Soviet model of economic planning. Industry, especially heavy industry, favored under plan.

Greater China—All of the territory of China.

Great Leap—See Great Leap Forward.

Great Leap Forward—Campaign beginning in 1958 and lasting through 1960 designated to accomplish at a greatly accelerated rate the economic modernization of the country, with an emphasis on industry. Often referred to as the Great Leap. An enduring institution of the campaign is the People's Commune (q.v.).

Great Proletarian Cultural Revolution—Official title of campaign (usually referred to as the Cultural Revolution), begun in 1966 and subsiding in 1969, to rekindle revolutionary fervor by inculcating Mao Tse-tung Thought (q.v.) and to eliminate revisionism (q.v.), associated by Maoists with PRC Chairman Liu Shao-ch'i and his supporters.

704

Han—*Also*, Han Chinese. Term used to designate Chinese ethnic group, which constitutes 94 percent of population; native speakers of Chinese (*q.v.*).

hsiang—Township; administrative village. Administrative unit approximately coterminous with traditional primary marketing area and, since mid-1960s, with the People's Commune (*q.v.*).

hsien—County, an administrative subdivision of a province or autonomous region.

Hundred Flowers Campaign—Government-sponsored initiative to permit greater intellectual and artistic freedom and variety. Introduced first into drama and other arts in mid-1956 under official slogan, "Let a hundred flowers bloom; let the hundred schools of thought contend," the movement spread to intellectual expression and, by early May 1957, was being interpreted as permission for intellectuals to criticize political institutions of regime. Movement halted abruptly at end of May 1957, at which time antirightist campaign was launched.

jinn—One of a class of spirits believed by Muslims to inhabit the earth, to assume various forms, and to exercise supernatural power.

kaoliang—A variety of grain sorghum, grown chiefly in North China and Manchuria. The seeds are used for food and in winemaking; and the stalks, for fodder, thatching, and fuel.

Long March—Famous yearlong trek, beginning in October 1934, carried out by Mao Tse-tung's Red Army (predecessor of People's Liberation Army) to escape government forces sent to suppress them. Over 100,000 people began overland trek from communist bases in Kiangsi Province and elsewhere in the south and, a year later, some 20,000 survivors reached Shensi Province in northwest, communist headquarters for the next decade.

Mahayana Buddhism—Literally, Buddhism of the Greater Vehicle. One of the two major sects of world Buddhism, established in first century A.D.; predominant sect in China, Korea, and Japan.

Manchuria—Geographic region from which Manchus (a Tungusic ethnic group that ruled China from 1644 to 1911) came. Most of Manchuria presently included in three northeastern provinces: Heilungkiang, Kirin, and Liaoning.

Mandarin—National language. In its spoken form, it is used by, and is intelligible to, roughly three-fourths of the population.

Mao Tse-tung Thought—Sayings and writings of Mao that serve as major source of national ideology.

National People's Congress—Highest popular assembly of PRC, elected in accordance with principles of democratic centralism (*q.v.*).

Outer China—Greater China (*q.v.*), minus China Proper (*q.v.*). Includes the three Manchurian provinces, Inner Mongolian

Autonomous Region, Tsinghai Province, Sinkiang Uighur Autonomous Region, and Tibetan Autonomous Region.

People's Commune—*See* Commune.

Politburo—Political Bureau. Policymaking group, consisting of approximately twenty-five persons, within Chinese Communist Party Central Committee. Politburo contains within it the Standing Committee—the handful of the most senior Party leaders—as well as other full and alternate membes.'

production brigade—Subdivision of a People's Commune (*q.v.*); above production team (*q.v.*).

production team—Subdivision within a People's Commune (*q.v.*), below production brigade (*q.v.*).

Red Guards—Teenage bands that first appeared in mid-1966 wearing armbands imprinted with words *Hung Wei Ping* (Red Guards) and carrying copies of the little red book, *Quotations from Chairman Mao*. Acting under leadership of Mao and his adherents, Red Guards were vanguard of Great Proletarian Cultural Revolution (*q.v.*).

"redness"—Political and ideological correctness, according to Maoist criteria.

revisionism—As used by Communists, term refers to political, economic, and social tendencies that stray rightward from orthodox Marxism-Leninism. The Chinese Communists have insisted that these tendencies are counterrevolutionary and that the Soviet Union is infected by this negative phenomenon.

"revisionist"—*See* revisionism.

SEATO—*See* Southeast Asia Treaty Organization.

Southeast Asia Treaty Organization (SEATO)—Eight-member regional collective security arrangement established in September 1954. Member nations are: Australia, France, New Zealand, Pakistan, Philippines, Thailand, United Kingdom, and United States.

tatzupao—Big character poster(s), placed on walls and other conspicuous places as part of public information and propaganda activities; became extremely prevalent during Great Proletarian Cultural Revolution (*q.v.*).

"theory of limited sovereignty"—*See* Brezhnev Doctrine.

work point—Unit of credit toward subsequent remuneration given to member of agricultural production team (*q.v.*) for completion of work for the collective account. Each assigned task carries an agreed norm, for which a satisfactory day's work will ordinarily result in earning of ten work points. Value of work point in given team is calculated at end of accounting period (usually annual), after first determining net assets available for distribution to team members. Net assets divided by total work points gives value of one work point. Payment is made in kind, cash, or combination of these.

Wu-han—Name used to refer to the tri-city complex of Wu-ch'ang, Han-yang, and Hankow that is situated at confluence of Yangtze and Han rivers.

yuan—The monetary unit; divided into ten chiao and 100 fen (*q.v.*). Exchange rate, as decreed by PRC, is 2.46 yuan equal US$1.00.

INDEX

Chiang Kai-shek (*see also* Republic of China): 1, 121, 466; biographical material, 5, 65, 71, 75, 79, 603, 604–605, 608
Chiang people: 110
chiao: 570
Chiaot'ung Polytechnic University: 463
Chieh Fang Jih Pao: 141, 361
Ch'ien San-ch'iang: 487
Chihli, Gulf of: 14, 18, 21
Chi-k'ou powerplant: 18
children: 83, 107, 139, 178; daughters, 159, 161, 162, 169; infanticide, 163; rights, 166, 171; sons, 159, 161, 164
Chile: 345, 347
Chin Ching-mai: 220
Chin dynasty: 39
Ch'in-huang-tao: x, 532
Ch'in state: 38, 39, 43, 45
China Association for Science and Technology: 483, 486
China Committee for the Promotion of International Trade: 533, 535
China News Agency: 361
China Ocean Steamship Agency: 389
China Pictorial: 362
China Press Agency: 365
Chinese Academy of Agricultural Sciences: 413
Chinese Academy of Medical Sciences: 187, 486
Chinese Academy of Sciences: 216, 301, 413, 457, 458, 467–478 *passim*, 480–482, 483–485, 487
Chinese checkers: 177
Chinese Communist Party: vii, 1, 32, 70, 71, 73, 76, 77, 276, 284–289, 289–291; agricultural policies, 397, 415, 419; Central Committee, 235, 241, 272, 276, 278, 279, 285, 287, 288; Congresses, 7, 288, 424, 472; crisis of leadership, 262, 268; labor unions and, 495, 505, 507, 508; membership, 123, 124, 127, 137, 139, 282; military affairs and, 614, 616, 620; role and function, 377, 378; science and technology, 467, 476, 477, 484
Chinese Communist Youth League: 7, 139, 141, 142, 193, 210, 287, 291
Chinese language (*see also* vernacular literature): equivalent of alphabetic order, 278; reform of, 70, 94, 96,

209; written, 35, 38, 43, 70, 94, 96, 211, 205
Chinese opera: 211, 217, 221
Chinese People's Association for Friendship with Foreign Countries: 301
Chinese People's Political Consultative Conference: 235, 289, 467
Chinese People's Soviet Republic: 609
Chinese People's Volunteers: 612
Chinese Renaissance. *See* New Culture Movement
Chinese Soviet Republic: 74, 234
Chinese Turkestan. *See* Sinkiang Uighur Autonomous Region
Chinese Welfare Association: 187, 188
Ch'ing dynasty: 5, 39, 51–53, 99, 215
Ching people: 111, 114
Chingpo people: 110, 111
Ch'iu Hui-tso: 279
Chi-Yu Banking Corporation: 570
chopsticks: 41
Chou En-lai: 7, 10, 75, 81, 447, 479, 543–544; biographical material, 121, 221, 289, 320, 323, 327, 328, 333, 339, 343, 603, 604; foreign policy, 82, 301, 303, 317, 319, 325, 332, 334, 337, 341, 342, 344; leadership, 241, 262, 271, 272, 273, 275, 277, **278**, 279, 284, 288; military affairs, 299, 316, 325, 631; Overseas Chinese, **330**
Chou dynasty: 39, 40–43
Christianity (*see also* Roman Catholicism): viii, 57, 58, 79, 82, 113, 145, 149, 150
Chu Hsi: 48
Chu Te: 74, 278, 603, 605, 606, 607, 609, 615
Ch'u Yuan: 216
Chuang people: 28, 91, 105, 106, 111; language, 97
Ch'un, Prince: 66
Chungking: 14, 23, 441, 446, 526; capital, 76, 352
Chung-kuo: 36
Ch'ung-ming Island: 19
civil aviation: 447, 543, 545, 551
civil servants: 41, 44, 51, 249, 585
civil service examinations: 2, 39, 46, 47, 52, 64, 117, 118, 194, 195
clan or lineage. *See* extended family
class structure. *See* social classes
climate: vii, 1, 13, 22–24

711

clothing: 113, 178–179, 181, 531

coal: 24, 434, 437, 441, 449, 450, 451, 455

coinage: *See* currency

collectively owned enterprises: 433

collectivization of agriculture (*see also* People's Communes): 80, 81, 82, 113, 266, 267, 268, 396, 414–422

Colombia: 347

Common Program: 198, 209, 235, 247, 314, 467, 580, 612, 619

communes. *See* People's Communes

communications (*see also* telecommunications): x, 62, 63

Communist Party. *See* Chinese Communist Party

Communist Youth League. *See* Chinese Communist Youth League

compradors: 59, 118, 125

concubinage: 159, 169, 170

Confucian classics: 48, 194, 211–212

Confucianism: viii, 3, 39, 44, 46, 61, 70; role in society, 142, 143, 144, 146, 251, 252

Congo (Brazzaville): 339, 340, 341

conscription: xi, 602, 614, 626, 627

constitution. *See* State Constitution

construction: 454, 456; cement plants, 435, 448

consumer goods: 382, 430, 437, 443, 445, 522, 526, 529

cooperatives: 189, 236, 384, 420; credit, 567, 568, 572; supply and marketing, 522, 523, 528, 530

copper: 434, 438, 450

corrective labor. *See* forced labor

cotton: 57, 387, 429, 524; crop, 396, 404, 408, 412; textiles, 447, 525, 531, 537

counterrevolutionary activities: 579, 580, 586, 593, 595, 598

courts: ix, 243, 591

credit: 385, 431, 542, 564, 565, 567, 572, 573, 574

crime and punishment (*see also* forced labor): 188, 579, 580, 589, 590, 591–599

crops (*see also* grain; industrial crops): ix, 23, 103, 106, 109, 112, 396, 412

Cuba: 311, 345, 347, 368

Cultural Relations with Foreign Countries, Commission for: 301

Cultural Revolution. *See* Great Proletarian Cultural Revolution

currency: 41, 43, 55, 564, 570

Czechoslovakia: 276, 312, 343, 344, 345, 368, 455, 477, 488

Dahomey: 340

Dairen. *See* Lu-ta

Dalai Lama: 107, 294, 321

death rate: 182

decentralization of government: 375, 376, 377, 385–388, 392, 393, 436, 525, 526

degrees, academic: 207

democratic centralism: 120–121, 291, 235, 254

Denmark: 342, 343, 535

department stores: 531

development plans: 236, 375, 412, 528; First Five Year, 81, 236, 266, 420, 435, 436, 470, 487, 500, 502, 512, 543; Second Five Year, 422, 429; Ten-Year Science Plan, 479; Third Five Year, 529; Twelve-Year Science Plan, 472, 473, 474

diet and nutrition: 101, 104, 177–178, 183, 395, 403, 405, 407, 531, 598

diplomatic recognition: 72, 79, 342, 345

disease and illness: 93, 103, 108, 110, 112, 143, 180, 182–183

divination: 108, 110

divorce: 166, 169

double cropping: 399, 401

Double Ten Day: 67

drama, traditional. *See* Chinese opera

Dream of the Red Chamber: 218

dynastic regimes: 39

Dzungaria basin: 16

East Germany: 343, 345, 368, 455, 488

economic planning: 267, 383, 386, 392–394, 520, 528, 558; role of government, 377–380

economy: ix, 8–9, 10, 373–394

Ecuador: 345, 347

education (*see also* higher education; private schools; vocational and technical schools; work-study school programs): viii, 3, 41, 46, 85, 124, 138, 139, 165, 192, 194–210; scientific education, 414, 457, 468, 469, 477

Egypt (United Arab Republic): xi, 337–338
electricity. *See* power generating
electronics: 438, 448, 457, 458, 490
elite class: 117, 127, 160, 162, 179 180, 194
embargoes on trade: 538, 540
employment (*see also* labor force): 206, 207, 216, 458, 501, 503
enemies of the people: 123, 125–127, 132, 150, 235, 264, 350, 515, 595
English language: 534
Ethiopia: xi, 341
ethnic groups (*see also* Han Chinese; minority nationalities): vii, 28, 33
Everest, Mount: 14, 16
exports: x, 231, 228, 386, 449, 520, 537–538; agriculture, 395, 409: industry, 442, 443, 447
extended family: 119, 141, 157, 160–161, 166–168; under communism, 171, 174

family system: 37, 83, 104, 115, 135, 151, 152, 157–171, 174
famine and food shortages: 77, 80, 83, 108, 266, 268, 269, 422, 431
fen: 570
Feng Ting: 152
fertilizers: x, 395, 397, 408; imports, 409, 537; manufacturing plants, 428, 435, 442, 443, 444
festivals: traditional, 146, 176, 223, 224
films: 225, 369–371, 559
financial system (*see also* banking system; budget): 571–575
Finland: 342, 343, 344
fiscal year: 557
fisheries: 25, 112, 399, 405
five goods: 151
Five Year Development Plans. *See* development plans
floods and droughts. *See* water conservancy
folk arts: 77, 223, 224, 225, 227–228
folk medicine: 146
folk religions: 38, 143, 144, 211
Foochow: 22, 57, 434
footbinding: 39, 49, 52, 169
Forbidden City: 227, 228
forced labor: 80, 188, 497, 501, 515–516, 543, 578, 590; reform through labor, 597–598

foreign aid programs. *See* assistance to foreign countries
foreign exchange earnings: 314, 394, 407, 409, 448, 541–542, 565; agriculture, 395, 404, 405; exports, 520, 538, 541
foreign influences: 45, 46, 48, 50, 53, 54–61, 462; students abroad, 466, 481; Western cultural influences, 118, 157, 217, 223, 224
foreign nationals: 57, 62, 592
foreign relations (*see also* border tensions and agreements): v, 62, 73, 280, 281, 293–295, 297–347, 520
foreign trade (*see also* Japan; Soviet Union): ix, x, 36, 46, 50, 51, 55, 56, 57, 63, 519, 520, 532–542, 569; government control, **387, 389, 393**; trading partners, 320, 326, 328–329, 330–331, 343, 345, 346–347, 538
forestry and timber: 179, **387, 399,** 406, 437; firewood, 407
Formosa Strait crises: 267, 305, 619, 620
Four Good Movement: 358, 617
Four Olds Movement: 258
Fourth Route Army: 77, 609
France: 63, 68, 69; trade with, 55, 57, 58, 343, 534, 538
Francis Xavier, Saint: 51
Fukien Province: xviii, 13, 55, 197, 366; industry, 436, 437, 546; language, 95; population, **27, 30, 313**
Fu-shun: 455
Fu-t'an University: 448

General Office for Internal Affairs: 582
Geneva Conferences: **82, 323–324, 332**
geomancy: 42
Germany (*see also* **East Germany;** West Germany): 63, 68, 69
Ghana: 339, 340
Ghenghis Khan: 104
Giles, Herbert A.: **97**
Giri, Varahgiri Venkata: 321
gold: 437, 542, 565, 571
Goloks: 294
government (*see also* Chinese Communist Party; decentralization of government; development plans; local government; National People's Congress): vii, 43, 65, 68, 69, 186–187, 632; chairmanship of

Hsu Shin-yu: 279
Hu Men River: 20
Hu Shih: 213, 218
Huai River: 17, 19, 50, 395, 411
Huang Hua: 337
Huang K'o-ch'eng: 616
Huang Yung-sheng: 275, 277, 279, 280, 630
Hui peoples: 28, 89, 91, 92, 100, 102, 103, 105, 106, 111
Huichow dialect: 95
Hu-k'ou power plant: 18
human hair: 538
Hunan Province: xviii, 13, 27, 74, 91, 256; industry, 438, 444, 450
Hundred Days: 463
Hundred Flowers Campaign: 82, 192, 222, 266, 267, 290, 349, 356, 363, 472
Hung Hsiu-ch'uan: 60
Hung society: 54
Hungary: 343, 345, 477
Hupeh Province: xviii, 13, 27, 438, 440, 449

I-ching (Book of Changes): 211
ideologies, political (see also Marxism-Leninism): 60, 67, 70, 250–254; common man, 37, 77; universal man, 48
Ignatiev, Nikolai: 59
Ili River: 21
imports: ix, 394, 404, 535–537; customs duties, 388, 560, 563; fertilizers, 409, 445; for industry, 433, 436; grain, 395, 408, 424
income: ix, 130, 135, 496, 512; cash payments, 571; family, 164, 165, 181, 189, 427, 428; per capita, 373, 519
India: 12, 47, 57, 82, 84, 519; border tension, 294, 619–620; diplomatic relations with, 298, 309, 319, 320–322; Soviet Union and, 311
Indonesia: 326–329; Chinese population, 30, 31, 55, 313
industrial crops (see also forestry and timber): 404–405
industry: ix, 62, 83, 206, 267, 380, 397, 433–456, 458; labor force, 495, 498–500, 502–503; productivity, 381, 496, 516, 517; research, 457, 467; safety measures, 515; wages, 510, 511, 512

infant mortality: 183
inflation: 78, 196
inheritance: 159, 169
Inner Mongolian Autonomous Region: vii, xviii, 13, 14, 25, 27, 87, 93, 247, 293, 390; atomic research sites, 488, 494; industry, 437, 441; radio and television, 366, 367
insurance: 189, 514, 568–569
intellectuals and scholars: 65, 80, 510, 579; politics and, 121, 198, 252; status, 43, 47, 116, 123, 124, 130, 168, 235
internal security (see also People's Liberation Army; police forces): xi, 577–591
international affairs. See foreign relations; United Nations
International Scientific Symposium: 480
investigative reports: 360
investment: 555, 564, 567, 568, 572; in agriculture, 424, 430; in industry, 382, 384, 556; Overseas Chinese, 569
Iraq: 338
iron and steel: 41, 470, 536; ore, 449, 453; pig iron, 439, 440; production, 437, 438–441, 442, 452
Irrawaddy River: 20, 21
irrigation (see also water conservancy): 18, 104, 106, 175, 395, 397, 403, 408, 410, 411, 455
Irtysh River: 20
Islam (see also Muslims): viii, 46, 50, 60, 144–145, 148, 292
Israel: 337
Italy: 304, 343, 345, 540

Japan: 30, 63, 65, 68, 368; aid from, 434, 445, 480; Chinese students in, 64, 67, 463, 464; North Korea and, 323; relations with, 51, 298, 315–318, 620; trade with, x, 317, 535, 538, 539, 540; war with, 69, 75
Joffe, Adolph: 604
Joint State-Private Bank: 564, 566
judicial system: viii-ix, 243, 591–594, 595
Jurched peoples: 49

K'aifeng: 39
K'ai-lan coal mines: 509
Kan language: 87, 89, 94, 95

Li Hung-chang: 64, 65
Li Li-san: 507
Li people: 97, 111, 114
Li Po: 221
Li Ta-chao: 213
Li Te-sheng: 281, 288
Li Tso-p'eng: 279
Liang Ch'i-ch'ao: 63
Liang Pin: 219
Liao Ch'eng-chih: 317
Liao Lu-yen: 417
Liao River: 15, 18
Liaoning Province: xviii, 13, 25, 27, 91; industry, 436, 437, 439, 449, 450, 451, 452
Liaotung peninsula: 21
Liberation Army Daily: 359
libraries: 61
Libya: 338
Lien-yun-chiang: x, 532
life expectancy: viii
light industry: 383, 438
limited sovereignty theory: 312
Lin Piao (*see also* Yeh Ch'un): 194, 200, 255, 258, 259, 603; foreign policy, 268, 270, 271, 274, 276, 277, 279, 280, 284, 288, 299, 324, military leader, v, 6, 615, 616–618, 625; successor to Mao, 237, 271, 273, 286
Lisu people: 97, 110
literacy: viii, 113, 197, 204, 209, 230, 504, 598; illiteracy, 230, 361, 369, 628
literature (*see also* vernacular literature): 43, 52, 70, 208, 220; classical, 211, 214, 216
Little Red Book. See *Quotations from Chairman Mao*
Liu Ning-yi: 508
Liu Pang: 44
Liu Po-ch'eng: 278
Liu Shao-ch'i (*see also* Wang Kuang-mei): 7, 141, 193, 200, 201, 239n, 241, 327; land distribution, 80, 419, 424; leadership, 84, 85, 256, 268, 270, 281, 357; Maoists and, 269, 272, 273, 274, 615
Liuchow peninsula: 21
livestock: 101, 104, 105, 106, 110, 111, 112, 174, 181, 430; breeding, 399, 405, 412; meat, 177, 178; slaughter by peasants, 82, 293
living conditions: 173–189
Lo Jui-ch'ing: 270

local government: 244–250; finance, 247, 555, 556, 562, 563, 574
Lolo people. *See* Yi people
Lon Nol: 334
Long March: 74, 75, 127, 606–607
Lop Nor test site: 491, 493, 494, 635
Lo-yang: 39, 438, 442, 443
L-T trade agreement: 317
Lu Hsun: 70, 153, 218
Lu P'ing: 363
Lu-Ting-i: 352, 353, 359
Lung Shu-chin: 294
Lungmen power plant: 18
Lu-shun: 22
Lu-ta (Dairen): x, 22, 532; manufacturing, 78, 444, 446, 453
Luxembourg: 345
Lysenko, Trofim: 407, 414

Ma-an-shan steelworks: 440
Macao: 13, 30, 51, 55, 533
machine industry: 437, 441–443, 446
malaria: 183
Malaysia: 30, 55, 327, 329–330; trade, 540, 541
Mali: 341
Malik, Adam: 328
Malraux, Andre: 343
Malta: 345
Manchuria: 12, 18, 22, 23, 87, 610; agriculture, 403, 406, 429; industry, 434, 500; Japanese invasion, 30, 74, 76; Russians and, 56, 59–60, 78, 310; settlement, 52, 400, 401
Manchus: 28, 51–68, 91, 100; dynasty, 5, 39, 215; language, 97, 99
Mandarin language: viii, 87, 89, 94, 95, 207
Manichaeism: 46
manual labor: 202, 250, 252, 289; prestige, 131, 136, 153
manufacturing: 433, 438–449, 454
Mao Tse-tung (*see also* Chiang Ch'ing; Marxism-Leninism): biographical material, 95, 122, 141, 196, 197, 211, 263, 272, 277, 474, 605–611 *passim*, 630; Chairman, v, 81, 236, 241, 266, 286; cult of personality, 151, 255–259, 264, 266, 272, 277; Cultural Revolution and, 271, 274, 275, 276; ideology, 77, 123, 125, 235, 357, 363, 366, 370, 375, 376; leadership, 1, 73, 79, 84, 85, 266,

268, 270, 273, 277, 278, 279, 284, 288; successor, 237, 271, 273, 286; **works listed, 255**

Mao Tse-tung Thought (*see also Quotations fom Chairman Mao; Selected Works of Mao Tse-tung*): 32, 85, 142, 155, 186, 213, 214, 248, 271, 287, 414, 507; agricultural policy, 374, 412, 420, 421; arts, 192, 193, 194; education, 197, 198, 200; foreign relations, 310, 321, 339; military policy, 601, 606, 607, 616, 624, 635; source of political values, 126, 130, 208, 234, 249, 254–259, 263–264; system of justice, 580, 589

Mao Tse-tung Thought Propaganda Teams: 186, 194, 202

Mao Tun: 218

Marco Polo: 39, 50

Marcos, Ferdinand: 334

marriage: 53, 106, 109, 111, 112, 141, 144, 154; remarriage of widows, 49, 161, 169, 171; selection of spouse, 157, 161, 166, 168, 169, 170

Marriage Law: 158, 170, 265

Marshall, George C.: 78

Marxist-Communist University: 197

Marxism-Leninism: 1, 2, 7, 35, 70, 77, 145, 191, 212, 234, 254, 257, 578

mass mobilization campaigns: 116, 129, 265, 290, 350, 354, 355–358

mass organizations: 117, 127, 141, 265, 350, 582, 585, 609; categories, 289–291; labor, 499, 509; religious, 146, 147, 148, 149, 150; scientific, 467; social, 176

mass trials: 594–595

Matsu Island: 83, 84

Mauritania: 341

May Day: 176, 177

May Fourth Movement: 69–70, 168, 195–196

May 7 cadre schools: 208, 209, 248, 271, 289, 508

medicine: 146, 184–188, 537; personnel, viii, 33, 140, 498; research, 187, 457, 458, 462, 466, 467, 474

Mekong River: 14, 20, 21, 333

memberships (*see also* **United Nations**): xi

Mencius: 48

Mencius (Meng-tzu): 42

merchant class: 36, 45, 46, 50, 51, 53

Mexico: 55, 345

Miao peoples: 28, 89, 105, 106, 111, 112; language, 97, 98

migrations (*see also* resettlement campaigns): 29, 59, 588

military academies: 65, 71, 604, 607, 627

Military Commission: 241

military missions: 301, 324, 341, 612

military rank; 128, 153, 614, 618

military regions: ix, 380, 621, 629

militia: xi, 124, 590, 602, 608, 614, 616, 627, 631, 632–633

millet: 399, 403

Min language: 87, 89, 94, 95

Min River: 20

mineral resources: 24, 434, 436; mining, 435, 348, 442, 449–453

Ming dynasty: 39, 50, 221, 226, 227, 228

ministries: 382, 383, 384, 522; listing, 242; research institutes, 458, 485, 486

Ministry of Agriculture and Forestry: **242, 243, 486, 563**

Ministry of Commerce: 382, 522, 525, 530, 563

Ministry of Communications: 242, 243, 545, 546

Ministry of Culture and Education: 242, 243, 365, 369, 475, 486

Ministry of Economic Relations with Foreign Countries: 242, 243, 301

Ministry of Finance: 388, 555, 557, 563, 564, 568

Ministry of Foreign Affairs: 301, 302

Ministry of Foreign Trade: 301, 522, 533

Ministry of Fuels and Chemical Industries: 242, 243

Ministry of Information: 360

Ministry of Internal Affairs: 242, 250, 582, 583

Ministry of Machine Building: 242, 243

Ministry of National Defense: 301, 482, 625, 629

Ministry of Posts and Telecommunications: 353

Ministry of Public Health: 32, 187, 486

Ministry of Public Security: xi, 581, 582, 587

Ministry of Trade: 521

nuclear test ban treaty: 491
nuclear weapons: 299, 434, 479, 487, 629
numerology: 42

O-chi-na River: 21
oil. *See* petroleum
Okinawa: 30, 317
On the Correct Handling of Contradictions Among the People (Mao): 125, 255
Open Door policy: 63
Opium Wars: 57–58
optical tools: 443
Ordos Plateau: 18
Outer Mongolia: 68, 78, 82, 325–326; border agreement, 84–85
Ou-yang Shan: 219
Overseas Chinese: 55, 67, 95, 120; Communism among, 302, 313; distribution of, 30, 326, 329, 334; dual nationality of, 327; mainland affairs and, 239, 361, 417, 429; number, 11, 26, 313–315; remittances from, 314, 315, 330, 542, 566; scientific recruitment among 469, 473
Overseas Chinese Affairs Commission: 301
Overseas Chinese Investment Corporation: 314, 569, 570

Pa Chin: 218
paddlefish: 25
Pai people: 97, 110
pai-kar: 403
painting: 226
Pakistan: 318–320, 321, 447, 540, 631; aid agreements, xi, 303; border with, 12, 84
palaces and temples: 227, 228, 229
Palaung people: 98
Palestinian guerrillas: 338
Pami people: 110
Pamir mountains: vii, 14, 15
Panama Canal: 347
Panchen Lama: 107, 294, 295
pandas, giant: 25
Paoans: 103, 105
pao-chia system: 121
Pao-t'ou: 436
paper: 406, 407, 437, 438, 449, 460; invented, 44, 226
paper tiger: 306
Paracel Islands: 21

Paris peace talks: 325
Pathet Lao: 332, 333
peaceful coexistence: 314, 333, 339; with India, 300, 301, 321
Pearl River: 14, 15, 20
peasantry: 2, 74, 129, 132; class, 44, 117, 119, 123, 133, 235; values, 121, 122, 160
peddlers: 519, 524, 528, 562
Pei River: 20
Peking man: 229
Peking Municipality: ix, 13, 17, 23, 27, 274, 408; banking and insurance, 565, 566, 568, 569; dialect, 94, 95; higher education, 185, 207, 464, 465, 475; history, 49, 50, 58, 72; industry, 436, 437, 440, 442, 445, 447, 448, 455; public information, 359, 363, 364, 367, 368; science in, 467, 479, 480; trade, 531, 533
Peking National University (Peita): 64, 69, 168, 195, 207, 208, 463, 466
Peking opera: 270, 280, 368
Pen-ch'i steelworks: 439, 440
P'eng Chen: 271, 272
P'eng Te-huai: 268, 270, 606, 612, 616
Penglung people: 110
People's Bank of China: 209, 382, 389, 555, 564–566, 570, 573
People's Communes: viii, 6, 25, 180, 246–247, 498, 526, 565; agriculture and, ix, 406, 422–428; communications, x, 366, 367; establishment, 83, 132, 134, 267; number, 396, 397; schools, 200, 204; security functions, 587; social organization, 174, 187, 188, 291
People's Congress. *See* National People's Congress
People's Daily: 359, 360
People's Liberation Army (PLA) (*see also* Red Army; Soviet Union used as model): vii, xi, 7, 79, 117, 509, 530, 601, 616–618; agriculture and, 397, 429, 615, 619, 624; Cultural Revolution and, 577, 582, 603, 624; leadership role, 117, 233, 261, 268, 270, 271, 275, 280, 284, 617, 626; police duties, 587, 590; political cadres, 128, 186, 187, 269, 281; Production and Construction Corps, 389–390; propaganda by, 220, 357, 358, 362; Red Guards and, 273, 274; schools and, 202, 206, 623; trans-

portation system and, 545, 546, 548–549

People's Police: xi, 583, 587–590, 591, 595

periodicals: 358, 359, 362; scientific, 457, 461, 462, 479

Peru: 345, 347

petroleum: 24, 437, 438, 443; oil refineries, 388, 452; oilfields, 434, 452; shortage, 336, 633; technology, 470, 474

Philippines: 30, 31, 55, 334

philosophy (see also ideologies, political): 41–43, 48, 212–214

pigs: 175, 387, 405, 419, 525; hog bristles, 522, 537

pigtail: 99

planning, governmental. See development plans

plastics: 443, 445

Podgorny, Nikolai: 326

Poland: 343, 344, 345, 368, 477, 488

police forces (see also militia; People's Police): 582, 587–591

police schools: 583, 589

Politburo: 7, 235, 285, 287, 288, 625; membership, 278; Standing Committee, 266, 271, 279, 287

political dynamics: 261–295

political parties (see also Chinese Communist Party; Kuomintang Nationalist Party): 289, 290

political reeducation. See thought reform

political system. See government

political values (see also ideologies, political): 142, 202, 250

polygamy: 104, 107, 111, 170

population (see also minority nationalities; Overseas Chinese): vii, 1, 11, 25–27, 30–33, 380; in agriculture, 24, 395; increasing, 33, 36, 54

porcelain: 44, 57, 225

ports and harbors (see also treaty ports): x, 22, 57

Portugal: 51, 55, 345

postal system: x, 62, 63, 353

posters. See wall newspapers

power generating: 179, 180, 403, 410, 453; hydroelectric, 18, 21, 435, 437, 438, 453–456

Pratas Islands: 21

prestige and status symbols (see also manual labor): 104, 111, 126, 127–131, 133, 137, 250; educated women, 162

prices: 180, 181, 387, 408, 559

primary schools: 197, 202, 204

printing: 46, 48

private ownership: businesses, 81, 115, 124, 236, 237; land, 84, 174, 181, 237, 239, 247, 256, 416, 423, 427–428, 525, 527, 528

private schools: 61, 149, 198

procuratorates: ix, 237, 238, 244, 591, 592, 593

production brigades: 246, 367, 396, 410, 419, 423, 424, 425

production teams: 246, 367, 396, 423, 424, 425

proletariat. See working class

propaganda and subversive activities: 146, 343, 349, 352–358; Department of Propaganda, 192, 194, 352, 359, 369

prostitution: 188

Protestants: 58, 62, 145

provinces (see also decentralization of government): ix, xviii, 25, 27, 244, 365, 484, 525, 583; budgets, 560, 562; government, 379, 392, 592, 596; labor unions, 506; transportation responsibility, 548

public information (see also newspapers; periodicals): 94, 97, 225, 349, 358–369

Pulang people: 110

Pumi people: 106

puppet theater: 224

Pu-yi, Emperor: 66, 68

Puyi people, 28, 106, 111, 113; language, 97

pyrite: 445

Quemoy Island: 83, 84

Quotations from Chairman Mao: 201, 255, 256, 357, 362

radio broadcasting: x, 351, 352; educational programs, 365; propaganda abroad, 328, 329, 330, 332, 337, 339; transmitters, 364, 365, 448; wired, 366

Radio Peking: 339, 344, 365

radiotelescope: 482, 458

railroads: x, 22, 387, 389, 399, 406, 407, 435, 446, 454, 543–549 *passim*
rainfall: vii, viii, 2, 13, 22, 23, 399–400, 403
ramie: 387, 404, 525
Rangoon: 274
rapeseed: 404, 412
rationing: 137; cloth, 178, 180, 447; consumer goods, 525, 526, 529, 531; food, 178, 407, 422
Razak, Tun Abdul: 330
"red and expert" (Mao): 198
Red Army (*see also* People's Liberation Army): xi, 74, 75, 76, 603, 607, 608, 610
Red Army University: 197
Red Detachment of Women: 222, 370
Red Flag: 359, 360
Red Guards: 7, 193, 201, 229, 315, 357, 363, 368; court system and, 243, 272, 273; effects on industry and transportation, 435, 544
Red Lantern: 222, 370
Red River: 14, 20, 21, 24
reform through labor. *See* forced labor
reincarnation: 107
religion (*see also* Buddhism; Christianity; folk religions; Islam, spirit religions): viii, 82, 88, 142–150
Republic of China (Nationalist China) (*see also* Kuomintang Nationalist Party): vii, 26, 31, 68, 70, 71, 76, 77, 79, 237, 343, 351, 415, 465, 521; African nations and, 303, 339; Asian nations and, 317, 318, 321; loyalties, 577; off-shore islands, 83, 84; propaganda against, 82, 366; seat in United Nations, 8, 297, 304, 306–310
research institutes: 413, 482–486, 490, 559, 561
resettlement campaigns (*see also hsia fang* campaigns): 30–31, 207, 210, 248, 276, 431, 502, 516; urban youths to farms, 131, 135–137, 370, 390
revolutionary committees: 245, 273, 274, 275, 276, 281, 283, 353, 379, 380, 481
revolutionary operas. *See* Peking opera
Ricci, Matteo: 51
rice: 24, 181, 392, 410, 412; crop, 175, 176, 177, 396, 399, 400, 401–402; exports, 536, 537; rice wine, 402

rich peasant class: 122, 123, 125, 132, 138, 416
rights of the individual (*see also* censorship; private ownership): 37, 480, 595; freedom of religion, viii, 145; voting, 125, 240, 245
rivers: 13, 17–21, 548
roads and highways: x, 543, 544, 545, 548–551
Roman Catholicism: 145, 149; missionaries, 50, 51, 56, 58, 62
Romania: 342, 343, 344, 345, 368, 477, 488
rubber: x, 330, 336, 541
rural areas (*see also* resettlement campaigns): 179, 181, 291, 455, 552, 565; credit cooperatives, 567, 572, 574; health care, viii, 33, 186; labor force, 497–498; migrations from, 29, 120, 504; public information, 351, 355, 361, 369; public security, 584, 586–587, 590; social system, 115, 118, 129, 132–135; taxes, 561–562; trade, 526, 529, 530, 532
rural free markets: 525, 527, 528, 529
Russia (*see also* Soviet Union): 55, 56, 58, 59, 63, 68; language, 366
Russo-Japanese war: 64

Salars: 103, 105
salt taxes: 560, 563
Salween River: 14, 20, 21
San-Men Gorge power plant: 456
satellites, earth: 278, 458, 636
Sato, Eisaku: 318
savings, personal: 181, 391, 512, 556, 565, 566, 572
schistosomiasis: 183
schools. *See* education
science and technology (*see also* nuclear development): 201, 457–494, 503; standardization of machine parts, 442
Scientific and Technological Commission: 216, 458, 476, 477, 483
scientific development plans: 472, 473, 474, 479
Scientific Planning Commission: 472, 475, 476
scientific research: 389, 413, 482–486, 559
sculpture: 227, 230–231
secondary schools: 197, 204

346; scientific cooperation, 474, 477–478, 481, 487–488; technical assistance from, 268, 367, 407, 436–437, 455, 456, 470, 613, 616, 635; United Nations and, 307, 308, 309

Soviet Union used as model: 230, 514; armed forces, 268, 601; Communist Party, 70, 71; Constitution, 82; economic development, 374, 383, 385, 392–393; labor organization, 495, 517

Soviet University: 197

soybeans: 396, 399, 403, 412

Spain: 55, 345

spirit religions (*see also* ancestor worship): viii, 108, 110, 111, 113

sports and recreation: 177, 284, 302, 370; table tennis matches, 305, 322, 368

Spratley Islands: 21

Spring and Autumn Period: 41

Spring Festival (New Year): 176

Ssu-ma Ch'ien: 214

standard of living (*see also* inflation): 173, 189, 390, 391

state capitalism: 236, 382

State Constitution (*1954*): 7, 82, 92, 233, 236, 247, 314, 514, 580, 595, 619, 625; freedoms under, 87–88, 145, 349, 515

State Constitution (1970 draft): 349, **425, 515, 580, 595, 619, 625**

State Council: 241–243, 555

State enterprises: **x, 433, 559, 561,** 565, 572, 573; profit factor, 559–560; **trading companies, 522, 533, 534**

state farms: ix, 389–390, 397, 400, 425, 428, 567

state-private enterprises: 433, 523

strikes: 509, 545

Students' Federation: 291

submarines: 631, 634, 635

subversive activities: 338, 339, 341, **347, 361, 366; agents from Taiwan, 577**

Sudan: 338

sugar: 404, 412, 438, 449, 525

Suharto: 328

Sui dynasty: 17, 46, 229

suicide: 142, 161, 356

Sukarno: 327, 328

Sun Yat-sen (*see also* Soong, Chingling): 120, 196, 414, 604; biographical material, 5, 66–68, 70, 71, 157

Sun Yat-sen University: 208

Sung Chiao-jen: 68

Sung dynasty: 39, 48, 184, 218, 226

Sungari River: 14, 18

surnames: 167

Swatow: 22, 23

Sweden: 342, 343

Switzerland: 342

Syria: 338

Szechwan Province: vii, viii, xviii, 13, 15, 22, 401, 406; Cultural Revolution in, 273, 281, 294; industry, 438, 441, 449, 452; language, 97; people, 27, 45, 91

table tennis. *See* sports and recreation

Tachai model commune: 135, 284

Tachen Islands: 82

Ta-ch'ing petroleum complex: 503

Tadzhik people: 89, 103, 105

Ta-hsueh Shan-Yun Ling mountains: 16

Tai people: 47, 89, 110, 111, 331; language, 94, 97, 98

T'ai Shan: 17

Taiping Rebellion: 60–61

Taiwan (*see also* Republic of China): 11, 21, 52, 55; language, 95

T'ai-Yuan: 436, 442, 444, 445

Takasaki, Tatsunosuke: 317, 540

Taking Tiger Mountain by Strategy: 370

T'ang dynasty: 39, 46, 226, 227, 229

T'ang-shan: 437

Tanzania: xi, 303, 339, 340, 341

T'ao Ch'ien: 216

T'ao Chu: 352

Taoism: viii, 42, 79, 142, 143, 146, 217, 229

Tarim River: 14, 16, 21, 103

Tatars: 105

tatzupao: 363–364

taxes: agricultural, 45, 429, 562; industrial, 559, 560, 561; pastoral, 430

tea: 47, 399, 404, 524, 525

teachers: 203, 204; training, 195, 206

telecommunications: x, 389, 552–553

television: 367–369

Television University: 368

temples and shrines: 146, 147, 165, 167

Teng Hsiao-p'ing: 7, 266, 271, 272, 273, 293
Teng Tzu-hui: 419, 420
Tengri Khan peak: 16
textiles (see also cotton): 437, 438, 442, 447–448
Thailand: 30, 31, 55
Thanat Khoman: 331
Thanglha Ri Range: 16
theater: 221, 222, 224, 225
thought reform: 265; political reeducation, 85, 136, 209, 234, 248; self-criticism meetings, 124, 133, 138, 142, 152, 254, 353, 590
three-anti campaign (Mao): 80
Three Kingdoms Era: 45
Three People's Principles (Sun): 67, 196
Three People's Solidarity Organization: 346
Tibetan Autonomous Region: vii, viii, xviii, 12, 13, 15, 47, 53, 79, 87, 293, 366, 438, 546; autonomy, 68, 247, 295; people, 27, 28, 91, 92, 97, 103, 105, 106–109; rebellion, 294, 321, 577; Sino-Indian agreement, 300
Tibetan Buddhism. See Lamaism
T'ien Han: 258
Tien Shan mountains: vii, 14, 15, 16
Tientsin, Treaties of: 58
Tientsin Municipality: ix, x, 13, 27, 359, 532; industry, 434, 436, 437, 442, 443, 446
Timor, Portuguese: 30
tin: 24, 438
Tito, Josip Broz: 342
tobacco: 387, 396, 404, 524
Tobago: 345
tombs: 228–229
topography: vii, 15, 400
tourism: 229
trade (see also foreign trade): 36, 46, 48, 50, 51, 53, 301, 382, 499, 519, 521–532
trade fairs. See Canton International Trade Fair
trade unions: 189, 193, 505–508, 517, 572
transliteration systems: 96–99
transportation (see also motor vehicles; railroads; waterways): 381, 394, 454, 499, 521, 543–553; economics, 386, 389, 551, 573; equip-

ment, 446–447; human and animal labor, 405, 543, 551
treaties and agreements (see also border tensions and agreements): xi, 57, 58, 69, 70, 77, 239, 294, 300, 318–319, 323; dual nationality of Chinese persons, 327; foreign trade, 317, 533, 535, 540; friendship, 316, 320, 322, 325, 327, 333, 335; with Soviet Union, 306, 310, 312, 470, 477, 478, 480, 487–488, 490
treaty ports: 57, 58, 351
Triad Society: 61, 67
T'sai Yuan-p'ei: 196
Tsangpo River: 14, 20, 21
Tseng Kuo-fan: 61, 64
Tsinan: 449
Tsinghai Province: vii, xviii, 12, 13, 17, 294, 488; industry, 438, 452; people, 27, 91
Tsinghua College: 464, 465, 466
Tsinghua University: 207, 208
Tsingtao: x, 22, 434, 532
Tsinling mountains: 12
Tsinling-Ta-pieh range: 16
Tsun-i Conference: 606
Tu Fu: 216, 220
T'u people: 103, 105
tuberculosis: 182
Tuchia people: 111, 114
Tulung people: 110
Tumen River: 18
T'ung Meng Hui: 66, 67, 68
T'ung people: 111, 114
Tung Pi-wu: 278, 281
Tung River: 20
Tungan Rebellion: 60
Tung-ch'i Polytechnic University: 463
Tungusic languages: 89, 98
Tunisia: 338
Turfan Basin: 14
Turkestan: 47
Turkey: 345
Turkic languages: 94, 98
typhoons: 23
tz'u: 217
Tz'u-hsi, Empress Dowager: 63, 65, 66

Uganda: 341
Uighurs (see also Sinkiang Uighur Autonomous Republic): 28, 47, 92, 102, 103–104, 294; language, 97, 98
Ulanfu: 293

Wu-han: industry, 436, 438, 440, 443; reactor, 490
Wu-han Incident: 274

yaks: 105, 106
Yalta Pact: 78
Yalu River: 14, 18
Yangtze River: viii, 14, 15, 17, 24, 25, 434, 474; valley, 22, 23, 45, 401, 404, 455; waterway, x, 19–20, 447, 547, 548
Yao people: 89, 98, 106, 111, 112
Yao Wen-yuan: 278, 280
Yeh Chien-ying: 279, 288, 489
Yeh Ch'un: 140, 279
Yeh Ting: 603
Yellow River: 15, 17, 18, 38, 88, 395, 474, 548; floods, 50, 60
Yemen: 82, 338
Yenan: 74
Yen-chi University: 100

Yenpien Korean Autonomous District: 100
Yi people: 28, 97, 106, 109–110
yin and *yang*: 42, 184
Young Pioneers Brigade: 193
youth: 133, 152, 157, 163, 270, 283; delinquency, 188; status of, 70, 159
yuan: 570
Yuan dynasty: 39, 49, 221
Yuan Shih-k'ai: 65, 68
Yueh language: 87
Yugoslavia: 342
Yukus: 103, 105
Yunnan Province: xviii, 13, 17, 22, 332, 333, 366, 406; industry, 438, 444, 445; people, 27, 91, 331
yurt: 101

Zambia: 303, 341
zinc: 434
Zoroastrianism: 46

PUBLISHED AREA HANDBOOKS

550–65	Afghanistan	550–58	Laos
550–98	Albania	550–24	Lebanon
550–44	Algeria	550–38	Liberia
550–59	Angola	550–85	Libya
550–73	Argentina	550–163	Malagasy Rep.
550–20	Brazil	550–45	Malaysia
550–61	Burma	550–161	Mauritania
550–83	Burundi	550–79	Mexico
550–96	Ceylon	550–76	Mongolia
550–159	Chad	550–49	Morocco
550–60	China, People's Rep. of	550–64	Mozambique
550–63	China, Republic of	550–35	Nepal, Bhutan and Sikkim
550–26	Colombia	550–88	Nicaragua
550–91	Congo (Brazzaville)	550–157	Nigeria
550–67	Congo (Kinshasa) Zaire	550–94	Oceania
550–90	Costa Rica	550–48	Pakistan
550–152	Cuba	550–46	Panama
550–22	Cyprus	550–156	Paraguay
550–158	Czechoslovakia	550–92	Peripheral States of the Arabian Peninsula
550–54	Dominican Republic		
550–155	East Germany	550–42	Peru
550–52	Ecuador		
550–150	El Salvador	550–72	Philippines
550–28	Ethiopia	550–162	Poland
550–29	Germany	550–160	Romania
		550–84	Rwanda
550–153	Ghana	550–51	Saudi Arabia
550–87	Greece		
550–78	Guatemala	550–70	Senegal
550–82	Guyana	550–86	Somalia
550–164	Haiti	550–93	South Africa, Rep. of
		550–95	Soviet Union
550–	Hungary	550–27	Sudan
550–151	Honduras		
550–21	India	550–47	Syria
550–154	Indian Ocean Territories	550–62	Tanzania
550–39	Indonesia	550–53	Thailand
		550–89	Tunisia
550–68	Iran	550–80	Turkey
550–31	Iraq		
550–25	Israel	550–74	Uganda
550–69	Ivory Coast	550–43	United Arab Republic
550–30	Japan	550–97	Uruguay
		550–71	Venezuela
550–34	Jordan	550–57	Vietnam, North
550–56	Kenya		
550–50	Khmer Rep. (Cambodia)	550–55	Vietnam, South
550–81	Korea, North	550–99	Yugoslavia
550–41	Korea, Rep. of	550–75	Zambia

*U.S. GOVERNMENT PRINTING OFFICE 1973—O513-727 (P037)